1892 The Homestead strike by the Amalgamated Association of Iron, Steel & Tin Workers at the Carnegie steel mills in Homestead, Pa., resulted in the death of several strikers and Pinkerton guards. The strike failed and the union was ousted from most mills in the Pittsburgh area.

1894 A strike of the American Railway Union led by Eugene V. Debs against the Pullman Co. was defeated by the use of injunctions and by Federal troops sent into the Chicago area. Debs and several other leaders were imprisoned for violating the injunctions, and the union's effectiveness was destroyed.

1898 Congress passed the Erdman Act, providing for mediation and voluntary arbitration on the railroads. The act also made it a criminal offense for railroads to dismiss employees or to discriminate against prospective employees because of their union membership or activity. This portion of the act was subsequently declared invalid by the United States Supreme Court.

1903 The Department of Commerce and Labor was created by an act of Congress (act of Feb. 14, 1903, 32 Stat. 825), and its Secretary was made a member of the Cabinet.

1905 The Industrial Workers of the World was organized in Chicago. The IWW advocated unions running economic institutions. It favored direct action, industrial unionism and the general strike.

1908 Section 10 of the Erdman Act applying to railroad employees, whereby the "yellow-dog" contract was outlawed and an employer was forbidden to discharge a worker for union membership, was declared unconstitutional. (*U.S.* v. *Adair.*)

1913 The United States Department of Labor was established by law. It included the Bureau of Labor Statistics (created in 1884 as the Bureau of Labor, see above), the Bureau of Immigration and Naturalization (created in 1891), and the Children's Bureau (created in 1912).

1914 The Clayton Act was approved, limiting the use of injunctions in labor disputes and providing that picketing and other union activities shall not be considered unlawful. Colorado militia sweeps a strikers' tent colony near Ludlow with machine gun fire and then proceeds to burn tents with people inside them. Thirty-nine men, women and children are killed. This is the culmination of a twenty-year class war in the Rockies.

1917 The "yellow-dog" contract was upheld and union efforts to organize workers party to such contract were held to be unlawful. (*Hitchman Coal & Coke Co.* v. *Mitchell.*)

1919 The Boston Police strike is snuffed out by the National Guard. Calvin Coolidge takes credit for breaking it and becomes a national celebrity. Congress praises a law making it a misdemeanor for police or firefighters to affiliate with unions.

1921 The Supreme Court held that nothing in the Clayton Act legalized secondary boycotts or protected unions against injunctions brought against them for conspiracy in restraint of trade. (*Duplex Printing Press* v. *Deering.*)

1924 Samuel Gompers, president of the AFL, died on December 13.

1926 The Railway Labor Act, passed on May 20, required employers to bargain collectively and not discriminate against their employees for joining a union. The act also provided for the settlement of railway labor disputes through mediation, voluntary arbitration, and fact-finding boards.

1930 The Railway Labor Act's prohibition of employer interference or coercion in the choice of bargaining representatives was upheld by the Supreme Court. (*Texas & N. O. R. Co.* v. *Brotherhood of Railway Clerks.*)

1932 The Anti-Injunction (Norris-La Guardia) Act prohibited Federal injunctions in labor disputes, except as specified, and outlawed "yellow-dog" contracts.

1933 Section 7(a) of the National Industrial Recovery Act guaranteed the right of employees to organize and bargain collectively through their representatives without interference, restraint, or coercion by employers. (Title I of act declared unconstitutional in *Schecter* v. *U. S.* on May 27, 1935).

1935 The National Labor Relations (Wagner) Act established the first national labor policy of protecting the right of workers to organize and to elect their representatives for collective bargaining.

The Committee for Industrial Organization (later the Congress of Industrial Organizations) was formed on November 9 by several AFL international unions and officials to foster industrial unionism.

1937 General Motors Corp. agreed to recognize the United Automobile Workers (CIO) as the bargaining agent for its members.

United States Steel Corp. recognized the steel Workers Organizing Committee as the bargaining agent for its members.

The National Labor Relations Act was held constitutional. (*NLRB* v. *Jones & Laughlin Steel Corp.*)

1940 A sitdown strike was held not to be an illegal restraint of commerce under the Sherman Anti-Trust Act in the absence of intent to impose market controls. (*Apex Hosiery Co.* v. *Leader.*)

(continued on rear endpaper)

CONTEMPORARY LABOR RELATIONS

Robert E. Allen / Timothy J. Keaveny

University of Wyoming

Addison-Wesley Publishing Company
Reading, Massachusetts
Menlo Park, California · London · Amsterdam · Don Mills, Ontario · Sydney

Library of Congress Cataloging in Publication Data

Allen, Robert E. (Robert Edward), 1946–
  Contemporary labor relations.

  Bibliography: p.
  Includes index.
  1. Industrial relations—United States. 2. Collective bargaining—United States. 3. Labor policy—United States. I. Keaveny, Timothy J. II. Title.
HD8072.5.A43 1983   331'.0973   82-11584
ISBN 0-201-00047-4

Copyright © 1983 by Addison-Wesley Publishing Company, Inc.

All rights reserved. No part of this publication may be reproduced. stored in a retrieval system, or transmitted, in any form or by any means, electronic, mechanical, photocopying, recording, or otherwise, without the prior written permission of the publisher. Printed in the United States of America. Published simultaneously in Canada.

ISBN 0-201-00047-4
ABCDEFGHIJ-DO-89876543

PREFACE

The nation's labor policy attempts to accommodate the often conflicting rights and interests of employees, unions, employers, and the public. While this is a difficult task, legislation, administrative rulings, and court decisions have yielded a labor policy that balances relatively well the divergent interests of the parties. To do this, tradeoffs have been made among the parties' conflicting rights, so that the needs of one party can be accommodated as much as possible with minimal adverse effects on the rights of others.

We faced an analogous balancing act when approaching this project. There were a number of concerns we wanted to address. While some were compatible with each other, others appeared to be in conflict. For example, our objective was to present a rigorous review of labor–management relations. Very often, readability is sacrificed for rigor. We wanted to avoid such a problem. It was important to build into the book the recent empirical research that has contributed greatly to our understanding of labor relations. At the same time, however, the "nuts and bolts," that is, the practices and procedures of labor relations, are an important part of an introduction to the discipline. Other aspects of labor relations we wanted to see reflected in the book included the contribution of the nation's labor policy, the implications for the parties associated with their interactions, and the history of the American labor movement. These various concerns are not necessarily incompatible. The challenge was to include meaningful discussions of them all while staying within the confines of a single-volume book.

The nation's balanced labor policy leaves each of the parties a little dissatisfied at least some of the time. We may be faced with a similar situation. Our effort to balance theory and practice, history and contemporary events, labor policy and union and management applications, as well as rigor and readability, was a challenging task. Although some tradeoffs had to be made, we hope you will find this book to be a useful, provocative introduction to labor–management.

The focus of this book is on private sector labor–management relations in the United States. Little attention was paid to labor relations in particular industries such as health care, agriculture, and professional sports. By keeping the discussion on a more general level, greater attention could be given to the major concerns of the field—union organizing, collective bargaining, and contract administration.

The impact of public policy on labor–management relations has been heavily emphasized. The evolution of public policy and the nation's basic labor legislation are each covered in separate chapters. Then, more detailed discussions of the nation's labor policy are presented in later chapters where appropriate. As examples, public policy affecting organizing campaigns, good faith bargaining, and grievance arbitration are thoroughly examined in the chapters concerned with these issues.

Throughout the book, we have attempted to be both descriptive and analytical. In a number of the chapters, you will find a "how to" component. For example, preparation for collective bargaining, costing out of labor agreements, and preparation for arbitration are major topics. Also, much empirical research has been reviewed and discussed. Several models have been developed. Throughout these discussions of theoretical and practical concerns, we have attempted to answer the question of why labor and management interact the way they do. Further, the implications of their interactions for the firm and the union and its membership emerge as major themes. However, since most readers are likely to be business students preparing for management careers, special attention has been given to the impact of labor relations on business organizations. In addition to a chapter on union structure and government, a separate chapter examines how management organizes itself to handle the labor relations function. Then, throughout the book, the ramifications of union organizing, collective bargaining, and contract administration are examined.

The importance of labor history to the understanding of contemporary labor relations emerges as another important theme. To promote a greater appreciation for the relationship between historical events and current affairs, relevant labor history is built into the substantive chapters. Where appropriate, the historical evolution of the issues of concern in the chapter is discussed before the current situation is examined. It is hoped this approach will make labor history more relevant and help improve the reader's understanding of contemporary labor relations.

While the primary concern of this book is with labor–management relations in the American private sector, a meaningful introduction to the discipline cannot ignore the public sector and international labor relations. Therefore, the final part of the book broadens the earlier perspective to include these two important topics.

Over the three years it has taken to complete this project, we have become indebted to many people who provided advice, assistance, and encouragement. Heartfelt thanks go out to the reviewers who conscientiously examined all or parts of the manuscript. Their comments and suggestions helped greatly. It is with pleasure that we acknowledge the contributions of Jim Dworkin (University of Minnesota), Dick Peterson (University of Washington), Lane Tracy (Ohio University), Charles Maxey (University of Southern California), Jim Martin (Wayne State University), Everett Kassalow (University of Wisconsin), James Scoville (University of Minnesota), M. D. Chaubey (Michigan Technological University), and John Jackson (University of Wyoming).

We are also indebted to a small cadre of able typists who helped at various stages of the project. Thanks go to Evelyn Smith and the typing pool of the Department of Business Administration, University of Wyoming, for helping with the preparation of much of the first draft. We also want to express our appreciation to those who typed parts of later drafts: Gloria Lacy, Joan Downham, Margaret Spangler, Stella Herrera, and Mary Keaveny. Special thanks go to Janis Jackson-Hill, management editor for Addison-Wesley. We are most grateful for her help and encouragement throughout this project. There are so many others who helped—graduate assistants, librarians, and students too numerous to name. Please accept our expression of gratitude for your cooperation.

We cannot fully express our appreciation to our families, Mary, Molly, Barry, Meghan, Patrick, and Barb. Their patience with our preoccupation with this project was more than we could reasonably expect. Thank you all for your support and encouragement.

Laramie, Wyoming   Bob Allen
1982   Tim Keaveny

CONTENTS

PART ONE   AN INTRODUCTION TO THE PARTIES   2

1: An Introduction to Labor Relations   4

Traditional Labor-Management Relations / Labor-Management Relations in a Period of Transition / What Is Labor Relations? / Why Study Labor Relations? / An Approach to the Study of Labor Relations / An Overview of the Text

2: The Evolution of Public Policy Toward Labor   30

Sources of Public Policy / Early Judicial Control of Trade Union Activities / Early Legislative Attempts / The Emergence of Statute Law / The Development of a Balanced Labor Policy / Regulation of Internal Union Affairs / The 1974 Amendments to the National Labor Relations Act / Labor Policies Affecting Public Policies

3: Labor Legislation: The Current Perspective   61

The National Labor Relations Act (as Amended) / The National Labor Relations Board / The Landrum-Griffin Act / Other Labor Relations Legislation

4: Union Structure, Government, and Politics   89

Relevant History / Functions of the Components in the Labor Movement / Government of National and Local Unions / Democracy in the Government of Unions / Change in Union Structure, Government, and Politics

5: Management Organization for Labor Relations   123

Role and Levels of Management / Management Attitudes Toward Unions / Relevant History / Current Management Organization for Collective Bargaining / Non-Union Organizations / Management Organization for Collective Bargaining When Employees Are Unionized / Emerging Issues

PART TWO   UNION ORGANIZING   154

6: Why Workers Organize   156

An Historical View of Why Workers Organize / The Formation of a Union / Why Workers Unionize: The Research Evidence / Trends in Union Membership / Should There Be a Change in the Goals of Union Negotiating Efforts?

7: How Workers Organize   185

Authorization Cards / The Certification Election Procedure / Summary

- Part Two Case Study: The Union Organizing Process   216

PART THREE THE COLLECTIVE BARGAINING PROCESS 231

8: Collective Bargaining: An Overview 232

Objectives of the Collective Bargaining Process / Characteristics of the Collective-Bargaining Relationship / Bargaining Power: The Moving Force / Strategy and Tactics of Negotiations / The Legal Requirements of Collective Bargaining

9: Collective Bargaining: From Preparation to Agreement 270

Early Preparation for Negotiations / Final Preparations for Bargaining / Union Preparation for Negotiations / From Initial Proposals to the Final Agreement / The Strike and Lockout / Activities in Support of Strikes

10: The Resolution of Bargaining Impasses 311

Techniques for Improving Collective Bargaining / Third-Party Efforts to Resolve Bargaining Impasses / Emergency Disputes / The Case for Free Collective Bargaining

PART FOUR COLLECTIVE-BARGAINING ISSUES 343

11: Wage Issues in Collective Bargaining 344

Determinants of Wage Levels / Relative Importance of Wage Determinants / Employee Pay Satisfaction / Establishing the Wage Structure

12: Supplemental Compensation Issues in Collective Bargaining 375

Public Policy on Wages / Public Policy on Employee Benefits / History of Supplemental Compensation / Common Fringe Benefits / Emerging Forms of Employee Benefits / Problems with Fringe Benefits / Costing Out a Labor Agreement

13: Institutional and Administrative Issues in Collective Bargaining 414

Administration and Institutional Issues / Instability in the Demand for Labor / Administrative and Institutional Issues and the Future

- Part Four Case Study: An Exercise in Negotiations 445

PART FIVE CONTRACT INTERPRETATION AND ADMINISTRATION 470

14: Contract Administration: Grievance Procedure 472

What Is a Grievance? / What Is a Grievance Procedure? / Functions of the Grievance Procedure / History of Grievance Procedures / Types of Grievances / Determinants of Grievances / Legal Status of Grievance Procedures / Recommendations for Effective Grievance Procedures

15: Grievance Arbitration 493

What Is Grievance Arbitration? / Grievance Arbitration and National Labor Policy / The Major Advantages of Grievance Arbitration / Moving from Grievance Procedure to Arbitration / The Arbitrability of Grievances / Preparing Your Case for Arbitration / The Arbitration Hearing / The Arbitrator's Decision / An Evaluation of Grievance Arbitration

- Part Five Case Studies: Arbitration Cases 528

PART SIX LABOR RELATIONS: AN EXPANDED PERSPECTIVE 534

16: Public Employee Collective Bargaining: An Overview 536

The Growth of Government Employment / Factors Inhibiting Public-Sector Unionism Prior to the 1960s / Factors Contributing to the Growth of Public-Employee Unionism / Differences Between the Public and Private Sectors / Similarities Between the Public and Private Sectors / Bargaining Arrangements in the Public Sector

17: Public-Sector Collective Bargaining: Legal Environment and Implications 571

Labor-Management Relations in the Federal Sector / Labor-Management Relations at the State and Local Levels / The Impact of Public Policy on Bargaining Outcomes

18: Union-Management Relations in Other Countries 600

Descriptions of Labor Relations in Other Countries / Multinational Collective Bargaining / Barriers to Multinational Bargaining / The Experience with Multinational Bargaining to Date / Alternative Union Strategies

19: The Future of the American Union Movement 630

Another Challenge / Relevant Trends and Forces / Employer Actions Having an Impact on Union Membership / Changing Workers' Values / Alternative Courses of Action / Organize More Workers

Name Index 655

Subject Index 658

Labor relations involve the interaction of three major groups: labor unions, the management staffs of employing institutions, and government agencies. Section I of this book introduces these three parties in the labor relations process. Chapter 1 describes the nature of the relationships between the parties and presents an overview of the book. By setting the nation's labor policy, government influences many aspects of labor-management relations; thus Chapters 2 and 3 are devoted to public policy concerns. Chapter 2 examines the evolution of labor policy, and contemporary labor law is reviewed in Chapter 3. After this discussion of the legal environment, attention turns to the other actors in the American system of labor relations. Chapter 4 examines the development of organized labor. Also, the basic characteristics of union structure, government, and politics are described. Management's pattern of organization for labor relations is presented in Chapter 5.

PART ONE

AN INTRODUCTION TO THE PARTIES

Chapter 1

AN INTRODUCTION TO LABOR RELATIONS

Gene Murdock worked in the maintenance department. As a result, his work took him throughout the plant. He always believed that auto workers complained about their jobs more than most other people. In recent months, Gene seemed to notice more grumbling about work than ever before. With over a quarter of the plant's production employees laid off and with periodic rumors of even more layoffs, it was not surprising that workers were upset. Occasionally, Gene heard talk that the slump in the automobile industry was so bad that the plant was going to close permanently. While Gene had been laid off three times since he joined the company, it had been only for a couple of weeks on each occasion. Each time, he knew he would be recalled to his job, but this was not the case anymore. The permanent loss of his job due to plant closure was an all-too-real possibility.

This morning it seemed that everyone was in an uproar. Over the weekend, Gene's union had started to renegotiate their labor agreement. The Sunday newspaper had said that the union was under pressure to make some concessions that would lower labor costs. Otherwise, unemployment in the industry would be likely to worsen. Everyone to whom Gene spoke seemed to have an opinion concerning what the union should do.

Gene knew that labor costs for cars assembled at his plant were several hundred dollars per car higher than those produced in Japan. He realized that if the American automobile industry was ever going to regain its competitive edge, the elimination of this labor cost differential would be necessary. One way to do so would be for his union to go back to the bargaining table and negotiate a giveback of their hard-earned wages and benefits.

So Gene understood why his union was now back at the bargaining table giving away previously negotiated wages and fringe benefits. Lower-paying jobs were better than no jobs at all. At the same time, however, Gene felt the need for higher wages, not lower wages. His dream of buying a house was all but gone because of current high interest rates. Everything he had to purchase was more costly now than last year. His gut tightened when he thought about trying to make ends meet with his lowered wage. He didn't even want to think about the fact that the wages the union and company were trying to lower had been obtained only after a lengthy strike two years ago. During the strike, he had spent all his savings and had had to borrow money from his parents just to pay the rent and feed his family. Now the union was giving back the wage increase obtained through that sacrifice. This didn't seem right.

Gene didn't like the idea of taking a lower wage. He also didn't like the prospect of losing his job if the plant were shut down. In his sarcastic moments, Gene hoped that the union officials were making good wages. No matter what they did, a sizable proportion of the union's membership was going to be upset. The union leadership was going to have to earn its keep this year.

Gene Murdock's union is one of many labor organizations in the automobile, steel, rubber, railroad, construction, and other industries that has negotiated concessions to help lower costs. Unions have been willing to renegotiate existing contracts and moderate future demands in order to help employers improve their financial status. By so doing, a union hopes that its members' job security will increase as the firm's economic position improves. In addition to lowering labor costs through less expensive contracts, a growing number of employers and unions are working together to solve problems of mutual concern. Union-management collaboration is addressing problems such as scrap reduction, changing technology, absenteeism, tardiness, and productivity improvement.

This trend toward more widespread cooperation differs from the traditional approach to labor-management relations in the United States. Customarily, unions always press for "more." To provide an ever-improving standard of living for their members, unions have sought higher wages, more fringe benefits, and a greater role in organizational decision-making each time a contract is renegotiated. Because the union's objectives are frequently incompatible with those of management, it is not surprising that traditional labor-management relations have been characterized by a high degree of conflict. Disputes tend to be resolved in favor of the party with the greater power. A union's ability to strike and a company's ability to withstand the strike are important factors influencing the relative power of the parties and their attainment of desired objectives.

The trend toward greater cooperation and less conflict between the parties suggests a period of transition for labor-management relations. Organized labor and employers are experiencing problems that are forcing them to reconsider their traditional patterns of interaction. For instance, in the 1940s after years of growth, union membership as a proportion of the labor force peaked and then began to decline. In recent years, a growing number of firms are aggressively fighting union organizing efforts. As already mentioned, many companies are expecting unions to relinquish previously negotiated benefits. Furthermore, unemployment among union members is higher now than in previous years.

Pressures on the labor movement have been intensified by adverse economic conditions. In recent years, a number of companies have faced financial hardships. The weak economic position of these firms is attributable to factors such as intensified foreign competition, outmoded plants and equipment, changing consumer tastes, and years of inadequate research and development. These problems are exacerbated by broader economic concerns such as high interest rates, slow economic growth, increasing energy costs, inflation, and unemployment. Taken together, these result in a relatively stagnant business environment in many sectors of the United States economy. Because of the multitude of problems facing both labor and management, the parties realize they cannot continue with "business as usual." Many professionals in the field of labor relations recognize there is a need to reevaluate the terms on which labor and management interact. As a result, the decade of the 1980s is likely to exhibit a number of labor practices that will mark a sharp departure from the historical approach to labor-management relations. This implies that some of the more conflict-ridden practices characterizing traditional labor-management relations will probably give way to more cooperative approaches. To fully comprehend contemporary labor relations, a two-step process is required. First, an understanding of traditional practices is necessary. This should then be complemented by an examination of efforts by the parties to resolve problems of mutual concern in a cooperative manner.

Before proceeding, it is important to understand the nature of the relationship between organized labor and management. The following section traces the evolution of the traditional approach to labor-management relations. The traditional approach emphasizes that both unions and employers have a vested interest in the success of an organization. The parties are under pressure to cooperate to the extent needed for the firm's survival. However, within this general framework, the objectives of organized labor and management are, to a degree, incompatible. It is therefore necessary to develop procedures for controlling and resolving the conflict the parties are likely to experience. In the next section, the trend toward greater labor-management cooperation will be discussed. As part of this discussion, the major forces pushing the parties toward cooperation will be identified. With this background in mind, the reasons for studying labor relations will be examined and an approach to its study presented. Concluding this chapter is an overview of the remainder of the text so that you will know what to expect from the rest of this book.

Traditional Labor-Management Relations

THE ADVERSARIAL RELATIONSHIP

When a group of workers decide they want union representation, many changes take place in their employer's organization. Much time will be spent later in this book examining these changes. One of the basic changes occurring in a company that becomes unionized is shared decision making. Prior to unionization, company management had the right to run the organization as they saw fit. After unionizing, management is obligated under the nation's labor laws to share with the labor organization decisions concerning wages, hours, and other conditions of employment. The shift from unilateral decision making to shared decision making can be the source of many problems as well as opportunities for labor and management.

The relationships between organized labor and management exhibit tension because the parties are pursuing objectives that are, to some degree, inconsistent. Labor and management have many long-run objectives in common because they have a shared interest in the firm's success. If a company is going to be able to provide stable employment opportunities for a union's members and offer improved wages and benefits, the company must be financially successful. Therefore, workers, their union, and management want the company to be successful. To help insure the success and survival of the firm, the parties are motivated to cooperate to some degree. However, the parties still have their own interests and objectives which may be in conflict. Workers are striving for higher wages while management is trying to minimize costs. Workers try to protect the status quo while management wants to be able to change production methods as needed without union resistance. Workers try to lessen their dependence on a firm by sharing in decisions affecting them. At the same time, employers try to protect their managerial discretion by retaining unilateral control over the work organization.

This pursuit of conflicting objectives, plus a simultaneous commitment to a firm's success and survival, have led to the development of an adversarial relationship between organized labor and management. The adversarial relationship has been described as follows:

> The two parties limit their *mutual* interests to the preservation and enlargement of the common pot which finances their respective factor shares. The parties recognize that wages and profits both require a prosperous enterprise. Beyond that, the relationship is dominated by a running dispute over the distribution of the enterprise's net proceeds between wages and non-wages. Management prefers the adversary relationship, because it fears that union collaboration will dilute management authority and thereby impair efficiency. The union prefers it that way, because the adversary relationship is most consistent with the maintenance of the union as a bargaining organization, and bargaining is what the union is all about.[1]

The basic assumption underlying the adversarial nature of labor-management relations is that the parties will be in conflict over at least some issues. This comes about as the parties pursue their self-interests. While one party attempts to achieve its objectives, it may prevent the other from reaching its goals. The resulting conflict must be resolved, or at least, contained. Disagreements between labor and management have been part of the labor relations scene since the inception of the American trade union movement. The following section examines the basis for labor-management conflict.

THE EVOLUTION OF THE RELATIONSHIP

The pre-Industrial Revolution period. The foundation of unionism and the field of labor relations rests in the potential conflict between the interests of employers and employees. If the objectives of employers and employees were the same; that is, if decisions benefiting employers also benefited their employees, unions would probably be unnecessary.

Prior to the industrial revolution in the United States, union-type activities existed but on a very limited scale. This was because the work environment was not characterized by widespread employer-employee conflict during the colonial period. To a degree, this situation was due to the nature of the product market.[2] Goods purchased and consumed in an urban area were produced locally. Because of limited transportation and communications, practically no competition from goods produced outside the locale was present. Also, much of the work performed was custom in nature;[3] that is, craftsmen made the product to specifications established by the customer. These factors allowed the prices of goods to be set high enough so that both the employer and employee could receive a satisfactory return for their efforts. The ability of employers to pass to the customer the higher costs associated with satisfactory worker wages tended to minimize employer-employee conflict.

Another factor dampening conflict between workers and their employers during the pre–industrial revolution period was that most workers could reasonably aspire to become self-employed. Freedom from having to spend one's entire work life employed by someone else could come about through two basic means. First, workers were able to acquire skills and set up their own businesses. Individuals learned their craft by serving an apprenticeship, during which time they helped and observed more experienced and skilled journeymen workers. When the apprentices' skills reached a certain level, they would become journeymen. As journeymen, the workers were able to become independent from the supervision of others. Because businesses tended to be small and without much equipment, it was possible for journeymen to establish their own operations with only limited capital. By so doing, individuals not wanting to work for someone else could become self-employed. The availability of free land during the colonial period was the second route to self-employment. Individuals wanting to be independent from urban areas and from the need to work for others could take advantage of the free land by becoming farmers.

The important point is that, prior to the industrial revolution, most workers wanting to be self-employed were able to do so. As a result, workers tended to identify with their employers rather than be in conflict with them.

The post–Industrial Revolution period. The American economy was changed dramatically by the industrial revolution. The introduction of the factory system in the early 1800s had several major implications, including:

- Large amounts of capital were needed to introduce the new, factory-based technologies. As a result, it was beyond the means of most workers to accumulate the money needed to open their own businesses. Some workers could still avoid employment in factories by acquiring land and becoming farmers. Most people, however, were destined to spend their work lives employed by others.
- The division of labor associated with the introduction of machinery changed the nature of the workforce. Rather than requiring skilled craftsmen to pro-

duce the goods demanded by society, large numbers of unskilled and semi-skilled workers were needed to tend the machines of the new technology.
- The new mass production technologies were more efficient than the small shops run by skilled craftsmen. As a result, goods produced by skilled craftsmen had a difficult time competing with products manufactured in factories.

As a result of these basic changes in the American economy associated with the industrialization process, the relationship between workers and their jobs changed dramatically. Gone were the days when most workers could realistically aspire to be self-employed, independent businessmen. Instead, most individuals would always work for others in the factories of America. With these changes, workers became dependent upon their employers for their livelihood.

The dependency relationship between workers and their employers fostered by the industrial revolution led to a conflict of interest between the two groups. This is not to say the goals of workers and employers were completely divergent. Employers needed workers willing to submit to managerial authority. At the same time, workers needed jobs available in factories to support themselves and their families. Consequently, it was within the self-interest of workers and employers to cooperate so that the firm could compete successfully in the product market. The finanacial success of the firm helped insure its survival and provided job stability for the employees. However, as previously discussed, some of the worker's goals, such as higher wages and greater job security, were incompatible with management's objectives. Efforts to resolve and control the conflict associated with incompatible goals led to the development of the union movement and the adversarial relationship between labor and management.

The American union movement emerges. The roots of the American union movement go back to the early years of the industrial revolution. It was not long before workers realized the "strength in numbers" principle applied to the job situation. Workers joined together, presenting management with a united front in order to get improved wages, benefits, and working conditions. These loose amalgamations of employees who banded together from time to time in the late 1700s and early 1800s to improve working conditions were the forerunners of today's labor unions.

From their beginnings up to the present time, unions have pressed for higher wages, improved benefits, and a greater participation in organizational decision making. Management's response has typically been to resist union intrusions into the running of the business. As a result, conflict has frequently developed between organized labor and management. As will be seen in later sections of this book, procedures have evolved that facilitate the resolution to the conflict inevitably developing between labor and management. While the conflict is not without bounds (both labor and management want the firm to be successful), disagreements between the parties are an essential component of traditional labor-management relations.

The adversarial relationship that has developed between the parties has been described in terms of an "armed truce".[4] This "armed truce" of traditional labor-management relations has the following characteristics:

AN INTRODUCTION TO THE PARTIES

- Management considers unions and collective bargaining to be a necessary evil.
- Labor's leadership views its main task to be the challenge and protest of managerial actions.
- The parties are in basic disagreement over the scope of collective bargaining and the issues subject to joint determination.
- Management and the union are rivals for the workers' loyalty.
- The relative power of the parties determines the ultimate results of their negotiations.
- Both labor and management want to establish orderly procedures for resolving conflict and to compromise differences between their respective positions.[5]

The adversarial relationship just described has been a basic characteristic of labor-management relations in the United States over the years because it has met the needs of the parties. Also, the adversarial principle has been tamed so that the resulting conflict can be controlled and resolved. On this point, it has been written:

> Indeed, the supreme achievement of western industrial relations has been its ability to come up with institutions that blunt the force of the adversary principle. These institutions include the trade union, professional management, arbitration, mediation, the welfare state, work-easing technologies, collective bargaining, and full employment.[6]

Much of the material in the chapters to follow examines the mechanisms developed by labor, management, and government to moderate the adversarial relationship.

Parties to the adversarial relationship (unions and management) are concerned with the distribution of revenues and decision-making authority. How will the revenues of the firm be divided between the workers and the owners of the company? Will management be able to make decisions unilaterally affecting work conditions or will such decisions be shared with the employees and their unions? Such questions point out the basic nature of problems facing labor and management. The parties are adversaries in a process determining the relative size of their shares—shares of revenue and shares of power. Over the years, the adversarial approach to labor-management relations has demonstrated its ability to handle the division of financial rewards and the establishment of power relationships.[7]

Labor-Management Relations in a Period of Transition

What happens to the adversarial relationship if the problems confronting labor and management do not concern issues such as the distribution of revenues or the relative power of the parties? These are issues that are typically viewed as involving the allocation of some fixed entity such as money or power between labor and management. Typically, whatever one party gains is at the expense of the other. For example, money allocated to the employees' pension program cannot be distributed to the stockholders as dividends. The workers' involvement in decision making usually lessens management's control over the matter.

However, a number of issues confronting labor and management do not involve the distribution of revenues or power. Some issues involve problems of concern to both workers and their employers. Foreign competition, changing technology, productivity improvement, the energy crisis, inflation, and rising unemployment are examples of problems that can jointly affect labor and management. See Exhibit 1.1 for a discussion of some major problems plaguing the United States economy. Exhibit 1.1 also presents some of the major challenges to labor-management relations associated with each trend. The response of the parties to such environmental challenges cannot usually be handled in the same way as distributive issues. Rather, a problem-solving approach is needed. In turn, problem solving requires greater cooperation between labor and management than usually characterizes their adversarial relationship.

EXHIBIT 1.1
Challenges to Labor-Management Relations

Inflation: Rapidly rising prices erode workers' purchasing power. At the same time, employers are faced with rising costs of materials and pressures to increase their products' prices. This, in turn, can jeopardize a firm's competitive position.

- Will large numbers of non-union workers be motivated to unionize in the belief that collective bargaining will lead to higher wages?
- Will labor and management negotiators be able to build sufficient protections for workers' purchasing power into labor agreement? Will the use of cost-of-living agreements that link wage increases to price increases continue to spread? Will the parties negotiate shorter contracts? If they negotiate more frequently, will this lead to an increase in the number of strikes; that is, situations in which employees refuse to work until management agrees with the union's terms?
- Will the government pass legislation limiting changes in wages and prices as part of an effort to break the continued wage-price spiral? How will the parties react to such government efforts? How will government efforts to control inflation such as high credit costs affect economic growth and workers' productivity? What is the impact of slow economic growth and lagging productivity on a firm's ability to meet worker demands for higher wages?

- Will the parties be able to work together to improve worker productivity; that is, each worker's output, so as to help allow wage increases to be granted without increasing labor costs?

Changing composition of the work force: Today's work force is very different from that which existed when trade unions initially gained prominence in the American economy during the 1930s and 1940s. More women are working, and workers tend to be better educated and are more likely to be employed in white-collar occupations. In other words, the white, male, blue-collar worker who has been the backbone of the American trade union movement represents a declining portion of the work force.

- Can unions develop organizing strategies needed to attract, on a widespread basis, females, minorities, college-educated, and professional employees?

AN INTRODUCTION TO THE PARTIES

EXHIBIT 1.1 *(Continued)*

- What affect, if any, will the changing composition of the work force have on union bargaining demands? Will there be a decreased emphasis on wages? Will attention shift to the negotiation of issues that will result in more challenging and satisfying jobs for workers? Will unions try to gain for workers a greater voice in managerial decision making?
- Will unions be confronted with internal problems as a result of a changing membership? Will the membership's increasing heterogeneity lead to more challenges to the union's leadership or more rejections by the rank-and-file union membership of contracts negotiated by the leadership?
- Will a larger involvement by women in the labor force lead to new union demands during collective bargaining such as pregnancy-related benefits and child care facilities?

Foreign competition: A number of American industries such as automobiles, electronics, and clothing are facing stiff competition from foreign-based operations. Since many foreign companies have lower costs, and frequently, more efficient technologies, such firms are able to compete effectively in the American market.

- Will labor unions be willing to make concessions such as delaying or foregoing negotiated benefits to help American businesses be more competitive?
- How will the technological changes needed to improve a firm's competitive position affect labor-management relations? Will labor and management negotiators be able to deal with the job insecurity and declining employment opportunities frequently associated with rapid technological change?
- Can labor-management cooperation lead to increased worker productivity so that firms can compete more effectively with foreign companies?
- What can labor, management, and government do to help buffer American workers and products from foreign competition?

Increased employer resistance to union organizing efforts: An increasing number of firms are striving to stay non-union. As a result, unions are likely to confront greater resistance to their organizing campaigns and are more likely to face greater employer support of employee attempts to disestablish the union.

- What can unions do to offset increased employer opposition to their organizing efforts?
- What can employers do to counteract a union's organizing campaign?
- How can public policy be modified to enhance or deter union organizing?
- How will trends such as the population shifting from northern parts of the country to the south and west where the union tradition appears weaker affect the union's organizing ability?

The energy crisis: Electricity, fuel oil, natural gas, and coal have dramatically increased in price in recent years. Also, the availability of some energy sources is unpredictable at certain times during the year. The energy problem is likely to persist for the foreseeable future. Both workers and management are affected by uncertain energy supplies and rising fuel costs.

- What can unions and employers do to minimize problems related to the energy crisis? Can changes in work schedules such as the four-day work week be negotiated to cut energy costs for both companies and employees?
- How will the parties react to possible technological changes intended to bring about energy savings? Will unions resist or support such changes? What can be done to help insure labor-management cooperation on energy conservation efforts?
- Will rising energy prices create new bargaining demands such as subsidized transportation?

The American economy is in a state of crisis. This crisis is creating problems that the traditional approach to labor-management relations cannot handle effectively. In response to these challenges, a new spirit of cooperation is being exhibited in many sectors of the economy. The forms cooperation takes range greatly depending on the nature of the problem. In the sections to follow, some of the major examples of labor-management cooperation will be briefly discussed.

CONCESSION BARGAINING

The American automobile industry is the most notable example of labor-management cooperation in the form of concession bargaining. Since the 1930s, the United Auto Workers (UAW) union and the automobile manufacturers have been strong adversaries. During the early 1980s, the slump in the industry which weakened the auto firms' financial positions and led to widespread unemployment among union members forced the parties to reevaluate their traditional approach to labor-management relations. In response to these problems, the UAW agreed to start negotiations months in advance of the old contract's expiration date because the problems were so severe that they had to be addressed as soon as possible. Also, the union allowed for the reopening of existing contracts to provide relief for ailing companies. Related to these changes was the recognition that the traditional approach which emphasized increasing wages and benefits had to give way to economic realities of the automobile industry. In response to the sales slump attributable to foreign competition and high interest rates, the union expressed a willingness to negotiate concessions so that the automobile companies would be more competitive. Concessions involve the giving up by a union of benefits it has already negotiated and which have been included in the labor agreement. For example, in the late 1970s, the UAW granted concessions amounting to over $600 million to help the financially beleaguered Chrysler Corporation.

More recently, other examples of cooperation in the automobile industry can be found. General Motors and the UAW attempted to negotiate lower wages and benefits to reduce labor costs. Then, the lower costs would be passed on to the customer in the form of lower prices. The hope was that lower automobile prices would stimulate sales, thereby improving the company's financial position and enhancing the workers' job security. An important part of this effort was a willingness by General Motors to open its books to an independent accounting firm to determine that labor cost savings were, in fact, passed on to the customers.[8] This willingness to share information, which traditionally was tightly controlled by management, represents a new form of bargaining behavior.[9] While these negotiations, which took place in January 1982, did not yield a new agreement, they did reflect a change in attitude by both labor and management. However, the UAW and Ford negotiated an agreement that saved the company hundreds of millions of dollars and enhanced worker job security. Later in 1982, the UAW and General Motors reached agreement on a new contract with lower labor costs.

AN INTRODUCTION TO THE PARTIES

UAW and Ford leaders sign the new agreement representing a new era of labor-management cooperation. In industries facing economic problems, such agreements may be needed to enhance the firm's financial position and increase the worker's job security.

While the labor-management relations in the automobile industry have received much media attention, unions in a number of other industries have demonstrated a willingness to experiment with more cooperative approaches to problems of mutual concern. Some unions have made major concessions to help improve the job security of their members. Deregulation of the airline industry and the air traffic controllers' strike caused financial hardships for several airlines. This led to the layoff of a number of union members. To enhance profitability and improve job security, the companies and the unions negotiated a number of givebacks or concessions. For example, during 1981, Braniff employees accepted a 10 percent pay cut. Continental Airlines pilots took a 10 percent cut in pay and agreed to forego a 9 percent raise scheduled for the following year. Pilots for United Airlines agreed to work rule changes that saved the company about $75 million. In exchange, the pilots received a no-layoff agreement from the company. In addition to the automobile and airline industries, concession bargaining has been used in the contruction, meat-packing, steel, railroad, and rubber industries.

While some unions have been willing (perhaps begrudgingly) to give back already negotiated wages and benefits, others have not had to go that far. However, they have had to moderate their demands when negotiating a new contract. In early 1982, the International Brotherhood of Teamsters and Trucking Management, Inc. (the trucking industry's bargaining organization) reached a new agreement. Because of trucking deregulation and depressed economic conditions, a number of trucking companies were financially hardpressed, and about 50,000 union truck drivers were unemployed. In an effort to improve conditions in the industry, the parties started negotiating early. The union was willing to drop some restrictive work rules in order to improve productivity in exchange for improved job security. The final contract was much less costly than the previous agreement.[10] It can be expected that other unions will also respond to depressed economic conditions by moderating their wage and benefit proposals.

QUALITY OF WORK LIFE

Traditional labor-management relations have focused on the establishment of wages, hours, and other terms and conditions of employment. The quality of work life (QWL) movement has expanded the range of subjects jointly determined by workers and management to include issues such as absenteeism, tardiness, improving relationships between workers and supervisors, productivity improvement, and technological change. The logic behind this approach is to improve worker satisfaction and productivity by getting workers more fully involved in the decision-making process. Until recently, QWL programs were more likely to be found in non-union organizations. However, a growing number of unionized firms are also getting involved in projects designed to improve the quality of work life.

Many unions were hesitant to participate in QWL programs. The concern was that management wanted union support in QWL programs in order to exploit the workers. There was also concern that greater cooperation with management would undermine the union's role in the organization. Furthermore, some union leaders feared that if the programs were successful and led to improved worker productivity, some employees would lose their jobs.[11]

Trust is a key ingredient for successful QWL programs. Therefore, it is necessary for the parties to build trust and eliminate suspicion about these joint efforts. Basic conditions for the development of a trusting relationship for the purposes of establishing QWL programs include:

- Workers must be insured the pace of their work will not increase as a result of any changes coming out of the QWL process.
- Workers will not be laid off as a result of the QWL process.
- Employee involvement in QWL activities should be voluntary.
- QWL programs should not affect the labor agreement between the company and the union.[12]

As unions and management have become more familiar with the preconditions for successful QWL programs, more and more joint union-management QWL programs have developed.

The focus of QWL programs is on problems of concern to both workers and management. By resolving such problems, both groups benefit. The typical approach is to develop committees composed of both workers and managers. These committees can address a wide range of problems, the resolution of which can lead to improved worker satisfaction and productivity.

The typical approach is to separate collective bargaining and the QWL process. Sometimes, the joint committees will be established by the labor agreement. However, the tough issues such as wages and fringe benefits are likely to be resolved through the traditional adversarial approach. The problems of mutual concern will be handled through joint committees. Why some issues continue to be handled traditionally and others with a more cooperative approach is not known at the present time.[13]

The use of joint labor-management committees focusing on QWL issues is not widespread in American industry at the present time. However, it has already been demonstrated that this approach can lead to decreased absenteeism and tardiness, improved product quality, reduced scrap, increased productivity, improved communications between workers and their supervisors, and enhanced job satisfaction. It is likely that a growing number of unions and companies will introduce QWL committees to increase worker involvement in the workplace.

The objective of the preceding discussion was not to provide a definitive discussion of the trend toward greater labor-management cooperation. More will be said about these issues later in the book. The point to be made is that the state of the economy has been a major factor causing the traditional adversarial relationship to be reconsidered. As long as industries are in trouble, unions and management are likely to explore new areas of collaboration.

This does not mean that the adversarial approach to labor-management relations will die. Where companies are not adversely affected by general economic conditions, traditional labor-management relations are likely to prevail. For example, in the fall of 1981, two divisions of American Standard and the United Electrical Workers were involved in an eight-week strike over the union's refusal to give back previously negotiated rights and benefits. It appears that where employers cannot prove their financial problems are severe, unions are unlikely to agree to major concessions.[14]

There are also doubts about whether this trend toward cooperation represents a permanent change in attitudes or simply a temporary "ceasefire" that will lapse when the economy improves. Over the years, the parties have relied heavily on the adversarial approach because it yielded results for both sides that they could not have otherwise achieved. Because of depressed economic conditions, traditional practices have not led to the desired results. Therefore, the parties have been willing to experiment with different approaches. It is possible that when the economy improves, the parties will move back toward their adversarial roles because these will prove useful once again.

At the present time, it is difficult to predict if the trend toward cooperation is temporary or permanent. It is probably safe to assume that some of the more cooperative approaches such as joint QWL programs will become a larger part of the industrial scene. The real uncertainty is how prevalent these practices will become. This means that students of labor relations will have to understand the traditional practices, procedures, attitudes, and beliefs characterizing the adversarial approach to labor-management relations. This is likely to be the dominant approach for the foreseeable future. It is also likely that the parties to labor relations will handle a greater number of issues more cooperatively than in the past. Therefore, it is also necessary to develop an understanding of the preconditions for cooperative behavior and the techniques available to the parties for taking advantage of these opportunities to cooperate.

What Is Labor Relations?

This book, then, is concerned with the study of the relationships that develop between organized labor and management. The term "labor relations" is frequently used to describe these relationships. However, since so many definitions of labor relations exist, it may be useful at this point in the book to define how the term is used herein.

The term labor relations has commonly been used to describe employee-employer relationships in both the union and non-union sectors.[15] This book, however, takes a narrower view of the field. Labor relations (also known as labor-management relations) will be treated here as the study of employee-employer relationships in the unionized portion of the economy. The primary thrust of the book is the examination of the relationships between the management of firms in the private sector and labor organizations representing the firms' employees. Since organized labor and management do not interact in a vacuum, the field of labor relations also includes the examination of the environment in which the parties operate. Elements of the environment affecting the nature of labor-managment relations include, for example, the nation's labor policy, technology of the workplace, attributes of the labor market, state of the economy, and social conditions.

As suggested in the preceding sections, labor-management relations are characterized by both conflict and cooperation. This is the basis of the adversarial relationship. A central focus of labor relations is the study of the attitudes, relationships, practices, and procedures developed by organized labor and management to resolve or, at least, control their conflict. As labor-management relations mature over the years, the parties are usually better able to work together to resolve their disagreements. Fewer problems lead to conflict and a larger number of issues are handled cooperatively. As noted earlier, this process has been hastened by the depressed economic conditions of the early 1980s. With time, a predominant pattern of accommodation develops in which the parties, without denying their differences, develop mechanisms for resolving their disagreements. As a result, labor-management cooperation is more prevalent today than in the past. Therefore, labor relations also involve the study of the conditions conducive to labor-management collaboration as well as the practices and procedures intended to facilitate cooperation.

Why Study Labor Relations?

Labor relations is a specialized field focusing on approximately 20 percent of the work force. While there are 102.5 million individuals in the labor force, only 20.2 million are represented by labor organizations.[16] In light of these facts, it is reasonable to ask why so much time and effort should be expended studying a relatively small proportion of the work force. The answer to this question rests with the notion that the impact of organized labor on the American economy is far broader than is implied by looking strictly at the number of unionized workers. This is the case for several reasons.

UNIONS ARE CONCENTRATED IN KEY INDUSTRIES

Unionized workers are not distributed evenly throughout industry. Rather, they are concentrated in the nation's basic industries. For example, over 75 percent of the transportation, construction, and mining industries are unionized. Between 50 and 74 percent of the workers employed in transportation equipment, primary metals such as steel and aluminum, and manufacturing are unionized.[17] Union participation in the determination of wages, benefits, and other working conditions strongly influences the efficiency and effectiveness of the basic industries constituting the backbone of the American economy.

PATTERNS ESTABLISHED BY UNIONS INFLUENCE NON-UNION SECTORS OF THE ECONOMY

The influence of unions on the economy is not limited to their impact on unionized firms. Non-union firms are affected by what goes on in unionized organizations. The trends and patterns established in the unionized sector of the economy "spill over" or influence the practices found in non-union firms. This occurs because there are pressures on non-union firms to match the wages, benefits and working conditions of unionized firms to be competitive in the labor market. Also, some non-union firms will match or exceed their unionized competitors as part of a strategy to remain non-union.

UNIONS ARE IMPORTANT POLITICAL FORCES IN THE AMERICAN ECONOMY

The impact of the American trade union movement is broader than its effect on industry. While unions concentrate their attention on collective bargaining, they also play a role in American politics. During an election campaign, labor organizations are capable of marshalling money and human resources in order to elect candidates supportive of labor's goals. In addition to these efforts, employee organizations also attempt to influence the legislative process through their lobbying activities. Representatives of organized labor are frequently consulted about public policy matters, serve on numerous committees and task forces, and fill administrative appointments in local, state, and federal government. Because of these diverse activities in the political arena, organized labor has the potential to influence the political decision-making process. While there is sharp disagreement concerning labor's impact on government and the policy-making process, trade unions have the potential to be a political force.

AN UNDERSTANDING OF LABOR RELATIONS CONTRIBUTES TO A BETTER INFORMED CITIZENRY

Even if an individual never has direct contact with a labor organization, the study of labor relations can significantly contribute to one's understanding of the American economy. On any given day, the newspaper or television newscasts will contain labor-related items. Recently, a local newspaper had, in one edition, articles concerning a breakdown in bargaining between firefighters and city negotiators; Polish worker unrest; violence associated with a strike by coal miners; complaints by postal worker union officials concerning delays in bargaining attributable to post office leadership; and a strike in major league baseball. This number of stories is not atypical. Because of the significance of labor-management relations to the American economy and political system, labor-related matters receive much attention from the news media. Therefore, the study of labor relations can also enhance one's understanding of current events.

An Approach to the Study of Labor Relations

Unlike some other disciplines, labor relations does not have a generally accepted theory or model around which its study can be built. Therefore, the study of labor relations can be approached in several different ways. John Dunlop's systems view of labor-management relations[18] is a useful place to begin discussion of the approach used in this book.

Dunlop's approach is helpful because it identifies the participants in the labor relations process as well as the outcomes of the process. The systems view also focuses attention on an important facet of labor relations—the interrelationships among the participants. Fig. 1.1 presents a diagram of Dunlop's systems approach.

Dunlop describes the major features of a systems approach in terms of:

- Three major participants (workers and their organizations; management and their representatives; and specialized government agencies such as the National Labor Relations Board).
- An ideology linking, to a substantial degree, the relationships among the participants. Dunlop defines an ideology as a "set of ideas and beliefs com-

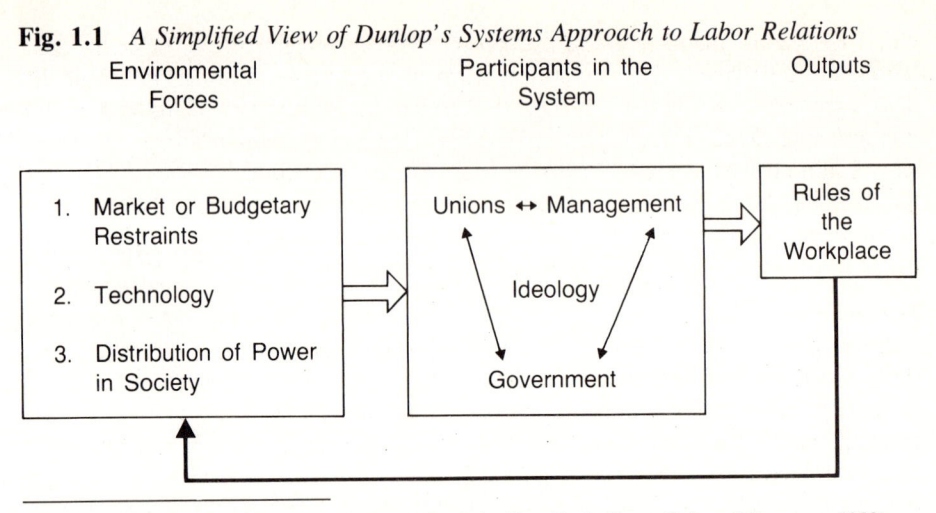

Fig. 1.1 *A Simplified View of Dunlop's Systems Approach to Labor Relations*

Environmental Forces	Participants in the System	Outputs

```
┌─────────────────────────┐      ┌─────────────────────┐      ┌──────────┐
│ 1. Market or Budgetary  │      │ Unions ↔ Management │      │ Rules of │
│    Restraints           │      │         ↕           │ ───▶ │   the    │
│ 2. Technology           │ ───▶ │     Ideology        │      │Workplace │
│ 3. Distribution of Power│      │         ↕           │      │          │
│    in Society           │      │     Government      │      │          │
└─────────────────────────┘      └─────────────────────┘      └──────────┘
            ▲                                                       │
            └───────────────────────────────────────────────────────┘
```

Source: John T. Dunlop, Industrial Relations Systems *(New York: Henry Holt and Company, 1958).*

monly held by the actors that helps to bind or integrate the system together as an entity."[19] As will be discussed in subsequent chapters, the ideology guiding labor-management relations in the United States has changed over the years.

- A context or environment in which the participants interact. While the environment can be defined by a number of different factors, Dunlop focused on three: market or budgetary constraints; technological characteristics of the workplace; and the distribution of power in the larger society.
- An output occurring as a result of the interaction of the participants. The output resulting from the interactions among labor, management and government is a network of rules governing the workplace and work community. This network of rules includes very diverse elements such as the nation's labor policy and the labor agreement establishing the major conditions of employment in a specific company.

THE PHASES OF LABOR RELATIONS

The Dunlop model describes a situation at a point in time. When labor-management relations are examined over time, three distinct phases can be identified. Before a union has the right to participate with management in establishing the rules of the workplace, the nation's public policy requires the union to be selected by a majority of the employees as their bargaining agent. Therefore, the first phase of the relationship between labor and management is the process by which the workers designate the union to represent them. Once the workers decide to have the union represent them, labor relations enters its second phase. In this phase, labor and management work through the negotiations process to jointly determine the major terms of employment, that is, the rules of the workplace. Once agreement is reached on the conditions of employment, labor relations enters its third phase. During the life of the labor agreement, the parties will have to resolve disagreements over the interpretation and application of the contract. During each phase of labor relations, the problems confronted by labor and management are basically different. The approaches for resolving the problems are also different. The following sections describe in more detail the nature of the problems and approaches for handling these problems in each of the three phases of the labor-management relationship.

The union-organizing process. Problems may develop involving organized labor and management over the union representation issue. Workers may believe their ability to secure desired benefits such as higher pay and improved benefits may be enhanced by union representation. At the same time, the employer may recognize that the employees' interest in unionism is the initial step in the erosion of management's unilateral control over the work organization. The problem concerns management's obligation to deal with the organization representing its employees. During the early years of the American trade union movement, much industrial strife and unrest was associated with union attempts to gain employer recognition. Because of these problems, government, through legislation, court decisions, and administrative rulings, began exercising control over the union-organizing process. Today, labor-management conflict over the union recognition issue and the tactics used to influence the workers' decision concerning union recognition are subject to regulation by the nation's labor policy.

Contract negotiations. The second phase of the relationship between labor and management occurs after the employer recognizes the union as the workers' bargaining agent. At this time, disagreements center on the role played by the union in the organization's decision-making processes. Typically, employers recognize the need to provide competitive wages, benefits, and levels of worker participation to attract, maintain and motivate an effective work force. However, employees, through their unions, may desire better wages and benefits and a louder voice in decision making than the employer is willing to offer voluntarily. Conflict may develop over how and to what extent employees through their union will share in the making of decisions influencing the workers' jobs. In the United States, collective bargaining has developed to accommodate the conflict that almost inevitably develops between labor and management over wages, benefits, and other conditions of employment. Through the collective bargaining process, a written agreement is developed that summarizes the negotiated settlement and identifies the subjects over which management has surrendered its right to make decisions unilaterally.

Contract interpretation and administration. The third phase of labor relations emerges after the written agreement is in effect. Differences of opinion between labor and management can develop over the interpretation or administration of the collective bargaining agreement. For example, the labor contract could specify that the employer must have "just cause" for discharging an employee. The company terminates an employee found sleeping on the job. The company contends that sleeping

Table 1.1 *Types of Conflict and Approaches for Resolving Conflict in Labor Relations*

Source of Conflict	Approach to resolving conflict
A question concerning the workers' desire for union representation exists; i.e., union presses for recognition while management resists the organizing efforts	Public policy (labor laws, court decisions, and administrative rulings) establishes procedures regulating labor and management behavior during organizing campaigns
Disagreements between labor and management concerning the rules of the workplace (wages, hours, and other working conditions)	Collective bargaining
Disagreements over the interpretation or application of an existing labor agreement	Grievance procedure with binding arbitration as established through collective bargaining

on the job provides just cause for discharge. The union claims it does not. In other words, the parties to the agreement disagree over the meaning of the term "just cause." It would be possible for the union to go on strike to pressure management into agreeing with the union's interpretation of the contract. However, such a practice would be highly disruptive to both the employer and employees. Stable, efficient, effective labor relations require a mechanism for resolving disputes arising during the life of the labor agreement without resorting to costly, disruptive strikes. The mechanism found in most labor agreements is a grievance procedure with arbitration.

This book will discuss each phase of labor relations. Also, the processes and procedures developed to minimize and resolve such conflict and promote cooperation are examined. Table 1.1 presents a summary of the three phases of labor-management relations and the general problem faced by the parties in each phase, and also identifies the major approaches for resolving each type of conflict.

An Overview of the Text

The chapters to follow are, in general, organized around the three phases of labor-management relations just discussed. Major sections of the book examine the nature of the problem characterizing each phase; the impact of the problems on workers, unions, management, government, and the public; and approaches to the resolution of the problems. However, before delving into the study of labor relations, it is necessary to have a good understanding of the participants (or actors, if using Dunlop's terminology) in labor relations—organized labor, management, and government.

SECTION I

The remainder of Section I examines these major parties to the labor-management relationship: government, organized labor, and management. The significance of the nation's labor policy for labor-management relations is underscored in Chapters 2 and 3. Chapter 2 reviews the evolution of the nation's policy toward labor relations.

A better understanding of today's labor policy can be obtained by knowing how this policy developed and why. The belief that knowing the historical development of an issue enhances one's understanding of the current state of affairs is one of the underpinnings of this book. Table 1.2 outlines the approach to labor history used here.

Table 1.2 *A Dialogue on the Study of Labor History as Part of a Book on Contemporary Labor Relations*

Almost any student	*The authors*
	Each of us has taught labor relations and collective bargaining for a number of years. A frequent complaint we hear from students is that labor history is boring and irrelevant.
Well, isn't it boring and irrelevant?	To many people, labor history is boring because it is considered irrelevant. To avoid this, it is necessary to link labor history with the contemporary scene. To make the topic interesting, it is necessary to establish its relevance.
How can this be done?	The approach in this book is to build into each chapter a discussion of the historical evolution of the major issues of concern in the chapter. With a historical perspective in mind, a better understanding of the contemporary issues can be obtained.
Why is a "historical perspective" so important?	To understand current events and be better able to predict what will happen in the future, it is necessary to understand the past. Today's events are not usually the results of happenstance. Typically, they are the result of a continual evolution, trial and error, and experimentation. Knowing the history or evolution of an issue provides us a more thorough understanding of the current situation.
That sounds good in principle. Can you give me some examples of how labor history improves my understanding of current events?	That's easy. You might wonder why unions generally resist the use of court injunctions in labor disputes. Today's reaction to the injunction is, to a degree, attributable to the oppression faced by trade unionists in the late 1800s and early 1900s as a result of widespread use of the injunction. Also, the American trade union movement is organized the way it is with power usually concentrated in the international unions because other forms of organization have been tried in the past and failed. Without knowledge of the past, the reasons unions look the way they do today might not be fully understood.

Table 1.2 *(Continued)*

Almost any student	*The authors*
Okay, an understanding of labor history will help my understanding of contemporary labor-management relations. How is labor history handled in this book?	Most labor relations books have a separate chapter on labor history. Then, elsewhere in the text, the contemporary issues are discussed. Only limited efforts are made to link the historical evolution of an issue with its current condition. It is not surprising that the relevancy of labor history is challenged.
	In this book, the historical dimensions of an issue are presented in the same chapter as the discussion of the contemporary situation. This allows the relationships between history and current events to be clearly established. Lessons from the past can be learned and their implications for the present and future fully appreciated.
That makes sense. Thanks.	Wait, there's more.
I was afraid of that.	We don't want to give the impression that labor history is of interest only because of its application to current events. Labor history is inherently interesting. It is a chapter of United States history about which most Americans have only limited knowledge. The American trade union movement has had more than its share of colorful individuals attached to it. The evolving labor movement had its victories and defeats, acts of courage, and despicable acts of violence. The people and events that make up the subject of labor history provide a fascinating view of American culture.

Chapter 2 provides a historical perspective on today's labor policy. The evolution of labor policy through its antilabor, laissez-faire, and prolabor phases and, finally, the development of a relatively balanced approach is presented. Chapter 3 focuses on the basic provisions of the nation's most important current labor laws. More detailed examinations of specific provisions of the laws are presented in later chapters along with discussions of how public policy influences the issues discussed in those chapters.

Chapters 2 and 3 are intended to point out the important role government, through its public policy toward labor, plays as a participant in the labor relations process. From an understanding of government's role and the legal environment, attention turns to the other participants—organized labor and management.

Chapter 4 examines union structure and government. After looking at the evolution of unions as organizations, the key elements of the unions' organizational structure are identified and their roles defined. This chapter also looks at some of the problems characterizing labor organizations such as racketeering, financial malfeasance, and rank-and-file membership apathy.

Labor relations are an important functional concern in unionized firms, much as finance, accounting, production, and marketing. They are an area of a firm's operation that can have important implications for the firm's success or failure. Chapter 5 examines different ways companies organize their resources to handle labor-management relations. It also delves into non-union firms and how they organize and operate to deal with employee relations.

To recapitulate, Section I provides an introduction to the three major participants in the labor relations process identified by Dunlop's systems approach—workers and their representatives (unions), management and government. Unions and management interact in a legal environment created by government actions including legislation, court rulings, and the actions of administrative agencies. The chapters in Section I provide an understanding of the participants so that the patterns of their interactions and areas of conflict and cooperation can be explored in subsequent chapters.

SECTION II

This section is concerned with the time period in which initial conflict between organized labor and management is likely to develop—the union organizing process. It is at this time unions encourage workers to designate the union as their representative in the collective bargaining process. At the same time, employers are likely to resist these organizing efforts. Chapter 6 examines worker attitudes toward unions and explores their motives with regard to the unionization issue. A model is presented to help identify and explain the factors influencing the workers' decision to unionize. Chapter 7 looks at the process through which workers desiring union representation can obtain it. This chapter reviews public policy regulating labor-management conflict during union organizing drives. It also reviews techniques used by unions to organize workers and management to resist union organizing efforts.

SECTION III

In general, if the majority of the workers in a unit desire union recognition, then the employer must bargain with the union over wages, hours, and other terms and conditions of employment. Typically, the union strives for better wages and conditions than would be voluntarily provided by the employer. Therefore, disagreements and conflict over these issues are likely to develop. Collective bargaining is the approach developed over the years by the parties and endorsed by the nation's labor policy for resolving disagreements over conditions of employment. Today, collective bargaining and efforts to make it work effectively are key components of labor relations. Because of the importance of collective bargaining to labor relations, Sections III and IV (six chapters) are devoted to its examination.

Collective bargaining has two major dimensions. It has a procedural aspect concerned with the theory, strategies, and tactics surrounding the negotiation of a collective bargaining agreement. There is also a substantive dimension. This is concerned with the subjects or issues over which the parties negotiate. When these topics are included in the labor agreement, they represent the output of the collective bargaining process. In Dunlop's terminology, they constitute the network of rules so important to labor relations. A sound understanding of labor relations requires knowledge of both the procedural and substantive aspects of collective bargaining.

Section III explores the procedural aspects of collective bargaining. Chapter 8 presents an introduction to collective bargaining. The objectives of collective bargaining are defined and the nature of the collective bargaining relationships examined. In addition to providing a theoretical overview of the collective bargaining process, and the role of the strike in the process, Chapter 8 also deals with the legal requirements of "good faith" bargaining. Chapter 9 builds on the overview provided in the preceding chapter and describes how these points can be applied; this chapter provides a detailed examination of how collective bargaining works in practice. Preparations for negotiations, contract ratification, and strikes are also discussed. The strike is an essential part of the collective bargaining process. Because of this, different aspects of the strike issue are discussed in each of the chapters in Section III. While strikes are an integral part of the collective bargaining process, they are expensive and inconvenient to all parties involved. Therefore, many labor and management representatives as well as government officials work to eliminate, or at least decrease, the likelihood that strikes will occur. Chapter 10 deals with techniques designed to improve bargaining so strikes are less likely. Also, alternatives to the strike are discussed.

SECTION IV

This section is concerned with the substantive aspects of collective bargaining. Chapter 11 examines a set of issues discussed almost every time labor and management sit down to negotiate a labor agreement—wages and salaries. This chapter looks at factors influencing the size of negotiated wage adjustments; procedures for establishing a wage and salary structure for a firm; and related wage issues such as shift differentials and overtime pay. The legislation affecting workers' wages is also reviewed in Chapter 11. Chapter 12 focuses on supplemental compensation, frequently referred to as fringe benefits. Factors associated with the rapid spread of fringe benefits are examined and different types of fringe benefits are discussed. Chapter 13 examines the third category of subjects bargained over by the parties—institutional issues. Major topics covered in this chapter include union security, managerial prerogatives, and seniority.

SECTION V

Attention shifts in this section from issues surrounding the negotiation of a labor agreement to the third phase of labor relations—administration of an existing contract. As previously discussed, labor and management are likely to disagree occasionally over the interpretation of their agreement. Section V examines the procedures developed to deal with disputes over the meaning of the contract. Chapter 14 is concerned with grievance procedures. A grievance procedure is a multistep process through which the parties attempt to resolve their disagreement. This chapter reviews different types of grievance procedures; presents a model useful for explaining why workers file grievances; and discusses ways the parties can make grievance procedures more effective. The last step of most grievance procedures is arbitration. Arbitration is used when labor and management cannot settle disagreements over the contract's interpretation on their own. The dispute is submitted to a neutral third party, known as an arbitrator, who makes a decision resolving the conflict. Chapter 15 examines grievance arbitration. The public policy affecting arbitration is discussed; the advantages and disadvantages of arbitration are reviewed; and procedures for preparing a case for arbitration are also presented.

SECTION VI

The first fifteen chapters of the book focus on private-sector labor relations in the United States. The book's final section expands this perspective considerably by examining labor relations in the public sector and international labor relations.

While there are many similarities between labor relations in the private and public sectors, there are also a number of dissimilarities. Chapter 16 provides an overview of public-sector labor relations. It examines factors contributing to union organizing in the public sector lagging behind the private sector and the causes for the rapid spread of public sector unionization since the 1960s. The chapter also examines the factors differentiating public- and private-sector labor relations and some of the major challenges to effective collective bargaining in the public sector. Chapter 17 examines the government policies affecting labor relations in the public sector. The evolution of public policy is discussed and the major features of current legislation reviewed. The chapter also discusses the effects of the collective bargaining process on the public sector.

With the growth of American multinational businesses and intensified foreign competition, an important link exists between labor relations in the United States and abroad. Chapter 18 deals with union-management relations in other countries. This chapter examines labor relations in several foreign countries. Then, efforts to achieve multinational collective bargaining are explored.

Thus, an attempt has been made to organize this book in a logical order that will enhance your understanding of labor relations. Attention now turns to an introduction to each of the major participants in the labor relations process. In Chapter 2, the emerging role of government and the evolution of the nation's labor policy are examined.

Discussion Questions

1. This chapter identified a number of trends likely to affect labor-management relations. Identify three other trends likely to be observed in the United States that could influence labor-management relations. What effects on labor-management relations could these trends have?
2. Who are the major participants in the labor relations process?
3. What types of problems are likely to develop between organized labor and management? In general, what devices have been developed to help control and resolve each type of conflict?

Notes

1. Jack Barbash, "The Ideology of Industrial Relations," *Proceedings of the Industrial Relations Research Association* (Madison: n.p., 1980), pp. 453–4.
2. John R. Commons et al., *History of Labour in the United States,* vol. 1 (New York: The Macmillan Co., 1918), p. 315.
3. Sanford Cohen, *Labor in the United States* (Columbus, Ohio: Charles E. Merrill Books, Inc., 1960), p. 71.
4. Jack Barbash, "Values in Industrial Relations: The Case of the Adversary Relationship," *Proceedings of the Industrial Relations Research Association* (Madison: n.p., 1981), p. 1.
5. Adapted material from pp. 20–21 in *Goals and Strategy in Collective Bargaining* by Frederick H. Harbison and John R. Coleman. Copyright, 1951, by Harper & Row, Publishers, Inc. Reprinted by permission of Harper & Row, Publishers, Inc.
6. Barbash, "Values in Industrial Relations," p. 3.
7. Ibid., p. 6.
8. "A Deal That Could Put a Brake on Car Costs," *Business Week,* 25 January 1981, p. 26.
9. "Tasting a New Kind of Power," *Business Week,* 1 February 1982, p. 16.
10. "What the Teamsters Pact Won't Do," *Business Week,* 1 February 1982, pp. 17–18.
11. "Quality of Work Life Catching On," *Business Week,* 21 September 1981, p. 76.
12. Irving Bluestone, "Quality-of-Work-Life Goals Fulfill Union Goals," *World of Work Reports,* December 1981, p. 91.
13. David Lewin, "Collective Bargaining and the Quality of Work Life," *Organizational Dynamics,* Autumn 1981, p. 44.

14. "A Bitter Standoff at American Standard," *Business Week,* 11 January 1982, p. 46.

15. Glenn W. Miller, review of *Labor Relations,* Arthur A. Sloane and Fred Witney, in *Industrial and Labor Relations Review* 31 (January 1978): 261.

16. U. S. Department of Labor, Bureau of Labor Statistics, *Handbook of Labor Statistics* (Washington, D. C.: Government Printing Office, 1980), p. 412.

17. U. S. Department of Labor, Bureau of Labor Statistics, *Directory of National Unions and Employee Associations* (Washington, D. C.: Government Printing Office, 1979), p. 66.

18. John Dunlop, *Industrial Relations Systems* (New York: Henry Holt and Company, 1958).

19. Ibid., p. 16.

Chapter 2

THE EVOLUTION OF PUBLIC POLICY TOWARD LABOR

Herm Tuttle has worked for Cramer Industries, a small automobile parts manufacturer, since 1931. He has been a member of the union since it organized the Cramer plant in 1937. Friday is Herm's last day on the job; he is retiring. While he is looking forward to retirement, he also has some concerns. He knows he is going to be able to keep busy and have a full life after leaving his job, so retirement doesn't concern him. He is worried about his union and its ability to continue to serve worker needs. The new people coming into the union don't seem to care about it. They don't want to work for the union. During a recent strike, many workers were unwilling to walk the picket line. Some even continued to work while the union was on strike. This never happened in the old days.

Didn't they remember the struggle of the older workers to build a strong union? Herm recalls something George Meany, long-time president of the AFL-CIO, said once while testifying before a Congressional committee: "Think back to the time when there were no job safety standards, no paid vacations, no sick leave, no pensions. Remember the company store, company towns, company unions, company politicians. . . ."

Herm remembers that the "good old days" were not particularly good for most American workers. He also remembers that things began to change after the Wagner Act was passed in 1935. He remembers how hard he and several of his old friends worked to establish the union. If those new people who thought that everything was okay and that they no longer needed the union knew what it was like before the union, they'd feel differently. Low wages, no fringe benefits, the fear of saying anything because you might be fired—the union changed all that. Those young guys would have different attitudes, if they only knew. . . .

A number of factors have shaped the evolution of the American union movement. Changing economic conditions, union structure and government, industrial composition and technology are all factors that have influenced union development. However, none of these has had as profound an effect on the evolution of American unions as the nation's public policy toward labor.

Herm Tuttle was aware of the impact of public policy on unions. Prior to passage of legislation protecting the employees' right to organize and engage in collective bargaining, he believed workers were employed under adverse conditions. After passage of protective legislation, many changes occurred in the United States economy. Unions began to play a much more prominent role. Millions of workers joined labor organizations. Collective bargaining spread rapidly in large part because of a change in the nation's labor policy.

Workers' rights to unionize and engage in collective bargaining were not always protected as they are today. Over the years, public policy toward labor has changed dramatically. Public policy and labor-management relations are closely intertwined. Consequently, the evolution of the American union movement has been strongly influenced by the national policy toward organized labor. Before examining today's public policy toward labor, the topic of Chapter 3, the evolution of this policy will be discussed. After reading this chapter, you should understand:

- The changing role played by the courts in the formation of the nation's labor policy.
- The relationship between the legislative and judicial branches of government and how this relationship influenced public policy.
- How public policy affected the ability of unions to organize and engage in collective bargaining.
- The major pieces of labor legislation and the role of each in the evolution of public policy.

Sources of Public Policy

Throughout the history of the American trade union movement, labor-management relations have been influenced by the nation's labor policy. The public policy toward labor has its roots in common law, statute law, administrative rulings and court decisions. Together, these constitute a large, relatively well-defined body of rules that comprise the nation's labor policy. This policy establishes the legal "ground rules" for labor-management relations in the United States.

During the early history of the American unions, the courts were the primary source of public policy. In the absence of labor legislation, the judiciary determined policy toward organized labor through the application of common-law rules. Common-law rules rely on judicial precedent. Over the years, the courts decide cases. From these decisions, legal principles or rules develop which are applied in later cases. The courts, through the application of common-law principles, exercised tremendous control over the trade union movement from its earliest days in the late 1700s to the early twentieth century.

Starting in the late 1800s and continuing to the present time, statute law emerged as the primary source of public policy toward labor. Statute laws are those passed by the legislative branch of government, such as the United States Congress. However, this fact did not preclude the judicial branch of government from influencing labor policy. Even though there was a decreased use of common-law rules, the courts still interpreted statute law. Laws passed by the legislative branch of government could be reinforced or legislative intent undone, depending on the court's interpretation of the statute. With the emergence of statute law as the basis for national labor policy, administrative agencies such as the National Labor Relations Board and the National Mediation Board were created to administer the laws. While administrative agencies are largely responsible for the day-to-day interpretation and administration of the labor laws, many of their decisions are subject to judicial review.

The purpose of this chapter is to trace the evolution of United States public policy towards labor unions. First, the influence of common law on trade union activities will be examined. Then, some of the early legislative attempts to regulate trade union activities and the reaction of the judiciary to these attempts will be reviewed. The third major section of the chapter will examine the emergence of statute law as the basis for contemporary United States public policy toward labor.

Early Judicial Control of Trade Union Activities

Unions similar to those existing today first developed in the United States in the late 1700s. These early unions were made up of skilled craftsmen in trades such as printing and shoe making and were a reaction to the rapidly developing industrial revolution. As trade developed during the post–Revolutionary War era, competition among merchants intensified. This created pressures on the merchants to lower prices, and in turn, lower the wages paid to journeyman craftsmen. At about the same time, the journeymen were beginning to feel competitive pressures from semiskilled workers.[1] For example, cheaper shoes were being produced in factories utilizing new technologies and a division of labor. Such factories employed lower-skilled, and therefore, lower-paid employees. As a result, skilled shoemakers had problems competing with less expensive, factory-made shoes.

Early trade union activities, such as strikes for higher wages, were designed to help maintain the favorable economic position historically held by skilled workers. It was not long before these activities fell under court review.

THE CRIMINAL CONSPIRACY DOCTRINE

Criminal conspiracy is a common-law doctrine developed in England and used to limit concerted trade union activities such as strikes. English judges believed that when workers acted in combination through an organization such as a union, these actions interfered with the free operation of the English economy. Employers who gave in to worker demands would be at a competitive disadvantage relative to other employers in the same industry. Similarly, if all English employers gave in to demands for higher wages, then the increased prices for English products would inhibit the sale of goods in world trade. In addition to the economic arguments supporting limits on the rights of workers engaged in concerted activities, there was the issue of property rights. English judges believed the owners of business had a property right in the ownership and control of their business. The owners had the right to operate their businesses free from interference by unions. This was the case even though it meant workers were denied their right to join with others and engage in activities such as striking for higher wages.[2]

The common-law doctrine of criminal conspiracy was developed to prevent the concerted activities of workers from interfering with the British economy and the rights of employers to run their businesses. A conspiracy has been defined as "a combination of two or more persons who band together to prejudice the rights of others or of society."[3] Since the unions' concerted activities infringed upon the rights of employers to run their businesses and interfered with the operation of the English economy, they were found to be criminal conspiracies.

The logic supporting the application of the criminal conspiracy doctrine to the activities of organized labor is not very compelling. Charles O. Gregory points out that:

- There is nothing illegal about a combination of workers.
- There is nothing illegal about workers desiring a better standard of employment.
- There is nothing illegal about an individual's refusal to work.[4]

However, when a group of workers refused to work, that is, went on strike to obtain higher wages, they were found guilty of a criminal offense. When the English courts examined the conflicting rights of striking employees and employers' rights to operate free from worker interference, the employers' rights prevailed.

THE PHILADELPHIA CORDWAINERS CASE

The English common-law doctrine of criminal conspiracy was first applied to union activities in the United States in 1806. The case was popularly known as the Philadelphia Cordwainers decision.[5] After some master shoemakers unilaterally reduced the price paid for boots, a group of journeymen shoemakers (known as cordwainers) demanded the old price be reestablished. This involved a price increase of 25¢ to 75¢ per pair (depending upon the type of boot involved). When the masters refused to agree with the demands, some journeymen shoemakers decided to strike. During the strike, eight journeymen were arrested. They were indicted for actions constituting "a combination and conspiracy to raise their wages."[6]

In a landmark decision, the striking journeymen shoemakers were found guilty of a criminal conspiracy. In this decision, the judge applied the doctrine of criminal conspiracy found in English common law. He stated:

> A combination of working men to raise their wages may be considered in a two-fold point of view: one is to benefit themselves . . . The other is to injure those who do not join the (combination) . . . The rule of law condemns both.[7]

As a result of this decision, a combination of working men to raise wages was viewed as a criminal conspiracy that could be suppressed by the state.[8] In other words, it became illegal for a group of workers to strike to obtain more favorable terms of employment. Consequently, strikes could not be used effectively as long as such actions were subject to prosecution as criminal conspiracies.

During the next thirty years, there were a number of other cases in which trade union members were charged with conspiracy. The use of the criminal conspiracy doctrine did not completely stop workers from striking to improve working conditions. However, trade union activities were limited by the doctrine's application.

COMMONWEALTH v. HUNT DECISION

In 1842, the *Commonwealth v. Hunt* [9] case was decided. This decision marked a change in policy with regard to the application of the criminal conspiracy doctrine to organized labor. In this case, a union went on strike to establish a closed shop. A closed shop is an arrangement in which all workers have to belong to a union before they can be employed. The union was charged with having "unlawfully, permissively, deceitfully, unjustly and corruptly conspired not to work for any master who employed any workmen not a member of their union. . . ."[10]

The trade unionists were found guilty for participating in a criminal conspiracy. The decision was appealed to the Massachusetts State Supreme Court. Upon appeal, the indictment against the union was dismissed. Chief Justice Lemuel Shaw reasoned that the indictment only charged that the workers tried to get all employees to become members of their union. Shaw concluded that such an objective was not illegal. He rendered a masterful decision by declaring that labor organizations could be legally formed and pursue legal objectives. At the same time, the decision continued to allow criminal conspiracy charges to be filed against union activities under certain conditions. If either the union's objectives were illegal or if the union employed illegal methods when pursuing its goals, the basis for criminal conspiracy charges was still present.

The impact of the *Commonwealth v. Hunt* decision has been described as follows:

> It enabled workers to organize themselves into unions. It removed the fear that they would be subjected to criminal proceedings for merely joining a labor union. It also enabled other labor organizations to encourage membership in their unions and to get strength from their unity as their refusal to work with non-members was held by Justice Shaw not to be unlawful. Labor unions secured legal approval of the "closed shop" principle, which immeasurably strengthened the ranks and enhanced their prestige.[11]

DOCTRINE OF LEGAL ENDS AND LEGAL MEANS

The significance of the *Commonwealth v. Hunt* decision cannot be overestimated. It marked the beginning of the end of the criminal conspiracy doctrine in labor disputes. The decision was the foundation for the application of a new legal principle—the doctrine of illegal means and ends. Given the considerable prestige of Justice Shaw as a jurist, other judges began examining the methods used by unions and their objectives. If a judge found either the means or the objectives illegal, a charge of criminal conspiracy could still be leveled.

Subsequent to *Commonwealth v. Hunt,* trade unionists would occasionally be charged as participants in criminal conspiracies. Since judges had considerable discretion when examining unions' means and objectives, criminal conspiracy charges could still be used to deter trade union activities. However, by the late 1880s, the courts were not relying very heavily on the criminal conspiracy doctrine. Several reasons have been cited for the declining use of the criminal conspiracy doctrine:

- It was not fast enough. Since trials lasted several days, the union had additional time to damage the employer through its concerted activities.
- It was becoming more difficult to get witnesses to testify against unions.
- It became more difficult to obtain juries willing to convict trade unionists under the criminal conspiracy doctrine.[12]

THE USE OF COURT INJUNCTIONS IN LABOR DISPUTES

A court injunction is a common-law device requiring a party to refrain from an act that would cause another party irreparable harm. Injunctions are issued by equity courts which handle specific types of legal problems. Equity courts get involved in situations where an action would cause damages for which a monetary award would be an insufficient remedy. The primary advantage of an injunction is that it can be used quickly and decisively to stop an action likely to cause irreparable harm. The court injunction is an important and effective legal device whose use has not been questioned in most situations. However, when applied to labor disputes, the injunction became a very controversial issue.

A basic assumption underlying the use of the injunction in labor disputes was that the employer has a right to do business. It was argued that concerted activities by unions such as picketing and strikes irreparably harmed the employer's business. Consequently, the union's actions could be stopped by means of an injunction. An injunction could be obtained from a judge without the need for a time-consuming hearing. Once issued, the injunction had the full backing of the court. Individuals violating the injunction would be subjected to punishment, including fines and imprisonment, at the discretion of the judge—usually without the benefit of jury trial.[13]

If an employer believed a threatened or actual strike could harm its property or jeopardize its right to do business, a court injunction could be obtained. An attorney would go to a judge with affidavits specifying acts the union and its agents had done or were about to do that would cause the employer irreparable harm. The complaint usually maintained that the only remedy for the situation would be an injunction banning the union's activities. The employer would usually request an *ex parte* temporary restraining order. *Ex parte* means that the injunction would be issued without notice of a hearing. As a result, the injunction would be granted based on the employer's complaint without benefit of hearing the union's position in the case. Commonly, the employer's attorney would draft a temporary restraining order that would be taken to a judge (frequently one with a known antiunion bias) to be signed. Occasionally, the judge would make changes in the restraining order as presented by the employer's attorney. However, it was more usual for the judge to sign the order as presented by the attorney.[14]

Frequently, the restraining order relied on very general language. For example, the persons subject to the injunction would be broadly defined. In the *Debs* case, the injunction was issued against the defendant "and all persons combining and conspiring with them and all other persons whomsoever."[15] Similarly, the behaviors limited by the injunction were stated very broadly. Very often, any behavior interfering with the employer's business was subject to the restraining order. In their classic examination of the use of the injunction in labor disputes, Frankfurter and Greene cite the following example of the language used in a restraining order:

> In the *Gompers Case,* the defendants were enjoined from "interfering in any manner with . . . the complaintant's . . . business," from "declaring or threatening any boycott," from referring to the complaintant as "unfair," from "in any manner whatsoever impeding, obstructing, interfering with or restraining the complaintant's business."[16]

As can be seen, the language of restraining orders tended to be vague and could be interpreted to limit behavior clearly legal outside the context of a labor dispute.

There were a number of procedural problems associated with the use of injunctions in labor disputes, including:

- The injunctions were issued without giving the union the opportunity to present its side of the dispute.
- Injunctions were issued without sufficient proof. Frequently, the only evidence that the employer's business was harmed or could be harmed would be provided by company witnesses.
- The injunction's language was usually quite vague.
- There were no procedures for the prompt appeal of an injunction by the union.
- The injunction had the effect of denying the individual accused of the crime a fair trial. For example, if a striker was charged with contempt of court for violating an injunction, the individual would be tried before the judge issuing the injunction, not a jury.[17]

Once a judge was convinced that the union's action would cause the employer irreparable harm, a restraining order would be issued. Then, any of the actions specified in the injunction would be forbidden until the court had the opportunity to conduct a hearing on the matter. The hearing would be held at some later point in time. At the hearing, the restraining order would be either made permanent or vacated. However, by that time the strike would usually be resolved. The restraining order gained time for the employer to take action against the union leaders. Also, the legal proceedings associated with the injunctions drained the union's resources, preoccupied its leadership, and demoralized the strikers. In sum, the strike would probably be lost either because the union leaders abided by the injunction or because they were fined and jailed for failing to adhere to the injunction's conditions. Consequently, the court injunction emerged as a very effective device for thwarting union organizing activities and decreased the usefulness of concerted union activities such as strikes, picketing, and boycotts.

THE "YELLOW DOG" CONTRACT

The "yellow dog" contract was another device that, when reinforced by the court injunction, was a very effective mechanism for limiting union organizing activities. A "yellow dog" contract was an agreement signed by a worker not to join a union. The employer would have the employee sign the agreement as a precondition of employment; that is, workers not signing the contract would not be hired. If a union attempted to organize employees who signed "yellow dog" contracts, the employer would seek an injunction to stop the union. The company would contend that the union was encouraging the employee to violate their "yellow dog" contract. The legality of this procedure was established in the *Hitchman Coal & Coke Co. v. Mitchell*[18] decision issued by the United States Supreme Court in 1917. Prior to the *Hitchman* decision, workers who signed a "yellow dog" contract probably felt no moral compulsion when they violated it. The effect of the contract was primarily psychological. However, after the *Hitchman* case, a decision to ignore the "yellow dog" contract constituted a violation of the law.[19]

From the beginning of the American union movement until the late 1800s, the courts were the primary source of public policy regarding organized labor. The legal environment created by the courts greatly inhibited trade union activity. As previously discussed, the injunction and the "yellow dog" contract severely limited the effectiveness of trade union activities. It has been argued that the courts sided with employers in labor-management disputes because judges and businessmen were from the same social class. To a degree, this could have been the situation. A better explanation for the antilabor judicial environment is found when the prevailing attitude of the courts with respect to individual rights is examined. It was believed that American society was rooted in individual freedom. Consequently, when individual freedom was threatened either by private groups or by government, the courts tended to intervene on behalf of individuals' rights.[20] When trade union activities interfered with an employer's right to do business free from union interference or the right of the non-union employees to be free from union control, it was not surprising that the courts intervened in favor of individual rights. The rights of the individual prevailed over the rights of the group.

Early Legislative Attempts

THE ERDMAN ACT

Although the courts were the primary source of public policy throughout the 1800s, some interest in trade union activities was expressed by the legislative branch of government during the 1890s. In 1898, the United States Congress passed the Erdman Act. This legislation was intended to protect interstate commerce by establishing and maintaining industrial peace in the railroad industry. Section 10 of the Erdman Act outlawed the "yellow dog" contract and made it illegal to discharge an employee for belonging to a labor organization. It was also illegal to blacklist railroad employees. Blacklisting was a practice in which the names of employees active in union affairs would be circulated among employers who would then refuse to hire them. Once workers were discharged for union activities, it was very difficult for them to regain employment due to the blacklisting practice. By making the "yellow dog" contract and blacklisting illegal and prohibiting the discharge of employees for union activities, the Erdman Act attempted to eliminate some major causes of strikes in the railroad industry.

While the scope of the Erdman Act was rather narrow since it only affected railroad workers, it was a definite advance in labor relations law. It recognized that the legislative branch of government had a role to play in protecting workers' right to organize and engage in collective bargaining. It also reflected an awareness that industrial peace could be enhanced and burdens to interstate commerce removed by the passage of labor legislation. In addition to the Erdman Act, fifteen states passed similar legislation protecting the rights of some workers to unionize.[21]

These early attempts to regulate labor relations through legislation were undone by the courts in *Adair v. U.S.* (1908).[22] The United States Supreme Court declared Section 10 of the Erdman Act unconstitutional because it deprived without due process the railroads' freedom to contract as insured by the Constitution's Fifth Amendment. It was also found that the commerce clause of the Constitution did not give Congress the authority to regulate contractual relations between employers and employees.[23] In other words, the railroads had the right to establish terms and conditions of employment. Similarly, employees had the right to sign "yellow dog" contracts or to find employment elsewhere if they did not want to sign the agreement. As expected, *Adair v. U.S.* had an adverse effect on unions operating in the railroad industry. According to Lieberman, "it *(Adair v. U.S.)* undermined the strength of the existing unions and served to discourage further unionization. More than that, it in effect encouraged the railroads in their practice of blacklisting workers who were suspected of being active in unionization."[24] In 1915, the state-level laws similar to the Erdman Act were declared unconstitutional by the United States Supreme Court in the *Coppage v. Kansas* case.[25]

As a result of the *Adair v. U.S.* and *Coppage v. Kansas* decisions, the early attempts to regulate labor relations by legislation proved futile. The Supreme Court refused to allow legislation to impinge upon the employer's right to engage in business free from interference. At about the same time Congress was attempting to protect the rights of employees to organize through the Erdman Act, another piece of legislation was passed which was interpreted by the Supreme Court as limiting trade union activities. This was the Sherman Anti-Trust Act.

UNIONS AND ANTI-TRUST LEGISLATION

The Sherman Act was passed in 1890. On the surface, the primary purpose of the legislation appeared to be the limitation of business activities interfering with interstate commerce. The intent of the Sherman Act was presented in Section 1 which stated:

> Every contract, combination in the form of a trust or otherwise, or conspiracy, in restraint of trade or commerce . . . is hereby declared illegal. Every person who shall make any such contract or engage in any such combination or conspiracy shall be guilty of a misdemeanor, and, on conviction thereof shall be punished by fine not exceeding five thousand dollars, or by imprisonment one year or by both punishments in the discretion of the court.

Although unions were not specifically mentioned in the Sherman Act, the intent of Congress to have the legislation include trade union activities was questioned. For a number of years, only business activities restraining interstate commerce were prosecuted under the Sherman Act. However, in 1901, a union attempt to organize a hat manufacturing company in Danbury, Connecticut, led to a court case in which the applicability of the Sherman Act to organized labor was examined.

The Danbury Hatters case. In 1908, the United States Supreme Court rendered its famous *Loewe v. Lawler* decision,[26] popularly known as the Danbury Hatters case.

EXHIBIT 2.1
A Secondary Boycott

A boycott is a refusal to do business with or handle the products of a particular company. When a dispute exists between the primary employer and primary union, this is known as a primary dispute. To increase pressure on the primary employer, the primary union pressures secondary employers to cease doing business with the primary employer. These secondary pressures constitute a secondary boycott. Secondary pressures could be exerted directly or through the secondary employer's unions. The secondary boycott was frequently used when the primary employer was able to keep operating despite the primary union being on strike. In an effort to shut down the primary employer's operation, the union could encourage secondary employers to stop providing raw materials and delivering or purchasing the primary employer's finished products. While the primary strike was unsuccessful, a successful secondary boycott could seriously affect the primary employer's business. As a result of the Danbury Hatters decision, secondary boycotts limiting the flow of commerce among states violated the Sherman Act.

Fig. 2.1 *Diagram of a Secondary Boycott*

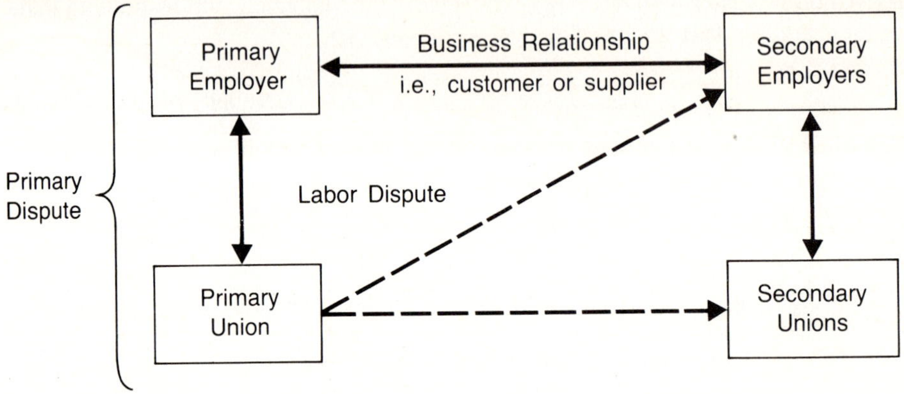

In this case, a company refused to recognize the union. In response, the union went on strike. To supplement the strike, the union initiated a secondary boycott of the company's hats. It did this by going to the hat company's customers and asking them not to purchase hats from the company involved in the labor dispute. It was also suggested the customers themselves might be boycotted if they refused to cooperate with the union's boycott request. The boycott was effective. There was a decrease in the demand for the company's hats. See Fig. 2.1 for a diagram of the secondary boycott technique. The company initiated court action contending that the union's activities constituted an illegal restraint of trade under the Sherman Act. An interesting feature of the Sherman Act is that violators can be required to pay triple damages. In this case, triple damages amounted to approximately $240,000.

In the Supreme Court's decision, the Sherman Act was interpreted to include trade union activities restraining interstate commerce. Writing for the majority, Chief Justice Fuller stated:

> In our opinion, the combination described in the declaration is a combination "in restraint of trade or commerce among the several states," in the sense that those words are used in the act, and the action can be restrained accordingly.
>
> And that conclusion rests on many judgments of this court, to the effect that the act prohibits *any combination whatever* to secure action which essentially obstructs the free flow of commerce between states, or restricts, in that regard, liberty of the trader to engage in business.[27] (emphasis added)

The impact of the Danbury Hatters decision on organized labor cannot be overestimated. Trade unions were denied use of the secondary boycott—a device capable of exerting tremendous pressure on recalcitrant employers. The Sherman Act was enforceable through civil suits providing for triple damages, criminal suits allowing both fines and imprisonment, and injunctive relief intended to stop activities restraining trade. Such enforcement placed severe limitations on trade union activities.

Strikes and boycotts restraining interstate commerce could be enjoined. Also, individual union members could be sued to recover triple damage rewards attributable to the violations of the Sherman Act by their union leaders.[28]

The Danbury Hatters decision prompted organized labor to work to remove union activities from the coverage of the anti-trust laws. These efforts, in part, led to passage of the Clayton Act.

The Clayton Act   The Clayton Act was passed by Congress in 1914. The portion of the legislation explicitly concerned with trade union activities was a response to the Danbury Hatters decision. With Section 6 and Section 20 of the Clayton Act, Congress attempted to exempt trade union activities from anti-trust legislation.[29] The text of Sections 6 and 20 is presented in Exhibit 2.2. Initially, organized labor was very

---

EXHIBIT 2.2
Sections 6 and 20 of the Clayton Act

Sec. 6. That the labor of a human being is not a commodity or article of commerce. Nothing contained in the anti-trust laws shall be construed to forbid the existence and operation of labor, agricultural, or horticultural organizations, instituted for the purposes of mutual help, and not having capital stock or conducted for profit, or to forbid or restrain individual members of such organizations from lawfully carrying out the legitimate objects thereof; nor shall such organizations, or the members thereof, be held or construed to be illegal combinations or conspiracies in restraint of trade, under the anti-trust laws.

Sec. 20. That no restraining order or injunction shall be granted by any court of the United States, or a judge or the judges thereof, in any case between an employer and employees, or between employers and employees, or between employees, or between persons employed and persons seeking employment, involving, or growing out of, a dispute concerning terms or conditions of employment, unless necessary to prevent irreparable injury to property, or to a property right, of the party making the application, for which injury there is no adequate remedy at law, and such property or property right must be described with particularity in the application, which must be in writing and sworn to by the applicant or by his agent or attorney.

And no such restraining order or injunction shall prohibit any person or persons, whether singly or in concert, from terminating any relation of employment, or from ceasing to perform any work or labor, or from recommending, advising, or persuading others by peaceful means so to do; or from attending at any place where any such person or persons may lawfully be, for the purpose of peacefully obtaining or communicating information, or from peacefully persuading any person to work or to abstain from working; or from ceasing to patronize or to employ any party to such dispute, or from recommending, advising, or persuading others by peaceful and lawful means so to do; or from paying or giving to, or withholding from, any person engaged in such dispute, any strike benefits or other moneys or things of value; or from peaceably assembling in a lawful manner, and for lawful purposes; or from doing any act or thing which might lawfully be done in the absence of such dispute by any party thereto; nor shall any of the acts specified in this paragraph be considered or held to be violations of any law of the United States.

pleased with the passage of the Clayton Act. Samuel Gompers, president of the American Federation of Labor, declared the Clayton Act as labor's "magna carta." The Clayton Act was intended to aid unions in two major ways:

- Prevent the indiscriminate use of injunctions by limiting the situations in which they could be issued and preventing the issuance of broad, sweeping injunctions.
- Declared trade union activities were not illegal combinations under the Sherman Anti-Trust Act.[30]

Unfortunately from organized labor's point of view, the victory associated with passage of the Clayton Act was relatively short-lived. The Clayton Act was interpreted by the Supreme Court very narrowly. As a result, most trade union activities were still subject to the nation's anti-trust legislation.

The Duplex Printing Press Co. v. Deering Decision.[31]   This decision was rendered in 1921 by the United States Supreme Court. In this case, the International Association of Machinists attempted to unionize the Duplex Printing Press Company by calling an organizational strike to demonstrate the extent of worker support for the union. However, this strike was ineffective. Only 13 out of approximately 300 employees joined the union. To buttress its organizational strike, the union instituted a secondary boycott. Unions operating in Duplex's major product market, New York City, refused to deliver, install, or service Duplex printing presses. In response to the boycott, the company requested and secured an injunction limiting the unions' boycott activities. However, upon appeal by the union, the injunction was vacated on the grounds that the secondary boycott was legal under Section 20 of the Clayton Act. Then, the company appealed this decision to the United States Supreme Court.

The Supreme Court ruled the Clayton Act did not provide organized labor a total exemption from anti-trust legislation. It was held that the secondary boycott limited the sale of Duplex presses in New York City and encouraged the sale of competitors' (who had agreements with the International Association of Machinists) presses. Relying on its Danbury Hatters decision as precedent, the Supreme Court ruled that the unions' boycott violated the Sherman Act. This decision was reached despite passage of the Clayton Act in the years between the Danbury Hatters and *Duplex Printing Press Co. v. Deering* decisions.

The court maintained that the Clayton Act only minimally changed the nation's anti-trust legislation as it affected organized labor. It reached this decision, in part, by providing a very narrow definition of Section 20 of the Clayton Act. As indicated in Exhibit 2.2, Section 20 stated that restraining orders could not be issued in disputes between "an employer and employees." This was interpreted to mean a company and its employees. Therefore, whenever nonemployees, such as trade unionists in New York supporting the Duplex boycott, became involved in the dispute, it would still be enjoinable under the Sherman Act.

The *Duplex v. Deering* decision was a major setback for organized labor. The protections thought to be extended by the Clayton Act evaporated with this decision. As a result, employers continued to apply for injunctions in situations where the union's activities restrained interstate trade.

The double standard. As a result of judicial interpretation, anti-trust legislation was applied to the activities of both business and organized labor restraining interstate commerce. However, the legislation was not applied equally. While a "rule of reason" was applied to the activities of business, no comparable rule was applied to the trade unions. When reviewing cases involving businesses, the Supreme Court differentiated between restraints of trade that were "reasonable" and "unreasonable." With this approach, not all business combinations restraining trade were considered illegal—only those that unreasonably did so. This created problems since the terms "reasonable" and "unreasonable" had no precise definitions. Therefore, it was not possible to interpret the meaning of the Sherman Act objectively.[32] However, it appears that the term "reasonable" was broadly defined when applied to businesses. As a result, a number of business activities restraining the flow of interstate commerce were found not to be violations of the Sherman Act.

The "rule of reason" approach to anti-trust cases was not similarly applied by the Supreme Court in restraint-of-trade cases involving unions. A clear example of the double standard is found in the application of the "rule of reason" in the *Coronado Coal Co. v. the United Mine Workers of America* decisions (1922 and 1925).[33] In this lengthy and involved case involving two appearances before the United States Supreme Court, the company established that a strike by union miners prevented 5,000 tons of coal from being produced daily. By stopping coal production, the union decreased the amount of coal in interstate commerce. In this case, little consideration was given to the amount of coal kept out of interstate commerce due to the strike. Taylor and Witney point out that "when the court concluded that a conspiracy existed to reduce the amount of coal in commerce, the conviction of the labor unions was assured. This same verdict would have been handed down, no doubt, regardless of the amount of coal in question."[34] There was no consideration by the court whether the restraint of trade was "reasonable" or "unreasonable" as in cases involving businesses.

In 1927, organized labor felt the full impact of the double standard. In the *Bedford Cut Stone Co. v. the Journeyman Stone Cutters' Association*[35] decision, the inconsistent application of the Sherman Act in cases involving unions and businesses was clearly demonstrated. A group of workers refused to handle stone quarried at sites in the Bedford-Bloomington, Illinois area. The purpose of this boycott was to pressure the mine operators to deal with the union. The Bedford Cut Stone Co. sought an injunction to stop the union from boycotting its product. The request for an injunction was denied. This decision was ultimately appealed to the United States Supreme Court. The Supreme Court decided that the boycott was an unreasonable restraint of trade that limited the shipment of stone products in interstate commerce. In an eloquent dissenting opinion, Justice Brandeis succinctly described the inconsistent application of the "rule of reason" and the resulting double standard in cases involving business and unions. Brandeis stated:

> If, on the undisputed facts of this case, refusal to work can be enjoined, Congress created by the Sherman Law and the Clayton Act an instrument for imposing restraints upon labor which reminds of involuntary servitude. The Sherman Law was held in the *United States v. United States Steel Corp.* . . . to permit capitalists to combine in a single corporation 50 percent of the steel industry of the United States dominating the trade through its vast resources. The Sherman Law was held in *United States v. United Steel Machinery Co.* . . . to permit capitalists to combine in another corporation practically the whole steel machinery industry of the country, necessarily giving it a position of dominance over steel manufacturing in America. It would, indeed, be strange if Congress had by the same act willed to deny members of a small craft of workmen the right to cooperate in simply refraining to work, when that course was the only means of protection against a combination of militant and powerful employers. I cannot believe that Congress did so.[36]

As a result of the Supreme Court's actions, the use of organized labor's traditional weapons in disputes such as strikes and boycotts was severely curtailed. In situations where it could be argued that a strike or boycott interfered with interstate commerce, an injunction could be issued under the Sherman Anti-Trust Act. Organized labor was equally concerned with the fact that the businesses received more favorable treatment under the anti-trust legislation than unions. These factors prompted labor to pressure Congress for legislative relief from the anti-trust laws and court injunctions.

The Emergence of Statute Law

During the late 1800s, labor leaders pressed for the passage of legislation limiting usage of anti-union employer devices such as blacklisting and the "yellow dog" contract. Also, there was interest in legislation limiting the involvement of the courts in labor-management relations and seeking an exemption from anti-trust legislation.[37] As already discussed, these early legislative attempts such as the Erdman Act and Clayton Act proved unsuccessful because they were either declared unconstitutional or interpreted narrowly by the United States Supreme Court. However, during the 1920s, legislative interest in labor relations increased. At about the same time, the attitude of the courts toward labor legislation became more supportive. As a result, statute law as the basis for United States labor policy became more important and the judiciary began playing a relatively less significant role.

The Railway Labor Act of 1926 was the first piece of federal legislation protecting employee rights to organize and engage in collective bargaining to stand the test of constitutionality. Over the following decade, several other pieces of legislation supportive of the collective bargaining process were passed. In a relatively few years, the antilabor legal environment created largely by the judiciary was supplanted by a prolabor public policy. This section will examine the major pieces of legislation making the transition from an antilabor legal environment to one supportive of union organizing and the collective bargaining process.

THE RAILWAY LABOR ACT OF 1926

The railways were a central part of the American economy in the 1920s. It was apparent that a stable, peaceful system of industrial relations was needed to prevent disruptive labor unrest in the railroad industry. A number of earlier attempts to write legislation to maintain labor peace in the railroad industry proved unsuccessful. In 1924, a new approach was taken. At the urging of President Calvin Coolidge, the railroad companies and unions worked out a procedure to bring about industrial stability. This proposal was the basis for the legislation passed by Congress in 1926.

The Railway Labor Act (RLA) relied very heavily on the collective bargaining process.[38] It specified that employees had the right to organize without employer interference and bargain collectively through representatives of their own choosing. Also, the railroad employers were required to bargain with their employees' representative. Only if the bargaining process broke down would the government become involved in a labor dispute.

Given the resistance exhibited by the courts in the past toward the regulation of labor relations by the federal government, there were serious questions about the constitutionality of the Railway Labor Act. In the *Texas and New Orleans Railroad Company v. Brotherhood of Railway and Steamship Clerks* case,[39] the company argued the Railway Labor Act was unconstitutional on the grounds that it impinged upon its First and Fifth Amendment rights. The company claimed these amendments allowed it to control decisions concerning the selection and discharge of employees. The Supreme Court rejected this argument, stating:

> The Railway Labor Act of 1926 does not interfere with the normal exercise of the right of the carrier to select the employees or discharge them. The statute is not aimed at the right of the employers but at the interference with the right of employees to have representatives of their own choosing. As carriers subject to the act have no constitutional right to interfere with the freedom of the employee in making their selections, they cannot complain of the statute on constitutional grounds.[40]

Additionally, the Supreme Court stated that Congress had the right to become involved in labor relations in the railroad industry because of the commerce clause of the Constitution. This is an argument that would be used in future years to provide a constitutional basis for federal regulation of labor relations.

Clearly, the Railway Labor Act marked a significant change in attitude toward labor relations by both Congress and the courts. While limited to the railroad industry, the RLA was more far-reaching than earlier legislative attempts. The legislation represented the federal government's endorsement of employees' right to organize and engage in collective bargaining. Collective bargaining was identified as the preferred method for resolving labor disputes. Also, the *Texas and New Orleans Railroad* decision established that the legislation was a valid exercise of congressional authority under the commerce clause of the Constitution. The Railway Labor Act marked the beginning of an era in which both Congress and the courts would be more protective of employees' right to organize and engage in collective bargaining. While this legislation was an improvement in the legal environment from organized labor's perspective, it affected a relatively small portion of the work force. This was because it was limited to the railroad industry. Also, the RLA was unresponsive to the major problems confronting trade unions: the court injunction and anti-trust legislation.

THE NORRIS–LA GUARDIA ACT

As a result of Supreme Court decisions such as *Duplex Printing Press Co. v. Deering* and *Bedford Cut Stone Co.*, organized labor lobbied for passage of legislation that would buffer unions from the court injunction and remove unions from the coverage of anti-trust legislation. These efforts finally paid off in 1932 when Congress passed the Federal Anti-Injunction Act, popularly known as the Norris–La Guardia Act. The factors leading to passage of the legislation are described in Section 2 of the Norris–La Guardia Act, presented in Exhibit 2.3.

Unlike the Railway Labor Act which extended and protected the rights of railway employees to organize free from employer interference and engage in collective bargaining, the Norris–La Guardia Act did not offer labor unions or their members any new rights. However, the legislation greatly changed the legal environment in which unions operated by placing sharp limitations on the ability of the federal courts to become involved in labor disputes. This was done by denying federal courts

---

EXHIBIT 2.3
Section 2 of the Norris–La Guardia Act

In the interpretation of this Act and in determining the jurisdiction and authority of the courts of the United States, as such jurisdiction and authority are herein defined and limited, the public policy of the United States is hereby declared as follows:

Whereas under prevailing economic conditions, developed with the aid of governmental authority for owners of property to organize in the corporate and other forms of ownership association, the individual unorganized worker is commonly helpless to exercise actual liberty of contract and to protect his freedom of labor, and thereby to obtain acceptable terms and conditions of employment, wherefore, though he should be free to decline to associate with his fellows, it is necessary that he have full freedom of association, self-organization, and designation of representatives of his own choosing, to negotiate the terms and conditions of his employment, and that he shall be free from the interference, restraint, or coercion of employers of labor, or their agents, in the designation of such representatives or in self-organization or in other concerted activities for the purpose of collective bargaining or other mutual aid or protection; therefore, the following definitions of, and limitations upon, the jurisdiction and authority of the courts of the United States are hereby enacted.

jurisdiction, and therefore, the ability to issue injunctions in most labor disputes. The Norris–La Guardia Act included a very broad definition of the term "labor dispute" to avoid problems found in the *Duplex v. Deering* decision which provided a narrow interpretation of the term. Section 13(c) of the Act specifies that the term "labor dispute" includes:

> Any controversy concerning terms or conditions of employment, or concerning association or representation of persons in negotiating, fixing, maintaining, changing or seeking to arrange terms or conditions of employment, regardless of whether or not the disputants stand in approximate relation of employer and employee.

The definition recognizes that organized labor has vested interest in employment even where the employees are not represented by unions. The rationale behind this broad definition has been stated as follows:

> In this definition of labor disputes and of cases arising out of labor disputes, Congress gave complete recognition to certain theretofore proscribed stranger activities of unions in the fulfillment of their heartfelt need to organize entire industries so that, by standardizing employment conditions throughout such industries, they could eliminate competitive hazard to already established standards in unionized units of such industries, presented by the undercutting effects of non-union wage and labor standard differentials.[41]

The Norris–La Guardia Act denied the courts their primary device for becoming involved in labor disputes—the injunction. It also made the "yellow dog" contract unenforceable in court. By so doing, employer attempts at deterring union organizing activities by use of the "yellow dog" contract were rendered practically useless.

The restrictions on the application of the Sherman Anti-Trust Act to labor disputes were upheld in *U.S. v. Hutcheson*.[42] In this decision, the court stated:

> The underlying aim of the Norris–La Guardia Act was to restore the broad purpose which Congress thought it had formulated in the Clayton Act but which was frustrated, so Congress believed, by unduly restrictive judicial construction. This was authoritatively stated by the House Committee on the Judiciary. "The purpose of the bill (Norris–La Guardia Act) is to protect the rights of labor in the same manner the Congress intended when it enacted the Clayton Act, October 15, 1914, . . . which act, by reason of its construction and application by the Federal courts, is ineffectual to accomplish that congressional intent." The Norris–La Guardia Act was a disapproval of Duplex Printing v. Deering and Bedford Cut Stone Co. v. Journeyman Stone Cutters Association. (case citations deleted)[43]

In summary, passage of the Norris–La Guardia Act did not provide unions and workers any additional rights. However, once federal courts were prevented from issuing injunctions in most labor disputes, unions were free to use tactics such as strikes and boycotts without judicial intervention. Additionally, the "yellow dog" contract, and to a large degree, injunctions issued under anti-trust legislation, were no longer major problems for organized labor. While it was still possible for unions

> **EXHIBIT 2.4**
> **Situations in Which Injunctions Can
> Still Be Issued in Labor Disputes**
>
> - As a result of the *Allen-Bradley v. Local Union No. 3* decision (325 U.S. 797, 1945), actions can be enjoined under anti-trust legislation if the labor organization combines with nonlabor groups to restrain interstate commerce.
> - Under the Labor-Management Relations Act, strikes found to threaten the nation's health and safety can be enjoined for up to eighty days. After that time, the injunction must be vacated.
> - Injunctive relief can be requested under Section 10(1) of the Labor-Management Relations Act in cases involving illegal secondary boycott activities, "hot-cargo" clauses, and organizational picketing.
> - When a union signs a "no-strike" agreement—i.e., an agreement not to strike during the life of the contract—an injunction can be issued if the union violates this agreement by striking (*Boys Market v. Retail Clerks*, 398 U.S. 235, 1970).
> - Certain acts of violence on a picket line can be enjoined.

to be charged with anti-trust violations, the situations were quite limited. See Exhibit 2.4 for a list of situations in which injunctions can still be issued. By restricting the use of injunctions in labor disputes, Congress created a "laissez-faire" environment in which labor and management were relatively free to interact without government intervention.

The government's "laissez-faire" or "hands-off" policy toward labor-management relations was rather short-lived. Shortly after passage of the Norris–La Guardia Act, additional legislation was enacted to protect the employees' rights to organize and engage in collective bargaining.

THE NATIONAL INDUSTRIAL RECOVERY ACT

The National Industrial Recovery Act (NIRA) was passed in 1933. This was a multifaceted piece of legislation intended to help the United States get out of a deep depression which had begun in 1929. As part of this effort, Section 7(a) addressed itself to labor legislation. This section declared that employees had the right to organize and engage in collective bargaining through representatives of their own choosing. Basically, Section 7(a) of the NIRA outlawed employer behaviors interfering with the collective bargaining process.

The NIRA was in existence for only two years. In the *Schecter Corp. v. U.S.*[44] decision (1935), the Supreme Court declared the NIRA unconstitutional. The Court concluded the legislation constituted an illegal delegation of power by Congress and exceeded Congress's authority to regulate interstate commerce. While Section 7(a) of the NIRA was not the subject of the *Schecter Corp. v. U.S.* decision, this important provision was invalidated when the legislation was struck down by the Supreme

Court. Despite the short life of the NIRA, its impact did not go unnoticed. This legislation represented an important change in the attitude of government toward labor unions. Instead of being laissez-faire, as was the Norris–La Guardia Act, Section 7(a) of the NIRA extended legal protections to workers' right to organize and engage in collective bargaining. However, the impact of the legislation was blunted since it contained very weak enforcement procedures. Shortly after the NIRA was declared unconstitutional, Congress passed new legislation that marked a complete break from the pre-existing attitude of government towards unions. With passage of the Wagner Act, Congress declared as national policy the encouragement of the practice and procedures of collective bargaining.[45]

THE WAGNER ACT

Even before the National Industrial Recovery Act was declared unconstitutional, Congressional efforts were underway to extend the philosophy of Section 7(a) of the NIRA and make it meaningful by establishing enforcement procedures. In 1935, the National Labor Relations Act (NLRA), also known as the Wagner Act, was passed. This legislation provided a permanent foundation for the protection of employee rights to organize and engage in collective bargaining.[46] Section 1 of the legislation identified its two major objectives:

- To promote industrial peace by encouraging the use of collective bargaining to resolve labor-management disputes rather than strikes or other forms of industrial unrest.
- By establishing equality of bargaining power between employees and employers, wage rates and purchasing power of workers could be increased. This would contribute to the prevention of recurrent business depressions.

It was apparent to the drafters of the legislation that the inequality of bargaining power between employers and employees not free to organize led to industrial unrest and contributed to economic instability. To remedy these problems, Section 1 of the Wagner Act declared it was public policy to encourage "the practice and procedure of collective bargaining by protecting the exercise by workers of full freedom of association, self-organization and designation of representatives of their own choosing for the purposes of negotiating the terms and conditions of employment or other mutual aid or protection." In other words, the full force of the federal government was placed behind the workers' right to organize and engage in collective bargaining.

It is not the purpose of this section to describe in detail the provisions of the NLRA. Since the act, as amended, is the cornerstone of today's national labor policy, the specific provisions of the legislation will be discussed in the next chapter. At this point, the provisions of the act will be described in general so the contribution of this important piece of legislation to the evolution of United States public labor policy can be fully understood.

To fulfill the objectives of the act, Section 7 specifies the rights of workers. This key provision states:

> Employees have the right to self organize, to form, join or assist labor organizations, to bargain collectively through representatives of their own choosing, and to engage in other concerted activities for the purpose of collective bargaining or other mutual aid or protection.

The NLRA was far more than a statement of employee rights. It also included provisions to implement and protect the rights outlined in Section 7. For example, Section 8 contained a list of unfair labor practices by employers. Unfair labor practices are limitations on employer behavior that interfere with the exercise of their employees' Section 7 rights. Under this section, employers were not allowed to form company-dominated unions, discriminate against employees because of their union activities, or refuse to negotiate with the employees' representative for collective bargaining.

In addition to encouraging collective bargaining by limiting employer behavior interfering with employees' Section 7 rights, the NLRA also established a procedure for determining whether employees wanted union representation. Prior to the passage of the NLRA, a union wanting to engage in collective bargaining would request an employer to recognize it as the employees' bargaining agent. If the employer agreed, bargaining would commence. However, employers were more likely to reject the union's request. Frequently, the union would call a strike to demonstrate worker support and to pressure the employer to bargain. Organizational strikes were very disruptive. They contributed greatly to the industrial instability characterizing labor relations prior to passage of the Wagner Act.

Section 9 of the NLRA instituted an administrative procedure for determining whether a union has support from the majority of employees. Under this procedure, a secret ballot election is held and the decision of the majority with respect to the unionization issue binds the minority. For example, if a majority of employees want union representation in collective bargaining, the union would negotiate a contract covering all employees. Through this process, the certification or representation election replaced the disruptive organizational strike as the primary mechanism for establishing a union's majority status in a bargaining unit. If the union wins the certification election, the employer has a legal obligation to engage in collective bargaining.

Unlike the National Industrial Recovery Act, the Wagner Act included provisions for enforcement. The National Labor Relations Board (NLRB) was created to administer the act. It was given the responsibility for implementing the act by conducting certification elections and preventing and remedying unfair employer labor practices. If the NLRB concluded that a violation of the act had occurred, it then had the power to order the offending party to cease and desist from the illegal behavior. Further, the NLRB could issue remedial orders. For example, an employer who committed an unfair labor practice by firing a worker for union activities could be ordered to rehire the illegally discharged worker. Also, the employer could be ordered to grant the discharged employee back pay for time lost due to the illegal discharge.

There were serious questions about the constitutionality of legislation giving the federal government an instrumental role in labor-management relations. Certainly, no provision in the United States Constitution specifically gave Congress the right to regulate labor relations. Section 1 of the act helped establish the constitutional basis for the legislation. Congress declared that the right to regulate labor relations rests on the commerce clause of the United States Constitution. Specifically, Section 1 states, in part:

> The denial by employers of the right of employees to organize and the refusal by employers to accept the procedure of collective bargaining lead to strikes and other forms of industrial strife or unrest, which has the intent or necessary effect of burdening or obstructing commerce by (a) impairing the efficiency, safety, or operation of the instrumentalities of commerce; (b) occurring in the current of commerce; (c) materially affecting, restraining, or controlling the flow of raw materials or manufactured or processed goods from or into the channels of commerce, or the prices of such materials in commerce, or goods in commerce; or (d) causing diminution of employment and wages in such volume as to substantially impair or disrupt the market for goods flowing from or into the channels of commerce.

It was not long before the constitutionality of the Wagner Act was tested. In the *NLRB v. Jones and Laughlin Steel Co.*[47] case, the company claimed, in part, that the Wagner Act was not applicable because its manufacturing facilities were intrastate in nature. Since the NLRB was limited to regulating interstate commerce, it did not have jurisdiction in the matter. By a narrow 5-4 margin, the Supreme Court provided very broad meaning to the concept of interstate commerce. In the *NLRB v. Jones and Laughlin Steel Co.* decision, the Supreme Court stated:

> Although activities may be intrastate in character when separately considered, if they have such a close and substantial relation to interstate commerce that their control is essential or appropriate to protect that commerce from burdens and obstructions, Congress cannot be denied the power to exercise that control.

With this interpretation of the commerce clause of the Constitution, the applicability of the National Labor Relations Act and the jurisdiction of the NLRB were broadly defined to provide the protection of Section 7 rights to a large proportion of the United States work force. The implications of this decision have been described as follows:

> Socially and legally, the Supreme Court's thin majority decision in this case revolutionized industrial relations in the U.S. and climaxed more than a century of labor history. The court placed a stamp of approval not only on the legal status of organized labor and the law to protect the workers' right to organize, but also on the *duty* of employers to deal in good faith with the authorized representatives of the workers concerning wages, hours and other conditions of employment. There could no longer be any question of the union's right to exist. The very interference with its existence by an employer through unfair labor practices became outlawed.[48]

IMPLICATIONS OF NLRA PASSAGE

Starting in the late 1930s and throughout the 1940s, there was rapid growth in trade union membership. A number of factors contributed to this growth, such as the competition between the American Federation of Labor and the Congress of Industrial Organizations. These were rival labor organizations which competed for workers from the late 1930s to 1955. The nature of these organizations and their competition will be discussed in detail in Chapter 4. Also, World War II created an environment conducive to union organizing. Additionally, a more favorable national labor policy created by the Wagner Act contributed to the success of union organizing during this time period.[49] Between 1935 and 1947, trade union membership increased from 3.7 million to 15.4 million.[50]

While the NLRA revolutionized labor relations in the United States by encouraging the use of collective bargaining to resolve labor-management disputes, life under this legislation was not without its problems. Over the years, a number of criticisms were leveled at the National Labor Relations Board and the legislation itself. It must be remembered that the Wagner Act was passed at a time when organized labor was relatively weak. In response to labor's "underdog" role, Congress passed a one-sided piece of legislation that severely limited management's behavior while leaving the weaker unions essentially unregulated. However, as a result of unions shedding their "underdog" status, legislation protecting unions without protecting employer rights, individual employees, and the public was subject to widespread criticism.

The major criticisms of the Wagner Act included:

- Powerful unions were abusing the rights of employers.
- Employers complained they could not get fair hearings before the NLRB since it served as both prosecutor and judge.
- The Wagner Act, as interpreted by NLRB, severely limited management's rights of free speech since anti-union statements during a union organizing campaign could be the basis for unfair labor practice charges.
- Individuals not wanting to join unions were subject to discriminatory treatment at the hands of some labor organizations.

In addition to these complaints, 1946 was characterized by a high level of strike activity. The dramatic increase in the number of strikes and work days lost due to labor disputes was attributed to the problems associated with the transition from a war-time to a peace-time economy and the removal of wage and price controls in effect during the war. This wave of strikes raised the question of whether the Wagner Act was, in part, the cause of this unrest. General dissatisfaction with labor organizations and the Wagner Act created pressures to amend the nation's basic labor legislation.

The Development of a Balanced Labor Policy: The Taft-Hartley Act

In 1947, Congress passed the Labor Management Relations Act, popularly known as the Taft-Hartley Act. Title I of this act contains an amended version of the National Labor Relations Act. The primary purpose of the Taft-Hartley amendments to the NLRA was to create legislation balancing the rights of unions, employers, and individuals. Additionally, the amendments recognized that the public had a stake in labor-management relations and needed protection from strikes threatening the nation's health and safety.

Section 1 of the National Labor Relations Act was modified to reflect the belief that, in addition to employer activities, union activities could also adversely affect interstate commerce. Section 1 states, in part:

> Experience has further demonstrated that certain practices by some labor organizations, their officers and members have the intent or necessary effect of burdening or obstructing commerce by preventing a free flow of goods in such commerce through strikes and other forms of industrial unrest or through concerted activities which impair the interest of the public in the free flow of such commerce. The elimination of such practices is a necessary condition to the assurance of the rights herein guaranteed.

As previously mentioned in conjunction with the Wagner Act, the details of the Taft-Hartley amendments will be discussed in detail in the next chapter. At this point the amendments will be discussed, in general, to demonstrate their contribution to the evolution of the nation's labor policy. The Taft-Hartley amendments brought about major changes in labor-management relations in the United States including:

- Section 7 was amended to protect the employees' right not to engage in union activities.
- A list of union unfair labor practices was added to Section 8. This included a list of union activities illegal under the act. For example, it was an unfair labor practice for a union to interfere with an employee's Section 7 rights, refuse to bargain, or charge excessive initiation fees or dues.
- Workers were allowed to decertify their unions.
- Employers were allowed to make anti-union statements during union organizing campaigns as long as they did not include threats of reprisal or promises of benefit.
- The NLRB was reorganized. An office was established responsible for the investigation and prosecution of violations of the act. A separate office decided whether the act had been violated. More will be said about the NLRB's organization in Chapter 3.

- Employers were no longer obligated to bargain with unions comprised of foremen and other supervisors.
- Procedures were included in the legislation to help settle strikes imperiling the nation's health and safety.
- Amendments outlawed the closed shop (a provision which requires the employer to only hire union members) and placed limitations on the union shop (a contract provision requiring a worker to join a union within a specified time after being hired).

With passage of the Taft-Hartley amendments, Congress attempted to create a more balanced labor policy—balanced in the sense that limitations were placed on trade union activity comparable to those limiting management activities under the Wagner Act. While equalizing the bargaining power by union and management was an important objective of the legislation, another goal was to protect individual employees from union pressures. The basic rights to organize and engage in collective bargaining extended by the Wagner Act were continued in the Taft-Hartley Act. However, the amendments recognized that employees have the right not to join a union and that this right needed protection from coercive union practices. Finally, the Taft-Hartley amendments attempted to protect the public from national emergency strikes. While not limiting the right of the parties to strike, the amendments included a procedure designed to encourage the prompt settlement of such disputes.

The National Labor Relations Act as amended by the Taft-Hartley Act provides the basis for the nation's current labor policy. In the years subsequent to the passage of the Taft-Hartley Act, relatively minor changes in a law affecting labor-management relations in the private sector have been enacted. However, in the decade subsequent to the Taft-Hartley Act, a number of problems concerning internal union affairs came to light. These problems led to passage of the Landrum-Griffin Act.

Regulation of Internal Union Affairs: The Landrum-Griffin Act

For a number of years prior to passage of the Landrum-Griffin Act, (formally known as the Labor-Management Reporting and Disclosure Act of 1959), the United States Senate was concerned with unethical and corrupt practices found in some labor organizations. Between 1954 and 1956, the Senate Subcommittee on Welfare and Pension Plans examined corrupt union practices. Again, between 1957 and 1959 the Senate Select Committee on Improper Activities in the Labor and Management Field (known as the McClellan Committee) conducted highly publicized hearings into illegal activities by a small number of labor organizations and their leaders.

During the course of these investigations, the McClellan Committee revealed a number of practices by unions and their leaders needing regulation. Although these practices were not widespread, they were significant enough to warrant congressional attention. Some of the problems relating to internal union affairs included:

- Lack of democratic procedures. Rank-and-file union members did not have the opportunity to select leaders or participate in decision making. Also, some dissident members were subject to violent acts designed to deter their opposition to the union's practices and leadership.
- Misuse of funds by some union leaders.
- "Sweetheart contracts"—an arrangement in which a union leader accepts bribes from the employer in order to negotiate weaker contracts (from the worker's viewpoint) but relatively inexpensive contracts from the employer's perspective.
- Some unions were closely aligned with organized crime.
- A number of shortcomings in the National Labor Relations Act, as amended by the Taft-Hartley Act, came to light.

In response to these revelations, Congress passed the Landrum-Griffin Act. In Section 2 of this legislation concerning the findings, purposes and policy of the legislation, the following was stated:

> The Congress further finds, from recent investigations in the Labor and Management field, that there have been a number of instances of breach of trust, corruption, disregard of the rights of individual employees, and other failures to observe high standards of responsibility and ethical conduct which require further supplementary legislation that will afford necessary protection of the rights and interests of employees and public generally as they relate to the activities of labor organizations, employers, labor relations consultants, and officers and representatives.

The Landrum-Griffin Act was passed to help alleviate some of the problems identified by the McClellan Committee. The act was a narrow piece of legislation intended primarily to regulate internal union affairs, not labor-management relations in general. Congress exercised control over internal union activities stating in Section 2(a) that:

> In order to accomplish the objectives of free-flow of commerce it is essential that labor organizations, employers, and their officials adhere to the highest standards of responsibility and ethical conduct in administering the affairs of labor organizations, employers, labor relations consultants, and their officers and their representatives.

The Landrum-Griffin Act regulated internal union affairs in a number of different ways. It established some protection designed to insure unions would be run democratically; it required unions to file with the Department of Labor copies of their constitution and by-laws and annual financial reports; elaborate reporting procedures were also required in an attempt to make labor racketeering and financial malfeasance more difficult; some types of convicted felons were precluded from holding union office; and a number of loopholes in the Taft-Hartley Act were closed. To enforce the act, punishment including fines, imprisonment, and civil suits could be applied against the offending party.

The Landrum-Griffin Act is basically different from the National Labor Relations Act, as amended. While the NLRA is designed to regulate labor-management relations, the Landrum-Griffin Act focuses on internal trade union activities. As a result of this later legislation, unions were no longer private organizations whose internal operations and financial affairs were the exclusive concern of their members. Once a union becomes a bargaining representative for a group of employees, it must open its internal union affairs to government scrutiny to help prevent abuses of the union's power. The major provisions of the Landrum-Griffin Act will be described in more detail in the following chapter.

The 1974 Amendments to the National Labor Relations Act

Since passage of the Landrum-Griffin Act, there have been several attempts to amend the National Labor Relations Act. For example, sweeping revisions of the nation's basic labor laws were proposed in the Labor Reform Act in 1977. All such attempts have failed except for the rather minor amendments passed in 1974. With these amendments, the coverage of the NLRA was expanded to include privately owned, nonprofit hospitals. In addition to extending coverage of the act to some hospitals, the 1974 amendments also included dispute resolution procedures and other protections to minimize the likelihood that labor disputes will interrupt the critical services offered by hospitals.

Labor Policies Affecting Public Employees

The National Labor Relations Act does not cover public employees—individuals employed by federal, state, or local government. The coverage of the act is limited to private-sector employees. The federal government, wholly owned government corporations, the Federal Reserve Bank and state and local political subdivisions are not employers within the meaning of the NLRA. Therefore, their employees are not subject to the act's protection.

Since passage of the Landrum-Griffin Act, the legislative basis for private-sector labor-management relations has been relatively stable. However, this has not been the case in the public sector. At the federal level, executive orders have been issued by Presidents Kennedy and Nixon governing union organization and collective bargaining in the federal sector. In 1978, the Civil Service Reform Act (Public

Law 95–454) was passed which, in part, provided a statutory foundation for labor organizing and collective bargaining for employees of the federal government. Similarly, many states passed laws extending collective bargaining rights to employees of state and local government. The evolution of labor policy with regard to labor-management relations in the public sector is basically different from that found in the private sector. The laws affecting public-sector labor relations will be discussed in detail in Chapters 16 and 17.

Summary

The purpose of this chapter was to trace the evolution of the nation's public policy toward organized labor. During the early years of trade union development, the courts played a major role in structuring United States labor policy. Initially, the criminal conspiracy doctrine was applied to trade union activities. As a result, employees were subject to criminal prosecution for engaging in concerted union activities. The criminal conspiracy doctrine gave way to "means-ends" tests in which the courts examined a union's objectives and the methods used to obtain those objectives. If either were found illegal, criminal conspiracy could still be applied. During the latter part of the 1800s, the court injunction emerged as a major device for limiting trade union activities. Later, the Sherman Anti-Trust Act was applied to trade union activities. As a result, union activities such as the strike and secondary boycott which interfered with the flow of goods in interstate commerce became illegal under the nation's anti-trust legislation. A legal environment largely determined by the courts persisted until the 1920s. At that time, statute law began to emerge as the basis for United States labor policy.

First, the Railway Labor Act provided employees in the railroad industry the right to organize and engage in collective bargaining. In 1932, the Norris–La Guardia Act limited the involvement of the courts in labor disputes by placing restrictions on their ability to issue injunctions. Then, the Wagner Act was passed revolutionizing labor-management relations in the United States.

The Wagner Act declared as public policy the encouragement of collective bargaining to resolve labor-management disputes. It stated that employees had the right to organize and engage in collective bargaining. Also, the National Labor Relations Board was created to implement and enforce the legislation. Passage of the Wagner Act helped create an environment conducive to rapid growth of trade unions during the 1930s and throughout the early 1940s.

The rapid growth of unionism was not without its problems. It became apparent that the Wagner Act which limited employer activities without restraining union behavior needed change. In the environment created by the Wagner Act, there was the potential for some unions to abuse their new-found strength. In 1947, the Taft-Hartley Act was passed. This legislation marked the beginning of a more balanced labor policy which attempted to protect the often conflicting rights of employers, employees, unions, and the public.

Twelve years later, the Landrum-Griffin Act was passed. This legislation was aimed at regulating internal union affairs in an attempt to insure trade union democracy and decrease the incidence of financial malfeasance and labor racketeering. Since passage of the Landrum-Griffin Act, the legislative framework for labor relations in the United States has remained relatively unchanged. While minor amendments to the act were passed in 1974, other attempts at more sweeping changes have failed to be passed by Congress.

While there have not been major changes in the law affecting labor-management relations in the private sector in recent years, this is not the case in the public sector. At the federal level, as well as at the state and local levels, executive orders have been issued and laws passed extending collective bargaining rights to some groups of public employees.

The primary thrust of this chapter has been the evolution of public policy affecting labor-management relations in the private sector. While this chapter has been historical in perspective, the next chapter will review some basic characteristics of contemporary labor policy in the private sector. A detailed examination of public-sector labor relations law will be handled in a later section of this book.

Discussion Questions

1. What is a court injunction? How were injunctions used in labor disputes? What effects did court injunctions have on labor-management relations?
2. What is a "yellow dog" contract? What effect did the "yellow dog" contract have on trade unions?
3. Why was it so important to organized labor that trade unions not to be subject to the nation's anti-trust laws?
4. How did the courts react to early legislative attempts to regulate labor-management relations? Cite two examples of court decisions which either reinforced or negated legislative attempts to regulate labor-management relations.
5. How did the courts regulate union activities prior to the 1920s? What effect did the Norris–La Guardia Act have on the legal environment in which trade unions operated? How did the Wagner Act affect the legal environment?
6. What was the basic purpose of the Landrum-Griffin Act? How does the Landrum-Griffin Act differ from earlier legislation such as the Wagner and Taft-Hartley Acts?
7. What is the significance of each of the following court decisions?
    a. *Philadelphia Cordwainers*
    b. *Commonwealth v. Hunt*
    c. *Hitchman Coal and Coke Co. v. Mitchell*
    d. *Adair v. U.S.*
    e. *Coppage v. Kansas*
    f. *Danbury Hatters*

g. *Duplex Printing Press Co. v. Deering*
h. *Coronado Coal Co. v. United Mine Workers*
i. *Bedford Cut Stone Co. v. Bedford Stone Cutters' Assoc.*
j. *Texas and New Orleans Railroad Co. v. Brotherhood of Railway and Steamship Clerks*
k. *U.S. v. Hutcheson*
l. *NLRB v. Jones and Laughlin Steel Co.*

Key Concepts

Criminal conspiracy doctrine
Doctrine of legal means and ends
Court injunction
"Yellow dog" contract
Common law

Statute law
Balanced labor policy
Secondary boycott
Double standard
Blacklisting

Notes

1. Thomas R. Brooks, *Toil and Trouble* (New York: Dell Publishing Co., 1971), pp. 15–16.
2. Charles O. Gregory, *Labor and the Law* (New York: W. W. Norton and Co., 1946), pp. 18–19.
3. Benjamin J. Taylor and Fred Witney, *Labor Relations Law,* 3rd ed. (Englewood Cliffs, NJ: Prentice-Hall, 1979), pp. 16–17.
4. Gregory, *Labor and the Law,* p. 19.
5. *Commonwealth (PA) v. Pullis* (1806).
6. Elias Lieberman, *Unions Before the Bar* (New York: Harper and Brothers, 1950), p. 4.
7. Recorder Moses Levy, *Commonwealth (PA) v. Pullis* (1806).
8. Lieberman, *Unions Before the Bar,* p. 15.
9. *Commonwealth (Mass.) v. Hunt,* 45 Mass. 4 (Metcalf) III, 1842.
10. Gregory, *Labor and the Law,* p. 28.
11. Lieberman, *Unions Before the Bar,* p. 27.
12. Taylor and Witney, *Labor Relations Law,* p. 23.
13. Gregory, *Labor and the Law,* p. 99.
14. Edwin E. Witte, *The Government in Labor Disputes* (New York: McGraw-Hill Book Co., 1932), p. 90.
15. *In re Debs,* Petitioner, 158 U. S. 564, 570 (1895), quoted by Felix Frankfurter and Nathan Greene in *The Labor Injunction* (Gloucester, MA: Peter Smith, 1963), p. 87.
16. Frankfurter and Greene, *The Labor Injunction,* p. 97.
17. Witte, *The Government in Labor Disputes,* pp. 107–8.
18. *Hitchman Coal and Coke Co. v. Mitchell,* 245 U. S. 229 (1917).
19. Lieberman, *Unions Before the Bar,* p. 93.
20. Neil W. Chamberlain and James W. Kuhn, *Collective Bargaining,* 2nd ed. (New York: McGraw-Hill, 1965), p. 265.
21. Taylor and Witney, *Labor Relations Law,* p. 143.

22. *Adair v. U. S.*, 208 U. S. 161 (1908).
23. Charles J. Morris, *The Developing Labor Law* (Washington, D. C.: BNA Books, 1971), p. 14.
24. Lieberman, *Unions Before the Bar*, p. 54.
25. *Coppage v. Kansas*, 236 U. S. 1 (1915).
26. *Loewe v. Lawlor*, 208 U. S. 274 (1908).
27. Ibid.
28. Lieberman, *Unions Before the Bar*, p. 67.
29. Morris, *The Developing Labor Law*, pp. 15–16.
30. Lieberman, *Unions Before the Bar*, p. 97.
31. *Duplex Printing Press Co. v. Deering*, 254 U. S. 443 (1921).
32. Taylor and Witney, *Labor Relations Law*, p. 55.
33. *Coronado Coal Co. v. The United Mine Workers of America*, 259 U. S. 344 (1922) and 268 U. S. 295 (1925).
34. Taylor and Witney, *Labor Relations Law*, p. 62.
35. *Bedford Cut Stone Co. v. Journeyman Stone Cutters' Association*, 274 U. S. 37 (1927).
36. Ibid.
37. Witte, *The Government in Labor Disputes*, p. 205.
38. Charles M. Rehmus, "Evolution of Legislation Affecting Collective Bargaining in the Railroad and Airline Industries," in *The Railway Labor Act at Fifty* (Washington, D. C.: U. S. Government Printing Office, 1977), p. 8.
39. *Texas and New Orleans Railroad Co. v. Brotherhood of Railway and Steamship Clerks*, 281 U.S. 548 (1930).
40. Ibid.
41. Gregory, *Labor and the Law*, p. 190.
42. *U. S. v. Hutcheson*, 312 U. S. 219 (1941).
43. Ibid.
44. *Schechter Corp. v. U. S.*, 295 U. S. 495 (1935).
45. Chamberlain and Kuhn, *Collective Bargaining*, p. 282.
46. Archibald Cox, Derek C. Bok, and Robert A. Gorman, *Labor Law*, 8th ed. (Mineola, NY: Foundation Press, 1977), p. 80.
47. *NLRB v. Jones and Laughlin Steel Co.*, 301 U. S. 1 (1937).
48. Lieberman, *Unions Before the Bar*, p. 201.
49. U. S. Department of Labor, *A Brief History of the American Labor Movement*, Bulletin 1000, revised (Washington, D. C.: U. S. Government Printing Office, 1970), p. 29.
50. Ibid., p. 65.

Suggested Readings

Berman, Harold J., and Greiner, William R. *The Nature and Functions of Law*, 3d ed. New York: The Foundation Press, 1972.

Brooks, Thomas R. *Toil and Trouble*, 2nd ed. New York: Dell Publishing Co., 1971.

Cox, Archibald. *Law and the National Labor Policy*. Los Angeles: University of California, Institute of Industrial Relations, 1960.

Dulles, Foster Rhea. *Labor in America*. 3d ed. New York: Crowell, 1966.

Goldman, Alvin L. *The Supreme Court and Labor-Management Relations Law*. Lexington, MA: D. C. Heath, 1976.

Millis, Harry A., and Clark, Emily C. *From the Wagner Act to Taft-Hartley*. Chicago: The University of Chicago Press, 1950.

Chapter 3

LABOR LEGISLATION: THE CURRENT PERSPECTIVE

Jana Matthews was the first female business agent in her union which represented clerks in the retail food industry. Although she had been interested in the business agent position for a couple of years, she didn't expect to be considered for such a job until she was older. The business agent servicing her store had a severe heart attack. It was not known whether he would ever return to work. Jana was pleased when she was nominated and elected to fill the business agent position.

Jana started working as a clerk in a grocery store on a part-time basis while she was in high school. After graduation, she began working full time. What started as a temporary position now appeared to be her career. While working as a grocery store clerk was a bearable job, she was glad to get elected to her new position. It was better-paid, and certainly more challenging, than her old position.

Because of Jana's experience in the retail food industry and the union over the years, she was comfortable with most of her new responsibilities. Her basic job was to service a number of retail grocery stores. She worked with union members to protect all the rights and benefits to which they were entitled under the labor agreement. While helping the union members was her basic responsibility, her job as business agent got her into a number of other areas.

Jana took Monday off. When she reported to the union offices on Tuesday morning, she was met by a pile of mail, internal memos, and telephone messages. Given how long it took to get caught up, she wondered if it was worthwhile taking a day off. A review of the "pile" on her desk reminded her of the varied nature of her job. She often thought that she was expected to be a labor lawyer. So many of the problems with which she dealt required her to have a basic understanding of labor law.

For example, there was a telephone message from Ron Olson, a clerk at a grocery store the union was trying to organize. He said he was fired for trying to help unionize the store. He wanted Jana to help him file an unfair labor practice charge with the NLRB. There was another phone message from the union steward at one of the larger supermarkets Jana serviced. The message stated that the truck drivers' union was picketing the store. The steward wanted to know if the clerks should respect the picket line or would that action violate the union's no-strike agreement. There was also a memo from the local union president reminding her of a meeting that afternoon to discuss an upcoming effort to unionize a new store. The store was an independent, i.e., a single store; not part of a chain. The store was quite small. The president wasn't even sure if it came under the jurisdiction of the National Labor Relations Act.

AN INTRODUCTION TO THE PARTIES

Jana had learned quite a bit about law in the six months since she had become a business agent. She still had lots more to learn. Next month she was starting a series of seminars intended to better acquaint her with the legal aspects of her job. She wondered if the store managers with whom she worked knew labor law as well as she did. She couldn't help but think her job would be much easier if they did.

While most organizations, both unions and companies, have labor attorneys available to them, it is important for union officers, line managers, and personnel and labor relations staff members also to have a good understanding of contemporary labor policy. All parties need to know their rights and obligations under the nation's labor laws. This chapter is designed to introduce you to the basic features of our major labor laws. It is hoped that while you learn the features of these laws, you will also recognize the complex and dynamic nature of the subject. When confronting legal problems, it is probably best to consult a labor attorney. The old adage that a person who represents himself has a fool for a client definitely applies to labor law. However, an understanding of labor law can help the manager or union official avoid legal difficulties and work with attorneys in the event that legal questions do arise.

One of the basic objectives of this book is to demonstrate that labor-management relations is a dynamic, ever-changing field. From the last chapter, you should appreciate the evolutionary nature of labor law. In this chapter, it is difficult to convey this same feeling of change since the basic purpose of this chapter is to describe the major pieces of labor legislation as they currently exist. While this chapter presents a rather static view of labor policy, that is, as it exists at a point in time, it should be remembered that NLRB and court decisions are rendered almost daily. These decisions are subtly changing the interpretation and administration of the nation's labor policy. Also, periodic revisions of labor law by Congress and state-level legislatures can be expected.

This chapter is designed to provide the reader with a basic understanding of the nation's labor law. Then, throughout the remainder of the book, the legislation will be discussed in greater detail as it pertains to specific subjects under discussion such as union organizing, collective bargaining and arbitration. To be more specific, this chapter has the following objectives:

- Identify the factors that determine the coverage of the National Labor Relations Act, as amended.
- Define the basic objectives of the NLRA, as amended, and employee rights created by this important piece of legislation.
- Describe the major provisions of the NLRA, as amended.

- Identify the major functions of the National Labor Relations Board (NLRB) and the primary functions of the NLRB's component parts.
- Describe the major provisions of the Landrum-Griffin Act.
- Present brief descriptions of the other major pieces of labor legislation and their basic objectives.

The National Labor Relations Act (as Amended)

From the previous chapter, it should be remembered that the Wagner Act was passed in 1935. It was designed to promote industrial peace and stability by encouraging the use of collective bargaining. In 1947, the Wagner Act was amended by the Labor Management Relations Act and again in 1959 by the Landrum-Griffin Act. Relatively minor amendments were also passed in 1974. Today, the National Labor Relations Act, as amended, provides the statutory base for a labor policy that encourages the use of collective bargaining to resolve labor-management disputes. Throughout the remainder of the book, whenever reference is made to the NLRA, you can assume it is the National Labor Relations Act, as amended by later laws, being discussed.

BASIC RIGHTS UNDER THE NLRA

The American trade union movement placed two major demands upon labor law. These demands are described in Exhibit 3.1. Section 7 is at the heart of the NLRA since it establishes as public policy the right to organize and engage in collective bargaining. It also protects workers' right to utilize economic weapons such as the strike and picketing, relatively free from government involvement. Section 7, as amended, states:

> Employees have the right to self-organization, to form, join, or to assist labor organizations, to bargain collectively through representatives of their own choosing, and to engage in other concerted activities for the purpose of collective bargaining or for other mutual aid or protection, and shall also have the right to refrain from any or all such activities except to the extent that such right may be affected by an agreement requiring membership in a labor organization as a condition of employment. . . .

Section 7 is a key provision since the major objective of many other provisions of the NLRA is to protect the rights established by Section 7.

AN INTRODUCTION TO THE PARTIES

> **EXHIBIT 3.1**
> **Basic Objectives of Labor Law**
>
> The American labor movement made two principal demands upon the law. One was for the right to form, join, and assist labor organizations and, through them, to bargain collectively with employers. The second was for the maximum freedom to use economic weapons—strikes, boycotts, picketing, and other concerted activities—to spread unionization and wring concessions from employers. Unionization and collective bargaining would have little value without the right to use these economic weapons, for although negotiation has its own compulsions, few "voluntary" agreements are executed in the absence of economic power. Concerted activities were also important methods of organizing new unions in the face of employer opposition. Without the right to strike, the genius of the American labor movement would be changed and, in consequence, we should have to revise our system of industrial relations.
>
> *Source:* Archibald Cox, Labor and the National Labor Policy *(Los Angeles: University of California, Institute of Industrial Relations, 1960), p. 2.*

UNFAIR LABOR PRACTICES

Sections 8(a) and 8(b) of the NLRA specify employer and union behaviors that are unfair labor practices. The prohibitions listed in these sections are designed to protect employees, employers, and unions from a number of different activities adversely affecting Section 7 rights.

Employer unfair labor practices. Section 8(a) lists five general categories of employer behavior illegal under the NLRA because they interfere with an employee's Section 7 rights. Section 8(a)(1) is a very broad provision making it an unfair labor practice for an employer "to interfere with, restrain or coerce employees in the exercise of their rights guaranteed by Section 7." An employer committing other unfair labor practices will usually be found to have also violated Section 8(a)(1). Actions depriving individuals of their Section 7 rights which are not specifically addressed in other parts of Section 8(a) may also constitute a violation of Section 8(a)(1). Examples of such violations include threatening employees with a decrease in benefits if they join a union, polling employees about their interest in a union, and granting wage increases with the intent of discouraging union membership.[1]

Section 8(a)(2) makes it an unfair practice for an employer "to dominate or interfere with the formation and administration of any labor organization or contribute financial or other support to it. . . ." This provision prevents employers from getting around the legislation by creating a "company union," that is, a union dominated or controlled by a company. It also prevents employers from giving one union preference over another.

Section 8(a)(3) makes it an unfair labor practice for an employer to discriminate "in regard to hire or tenure of employment or any term or condition of employment to encourage or discourage union membership...." Any number of acts can violate Section 8(a)(3) if the effect of the behavior is to encourage or discourage union membership. It has been stated that "an employer may discharge an employee for a good reason, a poor reason or no reason at all so long as the provisions of the National Labor Relations Act are not violated. It is, of course, a violation to discharge an employee because he engaged in activities on behalf of a union."[2] In addition to discharge, this provision forbids the refusal to hire, or the demotion of union sympathizers, or the shutting down of a plant in which there was a union organizing drive in order to "chill" unionism at other company plants.

It is a violation of Section 8(a)(4) for an employer "to discharge or otherwise discriminate against an employee because he has filed charges or given testimony under the act." The effectiveness of the legislation would be seriously weakened if employees could be subjected to employer discrimination for exercising their rights under the NLRA. Employers are prohibited from discharging, demoting, refusing to hire, or in any way discriminating with regard to working conditions against employees who file charges with the NLRB. Employees who testify as part of NLRB proceedings are afforded similar protections.

Section 8(a)(5) makes it an unfair labor practice for an employer "to refuse to bargain collectively with the representatives of the employees...." As will be discussed in Chapter 8 in regard to collective bargaining, employers must negotiate in "good faith" with the organizations selected by the employees to be their bargaining agent. Examples of 8(a)(5) violations include refusal to meet and confer at reasonable times, granting wage increases directly to employees while refusing to negotiate with the union or refusing to bargain over wages, hours, and other terms and conditions of employment. The significance of Section 8(a)(5) for labor-management relations is discussed in Exhibit 3.2.

Unfair union labor practices. When passed in 1935, the Wagner Act included the five unfair employer labor practices just described with no similar limitations on union activity. This was changed by the Taft-Hartley Act which included a list of six unfair union labor practices. The inclusion of unfair union labor practices recognized the need to limit union activities burdening or obstructing interstate commerce similar to the restraints placed on employers by the Wagner Act.[3] Like unfair employer labor practices, union practices are activities illegal under the NLRA because they interfere with employees' Section 7 rights. The Landrum-Griffin Act added a seventh unfair union labor practice.

Section 8(b)(1) makes it an unfair labor practice for a labor organization or its agents "to restrain or coerce (A) employees in the exercise in the rights guaranteed in Section 7 . . . or (B) an employer in the selection of his representatives for the purpose of collective bargaining or the adjustment of grievances." Union activities interfering with an employee's Section 7 rights, but not violating other unfair union labor practice provisions in Section 8(b) constitute potential violations of Section 8(b)(1)(A). Examples of activities that could violate Section 8(b)(1)(A) include: threatening employees who refuse to participate in a strike; engaging in acts of violence during a strike; or threatening employees with the loss of their jobs unless they

> **EXHIBIT 3.2**
> **The Significance of the Duty to Bargain**
>
> The historical significance of the duty to bargain cannot be exaggerated. In an early decision, the National Labor Relations Board noted that the protection to organization of employees given by the other unfair labor practices was intended to make possible the fostering of collective bargaining under Section 8(5). The Supreme Court, on a number of occasions, has also emphasized the importance of the duty to bargain. For example, the court has stated, "It was believed that the other rights guaranteed by the Act would not be meaningful if the employer was not under an obligation to confer with the union in an effort to arrive at the terms of an agreement." On another occasion the court took an even broader view, observing, "Enforcement of the obligation to bargain collectively is crucial to the statutory scheme."
>
> From a statistical and operational point of view, the duty to bargain has always played an important role in the administration of the Wagner and Taft-Hartley Acts. Second only to discriminatory discharge of employees, breach of this duty has always been a source of most employer unfair labor practices. Indeed, the proportion of charges alleging a violation of an employer's duty to bargain has recently increased to a point where it now constitutes about one-quarter of all cases. (*footnote deleted*)
>
> Source: *Reprinted from* The Government as a Source of Union Power *by Philip Ross by permission of University Press of New England. Copyright 1965 by Brown University.*

agree to support the union's organizing activities; or preventing nonstriking employees from reporting to work by mass picketing. 8(b)(1)(B) is violated if a union tries to restrain an employer's choice of a bargaining representative. For example, a union that insisted on negotiating with the owners of the company rather than the designated management representatives would be in danger of violating 8(b)(1)(B).

Section 8(b)(2) is violated if a union causes or attempts "to cause an employer to discriminate against an employee. . . ." There are two major ways a union can violate this provision. First, a union would violate this provision if it caused an employer, with whom it had a union shop provision, to discriminate against employees denied membership in the union for reasons other than failure to pay the uniform dues or initiation fees. In addition to such discrimination against the employee being in violation of Section 8(b)(2) by the union, the employer would probably violate Section 8(a)(3) for giving in to such pressures. Second, Section 8(b)(2) can also be violated if the union insists that an illegal union security clause be included in a labor agreement. For example, Section 8(b)(2) would be violated if a union demanded the employer only hire members of its organization. Such an arrangement would constitute a closed shop which is illegal under Section 8(a)(3). Insisting on a union shop clause in a right-to-work state would also probably violate Section 8(b)(2). While the parties can negotiate union security clauses in most situations, Section 14(b) of the NLRA allows states to pass laws prohibiting the inclusion of such clauses in labor agreements. States passing such laws are known as "right-to-work" states.[4] The right-to-work issue will be examined more fully in Chapter 13, which discusses union security.

Section 8(b)(3) makes it an unfair labor practice for a union "to refuse to bargain with an employer. . . ." This provision is analogous to Section 8(a)(5) which imposes a similar obligation to bargain on the employer. Like employers, unions are obligated to bargain "in good faith" over issues such as wages, hours, and other terms and conditions of employment. Union efforts to negotiate over illegal issues such as a closed shop could violate Section 8(b)(3). Also, the union has the same procedural requirements as employers. Failure to meet and confer at a reasonable time and place, or the refusal to put a contract into writing could lead to 8(b)(3) charges being leveled against a union.

Section 8(b)(4) is a very complex provision intended to prohibit strikes and other concerted activities aimed at employers and employees not directly involved in a labor dispute. In general, Section 8(b)(4) forbids unions from engaging in secondary boycotts. As discussed in the previous chapter, a secondary boycott usually involves:

1. A primary union.
2. A primary employer with which the union has a dispute.
3. A secondary employer neutral in the dispute between the labor union and the primary employer. The secondary employer could be a supplier or a customer of the primary employer. For example, on a construction site, a primary employer could be a subcontractor. If the subcontractor had a dispute with the union, the general contractor of the project would probably be a secondary employer.
4. Secondary employees who work for the secondary employers.

It should be remembered from Chapter 2 that a secondary boycott occurs when the primary union pressures a secondary employer and/or the secondary employees to join in their dispute with the primary employer. For example, a union could pressure a secondary employer to cease doing business with the primary employer. Or, the labor union could request secondary employees to refuse to handle the products of the primary employer. The purpose of such tactics is to increase the pressure on the primary employer to settle its dispute with the primary union.

Primary labor disputes, that is, those involving the primary union and the primary employer are not subject to extensive government control. The parties are relatively free to disagree to the extent allowed by their economic power. However, the primary disputants are not free to involve secondary employers and employees in their dispute. While not specifically utilizing the terms "primary boycott" or "secondary boycott," the NLRA bans the use of many secondary activities in Section 8(b)(4).

Fig. 3.1 indicates that Section 8(b)(4) has two major components. The first part of Section 8(b)(4) describes potentially illegal union activities. The latter part of the provision lists illegal union objectives. In general, unions or their agents engaging in

Fig. 3.1 *Components of Section 8(b)(4)*

Activities

8(b)(4)(i) states that a primary union cannot engage in or encourage secondary *employees* to strike or refuse to handle the products of a primary employer.

8(b)(4)(ii) states that a union cannot threaten, restrain or coerce secondary *employers*.

Objectives

8(b)(4)(A)—require a self-employed person to become a union member.

8(b)(4)(B)—force a person to stop using, selling or handling the goods or services of a primary employer.

8(b)(4)(C)—require an employer to recognize the union when the employer is already dealing with another union.

8(b)(4)(D)—force an employer to assign work to members of the union rather than some other labor organization.

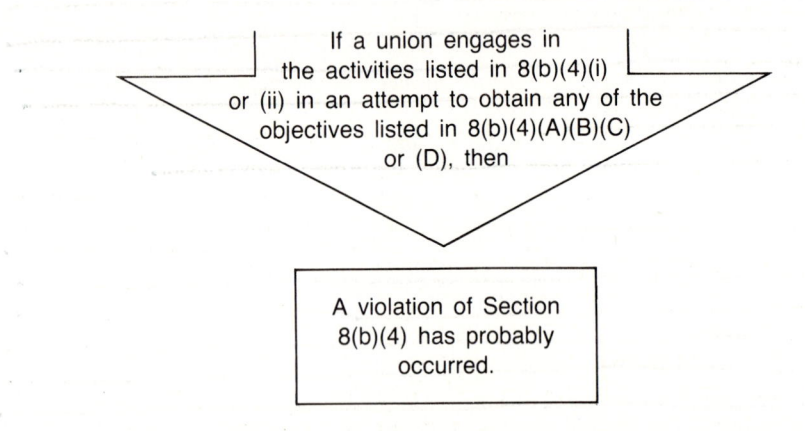

If a union engages in the activities listed in 8(b)(4)(i) or (ii) in an attempt to obtain any of the objectives listed in 8(b)(4)(A)(B)(C) or (D), then

A violation of Section 8(b)(4) has probably occurred.

the activities specified in Section 8(b)(4) in an attempt to secure any of the objectives listed will violate Section 8(b)(4). With this general overview of Section 8(b)(4) in mind, the details of the provision can now be examined.

Subsections 8(4)(i) and (ii) specify activities that are illegal if their intent is to secure the objectives listed in the provision. Subsection 8(b)(4)(i) states, in effect, that primary unions cannot engage in or encourage secondary *employees* to strike or refuse to handle or use the products of a primary employer. Subsection 8(b)(4)(ii) specifies that the primary union cannot threaten, restrain or coerce secondary *em-*

ployers. The ban on the activities listed in Section 8(b)(4)(i) and (ii) is not total. Those activities constitute an unfair labor practice only if the intent of the activities is to secure the objectives listed in Section 8(b)(4).

The four illegal objectives specified in Section 8(b)(4) are presented in subsections (A) through (D). These objectives are:

(A) Force or require a self-employed person to join a union.
(B) Force or require a person to stop using, selling, or handling or otherwise dealing with a primary employer. This is the "classic" secondary boycott situation.
(C) Force or require an employer to recognize or bargain with a particular labor organization when another union has already been certified as the employees' bargaining agent.
(D) Force or require an employer to assign work to members of a particular labor organization rather than some other labor organization. This is known as a jurisdictional dispute.

In summary, 8(b)(4) is a very complex provision designed to restrict secondary boycott activities. The provision does this by specifying in subsections 8(b)(4) (i) and (ii) certain secondary activities that are unfair labor practices if performed to help secure any of the objectives listed in Section 8(b)(4) (A) (B) (C) and (D).

Section 8(b)(5) makes it an unfair labor practice for a union to charge excessive or discriminatory initiation fees or dues in situations where the union has a union shop agreement. The legislation does not specify any limits for dues and initiation fees. However, Section 8(b)(5) does state that when deciding whether the union is charging excessively high amounts "the Board shall consider, among other relevant factors, the practices and customs of labor organizations in the particular industry, and wages currently paid to the employees affected." The NLRB decided that a union's $1000 initiation fee was both excessive and discriminatory. It was found that the $1000 fee constituted almost six weeks' pay and was twice the amount charged by a sister local in the same industry.[5] However, the NLRB has also decided that a $500 initiation fee was not excessive since it was in line with the fees charged by other unions in the same industry.[6] The NLRB reviews Section 8(b)(5) charges on a case-by-case basis to determine whether the union's dues or initiation fees are excessive or disciminatory.

Section 8(b)(6) is known as the antifeatherbedding provision. It is an unfair labor practice for a union "to cause or attempt to cause an employer to pay . . . for services which are not performed or not to be performed. . . ." Featherbedding is the practice of receiving pay for work that is neither performed by employees nor required by the employer. However, the featherbedding limited by Section 8(b)(6) is rather narrow since an unfair labor practice will not be found as long as some worker service is being provided the employer. This is the case even if the employer has no use for the service.[7]

Section 8(b)(7) places limitations on union picketing in certain situations. Under this provision, it is an unfair labor practice for a union to picket or threaten to picket an employer unless the union is currently certified as the employees' bargaining representative. This provision is designed to limit picketing by a minority union attempting to obtain members or to require the employer to recognize it. Similarly, the restrictions on organizational (also known as recognitional) picketing contained in Section 8(b)(7) would also apply to an uncertified union even if it represents a majority of the employees. A union picketing to force an employer to recognize it or to require the employees to select the union as their bargaining agent is in violation of Section 8(b)(7) if any of the following conditions exist:

- The employer has lawfully recognized another labor organization.
- There has been an NLRB certification election within the preceding twelve months.
- The picketing has been conducted without a petition for certification election being filed within a reasonable time, not to exceed thirty days.

OTHER MAJOR PROVISIONS CONTAINED IN SECTION 8

In addition to employer and union unfair labor practices, Section 8 contains several other major provisions. Section 8(c) is known as the "free speech" provision. It allows employers to make statements during the period preceding a certification election as long as the statements do not contain "threats of reprisal or force or promise of benefit." If such threats or promises are made, the employer can be guilty of an unfair labor practice. Prior to passage of the Taft-Hartley Act amendments, the view of the NLRB was that employers had no legitimate role to play in certification elections since the decision to unionize rested exclusively with the employees. However, this position was rejected by the Supreme Court. The Supreme Court ruled that employer speech which was not by its own terms coercive was protected by the First Amendment of the United States Constitution.[8] Section 8(c) can be viewed as a recognition by Congress that employers have a right to express their opinion concerning the unionization issue.[9]

Section 8(d) imposes on the parties the obligation to bargain in good faith; in addition to specifying the general obligation, it also imposes some procedural requirements on the parties such as meeting and conferring at reasonable times and reducing agreements to writing. The "good faith" bargaining requirements found in Section 8(d) will be discussed in more detail in Chapter 8.

Section 8(e) is concerned with "hot cargo" agreements. These are contract clauses in which an employer agrees not to do business with another employer. This was added to the NLRA by the Landrum-Griffin Act amendments in 1959. Specifically, Section 8(e) makes it an unfair labor practice for an employer and union to enter into an agreement in which the employer "ceases or refrains from handling, using, selling, transporting or otherwise dealing in the products of any other employer. . . ." Whereas Section 8(b)(4)(B) is concerned with such agreements which were the results of threats, coercion, or restraint, Section 8(e) makes it an unfair labor practice for employers and unions to voluntarily enter into "hot cargo" agreements. Two industries were exempted from Section 8(e): construction and garment manufacturing. In these industries, it is rather common to find contractual requirements specifying that when work is subcontracted, it will go to union shops only.

SECTION 9: REPRESENTATION ELECTIONS

The significance of Section 9 to the nation's labor policy cannot be overestimated. It declares that the representative designated by a majority of the employees in a bargaining unit will be the "exclusive representative of all employees in the unit for the purposes of collective bargaining. . . ." The principle of exclusive representation by the labor organization designated or selected by a majority of the employees is basic to our system of collective bargaining. Under this principle, the union as a representative of the majority speaks for all employees in the unit.[10] Exhibit 3.3 discusses the rationale behind the principle of exclusive representation.

Employees may gain union representation through three major ways. First, an employer can voluntarily recognize the union. Voluntary recognition may be granted if an employer is convinced a majority of the employees want union representation. Second, employers committing severe unfair labor practices during a union organiz-

---

EXHIBIT 3.3
The Principle of Exclusive Representation

Exclusive representation prevents an employer from playing the employees off against each other. By preventing an employer from dealing directly with employees, the doctrine of exclusive representation prevents an employer from taking advantage of some bargaining unit employees who might otherwise be subject to employer domination. Because of this doctrine, an employer cannot hire an employee on the condition that he accept working conditions less than those provided in the contract. Also, an employer cannot condition an individual employee's continued employment on his willingness to accept different conditions. An employer, for example, cannot tell an employee that because his work is slower he must accept lower pay. Under the doctrine of exclusive representation, an employer cannot enter into individual contracts with employees containing different provisions than the collective bargaining agreement. An individual employee cannot be forced to waive his contract rights. However, a contract may expressly permit individual bargaining on some subjects. Theatrical or sports collective bargaining agreements, for example, frequently provide only base pay rates and the employees may bargain individually for higher rates. In the absence of such exceptions, however, the contract determines the wages, hours, and working conditions for all employees.

Source: Bruce Feldacker, Labor Guide to Labor Law, 1980, p. 94. Reprinted with permission of Reston Publishing Co., a Prentice-Hall Co.

ing drive may be ordered by the NLRB to recognize and bargain with the union. Third, and most common, the NLRB conducts a representation (also known as a certification) election to determine whether a majority of the employees want union representation. Section 9 outlines general procedures for conducting union representation elections. Over the years, a multitude of NLRB and court decisions have provided detailed guidelines for the conduct of union certification elections. Section 9 is very important to our national labor policy because it substitutes an administrative procedure—the certification election—for the economic brute force of an organizational strike frequently used to demonstrate the union's majority status prior to passage of the NLRA. As a result of the certification election procedure outlined in Section 9, labor-management relations were greatly stabilized. Since Section 9 is so important to labor-management relations, this provision and its impact on union and employer behavior during the organizing process will be discussed in detail in Chapter 7.

SECTION 10: PREVENTION OF UNFAIR LABOR PRACTICES

The NLRB has two major functions under the National Labor Relations Act: conducting union certification elections as discussed in Section 9 and preventing and remedying unfair labor practices.

The authority to prevent and remedy unfair labor practices was granted to the NLRB by Congress in Section 10. This provision requires that persons alleging unfair labor practices have been committed file charges with the NLRB. In turn, the NLRB investigates the allegations. If the investigation indicates an unfair labor practice has occurred, then a formal complaint will be issued against the alleged violation. Fig. 3.2 outlines the basic procedures utilized by the NLRB to adjudicate unfair labor practice charges.

If it is concluded that an unfair labor practice has occurred, there are a number of remedies available to the NLRB. "Cease and desist" orders are the most common NLRB remedial orders. This is "an order directing a party found to have engaged in an unfair labor practice to cease and desist from a particular conduct found to be unlawful"[11] When remedying unfair labor practices, the NLRB's basic objective is to effectuate the purposes of the act; that is, protect the employees' rights to unionize and engage in collective bargaining. This objective requires the NLRB to go beyond the issuance of "cease and desist" orders when remedying some unfair labor practices. For example, if it is concluded an employer discriminated against several employees by discharging them for their union activities, it would not be enough to direct the employer to stop discriminating against employees. In this situation, a "cease and desist" order would be of little consequence to the workers already terminated. To protect the rights of the discharged workers, the NLRB has the authority to issue "make whole" orders. These are awards that "restore the discriminatee, as nearly as possible, to the economic position he would have enjoyed without the discrimination."[12]

When attempting to "make whole" an employee who suffered losses because of union or management unfair labor practices, the NLRB has been granted much

LABOR LEGISLATION: THE CURRENT PERSPECTIVE

Fig. 3.2 *Basic NLRB Procedures in Unfair Labor Practice Cases*

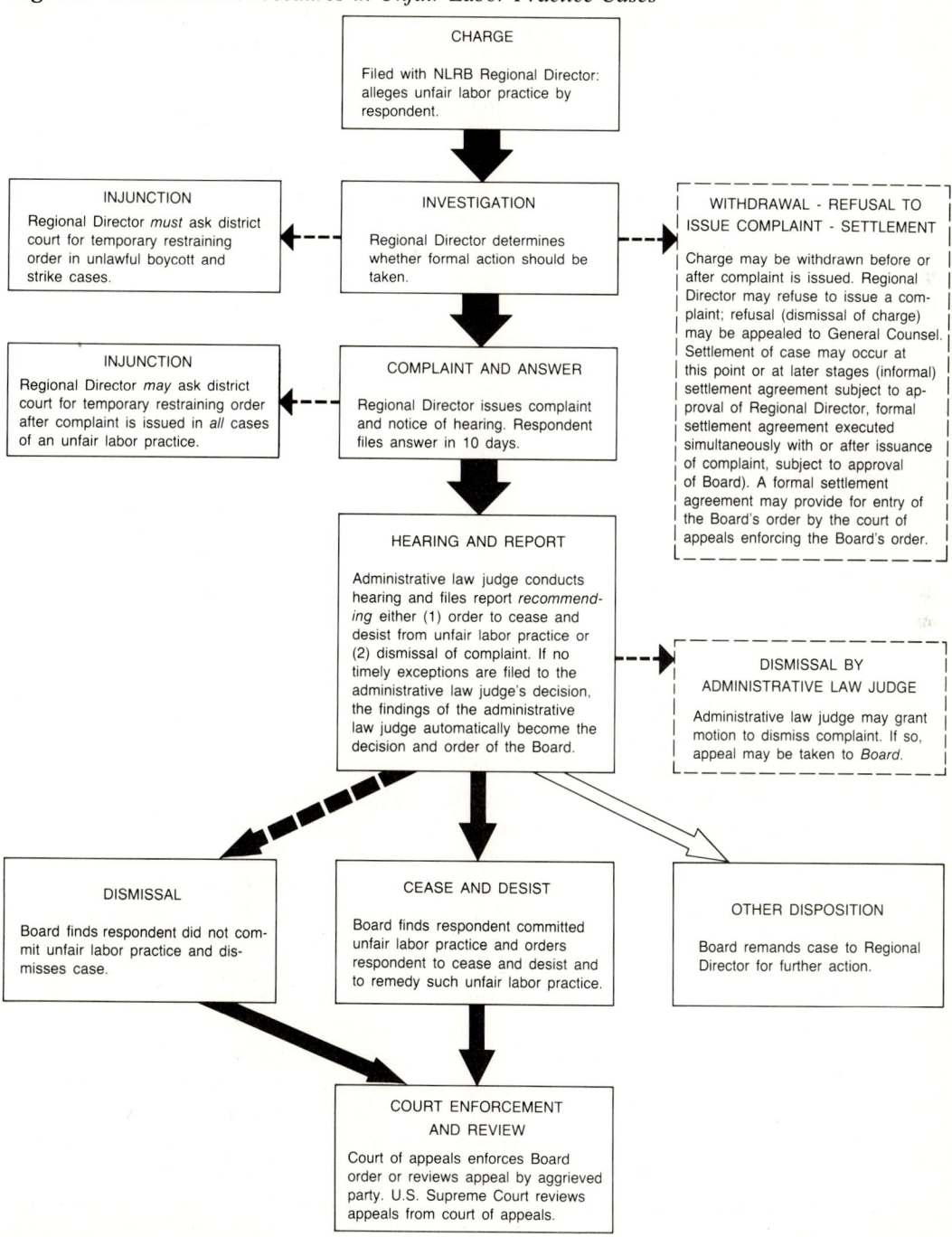

CHARGE
Filed with NLRB Regional Director: alleges unfair labor practice by respondent.

INVESTIGATION
Regional Director determines whether formal action should be taken.

INJUNCTION
Regional Director *must* ask district court for temporary restraining order in unlawful boycott and strike cases.

WITHDRAWAL - REFUSAL TO ISSUE COMPLAINT - SETTLEMENT
Charge may be withdrawn before or after complaint is issued. Regional Director may refuse to issue a complaint; refusal (dismissal of charge) may be appealed to General Counsel. Settlement of case may occur at this point or at later stages (informal settlement agreement subject to approval of Regional Director, formal settlement agreement executed simultaneously with or after issuance of complaint, subject to approval of Board). A formal settlement agreement may provide for entry of the Board's order by the court of appeals enforcing the Board's order.

COMPLAINT AND ANSWER
Regional Director issues complaint and notice of hearing. Respondent files answer in 10 days.

INJUNCTION
Regional Director *may* ask district court for temporary restraining order after complaint is issued in *all* cases of an unfair labor practice.

HEARING AND REPORT
Administrative law judge conducts hearing and files report *recommending* either (1) order to cease and desist from unfair labor practice or (2) dismissal of complaint. If no timely exceptions are filed to the administrative law judge's decision, the findings of the administrative law judge automatically become the decision and order of the Board.

DISMISSAL BY ADMINISTRATIVE LAW JUDGE
Administrative law judge may grant motion to dismiss complaint. If so, appeal may be taken to *Board*.

DISMISSAL
Board finds respondent did not commit unfair labor practice and dismisses case.

CEASE AND DESIST
Board finds respondent committed unfair labor practice and orders respondent to cease and desist and to remedy such unfair labor practice.

OTHER DISPOSITION
Board remands case to Regional Director for further action.

COURT ENFORCEMENT AND REVIEW
Court of appeals enforces Board order or reviews appeal by aggrieved party. U.S. Supreme Court reviews appeals from court of appeals.

Source: Bruce Feldacker, Labor Guide to Labor Law, *1980, pp. 14–15. Reprinted with permission of Reston Publishing Co., a Prentice-Hall Co.*

discretion. It has the authority to order an employer to reinstate an employee illegally discharged under Section 8. The employer can also be directed to compensate the employee for any losses incurred as a result of the illegal discharge. Similarly, a union found to have charged excessive or discriminatory initiation fees or dues under Section 8(b)(5) could be directed to reimburse the union member in the amount of the fee declared excessive. When determining remedies, the NLRB attempts to compensate individuals for actual losses attributable to the unfair labor practice. A remedy going beyond actual losses would probably be considered punitive. The NLRB's authority is to remedy unfair labor practices. It does not have the authority to formulate remedies that are punitive or, in other ways, do not effectuate the purposes of the act.

In addition to "cease and desist" and "make whole" orders, the NLRB has several other less frequently used remedies available to it. As will be discussed more fully in Chapter 7, the NLRB can direct an employer to bargain with a union even if the union fails to win a certification election. This can occur if the employer commits serious unfair labor practices during a union organizing campaign. Under Section 10(l), the NLRB can obtain a court injunction if a preliminary investigation indicates a violation of Sections 8(b)(4)(A), (B), or (C); or 8(e); or 8(b)(7) has occurred. Injunctive relief is not intended finally to resolve the unfair labor practice. Instead, injunctions are used to provide short-term relief while the NLRB deliberates the final resolution of the matter.[13]

While Section 10(l) requires the NLRB to seek injunctions in cases involving Sections 8(b)(4)(A), (B), (C); or 8(e); or 8(b)(7), Section 10(j) grants the NLRB discretionary power to obtain injunctive relief in other unfair labor practice cases. Finally, the NLRB has been granted special remedial powers in cases involving jurisdictional disputes, that is, violations of Section 8(b)(4)(D). If the parties cannot voluntarily resolve the matter involving the assignment of work to one of two or more unions claiming jurisdiction over the work, the NLRB decides the issue. Section 10(K) allows the NLRB to hear the matter and determine the dispute by assigning the work to one of the unions.

NLRB orders are not self-enforcing. If a party refuses to abide by an order, the NLRB must go to a federal district court and request a court order directing compliance. It is at this point that NLRB actions are subject to judicial review. The court's function is to review questions of law. Courts determine whether the NLRB interpreted the law properly. The courts will not, typically, question NLRB remedies for violations of the act since the Supreme Court has directed the lower courts not to substitute their judgment for the board's in matters involving the remedy for losses attributable to unfair labor practices. The assumption is that the NLRB has the expertise to best determine how violations of the act should be remedied.[14]

The purpose of this section was to describe the major provisions of the NLRA, as amended. While there are a number of other issues addressed in this key piece of federal labor legislation, a thorough examination of these topics is beyond the scope of this chapter. In the chapters to follow, the NLRA, as interpreted by the NLRB and court decisions, will be discussed as it is applied during the union organizing process, collective bargaining, and arbitration. Through this approach we hope to give you a better appreciation for the complex, dynamic nature of federal labor policy.

The preceding material concerning the NLRA contained many references to the NLRB, the federal agency responsible for administering the act. It is not possible to discuss the key provisions of the NLRA without discussing the enforcement agency. Section 7(a) of the National Industrial Recovery Act (NIRA) embodied a legislative philosophy similar to that found in the Wagner Act. However, Section 7(a) was destined for failure even before the NIRA was declared unconstitutional, largely because the legislation contained no meaningful enforcement mechanisms. The Wagner Act remedied this problem by creating the NLRB. Our attention now turns to an examination of the federal agency responsible for administration and enforcement of the NLRA.

The National Labor Relations Board

Section 3 of the NLRA created the National Labor Relations Board (NLRB) to administer the legislation and oversee the development of the labor policy under the act. Under the National Labor Relations Act, the NLRB has two functions:

- To determine by agency-conducted secret ballot elections whether employees want union representation in collective bargaining.
- To prevent and remedy unfair labor practices, whether by labor organizations or by employers.[15]

Fig. 3.3 presents an organizational chart for the National Labor Relations Board. As indicated in Fig. 3.3, the NLRB has two major components: the five-person board and the office of the general counsel. The board and the general counsel are independent of each other. Prior to the Taft-Hartley amendments in 1947, agents of the board would investigate alleged violations of the act. If there was evidence that a violation had occurred, the board would prosecute the charges. The same agency would then hear the charges and render a decision on the matter. This organizational structure in which the same agency investigated, prosecuted, and then judged the case was sharply criticized by employers. These criticisms led to a restructuring of the NLRB in the 1947 Taft-Hartley amendments. These amendments increased the size of the board from three to five members. Also, a new position was created—the office of the general counsel. This reorganization created one unit responsible for the investigation and prosecution of unfair labor practice charges (the office of the general counsel). Another unit within the NLRB was assigned the quasi-judicial responsibility for deciding whether an unfair labor practice had actually occurred (the five-person board). The major responsibilities of the board and the general counsel are discussed in greater detail below.

AN INTRODUCTION TO THE PARTIES

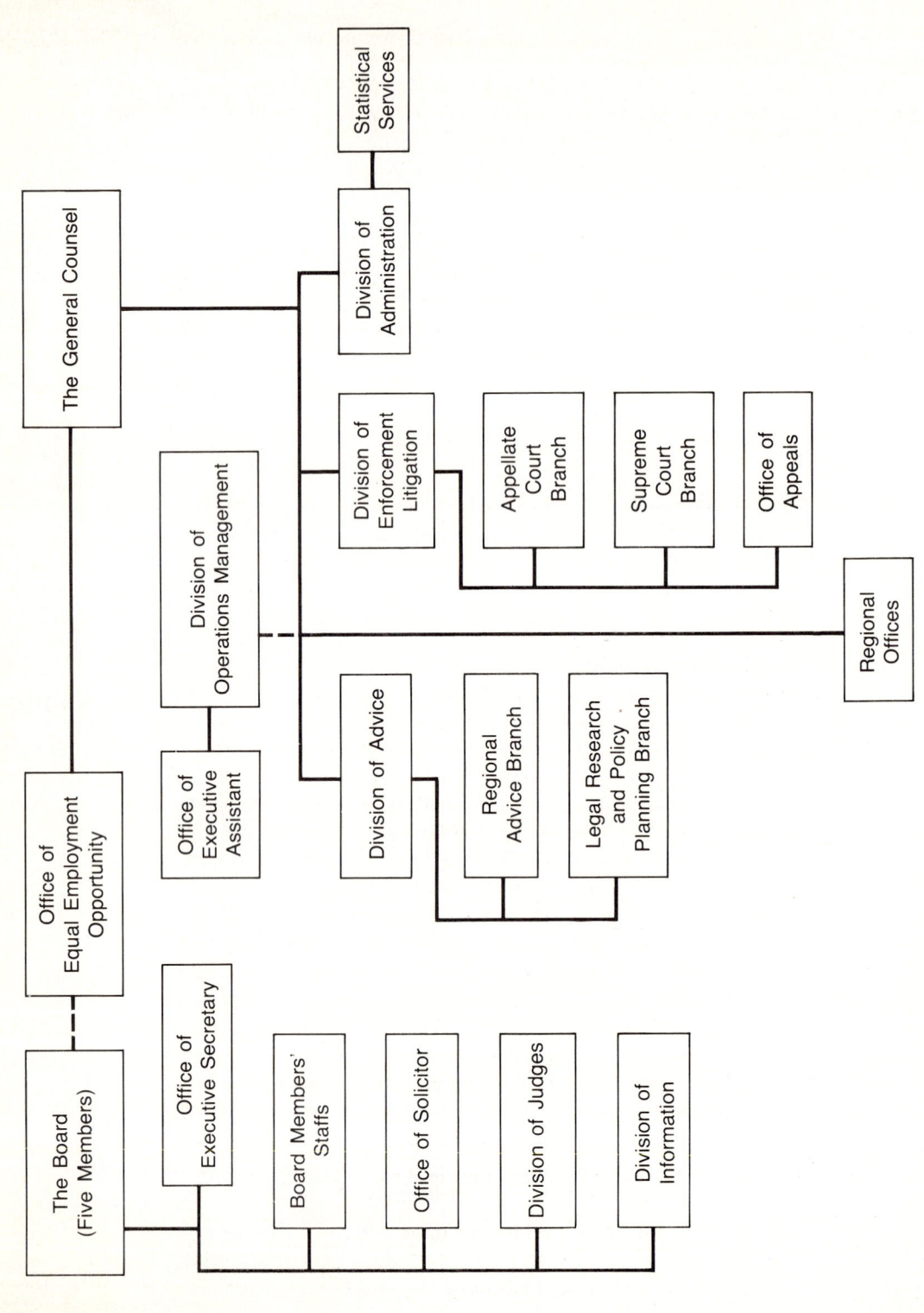

Fig. 3.3 *National Labor Relations Board*

THE BOARD

The Board is composed of five persons appointed by the president with the consent of the Senate for five year terms. The board plays a judicial function in the overall operation of the NLRB. While the general counsel investigates and prosecutes alleged violations of the act, the board decides the issues brought before it. Additionally, the board has responsibility for issues concerning certification elections. While most decisions in this area are delegated to regional directors, the board retains the right to review any decisions by regional directors involving certification elections.[16] Regional directors are in charge of the thirty regional offices located in major United States cities. Most cases examined by the NLRB are initiated at regional offices. More will be said about the role of the regional director later.

In more specific terms, the board has five basic functions:

- To prevent and remedy unfair labor practices.
- To determine whether employees want union representation in collective bargaining.
- To determine whether labor organizations have the authority to have union shop clauses in their collective bargaining agreements.
- To resolve jurisdictional disputes that have led to unfair labor charges being filed under section 8(b)(4)(D).
- To poll employees on the employer's last offer in national emergency dispute situations.[17]

THE GENERAL COUNSEL

Like the board, the general counsel is appointed by the president with the consent of the Senate. The general counsel serves a four-year term. It is the responsibility of the general counsel to administer the day-to-day operations of the NLRB and enforce the unfair labor practice provisions of the act. More specifically, the general counsel decides whether unfair labor practice charges will be prosecuted. This is a very important responsibility since the decision to prosecute an unfair labor practice charge rests exclusively with the general counsel and is not subject to board review. Also, the general counsel supervises all employees in the regional offices as well as most attorneys employed by the NLRB.[18] The office of the general counsel is responsible for the following activities basic to the operation of the NLRB:

- Seeks court injunctions as provided by the act.
- Supervises the actual conduct of the union certification elections.
- Seeks compliance with board orders.
- Applies to the courts for enforcement of board orders.
- Conducts employers' last-offer elections in national emergency disputes.[19]

While the board and the general counsel are the major components of the National Labor Relations Board, two other aspects of the NLRB's organization need to be discussed: the regional offices and the administrative law judges.

THE REGIONAL OFFICES

Organizationally, the regional offices are under the supervision of the general counsel. As previously mentioned, regional offices are located in major United States cities. Petitions for certification elections are filed with the regional offices. Similarly, charges that an unfair labor practice has occurred are also filed at a regional office.

Regional offices are supervised by regional directors. The regional director supervises a group of field agents. Field agents provide the initial investigation of petitions and charges filed with the NLRB. They have important responsibilities since the results of their investigations will be used by the regional directors, the board, and the general counsel as the basis for their decisions.[20]

ADMINISTRATIVE LAW JUDGES

Administrative law judges are involved with unfair labor practice cases. If the general counsel decides to prosecute, unfair labor practice charges will be initially heard by an administrative law judge who operates independently of both the general counsel and the board. These positions resemble those of federal district court judges. Administrative law judges are appointed for life and conduct their hearings like those in federal court. They serve a judicial function when deciding cases. In unfair labor practice proceedings, the case is prosecuted by an agent of the NLRB. The union or employer charged with committing the unfair labor practice provides its own legal counsel. The administrative law judge hears the case and renders a decision which can be appealed to the board.

In summary, the National Labor Relations Act is the major piece of labor legislation in the United States today. It is designed to protect employees' right to organize, engage in collective bargaining, and to utilize economic weapons such as the strike. The NLRA as interpreted by the NLRB and the courts has established the legal framework for labor-management relations in the United States. This section of the chapter was designed to provide an overview of the most important provisions of the NLRA. More detailed discussions of the legislation are found in subsequent chapters. The dynamics of labor-management relations examined in the chapters to follow cannot be discussed without looking at the legal environment and implications of the issues.

While the NLRA is primarily concerned with union-management relations, another major piece of labor legislation has a much narrower focus. The Landrum-Griffin Act is concerned with the regulation of internal union affairs. Attention now turns to an examination of the major components of the Landrum-Griffin Act.

The Landrum-Griffin Act

As discussed in the previous chapter, the Landrum-Griffin Act, also known as the Labor-Management Reporting and Disclosure Act, was passed in response to congressional concerns over the need to regulate internal union affairs. It is a relatively narrow piece of legislation intended to rectify problems concerning trade union democracy and corruption within the union movement.

TITLE I: BILL OF RIGHTS FOR MEMBERS OF LABOR ORGANIZATIONS

Title I is intended to insure minimum standards of internal union democracy. It provides that union members have the right to nominate candidates, vote in elections, attend the meetings, and participate in the deliberations of these meetings subject to reasonable rules and regulations. Title I states that union members have the right to meet freely and assemble. Also, individuals can express at meetings of the labor organization any of their views, arguments, or opinions. This portion of the Landrum-Griffin Act outlines procedures for membership participation in decisions concerning dues, initiation fees, and assessments. Additionally, the ability of the union to limit its members' rights to sue the organization or its officers was curtailed. Individuals can sue their union provided that the union's hearing procedures have been exhausted prior to initiating court action. Finally, Title I states that union members cannot be fined, suspended, expelled, or disciplined in any way (except for nonpayment of dues) without certain due-process standards being fulfilled. Before taking disciplinary action, Title I requires a union to present the member with charges in writing, give the individual a resonable time to prepare a defense to the charges, and provide the member a full and fair hearing.

TITLE II: REPORTING BY LABOR ORGANIZATIONS, OFFICERS AND EMPLOYEES OF LABOR ORGANIZATIONS, AND EMPLOYERS

As suggested by its label, Title II places extensive reporting obligations on unions, union employees and officers, and employers. Title II requires labor organizations to adopt a constitution and by-laws and to provide copies of each to the secretary of the Department of Labor. Unions must also report to the Department of Labor the names of officers, the initiation fees and dues required of its members, detailed descriptions of member qualifications, and descriptions of a number of internal union activities. These include the procedures for levying assessments, auditing financial transactions, disciplining officers, and ratifying labor agreements. Unions are also required to provide financial information such as their assets and liabilities, receipts of any kind and their source, salary figures and allowances paid to union officers and employees, and figures on any direct and indirect loans made to union officers and employees and to business enterprises.

In addition to the unions having to provide detailed reports, union officers and employees are also subject to reporting requirements. The primary objective of these requirements is to report financial information that could reveal a conflict of interest. Union officers and employees have to report any financial interest or business arrangement they or their family members have with companies in which the union represents or seeks to represent workers. For example, it is necessary to report transactions involving the stock or securities of firms with which the union has labor agreements. Also, if the union leaders or their families are involved with companies doing business with employers having labor agreements with the union, this also has to be reported.

Finally, employers have to report loans made to union officers, employees, or business enterprises. Also, employers must report payments to employees made in order to have them persuade other employees to exercise or not exercise their rights to organize and engage in collective bargaining. Similarly, any payment made with the intent of interfering with, restraining, or coercing employees in the exercise of their rights to organize and bargain must be reported. Persons willfully violating the reporting provisions of Title II are subject to both criminal and civil penalties. The violation of Title II requirements can be punished by fines up to $10,000 and imprisonment for not more then one year.

TITLE III: TRUSTEESHIPS

A trusteeship has been described as:

> A method of supervision and control whereby a parent organization suspends the autonomy of a subordinate body—a local union or intermediate unit such as a district council. The international union or central body has been delegated authority, in many labor organizations, to intervene if a subordinate unit is unable to fend for itself, cannot administer its collective bargaining contracts, or when other conditions which tend to weaken the organization exist.[21]

EXHIBIT 3.4
Abuses of Trusteeships

Five major abuses by some unions under investigation by the McClellan Committee were found particularly troublesome:

1. Some parent bodies imposed trusteeships without a legitimate basis for doing so.
2. Some parent organizations, having legitimately imposed a trusteeship, subsequently kept their subordinate body under trusteeship for too long a time (e.g., at the time of passage of the LMRDA, seventeen United Mineworkers' districts had been in trusteeship for over twenty years, and four more for more than ten).
3. The imposition and continuation of such trusteeships often went against the wishes of the rank-and-file members.
4. Trusteeships were at times used by the parent body as a means of looting local treasuries.
5. Some parent body officials used the votes of convention delegates from locals under trusteeship either to capture top office or to perpetuate themselves in office once elected. *(footnotes deleted)*

Source: Doris B. McLaughlin and Anita W. Schoomaker, *The Landrum-Griffin Act and Union Democracy* (Ann Arbor: University of Michigan Press, 1979), p. 127.

Typically, a trusteeship is established as a means for remedying a problem at the local level. Once the problem has been rectified, the trusteeship is abandoned and local control is re-established. While there are many sound reasons for the use of trusteeships, the procedure can be abused. Exhibit 3.4 summarizes some of the abuses of trusteeships uncovered by the McClellan Committee. Because of these types of problems, Title III of the Landrum-Griffin Act places restrictions on the use of trusteeships.

First, all trusteeships have to be reported within thirty days of their establishment and then semiannual reports must be provided to the Department of Labor for the duration of the trusteeship. Unions are required to report their reasons for establishing or continuing the trusteeship. Also, at the time the trusteeship is established, a full and complete report of the local financial conditions must be made. While in trusteeship, funds from the local cannot be transferred to the national. Additionally, the votes of delegates from locals in trusteeship at conventions or during the election of officers cannot be counted unless the delegates were chosen by a secret ballot of the local membership.

TITLE IV: ELECTIONS

Like Title I, Title IV is also concerned with providing minimum safeguards for internal union democracy. To this end, Title IV places some control over the union's election procedures. It specifies that national or international unions elect their officers at least once every five years. Title IV also requires these officers to be chosen either by secret ballot elections of the membership or at a convention where the delegates were chosen by secret ballot. Local unions are required to elect their officers not less than once every three years by secret ballot. Individuals have the right to participate in the election of union officers as long as they have fulfilled all the union's qualifications for membership.

TITLE V: SAFEGUARDS FOR LABOR ORGANIZATIONS

Title V recognizes that union leaders hold positions of trust within their organizations. This provision imposes on the union leadership fiduciary responsibility by stating that they have the duty to hold the union's "money and property solely for the benefit of the organization and its members and to manage, invest, and extend the same in accordance with its constitution and bylaws. . . ." Title V allows members to sue in order to recover damages or to secure an accounting in situations where it is alleged union leaders have failed to exercise properly their fiduciary responsibilities. Persons found embezzling or stealing union funds are subject to fines up to $10,000 and can receive up to five years in prison. To further encourage the financial accountability of union leaders, Title V requires union officers and employees to be bonded. Additionally, restrictions are placed on loans made by unions to their officers and employees. No officer or employee can be indebted to the union in excess of $2,000. Finally, Title V prohibits certain persons from holding union offices. Persons convicted of robbery, bribery, extortion or embezzlement, grand larceny, burglary, arson, violation of narcotics law, murder, rape, and assault with the intent to kill cannot serve as union officers. As originally passed, Title V also prohibited members of the Communist party from holding an office. However, in 1965, the United States Supreme Court declared this provision unconstitutional.[22]

TITLE VI: MISCELLANEOUS PROVISIONS

Under this section of miscellaneous provisions, places can be entered and records reviewed as part of an investigation into alleged violations of the act. Another part of Title VI outlaws extortionate picketing. This occurs when an employer is pressured to give an individual, such as a union official, money or other things of value as a condition of not picketing the employer's premises. Another major provision of Title VI makes it unlawful for a labor organization or its officers to punish by fining, suspending, expelling, or in any way disciplining union members for exercising their rights as provided by the act.

While Titles I through VI contain new legislation intended to regulate many aspects of internal union affairs and establish minimal standards for union democracy, Title VII contains amendments to the National Labor Relations Act. Important changes included closing loopholes in Section 8(b)(4) and the addition of Section 8(b)(7) to control organizational picketing.

Other Labor Relations Legislation

The focus of this chapter has been on two major pieces of legislation: the National Labor Relations Act, as amended, and the Landrum-Griffin Act. These laws provide the basis for regulating labor-management relations and collective bargaining in the United States. It should be noted, however, that several other pieces of legislation also affect labor-management relations in specific segments of the American economy. This section provides a brief overview of that legislation.

THE RAILWAY LABOR ACT

As discussed in the preceding chapter, the Railway Labor Act was passed in 1926 in response to the need to have stable labor-management relations in the railroad industry. Since its original passage, the coverage of the act has been expanded to include the air transportation industry.

This legislation extends to employees in the railroad and air transportation industries the right to organize and engage in collective bargaining. It created the National Mediation Board, which is responsible for determining whether employees desire union representation. While this responsibility for conducting certification elections is similar to that of the National Labor Relations Board, the powers of the National Mediation Board are broader than those of the NLRB. Section 6 of the Railway Labor Act outlines a procedure to be used by the parties when making changes in labor agreements that affect rates of pay, rules, or working conditions. As part of this process, the National Mediation Board attempts to facilitate a negotiated agreement by mediating disputes between employers and unions when their negotiations have failed.

In addition to the National Mediation Board, the Railway Labor Act also created the National Railway Adjustment Board. The National Railway Adjustment Board is composed of thirty-four members, seventeen employer representatives, and seventeen representatives from labor organizations. The purpose of this group is to resolve "disputes growing out of grievances or out of the interpretation or application of agreements concerning pay, rules, or working conditions. . . ."[23] The airline industry was exempted from the provisions establishing the National Railway Adjustment Board as the mechanism to handle disputes arising during the life of a labor agreement. Instead, management and unions in the airline industry developed their own grievance procedures similar to those found elsewhere in the private sector.

THE POSTAL REORGANIZATION ACT OF 1970

Like other federal employees, the rights of postal workers to unionize and engage in collective bargaining prior to 1970 were established by executive orders issued by Presidents Kennedy and Nixon. Under these executive orders, which are discussed in Chapter 17, labor unrest in the postal service became so widespread that it became apparent reform was needed. In 1970, the Postal Reorganization Act[24] was passed. The primary purpose of this legislation was to improve and modernize the postal service by creating an independent organization responsible for moving the mail. Chapter 12 of the Postal Reorganization Act focuses on employee-management relations. Under this legislation, questions concerning union representation are resolved by the National Labor Relations Board. A petition for a representation election can be filed by employees, by a labor organization acting on behalf of the employees, or by the postal service. The NLRB rules and regulations controlling representation issues were made applicable to the postal service. Additionally, the unfair labor practices found in Sections 8(a) and 8(b) of the National Labor Relations Act were made applicable to the postal service and its employees.[25] Thus, Chapter 12 of the Postal Reorganization Act applied a number of important features and administrative proceedings of the National Labor Relations Act to the Postal Service and its unions.

However, disputes arising during the negotiation of a new contract are handled in a different way under the Postal Reorganization Act than according to the procedures found in the National Labor Relations Act. Under the NLRA, collective bargaining disputes take place relatively free from government involvement. Under most circumstances, the parties are free to strike in the event they are unable to reach a mutually acceptable agreement. This is not the case under the Postal Reorganization Act. There is an absolute prohibition on the right to strike. Instead, procedures for resolving disputes by fact finding and arbitration have been substituted for the right to strike.[26] These topics are discussed later in the book.

STATE LABOR LAWS

Coverage of the National Labor Relations Act does not apply to organizations strictly intrastate in nature or those which do not significantly affect interstate commerce. The NLRB has established jurisdictional standards used to determine whether an employer affects commerce, and therefore, is covered by the NLRA. Between 1935 and 1947, a void existed in the nation's labor policy because the NLRB refused to get involved in disputes in interstate commerce that did not meet its jurisdictional standards. By not exerting jurisdiction, the disputes were not covered by federal law. Since the disputes involved interstate commerce, individual state laws could not be applied. As a result, a "no-man's land" existed in which labor disputes affecting interstate commerce that did not meet the NLRB's jurisdictional standards were not covered by either federal or state legislation. This problem was rectified with passage of the Taft-Hartley Act in 1947. Section 14(c)(2) allows states to assert jurisdiction over any labor dispute in which the NLRB has declined jurisdiction.

Over the years, a number of state laws have been passed to regulate those labor-management relations not subject to federal regulation. As would be expected, there is tremendous diversity in the content and enforcement of state labor laws. The diversity among state labor legislation and the inconsistencies with federal labor laws create some potential problems. With reference to this issue, Taylor and Witney state:

> It permits different labor relations policies within interstate commerce. Employers operating under a strict state law would face a competitive disadvantage over employers in a state with a weak or no organizational law. Likewise, inequitable treatment of employees from one state to another exists.[27]

PUBLIC SECTOR LABOR LAWS

So far, our concern has been with legislation affecting labor-management relations in the private sector (except for the postal service, which is quasiprivate). In addition to these laws, legislation has been passed at both the federal and state levels extending collective bargaining rights to many public employees. This legislation and its effects on labor relations and collective bargaining in the public sector will be discussed in Chapters 16 and 17.

Summary

The primary purpose of this chapter was to describe the National Labor Relations Act, as amended. Much more will be said about this key piece of labor legislation in subsequent chapters. In order fully to understand union organizing, collective bargaining, and arbitration, it is important to realize that these activities take place in a legal environment largely defined by the NLRA. While specific provisions of the NLRA will be discussed in greater detail in later chapters, this chapter was intended to provide an overview of the legislation.

Basically, the NLRA was passed to protect workers' right to unionize and bargain collectively with employers. Also, the NLRA protects the parties' right to utilize economic weapons such as strikes and picketing. Section 7 defines the basic rights established by the act. Other major provisions of the legislation are designed to effectuate the act's basic objectives. For example, Sections 8(a) and 8(b) contain unfair employer and union labor practices, respectively. In general, these are restrictions on employer and union activities interfering with employees' Section 7 rights. Similarly, Section 9 advances employees' Section 7 rights by establishing an administrative procedure for determining whether workers want union representation for the purpose of collective bargaining. By providing for a secret ballot election to establish a union's majority status, Section 9 precludes the need for unions to utilize disruptive organizational strikes as they seek employer recognition. Section 10 also protects employee Section 7 rights by granting to the NLRB the authority to prevent and remedy unfair labor practices.

Congress created the NLRB to administer this legislation. However, the NLRB does not have the authority to initiate actions. Parties must petition the NLRB to conduct certification elections. Also, individuals believing they are the victims of an unfair labor practice must file charges with the NLRB. Once a petition for an election or unfair labor practice charges are filed, the NLRB can take action.

The NLRB is composed of two major components. The five-person board serves a judicial function. It decides cases brought before it by the general counsel. The office of the general counsel is responsible for the day-to-day administration of the NLRB. An important part of these responsibilities is deciding whether complaints will be issued in unfair labor practice cases. In conjunction with this, the general counsel prosecutes parties allegedly committing unfair labor practices. It should be remembered that NLRB orders are not self-enforcing. If a party challenges a NLRB decision, the NLRB must go to a federal district court to get its decision enforced. Through this process, NLRB decisions are subjected to judicial review.

The NLRA is a prime example of the way our three-branch system of government works. Congress, the legislative branch, passed the NLRA. To administer the legislation, the NLRB was created. The NLRB is part of the executive branch of government. Finally, the judicial system has the authority to review the laws passed by the legislative branch, as it did with respect to the NLRA in the *NLRB v. Jones and Laughlin Steel Co.*[28] decision discussed in Chapter 2. The judicial system also has the authority to review NLRB decisions. If an NLRB decision is inconsistent with the purposes of the law, the judicial branch can set the decision aside.

The Landrum-Griffin Act was the other major piece of labor legislation reviewed in this chapter. While the NLRA, as amended, is a broad piece of legislation intended to regulate many aspects of labor-management relations, the Landrum-Griffin Act is a much narrower law. The primary intent of this legislation was to regulate internal union affairs. This was done by establishing minimum standards for union democracy and the election of union officers. Also, elaborate reporting requirements were established in an attempt to decrease corrupt practices by union leaders, management officials, and labor relations consultants. The Landrum-Griffin Act also includes a number of amendments to the NLRA designed to rectify problems with the law which became apparent since the last amendments were passed in 1947. The major NLRA amendments included tightening up on secondary boycotts [Section 8(b)(4)], "hot cargo" clauses [Section 8(e)], and restrictions on organizational picketing [Section 8(b)(7)].

We hope that this chapter has imparted an understanding of the complex nature of the nation's labor policy. Today's labor policy is composed of a number of different laws which have been interpreted by a large number of administrative rulings and court decisions. It is important to have an understanding of labor law in order to know your rights and responsibilities under this body of legislation. However, one should not hesitate to consult labor law specialists when uncertain about how to proceed in matters affected by the nation's labor policy.

Two chapters have been devoted to an examination of the nation's public policy toward labor, in order to underscore the importance of the legal environment in which labor and management interact. We hope that you now have an appreciation for the basic components of the nation's labor policy and the forces that have helped shape it over the years. With this background, attention can now turn to an examination of the principal parties in the labor-management relationship. Chapter 4 examines the structure and government of the American trade union movement, and Chapter 5 describes how management organizes to handle labor relations.

Discussion Questions

1. Under the nation's labor policy, what are the two major categories of labor legislation? What are the differences between these categories?
2. What factors led to the reorganization of the NLRB? What changes were made in the organizational structure of the NLRB as a result of Taft-Hartley amendments? What is the significance of these changes?
3. Under the NLRA, employees can be "made whole" for damages attributable to unfair union or management labor practices. However, there is no provision under the NLRA for punitive damages, compensation for mental anguish or the inconvenience of being improperly discharged. What are the advantages and disadvantages of amending the NLRA to allow the NLRB to grant punitive damages in unfair labor practice cases?
4. What factors led to passage of the Landrum-Griffin Act? Should the federal government have the right to regulate the internal affairs of private organizations such as trade unions?

Key Concepts

Unfair union labor practices
Company union
Right-to-work
Secondary boycott
"Hot cargo" clause
Jurisdictional dispute
"Free speech" provision
Featherbedding
Section 7 rights

Unfair employer labor practices
Exclusive representation
"Cease and desist" orders
"Make whole" orders
General counsel
Five-person board
Regional offices
Administrative law judges
Trusteeship

Notes

1. Stuart Rothman, *The Layman's Guide to Basic Law Under the National Labor Relations Act* (Washington, D. C.: National Relations Board, 1962), p. 78.

2. *Edward G. Budd Mfg. Co. v. NLRB,* U. S. Court of Appeals, (3d Cir. 1943), 138 F.2d 86.

3. Joseph P. Goldberg, "The Law and Practice of Collective Bargaining," in *Federal Policies and Worker Status Since the Thirties,* ed. Joseph P. Goldberg et al. (Madison, WI: Industrial Relations Research Association, 1976), p. 28.

4. The following states have "right-to-work" laws: Alabama, Arizona, Arkansas, Florida, Georgia, Iowa, Kansas, Louisiana, Mississippi, Nebraska, Nevada, North Carolina, North Dakota, South Carolina, South Dakota, Tennessee, Texas, Utah, Virginia, Wyoming.

5. *General Longshore Workers, I.L.A, Local 1419,* 186 NLRB 94.

6. *NLRB v. Television and Radio Artists, Local 804,* 315 F.2d 398 (1963).

7. *American Newspaper Publishers v. NLRB,* 345 U. S. 100 (1953).

8. *Virginia Power and Electric Co. v. NLRB,* 319 U. S. 533 (1943).

9. Bruce Feldacker, *Labor Guide to Labor Law* (Reston, VA: Reston Publishing Co., 1980), p. 81.

10. Ibid., p. 94.

11. Douglas M. McDowell and Kenneth C. Huhn, *NLRB Remedies for Unfair Labor Practices* (Philadelphia: University of Pennsylvania, Industrial Research Unit, 1976), p. 19.

12. Ibid., p. 81.

13. Ibid., p. 249.

14. Ibid., pp. 7–8.

15. *Thirty-Sixth Annual Report of the National Labor Relations Board* (Washington, D. C.: U. S. Government Printing Office, 1972), p. 4.

16. Kenneth C. McGuiness, *How to Take a Case Before the National Labor Relations Board,* 4th ed. (Washington, D. C.: Bureau of National Affairs, 1976), p. 26.

17. Ibid., pp. 26–7.

18. Ibid., p. 27.

19. Ibid., p. 27.

20. Ibid., p. 27.

21. Philip Taft, *Rights of Union Members and the Government* (Westport: Greenwood Press, 1975), p. 147.
22. *United States v. Brown,* 380 U. S. 278 (1965).
23. Railroad Labor Act, Section 3(i).
24. Public Law 91–375, 84 Stat. 719.
25. Fredrick C. Cohen, "Labor Features of the Postal Reorganization Act," *Labor Law Journal* 22 (January 1971): 47.
26. Ibid., p. 45.
27. Benjamin J. Taylor and Fred Witney, *Labor Relations Law,* 3d ed. (Englewood Cliffs: Prentice-Hall, 1979), p. 254.
28. *NLRB v. Jones and Laughlin Steel Co.* 301 U. S. 1 (1937).

Suggested Readings

Cox, Archibald, Bok, Derek C., and Gorman, Robert A. *Labor Law.* 9th ed. Mineola: Foundation Press, 1981.

Greenman, Russell L., and Schmertz, Eric J. *Personnel Administration and the Law.* 2d ed. Washington, D. C.: Bureau of National Affairs, 1979.

McLaughlin, Doris B., and Schoomaker, Anita W. *The Landrum-Griffin Act and Union Democracy.* Ann Arbor: University of Michigan Press, 1979.

McClellan, John L. *Crime Without Punishment.* New York: Duell, Sloan and Pearce, 1962.

McCulloch, Frank W., and Bornstein, Tim. *The National Labor Relations Board.* New York: Praeger Publishers, 1974.

Morris, Charles J. *The Developing Labor Law.* Washington, D. C.: Bureau of National Affairs, 1971.

Chapter 4

UNION STRUCTURE, GOVERNMENT, AND POLITICS

Erick Gaard, a student from a Western European country, is attending a large American university. He is majoring in business administration and is enrolled in an introductory labor relations course. During his years in the United States, he has read a good deal about American labor unions. Compared to unions in his homeland, American unions are strange organizations. Among the things he does not understand about American unions are:

- Why isn't there a labor political party in the United States that attempts to have unionists elected to office? Admittedly, the Democratic party and the union movement have close ties, but the Democrats are not a labor party. Furthermore, in the 1980 presidential election, some union leaders publically endorsed the Republican party's candidate for president.

- Why are American unions so committed to the capitalistic economic system rather than favoring a socialistic or communistic economic system? Some unions appear to be extremely anti-communistic.

- Why do American unions focus almost entirely on improving wages, benefits, and conditions of employment for union members in their current places of work? There appears to be relatively little emphasis on broad issues and social reform such as removing poverty or providing free medical care for everyone.

- Why is there almost exclusive reliance on the use of strikes, boycotts, and picketing applied to a specific employer or industry to secure goals? It would seem more sensible to rely on public opinion, favorable legislation and government intervention to achieve the desired ends.

- Why is the American union movement so fragmented? It appears that each union such as the Teamsters, Autoworkers, or Steelworkers is free to take whatever action it deems appropriate. It would seem that the union movement would be more effective if it were centralized and acted in unison.

89

Answers to Erick Gaard's questions as well as many other issues concerning the structure and government of American labor unions will be provided in this chapter. During the evolution of American unions, some of the approaches and directions he suggested were tried. Quite simply, they did not survive in America. Reasons for their failure will be suggested, as well as reasons for the evolution of our current system of unions. When you are finished studying this chapter you should:

- Understand the factors leading to the formation of national unions.
- Be able to describe the goals of the National Labor Union and the Knights of Labor and why these organizations ceased to exist.
- Know the principles upon which the American Federation of Labor (AFL) was based.
- Be aware of the events leading to the formation of the Congress of Industrial Organizations (CIO).
- Be able to discuss the issues that had to be resolved in order for the AFL and CIO to merge.
- Know the functions and structure of the American labor movement as it exists today.
- Understand the implications of leader oligarchy and member apathy.
- Be able to discuss some emerging issues in union structure and government.

The principal stages in the formation of American labor unions will be discussed in the first section of this chapter. The second section of this chapter will focus on the current structure, functions, and government of the elements in the American labor movement. Finally, current issues involving union structure and government will be addressed.

Relevant History

Early American trade unions were very different from modern unions. Several stages in the development of American unions can be identified. Additionally, key forces causing the nature of unions to change can be identified.

LOCAL CRAFT UNIONS

A labor union can be defined as a permanent employee association intended to protect and improve the employment conditions of its members. Such organizations came into existence in America at the end of the eighteenth century.[1] Earlier efforts by workers to protect and enhance their interests tended to be short-lived associations formed to respond to some crisis, e.g., a reduction in wages. These temporary organizations ceased to exist when the crisis passed. Crafts such as carpenters, shoemakers, and printers formed associations in Philadelphia, New York, and Boston in the late 1700s. Such associations were local in nature and typically sought to secure higher wages, enforcement of apprenticeship standards, and employment of union members.

Local union. These early unions were local in nature. They were formed in a particular city and did not seek to establish ties with associations in other cities. Such ties were not necessary because employers' product markets were local. A Boston printer did not compete with a Philadelphia printer in the product market.

Cooperation among unions within a city did not occur until 1827. At that time, the craft unions in Philadelphia joined together to form a city-wide group, a "city central" organization.[2] The "city centrals" attempted to elect local and state officials who would represent the interests of the working classes.

The first attempt at national worker organization stemmed from the "city central" movement. In 1834, representatives from "city centrals" in seven cities met to form the National Trades' Union.[3] However, the financial panic of 1837 led to a reduction in trade union activity and an end to the National Trades' Union. Until the 1930s this relationship between economic conditions and union membership held true. During poor economic conditions membership declined and during the good times, membership increased. With respect to the need for an association of city centrals, business was not competing on a national basis at this time. Consequently the National Trades' Union was ahead of its time.

THE EMERGENCE OF NATIONAL UNIONS

During the 1830s, extension of the product market beyond the community in which production took place was limited. Under these conditions the local trade union supplemented by the "city centrals" was sufficient to meet the objectives of trade union members.

National union. By the 1860s, the situation had changed dramatically, bringing about the need for national unions. At that time, a national union was the association of local unions for a given trade. Perlman describes the forces that operated to bring about national trade unions during the sixties.[4] By 1860, the most important east-west railway lines had been constructed. Means of transporting goods from the East coast to the Mississippi existed, and as a result product markets were no longer local. This was the most important factor leading to national labor unions.

The second factor, also stemming from the improved transportation system, was the increased geographic mobility of labor. This resulted in competition for employment between migratory journeymen and local trade union members. The national union was needed to limit competition for jobs on the part of geographically mobile journeymen.

The third cause was the formation of employer associations in which employers presented a united front to unions. Faced with the threat of an employer association, the logical reaction by local unions was to combine in a national union.

The final cause pointed out by Perlman was the factory system which led to a division of established trades. As a result, the need for skilled labor was reduced because employers could staff their factories with "green hands," or inexperienced workers that could be trained in a short time.

Between 1861 and 1865, thirteen national unions were formed.[5] Between 1865 and 1880, an additional fourteen national unions were formed. Some of these organizations have continued to the present day, e.g., the plasterers, cigarmakers, bricklayers, and masons.

NATIONAL LABOR FEDERATIONS

Federation. A labor federation is an association formed by national or local labor unions. The National Labor Union (NLU) was such an association. It was formed in 1866, in response to a perceived need for unification of labor groups throughout the country. The president of the NLU, William Sylvis, believed that producers' cooperatives were needed to free workers from the bonds of capitalism.[6] In a producers' or workers' cooperative, the work organizations are owned and managed by the workers. In addition, they receive the benefits or profits of the organization.

Syndicalism. The form of economic organization described above is also known as syndicalism. Sylvis was instrumental in the formation of several workers' cooperatives. However, they were not successful. Competitive pressures led to wage cutting and the employment of low-wage workers by the cooperatives. Notice that the cooperatives' practices were similar to those employed by management-operated organizations.

In addition to sponsoring producers' cooperatives the NLU supported various reform movements such as the abolition of convict labor and easy credit at low interest rates. The focus of the NLU was far removed from collective bargaining and an emphasis on workers' wages and employment conditions. As a result, the NLU lost member unions and effectively ceased to exist by 1872.

THE KNIGHTS OF LABOR

The second attempt to form a federation following the Civil War was the Noble Order of the Knights of Labor.[7] The Knights of Labor was founded as a local union in 1869 as a secret society. This was necessary to avoid blacklisting and other forms of retaliation by employers against workers because of their trade union activities. At the first national meeting in 1878, Uriah Stephens was elected Grand Master Workman. Shortly afterward, Stephens resigned and Terence V. Powderly succeeded him.

Like the National Labor Union, the Knights of Labor sought to replace the competitive economic system with an egalitarian system. Such a system attempts to achieve equality of economic, political, and social rights and privileges. Specific objectives included the eight-hour day; equal pay for equal work by women; abolition of child and convict labor; public ownership of utilities and the establishment of workers' cooperatives.[8] Powderly and other leaders of the Knights opposed seeking wage increases of a few cents per day. According to them, workers were entitled to the whole price of their labor. Further, the use of strikes to secure objectives was opposed. The use of reason and persuasion through educational and political means was preferred.[9]

Uriah Smith Stevens *Terence V. Powderly*

The Knights of Labor sought a form of unionism that included all workers, unskilled as well as skilled, in a single union.[10] The Knights accepted all workers regardless of trade, race, sex, or national origin. All were welcome except "bankers, stockbrokers, professional gamblers, lawyers and those who in any way derive their living from the manufacture or sale of intoxicating liquors." There were three organizational levels in the Knights of Labor. The basic unit was the local assembly. A group of local assemblies that were geographically close to each other made up a district assembly. The national assembly was comprised of all district assemblies and was headed by the Grand Master Workman. There were two types of local assemblies. A craft assembly was made up of skilled workmen of a single trade, e.g., tailors, carpenters, and so forth. A mixed assembly could include anyone who worked for a living, including employers and farmers. The unskilled and semiskilled factory workers were included in mixed assemblies. While the leaders of the Knights of Labor viewed the mixed local assembly as the ideal type, in 1882 the trade assemblies were more common by a ratio of three to one.[11]

While the leadership of the Knights opposed the use of strikes, the organization used such tactics very effectively. Following a major strike victory against the Wabash Railroad, membership increased from just over 70,000 in 1884 to 700,000 in 1886. With this rapid expansion, control and direction over the organization were lost. Because of these organizational problems and increased employer opposition, the Knights were involved in a series of strikes that were failures for the union. By 1890, membership had declined to about 100,000.

Without a doubt, the disastrous strikes involving the Knights of Labor contributed to the organization's decline. Another factor was the effort to include unskilled workers along with the skilled trades. Exhibit 4.1 reports the implications of attempting to incorporate such diverse groups into a single union.

> **EXHIBIT 4.1**
> **The Knights of Labor and Organization of the Unskilled**
>
> Their efforts (the Knights of Labor) to bring the unskilled workers within the fold of organized labor won only temporary success. However right in theory they may have been as to the importance of the organization of the unskilled, they were ahead of the times. The great mass of such workers, largely drawn from the ranks of the newly arrived immigrants, were separated by almost insuperable barriers of race, language and religion. Employers were quick to take advantage of every opportunity to stir up the friction and animosities that blocked any real cooperation. Moreover as the workers' ranks were constantly swelled by new arrivals, a tremendous reservoir of potential strikebreakers was always at hand to furnish cheap replacements for those who dared to take part in any union activity. The unskilled, industrial workers did not have in the 1880's either the cohesiveness or the bargaining power to make their inclusion in the organized labor movement practicable. In the face of unrelenting employer opposition it was not, indeed, until after the restriction of immigration in the 1920's and government support for labor organization in the 1930's that industrial unionism—with some few notable exceptions such as in coal mining—was successfully promoted.
>
> *Source:* Excerpt from page 127 of Labor in America: A History by Foster Rhea Dulles. *Copyright 1949, 1955, 1960, 1966 by Foster Rhea Dulles. (Thomas Y. Crowell) By permission of Harper & Row, Publishers, Inc.*

A more basic issue contributing to the Knights' demise involved the different inconsistent views of the organization's leadership and the members of trade assemblies. The trade assemblies wished to form autonomous district assemblies along craft lines.[12] Powderly opposed the formation of national trade districts, saying they were contrary to the basic principles of the Knights.[13] While the leadership was committed to sweeping social reform, the skilled workers sought to improve wages and conditions of employment. It has been argued that the Knights of Labor expired because it could not fulfill any function.[14]

THE AMERICAN FEDERATION OF LABOR

In 1881, representatives of several skilled trade unions met to form the Federation of Organized Trades and Labor Unions. About half of the representatives attending this meeting were members of Knights' trade assemblies. They were disenchanted with Powderly's "one big union" and the pursuit of social reform through legislative means.[15] The Federation organization sought an accommodation with the Knights of Labor that would permit autonomous national trade assemblies within the Knights. The final attempt to reach this agreement ended in failure in 1886. In that same year the American Federation of Labor (AFL) was formed, largely by organizations comprising the Federation of Organized Trades and Labor Unions. Samuel Gompers of the Cigar Makers Union was elected president.

Samuel Gompers

BASIC PRINCIPLES OF THE AFL

The basic principles forming the foundation of the AFL were craft union autonomy, exclusive jurisdiction and business unionism. Other principles underlying the formation of the AFL were avoidance of permanent alignments with a particular political party, the use of economic pressure to secure union objectives and unionization of skilled workers.

Autonomy of national unions. Gompers stated that earlier attempts to form a federation of unions had been unsuccessful because of a failure to recognize the right of the unions composing the federation to self-government.[16] He is quoted as saying, "The American Federation of Labor avoids the fatal rock upon which all previous attempts to affect the unity of the working class have split, by leaving to each body or affiliated organizations the complete management of its own affairs, especially its own particular trade affairs."[17]

Exclusive jurisdiction. The second key principle was that the AFL would permit only one national union for each trade. This is known as "exclusive jurisdiction." It attempts to avoid dual unionism which occurs when two or more unions seek to represent workers doing the same work. This had been a problem for a few years following the split with the Knights of Labor in 1886. The latter had formed local assemblies to compete with those trade unions that had left to join the AFL. Dual unionism enables an employer to play one union against another.

Business unionism. The principles just discussed focus on the organization of the AFL. Probably the key principle that set the AFL apart from the Knights was the AFL's commitment to business unionism. This principle concerns the goals of the AFL.

Adolf Strasser

EXHIBIT 4.2
Bread and Butter Unionism: Goals of the AFL

Question: You are seeking to improve home matters first?

Answer: Yes, Sir, I look first to the trade I represent . . . the interest of the men who employ me to represent their interests.

Chairman: I was only asking you in regard to your ultimate ends.

Witness: We have no ultimate ends. We are going on from day to day. We fight only for immediate objects—objects that can be realized in a few years.

In this often quoted testimony given by Adolph Strasser, president of the International Cigar Makers' Union before the Senate Committee on Education and Labor in 1885, we find the core of the philosophy that underlay the revival of trade unionism and was to inspire the formation of the American Federation of Labor. The new leaders of organized labor were not interested in the reformation of society through creation of a cooperative commonwealth. While they did not wholly abandon the humanitarian, idealistic goals of their predecessors, they prided themselves above all else on being "practical men." They were primarily concerned with the improvement of wages, hours and working conditions for their own trade union followers within the framework of the existing industrial system.

Source: Excerpt from page 150 of *Labor in America: A History* by Foster Rhea Dulles. *Copyright 1949, 1955, 1960, 1966 by Foster Rhea Dulles. (Thomas Y. Crowell) By permission of Harper & Row, Publishers, Inc.*

Exhibit 4.2 reports Adolph Strasser's perception of the goals of this approach to unionism. Along with Gompers, Strasser was a key figure in the formation of the AFL. In contrast to the Knights and the NLU which had become involved with attempts to change the basic economic system, the AFL accepted the capitalistic system and sought to improve the wages and working conditions of union members within that system.

Economic pressure. A fourth principle that set the AFL apart concerned the means relied upon to achieve goals. Recall that Powderly preferred to rely on education, persuasion, and legislation to achieve the goals of the Knights and discouraged the use of strikes. The AFL placed primary reliance on the use of economic pressure in the form of strikes and boycotts. Exhibit 4.3 describes the blending of the AFL goals and means.

Political involvement. Another factor setting the AFL apart was that it took a different position with respect to political involvement. Both the NLU and the Knights had become involved in the formation of a "workers" party. Through these political parties, an effort was made to elect their candidates to public offices. The AFL did not advocate the formation of a "labor" party or the establishment of any permanent alignment with an existing political party. Rather, the political strategy adopted by the AFL was to "reward labor's friends and defeat labor's enemies." The AFL supported the candidates for office who acted in the interest of trade unionism.

Skilled workers. Finally, the AFL focused on the unionization of skilled trades rather than including the semiskilled and unskilled, as had the Knights of Labor.

EXHIBIT 4.3
Business Unionism and the Use of Economic Pressure

The truth is that the outlook and ideals of this dominant type of unionism are those very largely of a business organization. Its successful leaders are essentially business men and its unions are organized primarily to do business with employers—to bargain for the sale of the product which it controls. It has found, however, by long and general experience that if it is to do business with the average employer or with associations of employers it must be prepared to fight. But throughout its history this fighting has been predominantly conducted with the purpose of forcing employers to recognize it as a business or bargaining entity. Its position and experience have been very much like that of a new and rising business concern attempting to force its way into a field already occupied by old established organizations in control of the market. Like the new business concern, it has had to fight to obtain a foothold. But to argue from this that it is organized for war is a complete "non sequitur." (a conclusion that does not follow)

Source: Robert Franklin Hoxie, Trade Unionism in the United States *(New York: D. Appleton and Company, 1928), pp. 336–37.*

There were exceptions; for example, mine workers were originally organized by the United Mine Workers, an AFL affiliate at the time. However, for the most part, the AFL did not seek to organize workers in other than skilled trades. If a union of unskilled or semiskilled workers requested such affiliation with the AFL, it was allowed to do so only when they had organized themselves and there were no jurisdictional disputes with craft unions. Exhibit 4.1 describes some of the problems involved in the unionization of unskilled and semiskilled workers. Basically, the diverse backgrounds of recent immigrants made it very difficult to achieve a united front. Then, if a unified position was achieved, it was easy for management to replace such workers with another group of recent immigrants.

These principles, with little or no modification, were to serve as the foundation of the AFL for many years. It was not until the mid-1930s that the focus on skilled trades would be seriously questioned. The principle of autonomy would not be modified until the mid-1950s. The business unionism focus coupled with the use of direct economic pressure as the means to secure improved conditions of employment continue to this day. The principle of exclusive jurisdiction has been retained to a large degree. However, because of the split between the AFL and the Congress of Industrial Organizations (CIO) and their later merger, some accommodation has been made with respect to this principle. The circumstances surrounding the changes and modifications in these principles are discussed later in this chapter.

INDUSTRIAL WORKERS OF THE WORLD

With the passing of the Knights of Labor, the craft assemblies affiliated with the AFL. But what happened to those seeking to organize the unskilled and semiskilled as well as those seeking basic change in the American economic system?

Among the latter were the syndicalists who formed the Industrial Workers of the World (IWW) in 1905. The "Wobblies" (IWW), modeled after the Knights of Labor, sought to organize all industrial workers (semiskilled and unskilled) into one big union. From its inception, the IWW had internal problems. A split existed between those committed to syndicalism and those seeking to improve the members' wages and conditions of employment within the existing economic system.

The IWW was successful in organizing workers for a limited period of time. Those organized were primarily casual workers in wheat fields, mines, and lumber camps.[18] The tactics of the IWW were particularly militant and violent. As a result, these aggressive tactics brought the IWW into public disfavor. During the First World War over 150 IWW leaders were jailed under wartime espionage laws.[19] Among them was "Big Bill" Haywood, a key figure in founding the IWW. Haywood jumped bail after his conviction and escaped to the Soviet Union where he died in 1928.

FORMATION OF THE CIO

By the 1930s, it was apparent that expanding employment was concentrated in mass production industries, i.e., the rubber and auto industries. In such industries, skilled workers were in the minority and the bulk of employees were semiskilled and unskilled. Consequently, the AFL, if it adhered to the principle of organizing only

William Haywood

skilled workers, would represent a smaller and smaller proportion of the labor force. At the 1934 AFL convention, a report was adopted which declared that new methods had to be developed for organizing workers who were difficult if not impossible to organize into craft unions, i.e., the semiskilled and unskilled workers in mass-production industries. The report directed the AFL Executive Council to charter or establish unions in the automotive, cement, and other mass production industries. This report also stated that the jurisdictional rights of existing trade unions were to be recognized.[20] The meaning to be attached to this statement by the executive council is described below.

Craft union and industrial union. At this point, it is necessary to make clear the distinction between a trade or craft union's jurisdiction and an industrial union's jurisdiction. A trade or craft union's jurisdiction is restricted to employees of a specific trade or occupation, e.g., carpenters, millwrights or cement masons. An industrial union's jurisdiction typically includes all employees in a particular industry, e.g., steel workers, rubber workers or auto workers, regardless of the workers' skills.

During the year following the 1934 convention, the AFL chartered unions in the rubber and auto industries. In defining the jurisdiction of these unions, certain skilled craftsmen and maintenance employees were excluded and placed under the jurisdiction of craft unions.

At the 1935 AFL convention, a report was submitted protesting the executive council's interpretation of the previous convention's declaration on industrial unionism. The report called for unrestricted charters of unions set up in mass-production industries. Under an unrestricted charter, skilled workers would not be excluded from the industrial union as had previously been done. The convention turned down the request for unrestricted charters. As a result of this decision, there was a split in the American labor movement. Exhibit 4.4 describes the basic positions taken by both sides in this debate over industrial unionism. Take special note of the eloquence with which John L. Lewis, president of the United Mine Workers, argued for unrestricted industrial unions.

John L. Lewis

EXHIBIT 4.4
Events Leading to the Formation of the
Congress of Industrial Organizations

The issue was placed fairly before the convention in majority and minority reports submitted by its resolutions committee. The former declared that since it was a primary obligation of the A.F. of L. "to protect the jurisdictional rights of all trade unions organized upon craft lines," industrial charters would violate the agreements that had always existed between the Federation and its craft affiliates. The latter insisted that in any industry where the work performed by a majority of the workers fell within the jurisdictional claim of more than one craft union, industrial organization was "the only form that will be acceptable to the workers or adequately meet their needs."

On the one side in this embittered controversy were William Green, cautiously following the policies bequeathed him by Samuel Gompers in spite of earlier advocacy of industrial unionism; the

EXHIBIT 4.4 *(Continued)*

hard-boiled and hard-hitting head of the carpenters, William L. Hutcheson, firmly resolved to keep all workers in wood or its substitutes within the comfortable fold of his own union; Daniel J. Tobin, the pugnacious leader of the teamsters who scornfully characterized the unskilled workers in the mass-production industries as "rubbish;" Matthew Woll, of the photoengravers, whose conservatism was exemplified by his role as acting president of the old and moribund National Civic Federation, and the dignified, scholarly John P. Frey, head of the Metal Trades Department of the A.F. of L. This was the Old Guard, ready to fight industrial unionism with all the weapons at its command.

Lewis led the insurgents and had the support of some of the most progressive and forceful labor leaders of the day. Among them were Charles P. Howard, calm, persuasive head of the Typographical Union and the actual author of the minority report; Phillip Murray, the somewhat retiring and soft spoken, but extremely able, "alter ego" of Lewis in the United Mine Workers; Sidney Hillman, the Lithuanian-born needle trades leader, who harbored a fund of nervous energy and ambition beneath his quiet manner and who had just brought the formerly independent Amalgamated Clothing Workers into the A.F. of L., and David Dubinsky, one of the shrewdest of trade unionists and president of the effervescent International Ladies' Garment Workers.

The debate among these chieftains over A.F. of L. policy continued for several days, the issue sharpened by attack and counterattack on the floor of the convention. Its peak was reached when Lewis, excoriating tactics that resulted in the new unions "dying like the grass withering before the autumn sun," vehemently assailed what he regarded as the betrayal of the promises made at the preceding convention.

"At San Francisco they seduced me with fair words," he thundered, "Now, of course, having learned that I was seduced, I am enraged and I am ready to rend my seducers limb from limb, including delegate Woll. In that sense, of course, I speak figuratively." He called upon the convention delegates to make a contribution to the welfare of their less fortunate brethren, to heed their cry from Macedonia, to organize the unorganized and make the Federation into the greatest instrument that had ever been forged to befriend the cause of humanity. And he solemnly warned that if they let slip this opportunity, the enemies of labor would be encouraged "and high wassail will prevail at the banquet tables of the mighty."

But for all his eloquence, his appeals and his warnings, Lewis was unable to make the delegates see why they should modify traditional policies. The majority were unmoved by the threat of being rended limb from limb, even figuratively. Their ears were closed to all cries from Macedonia. They were not disturbed by the picture of high wassail at the banquets of the mighty. When the final vote was taken, the program for industrial unionism went down to defeat through a vote of 18,024 to 10,933 in favor of the majority report of the resolutions committee favoring craft unions.

Shortly afterward an incident occurred which appeared to symbolize the break that this crucial vote meant. The details are somewhat obscure. But in the course of further wrangling over procedure, Hutcheson so far departed from parliamentary decorum as to call Lewis a term which bystanders identified as "bastard." The rejoinder of the miner's chieftain was an uppercut, with all the force of some 225 pounds behind it, which caught the equally burly czar of the carpenters squarely on the jaw. The assailants were separated and the danger of a free-for-all happily averted, but the altercation hardly served to placate feelings, already so touchy, in the two camps into which labor had been divided.

Source: Excerpt from pp. 293–95 of Labor in America: A History *by Foster Rhea Dulles. Copyright 1949, 1955, 1960, 1966 by Foster Rhea Dulles. (Thomas Y. Crowell) By permission of Harper & Row, Publishers, Inc.*

A few weeks after the 1935 convention, six AFL-affiliated unions formed the Committee for Industrial Organization (CIO). The objective of this committee, led by John L. Lewis, was to promote the unionization of workers in mass-production industries and encourage their affiliation with the American Federation of Labor. Later, four other unions joined the committee. The Executive Council of the AFL charged that the Committee for Industrial Organization promoted dual unionism by encouraging the formation of new unions to organize workers already within the jurisdiction of existing unions. The Committee for Industrial Organization was asked to disband. The unions involved refused to disband and were suspended from the AFL. Efforts at conciliation failed and in 1937, nine of the ten unions in the committee were expelled. Later that year, the Committee for Industrial Organization held a convention and formed a federation of unions named the Congress of Industrial Organizations (CIO). The CIO, as the AFL, was a loose federation of autonomous national unions.

AFL VERSUS CIO

The CIO unions successfully organized many giant corporations by 1941. In many cases, long bitter struggles took place before an employer recognized the union. Often, the workers used sit-down strikes. These are strikes in which the workers occupy the work place, making it impossible for an employer to hire strike breakers to operate the struck facility. The sit-down strike has since been ruled illegal because it is trespassing on private property. However, the sit-down strike was instrumental in organizing the automobile, rubber, textile, and glass industries.

Following the split with the CIO, the AFL departed from its policy of encouraging only craft unions, and chartered many industrial unions. Not to be outdone, the CIO chartered craft unions to compete with the AFL unions. As a result dual unionism existed for almost all kinds of work. AFL unions and CIO unions competed with each other for members in all trades and industries. The distinction between the two federations disappeared by 1940.

THE MERGER OF THE AFL AND CIO

Merger of the AFL and CIO took place in 1955. Before the merger was achieved, several problems had to be resolved. The principal issue was how to handle the jurisdictional disputes which stemmed from dual unionism. Initially, the AFL took the position that all CIO unions overlapping with existing AFL unions should be absorbed by the latter. The CIO demanded protection of its existing jurisdictions.

No-raiding agreement. This matter was handled by both groups agreeing to a "no-raiding" agreement. It stated that a union affiliated with one federation would not try to recruit members and organize a plant or shop where bargaining relations already existed with an affiliate of the other federation.

Another issue separating the AFL and CIO was the degree to which unions affiliated with the CIO were communist-dominated. In 1946, it was estimated there were eighteen such unions.[21] With the rapid growth that CIO unions had experienced in the late 1930s and 1940s, it had been relatively easy for communists to infiltrate the union movement and become union officials. It appeared that such leaders were willing to sacrifice the welfare of the membership in the interest of communist nations, especially the Soviet Union. Just following World War II, communist leaders and officials were so numerous that Taft wrote, "it was a question whether the anti-Communists in the CIO, could muster a majority."[22] However, in 1949 and 1950, eleven unions charged with communist domination were expelled by the CIO.[23] Most

Phillip Murray

William Green

George Meany

Walter Reuther

of the members of these unions were not sympathetic with their leaders and formed or joined unions affiliated with the AFL or CIO.

The leaders of the AFL and CIO played a role in delaying the merger. William Green of the AFL and John L. Lewis, later replaced by Phillip Murray of the CIO, would not agree to any compromise. In 1952, both Murray and Green died. Their replacements, George Meany of the AFL and Walter Reuther of the CIO, vigorously worked for unification, which occurred three years later. The 1955 convention of the AFL-CIO established the administrative structure and governing policies of the organization.

Structure and Government of the AFL-CIO

Fig. 4.1 presents a diagram of the structure of the AFL-CIO. The governing body of the AFL-CIO is the biennial convention. At the convention each union is entitled to representation in proportion to its membership. Between conventions, the executive officers, executive council, and general board handle the affairs of the federation. The executive officers are the president and the secretary-treasurer. The executive council includes the executive officers and thirty-three vice-presidents.

EXECUTIVE COUNCIL

Responsibilities of the executive council include evaluating legislation relevant to American labor unions and protecting the AFL-CIO from corrupt practices and communist influences. In this regard, the federation has more authority over affiliated unions than had been true under the principle of autonomy followed by the AFL. In 1956, George Meany said, "We have made it clear that union autonomy cannot be used as a cloak for corruption."[24] In its place is the doctrine of conditional autonomy which asserts that the AFL-CIO has the right to prescribe and control the constitutional and administrative practices of an affiliated union as a condition of association.[25] The reason for this change was that charges of corruption or communist domination against a union are highly visible and sometimes magnified by the press or members of Congress. It was believed that if the AFL-CIO presents an image of inaction, legislation harmful to the labor movement could be passed. Under the AFL-CIO constitution, the executive council has the right to investigate any affiliated union accused of wrongdoing. With the approval of two-thirds of the council, a union can be suspended if found guilty of corruption or subversion.

Other key responsibilities of the executive council include assisting unions in organizational activities, chartering new unions not in jurisdictional conflict with affiliated unions, and hearing appeals in jurisdictional disputes. These responsibilities are in keeping with the principle of protecting and preserving the jurisdiction of each member union.

UNION STRUCTURE, GOVERNMENT, AND POLITICS

Fig. 4.1 *Structure of the AFL-CIO*

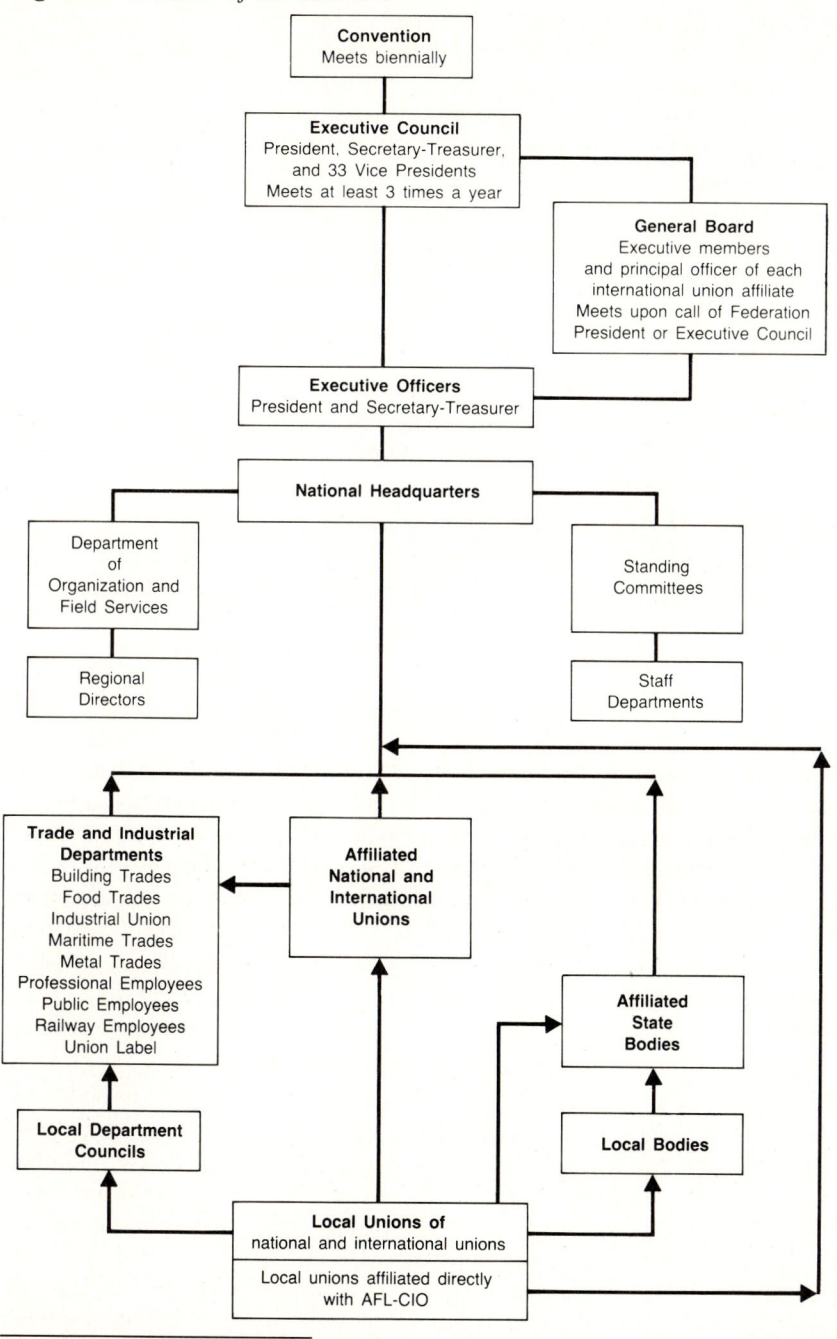

```
                    ┌─────────────────────┐
                    │     Convention      │
                    │  Meets biennially   │
                    └──────────┬──────────┘
                               │
                    ┌──────────┴──────────────────┐
                    │      Executive Council      │
                    │ President, Secretary-Treasurer,│
                    │   and 33 Vice Presidents    │
                    │  Meets at least 3 times a year│
                    └──────────┬──────────────────┘
                               │
                    ┌──────────┴──────────────────┐
                    │       General Board         │
                    │    Executive members        │
                    │ and principal officer of each│
                    │ international union affiliate│
                    │ Meets upon call of Federation│
                    │ President or Executive Council│
                    └─────────────────────────────┘

                    ┌─────────────────────┐
                    │  Executive Officers │
                    │ President and Secretary-Treasurer│
                    └──────────┬──────────┘
                    ┌──────────┴──────────┐
                    │ National Headquarters│
                    └──────────┬──────────┘
```

Department of Organization and Field Services — Regional Directors

Standing Committees — Staff Departments

Trade and Industrial Departments
- Building Trades
- Food Trades
- Industrial Union
- Maritime Trades
- Metal Trades
- Professional Employees
- Public Employees
- Railway Employees
- Union Label

Affiliated National and International Unions

Affiliated State Bodies

Local Department Councils

Local Bodies

Local Unions of national and international unions

Local unions affiliated directly with AFL-CIO

Source: U.S. Department of Labor, Directory of National Unions and Employee Associations, 1977 *(Washington, D.C., U. S. Government Printing Office, 1979), p. 2.*

To implement the no-raiding agreement which was critical for the merger of the federations, procedures for settlement of internal disputes were established. If a dispute takes place, the case goes to a mediator chosen from a panel composed of individuals within the labor movement. Should the mediator be unable to settle the dispute within fourteen days, it is referred to an impartial umpire chosen from a panel of "prominent and respected persons." The decision of the arbitrator takes effect five days after being reached unless it is appealed. An appealed decision is first referred to a subcommittee of the executive council which can dismiss the appeal or refer it to the entire executive council for a decision. The decision of the executive council is final.

GENERAL BOARD

The general board consists of the members of the Executive Council plus a principal officer from each affiliated union. It acts on matters referred to it by the executive officers or executive council and meets upon call by the president.

STANDING COMMITTEES AND STAFF

The president is authorized to appoint standing committees. They operate under the direction of the president. Committees are appointed for legislative, political, or other activities, e.g., civil rights, economic policy, and veterans affairs.

TRADE AND INDUSTRIAL DEPARTMENTS

The AFL-CIO constitution provides for nine trade and industrial departments. The function of these departments is to coordinate activities and facilitate communication among relevant national and international unions and organizing committees. For example, the building trades department serves as a means for seventeen AFL-CIO unions whose members are employed in the construction industry to deal with mutual problems. Among these problems are jurisdictional disputes between one union and another.

COMMITTEE ON POLITICAL EDUCATION (COPE)

COPE is the agency within the AFL-CIO structure which focuses on political activities. National unions have COPE departments and city centrals (local bodies in Fig. 4.1) have COPE committees. In addition, COPE has a unit in each state. In general, COPE attempts to coordinate and mobilize the political pressure generated by organized labor. It operates under the political policy which originally guided the AFL: reward your friends and punish your enemies (although it is true that COPE has traditionally supported Democratic party candidates).

Unions are prohibited from contributing dues money to political candidates. However, COPE does conduct campaigns to gather voluntary contributions for friends of labor and to arrange for the volunteers to work for the election of candidates.

AFFILIATED NATIONAL AND INTERNATIONAL UNIONS

A national union has collective bargaining agreements with different employers in more than one state and an international union is an American union which has members in Canada.[26] In our discussion of national and international unions, the term national union will be used for brevity. Such references apply equally to international unions; exceptions will be pointed out.

In 1977, there were 170 labor organizations classified as unions.[27] Of these, 106 were AFL-CIO affiliates. Membership of unions affiliated with the AFL-CIO made up about 77 percent of that year's total union membership. The unions not affiliated with the federation are independent national unions. Among them is the Teamsters, which is the largest American union. The main advantage for being affiliated with the federation is that such unions have exclusive jurisdiction for the type of workers each seeks to represent. As a result, competition from other affiliated unions is limited and the internal-dispute procedures come into effect where jurisdictional disputes occur. Independent unions do not have such protection. However, the Teamsters do not appear to have suffered.

The principle of autonomy, with the exceptions discussed above, still describes the relationship between the federation and member unions. The affiliated unions are quite autonomous in the conduct of their internal affairs.

LOCAL UNIONS

Local unions fall within two categories in the AFL-CIO: those chartered by a national union; and those not associated with a national union but affiliated directly with the federation. The latter are largely autonomous organizations, although the Executive Council does exercise some control over their internal affairs. The former are, on the other hand, controlled to a large extent by the parent national union. For example, a local union normally must obtain permission of the national union before going on strike. If a local strikes without permission, the national will usually withhold strike benefits.

AFFILIATED STATE AND LOCAL BODIES

The executive council is authorized to establish central bodies on a state or city basis. These are composed of locals of national unions and directly affiliated local unions. There are 50 state bodies, and in 1977, there were 745 local central bodies. These organizations perform functions parallel to the federation. They support legislation and candidates favorable to organized labor and educate the public concerning organized labor's position on issues.

Fig. 4.2 summarizes the relationships among the components of the American labor movement. The solid lines are intended to describe relationships in which one component is accountable to another. This occurs between independent and affiliated national unions and their chartered local unions. The dashed lines are intended to describe relationships which are autonomous, or largely so. This type of relationship

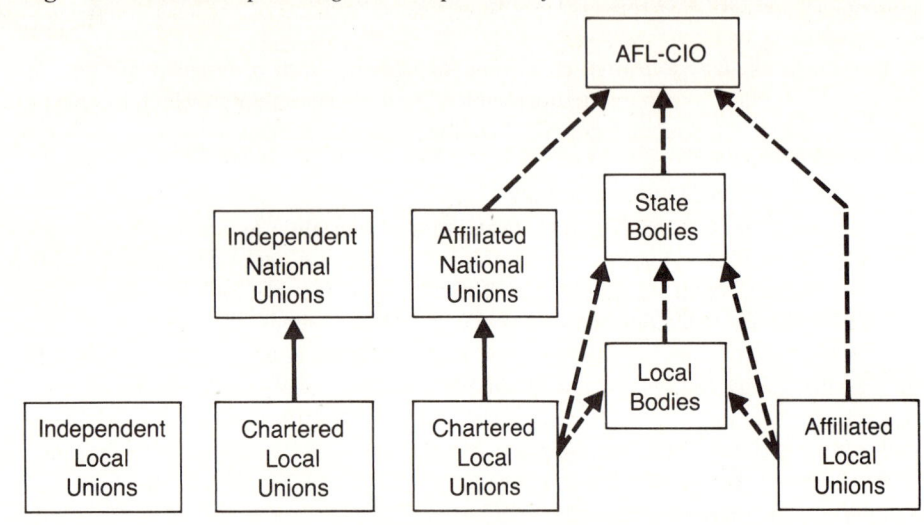

Fig. 4.2 *Relationship Among the Components of the American Labor Movement*

exists between the components associated with the AFL-CIO. Independent national unions and their chartered locals, as well as independent local unions, do not even have this loose relationship with state and local bodies or the federation.

Functions of the Components in the Labor Movement

As reflected in discussing the structure of the American labor movement, the basic components are the federation, the national union, and the local union. As indicated in the previous section, city and state centrals parallel the federation in that they are involved in political, educational, and representation activities.

FUNCTIONS OF THE AFL-CIO

The key functions served by the federation are a political and educational function; a coordinating function; a peacekeeping function; and an organizing function. The first involves lobbying in Congress on behalf of the American labor movement and insuring that labor's point of view is presented to the public. The second function concerns facilitating cooperation among unions representing workers in a particular industry or occupational classification. The peacekeeping function concerns the settlement of jurisdictional disputes. Finally, the federation promotes organization of nonunion workers. However, the primary responsibility for this acitivity is at the national union level.

The AFL-CIO is becoming increasingly involved in another function, promotion of free-trade union movements in foreign countries. The main reasons for this added concern are the rise in foreign trade and multinational corporations, as well as communist domination of foreign labor movements. Implications of these trends are discussed in Chapter 18.

FUNCTIONS OF THE NATIONAL UNION

A basic function of national unions is to organize the unorganized in a trade or profession in the case of craft unions, or in an industry in the case of industrial unions. The national union is the component of the union movement primarily responsible for recruiting more members. Typically, the process involves convincing the employees of a particular organization that it is in their best interest to join the union. When this happens, an additional local union is chartered or recognized by the national union. The employees of the organization would be members of the new local union.

Fig. 4.3 shows why it is in the interest of all employees in an industry or trade to organize the unorganized.

Fig. 4.3 *Demand for Union Labor in an Industry*

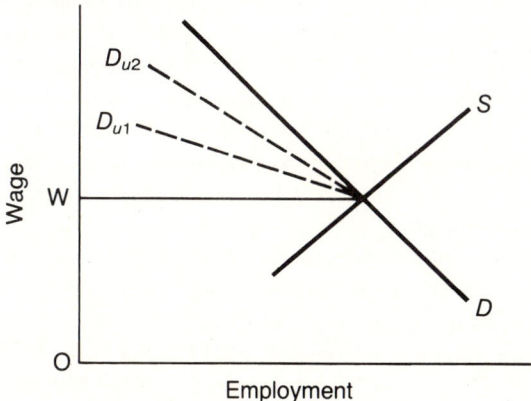

You can assume that a union will bargain over wages in a local market in the case of a local product-market industry, e.g., construction, or a national market in the case of a national product-market industry, e.g., textiles. D represents the demand for labor in the industry. D_{u1} and D_{u2} represent alternative levels of demand for union labor in the industry. As the proportion of the unionized labor force increases, the demand curve for union labor becomes more inelastic.* When the entire industry labor force is organized, the demand curve for union labor will coincide with the demand for labor in the industry (D). In Fig. 4.3, D_{u1} represents a low degree of

---

*Elasticity of the demand for labor refers to the change in employment associated with a given change in the wage rate. Suppose wages increased $1.00 per hour. If many layoffs take place as a result, it is an elastic demand. If few layoffs take place, it is an inelastic demand for labor. Comparing D_{u1} and D_{u2} in Fig. 4.3, the former is more elastic than the latter. In other words, a union's ability to secure higher wages for its members without jeopardizing their job security increases as unionization of the industry increases.

unionization in the industry, and D_{u2} represents a moderate degree. To varying degrees it is assumed in both cases that a union cannot push wages much above OW without causing layoffs at unionized firms. The reason for this is that unionized employers would have higher labor costs. When an attempt is made to pass along these increased costs, consumers will take their business to lower-priced non-union employers.

A second key function served by national unions is the negotiation of collective bargaining agreements. Several factors explain why the principal role in contract negotiation is typically performed by national rather than local union officials. First, as already pointed out in the discussion of relevant history, in those industries in which the product is easily transported to other geographic locations, it is necessary to have uniform wages and benefits among unionized employers in the industry. If this is not the case, the outcome is similar to that described in Fig. 4.3. The only difference is that customers will move from employers paying high union wages to employers paying low union wages because the price of the latter's products will be less due to lower operating costs.

Another reason for national officials playing a key role is that employers are often large organizations with several plants. Since a local typically represents employees at one location only, the bargaining expertise of those representing management is likely to be greater than that available from any one local union. When national officials who specialize in preparing for and negotiating collective bargaining agreements represent the local union, it is assumed that better contracts are obtained for union members. Also, a uniformity of conditions will prevail at all the employer's facilities. This is likely to be perceived as equitable by the workers. Also, the employer will have little incentive to transfer work from one plant to another in response to a more favorable labor agreement.

A third factor is that collective bargaining agreements, independent of organization size, are becoming increasingly complex. Both the number of issues negotiated and the complexity of those issues are increasing. The typical local union official is not qualified to negotiate the funding of complex fringe benefits such as medical insurance and pension plans. Consequently, it is necessary for the national to provide representatives with the necessary expertise.

Other functions served by the national can include representing a union member, or at least having a representative present at the final stage of the grievance procedure and in arbitration. Also, the national union provides strike benefits to members of a local out on strike. In addition, some national unions provide life and other insurance programs and retirement programs directly, rather than negotiating agreements in which employers provide these benefits.

FUNCTIONS OF THE LOCAL UNION

The main functions of the local union are negotiating the collective bargaining agreement and administering the agreement. With respect to the former function the role of local union officials relative to national representatives varies depending on the factors discussed in connection with national unions in the previous section. For example, local officials in a craft union such as the Carpenters and Joiners Union play a far more significant role during negotiations because of the local nature of the product market than local officials in an industrial union such as the United Auto Workers.

Local union officials are primarily responsible for insuring that the provisions of the collective bargaining agreement are adhered to by the employer. Again, there are differences between craft and industrial unions in performing this function. In a craft union local, a business agent is typically employed. One duty of the business agent is to insure that the contract is being followed. For example, the business agent for a carpenters' local might visit construction sites to insure that the contractor is employing union carpenters. In addition, a carpenter at each site is designated as the steward for the carpenters' union. If this person observes any violations of the agreement, and is unable to resolve the problem by talking to the foreperson, it will be turned over to the business agent.

The procedure for handling grievances in an industrial union local is different. In such locals, all members are typically employed by the same organization. They are not continually moving from employer to employer as in the construction industry. In situations where the employment relationship is more stable, the stewards are usually elected, e.g., one steward for each department. The stewards as a group make up the grievance committee, and the committee elects a chief steward. The department steward is initially responsible for handling a grievance. If he or she is unable to resolve the issue, the committee and chief steward will become involved. At the last step in the grievance procedure, the local union president will become involved in handling the grievance. Grievance procedures will be discussed in more detail in Chapter 14.

Government of National and Local Unions

The role of the convention and its relationship to the key executive positions in the AFL-CIO have been described. In this section the corresponding topics for the national and local union levels are addressed. Additionally, the issues of democracy in labor unions, member apathy, and responsiveness of union leaders to the interests of union members are discussed.

NATIONAL UNION GOVERNMENT

The supreme authority in national unions is the convention. Typically, the constitution, which specifies the procedures to be followed in governing a union, calls for a national convention annually or biannually. Each local union sends delegates to the convention. In most unions a system of proportional representation is used. This means that the number of delegates allocated to each local reflects the number of dues-paying members in the local. The delegates to the convention are elected by the local union members. Usually, local union officials are among those selected to attend the convention.

Decision making at the convention takes the form of debating and voting on resolutions, reports, and proposals submitted by committees and delegates. Later in the chapter democracy in unions will be discussed. In connection with that topic it is important to note at this point that national officials can have a great influence on the issues brought before the convention. This is because they typically select the members of the various committees reporting to the convention.

The principal national union officer is the president. Other key officials are the secretary-treasurer, vice-president or vice-presidents, and members of the executive board. The latter are ordinarily selected on a regional basis. The relationship between the president and the executive board varies. In some national unions, the president carries out the policies and decisions approved by the executive board and in others the president administers the affairs of the union subject to the approval of the executive board. Another arrangement can be that the national union president is free to administer the union without securing the approval of the executive board. The justification for the latter arrangement is that national union presidents must frequently make important decisions in a limited amount of time, and securing the approval of a committee spread across the country and responding to the problem in a timely fashion would be quite difficult.

National union officials are elected either directly by the general membership or by the delegates at the national union election. In this way, national union officials are ultimately responsible and accountable to the membership. The term of office for national officials varies, but the Landrum-Griffin Act specifies that elections of national officers must take place at least every five years.

LOCAL UNION GOVERNMENT

The members of a local elect their officers according to the by-laws of the local. The main officers are the president, vice-president, and secretary-treasurer. These elections usually involve the direct participation of the local members. Typically, the individuals filling these positions are employed alongside the other members of the local. As a result, good lines of communication usually exist between the local leaders and the local membership.

Turnover among elected local officials is frequent, relative to national officials. This suggests that the local union level is more democratic than the national union level. Reasons for the difference in turnover of officials by level will be discussed below.

Typically, local union officials fill their roles without compensation by the local. Apparently, the status and prestige received as a result of holding local union office is sufficient reward to motivate some union members to seek these positions. An exception to this practice is in craft union locals associated with the building trades. In these locals, a business agent is usually employed by the union. This individual is paid by the local and plays a key role in negotiating the union contract and insuring that it is followed.

Democracy in the Government of Unions

As they existed originally, American labor unions could be viewed as an example of a primitive form of democracy. "The membership meeting, the members in mass, constituted the legislative power. Administrative functions were vested in an executive board, elected by the members from their own midst."[28] Because of the close proximity between union leaders and their constituency and the active participation of the rank-and-file membership, the needs of the workers could be easily ascertained and acted upon by the union leadership. Under these circumstances, the union's stance in collective bargaining had to be responsive to the needs of the membership. If a gap developed between worker needs and union objectives in collective bargaining, the rank and file, through the democratic political process, would replace the incumbent officers with ones better able to meet their needs.

For a number of reasons, the democratic form of union organization did not persist and was replaced by a bureaucratic form. First, as unions grew in size, administrative problems developed that motivated a consolidation of authority and the establishment of procedures designed to promote orderly operations.[29] Second, bureaucratic centralization will tend to occur in one group when other organizations it is involved with become increasingly centralized.[30] Therefore, as industry became more concentrated and as the intervention of centralized governmental agencies became more frequent, the need for the consolidation of union administrative procedures resulted. Third, as a condition of union recognition, management bureaucracies began to demand "responsible union leadership." In this case, responsible leadership implies that the membership go along with agreements entered into by union leaders. To secure "responsibility," it may be necessary for the union leaders to develop mechanisms by which dissident union members are coerced into compliance with the leaders' decisions or disenfranchised so that their protest does not influence the union leadership's intended course of action. Finally, there has been an increase in the size and the scope of union activities which has resulted in the need for more elaborate services and specialization of some functions.[31] This has accentuated the need for a bureaucratic form of organization which can provide the expertise and administrative ability needed to satisfy the increased responsibilities and to offer additional services to the union's membership.

THE EFFECT OF BUREAUCRATIZATION ON LABOR UNIONS

As the bureaucratic form of organization replaced the democratic form, the seat of effective power changed. Legislative power gradually passed from the membership meeting to the union officials.[32] This passage of control from the rank and file to a group of paid full-time officials has had several implications. First, the concentration of the decision-making processes in the hands of a few individuals facilitates effective and efficient operation of a union. Second, this concentration introduces the possibility that labor leaders may abuse their positions of power; i.e., it is more possible for labor leaders to become unresponsive to membership needs and/or utilize the union's resources, which are in their trust, for personal gain. Third, the role of the rank-and-file membership in a union is greatly altered. The membership meeting becomes merely a plebiscitary body that votes for, and possibly against, proposals made by the union leaders.[33]

RANK-AND-FILE APATHY

As a result of the decreased importance of the membership meeting, the participation of the rank-and-file union member in union affairs has tended to decrease. The individual member may feel that the union leaders are being paid to run the union and, therefore, active participation is not necessary. Alternatively, the rank-and-file member may feel that because the decision making is concentrated in the hands of a few leaders, attempts at participation in union affairs are futile. Regardless of the reasoning, the effect is the same: a decline occurs in the number of union members actively participating in the decision-making processes of their union.

The decline in rank-and-file participation has been identified as the problem of member apathy. It is usually measured by the poor attendance at union meetings. Attendance at union meetings has been found to be in the range of 2 to 6 percent of total union membership.[34] Attendance was found to be higher in smaller unions and much higher at meetings covering such issues as strike votes, contract ratification, and the election of officers.[35]

The evolution of a bureaucratic structure and the ensuing decline in membership participation does not necessarily mean an end to democratic processes within labor organizations. As long as meaningful opportunities exist for membership participation in the formulation, ratification, and implementation of policy, the basis for union democracy still exists.[36]

OLIGARCHY AND LABOR UNIONS

Once a decline in rank-and-file participation occurs, factors become operative that may, in fact, remove from the membership any opportunity to exercise effective control over union policies and, therefore, bring about an almost total abolition of democracy.

Oligarchy. These factors have been identified as Michels's "iron law of oligarchy," which implies the domination of the electors by the elected. In bureaucratic organizations, power accumulates at the top, and as power accumulates an "iron law of oligarchy" is set in motion.[37] Exhibit 4.5 provides a description of the process by which this might occur.

Union oligarchy and the removal of leaders from membership control can become self-perpetuating because of the effect of the oligarchical form of organization on the democratic processes within a union. Once an oligarchy develops, the opportunity for the membership to become active greatly decreases. Turnover of union of-

> **EXHIBIT 4.5**
> **Iron Law of Oligarchy**
>
> As the leader becomes part of the hierarchy and secures the gratification and rewards of high office, his orientation towards his position will change. An ideology peculiar to the situation is constructed and maintenance of power becomes equated with the best means of achieving organizational goals. By this process the personal ends of the leader come to overshadow, may indeed replace, those of the organization. A leader may seek, and eventually achieve, emancipation from the membership and thus become independent of its control. In such situations the rule of the leader becomes absolute and power is exercised in an oligarchic manner.
>
> Source: Lois McDonald, Leadership Dynamics and the Trade-Union Leader *(Washington Square; New York University Press, 1959), p. 69.*

ficers decreases and access of all members to positions of power declines as well.[38] This situation develops for several reasons. Incumbent union officials may control the internal means of communication, thereby reducing the possibility for internal political conflict.[39] In addition, the primary source of leadership training is holding an elected office in the union. The average worker has little opportunity in other settings to learn the needed skills.[40]

RANK-AND-FILE RESPONSE TO OLIGARCHICAL CONTROL

The rank-and-file union member has a wide variety of needs to be satisfied by the union leadership and has certain expectations regarding administration of the union. In order to remain in office and maintain the strength of the union in collective bargaining, union officials must meet the basic expectations of the rank-and-file union member. This is necessary to maintain the allegiance of the rank-and-file members to the union and the leaders. In turn, allegiance determines, in part, the union's bargaining power. The ultimate economic weapon of the union is the strike. However, the strike can be employed effectively only when the members are willing to make substantial sacrifices for the welfare of the group.[41] Finally, as union bargaining power increases, the terms and conditions of employment agreed to during contract negotiations will be more favorable, which will tend to satisfy the needs of union members. As long as union leaders can satisfy worker needs, very seldom will the rank-and-file react against the absence of democratic practices within the union. Fig. 4.4 describes the circular relationship of these variables.

The presence or absence of rank-and-file participation and union democratic practices varies with the level of the union organization under examination. In general, participation by the rank and file is limited at the national level. The national convention tends to serve a "rubber stamp" function for decisions made by a

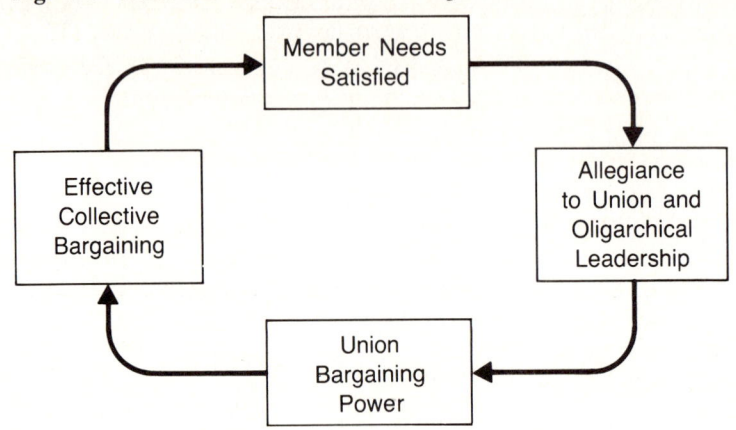

Fig. 4.4 *Rank-and-File Reaction to Oligarchical Leadership*

```
         Member Needs
          Satisfied
    ┌──────→ □ ──────┐
    │                ↓
 Effective        Allegiance
 Collective       to Union and
 Bargaining       Oligarchical
                  Leadership
    ↑                │
    └────── □ ←──────┘
          Union
         Bargaining
           Power
```

union's national officers and executive board. Incumbent officers are seldom opposed for re-election. This had led to long tenure in office for many national officers.[42] Only on rare occasions will there be a rank-and-file revolt against the national leaders, and these are precipitated only when the rank and file considers the union to be in a crisis situation. The defeat of incumbent president Tony Boyle in the 1972 United Mineworkers union election is an example of the potential for active rank-and-file participation in the affairs of a union at the national level. While Boyle was defeated, circumstances surrounding the election included: conviction of Boyle for misusing $49,000 in union dues; indictment of a Boyle associate for the murder of Joseph Yablonski, Boyle's opponent in the 1969 UMW presidential election; and widespread allegations that Boyle had authorized the murder.[43] The circumstances that lead to the defeat of an incumbent union president must be quite drastic and do not develop frequently.

At the local level, it is easier for union democracy to survive. This is not to say that participation rates are high or that an effective two-party political system is operating. However, there are a number of factors at the local level that allow the local union to approximate more closely a democratic organization. First, local leaders operate in close proximity to their constituents. It is easy for the rank and file to realize that local union leaders, relative to national leaders, are not representing the will of the majority. Second, local union meetings are more frequent and more conducive to rank-and-file involvement. Third, the skills needed to be a local union leader are not so great that it is impossible for inexperienced workers to run for office, and, if elected, to serve effectively. Finally, because most local unions are small, relative to national unions, and because local members are in close physical proximity, it is possible for opposition groups to form and for their ideas to be communicated to other members of the local.

Active participation in union activities has been emphasized as a basic characteristic of union democracy. Because of the relative ease of removing local union leaders from office, at the local level it is not necessary for members to attend meetings and vote on issues in order to influence the local officers. The desires of the quiescent members of the local must be considered when making decisions. They will remain inert only so long as they are satisfied with the decisions of the local leaders. The decision makers know this and try to act accordingly.[44]

Change in Union Structure, Government, and Politics

The issues of union democracy and member apathy have concerned students of the American labor movement for some time. Because these topics are central to the continued existence of unions as most now exist, these topics will continue to receive a great deal of attention. Other topics reflecting the dynamic nature of the union movement in the United States include union finances, union corruption, and union mergers.

UNION FINANCES

To finance the activities of a national union, members are required to pay an initiation fee when they join and monthly dues to remain in good standing. The amount of these fees and dues varies. A recent study of labor union fees and dues found that among the eighty-nine unions with set initiation fees, forty-five (just over half) charged less than $40.[45] Those twenty-nine unions charging more than $100 initiation fees were typically small unions representing professional workers, e.g., Directors Guild and football players. Monthly fees also vary by skill level and size of union. The dues rates for larger unions, both those affiliated with the AFL-CIO and independent unions, are typically less than $10 a month.[46]

The principal uses of these funds are to pay salaries of full-time officers, representatives, and clerical personnel. In addition, office space, supplies, and equipment must be rented and/or purchased. Other uses include payment of arbitration fees, building up the strike fund so that benefits can be paid when the union is on strike, preparation of union publications, conducting educational programs, and maintaining a retirement program for members.

There are restrictions on the ways in which unions can spend member dues and fees. Recent court decisions have made it necessary for some unions to adopt rebate plans which, if requested by a member, return the portion of one's dues that would have been spent on political activities. However, unions can continue to solicit voluntary contributions for political activities.

UNION CORRUPTION

During the early 1950s, George Meany attempted to reduce corruption in the American labor movement. In 1959, the Landrum-Griffin Act became law. As discussed in the previous chapter, this legislation focused on controlling corruption in unions.

Lane Kirkland

A recent report claims that union corruption is worse than ever.[47] It states that since 1973, about 450 union officers and employees have been convicted of serious labor-related crimes. In addition, twenty-two civil suits have been filed to recover stolen union-pension funds totalling over 170 million dollars.

It is contended that four unions have close ties with organized crime.[48] The unions are the Teamsters, the Laborers International Union, the Hotel and Restaurant Employees and Bartenders International Union, and the International Longshoremen's Association. The Teamsters were expelled from the AFL-CIO for corruption in 1958. Despite the current allegations concerning the Teamsters Union, it was recently invited to reaffiliate with the AFL-CIO. Lane Kirkland, AFL-CIO President, justified this action by arguing that the Landrum-Griffin Act took away from the federation the responsibility for controlling crime in American labor unions.[49]

This suggests that the AFL-CIO is no longer taking the position that the autonomy of member unions is conditional upon the absence of corrupt practices in the administration of internal national union affairs.

In 1978, the United States Department of Labor began a study of union corruption. This study identified certain characteristics shared by corrupt unions. They are typically decentralized and their members are employed by small firms and businesses. Additionally, the members tend to be unskilled, transient, immigrant, and underpaid. In view of these findings, it is predicted that corruption and racketeers will show up in unions representing farm workers in the years to come.[50]

UNION MERGERS

At the time of the AFL-CIO merger, it was anticipated that mergers of affiliated national unions would be quite extensive. George Meany and Walter Reuther are reported to have anticipated that the 135 affiliated unions would be reduced to 50.[51]

Several arguments for merging have been made. Among them are the need to join forces in order to present a stronger bargaining position to employers, to combine financial resources so that the necessary services and expertise can be made available to union membership, and to marshall sufficient resources and strength to lobby for legislation more effectively.[52]

The number of mergers hoped for by Meany and Reuther has not occurred. However, a total of fifty-seven mergers occurred between 1956 and 1977.[53] Most of these mergers have been classified as the joining together of basically similar unions.[54] As a result of these mergers, there has been a reduction in the number of jurisdictional disputes. Also, the merged unions have been better able to present a more united front in labor negotiations.

It has been suggested that during periods of rising costs and declining union memberships, an increase in the number of mergers can be expected.[55] As will be discussed in Chapter 6, union membership as a percent of nonagricultural employment has been declining since 1955. At this time, there is no reason to expect the trend in union membership to change. Consequently, mergers of unions and employee associations are expected to continue.

Summary

The early American unions were local craft or trade unions. It was not until employers became large and through improved systems of transportation were able to market goods at geographically distant locations that national unions developed. The Knights of Labor attempted to form a union for all workers. Leaders of the Knights wanted to achieve a more egalitarian economic system. Education and persuasion were to be the means of achieving the goals of the Knights. The American Federation of Labor offered alternative goals and means. The AFL sought immediate goals of improved wages and conditions of employment within the existing economic system. It respected the autonomy of member unions and encouraged the use of economic pressure to achieve goals. Further, the AFL focused on the unionization of skilled trades.

During the mid-1930s, some unions within the AFL were in favor of organizing employees of mass-production industries. A dispute arose concerning the means to achieve this end. As a result of this dispute, the Congress of Industrial Organizations was formed. The original objective of the CIO was to encourage the organization of mass-production industries. However, within a short time after the formation of the CIO, both the AFL and the CIO began chartering unions to compete with unions affiliated with the other federation. This competition between AFL and CIO unions continued until their merger in 1955.

The key organizational levels in today's union movement are the AFL-CIO, national unions, and local unions. Primary functions of the federation are lobbying on behalf of the union movement, educating the public concerning labor's point of view and resolving disputes among affiliated unions. Primary roles of a national union are organizing additional local unions within its jurisdiction and negotiating collective bargaining agreements for member local unions. The main functions of a local union are administering collective bargaining agreements and participating in the negotiation of agreements.

A number of problems are currently faced by the American labor movement. Among them are member apathy and oligarchy on the part of union leaders. In addition, there is evidence that corruption on the part of some union leaders is a problem. An additional phenomenon reflecting the changing nature of the movement is the continuing merger of national unions.

Discussion Questions

1. Why were the early American unions local unions? What factors brought about national unions?
2. What factors contributed to the failure of the National Labor Union and the Knights of Labor?
3. List and describe the principles upon which the American Federation of Labor was founded.
4. Why was the Committee for Industrial Organization formed and how did the Congress of Industrial Organizations come into being?
5. How has the problem of dual unionism been resolved by the AFL-CIO?
6. What is the relationship between the AFL-CIO and affiliated national unions, affiliated local unions, independent national unions, and independent local unions?
7. What are the key functions of the AFL-CIO, state and local bodies, national unions and local unions?
8. What is union leader oligarchy and how does it relate to rank and file member apathy? Why are these problems for today's union movement?
9. Is corruption a problem among union leaders today? Explain.
10. What are arguments for and against mergers of national unions?

Key Concepts

Syndicalism
Local union
National union
Federation
Autonomy of national unions
Exclusive jurisdiction

Dual unionism
Business unionism
Craft union
Industrial union
No-raiding agreement
Oligarchy

Notes

1. U. S. Department of Labor, *A Brief History of the American Labor Movement,* Bulletin 1000, revised (Washington, D. C.: U. S. Government Printing Office, 1970), p. 1.
2. Ibid., p. 5.
3. Ibid., p. 6.
4. Selig Perlman, *A History of Trade Unionism in the United States* (New York: The Macmillan Company, 1922), pp. 109–10.
5. U. S. Department of Labor, *A Brief History of the American Labor Movement,* p. 9.
6. Ibid.
7. Ibid., p. 13.
8. Ibid., p. 15.
9. Gerald N. Grob, "The Knights of Labor and The Trade Unions, 1878–1886," in *Readings in Labor Economics and Labor Relations,* 3rd ed., ed. Richard L. Rowan (Homewood, IL: Richard D. Irwin, 1976), p. 101.
10. Foster Rhea Dulles, *Labor in America: A History* (New York: Thomas Y. Crowell Company, 1949), pp. 126–27.
11. Norma J. Ware, *The Labor Movement in The United States, 1890–95* (New York: D. Appleton and Company, 1926), p. 158.
12. Grob, "The Knights of Labor and The Trade Unions, 1878–1886," p. 102.
13. Ibid., p. 103.
14. Philip Taft, *Organized Labor in American History* (New York: Harper and Row, 1964), p. 120.
15. Grob, "The Knights of Labor and The Trade Unions, 1878–1886," p. 103.
16. Taft, *Organized Labor in American History,* p. 117.
17. Ibid.
18. U. S. Department of Labor, *A Brief History of the American Labor Movement,* p. 23.
19. Thomas R. Brooks, *Toil and Trouble: A History of American Labor,* 2nd ed. (New York: Dell Publishing Company, 1971), p. 123.
20. U. S. Department of Labor, *A Brief History of The American Labor Movement,* p. 31.
21. *Communists in Labor Unions,* special report prepared for members of the Research Institute of America, 4 April 1946.
22. Taft, *Organized Labor in American History,* p. 624.
23. U. S. Department of Labor, *A Brief History of The American Labor Movement,* p. 47.
24. *AFL-CIO News,* 1 September 1956.
25. John Hutchinson, "George Meany and the Wayward," *California Management Review* 14 (1971).
26. Martin Estey, *The Unions: Structure, Development and Management,* 2nd ed. (New York: Harcourt Brace Jovanovich, Inc., 1976), p. 41.
27. U. S. Department of Labor, *Directory of National Unions and Employee Associations, 1977* (Washington, D. C.: U. S. Government Printing Office, 1979), p. 1.
28. Will Herberg, "Bureaucracy and Democracy in Labor Unions," in *Readings in Labor Economics and Labor Relations,* ed. Richard L. Rowan (Homewood, IL: Richard D. Irwin, Inc., 1972), p. 234.
29. Seymour M. Lipset, "The Political Process in Trade Unions: A Theoretical Statement," in *Freedom and Control in Modern Society,* ed. Monroe Berger, Theodore Abel, and Charles Page (New York: Octagon Books, Inc., 1954), p. 83.
30. Ibid., pp. 83–84.
31. Lois McDonald, *Leadership Dynamics and the Trade-Union Leader,* (Washington Square: New York University Press, 1959), p. 63.
32. Herberg, "Bureaucracy and Democracy in Labor Unions," p. 234.
33. Ibid., p. 234.
34. Leonard R. Sayles and George Strauss, *The Local Union,* (New York: Harcourt, Brace and World, Inc., 1967), p. 97.

35. Ibid., p. 98.
36. John R. Coleman, "The Compulsive Pressures of Democracy in Unionism," *The American Journal of Sociology* LXI (May 1956): 520.
37. S. M. Lipset, M. A. Trow, and J. S. Coleman, *Union Democracy* (New York: The Free Press, 1956), p. 4.
38. McDonald, *Leadership Dynamics and the Trade-Union Leader,* p. 69.
39. Lipset, "The Political Process in Trade Unions: A Theoretical Statement," p. 94.
40. Ibid., p. 89.
41. Ross Stagner and Hjalmar Rosen, *Psychology of Union-Management Relations* (Belmont, CA: Wadsworth Publishing Company, Inc., 1965), p. 68.
42. Martin Estey, *The Unions: Structure, Development and Management* (New York: Harcourt, Brace and World, Inc., 1967) p. 53.
43. "Tough Tony in Trouble?" *Time,* 4 December 1972, pp. 17–18.
44. Arnold S. Tannenbaum and Robert L. Kahn, *Participation in Union Locals* (Evanston: Row, Peterson and Company, 1958), pp. 168–69.
45. Charles W. Hickman, "Labor Organizations' Fees and Dues," *Monthly Labor Review* 100, no. 5 (May 1977): 20.
46. Ibid., p. 22.
47. "Union Corruption: Worse Than Ever," *U. S. News and World Report,* 8 September 1980, p. 33.
48. Ibid.
49. Ibid., p. 34.
50. Ibid., p. 36.
51. Arthur Goldberg, *AFL-CIO: Labor United* (New York: McGraw-Hill, 1956), p. 229.
52. Charles J. Janus, "Union Mergers in the 1970's: A Look at the Reasons and Results," *Monthly Labor Review,* October 1978, p. 13.
53. Ibid.
54. John Freeman and Jack Brittain, "Union Merger Process and Industrial Environment," *Industrial Relations* 16, no. 2 (1977): 180.
55. U. S. Department of Labor, *Directory of National Unions and Employee Associations, 1977,* p. 56.

Suggested Readings

Dulles, Foster Rhea. *Labor in America: A History*. New York: Thomas Y. Crowell Company, 1949.
Estey, Martin. *The Unions: Structure, Development and Management,* 2nd ed. New York: Harcourt Brace Jovanovich, Inc., 1976.
Perlman, Selig. *A History of Trade Unionism in the United States*. New York: The Macmillan Company, 1922.
Sayles, Leonard R. and Strauss, George. *The Local Union*. New York: Harcourt, Brace and World, Inc., 1967.
Taft, Philip. *Organized Labor in American History*. New York: Harper and Row, 1964.
U. S. Department of Labor, *A Brief History of the American Labor Movement*. Bulletin 1000, revised. Washington, D. C.: U. S. Government Printing Office, 1970.

Chapter 5

MANAGEMENT ORGANIZATION FOR LABOR RELATIONS

John Patrick was settling into his new job as Vice-President of Labor Relations for the United Manufacturing Company. He was hired to assume this job because top management of United had not been satisfied with the way the labor relations function had been managed by his predecessor. In recent years there had been a number of strikes at United's unionized plants, and day-to-day union-management relations were anything but cooperative. In addition, there were some non-union plants at which union organization efforts were increasing in intensity. The Chief Executive Officer had said that United wants "a stable operation" at all plants. He indicated that United was not in the union-busting business. If the employees at a plant wanted a union, that was okay with him, but he would prefer not to have any more unionized plants.

From what John had been able to learn from visits to the various United plants, the situation was as follows:

- At the plants already unionized, the employees appeared to be supporting the union. In addition, the union leaders appeared to be genuinely interested in representing the interests of the membership.
- At the non-union plants, union advocates were presently in the minority, but the number of employees favoring unionization appeared to be growing.

The Chief Executive Officer had assured John that top management would support whatever program was necessary to achieve stable union-management relations at the unionized plants and to prevent further union certification at the other plants. John's responsibility was to organize the labor relations department so that these goals could be attained.

AN INTRODUCTION TO THE PARTIES

The situation facing John is not unusual in that often some plants or locations are unionized while others are non-union. This chapter will explore alternative ways management organizes to deal with unions and to prevent further unionization. When you have completed this chapter you should:

- Be able to describe different categories of management attitudes toward and approaches to dealing with unions.
- Understand why management in the United States typically is opposed to unionization of an organization's workforce.
- Be aware of tactics used by management to resist unions during the 1800s and early 1900s.
- Know the basic approaches employed by management to remain non-union today.
- Be able to suggest why some organizations choose a positive approach to resisting unions and others choose a negative approach.
- Know how the labor relations function is commonly organized and who is typically responsible for various labor relations decisions when a union represents employees of an organization.
- Be able to describe the typical union-management working relationship and explain why management would assume an accommodative attitude toward a union.
- Be aware of trends that appear to be emerging in management's approach to dealing with unions.

The role of management in organizations and categories of management attitudes toward unions are topics addressed initially in this chapter. Then measures employed by management to resist unions during the nineteenth century and the early part of this century are discussed. The third section of the chapter focuses on current management tactics to limit unionization. The following section describes common ways in which the labor relations function is organized and decision-making authority is allocated when a union is present. Finally, an attempt is made to assess emerging trends in management's approach to unions.

The structure of the union movement in the United States and the functions served by the various levels of labor unions have been discussed in the previous chapter. This chapter concerns the organization of management for labor relations. This topic typically receives little attention in labor relations textbooks. We believe it deserves greater emphasis since management is one of the parties directly involved in collective bargaining. In addition, many students entering the labor force following college will have some contact with labor unions as members of management. Other students will be employed in labor relations or employee relations. For such students it is important to understand the standard ways in which management organizes to deal with unions.

MANAGEMENT ORGANIZATION FOR LABOR RELATIONS

Role and Levels of Management

Management is responsible for providing leadership and making decisions in work organizations. In the past, managers of American businesses were, quite often, also the owners. With the exception of small businesses, today's managers are typically not the owners. Rather, managers are employees hired to operate an organization on behalf of the owners.

Management of an organization is usually arranged in a hierarchy. Fig. 5.1 represents the levels of an organization.[1] At the lowest level are employees or workers. These individuals are not responsible for directing the work of others. Anyone above this level is typically referred to as part of management. Within management, three general groups are often identified.

Top-level managers are the chief executive officer of an organization and the vice-presidents. Managers at this level control the overall direction of the organization. They determine the basic goals of the organization and establish its policies. In addition, they play a key role in dealing with other organizations. They are not usually involved in the day-to-day operation of the organization. However, they do become involved in critical decisions involving the operation of the organization. As we shall see later in the chapter, top management plays the dominant role in dealing with unions.

Middle managers are responsible for establishing practices to implement policies of top management. They have specific areas of responsibility. Also, they manage other managers. They can range from department managers, to plant or store managers, to managers of major divisions of an organization. Fig. 5.1 presents a

Fig. 5.1 *Levels of Work Organizations*

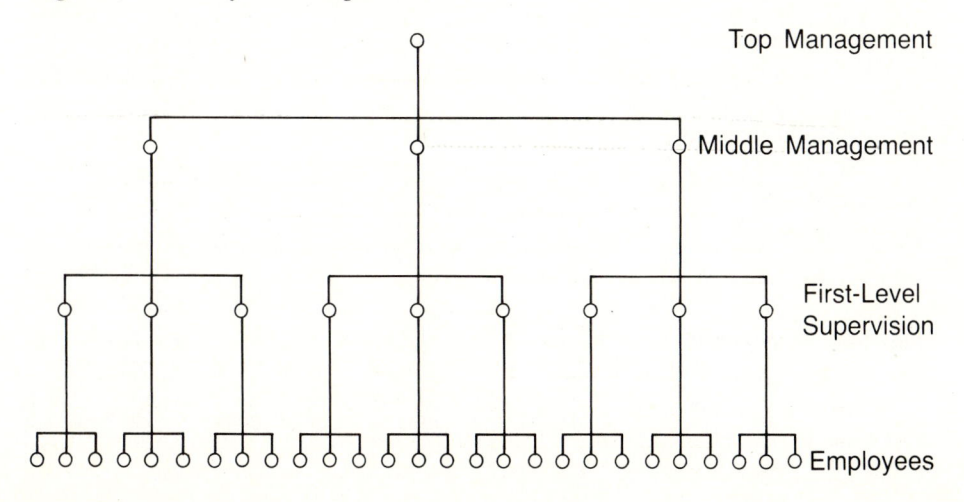

relatively simple organization. Actually, a large organization will have several levels within middle management.

First-level supervisors are primarily involved in implementing programs, procedures, and assignments received from middle management. They are the level of management that directs the work of the nonmanagerial workforce.[2] Consequently, first-level supervisors carry the primary responsibility for implementing an organization's labor relations programs and practices. They are the key communication link with employees and are the key figures in day-to-day implementation of a collective bargaining agreement.[3]

Management Attitudes toward Unions

Management can assume a number of different attitudes toward unions. Fig. 5.2 represents different possibilities. These categories are a modification of categories suggested by Selekman.[4] One can think of degrees of cooperativeness between managers and union leaders underlying these categories. However, this tends to be an oversimplification.

At one extreme is a management attitude that can be described as open hostility. It implies a determined effort to avoid dealing with any union. In management's efforts to avoid unions, open hostility implies a willingness to use almost any tool. Among techniques that employers have used during the history of labor relations in the United States are industrial spies to keep tabs on union activities and leaders,[5] armed guards supplied by such organizations as the Pinkerton Detective Agency,[6] and police as well as troops[7,8] to control and limit the effects of strikes.

Prior to passage of the National Labor Relations Act (NLRA), these tactics were used with some regularity. Since the NLRA was implemented, such strong-arm tactics have been used infrequently. Other techniques that are implied by this approach are the discharge of union activists and threats to the safety of union organizers. "Open hostility" implies a willingness to engage in illegal actions, to say nothing of practices involving questionable ethics.

Needless to say, if a union is certified in such a circumstance, management is continually seeking ways to get rid of the union. In addition, the employer may continue to engage in unfair labor practices by refusing to bargain with the union.

Fig. 5.2 *Management Attitudes Toward Unions*

Open Hostility	Controlled Hostility	Accommodation	Cooperation	Collusion

"Controlled hostility" implies a determination to avoid dealing with a union. However, it differs from "open hostility" in that it implies an adherence to the law. With respect to avoiding certification of a union, such managers would not engage in unfair labor practices. With respect to dealing with a certified union, such managers would be hard-headed bargainers. Management negotiators would try to limit union efforts to control or influence managerial decisions. However, a contract would be negotiated and meticulously followed.

Management assuming this attitude toward unions would recognize the legal right of a union to represent a company's employees. However, management would prefer not to have a union present and would be looking for ways to decertify the union. In attempts to do so, they would avoid charges of unfair labor practices.

The early years of a bargaining relationship between a union and an employer are likely to be characterized as a time of "controlled hostility." After a time, a softening of management's attitudes toward unions may take place. A major attitudinal change would be a recognition that the union will represent the employees for the foreseeable future and that efforts to decertify the union are fruitless.

"Accommodation" implies a willingness to deal with the union in such a way as to avoid unnecessary disagreements. There is a willingness to compromise when possible, to conciliate when necessary, and to tolerate at all times.[9] In a bargaining relationship characterized by accommodation, the focus is on the traditional issues of wages, fringe benefits, and administrative issues. Broader issues such as productivity do not enter the picture.

"Cooperation" involves another major shift in attitudes. Basically, it assumes an end to an "us versus them" attitude and the adoption of a "we" attitude. This "we" attitude implies a willingness to try to solve problems that adversely affect either party or both parties. It also implies a realization that both parties stand to gain from more efficient operations. Naturally, development of this attitude, as well as an attitude of accommodation, necessitates a similar attitude on the part of union leaders and members. Cooperative labor relations involves a concern for employee interests and welfare on the part of management and a concern for efficiency, elimination of waste, and advancing technology on the part of the union.

"Collusion" involves union-management relations that go beyond legitimate "cooperation." It implies a union-management relationship that adversely affects the legitimate interests of other employers, employees, the union membership, or the consuming public. For example, an employer may pay a bribe to union leaders in return for their agreement to a substandard or "sweetheart" labor contract. Often collusion implies that union leaders do not properly represent the interests of the union's membership.

WHY MANAGERS OPPOSE UNIONS

Management of an organization, both in the private and public sectors, makes decisions concerning the use of available resources. Typically, these resources are limited, in the sense that everyone in the organization cannot receive everything they would like to have. Management is responsible for representing the interests of the owners or of the taxpayers. As a result, it is inevitable that management's decisions will at times conflict with the wishes and interests of employees. In the long run, there may be little or no difference between the interests of owners (taxpayers) and employees. However, in the short run, conflicts are likely to occur.

When a union represents the employees of an organization, management's discretion in making decisions is less than when a union is not present. As will be apparent in later chapters, a collective bargaining agreement places constraints on a great many managerial decisions. In some cases, discretion on the part of management may be removed entirely. For example, when a reduction in the workforce is necessary, a labor contract is likely to specify that layoffs will be in reverse order of seniority. Management, on the other hand, would probably prefer to make such decisions in reverse order of merit, as determined by management.

THEORY X AND THEORY Y

Philosophies held by managers concerning the nature of the typical employee's attitude toward work can reinforce the belief that managers *should* be making decisions for employees. Douglas McGregor described two polar beliefs and assumptions made by managers concerning the motivation to work.[10] Traditional managerial attitudes were labeled Theory X and held that:

1. The typical employee dislikes work and will avoid it when possible.
2. Because of this dislike for work, most employees must be coerced, controlled, directed, or threatened in order to get them to put forth sufficient levels of effort to achieve organization goals.
3. The average worker prefers to be directed, wishes to avoid responsibility, has little ambition, and values security above all.

Alternatively, Theory Y is based on a more current view of employees in work organizations. It includes the following:

1. Work involving physical and mental effort is a natural thing for people to do. They do not inherently dislike work and it can be a source of satisfaction.
2. External control and threats of punishment are not the only means to bring about effort toward organizational goals. Employees will use self-direction and self-control to accomplish objectives to which they are committed.
3. In the right circumstances, the typical employee can learn to seek responsibility. Avoidance of responsibility, an absence of ambition, and an emphasis on security, according to McGregor, usually result from one's experiences in an organization.
4. The ability to exercise imagination and creativity in the solution of organizational problems is widely distributed in the workforce and has only been partially tapped by most work organizations.

> **EXHIBIT 5.1**
> **Management's Right to Direct the Workforce**
>
> The strike continued with no sign of either side yielding. During the month of August, President Baer, of the Philadelphia and Reading Railroad Company, gave expression to a few of his religious and sociological sentiments which made him a target for denunciation and ridicule. A photographer of Wilkesbarre addressed a letter to Mr. Baer appealing to him as a Christian to settle the miners' strike. Considering this an opportunity to reassure a religious man of his good intentions, Baer wrote the following interesting, though injudicious, letter:
>
> > I see you are evidently biased in your religious views in favor of the right of the workingman to control a business in which he has no other interest than to secure fair wages for the work he does. I beg of you not to be discouraged. The rights and interests of the laboring man will be protected and cared for, not by the labor agitators, but by the Christian men to whom God in His infinite wisdom, has given control of the property interests of the country.
>
> Source: Selig Perlman and Philip Taft, *History of Labor in the United States, 1896–1932*, vol. IV (New York: The MacMillan Company, 1935), p. 43.

Managers subscribing to Theory X are likely to adopt the view that it is necessary for management to direct and control the workforce in an authoritarian manner if organization goals are to be attained. Any interference from union leaders would be perceived as an infringement on the appropriate role of management. The company president referred to in Exhibit 5.1 displayed Theory X attitudes. His ideas also suggest the rather extreme position taken by some managers concerning the source of management's right to direct the affairs of an organization's workforce. The strike referred to occurred in 1902 and involved coal miners and coal operations, some of which were owned by the Philadelphia and Reading Railroad Company.[11]

Alternatively, a Theory Y attitude would imply the perception that it is proper for duly elected employee representatives to participate in decisions affecting terms and conditions of employment.

Relevant History

During the early 1800s, employer opposition to unions consisted of hiring non-union workers in place of union workers and of appealing to the courts to declare labor organizations illegal.[12] As discussed in Chapter 2, at that time American courts took the position that labor unions were "conspiracies in restraint of trade" and as such were illegal organizations. After *Commonwealth v. Hunt* (1842), conspiracy cases did not involve the legal status of unions per se, but the courts made use of the doctrine to restrain a number of union activities.[13] When the court believed that a union was seeking an unlawful objective or was using unlawful means to achieve a lawful objective, judicial action was undertaken to terminate the union activity. In fact, there were more labor conspiracy cases in the second half of the nineteenth century than in the first half.[14]

Strikebreakers. After 1880, the courts' use of the conspiracy doctrine in labor disputes decreased in frequency.[15] During the latter part of the nineteenth century, other management tactics came into use. The first to emerge was the widespread use of troops, police, and private security guards. The rationale for using armed forces was to protect private property. With management's attitude of "open hostility," and the ready availability of a pool of labor to replace strikers, it is not surprising that the use of troops and police resulted in violence.

LABOR VIOLENCE OF THE LATE NINETEENTH CENTURY

Many examples of violence, riots, and bloodshed that evolved from the circumstances described above are available. Exhibit 5.2 describes some of the events of the railroad strike of 1877. The strike began when railroad employees' wages were arbitrarily cut while high dividends were being paid to stockholders.[16] The strike halted the trains east of the Mississippi. Violence broke out in many American cities. July 1877 has been described as the bloodiest month in the history of the American labor movement.

EXHIBIT 5.2
The Railroad Strikes of 1877

The strikes, breaking out early in July, 1877, in protest against the wage cuts, were spontaneous. The first one was on the Baltimore and Ohio and it was at once followed by similar moves on the part of railway workers on the Pennsylvania, the New York Central and the Erie. Within a brief time all lines east of the Mississippi were affected, and the movement then spread to the Missouri Pacific, the St. Louis, Kansas and Northern, and other western lines. Railroad traffic throughout the country was interrupted and in sections completely paralyzed. As rioting flared up dangerously in Baltimore and Pittsburgh, Chicago and St. Louis, and even San Francisco, the country was confronted with its first industrial outbreak on a national scale. "It is wrong to call this a strike," the *St. Louis Republican* exclaimed, "it is labor revolution."

The strikers on the Baltimore and Ohio were the first to clash with authority at Martinsburg, West Virginia and order was restored at that point only after two hundred federal troops had been sent to the scene. Rioting on a much larger scale occurred in Baltimore. There the strikers stopped all trains, refused to allow them to move, and began to seize railroad property. When the militia, called out by the governor of Maryland, marched from their

EXHIBIT 5.2 *(Continued)*

armory to the railway station, a gathering crowd of workers and their sympathizers attacked them with brickbats, stones and clubs. The troops opened fire and broke for the station, but the rioters had had a taste of blood. They kept up the assault and set fire to the station. When police and firemen arrived, the mob for a time tried to prevent them from putting out the blaze but finally gave way. Disturbances continued through a wild and riotous night, and only the arrival of federal troops the next morning brought any real return of order. By then the toll of victims had mounted to nine persons killed, and more than a score (of whom three later died) gravely injured.

In the meantime a still more serious outbreak took place in Pittsburgh, where the strikers also stopped the trains and took possession of railway property. Here popular sympathy was wholly with the railway workers because of a deep seated resentment against the policies of the Pennsylvania. The local militia, openly fraternizing with the strikers, refused to take any action against them. The arrival of a force of 650 soldiers dispatched from Philadelphia to protect railway property, consequently precipitated a pitched battle in which the troops opened fire and after killing some twenty-five persons, and wounding many more, took over possession of the roundhouse and machine shops.

The infuriated strikers, their ranks swelled by miners, mill hands and factory workers, returned to the attack with arms seized from near-by gun shops and laid siege to the troops. As night fell, freight cars were set afire and pushed into the roundhouse until it too was blazing. The troops, surrounded by flames and nearly suffocated with smoke, fought their way out amid a hail of bullets and retreated across the Allegheny River.

The field was now left clear to what had become a mob of four or five thousand persons, swelled by hoodlums and tramps. Railway tracks were torn up, freight and passenger cars broken open, and what could not otherwise be destroyed, set afire. Some two thousand cars, the machine shops, a grain elevator and two roundhouses with one hundred and twenty-five locomotives went up in flames. The Union Depot itself was burned down. As the rioting continued unchecked, the more unruly and criminal elements broke into the liquor stores and began to pillage at will without regard to whose property they were robbing. They carried off furniture, clothing, provisions. . . .

It was not until after a weekend of drunken pillaging, in which the damage was estimated at from five to ten million dollars, that the police, reinforced by bands of armed citizens, began to restore some semblance of order. In the meantime, the entire state militia had been called out and following an emergency cabinet meeting, President Hayes ordered all federal troops in the Atlantic Department made available to cope with the emergency. Only when the regulars arrived in Pittsburgh was full protection finally accorded railway property.

Source: Excerpt from pp. 119–121 of *Labor in America: A History* by Foster Rhea Dulles. Copyright 1949, 1955, 1960, 1966 by Foster Rhea Dulles. (Thomas Y. Crowell) By permission of Harper & Row, Publishers. Inc.

Another violent incident occurred in 1886. Workers at the McCormick Harvester plant in Chicago were on strike. A clash between strikers and strikebreakers broke out. When police intervened to stop the dispute, four strikers were killed".[17] A protest meeting was held by the strikers and their supporters the next evening at Haymarket Square. About three thousand people attended. The meeting was practically over and the crowd dispersed when a police detachment of two hundred arrived. The police ordered the remaining workers to leave. Someone threw a bomb among the police. When it exploded, the police opened fire on the workers, who returned shots. Seven policemen and four workers were killed and over one hundred policemen and workers were injured.

In 1887–1888 there were a series of labor disputes in Pennsylvania involving coal miners and railroad employees. A congressional investigation of these disputes was extremely critical of the use of private armies in such disputes. "They report to nobody but the heads of the corporations employing them, from whom they get their orders and which they execute generally with a mailed hand."[18]

THE USE OF COURT INJUNCTIONS

The other tool that came into use by management during the late 1800s that was effective in frustrating union activities was court injunctions. It was the Pullman Strike that led to widespread use of court injunctions.[19] In 1894, the workers of the Pullman Car Company, under the leadership of Eugene V. Debs, struck because of a unilateral wage cut and the discharge of some union leaders. The strike against Pullman was having little effect on the company. Consequently, the railroads were asked to boycott the use of Pullman sleeping cars. The companies refused, resulting in a series of strikes against the railroads.

Court injunctions. Because the railroads were used to transport the mail of the United States, Federal officials requested and obtained an injunction ordering the union to cease striking the railroads. The Supreme Court upheld the use of injunctions in labor disputes. With this decision, court injunctions became a potent factor in labor-management disputes. By 1931 state and federal courts had issued a total of 1,845 labor injunctions.[20] Chapter 2 discusses the use of court injunctions to limit the effectiveness of union activities in depth.

PREVALENT MANAGEMENT ATTITUDES

It can be inferred from the practices of nineteenth-century employers described above that the prevalent management attitude toward unions was one of open hostility. The tactics used to resist unions during the late 1800s and during this century until the mid-1930s included yellow dog contracts, court injunctions, and anti-trust prosecution, as well as police and military force. These tactics indicate that open hostility toward unions continued into this century. It should be noted, however, that some industrialists were not so vehement in their opposition to unions. Exhibit 5.3 describes a few of these exceptions. It is curious that among the leaders of industry having moderate views toward unions were George Pullman and Andrew Carnegie, given the involvement of their organizations in the violent strikes. The Carnegie Steel Corporation was involved in the Homestead Strike of 1892. Private police, federal troops, and strikebreakers were used to break the strike. The manager of the Homestead plant was eager for a showdown with the union.[21] Perhaps the company's actions would have been different if Carnegie had personally been in charge.

> **EXHIBIT 5.3**
> **Moderate Management's Views Toward Unions**
>
> The new magnates were not given to worrying over employee relations, except possibly a few "paternalists," such as George Pullman. Mark Hanna, industrialist and politician, was the rare coal operator who saw no profit in fighting his workers. During the 1894 Pullman strike, Hanna outraged the members of the Cleveland Union Club by proclaiming that "a man who won't meet his men half way is a God-damn fool." And Andrew Carnegie's Scot Presbyterian soul was troubled. He went so far as to write: "The right of workingmen to combine and to form trades unions is no less sacred than the right of the manufacturer to enter into associations and conferences with his fellows. . . . My experience has been that trades unions upon the whole are beneficial both to labor and to capital." Carnegie even showed unexpected understanding about the reasons violence frequently broke out during strikes. "To expect that one dependent upon his daily wage for the necessities of life will stand by peaceably and see a new man employed in his stead is to expect much."
>
> Source: Thomas R. Brooks, Toil and Trouble 2nd ed. (New York: Dell Publishing Co., 1971), p. 87.

THE OPEN SHOP DRIVE

About the beginning of the twentieth century, the first signs of more sophisticated anti-union management tactics began to appear. Between 1900 and 1906, several employer associations committed to open shops were formed.[22]

Open shop drive. For some employer associations, it was enough to avoid closed shop agreements, while for other employer associations, an open shop was a shop that did not have any dealings with a union. Various tactics were used by these anti-union associations. Member employers were encouraged to maintain open shops and not become "traitors to their class" or "traitors to America."[23] Financial assistance was provided employers engaged in labor disputes. Blacklists were maintained and legislation sponsored by trade unions was opposed. Attempts were made to shape public opinion in the favor of the open shop. Constantly, the argument was made that society must protect the "right" of the non-union person to work in the place of his choice.[24]

WELFARE SECRETARIES

Another approach to counter the growth of trade unionism was the creation of the job of welfare secretary. Such positions in American companies began to emerge just prior to 1900.[25] The welfare secretaries were responsible for suggesting improvements in working conditions and for helping employees with such matters as housing, medical care, educational facilities, and recreational activities. It was largely from these positions that the "social welfare" or "social work" tradition in personnel management developed.

During the 1920s, the employee welfare dimension of personnel management received a great deal of emphasis. As will be pointed out in the next section, during the 1920s there was a major effort by American employers to resist unionism. This welfare emphasis was management's positive approach to discouraging the growth of unions.[26] These programs were discontinued during the Depression years.

THE AMERICAN PLAN

Anti-union efforts on the part of employers had normally been a part of the American economy but,

> Never before has America seen an open shop drive on a scale so vast as that which characterizes the drive now sweeping the country. Never before has an open-shop drive been so heavily financed, so efficiently organized, so skillfully generaled. The present drive flies all the flags of patriotic wartime propaganda. It advances in the name of democracy, freedom, human rights, Americanism.[27]

During the 1920s, management mounted an all-out effort to restrict the growth of unions. Prior to this period, American union membership tended to grow during periods of prosperity and stagnate or decline during periods of recession and depression. This was not the case during the 1920s. From a high of five million members in 1920, membership decreased to 3.6 million in 1929 and to 2.9 million by 1933.

American Plan. The goal of employers' associations of the 1920s was that industry be run on the "American Plan," i.e., referring to a shop that does not deal with unions.[28] A two-pronged approach was used. Some positive measures were used, as well as some less positive measures. Among the positive measures were employee welfare programs and company unions or "employee representation plans." Other measures such as blacklisting were also used. A more potent weapon was the use of the "yellow dog" contract. As discussed in Chapter 2, such contracts were held by the United States Supreme Court in the *Hitchman* case to be legally binding agreements.[29]

The effectiveness of "yellow dog" contracts, when coupled with readily available court injunctions, should be apparent. Typically, only a small percentage of employees in a plant might have agreed to such contracts. Even so, when union organizers attempted to organize the plant, the employer could contend to the court that such efforts threatened his interests in the contracts with such employees. The court would then issue an injunction prohibiting the union's organizing efforts—truly an effective anti-union tactic!

THE MOHAWK VALLEY FORMULA

The Mohawk Valley formula was an elaborate strikebreaking procedure. It was used when the objective of a strike was to force the employer to recognize and negotiate with the union. Breaking such a strike meant no collective bargaining and no union. This system of strikebreaking was devised by James H. Rand, Jr., president of Remington Rand.[30] By utilizing this formula, Rand was able to break strikes at six plants

> **EXHIBIT 5.4**
> **The Mohawk Valley Formula**
>
> The Mohawk Valley Formula was an elaborate strikebreaking scheme. Introduced by James Rand in the 1936 strikes of Remington Rand employees, it was later successfully utilized in the steel strike of 1937 and widely publicized as the Johnstown Plan. The elements in the "formula" have, of course, varied in its different applications. In essence, however, the original scheme comprised about nine steps: (1) conducting of a strike ballot by an employer, with misrepresentation of the issues involved and the strength of the union; (2) labeling the union leaders "agitators" and "radicals"; (3) economic pressure on the community, through threats to move the plant, in order to stimulate the formation of a citizens' committee by means of which public opinion could be crystallized against the strikers; (4) the amassing of a large police force to preserve "law and order" and intimidate the strikers; (5) emphasis on the violent aspects of the strike to hide the employment of strikebreakers; (6) the organization of a back-to-work movement accompanied by extensive advertising; (7) a theatrical opening of the struck plant; (8) the combined show of police force and pressure by the Citizens' Committee; (9) the complete cessation of publicity once the plant was operating at near-capacity.
>
> Source: Harry A. Millis and Royal E. Montgomery, Organized Labor (New York: McGraw-Hill Book Company, 1945), p. 612.

in 1936.[31] It was also used effectively to break the "Little Steel" strike in 1937. The scheme included efforts to isolate the union organizers from the rank-and-file union members, formation of local citizens' committees to promote back-to-work movements, maintenance or re-establishment of law and order, and a build-up of public opinion favorable to the employer's interests. Exhibit 5.4 describes the nine elements of the Mohawk Valley formula.

Current Management Organization for Collective Bargaining

Most of the management practices described in the previous section have been prohibited by legislation. Many managers continue to be hostile to unions, but will respect the law. Consequently, these and similar tactics are not typically used any longer.

The remainder of the chapter focuses on how management currently organizes to deal with unions. Two circumstances are addressed. First, what does the "union free" organization do to insure that it remains "union free"? Second, how does management organize its labor relations function when a union represents a part or all of its labor force?

AN INTRODUCTION TO THE PARTIES

Non-Union Organizations

Most people in the American labor force are not members of labor unions, as indicated by Fig. 5.3. About three of every four members of the non-agricultural labor force do not belong to unions. The "typical" employment situation is non-union. In view of this fact, what some employers currently do to remain non-union will be discussed. It should be recognized that in most organizations, steps are taken by management to prevent unionization.

Numerous approaches can be used to limit unionization. At one extreme, management tries to frustrate and impede such efforts. In terms of the expectancy model discussed in the next chapter, management takes steps that communicate the message to their employees that "The disadvantages of having a union will be high." This approach often leads to charges of unfair labor practices. This is known as the negative approach to remaining non-union. At the other extreme, management focuses on preventing the need for a union in the eyes of employees. Looking at this approach, using the expectancy model, management is trying to communicate the message, "No additional advantages will be available with a union." Label this the positive approach.

NEGATIVE APPROACH TO PREVENTING UNIONS

Firms using this approach attempt to make the costs of forming a union so great that a union will not be certified. To be effective, this approach necessitates that an employer be willing to ignore the National Labor Relations Act. For example, once a

Fig. 5.3 *Union and Non-Union Workers in the Non-Agricultural Sector of the Economy*

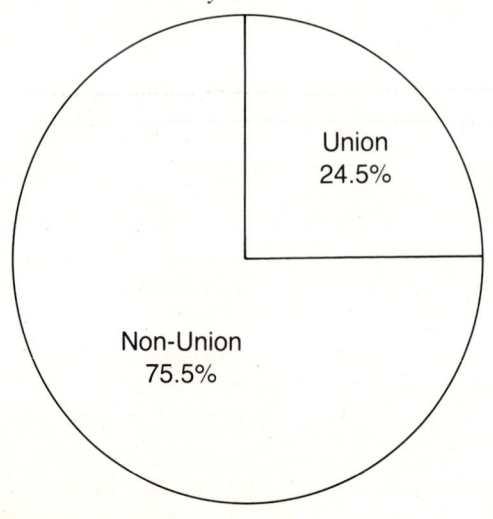

Union 24.5%

Non-Union 75.5%

union-organizing campaign is underway, one tactic is to discharge employees known to be sympathetic to the union. Other tactics that can be used are threatening to close the plant, threatening union sympathizers, "requesting" employees to spy on other employees that are union activists, denying overtime to union supporters, or transferring them to lower paying jobs.

Perhaps the best-known modern-day example of this approach to resisting unionization is J. P. Stevens. This organization is a textile manufacturer. Between 1963 and 1979, 147 charges of unfair labor practices against Stevens were processed by the National Labor Relations Board.[32] In 136 of these cases, Stevens was found guilty of violations of the National Labor Relations Act. Those practices listed above are among the unfair practices of which Stevens has been found guilty. Others include electronic spying on union organizers and firing employees who testified before the National Labor Relations Board.

Apparently, J. P. Stevens Co. is not an isolated case. The number of charges of unfair labor practices and the number found by the NLRB to be meritorius have more than doubled in recent years, with only a modest increase in the number of representation elections.[33] Also, in recent years, the number of unfair labor practices filed with the NLRB has increased at a rate of 7 to 10 percent annually.[34] It appears that non-union employers are more inclined to assume an approach of open hostility rather than controlled hostility. Why would an employer intentionally commit unfair labor practices?

According to the late George Meany, former president of the AFL-CIO, union busting is on the increase because it is cost effective.[35] He contended that employers have found that they can violate the law, pay the back wages ordered by the NLRB or the courts plus the lawyers' fees, and still be better off financially than when a union represents their employees. Because the penalty that the NLRB can impose in unfair labor practice cases is limited to awarding back wages, NLRB Chairman John H. Fanning has stated that the NLRB cannot deal effectively with the repeat offender.[36]

Another issue concerning the effectiveness of the current legislation is raised by the organization campaign involving the Textile Workers Union of America and the Darlington Manufacturing Company.[37] In 1956, a certification election was held, which the union won. There were charges of unfair labor practices during the organization campaign. The NLRB ruled that the employer was guilty of unfair labor practices. The NLRB ordered reinstatement with back pay for those employees affected by the unfair labor practices. The decision was appealed through the federal courts, to the United States Supreme Court. It was not until 1968 that reinstatement and the awarding of back pay began to take place. By this time many former employees affected by the decision could not be found. As late as 1974, carrying out the NLRB's decision was still not completed.

POSSIBLE REFORM MEASURES

The issue of whether committing unfair labor practices could be a cost-effective strategy was addressed in a recent study.[38] As indicated in Exhibit 5.5, it is reasonable to assume that an employer can secure economic advantages by ignoring the

> **EXHIBIT 5.5**
> **Cost-Effective Approach to Dealing with Unions**
>
> The results of this study indicate that under realistic conditions it is economically feasible for employers to secure economic gains by violating the National Labor Relations Act. The law needs reform to remove such disincentives for individual employer compliance.... In the past, the compliance system has been inadequate to the extent that some employers have found it profitable to commit unfair labor practices in order to forestall unionization. Those employers obeying the law because "it's the law" have faced a greater probability of incurring costs of unionization and may have been at a competitive disadvantage to employers who violated the law. Such inequities do not encourage compliance with the law and provide evidence of the need for labor law reform.
>
> *Source:* Reprinted from "Calculative Strategy Decisions during Union Organization Campaigns," by Charles R. Greer and Stanley A. Martin, Sloan Management Review, vol. 19, no. 2, p. 73, by permission of the publisher. Copyright © 1978 by the Sloan Management Review Association. All rights reserved.

National Labor Relations Act and engaging in some nineteenth-century labor practices. As a result, various changes have been recommended in the penalties that can be imposed by the NLRB. Among them are awarding double or triple backpay to employees unfairly discharged, barring violators from receiving federal contracts and fining repeat offenders.[39] Such proposals were rejected by Congress as recently as 1977 when the Labor Reform Act was not passed. However, it is quite possible that if the existing legislation is blatantly ignored by a large number of employers, changes will be made that will put more teeth in the law.

POSITIVE APPROACH TO REMAINING NON-UNION

The essence of the positive approach to remaining non-union is to provide employees with the benefits that could be expected if they were represented by a union. The number of publications focusing on this approach reflect the interest of non-union employers in such programs. Some examples are: "Making Unions Unnecessary"[40] and "Managing Without Unions."[41] A common theme of these publications is that any organization that gets a union deserves it. "No labor union has ever captured a group of employees without the full cooperation and encouragement of managers who create the need for unionization."[42]

A successful effort to prevent the need for a union has been compared to a three-legged stool.[43] Each leg is necessary to support the overall program as well as the other two legs. The three legs of the stool are: top management commitment, line management involvement, and personnel services support.

Top management of most non-union organizations will state that they are committed to remaining non-union. However, words are not sufficient. Meaningful procedures are necessary to demonstrate this commitment. For example, the organization may state that it has an "open door" policy in which employees have a right to appeal disciplinary actions to successively higher levels of management. This policy will not be meaningful until a procedure is in place which assures that an employee will receive a fair hearing if he or she chooses to exercise this right. Some non-union organizations have gone as far as establishing a grievance procedure with an outside arbitrator as the final step to insure the procedure is perceived as being fair.

Line management involvement is also critical to the success of a program to maintain a non-union shop. Among the skills that line managers should possess are:

- Tact in dealing with subordinates.
- The ability to use a participative management style.
- Communications skills.

Line management "is the organization" for most employees. If line managers are perceived to be fair, willing to let employees have a say in decisions affecting them and insure that employees know what is going on in the organization, employees will typically feel they can trust management.

Personnel services support is critical because it is this staff function that plays the key role in most programs affecting employees. Among these are:

- Providing wages and benefits comparable if not better than those available at union employers.
- Establishing transfer and promotion procedures that are based on merit and ability.
- Administering an objective and fair grievance procedure.
- Maintaining downward communications through such means as bulletin boards, a personnel policy manual, and an employee newspaper.
- Insuring effective upward communications through employee meetings, a suggestion system, employee attitude surveys, and employee counseling.

The interrelationship of the three legs of the stool is very important. As suggested above, if top management pays only "lip service" to the right of employees to appeal decisions of supervisors, the grievance procedure will not be effective. Among the things that could undermine the program are the refusal of higher levels of management to reverse unfair decisions of supervisors and permitting immediate supervisors to "get even" with subordinates who use the procedure. Similarly, problems that are pointed out through the upward communication system will typically go unsolved without the support of top management and the involvement of line management.

Employee committees. A word of caution is warranted concerning the use of employee meetings. In the past, some organizations have established committees composed of employee representatives. The function of these committees was to serve as a means of airing employee problems and complaints. In some cases, management discussed (perhaps negotiated) possible solutions to these issues with the employee committees. The position of the NLRB is that such committees, when composed of employee representatives, constitute company-dominated unions and are prohibited by the National Labor Relations Act.[44] A review of NLRB decisions concerning employee committees indicates that meetings should be scheduled by departments or some other manageable subdivision of the organization, with all employees in the group invited to attend. This affords every employee an opportunity to present and discuss his/her own personal grievances. Also, such meetings provide management with an effective vehicle for employee communications. The critical issue is the presence or absence of *employee representatives* meeting with management.

One authority on the positive approach sums it up by stating that the best approach to remaining non-union is to provide employees with the advantages they would expect from a union;[45] those advantages are fair wages and benefits, an effective grievance procedure, equitable promotion and transfer procedures, fair treatment by supervisors and open communications with management. Powell concludes by stating, "No employee in his right mind is going to call in unknown outsiders (union officials), and pay them $60 to $80 a year in dues from his family income, if he already enjoys the above advantages and has a harmonious relationship with and trusts his employer."[46]

WHICH APPROACH TO REMAINING NON-UNION?

The positive approach to remaining non-union has been used for many years. The earliest signs of this approach appeared with welfare secretaries at the turn of the century. Why have some employers chosen this approach while others have relied on suppression?

A number of factors appear to influence this choice. Probably the most important factor is the economic position of the organization. Advanced personnel management systems, competitive wages and benefits, as well as trained managers and supervisors are expensive. To support these programs, the organization must be profitable.

Alternatively, organizations that actively suppress unionization share several other characteristics. Among them are a social and political environment that is hostile to unions, low-wage unskilled workers with few employment alternatives, and a large supply of alternative employees.[47] These latter factors combine to make recruiting and training replacements a relatively inexpensive matter. Additionally, there must be a willingness on the part of management to engage in suppression tactics to remain non-union. As mentioned earlier, this approach has been labeled an attitude of "open hostility." Since the characteristics listed above are also associated with low-profit organizations in highly competitive industries, it is difficult to predict which is the cause and which is the effect. Perhaps if economic conditions were different, the negative approach to remaining non-union would not be used.

Management Organization for Collective Bargaining When Employees Are Unionized

When a part of an organization's workforce is represented by a union, management must organize for the purpose of negotiating and administering a collective bargaining agreement. A recent study by the Conference Board has made a great contribution to understanding how management organizes for collective bargaining.[48] Just under 700 organizations with at least part of their workforce unionized participated in the study.

DESCRIBING THE RELATIONSHIP

Fig. 5.4 reports the distribution of organizations with various proportions of their nonexempt workforce unionized. The terms "exempt" and "nonexempt" will be precisely defined in a later chapter. A loose definition of exempt is all professional, managerial, and administrative employees. All other employees are nonexempt.

Fig. 5.4 *Proportion of Nonexempt Workforce Unionized*

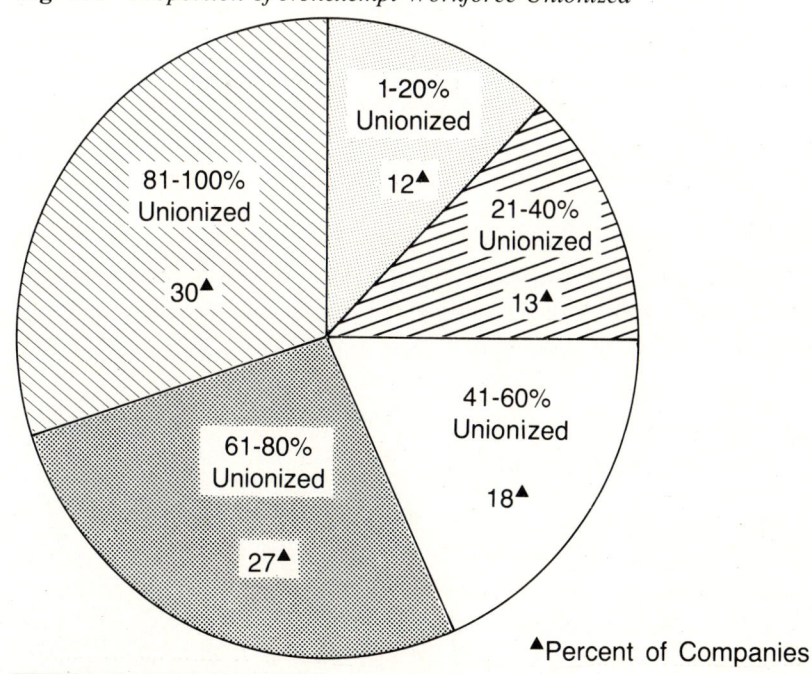

- 1-20% Unionized: 12 ▲
- 21-40% Unionized: 13 ▲
- 41-60% Unionized: 18 ▲
- 61-80% Unionized: 27 ▲
- 81-100% Unionized: 30 ▲

▲ Percent of Companies

Source: Audrey Freedman, Managing Labor Relations *(The Conference Board, Report No. 765, 1980), p. 2.*

As indicated by Fig. 5.4, there is a great deal of variation in the extent of unionization. However, over half of those organizations studied (57 percent) reported that at least 61 percent of their nonexempt workers were represented by unions.

As will be apparent later in this chapter, the proportion of the workforce that is unionized is important because management attitudes toward unions and management policies and practices appear to be different when an organization is highly organized relative to when it is minimally organized.

Organizations typically must negotiate with several unions. The median number of national unions dealt with is four.[49] One-fifth of organizations deal with twelve or more unions and one-fifth deal with only one union.

Another important aspect of describing the union-management relationship is the structure of the bargaining unit. Several possibilities exist in multilocation companies. The bargaining unit can be restricted to single locations, to several locations, or can be organization-wide. When bargaining is on a single-location basis, it is possible for the employer to reduce the impact of a strike at one location by increasing production at other locations. Consequently, it is in management's interest to restrict the scope of the bargaining unit as much as possible. The implications of the scope of the bargaining unit for labor-management relations will be discussed in more detail in Chapter 7. Among the unionized companies studied, 64 percent reported that "all or most" bargaining situations are single-plant units.[50] Twelve percent reported all or most bargains consisted of a two-tier system involving a multiplant "master" contract supplemented with single-plant local contracts. Eighteen percent reported that all or most bargaining relationships are under a single master contract. The remaining 6 percent bargain primarily on a multiemployer basis.

ORGANIZATION OF THE LABOR RELATIONS FUNCTION

The concepts of line and staff are used to describe authority relationships in organizations.[51] Line managers are those responsible and accountable for the accomplishment of an organization's primary objectives, i.e., producing the product or providing the service.

Staff authority. Staff managers usually provide advice and service to line managers in carrying out their work. Since line managers are accountable for the primary objectives of the organization, they typically have the final authority to make decisions.

There are differences in the type of authority that staff managers have in relation to line managers. The typical line-staff relationship is as described above. However, in some cases, because of specialized knowledge or expertise possessed by staff personnel, they may have the authority to give directions to line managers. Figs. 5.5 and 5.6 represent alternative staff authority relationships. The former presents the normal relationship in which the labor relations specialist reports to the line manager. For example, the plant labor relations manager may report to the plant manager. The labor relations manager would provide advice on matters concerning union-management relations, and the plant manager would have the final authority

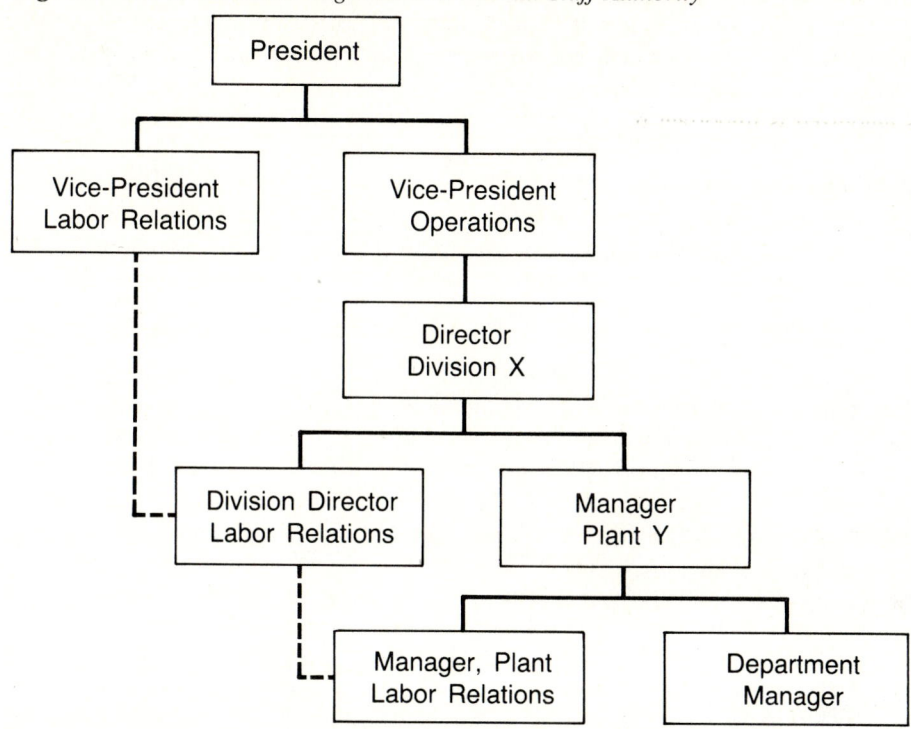

Fig. 5.5 *Labor Relations Organization: Normal Staff Authority*

```
                    ┌───────────┐
                    │ President │
                    └─────┬─────┘
         ┌────────────────┴────────────────┐
┌─────────────────┐              ┌─────────────────┐
│ Vice-President  │              │ Vice-President  │
│ Labor Relations │              │   Operations    │
└────────┬────────┘              └────────┬────────┘
         │                                │
         │                       ┌────────┴────────┐
         │                       │    Director     │
         │                       │   Division X    │
         │                       └────────┬────────┘
         │                ┌───────────────┴───────────────┐
         │        ┌───────────────────┐         ┌─────────────────┐
         └── ── ──│ Division Director │         │    Manager      │
                  │  Labor Relations  │         │    Plant Y      │
                  └─────────┬─────────┘         └────────┬────────┘
                            │                   ┌────────┴────────┐
                            │          ┌─────────────────┐ ┌──────────────┐
                            └── ── ── ─│ Manager, Plant  │ │  Department  │
                                       │ Labor Relations │ │   Manager    │
                                       └─────────────────┘ └──────────────┘
```

to make decisions. The labor relations specialists would be expected to insure that decisions adhere to labor relations policies and practices established at higher levels of the organization. This is represented by the dotted lines in Fig. 5.5.

Functional authority. Fig. 5.6 depicts the situation in which the labor relations staff has functional authority in labor relations matters. In such a case, labor relations specialists are directly responsible to the labor relations manager at the next higher organizational level.

In the majority of companies, the labor relations staff report to line managers, and have a "dotted line" relationship to their counterparts at the next higher level.[52] However, in about one-third of the companies studied, the plant labor relations staff report directly to higher-level labor relations managers.

STAFF RATIOS AND CAREER BACKGROUND OF LABOR RELATIONS EXECUTIVES

The most common ratio of labor relations specialists to unionized employees is one staff person per 200 to 400 union employees. However, about one in four organizations has one specialist for under 200 union employees.

AN INTRODUCTION TO THE PARTIES

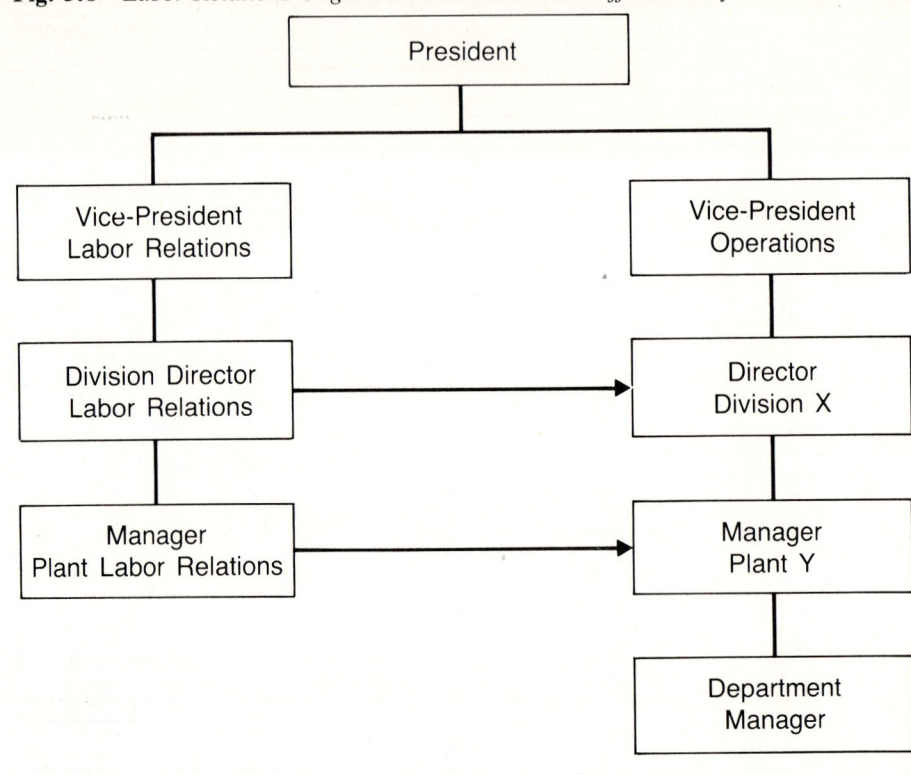

Fig. 5.6 *Labor Relations Organization: Functional Staff Authority*

```
                    President
                   /         \
       Vice-President        Vice-President
       Labor Relations        Operations
              |                    |
       Division Director  →   Director
       Labor Relations        Division X
              |                    |
           Manager       →      Manager
       Plant Labor Relations    Plant Y
                                   |
                               Department
                                Manager
```

Career progression in labor relations appears to depend on specialized experience and education. Four of five labor relations executives have spent their entire career in personnel or labor relations. Just under 60 percent of the top labor relations executives had college degrees in business, industrial relations, or economics.

RESPONSIBILITY FOR SPECIFIC FUNCTIONS AND DECISIONS

An important question is who is responsible for what kinds of decisions? This issue was also addressed by the Conference Board study. Table 5.1 provides an overview of the findings. It indicates the percentage of unionized organizations in which the function is performed or a decision is made by labor relations specialists rather than line managers.

Economic issues. Concerning cost decisions, the labor relations staff is usually responsible for developing an organization's proposals for wages and benefits. Additionally, the labor relations staff is usually responsible for recommending outside limits for the bargain as well as identifying the issues on which the company can

Table 5.1 *Responsibility for Specific Functions and Decisions*

Function or decision	Percent of companies (see note)
Cost decisions	
Developing wage position	82%
Developing pension and benefits position	85
Establishing outside limits	57
Determining strike issues	59
Approving wage items	23
Approving pensions and benefits	23
Approving outside limits	19
Approving strike issues	20
Approving complete package	21
Bargaining functions	
Background research	94
Developing initial benefit proposals	85
Developing initial wage proposals	82
Costing out union demands and management proposals	90
Conducting contract negotiations	88
Developing final contract language	94
Contract Administration	
Handling grievances and arbitration	85
Monitoring operations to anticipate problems and carry out policy	82

Note: The percentages indicate the proportion of companies in which the indicated function or decision is carried out by labor relations specialists as opposed to line management. The number of companies is 668.

Source: Audrey Freedman, Managing Labor Relations (The Conference Board, Report No. 765, 1980), p. 18.

expect a strike. Alternatively, line managers have final approval concerning: wages and benefits, approving outside limits on wages and benefits, approving strikes, and approving the package as a whole.

Centralized decision making. The level of line managers and labor relations specialists involved in these cost decisions should be noted. The line managers with final approval over the decisions listed above are usually chief executive officers (CEOs). If CEOs do not make these decisions, it is typically a decision made by a division-level manager. Almost never are such decisions made by plant managers. This is pointed out to emphasize that these labor relations decisions are centralized at the top level of management.

    Similarly, while the responsibility for developing the proposed company positions regarding wages and benefits and other issues is typically a staff function, it is high-level staff that is involved. The most common person assigned these responsibilities is the corporate vice-president of labor relations. Almost never are such responsibilities turned over to plant labor relations managers.

Bargaining responsibilities. Labor relations specialists are typically responsible for the various aspects of contract negotiations (see Table 5.1). Included are conducting the background research necessary in preparing for negotiations, developing the initial company position, costing out union demands, actual contract negotiations, and determining the actual contract language.

Contract administration. Handling grievances and arbitration is typically the domain of the labor relations specialist. In addition, labor relations specialists are typically responsible for monitoring labor relations operations in an attempt to anticipate problems and to insure that established policies are being followed.

MANAGEMENT ATTITUDES AND PHILOSOPHY

The complexities in identifying management attitudes and philosophy toward unions are apparent from the Conference Board study. Respondents were asked to describe their company policy toward unions. Many respondents indicated that it was difficult to state *a* company approach to unions. The following exerpts from one company's response indicate why it may be difficult to identify a policy:[53]

"There are over 500 contracts covering 25,000 employees. . . ."

"We deal with over 35 international, national and independents labor unions in the United States. . . ."

"We deal with 75 separate local labor unions; each day approximately 70 labor contracts are in various stages of contract negotiations."

With this warning concerning the possibilities of oversimplification, a review of some highlights of the Conference Board study concerning the nature of company attitudes toward unions will be given. Unionized companies were asked:[54]

Which is the more important role of the labor relations function in your company?

Keeping as much of the company nonunion as possible
or
Achieving the most favorable bargain possible.

About two of three companies selected the latter alternative and one of three selected the former. Responses to this question were closely related to the proportion of the nonexempt workforce that is represented by unions (see Fig. 5.4). Among those companies in which fewer than 20 percent of the workers are unionized, over 90 percent said union containment is more important. Alternatively, among those companies in which 61 percent or more of the workforce is unionized, about 10 per-

Table 5.2 *Union-Management Relationships*

Statement	Number	Percent agreement
■ The union is effective in bringing up genuine employee concerns reflecting employee priorities.	657	88%
■ The union's negotiators are skilled and well prepared.	654	62
■ The union leaders and management officials try to cooperate with each other as much as possible.	652	80
■ The relations between the union leaders and management officials are hostile.	654	9
■ The union leaders and management officials distrust one another.	654	27
■ The union leaders and management officials try to weaken each other's power.	654	27

Source: Audrey Freedman, Managing Labor Relations *(The Conference Board, Report No. 765, 1980), pp. 57, 59.*

cent said union containment is more important. Answers to this question indicate that when about a third or more of an organization's nonexempt employees are unionized, the top priority usually shifts from containing unionization to bargaining and dealing with unions.

In this same study, several questions were asked concerning the nature of the relationship between management and unions. Respondents were asked to describe the relationship with the union in its largest bargaining unit. Table 5.2 reports the statements used in the study and the percent responding "agree" or "strongly agree."

The pattern of responses presented in Table 5.2 suggests that an atmosphere of hostility is relatively rare, whereas an atmosphere of accommodation is relatively common. This is reflected by the 80 percent agreement to the statement "union leaders and management officials try to cooperate." Exhibit 5.6 reports one company's explanation for assuming an accommodative position.

Emerging Issues

The previous section suggests that the typical established union-management relationship can be described as cooperative or accommodative. However, there are signs that organizations with the goal of containing unionism are increasing their efforts to achieve this objective. The number of publications in recent years suggesting management strategies for winning a decertification election[55] or ousting a union[56] reflect this pattern.

A "hardball" approach toward decertification appears to be developing.[57] With this strategy, management refuses to agree to union wage demands during negotia-

> **EXHIBIT 5.6**
> **Union-Management Cooperation**
>
> One management source described its coexistence policy in these pragmatic terms:
>
> > It is practically impossible to build a satisfactory union-company relationship if union officials feel that the company is out to 'get' them, or to destroy the union. Once we have made up our minds that the union is here to stay, it is best to recognize the political aspects of union leadership. We cannot afford to behave one day as though we want to destroy the union and its leaders and then try to obtain their cooperation the next day. We must consistently recognize the role of the union as the legal and proper representative of employees in a certified bargaining unit. This can be done while at the same time requiring acceptance by the union of management's responsibility to manage the business.
>
> Source: Audrey Freedman, Managing Labor Relations (The Conference Board, Report No. 765, 1980), p. 58.

tions. When the union strikes, replacements for the strikers are hired. Then the new workforce composed of replacements and nonstriking union members petition the National Labor Relations Board for a decertification election. It is illegal for management to encourage the latter step, but this step is fairly predictable given the composition of the workforce. In a recent strike involving a Colorado employer, the union apparently avoided this outcome. When the employer announced a decision to hire replacements for strikers and 1800 applications for employment were received for the jobs of the 950 strikers, the strikers decided to return to work under the terms of the old contract.[58]

In the construction industry, another approach to reducing unionization is being used. It is labeled "double-breasted" shops. Construction companies create a new division or subsidiary company that is nonunion.[59] This permits establishing wage scales below union levels, providing less costly fringe benefits and more flexible work assignments. Additionally, work is not interrupted by strikes. The success of this strategy depends on the subsidiary being classified as a legally separate entity.

Referring to the discussion of management philosophy and attitudes toward unions, while the majority of employers can be viewed as accommodative, some are most certainly committed to containing and reducing unionization. The factors that appear to be related to a policy of containment are a low rate of unionization of the current workforce and the possibility of substantially lower labor costs without unionization.

This discussion of emerging issues is not complete without noting signs of increased cooperation between unions and management. In some Western European countries employee representatives sit on the board of directors of corporations. This is known as co-determination, a subject discussed in greater detail in Chapter 18. The possibility of implementing such representation in the United States has been explored.[60] In May 1980, Douglas A. Fraser, president of the United Auto Workers, became a member of Chrysler Corporation's board of directors.[61] Admittedly, the Chrysler situation in 1979 and 1980 was unique, but some labor leaders expect to see more union leaders serving in such roles.[62]

At the grassroots level of union-management cooperation, there appears to be renewed interest in the Scanlon Plan.[63,64,65] In Chapter 11, the Scanlon Plan will be examined in detail. For our current discussion, it is sufficient to say that the Scanlon Plan focuses the attention of workers and management on improving productivity and relies on union-management cooperation to achieve this goal.[66]

Summary

Management is responsible for making decisions concerning the allocation of resources in an organization. In doing so, it is expected to reflect the interests of owners (private sector) or taxpayers (public sector). At times the interests of owners or taxpayers will conflict with the interests of employees. When a union represents the employees, management's flexibility to make decisions is reduced. Consequently, management typically prefers not to have a union representing the organization's employees.

Management can take several different stances with respect to unions. In resisting unions, an organization can engage in illegal and unethical practices. Alternatively, an organization can attempt to remove the need for a union through progressive personnel policies. When a union represents employees of an organization, management can try to undermine the union, hoping for decertification, or management can accept the union and try to work effectively with the union.

During the 1800s, management typically relied on some combination of the courts, armed force, and strikebreakers to resist unions. About the turn of the century some organizations began using positive measures to try to remove the perceived need by employees for unions. These programs were the predecessors of the personnel management function.

Modern-day management tactics to remain non-union are basically similar to the alternatives used in the early 1900s. Some organizations use a negative approach which includes such tactics as discharging union activists. Other organizations use a positive approach which relies heavily on progressive personnel management practices to remove the need for a union. Concerning the former approach, there is some evidence that it is cost effective in view of the limited penalties that can currently be imposed by the NLRB on employers for engaging in unfair labor practices.

The typical union-management relationship is complex. It usually involves several unions representing employees at different plants or locations. Decisions concerning the labor relations function are highly centralized. Final authority to make decisions on economic matters is usually held by the chief executive officer. The responsibility to develop alternative proposals and to conduct negotiations is usually that of the vice-president for labor relations. Given the emphasis on conflict in most labor relations textbooks, it is surprising that most companies describe the relationship between labor relations specialists and union leaders as cooperative.

Discussion Questions

1. What are alternative approaches management can take in dealing with unions?
2. Why does management usually resist unionization?
3. List and discuss tactics used by management to resist unions during the 1800s and early 1900s.
4. Describe the negative as well as the positive approaches to remaining non-union used by modern day managers. What factors appear to influence the choice between these approaches.?
5. How is the labor relations function organized in unionized organizations? Discuss reporting relationships as well as decision making responsibility.
6. Describe the typical union-management working relationship and discuss factors that appear to influence this relationship. Why would management ever assume an accommodative or cooperative attitude toward a union?
7. What trends appear to be emerging in management's approach to unions?

Key Concepts

Strikebreakers
Court injunctions
Open shop drive
Company unions
American Plan
Mohawk Valley formula

Employee committees
Centralized decision making
Staff authority
Functional authority
Double-breasted shops

Notes

1. James L. Gibson, John M. Ivancevich, and James H. Donnelly, Jr., *Organizations: Structure, Processes, Behavior* (Dallas, TX: Business Publications, Inc., 1973), p. 117.

2. John H. Jackson, and Timothy J. Keaveny, *Successful Supervision* (Englewood Cliffs, N. J.: Prentice-Hall, Inc., 1980), pp. 5–9.

3. Ibid., pp. 351–52.

4. Benjamin M. Selekman, "Varieties of Labor Relations," *Harvard Business Review* 27 (1949): 175–99.

5. Thomas R. Brooks, *Toil and Trouble: A History of American Labor* (New York: Dell Publishing Co., 1971), pp. 146–47.

6. Ibid., p. 90.

7. Ibid., pp. 128–29.

8. Ibid., pp. 190–91.

9. Selekman, p. 185.

10. Douglas M. McGregor, *The Human Side of Enterprise* (New York: McGraw-Hill, 1960).

11. Selig Perlman and Philip Taft, *History of Labor in The United States, 1896–1932,* vol. IV (New York: The MacMillan Company, 1935), pp. 42–43.

12. U. S. Department of Labor, *A Brief History of the American Labor Movement,* Bulletin 1000, U.S. Government Printing Office, Washington, D.C. (1970), p. 3.

13. B. J. Taylor, and F. Witney, *Labor Relations Law,* 3rd ed. (Englewood Cliffs, N. J.: Prentice-Hall, Inc., 1979), p. 22.

14. Ibid.

15. Ibid., p. 23.

16. Foster Rhea Dulles, *Labor in America: A History* (New York: Thomas Y. Crowell Co., 1949), p. 118.

17. Ibid., p. 124.

18. Philip Taft, *Organized Labor In American History,* (New York: Harper & Row, 1964), p. 105.

19. Taylor and Witney, pp. 30–31.

20. Ibid., p. 31.

21. Brooks, p. 89.

22. Harry A. Millis and Royal E. Montgomery, *Organized Labor* (New York: McGraw-Hill Book Company, 1945), p. 96.

23. Ibid., p. 97.

24. Ibid.

25. John B. Miner, and Mary Green Miner, *Personnel and Industrial Relations,* 3rd ed. (New York: MacMillan Publishing Co., 1977), p. 28.

26. Ibid., p. 31.

27. S. Zimand, *The Open Shop Drive* (New York: Bureau of Industrial Research, 1921), p. 5.

28. Taft, p. 364.

29. *Hitchman Coal Co. v. Mitchell,* 245 U. S. 229 (1917).

30. Taylor and Witney, p. 134.

31. Ibid.

32. Amalgamated Clothing & Textile Workers Union, *J. P. Stevens Boycott Fact Sheets,* 770 Broadway, New York, NY 10003.

33. Alan Kistler, "Companies Break the Law to Break Unions," *Readings in Labor Economics and Labor Relations,* 4th ed., ed. R. L. Rowan (Homewood, IL: Richard D. Irwin, 1980), pp. 109–11.

34. John H. Fanning, "We Are Forty—Where Do We Go," *Labor Law Journal* 27, (January 1976): 3–10.

35. George Meany, "The Case For Labor Law Reform," *AFL-CIO American Federationist* 84 (April 1977): 2.

36. Fanning, pp. 3–10.

37. Phillip Sparks, "The Darlington Case: Justice Delayed Is Justice Denied," *Labor Law Journal* 26 (December 1975): 759–66.

38. Charles R. Greer, and Stanley A. Martin, "Calculative Strategy Decisions During Union Organization Campaigns," *Sloan Management Review* (Winter 1978): 73.

39. Ibid.

40. Charles L. Hughes, *Making Unions Unnecessary* (New York: Executive Enterprises Publications Co., 1976).

41. M. Scott Myers, *Managing Without Unions* (Reading, MA: Addison-Wesley Publishing Co., 1976).

42. Hughes, p. 1.

43. Randall Brett, "No Need for a Union Today," *The Personnel Administrator* March, 1979, p. 23.

44. Harry Sangerman, "Employee Committees: Can They Survive Under the Taft-Hartley Act?" *Labor Law Journal*, October 1973, pp. 684–91.

45. L. B. Powell, *How to Handle a Union Organizing Drive: A Supervisor's Handbook* (Los Angeles, CA: Libby's Lithograph Co., 1968), pp. 91–92.

46. Ibid.

47. Thomas A. Kochan, *Collective Bargaining and Industrial Relations* (Homewood, IL: Richard D. Irwin, 1980), p. 184.

48. Audrey Freedman, *Managing Labor Relations* (The Conference Board, Report No. 765, 1980).

49. Ibid., p. 2.

50. Ibid., p. 4.

51. John H. Jackson and Cyril P. Morgan, *Organization Theory: A Macro Perspective For Management* (Englewood Cliffs, N. J.: Prentice-Hall, Inc., 1978), pp. 143–44.

52. Freedman, p. 27.

53. Ibid., pp. 4–5.

54. Ibid., p. 5.

55. Woodruff Imberman, "How to Win a Decertification Election," *Management Review,* September 1977, pp. 26–39.

56. William E. Fulmer, "When Employees Want To Oust Their Union," *Harvard Business Review,* March-April 1968, pp. 163–70.

57. Douglas Martin, "Labor Nemesis: When the Boss Calls in This Expert, the Union May Be in Real Trouble," *Wall Street Journal,* 19 November 1979, pp. 1, 22.

58. J. Ruhl, "Colorado Employers Tougher With Unions: Labor Losing Clout and Members in the Battle for Workers," *Rocky Mountain News,* 20 January 1980, p. 60.

59. Tim Bornstein, "The Emerging Law of the 'Double-Breasted' Operation in the Construction Industry," *Labor Law Journal* 28 (February 1978):77–79.

60. T. Mills, "Europe's Industrial Democracy: An American Response," *Harvard Business Review* 56, no. 6 (1978): 143–52.

61. "More Unions Knocking at Boardroom Doors?" *Industry Week,* 12 November 1979, pp. 19–21.

62. Ibid.

63. J. W. Driscoll, "Working Creatively With A Union: Lessons from the Scanlon Plan," *Organizational Dynamics* 8, no. 1 (1979): 61–80.

64. B. E. Moore, and T. L. Ross, *The Scanlon Way To Improved Productivity: A Practical Guide* (New York: John Wiley and Sons, 1978).

65. J. Kenneth White, "The Scanlon Plan: Causes and Correlates of Success," *Academy of Management Journal* 22, no. 2 (1979): 292–312.

66. Moore and Ross, p. 1.

Suggested Readings

Brooks, Thomas R. *Toil and Trouble: A History of American Labor*. 2nd ed. New York: Dell Publishing Co., Inc., 1971.

Freedman, Audrey. *Managing Labor Relations*. Conference Board, 1980.

Greer, Charles R., and Martin, Stanley A. "Calculative Strategy Decisions during Union Organization Campaigns." *Sloan Management Review* (Winter 1978): 61–74.

Myers, M. Scott. *Managing Without Unions*. Reading, MA: Addison-Wesley Publishing Co., 1976.

Taft, Philip. *Organized Labor in American History*. New York: Harper and Row, 1964.

The system of American labor relations is intended to facilitate the resolution of conflicts that inevitably develop between labor and management. As previously discussed, when a relationship between a union and a company is examined over time, three different phases of labor-management relations can be identified. For each period, different problems can develop and different mechanisms to help resolve the problems are used. The first phase begins when a union attempts to organize a company's workforce. The parties enter the next phase of the relationship when they work to establish the terms and conditions of employment. This involves the negotiation and periodic renegotiation of the collective bargaining agreement. The successful negotiation of a labor agreement does not end the potential problems the parties are likely to have. No matter how hard the parties try to avoid disagreements during the life of the contract, problems may arise over the day-to-day interpretation and administration of the agreement.

This section examines the first phase of labor relations—the union organizing process. The union's attempt to organize a group of workers is likely to elicit resistance from the employer. In the section to follow, two dimensions of the union organizing process are examined. First, Chapter 6 looks at factors influencing the workers' decision to unionize. As the proportion of representation elections won by unions declines, interest in obtaining a better understanding of the factors affecting the workers' choice of a bargaining agent has intensified. Then, Chapter 7 reviews the process by which workers select a labor organization to represent them in collective bargaining. As previously discussed, the regulation of conflict between labor and management during the union organizing process is one of the basic objectives of our national labor policy. Chapter 7 focuses on the contemporary policy affecting union and management behavior intended to influence employees' selection of a collective bargaining representative.

PART TWO   UNION ORGANIZING

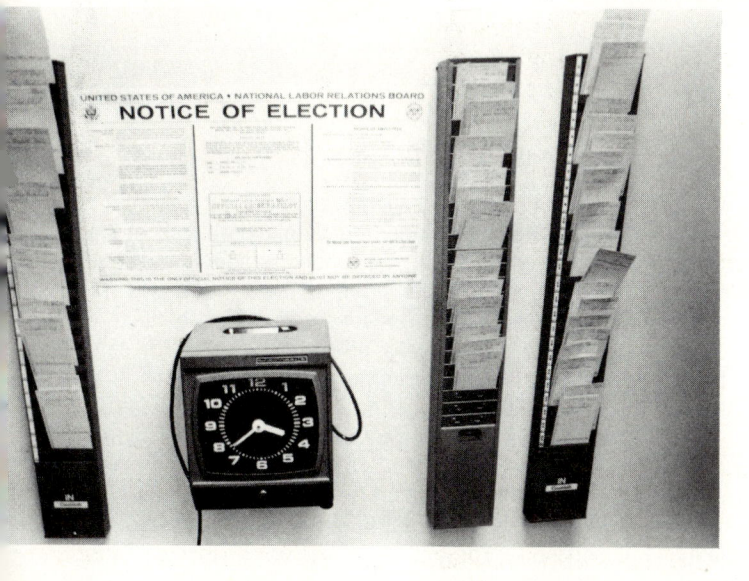

Chapter 6

WHY WORKERS ORGANIZE

Georg Creamovich, Don Swab and Mark Walls were old friends. Regularly they would get together at Herb's Place and tip a few. Creamovich had been raised in a family that was prounion. In fact his grandfather had been a union activist in the iron mines of northern Minnesota during the early 1900s. One reward for his efforts was being blacklisted by the mining companies. The only job he could get in the mining town where he lived was at the parochial school working as a maintenance man.

Creamovich was a union member, while Swab and Walls were not union members. During these meetings at Herb's the conversation usually got around to union membership at some point. Creamovich would encourage them to take the lead in forming unions where they worked. Walls worked for National Furniture Manufacturing and Swab worked for American Wood Products. The following are characterizations of working conditions at each company, as viewed by Walls and Swab respectively.

National Furniture Manufacturing produced wooden furniture. The production employees at National are skilled and semiskilled workers. They are not represented by a union. Most of them are satisfied with the type of work they perform. The work involves a challenge and is not highly repetitious. However, there are some problems at National. Most production workers feel they could earn more at other firms in the community. This feeling is justified because wages and benefits at National are typically below the median for comparable jobs in the community.

First-line supervisors are also a concern in the minds of many production workers at National. Personnel decisions are decentralized and there are virtually no written personnel policies. As a result, different standards are used by first-level supervisors. For example, one supervisor will suspend an employee for a day when he or she is absent without a valid reason. On the other hand, another supervisor will not take such action unless an employee is absent at least five days.

American Wood Products also manufactures wooden furniture. As at National, the employees are not unionized. Unlike National Furniture Manufacturing, however, the production jobs at American have been simplified so that there are no skilled positions. The duties performed by those in most jobs are learned in a short time and are repetitive. There is very little challenge in the work and production workers are supervised closely. If any problems or questions arise, a supervisor deals with them. Most production employees at American are dissatisfied with the nature of their work.

Consistent with the nature of the production jobs, personnel policies and practices at American are centralized and are applied in a consistent manner throughout the organization. In addition, American insures that its wages and fringe benefits are at or above the median for comparable jobs in the community. As a result, production workers are satisfied with their compensation and the personnel practices at American.

Based on the descriptions of working conditions in these companies, when you finish studying this chapter you will be able to predict which company's workforce is most likely to support the formation of a union. In addition you should:

- Be able to describe issues surrounding the formation of unions during the late 1700s and the 1800s.
- Understand how Maslow's need hierarchy, expectancy theory and equity theory can be used to analyze the decision to support or oppose representation by a union.
- Be aware of research findings pertaining to the relationship between attitudes toward unions (or the decision to vote for a union) and:
  a. The relative importance of intrinsic and extrinsic job dissatisfaction.
  b. Dissatisfaction with management decisions and perceptions of worker influence on management decisions.
  c. Perceptions of union instrumentality.
  d. Feelings of equitable treatment.
- Know trends in union membership and in results of certification and decertification elections.
- Be able to suggest a course of action that unions might follow to improve their ability to attract and retain members.

An Historical View of Why Workers Organize

Studying the circumstances surrounding the formation of unions during the early years of the American union movement provides an historical view of why workers organize. In this section selected events, working conditions, and issues in the development of American unions are described.

THE CORDWAINERS AND EFFORTS TO AFFECT WAGES AND PROTECT JOBS

The first American union that continued in existence for a number of years was the Federal Society of Cordwainers.[1] The circumstances surrounding the formation of the Cordwainers and the practices of such groups provide an historical view of why workers organize. It was the custom for the Cordwainers and other unions of that era to call a meeting of those working in the particular trade to discuss the wage to be requested of their employers. Then a representative or representatives of the trade association or union would visit each of the employers and ask them to agree to the wages that had been agreed upon at the meeting of those working in the trade.

Another issue that early unions in the United States were concerned about was the hiring of workers who had not completed the full apprenticeship period.[2] The journeymen felt that these individuals lowered the work standards of the trade and increased the supply of labor. Typically the "half-way" journeymen were willing to work for rates below those established by the journeymen union members. Consequently, a second typical request was for employers to give preference in employment to members of the union who had completed the full apprenticeship period.

According to Taft[3] the first recorded collective bargaining in the United States was the negotiations between the Philadelphia Cordwainers and their employers in 1799. These negotiations followed a lockout that occurred when union members refused to accept a wage cut. A committee of union members met with a group of employer representatives and were able to arrive at a compromise solution to the dispute.

In 1805, the Philadelphia Cordwainers went on strike to achieve higher wages. It was this strike that led to the indictment of the Cordwainers for conspiracy to raise wages. Other examples of skilled trades engaging in collective bargaining and collective activity to pursue similar kinds of goals are described by Taft.[4] The central theme of descriptions of early American unions is that workers organized to protect their jobs and secure higher wages.

OTHER ISSUES ARE ADDED

While in very early years union bargaining efforts focused on wages and job security, events of the 1800s and early 1900s resulted in a shift in focus. Other issues were added to the list of union concerns. Included were efforts to reduce the length of the work day and to increase the standards of safety in employment. It is estimated that the normal work week in 1890 was about sixty hours. However, there were several trades in which it is estimated the normal number of hours worked per week was seventy-two or more.[5] Somers and Somers[6] estimate that the peak in industrial accident rates was reached during the first decade of this century. In the year ending June 30, 1907, 4,534 workers were killed in railroading, and 2,534 men were killed in bituminous coal mines.[7] The total occupational death toll in 1908 is placed at between 30,000 and 35,000.[8]

Exhibit 6.1 provides a compilation of facts concerning working conditions at the turn of the century. In light of these facts it is hardly surprising that workers

> **EXHIBIT 6.1**
> **Working Conditions at the Turn of the Century**
>
> Here are a few cold figures:
> 1. *Wages*. The *average* annual earnings of American workers . . . were something like $400 or $500 a year. For unskilled workers they were somewhat less—under $460 in the North, under $300 in the South. A standard wage for an unskilled man was a dollar and a half a day—when he could get work. That qualification is important: one must bear in mind that according to the census of 1900, nearly 6½ million workers were idle (and therefore, in most cases, quite without income) during some part of the year; that of these, nearly 2 million were idle four to six months out of the twelve.
> 2. *Hours*. The average working day was in the neighborhood of 10 hours, six days a week: total, 60 a week. In business offices there was a growing trend toward a Saturday half holiday, but if anybody had suggested a five-day week he would have been considered demented. At the time when the International Ladies' Garment Workers Union was established in 1900, the hours in this trade, in New York, were 70 a week.
> 3. *Child labor*. Among boys between the ages of 10 and 15, no less than 26 percent—over a quarter—were "gainfully employed"; among girls in the same age groups, 10 percent were. Most of these children were doing farm work, but 284,000 of them were in mills, factories, etc., during years in which, in any satisfactorily arranged society, they would have been in school.
> 4. *Accidents*. The standards of safety were curiously low from our present-day point of view. Consider this set of facts: in the single year 1901, one out of every 399 railroad employees was killed, and one out of every 26 was injured. Among engineers, conductors, brakemen, trainmen, etc., the figures were even worse than this: in that single year, one out of every 137 was killed.
>
> *Source*: Abridged material from pages 55–57 in *The Big Change: America Transforms Itself 1900–1950* by Frederick Lewis Allen. Copyright, 1952, by Frederick Lewis Allen.

wanted to reduce the number of hours worked per day, increase the safety standards of American industry, and seek to provide some protection in the form of insurance when a worker was injured or killed. Unions were a vehicle to aid workers in attaining these goals.

MORE RECENT ISSUES

Slichter, Healy, and Livernash[9] state that the origin of a union in many organizations resulted from employee perceptions that the company has been arbitrary and discriminatory in meting out discipline. The presence of a union offers protection against unfair disciplinary treatment. A union is present on a daily basis ready to pursue grievances relating to alleged unfair discipline.

Exhibit 6.2 reports the results of research conducted during a union organization campaign in the early 1940s. Factors influencing employee opinions concerning

> **EXHIBIT 6.2**
> **Why Workers Join Unions**
>
> The worker reacts favorably to union membership in proportion to the strength of his belief that this step will reduce his frustrations and anxieties and will further his opportunities relevant to the achievement of his standards of successful living.
>
> He reacts unfavorably in proportion to the strength of his belief that this step will increase his frustrations and anxieties and will reduce his opportunities relevant to the achievement of such standards.
>
> Source: W. Wright Bakke, "Why Workers Join Unions," Personnel, *July 1945 (New York: American Management Association, Inc., 1945), p. 37.*

the union are reviewed. Included are opportunities for promotion, nature of supervision, communication with supervisors, and opportunities to present grievances.

This brief historical review of factors pertaining to the formation of unions and of union activities provides some clues concerning why workers organize. In the next section we will present an explanation of the underlying causes and processes involved in a worker's decision to support the formation of a union.

The Formation of a Union

COALITION

A coalition is a group of individuals who find that by acting together they are able to achieve their individual goals.[10] A union can be viewed as a coalition. It is a group of employees who find that they can better attain such goals as were discussed in the previous section by acting together. Viewing unions as coalitions helps to clarify the question we are addressing: which employee goals are associated with the formation of a union?

EMPLOYEE GOALS AND NEEDS

Viewing a union as a coalition formed to facilitate the attainment of goals of individuals within a group raises the issue of what are common goals of individuals in a work organization. Before the discussion of common goals of workers, a distinction must be made between goals and needs and the relationship between them.[11] All individuals have needs. When needs are not met, they set off tensions within a person. A goal is something that a person believes will remove that tension and satisfy the need or needs causing the tension. Since needs are associated with goals, we must identify basic categories of employee needs. One attempt to identify categories of human needs is provided by Maslow.[12]

HIERARCHY OF NEEDS

Fig. 6.1 lists the categories of needs as proposed by Maslow. He suggests that these needs are organized in a hierarchy such that basic needs must be satisfied before higher needs become important. For example, physiological needs must be satisfied before safety needs become important to a person. As physiological needs are satisfied, safety needs emerge in importance for a person. In turn, a person's safety needs must be satisfied before his or her social needs become important. There are two principal implications of this hierarchy notion. First, even though a need may not be satisfied, if it is not important to a person, it will not be a major determinant of that individual's behavior. Second, the category of need lowest in the hierarchy that is not satisfied will be important to a person and will be a major determinant of that person's behavior.

Originally Maslow suggested there were five steps or stages to this "satisfaction of a need—emergence of the next need" process. More recent work involving Maslow's categories suggests that it is more accurate to think of two or three steps in the hierarchy.[13] According to the two-step view, physiological and safety needs make up one category and social, esteem, and self-actualization needs make up the other category. With respect to the hierarchial importance of these needs, the lower-level physiological and safety needs must be satisfied before the higher-level social, esteem, and self-actualization needs become prime determinants of an individual's behavior. However, no predictions are made about which of the second-level needs will come into play once the lower-order needs are satisfied. Lawler states that it is clear that needs exist on at least these two levels, but it is not certain whether it is better to think in terms of three categories: physiological and safety; social; and esteem and self-actualization.[14]

Fig. 6.1 *Maslow's Categories of Needs*

Low   1. Physiological needs: e.g., hunger, thirst, rest.
         2. Safety needs: e.g., avoid situations involving injury and death and situations involving uncertainty, injustice, and unfairness.
         3. Social needs: the need to relate and interact with others.
         4. Esteem needs: the desire for a high evaluation of oneself (self-respect) and the respect of others.
High   5. Self-Actualization needs: the desire to become what one is capable of being, self-fulfillment or growth. *"BE All that you can be."*

Source: Adapted from A.H. Maslow, "A Theory of Human Motivation," Psychological Review *50 (1943): 370–96.*

Another taxonomy of needs has been proposed by Alderfer.[15] According to this view there are three need categories: existence, relatedness, and growth. Existence needs include all physiological and material desires. Such needs correspond to Maslow's physiological and most safety needs. Relatedness needs involve interpersonal relationships with others. These needs correspond to Maslow's social needs and certain safety needs. Growth needs pertain to one's creative efforts and personal growth on the job. These needs are comparable to Maslow's self-actualization and esteem needs.

The modifications in Maslow's hierarchy that have been suggested by research result in a revised hierarchy very similar to Alderfer's theory. Some writers suggest that the latter provides a clearer understanding of employee motivation.[16]

EXPECTANCY MODEL

The above discussion indicates what employees want from work. However, it does not explain why employees would favor forming a union or would vote for a union in an election. This behavior can be explained using an expectancy model. Vroom has stated that the choices a person makes depend on the outcomes that are expected to follow from the choice or behavior and the individual's feelings or preferences concerning these outcomes.[17] A great deal of research has stemmed from Vroom's work. Several reviews of this research are available.[18,19,20] The key concepts of the expectancy model are represented in Fig. 6.2. Since most research on the expectancy model has focused on the motivation to work, Fig. 6.2 focuses on this choice in behavior. The model hypothesizes that such employee choices depend on three types of perceptions. One perception is the *valence* or feelings attached to the outcome that can follow from different levels of job performance. Valences can be positive, neutral, or negative. Positive valences attached to an outcome imply that a worker likes the outcome. Neutral feelings imply that a worker does not care one way or the other about the outcome. Negative valences mean that a worker would prefer to avoid the outcome. For example, a worker may have positive feelings toward a 10 percent pay increase, not care one way or the other about increases in pension benefits, and wish to avoid being discharged.

A second perception is labeled *expectancy*. This refers to an employee's estimate that changes in his or her effort will lead to changes in performance. For example, will an increase in one's effort improve one's job performance? An employee's ability to influence performance by changing his or her effort could be limited because of one's skills. If a person's job skills are limited, an increase in effort will probably not improve his or her job performance. In addition one's ability to influence one's job performance may be limited by environmental factors, e.g., job performance and productivity could depend on group effort and cooperation. One individual's effort could have little or no impact on these factors.

The third perception is termed *instrumentality*. It pertains to the likelihood that different levels of performance will lead to certain outcomes. For example, a 10 percent raise may be more likely to follow from high performance than from typical performance. Alternatively, discharge may be more likely to follow from typical performance than from high performance.

Fig. 6.2 *Expectancy Model of Motivation to Work*

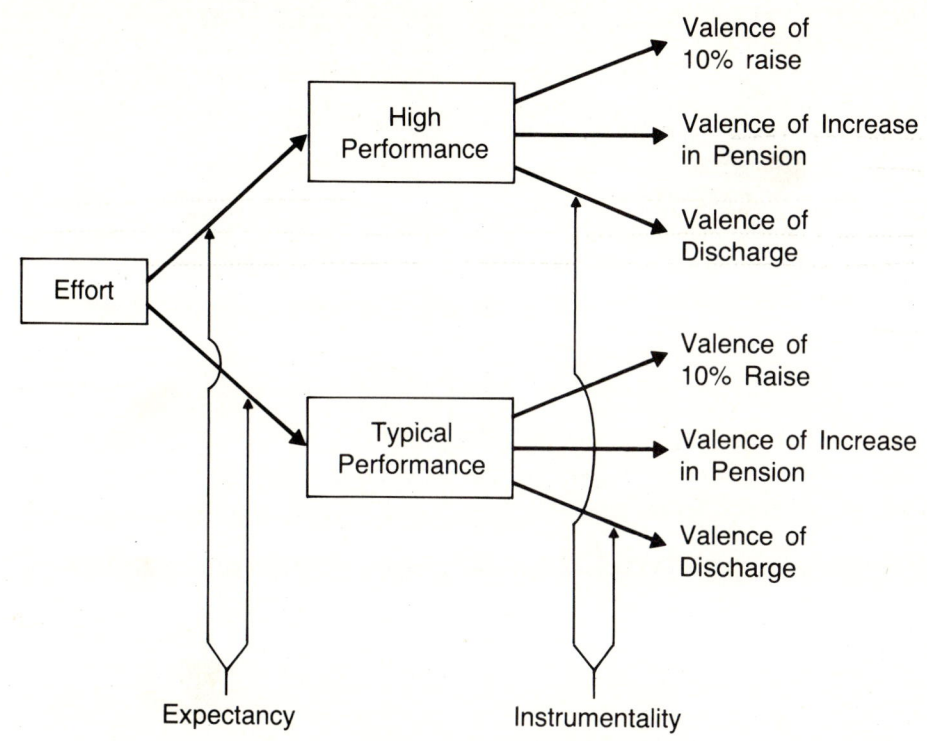

```
                          ┌──────────────┐ ──→ Valence of
                       ↗  │    High      │      10% raise
                          │ Performance  │ ──→ Valence of Increase
                          └──────────────┘      in Pension
                                          ──→ Valence of
   ┌────────┐                                   Discharge
   │ Effort │
   └────────┘              ┌──────────────┐ ──→ Valence of
                       ↘  │   Typical    │      10% Raise
                          │ Performance  │ ──→ Valence of Increase
                          └──────────────┘      in Pension
                                          ──→ Valence of
                                                Discharge

        Expectancy              Instrumentality
```

The model predicts that the greater the positive valence attached to outcomes and the greater the expectancy and instrumentality perceptions associated with a level of performance, the greater the motivation to perform at that level. It is assumed that an individual will choose the alternative level of performance that has the greatest positive force or utility.

THE DECISION TO SUPPORT OR OPPOSE A UNION

Fig. 6.3 presents a model of a worker's decision to support or oppose a union. This model is an adaptation of the expectancy model presented in Fig. 6.2. The employee's decision concerning job effort in Fig. 6.2 corresponds to the decision concerning effort to support or oppose a union. The result of one's efforts in Fig. 6.2 is the level of job performance and in Fig. 6.3 it is the presence or absence of a union. At the right of each figure are the outcomes that could follow from job performance in the former figure and that could follow from the presence or absence of a union in the latter figure.

Valences are attached to the outcomes that could follow from having a union or not having a union, just as valences are attached to outcomes that could follow from levels of job performance. Similarly, valences associated with the various outcomes can be positive, neutral, or negative.

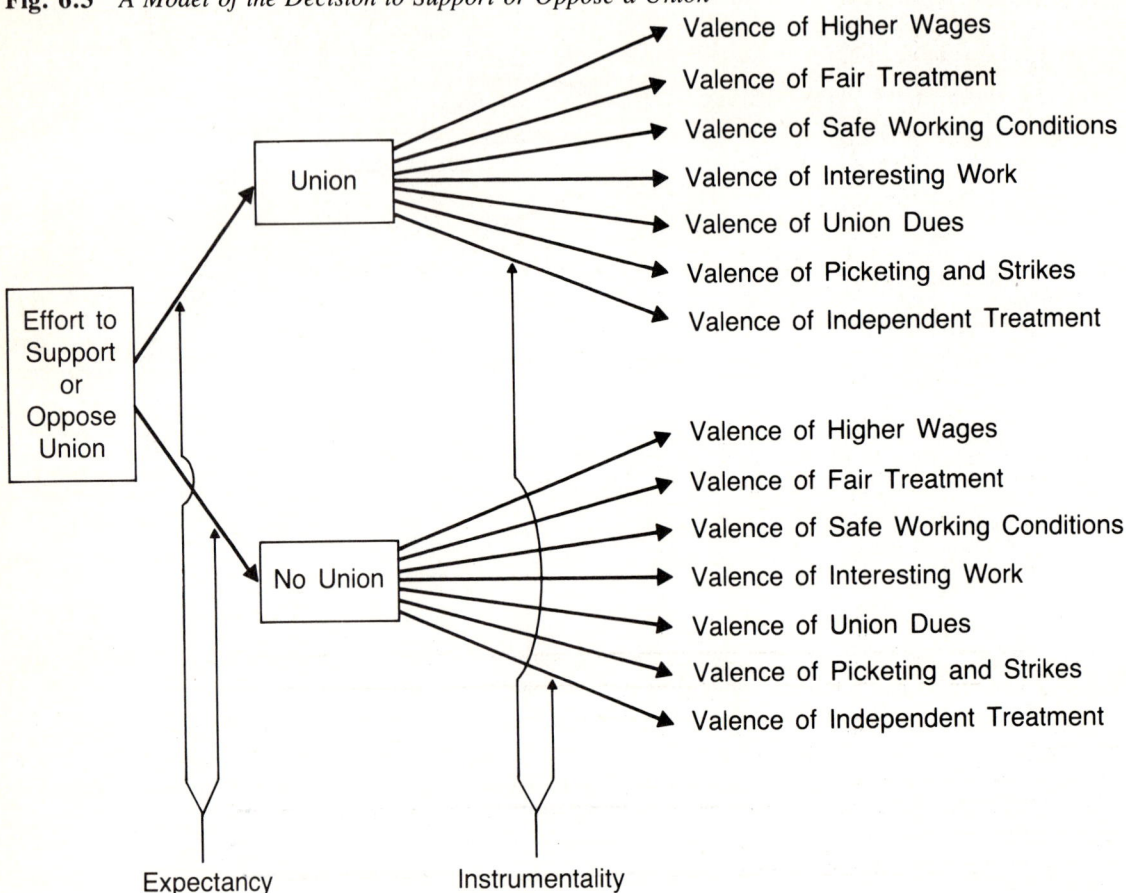

Fig. 6.3 *A Model of the Decision to Support or Oppose a Union*

```
                              → Valence of Higher Wages
                              → Valence of Fair Treatment
                              → Valence of Safe Working Conditions
                   ┌───────┐  → Valence of Interesting Work
                   │ Union │  → Valence of Union Dues
                   └───────┘  → Valence of Picketing and Strikes
                              → Valence of Independent Treatment
┌──────────┐
│ Effort to│
│ Support  │
│   or     │
│ Oppose   │
│  Union   │
└──────────┘
                              → Valence of Higher Wages
                              → Valence of Fair Treatment
                   ┌────────┐ → Valence of Safe Working Conditions
                   │No Union│ → Valence of Interesting Work
                   └────────┘ → Valence of Union Dues
                              → Valence of Picketing and Strikes
                              → Valence of Independent Treatment

     Expectancy        Instrumentality
```

Expectancy perceptions are also assumed to enter into the discussion to support or oppose a union. In this context it refers to an employee's estimate that his or her effort regarding the union will have an impact on whether or not there is a union. As with job performance, a single worker's efforts may have little impact on whether or not a union represents a group of workers. We assume that expectancy perceptions are particularly significant in explaining an individual worker's efforts when that person's attitude toward a union is at odds with the attitude of the majority of co-workers. For example an individual worker may prefer to have a union but expend no effort to form a union because most co-workers oppose being represented by a union.

In Fig. 6.3 instrumentality refers to the likelihood that having a union or not will lead to various outcomes. The meaning of instrumentality in both figures is very similar.

The outcomes that could follow from the presence or absence of a union listed in Fig. 6.3 represent a partial list. Many other outcomes could be included. Examples include fringe benefit levels, employment security, ability to lodge grievances about employment conditions without fear of retribution, and participation in decisions affecting one's working conditions.

Among those outcomes listed in Fig. 6.3 we have included some to which most workers attach positive valences, e.g., higher wages and fair treatment. We have also listed outcomes to which most workers would attach negative valences, i.e., paying union dues, striking, and picketing.

The instrumentality estimates associated with these outcomes are likely to be different. For example, employees may perceive that a union is likely to be instrumental in obtaining higher wages, fair treatment, safe working conditions, payment of union dues, and participation in strikes and picketing. It may be perceived that having a union or not having a union will make no difference concerning the likelihood of having interesting work. Finally, it is probable that workers will perceive that the ability of an individual worker to deal independently with management about conditions of employment will be virtually eliminated by having a union.

It is predicted that the greater the positive valence attached to outcomes and the greater the expectancy and instrumentality estimates associated with having a union, the greater the motivation to support a union. Following this reasoning, as the motivation to support a union becomes greater, the effort expended in support of a union is expected to increase.

WHICH OUTCOMES ARE VALENT?

Before one can predict if workers will support or oppose a union with the model presented in Fig. 6.3, three kinds of information are necessary: instrumentality perceptions, valences attached to the outcomes perceived to follow from the presence or absence of a union, and expectancy perceptions. Several studies have been reported that enable one to infer which outcomes workers perceive to be attainable when employees are represented by a union. These will be reviewed in the next section of this chapter.

The issue of explaining which outcomes will be highly valent or important is addressed in this section. Two approaches to providing an explanation for this issue will be explored. Inferences can be drawn from equity theory and inferences can be derived from Maslow's need hierarchy.

EQUITY MODEL

According to equity theory individuals make comparisons between what they receive in an employment situation and the inputs or investments they put into the situation.[21] In the terminology of equity theory, outcomes refer to the things received as a result of employment and inputs are investments in a work situation. Examples of outcomes include wages, fringe benefits, working conditions, treatment by supervisors, job security, and interesting work. Examples of inputs include a person's skills, training, education, seniority, and merit or job performance.

Specifically, the equity model states that an individual compares one's own outcomes relative to one's own inputs with the outcomes and inputs of others. Fig. 6.4 represents this comparison. An employee is predicted to feel that an employment

Fig. 6.4 *Equity Theory*

$$\frac{\text{Self Outcomes}}{\text{Inputs}} \quad \text{compared with} \quad \frac{\text{Other Outcomes}}{\text{Inputs}}$$

If ratio for self exceeds ratio for other, feel overpaid.
If ratio for self equals ratio for other, feel equitably treated.
If ratio for self is less than ratio for other, feel underpaid.

situation is fair or equitable if these ratios are equal. For example an individual will feel fairly treated when it is perceived that the other person has wages and working conditions that are the same or nearly the same as one's own and that the other person is the same with respect to factors as skill, seniority, training, effort, and performance. It is possible that one will conclude that his or her ratio is more favorable than the ratio of another person. In this case, the person will feel overpaid or overcompensated. Research on equity seldom finds persons who report feeling overpaid. Possibly such individuals change the person with whom they are comparing themselves. It is assumed that the new comparison person will be selected in such a way that feelings of equity will be achieved.

When making the comparisons described by the equity model, the remaining possibility is that one concludes his or her ratio is less favorable than the other person's ratio. Such an individual will feel underpaid. In this case it is predicted that the person will be dissatisfied and will seek to restore feelings of equity. For example, the employees of a company that pays lower wages and provides fewer benefits than other companies provide employees with similar skills and working conditions are predicted to be dissatisfied with their wages and benefits. Also these outcomes will be valent or very important to them.

A number of possible ways can be used to try to restore equity, when a person feels undercompensated. One is to reduce job effort and performance. Another is to try to influence the outcomes received. In the above example employees of the low-wage company could quit and seek employment at one of the organizations providing a higher level of compensation. Research on labor mobility suggests that economic issues such as wages, benefits, and employment stability are often the reasons for changing employers.[22] This research also makes clear that members of the labor force are often successful in raising their compensation through such moves.[23]

Another approach to influencing outcomes in this example is for the employees of the low-wage company to form a union. Historically American trade unions have focused on such issues as compensation and job security. If most employees of such an employer believe that a union could improve their wages, they are likely to support a union.

The central issue we are addressing in this section is explaining which outcomes will be highly valent or important in the minds of workers. We posit that those outcomes which are present to a lesser degree in one's place of employment than in other places of employment will be highly valent. An implicit assumption of the preceding statement is that the other places of employment should, in the workers' minds, be compared with their place of employment. For example, these other companies may be in the same industry or may employ workers with similar skills.

NEED DEPRIVATION-NEED IMPORTANCE

Another indication of which outcomes will be perceived as important by employees is provided by research on Maslow's hierarchy. The available evidence makes clear that when the amount of reward associated with a particular need is reduced, that need becomes very important to the individual.[24] This implies that if an organization reduces the amount of an outcome provided, that outcome will become very important or highly valent to the persons affected by the change. For example, if an organization reduces wages or fringe benefits or during times of rapid inflation fails to raise wages at a rate sufficient to maintain real income, it is likely that such factors will be dominant outcomes for that organization's employees.

Why Workers Unionize: The Research Evidence

In recent years a substantial number of studies have sought to identify worker attitudes and opinions associated with favoring the formation of a union. That literature is reviewed in this section. These studies have been grouped in the following categories and the relationships between the attitudes addressed in each type of study and the decision to support a union are reviewed. The categories are:

1. The relative importance of extrinsic job satisfaction compared to intrinsic job satisfaction.
2. Employee participation in decision making and the distribution of power between employees and management.
3. Perceptions of instrumentality of unions for attaining selected outcomes.
4. Perceptions of equitable treatment.

EXTRINSIC AND INTRINSIC JOB SATISFACTION

Extrinsic job conditions refer to the job context or work environment.[25] Examples include job security, salary, fringe benefits, working conditions, quality of technical supervision, and quality of interpersonal relations with supervisors and co-workers. Intrinsic job conditions refer to the content of the job.[26] Examples include opportunities for achievement, responsibility associated with the job, recognition, advancement, and personal growth and development. Referring back to the revised Maslow need categories, extrinsic factors are outcomes that correspond to the satisfaction of lower-order needs. Alternatively, intrinsic factors are outcomes associated primarily with the satisfaction of higher-order needs.

The available evidence relating attitudes toward work and attitudes toward unions suggests that overall job satisfaction is negatively associated with the perceived need for a union. With respect to the relative importance of satisfaction with intrinsic and extrinsic factors, studies have typically found the latter to dominate. Getman et al.[27] related measures of job satisfaction to self-reported vote in certification elections. Their data suggest that satisfaction with such factors as wages and job security are most strongly associated with voting behavior. Alternatively, satisfaction with the nature of work was not as strongly correlated with voting behavior in certification elections. Schriesheim[28] also studied employees involved in a certification election. The focus of his study was to compare the association between voting behavior and satisfaction with such factors as job security, pay, working conditions, and company policy as opposed to satisfaction with independence, variety, creativity, and opportunity for achievement. Schriesheim's conclusion was that while prounion voting was related to the latter measures of intrinsic job satisfaction, it was more strongly related to the measures of economic satisfaction. Kochan[29] studied a nationwide sample which included both white-collar and blue-collar employees. He reports that overall about one-third of those employees not presently union members were in favor of unionization. About 39 percent of the blue-collar workers supported unionization compared to 28 percent of the white-collar workers. Kochan concludes that those who reported problems with inadequate income, fringe benefits, and health and safety hazards on their jobs were more likely to support a union.

DIFFERENCES BETWEEN WHITE-COLLAR AND BLUE-COLLAR WORKERS

Kochan compared white-collar and blue-collar workers. Among blue-collar workers dissatisfaction with extrinsic factors was more strongly related to favoring a union. However, dissatisfaction with intrinsic factors such as nature of work was more strongly associated with the inclination to form a union among white-collar workers.

Many studies of the relationship between job satisfaction and support of unions have relied upon college professors as subjects. As college professors make up a subset of white-collar members of the labor force, results of these studies will be reviewed. Bigoness[30] found a negative relationship between the perceived need for a union and satisfaction with the nature of work, promotional opportunities, pay, supervision, job involvement, and salary. When the relative importance of these different variables was compared it was found that satisfaction with work, pay, and promotions had the most important influence on attitudes toward collective bargaining. Allen and Keaveny[31] report that intrinsic job satisfaction was significantly related with the perceived need for a union, as were measures of satisfaction with economic variables. When intrinsic job satisfaction and extrinsic job satisfaction were considered at the same time, it was found that satisfaction with economic factors had the greatest relationship with the perceived need for a union.

Most studies comparing the relative importance of intrinsic and extrinsic job satisfaction in determining attitudes toward a union among white-collar workers have focused on college professors. While college professors are a subset of white-collar members of the labor force, you should be careful in making generalizations about all white-collar workers based on this small group. Kochan's results are based on a random sample of the American work force. Consequently, his results are probably more representative of the relative importance of intrinsic and extrinsic job satisfaction in determining attitudes toward unionization among white-collar employees.

Among blue-collar workers, the research indicates that satisfaction with extrinsic job factors bears a stronger relationship to attitudes toward formation of a union. However among white-collar employees, satisfaction with intrinsic factors may be more important in determining attitudes toward unionization. A possible explanation for this difference is suggested below.

SATISFACTION WITH ADMINISTRATIVE PROCEDURES

The relationship between satisfaction with decisions made by administrators and interest in unionization has been studied. It appears that satisfaction with administrative decisions affecting employees is negatively related to attitudes toward unions.[32,33] The studies have been of college faculty. One study found that satisfaction with representation of faculty interests in campus administration and with the personnel decision-making system was more associated with support for collective bargaining than was satisfaction with salaries and fringe benefits.[34] In a second study, distrust of administrative decision making and dissatisfaction with work content were significantly related to prounion voting in a representation election.[35] The former variable had a much stronger relationship with voting for the union than the latter variable. When considered at the same time as distrust of administrative decision making and dissatisfaction with work content, dissatisfaction with economic issues was not related to voting for the union.

In a third study of college faculty, the anticipated relationship between future job performance and future salary increases was inversely related to the perceived need for a union.[36] Trust in administrative decisions was not measured in this study. However, we assume that a perceived breakdown in the relationship between job performance and pay raises would be associated with distrust in administrative decisions.

Kochan's study of a representative sample of the American labor force provides further evidence concerning the importance of workers' perceived ability to influence management decisions.[37] Among blue-collar workers, as the difficulty in getting management to make changes concerning job-related problems increased, support for unionization increased. Among white-collar workers, union support was significantly related to the desire to participate in decisions concerning one's job.

Viewing the entire sample, most workers who both wanted greater participation in decisions and felt that it was difficult to get management to make changes pertaining to their jobs supported unionization.

Taken together these studies indicate that satisfaction with administrative decisions is an important variable influencing attitudes toward unionization. The latter study also indicates that among white-collar workers the desire to participate in decisions is a potent determinant of union support.

INSTRUMENTALITY OF UNIONS

Fig. 6.3 presented a model of the decision to support or oppose a union. That model suggests that the importance of outcomes that are associated with the presence or absence of a union influences this choice. The previous section reviews research which indicates that extrinsic job dissatisfaction among blue-collar workers and possibly both intrinsic and extrinsic job dissatisfaction among white-collar workers are associated with supporting a union.

The model in Fig. 6.3 also suggests that perceptions of the instrumentality of unions for attaining outcomes will influence workers' support of a union. Some research has been completed that focuses on the relationship between instrumentality perceptions and union support. A study of registered nurses at the time of a certification election found perceived union instrumentality to be strongly correlated with both the intent to support the union and actual vote in the certification election.[38] In this study union instrumentality measured the extent to which the presence of a union would result in improved extrinsic outcomes of pay, fringe benefits, working conditions, supervision, and fair treatment.

Kochan also studied the relationship between instrumentality and propensity to join a union.[39] He studied a nationwide random sample of the American labor force. His measure of union instrumentality also focused on extrinsic job factors. As in the study cited above, perceived instrumentality was associated with support of a union. It should be noted that supporting a union was more closely related to instrumentality than to either extrinsic or intrinsic job satisfaction. This was true among both white-collar and blue-collar workers.

The view that unions are effective at improving the working conditions of their members is widespread. Kochan's study found that 4 out of 5 workers agreed that unions improve wages and job security of their members as well as protect workers against unfair management practices. The respondents were about equally divided as to whether the benefits of being represented by a union are worth the dues charged for membership.

The notion of union instrumentality may provide an explanation of why dissatisfaction with intrinsic factors is related to interest in unionization among white-collar workers but not among blue-collar workers. It is possible that unions which organize white-collar workers focus more on improving intrinsic conditions of work than do unions whose membership is composed predominantly of blue-collar workers. As a result, white-collar workers dissatisfied with intrinsic factors are more likely to turn to a union in an effort to improve intrinsic aspects of their work.

UNION INFLUENCE ON WAGES AND FRINGE BENEFITS

The preceding section reported information about worker opinions concerning the instrumentality of unions. Empirical evidence is available concerning two aspects of the instrumentality of unions: the influence of unions on wages and on fringe benefits.

A study using data collected by the U. S. Bureau of the Census from over 38,000 workers in 1976 estimated the impact of unions on direct wages.[40] Wages were adjusted for a wide range of variables that influence wages, e.g., age, sex, education, location of employment, occupation, and industry. After adjusting wages for these worker characteristics, among men the wage advantage for union workers over non-union workers was $.90 per hour. After similar adjustments in the wages of women, the wage advantage for female union workers over female non-union workers was $.60 per hour.

In 1977, the results of an investigation of union fees and dues were published.[41] This study reported that in approximately three of four unions, whose membership includes over 75 percent of unionized Americans, the national union portion of monthly dues was less than $6.00 per month. This suggests that the wage advantage associated with union membership more than offsets the costs of union dues.

Other studies have presented evidence of the impact of unions on employee compensation. Census data from 1950, 1960, and 1970 demonstrate that in heavily unionized states, family income is more evenly distributed.[42] Stated in a different way, the incidence of low income families in a state is inversely related to the percentage of the labor force which is unionized.

Evidence concerning the dispersion of wage figures across unionized employers and within unionized places of employment provides further support for the instrumentality of unions: unions do reduce the dispersion of earnings both within and across places of employment.[43] Other things being equal, the data indicate that the dispersion of earnings is lower among organized blue-collar workers than among non-union blue-collar workers. This implies that on the average, the low-wage non-union worker stands to gain more from unionization. Further, the dispersion in average wages paid by unionized employers is less than among non-union employers. Finally, the wage differential between blue-collar and white-collar employees is smaller among unionized employers than among non-union employers.

The effects of unionism on fringe benefits have also been studied. The evidence shows that unions increase the level of fringe benefits provided by employers.[44] The principal effect appears to be in the form of better pension; vacation; and life, accident, and health insurance benefits. In addition, stated in percentages, the impact of unions on fringe benefits exceeds the impact of unions on wages. This suggests that focusing solely on the wage effect of unions understates unions' effect on total compensation.

In summary, the empirical data concerning the impact of unions on wages and fringe benefits support workers' perceptions of union instrumentality concerning wages. Unions do in fact improve wages for most workers, particularly low-wage workers. Further, it appears that workers' perceptions are in error because they underestimate the magnitude by which the wage-and-fringe-benefit advantage of unionized employment over non-union employment exceeds the cost of union dues.

FEELINGS OF EQUITY

Dissatisfaction with wages and fringe benefits can occur because they are perceived to be below some acceptable standard. This is reflected by the expectation that employees should receive a "living wage." In addition, dissatisfaction with wages and benefits can stem from the way in which they are administered. Employees wish to receive wages that are equitable relative to the wages received by other workers. This is reflected by the phrase "fair wage." Perceived inequity in the administration of wages, as well as a wide range of other work related decisions, leads to dissatisfaction with the particular outcome.

In a national sample of white-collar workers, the extent to which wages were believed to be inequitable relative to other people doing similar work was positively related to the willingness to unionize.[45] Among blue-collar workers, feelings of pay inequity were not related to willingness to form a union; however, dissatisfaction with income level was significantly related to union support.[46] Among a sample of college professors, perceived inequity in salary increases was significantly related to the reported need for a union.[47]

Trends in Union Membership

The bottom line in judging the effectiveness of the union movement in contributing to the satisfaction of worker needs is to study trends in the number of union members. If unions are judged to be the most effective means for workers to achieve outcomes that are important to them, then union membership will be growing in absolute numbers as well as percentage of the labor force. Table 6.1 reports total union membership and union membership as a percent of nonagriculture employment for selected years. The data indicate that in absolute numbers of members, unions have been growing since 1930. In 1976, total union membership in the United States was 19,634,000. If one includes members of employee associations such as nurses associations and teachers associations, then total membership in employee organizations was 22,662,000 in 1976.[48]

These figures suggest that the union movement is alive and well in the United States. However, more recent data indicate that the absolute number of union members declined between 1978 and 1980.[49] Evidence that all is not well with the American labor movement is found when one focuses on union membership as a percent of nonagriculture employment. Table 6.1 shows that union membership as a percent

Table 6.1 *Union Membership in the United States: Selected Years 1930–1976*

Year	Total membership (thousands)	As percent of Nonagricultural employment	Year	Total membership (thousands)	As percent of Nonagricultural employment
1930	3,401	11.6	1955	16,802	33.2
1935	3,584	13.2	1960	17,049	31.4
1940	8,717	26.9	1965	17,299	28.4
1945	14,322	35.5	1970	19,381	27.3
1950	14,267	31.5	1975	19,611	25.5
			1978	20,246	23.6

Source: U.S. Department of Labor, Bureau of Labor Statistics *Handbook of Labor Statistics 1980*, Bulletin 2070 (U.S. Government Printing Office, Washington, D.C., December, 1980), p. 412.

of nonagriculture employment reached a peak in 1955 and has been declining since that time. In 1978 the figure was 23.6 percent which was the lowest since 1937 when union membership as a percent of nonagriculture employment was 22.6 percent.[50,51]

CHANGING INDUSTRY COMPOSITION

Different factors are contributing to the decline in union membership as a percent of nonagriculture employment. One factor is the trend in employment by industry. Table 6.2 reports the distribution of nonagricultural employment by major sectors of the economy. Inspection of Table 6.2 shows that certain sectors of the economy have been declining as a percent of total employment. Examples are mining, contract construction, manufacturing, transportation, communications, and public utilities. On the other hand, some sectors of the economy have been maintaining or expanding their proportion of total civilian employment. Examples include retail trade, finance, insurance and real estate, and other services. The latter include employment in hotels and restaurants, recreational services, and medical services.

The significance of these trends is that the sectors of the economy that have been declining as a percent of total civilian nonagriculture employment are those sectors where unions have been most effective in organizing members. Alternatively, those sectors of the economy which have been holding their own or have been expanding as a percent of total employment are the parts of the economy in which unions have been relatively unsuccessful in organizing members. For example, contract construction and transportation are industries in which 75 percent or more of employees are union members and communications, mining, and manufacturing are industries in which the percent of unionized employees is between 50 and 75 percent.[52] Alternatively industries in which fewer than 25 percent of the employees are unionized include service, finance, and wholesale and retail trade. These figures indicate that unions have not been effective in organizing those industries in which increases in employment have been concentrated.

Table 6.2 *Nonagriculture Employment Distribution By Major Sector, Actual and Projected, Selected Years 1959–1990*

Sector	1959	1968	1973	1977	1980	1985	1990
			(Percent distribution)				
Government	13.02	15.55	16.12	16.73	16.06	15.48	15.09
Mining	1.23	.83	.79	.95	1.01	.97	.92
Contract Construction	5.93	5.18	5.59	5.15	5.15	5.10	4.96
Manufacturing	27.39	26.31	23.89	21.86	21.76	21.13	20.59
Transportation, Communication, and Public Utilities	6.83	5.94	5.71	5.33	5.28	5.06	4.88
Wholesale and Retail Trade	22.16	21.44	22.33	23.03	23.64	23.78	23.60
Finance, Insurance, and Real Estate	4.64	4.82	5.20	5.38	5.38	5.61	5.77
Other Services	14.64	16.74	17.90	19.47	20.10	21.53	23.06
Private Household	4.15	3.20	2.45	2.11	1.62	1.33	1.13
Total Civilian Nonagricultural Employment*	62,072	72,173	85,202	90,793	98,787	108,929	115,981

Source: Adapted from: Valerie A. Personick, "Industry Output and Employment: BLS Projections to 1990," *Monthly Labor Review 102* (April 1979): 3–14.

*In thousands.

EMPLOYER EFFORTS TO REDUCE THE PERCEIVED NEED FOR A UNION

Another factor contributing to the decline in union membership as a percent of total nonagriculture employment is that employers may be more effective in reducing the need for a union as perceived by employees. Several organizations and consulting agencies make available to employers programs and strategies designed to achieve this objective. One publication of this type argues that through progressive personnel policies an organization can remove the sources of employee dissatisfaction and thereby remove the motivation to form a union.[53]

The above material which discusses the relationship between dissatisfaction with extrinsic factors and distrust of management decisions indicates that if an employer has personnel policies and practices that are perceived to be fair by employees, the employer has removed many of the sources of dissatisfaction that appear to lead to the formation of a union.

TRENDS IN DECERTIFICATION ELECTIONS

Further evidence that unions are finding it more and more difficult to organize additional bargaining units is presented in Table 6.3. It reports the number of certification elections and decertification elections for selected years between 1950 and 1978. The data indicate that the number of both certification and decertification elections has been increasing since 1950. The data also indicate that the percentage of both certification and decertification elections won by unions is decreasing. In 1950 unions won about three out of four certification elections, whereas in 1978, unions won fewer than one-half. On the other hand, in 1950 unions won about one-third of all decertification elections while in 1978 the ratio was just over one in four.

Krislov[54] suggests that the increase in decertification elections poses no major threat to unions. However, the fact remains that the number of decertification elections is increasing and the number of decertification elections being lost by unions is also increasing.

Some evidence concerning the reasons for decertification is available.[55] Interviews with employers, government officials, and union officers suggest that among the factors explaining why some employees choose to support union decertification is failure of unions to meet the expectations of their membership. For example, employees may expect to receive greater wage increases and fringe benefit improvements than unions are able to deliver. Another factor explaining the decision of some workers to vote in favor of decertification is that the costs of union membership are underestimated. The main "unexpected" cost appears to be the interruption of earnings which results from a strike. Referring back to the model presented in Fig. 6.3,

Table 6.3 *Trends in Union Certification and Decertification Elections*

Year	Number of elections resulting in certifications	Percent of certification elections won by union	Number of decertification elections	Percent of decertification elections won by union
1978[a]	8240	46.0	807	26.4
1975[b]	8577	48.2	516	26.6
1970[c]	8074	55.2	301	30.2
1965[d]	7776	60.2	200	36.0
1960[e]	6380	58.6	237	31.2
1955[f]	4215	67.6	157	35.0
1950[g]	5619	74.5	112	33.0

a. *Forty-Third Annual Report of the National Labor Relations Board* (Washington, D.C.: U. S. Government Printing Office, 1979), Table 13, pp. 266–8.
b. Fortieth Annual Report . . ., (1976), Table 13, pp. 232–5.
c. Thirty-Fifth Annual Report . . ., (1971), Table 13, pp. 178–81.
d. Thirtieth Annual Report . . ., (1966), Table 13, pp. 197–9.
e. Twenty-Fifth Annual Report . . ., (1961), Table 13 and 14, pp. 190–3.
f. Twentieth Annual Report . . ., (1956), Table 13 and 14, pp. 180–82.
g. Fifteenth Annual Report . . ., (1951), Table 15 and 16, pp. 232–4.

original instrumentality estimates about higher wages and fringe benefits and the chances of a strike when represented by a union may be substantially revised as a result of actual experience. As a result one may shift from supporting the union to opposing it. When a decertification election is lost by a union, it is implied that a majority of the employees in the bargaining unit have concluded that their net advantage or greatest advantage is to be without a union, or at least without the particular union.

The relationship between the outcome of decertification elections and other variables has been studied. Bargaining-unit size, the nature of the employer-union bargaining relationship, and union involvement in the campaign prior to the election are all related to the outcome of decertification elections.[56] The establishment of a small unit may place a union at a disadvantage because of the difficulties and cost of providing the level of services deemed appropriate by the members of the unit. Further, it is easier for management to improve employee relations in a small unit.

Failure to develop a positive union-management relationship appears to contribute to decertification. If the union and employer do not establish such a relationship within a few years, it appears that employees may become frustrated and dump the union.

Campaign involvement by the union also influences the support received by the union in a decertification election. The available evidence indicates that if a union chooses not to campaign, it is almost certain to be decertified.

Decertification elections involving more than one union should be distinguished from those involving only one union. In the latter situation, unions are decertified in about 3 of 4 elections, while in the former case, the incumbent wins just under one of two elections.[57] Further, in fewer than 2 percent of elections involving more than one union do the voters select not to be represented by any union. Apparently in such situations members of the bargaining unit use the decertification process to seek better union representation or to cause incumbent unions to pay better attention to the members of the bargaining unit.

The relationship between economic conditions and the incidence of decertification elections has been studied. The number of elections resulting in decertification is positively related to both changes in the cost of living and unemployment.[58] This suggests that dissatisfaction with a union spreads as the cost of living and unemployment rates increase, leading union members to the conclusion that their union is not effective in representing their interests. The relationship between change in employment level and the incidence of decertification elections is negative. This implies that when alternative employment opportunities are expanding, those dissatisfied with the union change jobs rather than seek decertification.

Should There Be a Change in the Goals of Union Negotiating Efforts?

Sheppard and Herrick studied the values of American workers and conclude that if anything sets young workers apart it is their antiauthoritarianism.[59] They predict that as these young workers grow older their antiauthoritarianism will not diminish. As a result it is anticipated that our institutions will be modified to accommodate the changing values of the work force. The principal conclusions of the study relevant to this discussion are: young workers place substantially more importance on interesting work and on the opportunity to develop their own abilities; and with regard to traditional bread-and-butter issues such as pay, job security, and fringe benefits, age appeared to make no difference. All age groups seemed to be equally interested in these bread-and-butter issues.

Referring back to the model presented in Fig. 6.3, this difference in values implies that the perceived advantage of being represented by a union can be increased if unions are instrumental in providing intrinsic rewards.

Union leaders are in a dilemma with respect to this issue. Survey evidence concerning what union members believe should be the focus of union efforts in representing the membership supports the position that union members want their union to focus on bread-and-butter issues. Kochan[60] reports that union members believe unions should place most emphasis on wages and fringe benefits and effective handling of grievances. Alternatively, they indicated that unions should place relatively little emphasis on achieving such goals as more interesting work and achieving a greater say in decisions concerning their jobs. However, it should be pointed out that while issues pertaining to intrinsic job factors were ranked low compared to issues concerning extrinsic job factors, about 60 to 75 percent of union members wanted their unions to exert some or a lot of effort in improving the quality-of-work aspects of their jobs. This suggests that while workers still view unions as representatives of their economic interests, they are looking for an expansion of union activity into the quality of work life.

Other studies have also found that union members place greater importance on the traditional economic and security issues and believe that union leaders should place greater emphasis on the attainment of these objectives.[61,62] Even among college professors it appears that most faculty favor focusing bargaining efforts on traditional trade-union issues such as pensions, fringe benefits, and salaries, and relegating issues concerning control of the university and other academic issues to existing administrative procedures.[63] On the other hand a study of registered nurses suggests they attach more importance to bargaining issues pertaining to intrinsic work issues.[64] Further evidence that union members want unions to become involved in such issues is provided by a study of unionized railroad workers. In this study about nine of ten workers felt that their union should address intrinsic work factors either through traditional collective bargaining procedures or through joint union-management programs.[65]

A survey of union leaders concerning the issues most important to union members indicates that in their opinion intrinsic rewards such as challenging and interesting work are ranked lower than economic issues by the union membership.[66] However, the same survey does suggest that some union leaders are introducing such issues into contract negotiations. Table 6.4 reports the proportion of high-ranking union officials and union stewards who report having bargained with respect to selected issues concerning intrinsic aspects of work. About one-fifth to one-third of the union officials surveyed reported having negotiated with respect to the issues listed. The extent to which unions should become involved in negotiating such issues is a

Table 6.4 *Incidence of Bargaining with Respect to Intrinsic Aspects of Work*

Issue	Union officials (percent)	Union stewards (percent)
Right to change job assignment at same pay (job rotation)	37%	32%
Free skills training	37	30
Full utilization of skills and education	22	16
Chance to participate in management decisions	23	10
Degree of freedom to make decisions about one's work	23	9
Variety in duties	19	12

Source: Adapted from Harold L. Sheppard and Neal Q. Herrick, *Where Have All The Robots Gone? (New York: The Free Press, 1972) p. 185.*

EXHIBIT 6.3
A Union Leader Looks at Job Enrichment

"If you want to enrich the job, enrich the pay check. The better the wage, the greater the job satisfaction. There is no better cure for the 'blue collar blues.'"

If you want to enrich the job, begin to decrease the number of hours a worker has to labor in order to earn a decent standard of living. Just as the increased productivity of mechanized assembly lines made it possible to decrease the work week from 60 to 40 hours a couple of generations ago, the time has come to translate the increased productivity of automated processes into the kind of enrichment that comes from shorter work weeks, longer vacations and earlier retirements.

If you want to enrich the job, do something about the nerve-shattering noise, the heat and the fumes that are deafening, poisoning and destroying the health of American workers. Thousands of chemicals are being used in work places whose effects on humans has never been tested. Companies are willing to spend millions advertising quieter refrigerators or washing machines but are reluctant to spend one penny to provide a reasonably safe level of noise in their plants. And though we are now supposed to have a law that protects working people against some of the more obvious occupational hazards, industry is already fighting to undermine enforcement, and the Nixon Administration has gone along with them by cutting the funds that are needed to make it effective.

Source: William W. Winpisinger, "Job Enrichment—Another Part of the Forest," *Industrial Relations Research Association Series: Proceedings of the Twenty-fifth Anniversary Meeting,* ed. Gerald G. Somers, *(Industrial Relations Research Association, Madison, WI, 1973), pp. 156–57.*

matter of dispute. Exhibit 6.3 provides an illustration of one labor leader's point of view.

The extent to which unions can be expected to push for improvement in the quality of work life depends in part on the nature of the bargaining relationship. If it is an adversary relationship in which management makes decisions and the union initiates a grievance if the membership is dissatisfied with the decision, it will be difficult for unions to become involved in negotiating improvements in the quality of work.

Strauss[67] has suggested that unions have historically participated in decisions that involve making choices between goals and objectives of different groups within the membership. He argues that there is a basic parallel between negotiating improvements in the quality of work life and negotiating improvements in health and safety standards. His suggestion is that union management committees be created to discuss such issues outside the normal bargaining relationship.

Summary

In reviewing motivation theories that are relevant to a discussion of why workers support a union we have attempted to address three issues:

- Which employee needs or goals may be relevant?
- Which are the principal variables that enter into the decision to support or oppose a union?
- Why are some needs or outcomes related to the satisfaction of these needs very important to some workers and comparatively unimportant to other workers?

A revised version of Maslow's hierarchy has been suggested as a way to address the first issue. A two- or three-category taxonomy of needs appears to exist. In the two-step version, physiological and security needs compose one category and social, esteem, and self-actualization needs compose the other. In the three-step system, social needs make up a separate need category.

An adaptation of expectancy theory is suggested as a model of the variables entering into the decision to support or oppose a union. The variables are valences attached to outcomes, expectancy perceptions, and instrumentality perceptions. The latter perception refers to workers' estimates of the outcomes which follow from having a union represent workers' interests. The former pertains to the importance attached to the potential oucomes.

The final issue is predicting which outcomes will be valent or important to a group of workers. The equity model provides one approach to explaining who will feel unfairly treated and as a result will be dissatisfied with selected outcomes. This model assumes that employees compare their outcomes and inputs with the outcomes and inputs of others. When an employee perceives that he or she is receiving less than is equitable, dissatisfaction occurs. As dissatisfaction with a particular outcome increases, it becomes more important to that person.

Based on research concerning Maslow's theory, it is expected that when lower-order needs are not satisfied they will be perceived as important needs. Hence, outcomes associated with the satisfaction of these needs will be highly valent. Alternatively when these needs are satisfied, these needs and the associated outcomes will be less important. Further, if the satisfaction of lower-order needs is interrupted, they will increase in importance, as will the outcomes associated with their satisfaction.

Research pertaining to why workers organize has focused on selected issues. These are attitudes toward unions and the relative importance of intrinsic and extrinsic job satisfaction; the distribution of decision-making power between employees and management, and trust in management; perceptions of union instrumentality; and perceptions of equity.

Among blue-collar employees, the evidence indicates that dissatisfaction with extrinsic work factors bears a stronger relationship with favoring a union than does dissatisfaction with intrinsic factors. Among white-collar workers the evidence is mixed. However, the weight of the evidence indicates that dissatisfaction with intrinsic factors may be more important than dissatisfaction with extrinsic factors in explaining prounion attitudes.

Feelings of distrust toward management decisions are also positively related to favoring a union. Similarly dissatisfaction with management decisions and perceived lack of influence on management decisions are correlated with favoring a union.

Perceptions of union instrumentality may bear the strongest relationship to attitudes concerning unionization. Employees who believe that unions lead to higher wages and benefits as well as protection from unfair treatment by management are likely to favor representation by a union. Studies comparing wages and benefits of union and non-union workers demonstrate that unions are instrumental in securing better rates of compensation for their members.

Finally, perceptions of inequitable compensation are related to favoring a union.

Union membership as a percent of the nonagricultural labor force has been declining since 1955. The percent of both certification and decertification elections won by unions have been declining since 1965. These facts suggest that all is not well for the union movement in the United States. In connection with these trends it has been suggested that unions should change their bargaining goals so that more emphasis is placed on improving intrinsic work factors. The available research evidence does not make it clear that this will have a positive effect on union membership.

Discussion Questions

1. What goals were commonly sought by unions during the late 1700s and early 1800s?
2. Describe working conditions that may have contributed to worker interest in unions during the late nineteenth century and the early twentieth century.

3. Analyze the decision to support or oppose a union using an expectancy model.
4. Discuss why job outcomes, i.e., wages or job security, may be more important to some workers than others and why a given worker may attach more importance to an outcome at one point in time than another point in time.
5. What is the relative importance of dissatisfaction with extrinsic factors and intrinsic factors in explaining worker attitudes toward unions?
6. What is the relationship between employee perceptions of the need for a union and perceptions of decision making by management, as well as perceptions of union instrumentality?
7. Is all well for the union movement in the United States? Explain your position.
8. Suggest a course of action that unions could follow that might improve their ability to attract and retain members.

Key Concepts

Coalition
Extrinsic work factors
Intrinsic work factors
Union instrumentality

Valence
Inequity
Need deprivation-need importance

Notes

1. Phillip Taft, *Organized Labor in American History* (New York: Harper and Row, 1964), p. 5.
2. Ibid., pp. 6–7.
3. Ibid., p. 7.
4. Ibid., pp. 6–11.
5. J. Kuczynski, *A Short History of Labour Conditions Under Industrial Capitalism in the United States of America 1789–1946* (New York: Barnes and Noble, 1973).
6. Herman M. Somers and Anne R. Somers, *Workmen's Compensation* (New York: John Wiley and Sons, Inc., 1954), p. 9.
7. Arthur H. Reede, *Adequacy of Workmen's Compensation* (Cambridge: Harvard University Press, 1947), p. 345.
8. Frederick L. Hoffman, "Industrial Accidents," Bulletin of the Bureau of Labor Statistics, p. 418, cited in J.G. Turnbull, C.A. Williams, and E.F. Cheit, *Economic and Social Security,* 4th ed. (New York: Ronald Press, 1973), p. 283.
9. Sumner H. Slichter, James J. Healy, and E. Robert Livernash, *The Impact of Collective Bargaining on Management* (Washington, D. C.: The Brookings Institution, 1960), p. 624.
10. Ross Stagner and Hjalmar Rosen, *Psychology of Union-Management Relations* (Belmont, CA: Wadsworth Publishing Co., 1965), p. 59.
11. Ibid., pp. 21–24.
12. Abraham H. Maslow, "A Theory of Human Motivation," *Psychological Review* 50 (1943): 370–96.

13. Edward E. Lawler, *Pay and Organizational Effectiveness: A Psychological View* (New York: McGraw-Hill Book Co., 1971), p. 28.

14. Ibid.

15. Clayton P. Alderfer, *Existence, Relatedness and Growth* (New York: Free Press, 1972).

16. Andrew D. Szilagyi and Marc J. Wallace, *Organizational Behavior and Performance,* 2nd ed. (Santa Monica, CA: Goodyear Publishing Co., 1980), pp. 105–15.

17. Victor H. Vroom, *Work and Motivation* (New York: John Wiley and Sons, 1964).

18. John P. Campbell and Robert D. Pritchard, "Motivation Theory in Industrial and Organizational Psychology" in *Handbook of Industrial and Organizational Psychology,* ed. Marvin D. Dunnette (Chicago, Rand McNally Publishing Co., 1976), pp. 63–130.

19. Herbert G. Heneman III and Donald P. Schwab, "Evaluation of Research on Expectancy Theory Predictions of Employee Performance," *Psychological Bulletin* (1972): 1–9.

20. Herbert G. Heneman III and Donald P. Schwab, "Work and Rewards Theory" in *ASPA Handbook of Personnel and Industrial Relations,* eds. Dale Yoder and H.G. Heneman, Jr. (Washington, D. C.: Bureau of National Affairs, 1979), Section 6, pp. 1–22.

21. J. Stacy Adams, "Inequity in Social Exchange," in *Advances in Experimental Social Psychology,* vol. 2, ed. L. Berkowitz (New York: Academic Press, 1965), pp. 272–83.

22. Herbert S. Parnes, *Research on Labor Mobility* (New York: Social Science Research Council, Bulletin 65, 1954), pp. 144–90.

23. Ibid.

24. Mahmood A. Wahba, and L.G. Bridwell, "Maslow Reconsidered: A Review of Research on the Need Hierarchy Theory," *Organization Behavior and Human Performance* 15 (1976): 212–40.

25. Szilagyi and Wallace, p. 110.

26. Ibid., p. 111.

27. Julius E. Getman, Stephen B. Goldberg, and Jeanne E. Herman, *Union Representation Elections: Law and Reality* (New York: Russell Sage Foundation, 1976), pp. 53–72.

28. Chester A. Schriescheim, "Job Satisfaction, Attitudes Toward Unions, and Voting in a Union Representation Election," *Journal of Applied Psychology* 63 (1978): 548–52.

29. Thomas A. Kochan, "How American Workers View Labor Unions," *Monthly Labor Review* 102 (April 1979): 23–31.

30. William J. Bigoness, "Correlates of Faculty Attitudes Toward Collective Bargaining," *Journal of Applied Psychology* 63 (1978): 228–33.

31. Robert E. Allen and Timothy J. Keaveny, "Correlates of University Faculty Interest in Unionization: A Replication and Extension," *Journal of Applied Psychology* 66 (October 1981): 582–88.

32. Peter Feuille and J. Blandin, "Faculty Job Satisfaction and Bargaining Sentiments: A Case Study," *Academy of Management Journal* 17 (1974): 678–92.

33. T.H. Hammer and M. Berman, "The Role of Noneconomic Factors in Faculty Union Voting," *Journal of Applied Psychology* (1981): 415–21.

34. Feuille and Blandin, pp. 678–92.

35. Hammer and Berman, pp. 415–21.

36. Allen and Keaveny, pp. 582–88.

37. Kochan, pp. 23–31.

38. Thomas A. DeCotiis, and J. Y. LeLouarn, "A Predictive Study of Voting Behavior in a Representation Election Using Union Instrumentality and Work Perceptions," *Organizational Behavior and Human Performance* 27 (1981): 103–18.

39. Kochan, pp. 23–31.

40. Joseph R. Antos, Mark Chandler, and Wesley Mellow, "Sex Differences in Union Membership," *Industrial and Labor Relations Review* 33 (January 1980): 162–69.

41. Charles W. Hickman, "Labor Organizations Fees and Dues," *Monthly Labor Review* 100 (May 1977): 19–24.

42. Thomas Hyclak, "Unions and Income Inequality: Some Cross-State Evidence," *Industrial Relations* 19 (Spring 1980): 212–15.

43. Richard B. Freeman, "Unionism and the Dispersion of Wages," *Industrial and Labor Relations Review* 34 (October 1980): 3–22.

44. Richard B. Freeman, "The Effect of Unionism on Fringe Benefits," *Industrial and Labor Relations Review* 34 (July 1981): 489–509.

45. Kochan, pp. 23–31.

46. Kochan, pp. 23–31.

47. Allen and Keaveny, pp. 582–88.

48. U.S. Department of Labor, Bureau of Labor Statistics, *Directory of National Unions and Employee Associations,* Bulletin 2044 (Washington, D.C.: U.S. Government Printing Office, December 1979), p. 61.

49. "Union Labor Fortunes Appear at Lowest Ebb," *Denver Post,* 11 October 1981, p. 50.

50. U.S. Department of Labor, Bureau of Labor Statistics, *Directory of National Unions and Employee Associations.*

51. U.S. Department of Labor, Bureau of Labor Statistics, *Handbook of Labor Statistics 1980,* Bulletin 2070, (Washington, D.C.: U.S. Government Printing Office, December 1980) p. 412.

52. U.S. Department of Labor, Bureau of Labor Statistics, *Directory of National Unions and Employee Associations,* p. 70.

53. Charles L. Hughes, *Making Unions Unnecessary* (New York: Executive Enterprises Publications Co., 1976), pp. 13–14.

54. Joseph Krislov, "Decertification Elections Increase but Remain No Major Burden to Unions," *Monthly Labor Review* 102 (November 1979): 30–32.

55. I. Chafetz and C.R.P., Fraser, "Union Decertification: An Exploratory Analysis," *Industrial Relations* 18 (Winter 1979): 59–69.

56. William E. Fulmer and T.A. Gilman, "Why Do Workers Vote for Union Decertification?" *Personnel* (March-April 1981): 28–35.

57. John C. Anderson, Gloria Busman, and Charles A. O'Reilly III, "What Factors Influence the Outcome of Decertification Elections?" *Monthly Labor Review* 102 (November 1979): 32–36.

58. John C. Anderson, Charles A. O'Reilly III and Gloria Busman, "Union Decertification in the U.S.: 1947–1977," *Industrial Relations* 19 (Winter 1980): 100–7.

59. Harold L. Sheppard and Neal Q. Herrick, *Where Have All the Robots Gone?* (New York: Free Press, 1972), pp. XX, 122–43.

60. Kochan, pp. 23–31.

61. Thomas A. Kochan, David B. Lipsky, and Lee Dyer, "Collective Bargaining and the Quality of Work: The Views of Local Union Activists," *Industrial Relations Research Association Series, Proceedings of the 27th Annual Winter Meeting,* eds. J.L. Stern and B.D. Dennis, (1974), pp. 150–62.

62. Graham L. Staines, and Robert P. Quinn, "American Workers Evaluate the Quality of Their Jobs," *Monthly Labor Review* 102 (January 1979): 3–12.

63. Allen M. Ponak and Mark Thompson, "Faculty Attitudes and the Scope of Bargaining," *Industrial Relations* 18 (Winter 1979): 97–102.

64. Allen M. Ponak, "Unionized Professionals and the Scope of Bargaining: A Study of Nurses," *Industrial and Labor Relations Review,* 34 (April 1981): 396–407.

65. William H. Holley, Hubert S. Feild, and James C. Crowley, "Negotiating Quality of Worklife, Productivity and Traditional Issues: Union Members' Preferred Roles of Their Union," *Personnel Psychology* 34 (1981): 309–28.

66. Sheppard and Herrick, pp. 181–183.

67. George Strauss, "Managerial Practices" in *Improving Life at Work,* eds. J.R. Hackman and J.L. Suttle (Santa Monica, CA.: Goodyear Publishing Co., 1977).

Suggested Readings

Allen, R.E. and Keaveny, T.J. "Correlates of University Faculty Interest in Unionization: A Replication and Extension." *Journal of Applied Psychology* 66 (October 1981): 582–88.

Antos, J.R., Chandler, M. and Mellow, W. "Sex Differences in Union Membership." *Industrial and Labor Relations Review* 33 (January 1980): 162–69.

Chafetz, I. and Fraser, C.R.P. "Union Decertification: An Exploratory Analysis," *Industrial Relations* 18 (Winter 1979): 59–69.

DeCotiis, T.A. and LeLouarn, J.Y. "A Predictive Study of Voting Behavior in a Representation Election using Union Instrumentality and Work Perceptions." *Organizational Behavior and Human Performance* 27 (1981): 103–18.

Freeman, R.B. "The Effect of Unionism on Fringe Benefits," *Industrial and Labor Relations Review* 34 (July 1981): 489–509.

Freeman, R.B. "Unionism and the Dispersion of Wages," *Industrial and Labor Relations Review* 34 (October 1980): 3–22.

Getman, J.G., Goldberg, S.B., and Herman, J.E., *Union Representation Elections: Law and Reality*. New York: Russell Sage Foundation, 1976, pp. 53–72.

Kochan, T.A. "How American Workers View Labor Unions," *Monthly Labor Review* 102 (April 1979): 23–31.

Sheppard, H.L. and Herrick, N.O. *Where Have All The Robots Gone?* New York: Free Press, 1972.

Chapter 7

HOW WORKERS ORGANIZE

Art Payton drives a truck for City-Wide Distributors, Inc., a firm that sells a wide variety of goods to retail supermarkets. Art is one of 23 drivers who make deliveries from the firm's warehouse to its customers throughout the Denver metropolitan area. For the last several months, a number of drivers have been complaining about their wages and fringe benefits. City-Wide's truck drivers are paid $1.00 per hour less than the unionized drivers employed by other warehouses in Denver. Just last week, Art's best friend at work, Bud Roberts, was fired for allegedly not turning in all the day's receipts. He was discharged despite his denials of any wrongdoing.

As a result of the relatively poor wages and fringe benefits as well as the arbitrary discipline and discharge practices revealed by Bud's firing, the drivers are very upset. Although Art has never belonged to a union, he has heard that a union can bring about higher wages, fringe benefits, and job security. He talks with some of the other drivers. Of the 23 drivers, at least 13 agree with Art that unionizing might bring about the job changes they want. The question now is: How can they get a union to represent them in collective bargaining with City-Wide Distributors, Inc.?

You can see that Art Payton and the other City-Wide drivers are facing some of the issues discussed in Chapter 6. In this chapter, we will see how workers select a union to represent them in collective bargaining. The focus will be on the sequence of events that begins when workers express interest in unionizing and ends either when the employer incurs an obligation to engage in collective bargaining with the union or when the workers reject unionization. After studying this chapter, you should be able to:

- Explain what an authorization card is and how authorization cards are used in union organizing campaigns.
- Describe the limitations on union and management behavior during the time period when workers are being solicited to sign authorization cards.

185

UNION ORGANIZING

- Discuss the process by which the NLRB determines whether a union represents a majority of the workers for the purpose of collective bargaining.
- Analyze NLRB policies concerning union and management conduct during a union certification election campaign.
- Describe how NLRB certification elections are conducted.

The process by which employers select a collective-bargaining representative is one of the primary concerns of the nation's labor policy. The National Labor Relations Act (NLRA), passed in 1935, established an administrative procedure for determining whether employees want union representation. One of the basic objectives of this act was to eliminate disruptive organizational strikes by providing an alternative method. Over the years, legislation, NLRB rulings, and court decisions have established the processes by which workers can obtain union representation.

Section 9(a) of the NLRA states that a union selected by a majority of the employees will be the exclusive representative of all employees in a unit for the purpose of collective bargaining. The NLRA does not, however, specify how the majority status of the labor union will be established. The union's majority status can be determined in two basic ways: voluntary recognition and through the NLRB's certification election procedure. Regardless of the approach taken, the process of selecting a bargaining representative begins with the union solicitation of signed authorization cards.

Authorization Cards

At the outset of a union organizing drive, the labor organization attempts to get as many workers as possible to sign authorization cards. An authorization card is a document indicating that an employee wants to be represented by a labor organization in collective bargaining. By signing such a card, employees designate a union to represent them with their employer.[1] It is also possible for workers to authorize the labor organization to represent them in collective bargaining by actually applying for membership in the union or by signing a petition designating the union as their bargaining agent. However, authorization cards are most likely to be used early in an organizing campaign to determine the degree to which the workers are interested in unionism.

USES OF AUTHORIZATION CARDS

Labor organizations typically work hard to get employees to sign authorization cards because the cards can be used in a number of different ways. First, workers' interest in unionization, as indicated by their willingness to sign authorization cards, can be used to assess the effectiveness of the union's organizing effort. Since organizing consumes union time and money, an early appraisal of the potential to organize a particular group of workers can lead to a more efficient allocation of union resources.

Second, a union can request an employer to bargain based on signed authorization cards. As mentioned earlier in this chapter, Section 9(a) of the NLRA, as amended, specifies that the representative selected for collective bargaining by a majority of employees in a unit will be their exclusive representative for the purposes of collective bargaining. However, the act does not specify how the majority status of the labor organization will be established. While the NLRB prefers the union's majority status be established through the NLRB certification election procedure,[2] the NLRA also allows for voluntary recognition. When a union secures authorization cards from a majority of employees in a unit considered appropriate for collective bargaining, the union can request the employer to recognize it as the employees' bargaining agent. Typically, when the union requests recognition, it will offer to prove its majority status. This can be done by allowing the employer or an impartial third party acceptable to both the union and the employer to compare the signed authorization cards with the company's payroll records in order to determine whether a majority of the employees designated the union as their bargaining agent. If it is established that a majority of the employees designated the union as their bargaining agent, then the employer is obligated to bargain with the union. Failure to do so could lead to charges that the employer violated Section 8(a)(5) of the NLRA.

The third reason for the union getting employees to sign authorization cards is that the NLRB requires a showing of interest to see if a question of representation exists. For a union to secure an NLRB election, at least 30 percent of the workers in the bargaining unit must designate the union to be their bargaining representative. This is an administrative requirement intended to keep the NLRB from getting involved in certification election proceedings where only a small proportion of employees are interested in unionization.

Finally, authorization cards can be the basis for the NLRB certifying the union as the employees' bargaining agent even though the union does not win the certification election. It is possible for the union to secure authorization cards from a majority of the employees, and then request the employer's recognition. While the employer has the right to question the union's claim of majority status and insist that the issue be resolved by an NLRB election,[3] it cannot engage in serious unfair labor practices that prevent the employees from making a free choice in a certification election.

If an employer refuses to recognize a union's claim of majority status based on signed authorization cards, and then commits serious unfair labor practices that inhibit the employees' uncoerced selection of a bargaining agent, the NLRB can order the employer to bargain with the union. In *NLRB v. Gissel Packing Co.*, the United States Supreme Court ruled that if the NLRB finds:

> that the possibility of erasing the effects of past (employer unfair labor) practices and ensuring a fair election (or a fair rerun) by use of traditional remedies, though present, is slight and that employee sentiment once expressed through cards would, on balance, be better protected by a bargaining order, then such an order should issue.[4]

As can be seen, the policy set forth in the *Gissel Packing* decision provides unions an incentive to secure signed authorization cards from a majority of the workers in the bargaining unit. Even though a union loses the certification election, the signed cards can be the basis for a bargaining order in the event the employer engages in unfair labor practices.

THE AUTHORIZATION CARD CAMPAIGN

According to a study by Getman, Goldberg, and Herman, the theory behind the use of authorization cards is that employees signing cards want the union to represent them and workers not signing the cards either do not want union representation or are uncertain.[5] The use of authorization cards, especially as the basis for a bargaining order, has been sharply criticized because the cards are potentially unreliable indicators of support for union representation. Workers may sign authorization cards because of peer pressure, to avoid being bothered, or in order to get an election; not because they want the union as their bargaining agent. However, research on this topic suggests that card signing is an accurate indicator of employee choice at the time the card is signed.[6]

MANAGEMENT RESPONSE TO THE AUTHORIZATION CARD CAMPAIGN

Because of the multiple uses for authorization cards, the cards are a critical part of the union's organizing effort. Consequently, it is quite likely the employer will resist the authorization and campaign. One way an employer can stifle the union's activities is to limit the union organizers' access to the work place. Since the work place is the single best place for organizing to take place, employers have attempted to limit union organizing on company property.

BANS ON DISTRIBUTION OR SOLICITATION

Many companies have no-distribution or -solicitation rules intended to prohibit on company time and property the distribution of literature and the solicitation of funds or support for various causes. Such rules are intended to prevent employees from being harrassed while at work and to insure that solicitation and distribution of literature do not interfere with the firm's efficiency. These rules can be justified in terms of the employer's right to exercise control over its property. However, problems develop when no-distribution or -solicitation rules are applied to union organizing efforts. Under the national labor policy, bans on solicitation and distribution may have to be modified to accommodate union organizing.

An employer could try to inhibit union organizing by applying no-distribution or -solicitation rules to stop union organizers from handing out literature or requesting workers to sign authorization cards on company premises. The NLRB's policy on no-distribution or -solicitation rules, as applied to union organizing campaigns, is the result of several NLRB and court decisions. Under the NLRB's policy, a distinction is drawn between employee and nonemployee union organizers. In its *Republic Aviation Corp. v. NLRB* decision,[7] the Supreme Court endorsed the NLRB's policy that no-distribution or -solicitation rules cannot limit employee organizing efforts. In general, employees can solicit others to sign authorization cards and can distribute union literature on company premises in nonwork areas during nonworking hours. To stop employees from union organizing activities such as soliciting signatures on authorization cards, an employer would have to demonstrate that the activities interfere with production or its ability to maintain plant discipline. A subsequent decision extended this rule to include situations in which employees were being paid for nonwork times.[8] As a result, employers cannot apply no-distribution and -solicitation rules to employee union organizing efforts during paid lunch periods and rest breaks.

Union organizing efforts by nonemployees such as union business agents or international representatives are handled differently under the national labor policy. In the *NLRB v. Babcock and Wilcox*[9] decision, the Supreme Court ruled that an employer can limit the distribution of union materials by nonemployee organizers on company-owned property as long as two conditions are met:

- Reasonable alternative means by which the union can communicate its message to the employees are available.
- The company does not discriminate against the union by denying it the opportunity to distribute literature and solicit support while allowing others such as representatives from charitable institutions the right to do so.

As long as the employer uniformly applies its no-distribution or -solicitation rule and the union organizers have alternative ways to contact the workers such as through newspaper and radio advertisements, an employer can deny nonemployee union organizers access to company-owned property. This is the case even if the company-owned property is quasipublic in nature such as a shopping mall[10] or parking lot.[11]

LIMITATIONS ON UNION BEHAVIOR

National labor policy recognizes the importance of unions having access to workers during authorization card campaigns. However, there are limitations on union behavior during this time period. In order for the union to use the authorization cards to support its petition for a certification election or a request for voluntary recognition, the following conditions must be met:

- The authorization cards must designate the union as the worker's bargaining representative and not state that the card's sole purpose is to request an election. In other words, the card must unambiguously state its purpose. The board has gone so far as to accept dual-purpose cards, that is, cards designating the labor organization as bargaining agent and requesting an election.[12] Fig. 7.1 presents an example of a single-purpose card.
- The signatures on the authorization cards must be timely. Cards are considered "stale" if they are the result of some previous organizing efforts. Such

Fig. 7.1 *Facsimile of a Single-Purpose Union Authorization Card*

YOUR RIGHTS UNDER THE LAW

The National Labor Relations Act (Taft-Hartley and Landrum-Griffin) provides the following:

Sec. 7. Employees shall have the right to self-organization, to form, join or **assist** labor organizations, to bargain collectively through representatives of their own choosing, and to engage in concerted activities, for the purpose of collective bargaining or other mutual aid or protection.

The law says that you have a RIGHT TO FORM A UNION.

The law says you have a RIGHT TO A UNION CONTRACT.

The law says that your ADMINISTRATOR OR SUPERVISORS CAN'T FIRE YOU OR HURT YOU IN ANY WAY FOR ORGANIZING OR JOINING A UNION.

If you're working, YOU BELONG in the Union that will work to improve conditions and win security for all workers at your work place.

For additional information call Wheat Ridge 303-425-0897
Toll Free Colo. 1-800-332-7735
Wyoming 1-800-442-3273

FOLD HERE AND GLUE DOWN THE FLAP

UNCLE SAM SAYS...
IT'S OK TO ORGANIZE

YOUR RIGHTS TO ORGANIZE ARE GUARANTEED UNDER SECTION 7 OF THE NATIONAL LABOR RELATIONS ACT, AND PROTECTED BY THE NATIONAL LABOR RELATIONS BOARD, AN AGENCY OF THE UNITED STATES FEDERAL GOVERNMENT.

Fill out the attached authorization card and mail it TODAY!

FOLD HERE

UNITED FOOD & COMMERCIAL WORKERS LOCAL #7
CHARTERED BY UFCW AFL/CIO CLC

Desiring to enjoy the rights and benefits of collective bargaining

I, _____
(Full Name) (Please Print)

employee of the _____
(Firm Name) (Please Print)

Employer Address _____ Store No. _____
(Please Print)

Employed as _____ Dept. _____
(Job Title) (Please Print)

Home Address _____ Phone _____

_____
City   State   Zip

hereby authorize UFCW International Union, AFL-CIO, CLC or its chartered Local Union to represent me for the purpose of collective bargaining, respecting rates of pay wages, hours of employment, or other conditions of employment, in accordance with applicable law.

_____
(Date)   State   (Signature of Employee)

20

cards are not indicative of the employees' attitude concerning the current organizing effort. The NLRB established its "stale card" rule in the *Surpass Leather Co.* decision[13] by accepting only cards signed within a reasonable time period prior to the union's use of the cards to request voluntary recognition.
- Unions cannot use authorization cards signed by employees who also signed cards designating another union to represent them. It is up to the union to produce sufficient evidence to establish that employees signing two cards desired exclusive representation by the union involved in the proceeding.[14]
- A union must guard against verbally misrepresenting the cards during the authorization card campaign. If the NLRB finds that the cards have been misrepresented, it can refuse to consider those cards as support for a certification election or voluntary recognition. For example, a union organizer cannot tell an employee that the sole purpose for signing an authorization card is to secure a certification election.[15] An organizer does not have to use the words "only purpose" or "sole purpose." If the intent of the card solicitor is to create the belief that the only purpose of the card is to get an election, the NLRB will consider the card invalid regardless of the words used.[16]
- The union must refrain from threatening or coercing employees into signing authorizations. As will be seen later, employee free choice is the basic theme of the NLRB's policy toward union election campaigns. This principle also applies to authorization card campaigns. Employees should be able to freely and voluntarily designate the union as their bargaining agent or refrain from doing so.

The Certification Election Procedure

At some point during the authorization card campaign, a union will either abandon the organizing effort for lack of support or will proceed with its organizing activities. As previously discussed, a union obtaining signed authorization cards from a majority of the employees can request voluntary recognition from the employer. However, if the employer has "good faith" doubts about the union's majority status, it can insist that the issue be resolved by an NLRB-conducted representation or certification election. The terms "representation" and "certification" election will be used interchangeably. Fig. 7.2 outlines the sequence of events surrounding the representation election procedure.

ELECTION PETITION

In order for the NLRB to conduct a certification election, some party must request or petition the NLRB to do so. It is important to remember that the NLRB does not have the power to determine the bargaining representative or investigate union claims

UNION ORGANIZING

Fig. 7.2 *Sequence of Basic Events Comprising the Certification Election Procedure*

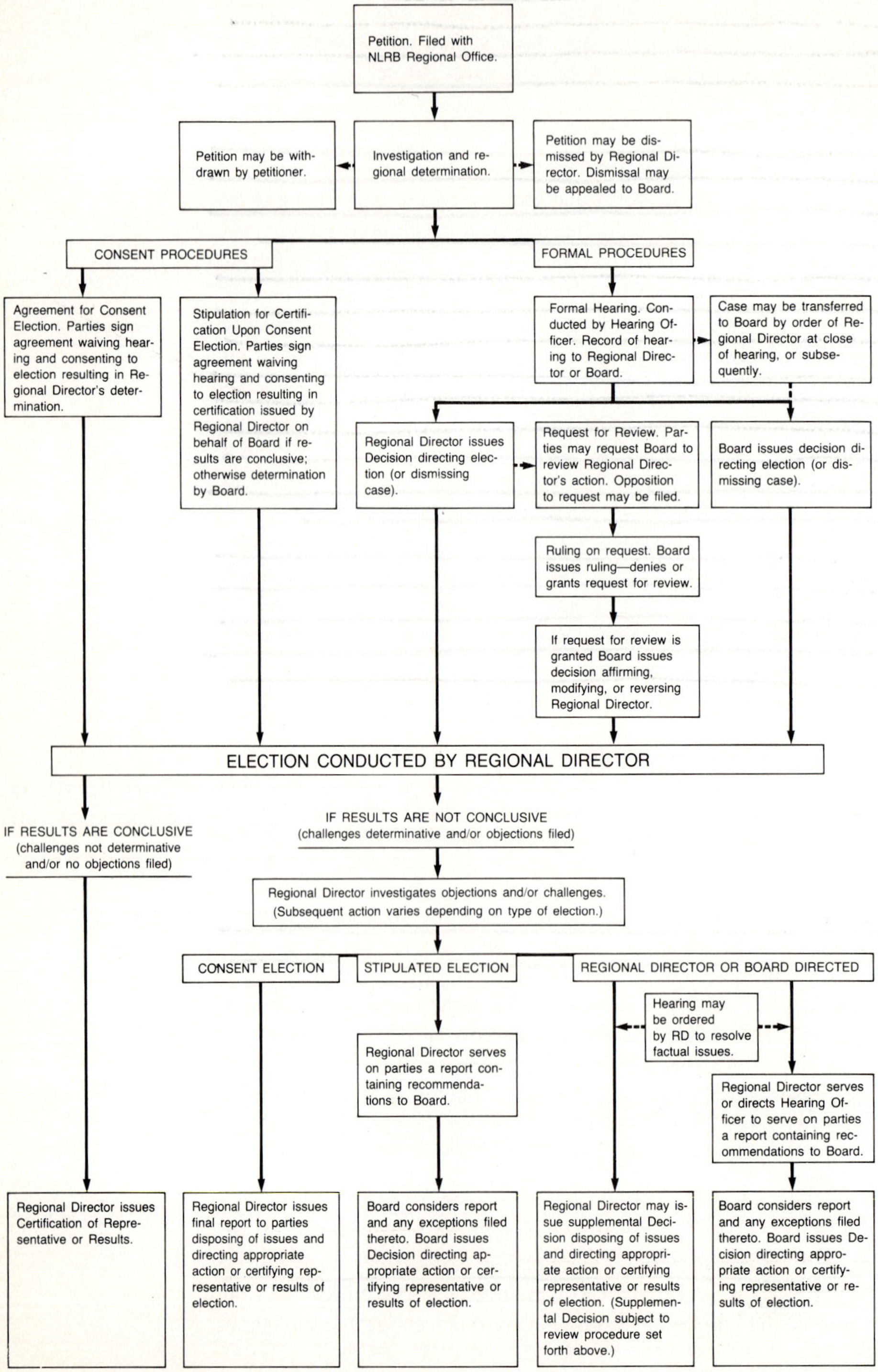

of majority status on its own initiative.[17] It is necessary for an election petition to be filed. A petition is a formal request addressed to the NLRB to determine whether a majority of employees in a bargaining unit wish to be represented by a particular labor organization for the purposes of collective bargaining.[18] A petition for an NLRB-conducted certification election can be filed by:

- An employee or a group of employees.
- A labor organization acting on behalf of the employees.
- An employer.

If the petition is filed by employees or on their behalf by a labor organization, the petition must be accompanied by a showing of interest or support by employees desiring union representation (at least 30 percent). Also, the petition must state that the employer declined to recognize the labor organization. If the employer files the petition, the petition must state that one or more labor organizations has requested to be the employees' exclusive bargaining representative.[19] Fig. 7.3 is a facsimile of an NLRB petition for an election.

NLRB INVESTIGATION

Once a petition for an election is filed, the situation must be investigated by the NLRB to determine whether a question of representation exists that can be resolved by a certification election. The NLRB investigation is designed to determine:

Jurisdiction. The NLRB has the jurisdiction to conduct an election only in enterprises affecting interstate commerce as defined in Section 2 of the NLRA.

Showing of interest. As previously discussed, it is NLRB practice to require a showing of interest by at least 30 percent of the employees in an appropriate bargaining unit if the election is petitioned by employees or a union. If the NLRB investigation shows that there is less than a 30 percent showing of support, it typically will not direct an election to take place.

Question of representation. In order for an election to be ordered a question of representation must exist. For example, if a union requests recognition by an employer and the request is denied by the employer, the NLRB will usually conclude a question of representation exists.

Appropriateness of the bargaining unit. One of the key determinations made by the NLRB concerns the appropriateness of the bargaining unit. This decision identifies the workers able to vote in the certification election, and therefore, the employees the union seeks to represent. The factors considered by the NLRB when deciding the appropriateness of the bargaining unit will be discussed later in this chapter.

Qualifications of the employee representative. According to Section 2(4) of the NLRA, any individual or labor organization can serve as the employees' representative in collective bargaining. However, supervisors and other management representatives cannot be the employees' representative. The key point is whether the labor organization will effectively represent all the employees in the bargaining unit. Ab-

UNION ORGANIZING
194

Fig. 7.3 *Facsimile of an NLRB Petition for an Election*

FORM NLRB-502　(11-64)　　UNITED STATES OF AMERICA　　FORM EXEMPT UNDER
　　　　　　　　　　　　　NATIONAL LABOR RELATIONS BOARD　　44 U.S.C. 3512

PETITION

	DO NOT WRITE IN THIS SPACE
	CASE NO.
INSTRUCTIONS.—Submit an original and four (4) copies of this Petition to the NLRB Regional Office in the Region in which the employer concerned is located. If more space is required for any one item, attach additional sheets, numbering item accordingly.	DATE FILED

The Petitioner alleges that the following circumstances exist and requests that the National Labor Relations Board proceed under its proper authority pursuant to Section 9 of the National Labor Relations Act.

1. Purpose of this Petition *(If box RC, RM, or RD is checked and a charge under Section 8(b)(7) of the Act has been filed involving the Employer named herein, the statement following the description of the type of petition shall not be deemed made.)*
(Check one)

☐ RC-CERTIFICATION OF REPRESENTATIVE —A substantial number of employees wish to be represented for purposes of collective bargaining by Petitioner and Petitioner desires to be certified as representative of the employees.

☐ RM-REPRESENTATION (EMPLOYER PETITION)—One or more individuals or labor organizations have presented a claim to Petitioner to be recognized as the representative of employees of Petitioner.

☐ RD-DECERTIFICATION — A substantial number of employees assert that the certified or currently recognized bargaining representative is no longer their representative.

☐ UD-WITHDRAWAL OF UNION SHOP AUTHORITY—Thirty percent (30%) or more of employees in a bargaining unit covered by an agreement between their employer and a labor organization desire that such authority be rescinded.

☐ UC-UNIT CLARIFICATION—A labor organization is currently recognized by employer, but petitioner seeks clarification of placement of certain employees: *(Check one)* ☐ In unit not previously certified
　　　　　　　　　　　　　　　　　　　　　　　☐ In unit previously certified in Case No. _____.

☐ AC-AMENDMENT OF CERTIFICATION—Petitioner seeks amendment of certification issued in Case No. _____.
　　Attach statement describing the specific amendment sought.

2. NAME OF EMPLOYER	EMPLOYER REPRESENTATIVE TO CONTACT	PHONE NO.

3. ADDRESS(ES) OF ESTABLISHMENT(S) INVOLVED *(Street and number, city, State, and ZIP Code)*

4a. TYPE OF ESTABLISHMENT *(Factory, mine, wholesaler, etc.)*	4b. IDENTIFY PRINCIPAL PRODUCT OR SERVICE

5. Unit Involved *(In UC petition, describe PRESENT bargaining unit and attach description of proposed clarification.)*

Included

Excluded

6a. NUMBER OF EMPLOYEES IN UNIT:

PRESENT _____

PROPOSED (BY UC/AC)
_____

6b. IS THIS PETITION SUPPORTED BY 30% OR MORE OF THE EMPLOYEES IN THE UNIT?*
☐ YES ☐ NO
*Not applicable in RM, UC, and AC

(If you have checked box RC in 1 above, check and complete EITHER item 7a or 7b, whichever is applicable)

sent any proof that the labor organization will not represent all the employees, the NLRB will typically consider the labor organization as qualified and direct an election (assuming the other conditions are also met).

Contract and election bars. There are several other factors the NLRB considers before directing an election. In situations where the employer has a valid contract with another union covering the same group of workers as discussed in the petition, the NLRB will usually not order an election. This is known as a contract bar. An

Fig. 7.3 *(Continued)*

7a. ☐ Request for recognition as Bargaining Representative was made on .... and Employer
(Month, day, year)
declined recognition on or about .... (If no reply received, so state)
(Month, day, year)

7b. ☐ Petitioner is currently recognized as Bargaining Representative and desires certification under the act.

8. Recognized or Certified Bargaining Agent *(If there is none, so state)*

NAME	AFFILIATION
ADDRESS	DATE OF RECOGNITION OR CERTIFICATION

9. DATE OF EXPIRATION OF CURRENT CONTRACT, IF ANY *(Show month, day, and year)*	10. IF YOU HAVE CHECKED BOX UD IN 1 ABOVE, SHOW HERE THE DATE OF EXECUTION OF AGREEMENT GRANTING UNION SHOP *(Month, day, and year)*

11a. IS THERE NOW A STRIKE OR PICKETING AT THE EMPLOYER'S ESTABLISHMENT(S) INVOLVED? YES ...... NO	11b. IF SO, APPROXIMATELY HOW MANY EMPLOYEES ARE PARTICIPATING?

11c. THE EMPLOYER HAS BEEN PICKETED BY OR ON BEHALF OF ...., A LABOR
(Insert name)
ORGANIZATION, OF .... SINCE ....
(Insert address) *(Month, day, year)*

12. ORGANIZATIONS OR INDIVIDUALS OTHER THAN PETITIONER (AND OTHER THAN THOSE NAMED IN ITEMS 8 AND 11c), WHICH HAVE CLAIMED RECOGNITION AS REPPRESENTATIVES AND OTHER ORGANIZATIONS AND INDIVIDUALS KNOWN TO HAVE A REPRESENTATIVE INTEREST IN ANY EMPLOYEES IN THE UNIT DESCRIBED IN ITEM 5 ABOVE. (IF NONE, SO STATE.)

NAME	AFFILIATION	ADDRESS	DATE OF CLAIM *(Required only if Petition is filed by Employer)*

I declare that I have read the above petition and that the statements therein are true to the best of my knowledge and belief.

....
(Petitioner and affiliation, if any)

By ....
(Signature of representative or person filing petition) *(Title, if any)*

Address ....
(Street and number, city, State, and ZIP Code) *(Telephone number)*

WILLFULLY FALSE STATEMENT ON THIS PETITION CAN BE PUNISHED BY FINE AND IMPRISONMENT (U.S. CODE, TITLE 18, SECTION 1001)

GPO 924 938

election bar is said to exist if the NLRB refuses to order an election because another election has been held in the same bargaining unit within the previous twelve months. This policy was established by Section 9(c)(3) of the NLRA.

THE APPROPRIATE BARGAINING UNIT

The appropriateness of the bargaining unit is the issue most likely to be contested in a representation election case. While the union will claim to represent a given group of workers, the employer could argue that another group of employees is more appropriate. The manner in which the bargaining unit is defined can affect the outcome of the election as well as the collective bargaining relationship that develops between the parties. For example, a union could state the appropriate bargaining unit is all the production and maintenance workers at an employer's Milwaukee, Wisconsin, plant. The employer could either agree with the union or propose that some other unit should be created such as the production and maintenance workers at all its plants, regardless of location. This is a tough decision. Pressing for the inclusion of workers at other plants could make the union's organizing effort much more difficult especially if the other plants are less interested in unionization. However, the influence of the union will be much greater if it wins the election in the larger, employer-proposed bargaining unit. At the same time, the union is likely to try to limit the unit to cover only the work group that has expressed greatest interest in organizing. By so doing, the union increases its chances of winning the election.

The NLRA provides little guidance on this issue of the appropriate bargaining unit. Section 9(b) directs the NLRB to establish bargaining units that will "assure employees the fullest freedom in exercising rights guaranteed by the Act. . . ." It then provides that the NLRB cannot include professional employees in bargaining units with nonprofessional employees unless a majority of the professional employees vote to be included in the unit (Section 9(b)(1)). Section 9(b)(3) prevents the NLRB from including plant guards and other employees hired to protect the employer's property in bargaining units composed of other categories of workers. Also, supervisors cannot be included in the bargaining unit.

Given the lack of legislative guidelines, it is necessary to review NLRB and court decisions to determine the factors considered when determining an appropriate bargaining unit. The basic objective of the NLRB is to establish bargaining units that will enhance the effectiveness of the collective bargaining process. To a large degree, this can be done by including in the bargaining unit workers having common employment interests, that is, similar interests with respect to wages, hours, and other terms and conditions of employment. When determining the commonality of interests among the employees, and therefore, the appropriateness of the bargaining unit, the NLRB considers a number of factors. The general criteria for determining the appropriate bargaining unit were stated by the NLRB in its *Continental Baking*[20] decision and include:

- Mutuality of interest with respect to wages, hours, and working conditions as determined by a review of the duties, skills, and working conditions of the employees involved.
- Existing bargaining history—traditional patterns to union organizing as found in the industry involved, or in other situations involving the same union and employer, will be examined to obtain information concerning whether a particular bargaining unit will be effective.
- In situations where one of two bargaining units could be equally appropriate, the desires of the employees will be considered. Under the *Globe Machine and Stamping Co.*[21] doctrine, the appropriate bargaining unit will be established by the results of a self-determination election in which the employees will select the one they prefer from equally appropriate bargaining units.

- Where the employer has a number of different plants or stores located in diverse geographical locations, the NLRB must decide whether the appropriate bargaining unit is made up of a single plant or all the plants. When deciding between a single or multiplant unit, the NLRB will emphasize bargaining history. If there was a multiplant bargaining unit in the past, the NLRB is likely to continue that practice in later organizing efforts. Alternatively, if early organizing was on a single-plant basis, the NLRB is likely to extend that practice by deciding a single unit is proper.[22] In addition to bargaining history, the NLRB considers the physical proximity of the units. If the plants are quite far apart, the board may consider them too far removed to allow for effective bargaining by a single unit.[23]

- The relations among employees at the different units is another factor considered by the NLRB when deciding between single or multiplant bargaining units. In organizations where the employees of two different units have been frequently transferred or subject to the same supervision, the NLRB has established multiplant units rather than separate bargaining units for two plants. It was reasoned that the transfer of employees and common supervision are indicative of a common operation.[24]

- The centralization of the employer's labor relations function is also considered by the NLRB. If each individual unit is largely responsible for its own labor relations, this would favor single-plant bargaining units. However, where labor relations are highly centralized, a multiplant unit is likely to be considered more appropriate.

- The NLRB gives weight to the extent of union organization. While this cannot be the factor controlling the decision concerning the appropriate bargaining unit as a result of Section 9(c)(5) of the NLRA, it is a variable that can be given some weight. Extent of union organization refers to the proportion of an employer's work force that is unionized. For example, a union may be able to organize a single plant but not the employer's entire multiplant operation. In such a situation, the NLRB may support the union's request for a single plant rather than a multiple-plant bargaining unit as long as other factors such as the employer's administrative organization and the physical proximity of the individual units also support the single unit.

As can be seen, the NLRB's decision concerning the appropriate bargaining unit takes a number of complex variables into consideration. The board has been criticized for identifying a number of factors as opposed to a single factor for determining the appropriateness of a bargaining unit. However, the NLRB's objective is to establish a bargaining unit that will facilitate the development of a good collective bargaining relationship. It has assumed that this can best be accomplished by establishing bargaining units composed of workers with common interests with respect to wages, hours, and other terms of employment. Since a number of factors influence the commonality of worker interests, it should not be surprising that the NLRB considers a number of variables when establishing bargaining units.

NLRB ELECTION ORDERS

If the NLRB's investigation indicates the conditions for an election have been met, the NLRB will try to get the parties to agree to resolve the question of representation through informal election procedures.[25] The parties have two alternatives that will lead them to an NLRB election but will avoid the need for formal NLRB hearings. The two procedures are: consent election agreements and stipulations for certification. Fig. 7.4 outlines the informal election procedure as well as the formal procedures to be discussed later.

Informal election procedures. Consent election agreements are most likely to be used in uncomplicated cases. With this procedure, the unions and management agree on the time and place for the election, the choices to be found on the election ballot, and a method for determining who is eligible to vote. Also, the parties agree to be bound by the NLRB regional director's decisions on questions arising out of the election such as the eligibility of voters, challenged ballots, and objections to election procedures. In consent elections, union and management give up the right to appeal to the five-person board in Washington, D. C. the decisions of the regional directors concerning election issues.

The stipulations for certification procedure (stipulated elections) are similar to the consent-election procedure with one major difference. Rather than being bound by the regional director's decisions on questions pertaining to issues such as challenged ballots and objections to the election, the parties retain the right to have such questions finally determined by the board in Washington, D. C.

Formal election procedures. In the event that either or both of the parties do not agree to one of the informal election procedures, a formal procedure will be used. This means a public hearing will be conducted by the NLRB during which the parties can present information relevant to the representation question. The record of the proceeding is forwarded to the regional director who, after studying it, will either direct an election or dismiss the petition for the election. If an election is ordered, this is known as a directed election. In this procedure, the regional director decides a number of issues resolved by the parties in the informal election procedures. For example, the regional director establishes the appropriate bargaining unit, who is eligible to vote at the time and place of the election. Directed election procedures are most likely to be used in complicated cases or in situations where one party, usually management, is attempting to delay the certification election.

Expedited elections. In addition to consent, stipulated, and directed elections, there are also expedited elections. Expedited elections are used in situations where the union has engaged in organizational or recognitional picketing. If a petition for an election is also filed, the NLRB must order an election and certify the election as specified in Sections 8(b)(7)(C) of the NLRA. Under this procedure, certification elections are usually conducted sooner than under the other procedures since a showing of support is not required and no NLRB hearings are conducted.

Regardless of the procedure used, the NLRB election order will probably trigger an intensification of the union's organizing efforts. The union is likely to work harder at encouraging workers to vote for union representation. At the same time,

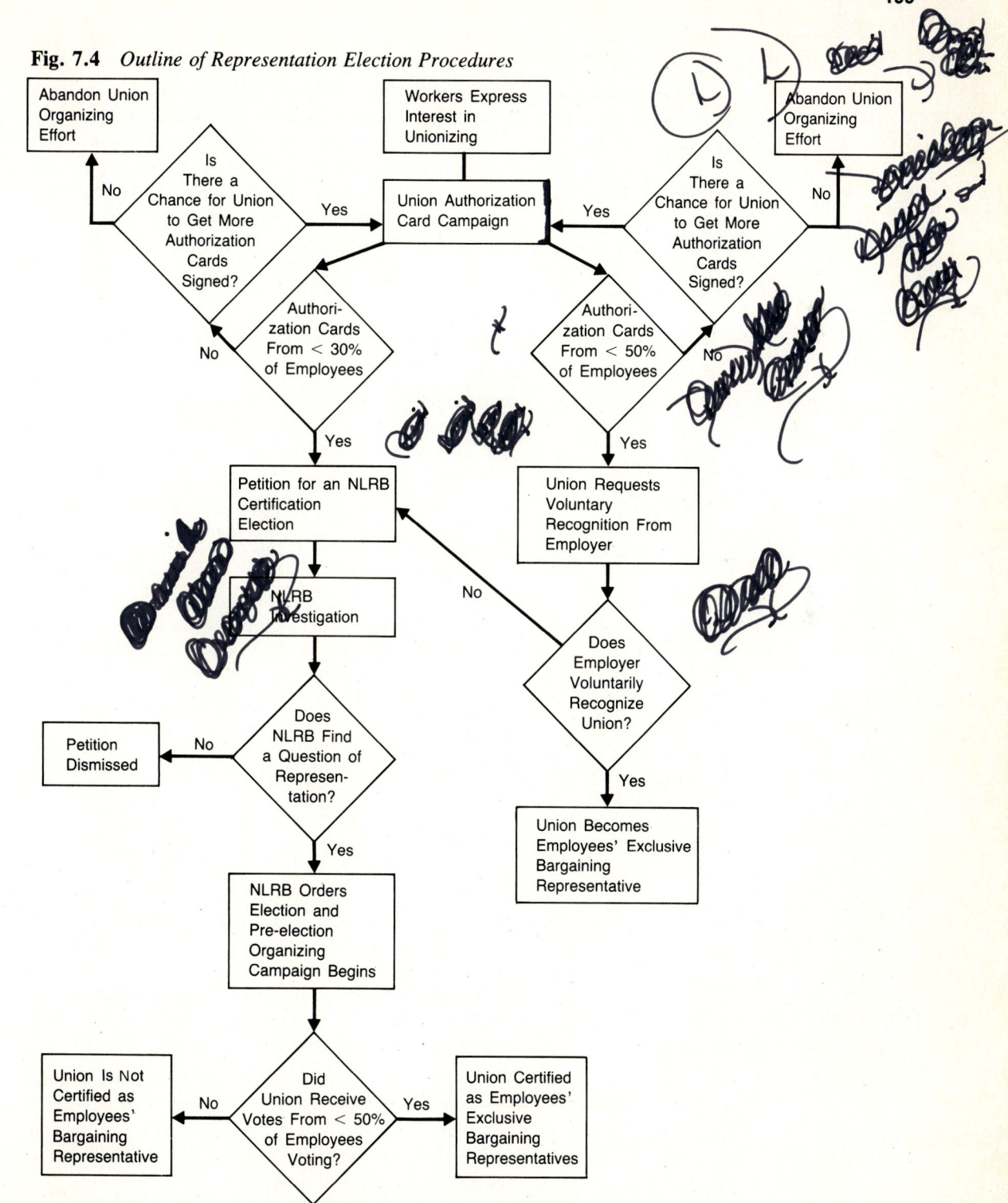

Fig. 7.4 *Outline of Representation Election Procedures*

the employer will be attempting to counteract the union's organizing efforts. The time period preceding the election can be very difficult for the workers, the union, and management. This is because the selection of a collective bargaining representative has important consequences for all the parties. To protect the workers' rights during this highly emotional period, the NLRB has developed a number of policies regulating the behavior of the parties during the pre-election period. The next section reviews the national labor policy affecting union organizing campaigns. The implications of these policies for union and management activities during the pre-election period are also discussed.

CONDUCT DURING THE PRE-ELECTION PERIOD: AN OVERVIEW OF THE POLICY

The time period beginning with the NLRB's ordering a certification election and ending with the election is characterized by many limitations on both union and management behavior. The NLRB outlined the basic guidelines for behavior during this pre-election period in its *General Shoe Corp.*[26] decision. The intent of the national labor policy is to insure that certification elections are conducted under "laboratory conditions" in which the employees are able to make a free and uncoerced choice in the selection of their bargaining agent. The NLRB stated:

> Conduct that creates an atmosphere which renders improbable a free choice in an election may invalidate the election even though such conduct may not constitute an unfair labor practice. . . . "In election proceedings, it is the Board's function to provide a laboratory in which an experiment may be conducted, under conditions as nearly ideal as possible to determine the uninhibited desires of the employees. . . ."[27]

Under the *General Shoe* doctrine, when union or management behavior is not consistent with the tenets of "laboratory conditions," the NLRB can order another election. Alternatively, the NLRB can even certify the union as the workers' bargaining agent if a majority have signed authorization cards under the previously discussed *Gissel* doctrine. Over the years, the NLRB has applied the *General Shoe* doctrine when it appeared that employer or union conduct during the pre-election period interfered with the employees' right to a free and uncoerced choice in the certification election. The major factors affecting employer and union behavior during the pre-election period will now be discussed.

EMPLOYER BEHAVIOR DURING THE ORGANIZING CAMPAIGN

Most employers operate on a non-union basis. It is safe to say that most non-union employers would prefer to stay that way. Therefore, the employer will usually respond to the union's organizing effort by conducting a campaign of its own to counteract the union's activities. The question becomes: How far can an employer go when expressing its views on the union's organizing efforts?

Section 8(c). Employers are not free to say whatever they want to express concerning the union. Section 8(c) of the NLRA and court decisions involving this provision have placed limits on the employer's response to the union. Section 8(c) states:

> The expressing of any views, argument, or opinion, or the dissemination thereof, whether in written, printed, graphic or visual form, shall not constitute or be evidence of an unfair labor practice under any provisions of this Act, if such expression contains no threat of reprisal or force or promise of benefit.

Section 8(c) is commonly known as the "free speech" provision and was added to the NLRA by the Taft-Hartley amendments. Remember from Chapter 3 that prior to the inclusion of Section 8(c) in the NLRA, the NLRB had sharply limited employer speech during organizing campaigns. Section 8(c) was added to the legislation to insure that employers had the right to speak freely on the issue of unionism as long as employees were not threatened or offered positive inducements not to vote for the union.

There is a fine line of distinction between legal antiunion statements and threats or promises of benefit. Perhaps, some examples of legal and illegal activities would be useful. An employer and its supervisors are free to:

- Tell employees that the employer does not want or need a union.
- Tell employees that they have the right under the law not to join the union and that they cannot be forced to join the union.
- Employees can be reminded of the benefits they are receiving and their benefits can be compared with those provided by unionized firms.
- Employees can be told about the disadvantages of being a union member such as dues, initiation fees, and the potential loss of income resulting from strikes.
- Employees can be advised that the company's policies with respect to pay changes, promotions, and transfers will be continued.[28]

Employers are free under Section 8(c) to say anything as long as the statements do not involve a threat or a promise. However, some employer statements can be used to support unfair labor practice charges. Examples of statements likely to violate the tenets of Section 8(c) include:

- Promises to employees they will receive pay increases, promotions, better working conditions, and other improved benefits if they refuse to join the union or vote against it.
- Threats of job loss or reduced wages or threatening or intimidating language designed to deter the employees' support for the union.

While Section 8(c) is concerned with employer statements during union organizing campaigns, there are also limitations on management's overt behavior. In other words, an employer and its representatives must avoid practices that could prevent employees' free and uncoerced choice in the certification election.

Interrogation and polling. It is understandable that an employer would want to know how the workers feel about the union's organizing effort. To obtain this information, the employer may talk to individual employees about their union attitudes. The NLRB has been concerned about such activities since it is not possible for employers to "discriminate against union adherents without first ascertaining who they are."[29] At one point in time, the NLRB viewed all employer interrogations of workers concerning their attitudes toward the union illegal. However, the NLRB liberalized its position and ruled that interrogations would be legal *prior* to the direction of a certification election as long as:

- The employer's reason for interrogating the employees was to verify the union's claim it represented a majority of the employees.
- The employees were told the purpose of the interrogation.
- The employees were given assurances against reprisals.
- The employees were polled by secret ballot.
- The questioning took place in an environment free from employer hostility to union organizing.[30]

However, once the NLRB directs an election, polling and interrogation are inappropriate. The NLRB reasons that questions concerning the union's status should be resolved by the election. Consequently, there is no need for an employer to poll workers once an election has been ordered.

Discrimination. Employers must avoid discriminating against employees because of their union organizing activities. In the *Edward G. Budd Mfg. Co. v. NLRB* decision, it was stated that:

> An employer may discharge an employee for a good reason, a poor reason or no reason at all so long as the provisions of the National Labor Relations Act are not violated. It is, of course, a violation to discharge an employee because he has engaged in activities on behalf of a union.[31]

Discrimination against an employee for union activities adversely affects the worker involved and can instill fear in other employees that their support of the union could jeopardize their jobs as well. Since this is not consistent with the NLRB's objective that workers be able to make a free and uncoerced choice in a representation election, discriminatory employer behavior during the pre-election period will be the basis for unfair labor practice charges and for setting aside the election results. To avoid these consequences, employers should not engage in behavior such as:

- Assigning or transferring employees to less desirable jobs because of their union organizing activities.
- Disciplining or discharging employees for union activities during nonwork times.[32]
- Closing the plant that the union is trying to organize in order to "chill" unionism at other plants operated by the employer.[33]

Promises of benefit. It is probably quite obvious why the NLRB would limit employer threats of reprisal and other discriminatory activities. The limitations on employers with respect to offering and actually granting benefits to employees in order to induce them not to support the union may be less apparent. In *NLRB v. Exchange Parts Co.*,[34] the Supreme Court examined a case in which the employer announced it would give the workers an additional holiday, use a new vacation schedule, and implement a new method for computing overtime. The changes were intended to influence the results of the certification election. The Supreme Court held that the employer had committed an unfair labor practice [violated Section 8(a)(1)] and that the election should be set aside. The Supreme Court reasoned that:

> The danger inherent in well-timed increases in benefits is the suggestion of a fist inside the velvet glove. Employees are not likely to miss the inference that the source from which the future benefits must flow and which may dry up if it is not obliged.[35]

It is not as if any benefit granted during a union organizing drive will be found to destroy "laboratory conditions." If the change in benefits, such as an annual wage adjustment, was regularly scheduled to occur during the pre-election period, the change would not serve as the basis for an unfair labor practice charge. However, the burden is on the employer to demonstrate that the benefits were granted during the union organizing drive for reasons unrelated to the upcoming election. A number of practices have been found to violate the national labor policy when the employer cannot establish that the changes were unrelated to the election. Examples of such activities include:

- A multiplant employer increasing wages in a plant where a union election took place and not doing so in other plants.
- Establishing a safety committee having employee representation and implementing some of the committee's recommendations.
- Changing the regular pay day by moving it up to the day before the certification election.
- Announcing the establishment of a profit-sharing plan during the pre-election period.

Other factors affecting employer behavior. In most situations, the employer is free to carry its legal antiunion message to the employees. The employer can go so far as to conduct meetings on the company premises and on company time. These are known as "captive audience" speeches. The employer is also free to deny the union's request for an opportunity to reply to the statements made during the "captive audience" speech.[36] However, under the *Peerless Plywood*[37] decision, the employer cannot conduct a "captive audience" speech during the twenty-four hours preceding the certification election. Violation of the "twenty-four hour rule" can be the basis for setting an election aside. Exhibit 7.1 discusses a legislative proposal that was intended to give unions a greater opportunity to counteract employer "captive audience" speeches.

> **EXHIBIT 7.1**
> **Should Unions Have Equal Access to Employees?**
>
> The ill-fated Labor Reform Act of 1977 addressed itself to the issue of equal access for unions. The legislation proposed, in effect, that if an employer conducts a "captive audience" speech, the union would have an opportunity to also address the employees on the company's premises and on company time.
>
> Unions argued that this legislative change was necessary since employers have a distinct advantage by being able to talk to employees during work hours. It was contended that the work place provided the best opportunity to discuss union organizing. By being able to conduct "captive audience" speeches, employers have an inappropriate amount of control over the dissemination of information at the work place.
>
> Opponents to granting unions greater access to the work place argue that union organizers already have access if no other reasonable means for contacting employees exist. This policy was the result of the *NLRB v. Babcock and Wilcox* decision. Furthermore, unions can contact employees at their homes or at union-called meetings. Also, employees can engage in union organizing activities at the work place during non-work times in non-work locations. While unions can contact workers at home or union meetings and through the mail, the employer's only real access to employees is at the work place. Opponents to granting unions greater access contend that doing so would destroy the relative balance of power between labor and management during the union organizing process.
>
> Since the Labor Reform Act of 1977 was not passed by Congress, unions were not granted equal access to the work place. As a result, employers can hold "captive audience" speeches as long as the "twenty-four hour rule" is not violated.
>
> Should the nation's labor policy be amended to allow unions greater access to the work place during the certification election process?

UNION BEHAVIOR DURING THE PRE-ELECTION PERIOD

Once the NLRB orders a representation election, the primary task for the union is to convince a majority of the voting workers in the bargaining unit to vote for union representation in the upcoming election. It is quite possible that the union did not confront serious opposition from the employer during the authorization card campaign. However, the period between the election order and the representation election will most likely be characterized by active employer opposition. Like the employer, the union is also responsible for maintaining "laboratory conditions." Behavior found to interfere with workers' ability to make a free and uncoerced choice in the certification election can be the basis for setting the election aside.

It is important for a union to be able to take its message to the workers. While the work place is probably the best location for union organizing efforts to take place, it is also important for the union to be able to contact employees at home. This process has been greatly facilitated by the NLRB's *Excelsior Underwear*[38] rule which requires an employer to submit a list of employee names and addresses to the NLRB (which, in turn, makes the list available to the union) within seven days of the election order. In addition to contacting employees at home, the union can distribute handbills and have employees wear union buttons or tee-shirts in order to publicize its organizing effort.

Union organizers are not able to engage in practices that interfere with employee free choice. Examples of such illegal behaviors include:

- Threatening employees with physical harm if they do not vote for the union.
- Threatening employees with expulsion from the union and the loss of their jobs if they supported another union in an upcoming election.[39]
- Serious acts found to violate Section 8(b)(1) of the NLRA could provide grounds for setting an election aside.

In addition to limiting acts likely to coerce employees into supporting the union, the national labor policy also prevents unions from using positive inducements that might affect employee free choice. For example, in *NLRB v. Savair Manufacturing Co.*,[40] the United States Supreme Court ruled that unions cannot use as an organizing tool an offer to waive initiation fees for employees who recognized the union as their bargaining agent prior to the election. However, if the offer to waive initiation fees or dues is extended to all workers in the bargaining unit, regardless of how they vote in the election, national labor policy is not violated.[41] Additionally, union organizers must be careful about other economic inducements offered workers during the organizing campaign. Union victories have been set aside where the union offered free life insurance to employees becoming members and where potential voters were given five-dollar gift certificates.[42]

ISSUES DISCUSSED DURING ORGANIZING CAMPAIGNS

Now that we have a general understanding of the factors influencing union and management actions during an organizing campaign, attention can turn to the examination of the issues discussed by the parties during the campaign. As part of a larger study, workers were requested to recall the issues discussed by union and management during organizing campaigns. While the average campaign included approximately thirty issues raised by the company, there were only six company issues remembered by 30 percent or more of the employees:

- Improved conditions are not dependent on unionization.
- A new company or management has recently taken over.
- Plant closing or moving may follow unionization.
- The financial costs associated with unionism such as dues are greater than the benefits.
- The union is an outsider that will interfere with the efficient operation of the firm and harm employee-employer relationships.
- Some existing benefits may be lost as a result of unionization.[43]

When questioned about union campaign themes, only three issues were recalled by more than 30 percent of the employees:

- The union will improve the currently unsatisfactory wages.
- The union will prevent unfairness by setting up a grievance procedure and seniority system.
- The union will improve generally unsatisfactory working conditions.[44]

CHANNELS OF COMMUNICATION USED IN UNION ORGANIZING CAMPAIGNS

In order to communicate information about the campaign issues to the employees, both the company and the union have three major techniques available to them: written materials, group meetings, and individual contacts. Written materials play an important role in organizing campaigns. Getman, Goldberg, and Herman report that 92 percent of the employees in the elections studied recalled receiving some or all of the employer's material. Similarly, approximately 85 percent of the workers remembered receiving some or all of the union's written materials. It was also revealed that workers who received written materials from the union and company were more familiar with the campaign issues than those who did not.

Meetings were used more frequently than written materials by both the union and management to communicate with the employees. In more than 90 percent of the elections, union and management relied on group meetings. It appears that the company is at a noticeable advantage when it comes to using group meetings, since the employer can call a meeting on the company premises and on company time. The union must hold meetings away from the workplace and during nonwork hours. Getman, Goldberg, and Herman report that the employer was much more successful in getting employees to attend meetings than the union. Where company meetings were used as part of an organizational campaign, 83 percent of the employees reported attending one or more company-sponsored meetings. This compares with only 36 percent of the employees attending union meetings. As with written materials, attendance at union and company meetings was associated with a greater familiarity with the campaign issues.

Personal contacts are the third major technique for familiarizing workers with campaign issues. Companies are most likely to use low-level supervisors to communicate with individuals or small groups of workers. Prounion employees and nonemployee organizers such as international representatives are most likely to interact with individuals to convey the union's message. While personal contacts have been found to increase workers' familiarity with campaign issues, this technique appears to be relatively less effective than written materials and group meetings.

CAMPAIGN PROPAGANDA

During the union organizing campaign, there is the possibility that either the union or management will make statements or distribute written materials containing exaggerations or completely untruthful information. It is possible that such campaign propaganda could infringe upon the employees' free choice in the upcoming certification election. In the past, the NLRB has ruled that employer and union misrepresentation of facts during the pre-election period could destroy "laboratory conditions," and therefore, could provide the basis for setting an election aside. Under this policy, the board would review campaign propaganda. If it was found that significant facts were misrepresented at a time so late in the campaign that the other party would not have an opportunity to make an effective reply, the election would be set aside. This view was known as the *Hollywood Ceramics* doctrine.[45]

The board's approach to cases involving pre-election misrepresentations has changed several times in recent years. In 1977, the position taken in *Hollywood Ceramics* was reversed in the board's *Shopping Kart Food Market, Inc.*[46] decision. It was ruled that the board would no longer review the truth or falsity of campaign statements. This new policy was short-lived. *Shopping Kart* was reversed in 1978 by the board's *General Knit of California*[47] decision. In this case, the board returned to its *Hollywood Ceramics* policy. As a result, the NLRB would review the content of pre-election campaign statements. Substantial misrepresentations could provide grounds for setting an election aside once again.

In August 1982, the board changed its position on this issue for the third time in five years. In *Midland National Life Insurance Co.*,[48] the board abandoned its *Hollywood Ceramics* doctrine and reverted to the position put forth in the *Shopping Kart Food Market* decision. Therefore, the NLRB will no longer set aside elections because of misleading campaign statements. This means that employees will have to be able to determine the truth or falsity of campaign propaganda. Under this recently stated policy, the board will review misleading campaign statements in only two situations:

- where the misleading statements improperly involve the NLRB and its processes, and
- where employees are unable to recognize propaganda for what it is because of the use of forged documents.

The NLRB will, however, set elections aside where campaign themes appeal to racial prejudice. In *Sewell Manufacturing Co.*, the NLRB found that racial appeals tended to create confusion and fear that could destroy "laboratory conditions." The NLRB stated that:

> Appeals to racial prejudice on matters unrelated to the election issues or to the union's activities are not mere "prattle" or puffing. They have no place in Board electoral campaigns. They inject an element which is destructive of the very purpose of an election. They create conditions which make impossible a sober, informed exercise of the franchise. The Board does not intend to tolerate as "election propaganda" appeals or arguments which can have no purpose except to inflame the racial feelings of voters in the election.[49]

If it is concluded after an examination of campaign literature that the racial themes were intended to confuse the situation and arouse racial prejudices, it is quite likely the election will be set aside. However, where the literature was designed to encourage racial pride or where racial themes were an important campaign issue having implications for the advantages and disadvantages of unionizing, the NLRB will not set the election aside.

THE IMPACT OF ORGANIZING CAMPAIGNS

Much has been said about the efforts of the NLRB to insure that workers have the opportunity to make a free and uncoerced choice in union certification elections. Again as shown in the work of Getman, Goldberg, and Herman, the basic assumptions underlying the NLRB's approach to union organizing campaigns can be identified. These assumptions are listed in Exhibit 7.2.

In order to determine the effect of the pre-election campaign on employee voting behavior, Getman, Goldberg, and Herman studied thirty-one union certification elections and interviewed over 1200 employees involved in the elections. This study revealed that workers do not pay close attention to campaign issues. On average, employees could remember only 10 percent of the company's campaign issues and 7 percent of the union issues.[51] Also, unlawful employer campaign tactics did not appear to compel employees to vote against union representation. A greater loss of union support was not found in election situations exhibiting unlawful campaigning relative to the elections where illegal tactics were not used. The most interesting finding of this study was that relatively few workers changed their position on unionism during the pre-election campaigns. A substantial proportion (approximately 80

EXHIBIT 7.2
Assumptions Reflected in Board Regulation of Campaign Tactics

1. Employees pay attention to the campaign.
2. Employees will interpret ambiguous employer statements as threats or promises.
3. Employees know little about labor-management relations or the effect of unionization on such relations.
4. The employee's pre-campaign intent to vote for or against union representation is weak and can be easily altered by the campaign.
5. The union does not have an adequate opportunity to communicate with the workers when there exists an imbalance in the opportunities for organizational communication. Therefore, the union should have the same opportunity to communicate with the workers as the employer.
6. The signing of authorization cards is not a clear expression of the worker's desire for union representation. A certification election is the preferred method for resolving questions of union representation.

Source: Julius Getman, Steven Goldberg, and Jeanne Herman, Union Representation Elections: Law and Reality *(New York: Russell Sage Foundation, 1976), ch. 1.*

percent) of the employees voted after the organizing campaign in the same way they would have voted before the pre-election campaign. Only 13 percent of the employees "changed their minds," that is, voted in the election contrary to their original intent. Another 6 percent went from being undecided prior to the pre-election campaign to making a decision in the election. It may appear that pre-election campaigns are relatively ineffective in changing worker attitudes toward union representation. However, the votes of workers who changed positions during the pre-election campaign determined nine of the thirty-one (29 percent) elections studied.

THE ELECTION AND LATER

To this point in the chapter, our major concern has been with union and management activities during the time period leading up to a representation election. Attention can now turn to the election itself and the NLRB orders issued after the election.

The election. Certification elections are conducted by representatives of the NLRB. Typically, an area or areas within the work organization are designated as the polling place. Also, times during working hours the polls will be open are specified. During the election, which is by secret ballot, both union and management have the right to have observers watch the proceedings. Fig. 7.5 is an example of a ballot used in an NLRB certification election.

Challenged ballots. A list of workers eligible to vote in the election is available at the polling places. If a person whose name is not on the list tries to vote, that individual will be challenged. The challenge to the person's right to vote in the election can be made by the NLRB representative, the union observer or the management observer. Frequently cited reasons for challenging the eligibility of a voter are that the person is a supervisor or the individual's job is not in the bargaining unit. Voters who are challenged will be given an envelope in which to place their ballot after voting. Challenged ballots are counted only if there is a sufficient number to affect the outcome of the election. For example, after a count of the ballots, there could be twenty-five votes for union representation and twenty votes against it. If there were only two challenged ballots, those votes would not affect the election results even if both were cast in opposition to union representation. If, however, there were ten challenged ballots, those votes could affect the election's outcome. In this situation, an NLRB representative would study each challenge to determine whether the individual had the right to vote. Only the ballots of the challenged voters found eligible to vote are counted and added to the other ballots.

After the polls close, the ballots are counted and challenged ballots are resolved. Once this is done, the results of the election are announced and the election is over. If the union secured votes from a majority of the voters in the election, it will be declared the winner. If, however, there is a tie vote, or less than half of the employees voted for union representation, the union will have lost the certification election.

Run-off elections. On every ballot, the employees will have at least two choices: a union or no union. In some situations, there will be more than one union on the

Fig. 7.5 *Sample Ballot Used in an NLRB Representation Election*

```
================================================================
                    UNITED STATES OF AMERICA
                 National Labor Relations Board
              OFFICIAL SECRET BALLOT
                    FOR CERTAIN EMPLOYEES OF
                       XXXXXXXXXXXX, INC.
                         XXXXXXXX, XXX
================================================================
     Do you wish to be represented for purposes of collective bargaining by -

               XXXXXXXXXXXXXXXXXXXXXXXXXXXXXX
                      LOCAL NO. X, AFL-CIO


================================================================
              MARK AN "X" IN THE SQUARE OF YOUR CHOICE
================================================================


              YES                              NO
              □                                □


================================================================
```
        DO NOT SIGN THIS BALLOT. Fold and drop in ballot box.
      If you spoil this ballot return it to the Board Agent for a new one.

ballot. This means the employees will have at least three options: vote for union #1, union #2 or vote for no union. It is possible that none of the options will receive a majority vote. Under these circumstances, the two choices receiving the greatest number of votes will be placed on the ballot in a second election to be held at a later date. This is known as a run-off election.

Objections to the election. Within five days of the election, objections to the election can be filed with the regional director of the NLRB. Objections fall into two major categories: objections to the conduct of the election and objections concerning conduct affecting the results of the election.[54] Objections to the conduct of the election are primarily concerned with the environment in which the election took place. In other words, these are questions involving election procedures. Examples of such objections include:

- Electioneering too close to the polls.
- Polls closing too early.
- Union or management observers not present when the ballot box was opened.

- Polling place failing to provide voters sufficient privacy in which to cast their secret ballots.

Objections concerning conduct affecting the election involve the behavior of the parties on election day that could have influenced voting behavior. Examples of this type of objection include:

- Supervisors kept the polling place under surveillance to determine who voted and who did not.
- Supervisors were "hanging around" the polling place.
- Employees were told on the election day that there would be "trouble" if the union won the election.
- An employee handed out a sample copy of the ballot with an "X" in the "NO" box.[55]

Once the objections are filed with the regional director, the other party will be notified and given the opportunity to respond to the charges. After receiving the response from the other party, the regional director makes a decision on the objections. If the union wins the election, and if the regional director concludes the objections are without merit, a certification of representative will be issued. This designates the union as the exclusive bargaining representative of the employees in the bargaining unit. If the union loses the election, no such certification will be issued. Instead, a certification of results will be issued. This is a notification from the NLRB reporting that the union was not supported by a majority of the employees voting.

The regional director could conclude that the objections have merit and set the election results aside. If the regional director believes that infractions have not permanently destroyed "laboratory conditions," a second or re-run election will be directed. However, if it is concluded that the employer's unfair labor practices were severe enough to preclude a fair election at a future time, a bargaining order could be issued. It should be remembered from earlier in the chapter that if it is found that illegal employer behavior caused the union to lose its majority as indicated by authorization cards, the union could be designated as the employees' bargaining agent even if it lost the election.

Decisions of the regional director can be appealed to the five-member board. The board can certify the election results thereby ending the case, order a new election, or designate the union as bargaining agent based on its authorization card majority. If one of the parties still disagrees with board action, it cannot directly appeal the case in federal court. Only final board orders can be challenged in the federal courts. Since orders in representation cases are not considered final, they cannot be appealed. Parties desiring judicial review of board orders in certification election proceedings will usually have to commit an unfair labor practice. As part of the adjudication of the unfair labor practice charges, it will be possible to obtain judicial review of the certification election procedure. For example, if an employer thought the board erred in certifying the union, it could refuse to bargain with the union. In response, the union would probably file charges that the employer was committing an unfair labor practice by violating Section 8(a)(5) of the NLRA. Board orders in unfair labor practice cases are final. Consequently, they are subject to judicial review. As the federal court reviewed the order concerning the refusal-to-bargain charge, it would also examine the certification procedure leading to the bargaining order.

The bargaining order. As previously mentioned, the NLRB will issue a certification of representative if the union wins the election. This notice acknowledges the union victory and designates the union as the exclusive representative of the employees in the bargaining unit. The notice will also identify the bargaining unit represented by the union.

At this time, the employer has the obligation to engage in good faith collective bargaining with the union. Under the election bar rule, the parties will have twelve months in which to attempt to negotiate a collective bargaining agreement without other certification elections being held in the bargaining unit. If the union loses the election, the employer is assured of a twelve-month union-free environment by the election bar rule.

Summary

This chapter examined the process by which a union attempts to organize a company. In most situations, the union will initiate its organizing effort by encouraging workers to sign authorization cards designating the union as the employees' bargaining agent. Once authorization cards have been signed by a significant portion of the workers, the union will request the employer to recognize it as the employees' bargaining representative. However, if the employer has "good faith" doubt concerning the union's majority status, the question of representation will be resolved by an NLRB-conducted certification election.

After the NLRB directs a certification election to take place, both labor and management are subject to a number of restraints imposed on their behavior by national labor policy. The basic objective of labor policy during the pre-election period is to create an environment that allows employees to make a free and untrammelled decision concerning union representation. Union and management behavior found to interfere with employee free choice can be the basis for setting election results aside.

Throughout the pre-election period, the union organizers will be working to convince employees that unionism is within the workers' self-interest. Similarly, management will be striving to counteract the union's organizing effort and will try to convince employees that the costs of unionizing outweigh the benefits. To carry its message to the workers, both labor and management rely on written materials, group meetings, and personal contacts.

The culmination of a union organizing drive is usually an NLRB-conducted certification election. By means of a secret ballot, employees determine whether the union will represent them in collective bargaining. If a majority (one over half) of the workers voting favor union representation, the NLRB will designate the union as the employees' exclusive bargaining agent. Failure by the union to obtain a majority of the votes usually means the employees will not have a collective bargaining agent.

After the representation election, conflict between labor and management over the issue of union organizing is resolved, at least temporarily. If the union loses the election, another election cannot be held for one year. The employer will continue to operate on a non-union basis during that time. Union victory in the certification election significantly changes the nature of the relationship between the employees and their employer. The employees, through their union, have the right to negotiate over wages, hours, and other terms and conditions of employment.

As the parties enter the bargaining relationship, the nature of the conflict between them changes. They are likely to disagree over the conditions of employment proposed by the union and those offered by management. Collective bargaining is the process used to resolve disagreements over terms and conditions of employment. The section to follow will examine the collective bargaining process as practiced in the United States.

Discussion Questions

1. What is an authorization card? How are authorization cards used during the union organizing process? Should the NLRB exercise more or less control over unions as they attempt to get workers to sign authorization cards?
2. Should employers be required by the NLRB to allow the union to address workers concerning the benefits of unionism on company property and on company time?
3. What factors influence the NLRB's definition of an appropriate bargaining unit? What is the significance of the NLRB's decision concerning the appropriate bargaining unit to the union? To management?
4. What channels of communication are available to unions and management when trying to influence the workers' vote in a certification election? How successful are union and management campaign tactics in influencing the workers' decision in a representation election?
5. What is the significance of each of the following NLRB or court decisions:
   Linden Lumber Division, Summer and Co.
   NLRB v. Gissel Packing Co.
   Republic Aviation Corp. v. NLRB
   Pure Oil Co.
   NLRB v. Babcock and Wilcox
   Continental Baking
   General Shoe Corp.
   Edward G. Budd Mfg. Co. v. NLRB
   NLRB v. Exchange Parts Co.
   Peerless Plywood Co.
   Excelsior Underwear, Inc.
   Savair Manufacturing Co.
   Midland National Life Insurance Co.
   Sewell Mfg. Co.

Key Concepts

Authorization card
Voluntary recognition
Showing of interest
No-distribution or -solicitation rules
Election petition
Election bar
Contract bar
Consent election

Stipulated election
Directed election
Expedited election
"Twenty-four hour rule"
Run-off election
Challenged ballots
Certification of representative
Certification of results

Notes

1. S. I. Schlossberg and F. E. Sherman, *Organizing and The Law,* rev. ed. (Washington, D. C.: Bureau of National Affairs, 1971), p. 50.
2. *Aaron Bros.,* 158 NLRB 1077 (1966).
3. *Linden Lumber Division, Summer and Co. v. NLRB,* 419 U.S. 301 (1974).
4. *NLRB v. Gissel Packing Co.,* 395 U.S. 575 (1969).
5. J. G. Getman, S. B. Goldberg, and J. B. Herman, *Union Representation Elections: Law and Reality* (New York: Russell Sage Foundation, 1976), p. 131.
6. Ibid., p. 132.
7. *Republic Aviation Corp. v. NLRB,* 324 U.S. 763 (1945).
8. *Pure Oil Co.,* 75 NLRB 539 (1947).
9. *NLRB v. Babcock and Wilcox,* 351 U.S. 105 (1956).
10. *Hudgens v. NLRB* 424 U.S. 507 (1976).
11. *Central Hardware Co. v. NLRB,* 407 U.S. 539 (1972).
12. *Thirty-Second Annual Report of the National Labor Relations Board* (Washington, D. C.: U. S. Government Printing Office, 1968), p. 101.
13. *Surpass Leather Co.,* 21 NLRB 1258.
14. *Bendix Westinghouse Air Brake Co.,* 161 NLRB 789.
15. *Cumberland Shoe Corp.,* 130 NLRB 394 (1961).
16. *Swan Super Cleaners,* 384 F. 2nd 609 (6th Cir. 1967).
17. K. D. McGuiness, *How to Take a Case Before the National Labor Relations Board,* 4th ed. (Washington, D. C.: Bureau of National Affairs, 1976), p. 49.
18. Ibid., p. 49.
19. *A Layman's Guide to Basic Law Under the National Labor Relations Act* (Washington, D. C.: U. S. Government Printing Office, 1966), p. 10.
20. *Continental Baking Co.,* 99 NLRB 777 (1952).
21. *Globe Machine and Stamping Co.,* 3 NLRB 294 (1937).
22. Schlossberg and Sherman, *Organizing and the Law,* p. 138.
23. *Sav-On Drugs, Inc.,* 138 NLRB 1032 (1962).
24. Schlossberg and Sherman, *Organizing and Law,* p. 138.
25. McGuiness, *How to Take a Case Before the National Labor Relations Board,* p. 93.
26. *General Shoe Corp.,* 77 NLRB 124 (1948).

27. Ibid.
28. L. Jackson and R. Lewis, *Winning NLRB Elections: Management Strategy and Preventative Programs* (New York: Practising Law Institute, 1972), pp. 53–54.
29. *Cannon Electric Co.*, 151 NLRB 1465 (1965).
30. *Struknes Construction Co.*, 165 NLRB 1062 (1967).
31. *Edward G. Budd Mfg. Co. v. NLRB*, 138 F.2d 86 (3rd Cir. 1943).
32. Jackson and Lewis, *Winning NLRB Elections*, p. 55.
33. *Darlington Mfg. Co. v. NLRB*, 397 F2d 760 (4th Cir. 1968).
34. *NLRB v. Exchange Parts Co.*, 375 U.S. 405 (1964).
35. Ibid.
36. *Livingston Shirt*, 107 NLRB 400 (1953).
37. *Peerless Plywood Co.*, 107 NLRB 427 (1953).
38. *Excelsior Underwear, Inc.*, 156 NLRB 1236 (1966).
39. *Vickers Inc.*, 152 NLRB 793 (1965).
40. *Savair Manufacturing Co.*, 414 U.S. 270 (1973).
41. *Gilmore Industries Inc.*, 140 NLRB 100 (1962).
42. Schlossberg and Sherman, *Organizing and the Law*, p. 215.
43. Getman, Goldberg, and Herman, *Union Representation Elections*, pp. 78–79.
44. Ibid., pp. 80–81.
45. *Hollywood Ceramics Co.*, 140 NLRB 221 (1962).
46. *Shopping Kart Food Market, Inc.*, 228 NLRB 190 (1977).
47. *General Knit of Calif., Inc.*, 239 NLRB 101 (1978).
48. *Midland National Life Insurance Co.*, 263 NLRB ____, No. 24, to be reported (1982).
49. *Sewell Mfg. Co.*, 138 NLRB 66 (1962).
50. *Archer Laundry Co.*, 150 NLRB 73 (1962).
51. Getman, Goldberg, and Herman, *Union Representation Elections*, p. 109.
52. R. W. Merry, "Labor Law and Union Organizing," *Wall Street Journal*, 19 April 1978.
53. "Labor Comes to a Crossroads," *Time*, 4 September 1978.
54. Lewis and Jackson, *Winning NLRB Elections*, p. 170.
55. Ibid., p. 170.

Suggested Readings

Getman, Julius G.; Goldberg, Steven B.; and Herman, Jeanne B. *Union Representation Elections: Law and Reality*. New York: Russell Sage Foundation, 1976.
Ground Rules For Labor and Management During Organizing Drives. Englewood Cliffs: Prentice-Hall, 1978.
Hunt, James W. *Employer's Guide to Labor Relations*, rev. ed. Washington, D. C.: Bureau of National Affairs, 1979.
Jackson, Louis and Lewis, Robert. *Winning NLRB Elections: Management's Strategy and Preventative Programs*. New York: Practising Law Institute, 1972.
McGuiness, Kenneth C. *How To Take a Case Before the National Labor Relations Board*, 4th ed. Washington, D. C.: Bureau of National Affairs, 1979.
Schlossberg, Steven I. and Sherman, Fredrick E. *Organizing and the Law*, rev. ed. Washington, D. C.: Bureau of National Affairs, 1976.

Part Two
Case Study

THE UNION ORGANIZING PROCESS

Downtown Art Metal, Inc.

(A)

Downtown Art Metal (DAM) Inc. is a small manufacturer of ornamental lawn furniture operating in Cleveland, Ohio. Its only product line is composed of decorative lawn chairs, loveseats, tables, and birdbaths. The basic manufacturing process is to cast the component parts from iron. Then, the parts are welded together and painted. The finished products are sold to several companies which, in turn, distribute them to a number of department stores, lumber yards, and nurseries. While DAM, Inc. manufactures a high quality, long-lasting, and attractive product line, it has fallen on hard times financially in recent years. Most new homes have small yards which do not have much room for lawn furniture. Also, high housing costs have prevented many homeowners from spending large amounts on decorative lawn furniture. As a result, there has been a substantial decline in demand for DAM, Inc.'s product. DAM, Inc. has barely broken even for the last few years after being a relatively profitable firm for over thirty years.

DAM, Inc. was founded in 1946 by Peter Wilson. During World War II, Wilson worked for a small company that did metal casting on a subcontracting basis for several larger firms with military contracts. After the war, the company could not survive without the military business. Wilson was able to purchase the building and equipment at a bankruptcy sale.

Wilson knew the company had the equipment to make decorative lawn furniture. His grandmother had a set of cast iron lawn furniture which he thought was most attractive. When Wilson attempted to purchase a similar set, he found it very difficult to find one. That is when he decided a demand for such a product existed if the furniture could be high quality but reasonably priced.

The transition from producing war goods to lawn furniture went much smoother than Wilson ever thought possible. Not only was he very familiar with the plant and its equipment, he was able to hire some key employees who had worked for the old company. By December 1946, DAM, Inc. was producing its line of distinctive lawn furniture. At this time, it was employing twenty-six workers.

Wilson had been right. There was a market for his line of lawn furniture. The business grew rapidly. In 1950, Wilson's son, Doug, entered the business. Doug Wilson had been in the army during World War II. Upon discharge, he went to college on the GI Bill. After receiving a bachelor's degree in business administration, he began working for DAM, Inc. as the office manager. Over the years, Doug Wilson worked in a number of administrative positions. In 1962, he was vice-president of administration. His father was responsible for all aspects of the manufacturing process. By 1962, employment in the foundry had increased to 153 production and maintenance workers. An additional 24 employees worked in the company's offices.

While things were going well for the business, things were not going well for the Wilson family. In January, 1963, while vacationing in St. Petersburg, Florida, the older Wilson suffered a heart attack and died. As a result, Doug Wilson became the sole owner and chief executive officer of DAM, Inc. Although Doug Wilson was an astute businessman, he never paid close attention to the manufacturing aspects of the firm.

1963 was a difficult year. Wilson had to hire two vice-presidents, one to fill his old position of vice-president for administration and another to serve as vice-president for production. Once the administrative void created by his father's untimely death was filled, DAM, Inc. stabilized. While the business continued to grow, the growth rate during the 1960s was much slower than that of the previous decade. By 1970, the firm was in a "no growth" situation. While profits were acceptable and the firm was sound financially, it became readily apparent to Wilson that the market for ornamental lawn furniture was not what it used to be. By 1980, sales had started to decline. For the first time in the company's thirty-four-year history, DAM, Inc. lost money. In response to the weakening demand for the company's product, DAM, Inc. had to "tighten its belt."

The relationship between the Wilson family and the DAM, Inc. work force had always been good. Peter, and later Doug Wilson always tried to be fair to their employees. In 1948, there was some labor unrest. The International Association of Iron Handlers (IAIH) attempted to organize the DAM, Inc. workforce. However, the IAIH was overwhelmingly defeated in an NLRB-conducted certification election. Since that time, DAM, Inc. paid wages and fringe benefits comparable to other firms within iron molding industry.

In 1980, with the impending financial crisis associated with the decreased demand for ornamental lawn furniture, DAM, Inc. management decided to decrease the size of its operation, and in general, lower its costs of doing business. The company decreased the workweek from five to four days during certain weeks of the year, dropped the life insurance coverage for the hourly employees and changed its health insurance coverage from family to single coverage. Workers wanting family health insurance coverage had to pay an additional $35.00 per month. Also, the company had always granted annual wage increases comparable to the change in the cost of living in the Cleveland area. The workers were told that if the company was to survive, everybody would have to make sacrifices. This meant that the employees would not receive the pay increase they were expecting.

At first, the worker response to the cost-cutting program was rather favorable. Many of the workers were long-term employees who appreciated the fair and equitable treatment they had received over the years. During 1980, however, worker attitudes started to change. Initially, it was the younger workers who were most critical of the company's actions. The shortened workweek and the decrease in insurance benefits hit this group the hardest. Also, rumors were spreading that all workers with less than five years seniority would be laid off. Given the unemployment rate in Cleveland of around 10 percent, many younger workers were concerned about their re-employment potential. During the later part of 1980 and early 1981, there was more and more grumbling about their wages falling behind workers in similar jobs for other employers in the Cleveland area. Although Mr. Wilson tried to assure the workers that the cutbacks were temporary, the workers were still very upset about their decreasing purchasing power and job security. While a few workers quit, most were afraid they would not be able to find jobs elsewhere.

In September, 1980, several long-service employees met with Doug Wilson. They told Wilson that the discontent had spread from the younger workers to a number of the more senior employees. Wilson was also told that for the first time since the late 1940s, the workers were talking about unionizing. Even though nobody had contacted a union, the workers reported that they would not be the least bit surprised if a union got involved in the near future.

UNION ORGANIZING

Exhibit 1
Map of Area Surrounding DAM, Inc. Plant

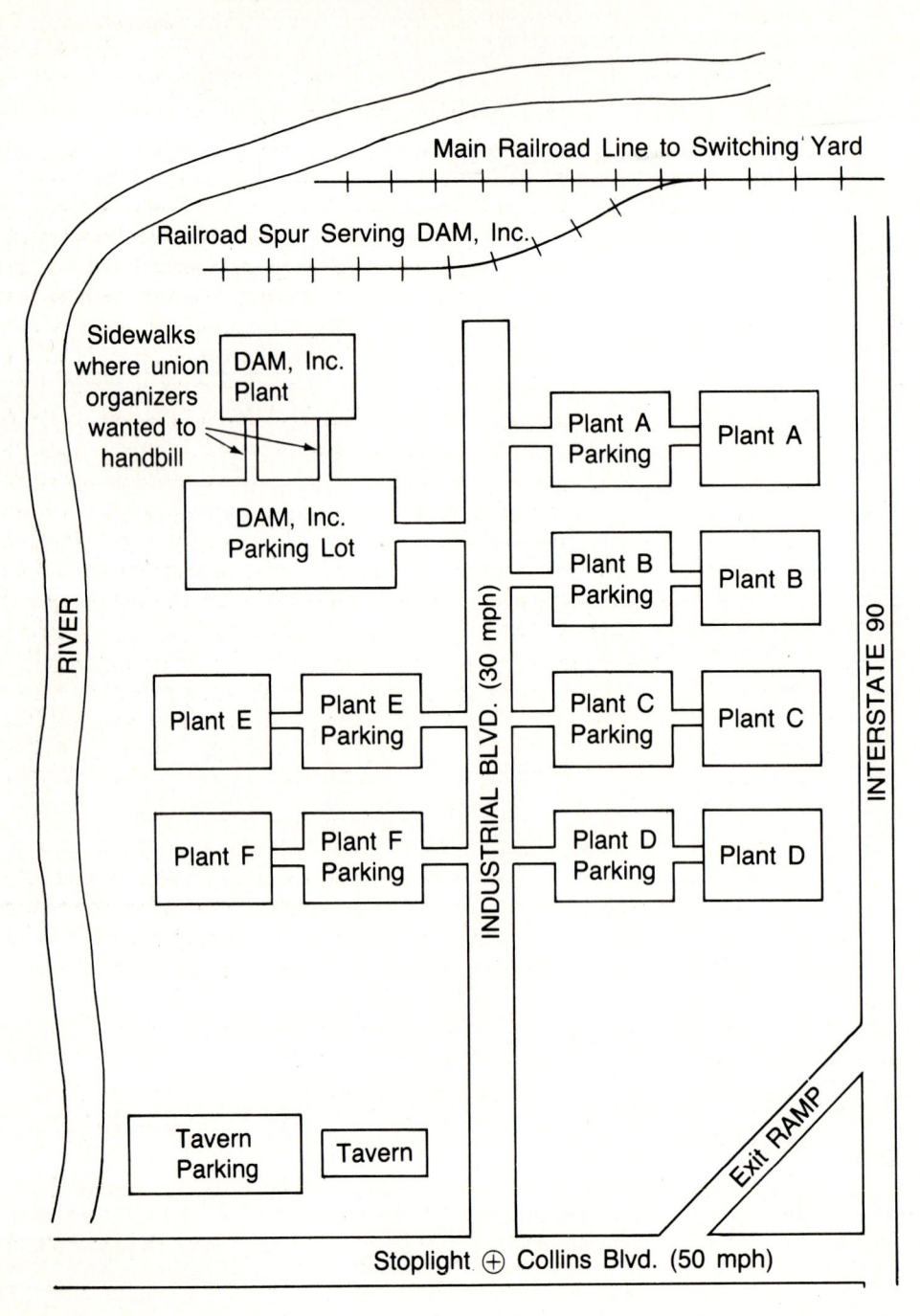

DISCUSSION QUESTIONS

1. What factors are most likely to motivate employees to unionize? Are the conditions in DAM, Inc. conducive to union organizing?
2. If Doug Wilson wanted to keep DAM, Inc. non-union, what would you propose he do?
3. If you were a DAM, Inc. employee who thought that unionization would be beneficial, what would you do to help bring about union organization?

(B)

On the morning of February 2, 1981, as the DAM, Inc. employees were walking from the parking lot to the plant, they were met by two men distributing handbills and union authorization cards. The men were Scott Thompson and Ronald Corbett, international representative for the Brotherhood of Iron Molders and vice-president, Local 112 of the Brotherhood of Iron Molders, respectively.

When Doug Wilson had arrived at work that morning, he was quite surprised to see the beginning of a union organizing attempt. To his knowledge, there had been little discussion concerning union organizing at DAM, Inc. for the last several months. Wilson was not pleased with the thought of union literature being passed out by non-employees on privately owned company property. It was bad enough that the union was trying to organize his workforce.

Wilson called the company attorney, Jack Wallace, to see if anything could be done to remove the union organizers from the company's property. After reminding Wilson that he was not a labor lawyer, Wallace responded that if the organizers were not employees of the firm, they could be asked to leave since they were trespassing on company property.

After talking to Wallace, Wilson went outside and told the union organizers, Corbett and Thompson, that they had to leave the premises. Corbett responded that they did not have to go since they had no better way to contact DAM, Inc. employees. Wilson said that he wasn't too concerned about their problems; that they were trespassing; and that if they didn't leave he would call the police. Corbett and Thompson said they would go but that they would be back.

Upon returning to the union office, Thompson and Corbett reviewed their organizing effort at DAM, Inc. and the conditions under which handbilling and the distribution of authorization cards were taking place. Exhibit #1 is a map of the area surrounding the DAM, Inc. plant. After this review, Thompson and Corbett decided the only reasonable place to distribute union literature was near the parking lot. Also, they believed they had no better way to contact the employees about their organizing effort at the DAM, Inc. plant. Corbett decided to summarize the situation in a letter to Doug Wilson. Corbett's letter to Doug Wilson is presented as Exhibit #2.

Wilson received Corbett's letter on February 6, 1981. His first reaction was to ignore it. He believed as owner of the property, he had the right to deny anyone he wanted, including union organizers, access to it. After this initial reaction, he decided to send the letter to Jack Wallace, the company attorney, for legal opinion before taking any action.

DISCUSSION QUESTIONS

1. Referring to Corbett's letter (Exhibit #2), was the personnel department obligated to provide Corbett the list of names and addresses as requested?
2. Assuming everything in Exhibit #2 is true, if you were Jack Wallace, the company attorney, what would you recommend concerning the distribution of union literature on company property? Why?
3. This case is an example of conflicting interests. On the one hand, the company has property rights. On the other hand, the employees have rights to organize. In this case, whose rights should take priority? Why is this such a difficult issue to resolve?

(C)

On March 15, 1981, Doug Wilson received a telephone call from Scott Thompson, International Representative for the Brotherhood of Iron Mold-

Exhibit 2
Letter from Ron Corbett to Doug Wilson

Brotherhood of Iron Molders
Room 714, Union Hall
1411 Freedom Place
Cleveland, Ohio

February 2, 1981

Mr. Douglas Wilson
Downtown Art Metal Inc.
411 Industrial Avenue
Cleveland, Ohio

Dear Mr. Wilson:

Earlier today, you requested Scott Thompson and me not to distribute union literature on your company's grounds. After a complete review of our activities, it is my opinion that Mr. Thompson and I were within our rights under the National Labor Relations Act to take our organizing efforts on to your company's property. Let me acquaint you with the circumstances which caused me to reach this conclusion:

1. I contacted your personnel office and requested a list of employee names and addresses. The request was denied.

2. I tried to write down license plate numbers and obtain names through the state motor vehicle bureau. Since many workers carpool or take the bus to work, this effort proved futile.

3. Traffic congestion as workers arrive at and depart from the plant made it very difficult to give out union literature while standing in the street.

4. As you are aware, your workers live throughout the Cleveland metropolitan area. It is my understanding that while many (approximately 40 percent) live in Cleveland, the rest live in the suburbs and neighboring towns. Several workers commute as far as 50 miles each day. Because the workers live in such a geographically diverse area, it would be almost impossible for the union to reach the workers through newspaper or radio advertising.

In conclusion, for the above reasons, I feel that representatives from my union have the right to distribute literature on company property. I request that union representatives be allowed to do so without being harassed by company officials. I will assure you that we will not litter company grounds or interfere with the efficient operation of your plant. Since I strongly believe that efforts to stop our handbilling and distributing authorization cards on company property seriously interfere with the employees' Section 7 rights, it is quite likely that unfair labor practice charges will be filed if union representatives are forced off company grounds in the future.

Sincerely,

Ronald Corbett

Ronald Corbett
Vice President, Brotherhood of Iron Molders, Local 112

ers. Thompson requested they meet later in the day to discuss the union's organizing effort at the DAM, Inc. plant. Wilson agreed to meet with Thompson at 4:30 p.m. on that day.

After the introduction and some brief small talk concerning Cleveland's financial woes, the weather, and the upcoming baseball season, Wilson and Thompson got down to business. Their discussion went as follows:

Thompson: As you know, Doug, the Brotherhood of Iron Molders has been seriously trying to organize your plant for about the last six weeks.

Wilson: How could I not be aware of that? This little company has enough problems without having to fight the union in an election campaign.

Thompson: My union doesn't want a fight. We have already received authorization cards from a majority of the workers in the unit. We request that you recognize the union voluntarily. That will save us both the hassle of having to have an NLRB-conducted election.

Wilson: What do you consider the appropriate bargaining unit to be?

Thompson: It seems to us that all production and maintenance employees should be in the unit and the supervisors, clerical, shipping-and-receiving people, and the plant guards should be excluded from it.

Wilson: Well, I agree that the clerical employees, supervisors, and plant guards shouldn't be in the unit, but certainly, the workers in shipping and receiving should be. You know they work very closely with the employees in production. In fact, there have been a number of transfers between production and shipping. They eat lunch together, carpool together. It's all one big happy family out there in the plant.

Thompson: Wait a second. You know that some of your most loyal "hands" are in the shipping and receiving department. There's no way we are going to be able to organize them.

Wilson: That's your problem, Scott. It's bad enough that you are "hell bent" on organizing a company having serious financial problems like mine. I'm certainly not going to stand by and let you fragment this little company into different bargaining units.

Thompson: Does this mean you won't voluntarily recognize the union?

Wilson: You're real sharp, Scott. You can get to the heart of the matter real quick. Since we don't agree on the unit, it's probably better for you to petition for an NLRB election to resolve the bargaining unit issue and the question of representation.

Thompson: You're making a mistake by going to an election. An election is likely to cause us both a lot of problems.

Wilson: Let's get it straight. We disagree on the bargaining unit issue. That's one problem. There's an even more basic issue. You claim to have signed authorization cards from a majority of the employees. Even if we agreed on the bargaining unit, I have serious doubts about your card majority. I've heard all sorts of stories about how you got the employees to sign the cards.

Thompson: What kind of stories have you heard?

Wilson: I've heard that some workers were told they had to sign the cards in order to get an NLRB election. I was also told that a couple of workers were threatened that they would be in "trouble" if they didn't sign the cards. I heard that old Frank, the Greek fellow who doesn't read English very well, was told he was signing a card that would allow him to attend a union picnic next summer. Frank wasn't designating the union to be his bargaining agent. He thought he was signing up for a picnic.

Thompson: That's not my approach to getting employees to sign authorization cards. You can be sure I'll investigate your allegations.

Wilson: That's not a bad idea.

Thompson: This is your last chance. Will you voluntarily recognize the union?

Wilson: Hell, No! There's the door. Close it on your way out.

After Thompson left, Doug Wilson wondered if he had taken the proper action. Not only was he concerned about rejecting the union's request for voluntary recognition, he also questioned whether he should have been so sarcastic and antagonistic toward Scott Thompson.

DISCUSSION QUESTIONS

1. Determining the appropriate bargaining unit is an important issue. Assuming the union petitioned for an election, what criteria would the NLRB consider when deciding on the appropriate bargaining unit? Do you think the NLRB would accept the union's or the company's position?
2. What is an authorization card? How are authorization cards used? Assuming Thompson's allegations concerning union tactics to get workers to sign authorization cards are true, would the NLRB use the cards as proof of the union's claim of majority status? Why?
3. Did Wilson err by being sarcastic and openly antagonistic toward Thompson? Why?
4. Did Wilson have sufficient grounds for denying the union's request for voluntary recognition and insisting on a certification election?

(D)

Since DAM, Inc. refused to voluntarily recognize the Brotherhood of Iron Molders as the employees' exclusive bargaining agent based on its authorization-card majority, the union petitioned for an NLRB-conducted certification election. After an investigation, the NLRB decided the appropriate bargaining unit would include the production and maintenance employees, as well as workers in the shipping and receiving department. On April 12, 1981, the NLRB established June 15, 1981 as the date for the election.

Once the election was ordered, both union and management began their efforts to influence the workers' votes in the upcoming election. The union held several organizing meetings in the back room of a tavern located near the plant. Similarly, the company had a meeting on company time and on the company premises. All employees had to attend the meeting. The union requested the opportunity also to meet with employees on company time and property. However, the request was refused. Also, the company sent two letters to the employees' homes responding to issues raised by the union. While the union and management were actively involved in the certification election campaign, there were no serious problems until April 26, 1981.

Early in the campaign, most union activities were away from the plant. With the exception of handbilling in the DAM, Inc. parking lot (the subject of Exhibit 1) the Brotherhood of Iron Molders, Local 112 did little to press its campaign at the workplace. However, the union organizers thought they had too low a profile in the campaign, so the decision was made to increase publicity and organizing efforts at the plant. This decision lead to a series of confrontations between prounion employees and DAM, Inc. management.

The first incident took place at approximately 11:45 a.m. on April 26, 1981. Approximately fifty employees were seated in the company cafeteria having lunch. DAM, Inc. employees receive a half-hour unpaid lunch break. Since seating capacity in the lunch room is limited, approximately one-third of the production and maintenance staff will be eating at any time around the noon hour.

In the cafeteria on that day, Jack Johnson, a strong union supporter, was distributing a handbill announcing another union meeting. Occasionally, he would stop to talk with employees. After using approximately fifteen minutes of his lunch break to publicize the union's organizing effort, Johnson was summoned to report to Larry Haley, the shop foreman.

In Haley's office, the following conversation took place:

Haley: You should know better, Johnson, than to solicit on company premises.
Johnson: What are you talking about?
Haley: DAM, Inc. has a rule that has been uniformly applied for the last eleven years designed to keep employees from being harassed by people soliciting for various and sundry causes. The rule states: "Soliciting will not be permitted in the factory, cafeteria, or offices." The rule applies to union organizing efforts.
Johnson: Oh yeah. I'm familiar with that but I thought it was intended to stop Girl Scouts from selling us cookies.
Haley: Don't try to be funny! I could have you suspended for breaking the no-solicitation rule. I'm not going to do that. Consider this a warning. The next time you or any of your prounion cronies try to get more workers to join your cause while on company property, you will be suspended.
Johnson: You can't do that. I have a right to solicit during my nonworking time. Don't forget, we aren't being paid by the company during lunch.
Haley: Since when did you get your law degree? You heard what I said. No more soliciting while you're at work.
Johnson: We'll see what the union says about this. I'll be back to discuss this with you after I talk with the union.

After work that night, Johnson called Scott Thompson, the union's international representative, and related his conversation with Mr. Haley. Thompson said he would talk to Tom Bushley, the union's attorney and then get back with Haley.

The very next day, April 27, 1981, another incident took place. Four workers, without union approval, had had tee-shirts made up. The front of the shirt said "This company is *no* DAM good." The following was printed on the back: "Doug Wilson doesn't give a DAM." On these shirts, the workers wore buttons stating simply "Vote for Local 112."

At about 9:30 a.m., Larry Haley called all four employees into his office. He told them that several employees found their tee-shirts offensive. They could either remove the shirts or go home. They were not welcome back at the plant until they decided not to wear the shirts. Haley reminded them that they would not be paid if they left. The employees told Haley that they had worn the tee-shirts as a joke. They thought the shirts were funny and did not think the shirts would offend anyone. Haley said that union organizing was not a joke. He also reiterated his ultimatum; either take off the shirts or go home. All four decided to leave work.

As soon as they left the plant, they called Scott Thompson to report what had happened. Thompson asked if the shirts interfered with production. The workers reported that while there had been several comments and a few jokes made when they first got to work, no one said anything after that. It was their opinion that production wasn't affected at all by the shirts. Thompson said he would check into the situation and get back with them. He also suggested they return to work the next day, but not wear the shirts again until the problem was resolved.

Later in the day on April 27, 1981, Haley had another confrontation with a group of prounion employees. At approximately 3:35 p.m. as the workers punched out at the end of the day, three union supporters were handing out union literature. One of them had a megaphone through which he was encouraging the workers to attend a union meeting in order to learn more about the benefits of joining the union.

Haley came out of his office and pulled the three union supporters aside. He told them if they didn't keep the union organizing efforts quieter, he would have to fire them. Since the workers didn't know if they could be discharged for what they were doing, they curtailed their orgainizing efforts and went home. Again, Scott Thompson was called. Thompson thanked them for the information and told them he had a meeting with Tom Bushley later that evening. Thompson and Bushley met that evening to discuss Haley's behavior of the last two days.

DISCUSSION QUESTIONS

1. Did the company illegally interfere with the union's organizing effort by requiring the employees to attend a company-sponsored meeting on company time while denying the union the same opportunity?
2. Despite the no-solicitation rule, did Jack Johnson have the right to solicit during his lunch hour? Why? Would your answer be any different if Johnson had been on a company-paid lunch break? Why?
3. Did the company have the right to tell the four employees to either remove the shirts or go home?
4. Did Haley's action with regard to the tee-shirts represent an interference with the employees' rights under the NLRA or was it simply an attempt by Haley to maintain order and discipline at the plant?
5. Did Haley's threat to discharge the employees who were using the megaphone violate the employees' rights under the act?
6. What standards of conduct does the NLRB require during the pre-election period? Did any of Haley's actions violate the NLRB's standards for pre-election conduct?

(E)

On May 14, 1981, Doug Wilson, owner and president of DAM, Inc. was working in his office at the plant. At approximately 9:15 a.m., he received a telephone call from Dan Berry, the company's vice-president for administration. Berry had been assigned the task of monitoring the union's organizing effort and overseeing the company's anti-union campaign. Berry wanted to show Wilson a handbill union organizers had given to workers attending a union-sponsored picnic held the previous afternoon. Wilson told Berry to come to his office right away. Once in Wilson's office, Berry gave Wilson the handbill. A copy of the handbill is presented as Exhibit 3.

Wilson examined the handbill for a few minutes. His reaction was that while it accurately reflected DAM, Inc.'s position, it appeared seriously to overstate the wages and benefits being offered by the other firms. Berry agreed with Wilson's appraisal. However, to make sure, he said he would contact the firms mentioned on the handbill to determine whether the information was accurate.

That afternoon, Berry called the personnel managers at each of the companies listed on the union's handbill. The information he received from these telephone calls is summarized in Exhibit 4. After reviewing the data, Berry concluded that the union had accurately portrayed the life and medical insurance benefits as well as the grievance procedures. However, the union seriously overstated the wages paid by the other firms and the length of the paid vacations. Now that he had the information, Berry was not sure what to do with it. He decided to think about it overnight.

The next morning Berry met with Wilson to review his findings. Wilson was very upset. To this point on the campaign, the union had worked hard to convince the workers to vote for it in the election. The distorted information on the handbill was the first indication that the union was using deceitful practices in its organizing effort. Wilson asked Berry how the company should respond to the handbill.

Berry recommended that the company do nothing until after the election. If the union won the election, the company should then file objections with the NLRB claiming the union used illegal election propaganda. Berry was confident that when the NLRB saw the deceptive nature of the handbill, they would set the election aside and order a new one.

DISCUSSION QUESTIONS

1. What role does the NLRB play in the evaluation of misleading campaign statements?
2. Should Wilson follow Berry's advice? Why? If you decide Wilson should reject Berry's advice, what course of action would you propose?

Exhibit 3
Handbill Distributed by the Brotherhood of Iron Molders to DAM, Inc. Employees

ATTENTION DAM, INC. WORKERS

You have known for a long time that the company has been screwing you with a vigor not seen in the Cleveland area since the 1930s. While the fat cats (Wilson and the bunch of lackeys he calls his managers) keep getting richer, the serfs (we mean employees) of DAM, Inc. have had their pay and benefits fall farther and farther behind those received by other employees in the iron molding industry.

Unite! Unionize! Get what you deserve! Look at the figures below. See how bad you are being treated. Vote for the Brotherhood of Iron Molders on June 15, 1981 if you want the wages and benefits you deserve.

	DAM, Inc.	Duckwell Iron Works	Lewis Iron and Steel*	Reed Iron Products*
Hourly wage—Laborer	$4.25	$4.75	$6.95	$6.95
Hourly wage—Painter	$4.37	$5.25	$7.45	$7.45
Hourly wage—Grinder	$4.51	$5.65	$8.00	$8.00
Hourly wage—Welder	$4.87	$6.10	$8.75	$8.75
Weeks paid vacation	2	3	5	5
Life insurance	No	Yes	Yes	Yes
Medical insurance	Single-coverage	Single-coverage	Family plan	Family plan
Grievance procedure	No	No	Yes	Yes

*Employees represented by the Brotherhood of Iron Molders

Exhibit 4
Summary of Data Collected by Berry

	Duckwell Iron Works	Lewis Iron And Steel	Reed Iron Products
Hourly wage—Laborer	$4.25	$4.50	$4.50
Hourly wage—Painter	$4.50	$5.25	$5.25
Hourly wage—Grinder	$4.75	$5.35	$5.35
Hourly wage—Welder	$5.50	$5.75	$5.75
Weeks paid vacation	2	3	3
Life insurance	No	Yes	Yes
Medical coverage	Single-coverage	Family plan	Family plan
Grievance procedure	No	Yes	Yes

(F)

Scott Thompson, the union's international representative, was really mad. He had just played a tape recording of a speech made by Doug Wilson, president of DAM, Inc. to the DAM, Inc. employees. Throughout the pre-election campaign, DAM, Inc. had relied quite heavily on captive audience speeches. Up until the most recent one, which was delivered on May 31, 1981, Wilson had always spoken on rather noncontroversial issues. In one speech he talked about the importance of loyalty.

Exhibit 5
Verbatim Transcript of Wilson's May 31, 1981, Captive-Audience Speech

Thank you all for coming to this afternoon's meeting. This session represents part of my continuing effort to help you vote intelligently in the upcoming union certification election. I'll make my statements as brief as possible.

As you are probably aware, the union has promised to increase your wages and improve your fringe benefits. The union has clearly and repeatedly stated that if chosen as your bargaining agent, they will bring your wages in line with other firms also represented by the Brotherhood of Iron Molders. What they had not told you is where the money to fund the contract will come from. The union will not generate more sales for DAM, Inc. The union will not be able to increase your productivity. The union will not increase the revenues of this firm.

A number of you have been with DAM, Inc. for many years. I, and before me, my father, have always tried to offer competitive wages and fringe benefits. Do you think I have enjoyed watching your wages and benefits fall behind those offered by our competitors? It has been with great concern that your economic position has eroded in the last couple of years. It has happened only as a last resort.

The union has promised you dramatic improvements in your wages and fringe benefits. I sincerely wish that DAM, Inc. could afford to agree with the union but as you are all aware, you can't get blood from a turnip. The union has failed to answer the basic question: where will the money come from to fund the contract they say they will bring to you?

As many of you are probably aware, DAM, Inc. has lost money in each of the last two years. Things aren't looking much better for this year. If our current projections are accurate, we will lose approximately $200,000 this year. For how long can DAM, Inc. operate at a loss? As owner and president of the firm, I am probably in the best position to answer that question. Unequivocally, I can state that if things don't improve in the near future, the firm which my father started will no longer be. While there is a chance we will turn the corner and be able to survive, I can assure you this will not happen if the union is voted in. DAM, Inc. will shut its doors and all of you will be out of a job if the union is voted in. We are doing the very best we can with respect to your wages and benefits. If we could offer you more, we would. Even if the union moderated its position and asked for less than what they are currently telling you that you will get, we cannot afford it. The union dooms this company and dooms your future with it. I urgently request that you be patient and work with us to turn DAM, Inc. around. Together we have a chance to make this company survive, and thereby, insure your future economic security. If the union is voted in, I'll probably be seeing you at the unemployment office.

I don't like speaking this way. But, I think you should be aware of the economic realities of the situation and be prepared to live with the consequences of your acts. While I would prefer to continue operating non-union, I am willing to respect your wishes if you feel unionism is within your self-interest. Unfortunately, DAM, Inc. does not have the economic wherewithal to meet the demands being discussed by the union. A vote for the union will mark the end of DAM, Inc.

In another, Wilson just outlined the NLRB's procedure for conducting a certification election. However, Wilson's speech on May 31, 1981, went much further. Thompson even thought that Wilson committed a serious unfair labor practice as a result of his most recent speech.

There was no chance that Wilson had been misquoted in his May 31, 1981, speech. An employee tape recorded the entire meeting. Exhibit 5 is a verbatim transcript of Wilson's speech.

Thompson was quite confident that Wilson had gone beyond the bounds of permissible employer speech outlined in Section 8(c) of the NLRA. To Thompson, it appeared that Wilson threatened to close the plant if the employees voted for the union. Thompson wondered if he should file unfair labor practice charges.

DISCUSSION QUESTIONS

1. What is the purpose of Section 8(c) of the NLRA?
2. There is a very fine line of distinction between an illegal threat and a lawful prediction. Did Wilson's speech constitute a threat or was it a legal prediction? Why?
3. What factors are considered by the NLRB when differentiating between a threat and a prediction? Do you think the NLRB would find that Wilson committed an unfair labor practice with his speech of May 31, 1981? Why or why not?

(G)

The certification election at DAM, Inc. in which the employees would either accept or reject the Brotherhood of Iron Molders as their bargaining agent was only one day away. The union organizing campaign which had been going on since April 12, 1981 when ordered by the NLRB had its ups and downs. While most union and company campaign tactics had been very open and honest and intended to allow the workers to make a free and informed choice, events had occasionally transpired of questionable legality. The lively contested pre-election campaign lasted right up to election day.

On the day before the election, June 14, 1981, the workers were faced with an unusual scene as they arrived at work. The union had rented a sound truck that was parked in the street in front of the DAM, Inc. plant. Over the truck's loudspeakers, music was playing. Occasionally, the music would be interrupted, and verbal appeals for the workers to vote for Local 112 in the election were made. The appeals lasted no more than fifteen seconds each. Once made, the music was resumed. Since June 14, 1981 was a hot, muggy day, the windows in most of the plant were open. Throughout the day, the music and the periodic appeals to vote could be heard throughout the plant.

At 3:00, all employees were told by their supervisors to stop working and report to the company cafeteria. Once the workforce was assembled, Mr. Wilson began to address the group. In his speech, Wilson discussed the voting procedures in certification elections and reminded the workers of the firm's poor economic position. He encouraged the employees to work with the DAM, Inc. management to help the firm improve its economic position and not against it by voting for the union. By the end of his twenty-minute speech, Mr. Wilson was very emotional in his appeals for worker support and loyalty to the firm which had treated them so well over the years. When finished speaking, he told the workers they could go home, ten minutes before their normally scheduled quitting time.

When Wilson returned to his office, Scott Thompson, the union's international representative, was waiting to talk with him. Their converstion went as follows:

Thompson: When I stopped by this afternoon, it was just to "touch ground" with you prior to the election. I thought we could discuss who the election observers would be and I wanted to see the polling area. I was very sur-

Wilson: prised to see you were giving a speech that workers were required to attend on the eve of the election.

Wilson: What's wrong with that?

Thompson: Did you ask your attorney if it was OK to give the speech today?

Wilson: No, it didn't seem necessary. Did I do something wrong?

Thompson: I don't want to nit-pick but it's an unfair labor practice for an employer to make a captive-audience speech during the twenty-four hours preceding a certification election.

Wilson: My speech was no different than the union's sound truck blasting away all day outside the plant.

Thompson: I think there is a major difference between the two activities. But this is the type of situation that the NLRB will have to resolve.

DISCUSSION QUESTIONS

1. What is the NLRB's policy concerning election speeches made during the twenty-four-hour period preceding the election?
2. If the union filed unfair labor practices because of Wilson's speech the day before the election, do you think the NLRB would conclude a violation of national labor policy had taken place?
3. Did the union's use of a sound truck violate the NLRB's policy on speeches during the twenty-four-hour period preceding an election?

(H)

On June 15, 1981 the certification election at DAM, Inc, in which the workers would accept or reject the Brotherhood of Iron Molders as their bargaining representative went ahead as scheduled. A portable canvas polling booth had been set up by the NLRB in the hall outside the company cafeteria. The polling place was open from 7:00 a.m. to 3:30 p.m. The election went smoothly. There were no challenged ballots and no incidents took place that could cause the election to be set aside.

After the polls were closed, the NLRB agent who had supervised the election took the ballot box to a conference room. In the presence of union and company observers, the board agent opened the box and proceded to count the ballots. When the ballots were counted, the union had lost the election. A total of 75 workers voted for union representation and 100 voted against it.

When Scott Thompson, the union's international representative, heard the election results, he was very disappointed. He contacted Tom Bushley, the union attorney. Thompson wanted to review the entire pre-election campaign with Bushley to determine whether the union had grounds to file objections to the election or unfair labor practice charges.

After discussing the campaign and election, Bushley decided there were not sufficient grounds to file objections to the election. However, it appeared that illegal employer actions had caused the union's majority as indicated by signed authorization cards to be eroded. Bushley said he would file unfair labor practice charges with the NLRB's regional office the next day.

That evening, Bushley sat down to list the employer violations he thought had occurred during the union's organizing campaign. The list included:

1. The company's enforcing a uniform no-solicitation rule (D).*
2. Sending workers home for wearing pro-union tee-shirts (D).
3. Threatening to fire workers for union organizing activities (D).
4. Threatening to close the plant if the union won the certification election (F).
5. Conducting a captive-audience speech within twenty-four hours of the election (G).

*The letters in parentheses refer to the case in which the incident took place.

DISCUSSION QUESTIONS

1. For each of the five issues raised by Bushley, do you think the NLRB would conclude the behavior constituted an unfair labor practice? Be sure to cite cases to support your position.
2. Assuming the NLRB found the company committed unfair labor practices during the union organizing campaign, what would the appropriate remedy be in this case? In Part C, Wilson charged that a number of illegal practices had been used by the union to get the workers to sign an authorization card. How would the truth or falsity of these allegations affect the NLRB's remedy in this case?

Once a union has been certified as the employees' collective bargaining representative, the relationship between labor and management enters a new phase. A certified union has the right to participate in the determination of wages, hours, and other conditions of employment. It is likely that the parties will disagree over such issues. Collective bargaining is the process through which labor and management try to resolve their disagreements over the conditions of employment. Through the give-and-take of collective bargaining, labor and management negotiators jointly determine the "rules of the workplace." When put into writing, these rules become the collective bargaining agreement.

This section contains three chapters. Chapter 8 provides an overview of the collective bargaining process. It defines collective bargaining, discusses the dynamics of the relationship, and reviews the national labor policy as it affects the collective bargaining relationship. Chapter 9 presents a "nuts and bolts" approach to collective bargaining. It is primarily concerned with how the parties prepare for the negotiation of a labor agreement. Chapter 10 is concerned with dispute resolution. The vast majority of labor agreements are negotiated by the parties without outside intervention and without having to resort to a strike. However, situations do arise in which the parties may need help from outsiders such as mediators and arbitrators to conclude their negotiations successfully. Chapter 10 will review the roles played by these third parties. Occasionally, the union and management are unable to reach agreement and resort to the strike. Chapter 10 will also examine the role of the strike weapon in the collective bargaining process.

PART THREE THE COLLECTIVE BARGAINING PROCESS

Chapter 8

COLLECTIVE BARGAINING: AN OVERVIEW

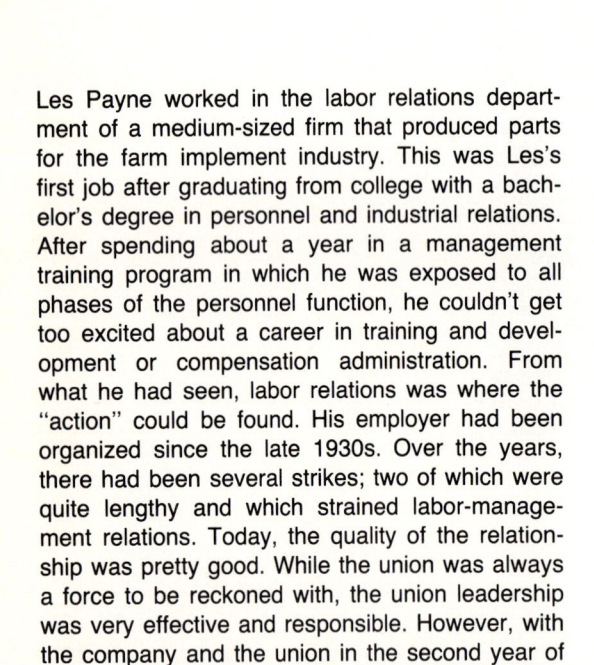

Les Payne worked in the labor relations department of a medium-sized firm that produced parts for the farm implement industry. This was Les's first job after graduating from college with a bachelor's degree in personnel and industrial relations. After spending about a year in a management training program in which he was exposed to all phases of the personnel function, he couldn't get too excited about a career in training and development or compensation administration. From what he had seen, labor relations was where the "action" could be found. His employer had been organized since the late 1930s. Over the years, there had been several strikes; two of which were quite lengthy and which strained labor-management relations. Today, the quality of the relationship was pretty good. While the union was always a force to be reckoned with, the union leadership was very effective and responsible. However, with the company and the union in the second year of a three-year contract, things were bound to heat up as contract-negotiations time approached. No doubt about it, labor relations was where the action was. So when the opportunity presented itself after his training was completed, Les joined the labor relations staff.

Les started his new job investigating grievances and doing some of the research needed to prepare for arbitration. However, he was not going to be doing this for long. He had been told that he would be brought into the process of preparing for collective bargaining in some capacity in the near future. Les had some reservations about working on the upcoming negotiations. He didn't want to broadcast the fact that he knew very little about labor negotiations. While he had taken a collective-bargaining class in college, he didn't have a good understanding of the collective-bargaining process.

To Les, the collective-bargaining process was like a black box. He had noticed that the local town newspaper would run articles announcing the beginning of negotiations. At some later time, he would read that the workers were on strike. Alternatively, the newspaper would run an article announcing that an agreement had been reached. It seemed to Les that these agreements were always reached just minutes before the old contract was to expire. The pictures accompanying these articles always seemed to include exhausted-looking but smiling union and management negotiators.

From watching the local news media, Les was aware of negotiations occurring at plants in the area. Coverage was usually provided at the later stages of negotiations, especially if a strike occurred. But what happened between the beginning and the end of negotiations? Les didn't have a good idea of what went on during contract negotiations. More important, he didn't know why collective bargaining looked the way it did.

The thoughts of getting involved in the upcoming negotiations made Les feel incompetent. While feeling insecure, he knew he would learn a lot in the year to come.

It is not surprising that Les had uncertainties about the upcoming negotiations. It is difficult to develop an intensive understanding about a specific round of collective-bargaining negotiations without actually observing the process. There are approximately 178,000 separate labor agreements in the United States.[1] It is probably safe to say that no two sets of negotiations leading up to these contracts were the same. While a tremendous diversity of behaviors is exhibited in the bargaining room, the objectives of the parties and the factors influencing the outcomes of the collective-bargaining process are quite similar. This chapter is designed to provide an overview of collective bargaining as practiced in the United States. To this end, the objectives of the process, the characteristics of the collective-bargaining relationship, the factors influencing the outcomes of the process and the legal restraints on labor negotiations will be discussed.

More specifically, after studying this chapter you should be able to:

- List the three basic objectives of the collective-bargaining process.
- Enumerate the basic characteristics of the collective-bargaining relationship.
- Discuss bargaining power and the factors influencing the relative bargaining power of labor and management.
- Briefly describe Walton and McKersie's behavioral theory of labor negotiations.
- Explain what the legal requirements of "good faith" bargaining are.

Objectives of the Collective Bargaining Process

As discussed in Chapter 1, something like an armed truce exists between labor and management. Their relationship is characterized by conflict. However, this conflict usually takes place within bounds. Both groups have a vested interest in developing a prosperous organization. This is because both profits and wages are paid out of a firm's revenues. Also, both labor and management are, to a degree, dependent upon each other. The union is dependent on the firm for jobs. It has been said that a union is to a business as a fish is to water. Without one, you cannot have the other. An employer is less dependent on a union than vice versa. Certainly, a business can survive without a union. However, the employer needs an efficient workforce at a minimal cost. The union has the ability to withhold workers' services through strikes and other sanctions. Therefore, it is within the self-interest of the unionized employer to cooperate with the labor organization to the extent needed to attract and maintain an efficient workforce.

Within these general boundaries, labor and management are free to disagree over a wide range of issues. It is quite likely that unions will seek wages, benefits, and a role in decision making more costly and restrictive of managerial prerogatives than most employers will voluntarily offer. Collective bargaining is the process through which labor and management negotiators resolve their disagreements over wages, hours, and other terms and conditions of employment.

While the specific issues over which conflict can arise are diverse, it is possible to identify three broad categories on which parties seek agreement through collective bargaining:

- Collective bargaining is a system for determining workers' compensation including both wages and fringe benefits. As a result, collective bargaining helps determine the distribution of the "economic pie" between capital and labor.
- Collective bargaining is a procedure for establishing, revising, and administering the rules of the workplace. In addition to governing wages and fringe benefits as just mentioned, collective bargaining may address a wide range of issues important to both management and the workers. The rules of the workplace negotiated by the parties may specify the duties and responsibilities of the workers. Closely related to this, the disciplinary actions associated with employees not fulfilling their responsibilities may also be determined through collective bargaining. Other rules of the workplace define the workers' rights associated with employment by the company.[2] It must be emphasized that the parties are not in conflict on all issues addressed during collective bargaining. Collective bargaining can also be a process through which problems of mutual concern can be addressed. For example, difficulties concerning plant safety and workers' skill development can be handled through the bargaining process.
- Collective bargaining is a method for resolving disputes arising during the life of the labor agreement. Most labor contracts include a grievance procedure that provides a mechanism for solving problems related to the interpretation or administration of the contract. Such disputes inevitably arise during the life of a labor agreement.[3] Most labor contracts include grievance procedures with arbitration to handle disputes over the meaning of the agreement. These topics will be discussed in Chapters 14 and 15.

Characteristics of the Collective-Bargaining Relationship

When the parties engage in collective bargaining, they enter into a relationship through which they will attempt to resolve conflicts over issues such as wages, hours, and fringe benefits. This relationship has a number of characteristics that can influence both the content and style of the interactions between labor and management representatives. The collective-bargaining relationship has been described in terms of a number of characteristics that will be discussed below.[4]

COLLECTIVE BARGAINING INVOLVES GROUP RELATIONSHIPS

In a general sense, the collective-bargaining relationship involves two major groups, the union and management. However, it is important to recognize that a union is a political organization composed of a number of subgroups. These groups can form along a number of different dimensions such as skilled and unskilled, old and young workers, and males and females. Typically, the various subgroups have some interests unique to themselves and have objectives that could clash with the goals of the other subgroups. Similarly, management is characterized by a number of subgroups such as line supervisors, financial staff, and personnel and industrial-relations department employees.

The group aspect of the collective-bargaining relationship has a number of implications, especially for the union and its membership. The most obvious consideration is that by forming a group (the union), employees realign their bargaining power. While working as individuals, employees may have been ineffective when they tried to bring about changes in their conditions of employment. However, unionizing better enables them to pressure management into making changes. The power associated with organizing has been described as follows:

> It is by mobilizing their power—economic, political, and moral—that workers and their leaders compel management in the first instance to deal with them and then to grant, in whole or in part, the demands which they make upon the corporation. It is by countering with power—economic, political, and moral—that corporate management determines how much and to what extent it will deal with its employees through organized unions, and, once it deals with these unions, how much of the demands it will grant, consistent with the necessity of maintaining competition, efficiency, and freedom to conduct the enterprise. Indeed, management often finds it necessary to make proposals of its own to the unions.[5]

The transition from individual bargaining to bargaining through a group is one of the moving forces behind the urge to organize and the desire to engage in collective bargaining. Without the power generated by the group (the union), employers would have little incentive to negotiate over conditions of employment.

In addition to realigning the relative power of employees vis-à-vis management, the group aspect of the collective-bargaining relationship has a number of other implications for the parties. First, the union leadership will have to reconcile the many and often conflicting goals and objectives of the union's constituent subgroups. As a result, the union leadership may experience political problems within their organization that can spill over and affect the collective-bargaining relationship with management.

Second, in most collective-bargaining situations, the collective bargaining agreement allows some employee subgroups to be discriminated against relative to other subgroups. For example, seniority clauses usually give longer-service employees greater job security than workers with fewer years of service. To a degree, this can intensify the union's political problems discussed above. It also requires that the parties go to great lengths to clearly specify the rights of workers and the requirements for receiving those rights. There is a need to establish standardized rules and regulations. This will help workers understand what their rights are, and perhaps, why they have fewer rights and benefits than other employee subgroups. When the rules and regulations governing the conditions of employment are reduced to paper, the result is a collective-bargaining agreement. Once the labor agreement is in effect, management's flexibility is severely limited. No longer is management free to do as it pleases. Instead, many managerial decisions will be governed by the labor agreement.

COLLECTIVE BARGAINING INVOLVES A CONTINUOUS RELATIONSHIP

One of the common misconceptions about collective bargaining is that it occurs every several years when it is time to renegotiate a labor agreement. While contract negotiations are an important aspect of the collective-bargaining relationship (and the one that receives the most attention by the news media), it must be recognized that the parties interact with one another on a daily basis throughout the life of the contract. Since it is necessary to resolve conflicts over the interpretation or administration of the labor agreement day in and day out, the union and management remain parties to the collective-bargaining relationship throughout the life of the agreement. Exhibit 8.1 discusses the continuous nature of the collective-bargaining relationship.

The importance of the continuous nature of collective bargaining to the relationship between the parties cannot be overstated. It is this aspect of the relationship that forces the parties to consider the longer-run implications of their actions. Behavior during contract negotiations can influence the parties during the life of the contract. Deceitful practices or attacks on the other bargainer's personal integrity exhibited during the heat of the union's organizing campaign are not likely to be forgotten once the union is certified. The hostilities and animosities generated during the unionizing effort may inhibit the parties' ability to successfully negotiate their first contract. Similarly, a cooperative attitude by labor and management during contract negotiations may spill over and facilitate the amicable handling of disputes during the life of the contract.

> **EXHIBIT 8.1**
> **The Continuous Nature of the Collective-Bargaining Relationship**
>
> Collective bargaining involves, first, the negotiation of a general agreement as to terms and conditions of employment and, second, the maintenance of the parties' relations for the period of the agreement. The first process is the dramatic one which catches the public eye and which is sometimes mistaken to be the entire function of collective bargaining. But in fact, it is to labor relations approximately what the wedding is to domestic relations. It launches the parties on their joint enterprise with good wishes and good intention. The life of the enterprise then depends on continuous, daily cooperation and adjustment.
>
> From this point of view, the heart of the collective agreement—indeed, of collective bargaining—is the process for continuous joint consideration and adjustment of plant problems. And it is this feature which indicates the great difference between the collective labor agreement and commercial contracts generally. The latter are concerned primarily with ''end results''; the former, with continuous process.
>
> *Source:* Harry Schulman and Neil W. Chamberlain, Cases on Labor Relations *(Mineola, NY: Foundation Press, 1949), p. 3.*

The important point is that the union organizing process, contract negotiations, and grievance handling cannot be viewed as isolated events. What goes on in one phase of the collective-bargaining relationship is likely to influence the relationship at a later time. Consequently, when deciding on a course of action, it is necessary to consider the longer-run implications of the decision as well as the more immediate ramifications. While it may be tempting for bargainers to exercise their power fully during negotiations, it may be better to exercise restraint since the parties have to live together after the agreement is signed. This suggests that the continuous nature of the collective-bargaining relationship has the potential to serve as a moderating force. It is a factor tending to move the parties toward more cooperation and harmony as opposed to open aggression and hostility.

COLLECTIVE BARGAINING IS A DIVERSIFIED RELATIONSHIP

The nature of the collective-bargaining relationship is a function of a number of different variables such as:

> The technology employed by the firm—labor or capital intensive. This factor could influence the company's ability to keep operating during a strike by using supervisors or by hiring replacements for strikers.
>
> Product market considerations which could influence the ability of the firm to pass higher costs on to the consumer by raising prices.

Labor market factors such as the unemployment rate and the mobility of workers. For example, if unemployment was low, an employer may have a difficult time hiring replacements for strikers. At the same time, striking employees would be more likely to find part-time employment, thereby increasing their ability to stay out on strike.

The firm's administrative structure (e.g., centralized versus decentralized) could influence the rate with which grievances are settled. In a highly centralized company, grievances may have to be handled at higher organizational levels than in a decentralized firm. As a result, it may take longer for grievances to be resolved.

Union politics could influence the relationship since political problems within the labor organization could interfere with the leadership's ability to negotiate with management.

Public policy differentially affects the various industries. While a nationwide railroad strike could elicit government intervention, it is unlikely that a nationwide shut down of furriers would draw much attention from government.

Tradition is a factor which can either promote or inhibit a sound collective-bargaining relationship. For example, the United Mine Workers Union has a long tradition of "no contract, no work." Management knows that if an agreement is not reached by the contract's expiration date, a strike will follow.

Because bargaining units can differ with respect to one or more of these variables, tremendous diversity in collective-bargaining relationships is found in the United States. Consequently, labor and management will have to strive to establish a relationship that works, given their situation. It will probably be difficult for the parties to draw too extensively from the experiences of other bargaining units when defining the terms of their relationship.

COLLECTIVE BARGAINING IS AN EVOLUTIONARY OR DYNAMIC RELATIONSHIP

The quality of the collective-bargaining relationship is not static. It will change over time. As long as the collective-bargaining relationship is determined by the interactions of a number of different variables, a change in any one of the variables can alter the basic characteristics of the relationship. This means that the parties will have to work continually to redefine the terms of their interactions as their environment changes. The parties need to recognize that practices that were effective in the past may be ineffective in the future. Also, it cannot be assumed that a solid collective-bargaining relationship will persist over time. The parties cannot ignore the quality of their relationship. They will have to work at maintaining or improving it in light of an ever-changing environment.

COLLECTIVE BARGAINING IS AN ESSENTIALLY PRIVATE RELATIONSHIP

As has already been discussed, a number of pieces of legislation help define the environment in which the parties interact. While the parties are largely free to define the terms of their interaction, they cannot ignore the public policy. As previously discussed, the national labor policy establishes many of the rules of conduct under which the parties interact. However, the determination of most substantive matters such as wages and fringe benefits are left to the negotiations between labor and management.

In summary, the parties enter into a collective-bargaining relationship to resolve conflicts inevitably developing between labor and management. This relationship has a number of characteristics influencing the nature of the interactions between the parties. Periodically, labor and management attempt to redefine the terms of their agreement. Each side has a set of objectives it seeks. Each side knows it will not be able to secure its objectives totally. Through the process of negotiations, the parties will explore a wide variety of alternative settlements. From all the alternative settlements available to the negotiators, they will find one that is mutually acceptable. Our attention now turns to an examination of an approach that will identify the factors influencing the nature of the final agreement.

Bargaining Power: The Moving Force

Why does the final agreement take the form that it does? In some situations, management appears to more fully achieve its objectives. In other situations, the terms of the final agreement indicate the union was better able to meet its bargaining goals. To a substantial degree, the form of the final agreement reflects the relative bargaining power of the parties. The view taken here is that bargaining power is the effective force behind the whole collective-bargaining relationship and the process of intergroup agreement.[6]

THE AREA OF INTERDEPENDENCY

For the purpose of simplicity, it is assumed that the union and management are negotiating a contract to encompass one issue—a wage rate to be paid to a homogeneous work force. The range of possible wage rates on which the parties could agree is bounded at the lower end of the continuum by the governmentally imposed minimum wage. Theoretically, no upper limit to the wage settlement exists.

In practice, however, there is a relatively limited range to the possible wage rate increases acceptable to the parties. The lower limit to the range of possible settlements is marked by the employer's estimate of the lowest wage rate needed to attract, maintain, and motivate a work force of a desired quality. An upper limit to the range of possible settlements is also present above which the union will not press. The union recognizes that at some wage rate, labor costs become so high that the employer will automate, relocate, or even go out of business. In other words, unions must be concerned about the unemployment of their membership as they press for wage increases. With these ideas in mind, two points can be identified that define the area of interdependency; the most fundamental limit to union-management conflict.[7] Fig. 8.1 depicts the boundaries to the area of interdependency. Given this

THE COLLECTIVE BARGAINING PROCESS

Fig. 8.1 *Area of Interdependency*

```
                Area of Interdependency
                  ⏞
                ──┼──────┼── continuum of wage settlements
                  a      b
```

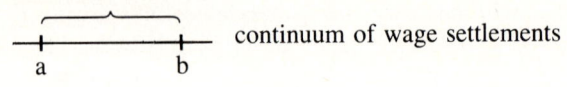

a—This point represents a wage rate below which the employer will not press for fear of being unable to attract, maintain, or motivate a work force of desired quality.

b—This point represents a wage rate above which the union will not press for fear of creating unemployment for its membership.

definition of the area of interdependency, settlement will not take place outside this range. To determine where the settlement will take place within this range, additional information is needed.

SETTLEMENT RANGE

Within the area of interdependency, two additional points known as resistance points can be identified. The union's resistance point can be defined as the wage rate below which the union would rather strike than accept. Similarly, management's resistance point is a wage above which it would take a strike rather than accept. In other words, the union's resistance point is the best agreement (lowest wage) the company can hope to attain while avoiding a strike. Management's resistance point is the best contract (highest wage) the union can receive without having to strike.

The union and management resistance points define the settlement range. If management's resistance point (MRP) is greater than the union's resistance point (URP), there is a positive settlement range as indicated in Fig. 8.2. Within a positive settlement range, any contract value is more acceptable to both parties than a strike, and therefore, agreement is possible.

Fig. 8.3 depicts a negative settlement range in which management's resistance point (MRP) is lower than the union's (URP). In this situation, the likelihood of a strike is very great unless one or both of the parties alter their resistance points. As

Fig. 8.2 *Positive Settlement Range*

```
              Positive Settlement Range
                   ⏞
                ──┼──────┼── range of contract values
                  URP    MRP
```

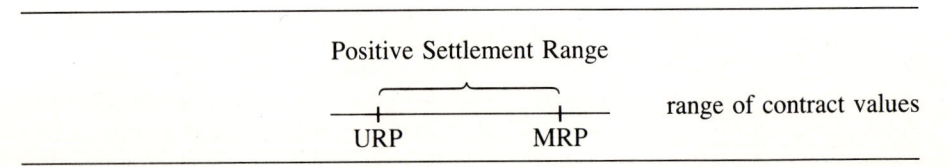

Fig. 8.3 *Negative Settlement Range*

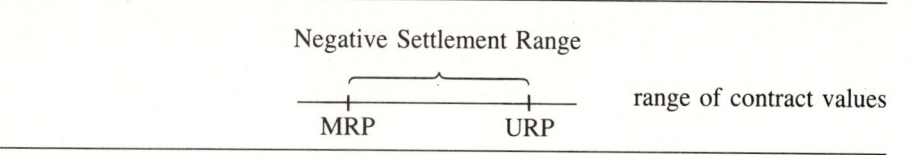

```
                  Negative Settlement Range
                  ⌒‾‾‾‾‾‾‾‾‾‾‾‾‾‾‾⌒
          ────────+───────────────+────────  range of contract values
                 MRP             URP
```

can be seen from Fig. 8.3 and the definition of resistance points, management would rather take a strike than pay a wage greater than MRP and the union would rather strike than take a wage lower than URP. Unless the parties alter their positions during the course of negotiations, a strike is most likely.

A DEFINITION OF BARGAINING POWER

Given the definition of a positive settlement range, it is known that a number of possible settlement points are available. From these values comprising the settlement range, the task for both union and management negotiators is to reach an agreement as close to the other bargainer's resistance point as possible. By so doing, the bargainer will achieve the best agreement possible without having a strike. Within the settlement range, it is the relative bargaining power of the parties as well as their negotiating ability that determines where the final settlement will be.[8]

Bargaining power can be defined as the ability to secure another's agreement on one's own terms.[9] In other words, the union's bargaining power is management's willingness to accept the union's demands. Similarly, management's bargaining power can be viewed in terms of the union's willingness to accept management's demands. The question now becomes: What factors influence the parties' willingness to accept terms proposed by the other side? The answer to this question rests in an examination of each bargainer's costs of disagreeing with the other bargainer's demands relative to the costs of agreeing with them.

Fig. 8.4 summarizes this view of bargaining power. This approach focusing on each bargainers' costs of disagreeing relative to the costs of agreeing does not allow

Fig. 8.4 *Management and Union Bargaining Power*

$$\text{Management's Bargaining Power} = \frac{\text{Union's Costs of Disagreeing with Management's Terms}}{\text{Union's Costs of Agreeing with Management's Terms}}$$

$$\text{Union's Bargaining Power} = \frac{\text{Management's Costs of Disagreeing with Union's Terms}}{\text{Management's Costs of Agreeing with Union's Terms}}$$

for a definitive determination of where within the settlement ranges the final agreement will take place. However, this approach does allow for attention to be focused on the forces motivating the parties to make concessions to the other bargainer or to refuse to accept the other's demands. Also, a better understanding of the strategies and tactics observed during negotiations is facilitated by this approach. Much of what goes on during preparations for negotiations and during the bargaining process itself is intended to manipulate costs of agreeing and disagreeing.

COSTS OF AGREEING

When discussing bargaining power, the term "cost" is used in a very general sense to describe a disadvantage. A disadvantage can be either economic or noneconomic; that is, costs that can be measured in terms of dollars as well as those that cannot. It has been pointed out that:

> The sort of balancing of costs which is contemplated in the definition of bargaining power does not require measurement of costs in any arithmetical sense, however, the balancing of incommensurable items may be accomplished in the same way that oranges may be balanced against apples on a consumer's indifference map. What these costs of agreement and disagreement may be to the bargainers cannot be known precisely enough to permit balancing, except through the exploratory process of negotiations. Through negotiating the feasible and infeasible, combinations become apparent.[10]

COSTS OF DISAGREEING

The strike is the primary mechanism used by a union to impose costs on an employer for refusing to accept the union's terms. It has been a long-held view that the essence of a union's bargaining power is the ability to "hurt" the employer. In its simplest form, a union's bargaining power is determined by its ability to impose costs on management by withholding the workers' services through the strike mechanism. Consequently, the ability of the parties to strike from the union's perspective and take a strike from management's perspective is a major determinant of their relative bargaining power. While the union seeks to increase the effectiveness of the strike, the employer endeavors to minimize the adverse effects of the strike on its operation.

FACTORS INFLUENCING THE UNION'S ABILITY TO STRIKE

Although the strike weapon will be discussed again in Chapter 9, a number of aspects of strikes will be examined now and related to the bargaining power of the parties. There are several factors within the control of the union that can influence its ability to strike and impose costs on the employer for refusing to accept its conditions. Examples include:

Internal union politics. It is important for the union leadership to minimize factional disputes within their organization. By so doing, they can increase the likelihood that a substantial proportion of the membership will abide by their call to strike. Also, unity will decrease the probability, once on strike, that groups will return to work prior to an agreement being reached.

Strike funds. The union can increase the ability of its membership to engage in a prolonged strike by providing workers with some compensation during the strike. By accumulating a large strike fund through the collection of membership dues and lining up financial support from other labor organizations, the union can minimize the adverse economic consequences of striking. Additionally, the union can assume the cost of insurance programs offered by the employer that would otherwise lapse during a strike. This should help insure the workers some measure of economic security while away from the job.

Financial responsibility on the part of the membership. To a large degree, a union's ability to engage in a lengthy strike is a function of the workers' ability to survive financially while on strike. To facilitate this, the union could keep its membership informed about their eligibility for food stamps and other state and federal aid. The union could also encourage local merchants and banks to extend credit to striking employees. In the longer run, unions can help their members prepare for strikes. By encouraging members to save some of their income while working or by providing financial counseling, the union can help insure that the membership will have some savings to help buffer them from the financial problems often experienced during a strike.

Other unions' willingness to honor the picket line. Such action could prevent the delivery of raw materials or the shipping of finished products. As a result, the employer may not be able to operate during the strike, thereby increasing its costs associated with the strike.

FACTORS INFLUENCING MANAGEMENT'S ABILITY TO TAKE A STRIKE

While there are some factors within the union's control that increase its ability to strike and impose costs on management, management has alternatives available to it to help immunize itself from the strike. Some of these actions include:

Increased inventories in anticipation of a strike. Prior to the strike, the employer can build up inventories so that the strike will not adversely affect their customers. If the firm can ship products or if the customers can work from inventories during the strike, the union's strike activity will be relatively less disruptive than if inventories were not available.

Trained supervisors to run the facility. This option is particularly relevant for organizations that are automated or capital-intensive such as a telephone company or oil refinery. By being able to keep the organization operational, the strike will have less impact on the revenues of the firm than if it was entirely shut down.

Improve the financial position of the firm. The primary intention of most strikes is to create financial hardships by interrupting the revenues of a firm by stopping production. To help stabilize the financial position of the firm during a strike, several options are available to the employer. It is possible to line up short-term loans from a bank or other type of lending institution. Alternatively, in anticipation of a strike, a firm could increase its short-term financial reserves. For example, management could defer long-term investments in capital goods such as equipment or facilities; investing instead in short-term investments such as treasury bills. In the event of a strike, the firm could then offset the loss in revenues by liquidating its short-term reserves.

Strike insurance. Strike insurance can be viewed as an employer's mutual-aid pact. Employers can contribute to a fund from which payments are made to individual companies while on strike. Alternatively, employers can enter into a formal agreement through which a proportion of the increased revenues earned by firms in the industry not on strike and attributable to increases in business caused by the strike are returned to the firm on strike. Another approach is for employers to purchase insurance from an insurance company. In the event of a strike, the insurance company pays the struck employer some predetermined sum of money. This approach

Strike insurance can prolong strikes. The strike interrupting the 1981 baseball season did not end until the strike insurance purchased by the ball club owners expired.

was taken by baseball club owners during the 1981 baseball strike. In anticipation of a strike, the owners contributed 2 percent of their gross receipts into a fund that was ultimately valued at $15 million. They also purchased a 50 million dollar business interruption insurance policy from Lloyds of London for two million dollars. The insurance plan was designed to take effect after 150 games were missed. The plan compensated club owners at a rate of $100,000 per game not played due to a strike. Up until the time the insurance policy began compensating the owners, they were able to draw funds from their $15 million strike fund.[11]

Strike insurance appears to increase the firm's ability to stay out on strike. The airline industry worked under the Mutual Aid Agreement (MAA) for approximately twenty years (from 1958–1978). As the benefits paid to firms on strike became more generous, the length of strikes in the industry tended to increase.[12] Because of the disruptive effect of the MAA, Congress placed stringent limitations on the strike insurance plan in the Airline Deregulation Act of 1978.

It is interesting to note that in the 1981 baseball strike, little progress was made toward a settlement until the $50 million strike insurance plan was about to run out. Ironically, the baseball players ratified the new agreement on the same day the club owners' strike insurance plan expired.

OTHER FACTORS INFLUENCING THE PARTIES' ABILITY TO STRIKE AND TAKE A STRIKE

In addition to factors largely within the control of either union or management, a number of other factors beyond the control of the parties to the labor dispute affect their ability to strike and take a strike. To a degree, these are environmental factors such as:

Labor market conditions. Under loose labor market conditions, that is, relatively high unemployment, an employer could hire replacements for the strikers to keep the facility operational, thereby minimizing the effects of a strike. Such a tactic would be much more difficult for an employer to utilize if unemployment was relatively low. However, in tight labor markets, that is, with low unemployment rates, a union's ability to strike could be enhanced. This is because the availability of part-time or alternative full-time employment for the workers on strike could lengthen the time they could afford to stay out on strike.

Product market considerations. When looking at the strike weapon, consideration must be given to the nature of the product market in which the firm competes. If the industry is highly competitive, a firm on strike could permanently lose customers to the competition. Knowledge of the long-term loss of revenues due to a decrease in customers could increase management's costs of disagreeing with the union. Alternatively, if the firm offers a product or service for which there are no acceptable substitutes available, the loss of revenues attributable to the strike will not be permanent. Instead, they will be deferred to a time when production is re-established. Knowledge that the revenues are not permanently lost, only deferred, decreases the effectiveness of the strike.

The nature of the workers involved. If the workers involved in the labor dispute hold key positions within the firm, the strike could disrupt the entire operation. Chamberlain and Kuhn cite the example of powerhouse employees. If the small number of powerhouse employees go on strike, the entire facility could be shut down. Consequently, the cost of disagreeing with the union's demands could be substantial.[13] If, however, the firm could operate without the striking workers or if the employees involved in the labor dispute could be easily replaced, then the employer is relatively immune from the strike.

PROCEDURAL FACTORS INFLUENCING THE PARTIES' ABILITY TO STRIKE AND TAKE A STRIKE

Procedural issues negotiated by the parties can also affect their ability to strike or take a strike. Procedural issues concern factors such as the timing of strike activities as well as the definition of who are the participants in the labor dispute. Examples of procedural issues include:

The contract's expiration date. Since the purpose of a strike is to impose economic costs on an employer while minimizing the financial burden on the striking workers, the contract expiration date is a key concern. Unions will endeavor to have the contract expire during the employer's peak season such as early summer in the construction industry, or early fall (to coincide with new model introductions) in the automobile industry. The employer's costs of disagreeing are relatively lower if the strike happens to coincide with the company's off season. Also, the union will try to make sure the contract does not expire at a time that is inconvenient to its membership. For example, it is unlikely for a union to support a contract expiration date coinciding with the Christmas holidays, when the rank-and-file membership can least afford to strike.

A common expiration date. The ability to strike an individual plant is, to a degree, a function of the effect of the strike on the rest of the firm, or perhaps, the industry. For example, a union striking a single plant of a large, multiproduct firm such as General Electric is likely to impose relatively minor costs on the firm. However, if the unions at all General Electric plants could strike at the same time because of a common expiration date, then the company's costs of disagreeing would increase substantially. Similarly, if a union could shut down an entire industry by having a common expiration date on contracts with the firms in that industry, greater economic pressures could come to bear on the employers.

It should be recognized that there are also problems for a union associated with the common expiration date. Instead of having a portion of its membership on strike, all the workers would be away from the job. Consequently, a strike fund would not go as far and "staying power," that is, the ability of the union members to engage in a long strike, would be diminished. One probable reason why the United Automobile Workers negotiate with one auto manufacturer at a time is that, in the event of a strike, only a portion of its membership would be tapping the strike fund.

Composition of the bargaining team. Under certain circumstances, it may be within the self-interest of the union and management to coordinate its bargaining efforts with others. For example, when a number of unions engage in collective bargaining with a large employer with diverse product lines, some coordination among the unions could be useful. Similarly, in industries such as trucking where a large number of relatively small employers deal with the large, powerful International Brotherhood of Teamsters, the development of multiemployer bargaining teams could enhance the employers' bargaining power.

When one side of the bargaining relationship is unified while the other is not, there is the chance for the large union or employer to use "divide and conquer" tactics. It has been written that:

> When each union bargains separately with the same employer, experience shows that management will often take advantage of this situation and play off one union against the other, or the multiplicity of negotiations and expiration dates may produce a chaotic, unmanageable bargaining relationship. In either case, the members of unions in the company suffer.[14]

Similar tactics can be directed against small employers by unions. When the Teamsters were trying to obtain a nationwide master labor agreement during the early 1960s, employers developed multiemployer bargaining in an effort to resist union pressures. When discussing the movement toward a national agreement, it was stated:

> Hoffa's most successful bargaining technique appears to have been based on a divide and conquer strategy. These strike threats were selective and never included all employers in an area. In most cases, although association bargaining existed, individual truckers have been found who were willing to sign before the association had agreed (even when these truckers were represented by the association), with the result that the truckers respect the union and Hoffa and direct their ill will at their fellow truckers.[15]

To decrease the likelihood that one side will exploit the other side's "weakest link," employers and unions can alter the structure of their bargaining teams. When several unions enter into a cooperative effort to make their bargaining with a large employer more effective, this is known as coordinated or coalition bargaining. This form of bargaining was originally utilized by a group of eight unions that were negotiating with General Electric and Westinghouse in 1966. The objectives of the coalition of unions were described as follows:

> The IUE and seven other international unions whose locals also had agreements with General Electric formed a Committee on Collective Bargaining (CCB). This was an outgrowth of the union's dissatisfaction with the traditional separate negotiations between the company and the different unions, in which the unions believed General Electric was playing each union against the other. The avowed purposes of the members of CCB were to coordinate bargaining in 1966 with GE and its chief competitor, Westinghouse, to formulate national goals and otherwise support one another.[16]

When a number of employers enter into negotiations with a national union, this is known as multiemployer bargaining. Such an arrangement leads to a master agreement defining the basic conditions of employment. Then, subsidiary agreements can be negotiated between local unions and individual companies to handle specific problems.[17]

In sum, the strike or the threat of a strike is the primary device by which union and management costs of disagreeing can be influenced. A strike causes the union membership to lose income while the employer loses production and revenue. The cost of disagreeing with the terms offered by the other bargainer, and therefore, the parties' bargaining power can be influenced by a number of factors discussed above that affect a union's ability to strike and an employer's ability to take a strike.

COSTS OF AGREEING

The cost of agreeing with the other bargainer's demands is the other major determinant of bargaining power. One of the interesting aspects of the definition of bargaining power used herein is that bargaining power is relative to what is being bargained. For example, if a union proposed an excessively large change in wages, its bargaining power would be weakened because of management's high cost of agreement. In other words, management is unlikely to agree to the union's demand, and therefore, the union's bargaining power is diminished. If, on the other hand, the union proposed a very modest wage increase, its bargaining power would be enhanced since management would be willing to accept the union's terms. Hopefully, it can be seen that bargaining power varies with the demands.

The costs of agreeing can be placed into three categories: (1) direct costs of agreement; (2) secondary costs of agreement; and (3) nonmarket costs of agreement.[18]

Direct costs of agreement. The direct costs of agreement are the specific costs attributable to the contract provisions for the workers in the bargaining unit. These costs include matters such as wage increases, additional holidays, and longer vacations. The greater the gap between the cost of the union's proposals and the employer's bargaining objectives, the greater the direct costs of agreement.[19] Not only must the cost of the contract terms be considered, the duration of the provisions should be built into the deliberations. Typically, once a provision is written into a labor agreement, it is there to stay. Consequently, the cost of agreement should include the costs for the contract period as well as for some indefinite future periods.

Secondary costs of agreement. The direct costs of agreement are those associated with the contract terms involving the workers subject to the labor agreement. Secondary costs are attributable to the increased benefits received by the company's other employees not working under the contract. For example, it is quite likely that benefits received by one union will have to be extended to other unions bargaining with the company. Also, the improvements will have to be extended to nonunion workers such as clerical employees, supervisors, and higher levels of management.

Nonmarket costs of agreement. Nonmarket costs are those that typically cannot be expressed in economic terms. They usually involve matters of principle. Union security clauses and check-off of union dues provisions are examples of bargainable issues that have few, if any, economic costs but could be the subject of much disagreement because of the nonmarket costs. It is possible for management to oppose such provisions because they interfere with the personal freedom of their workers, not because of the economic costs associated with issues. Although it is not possible to build nonmarket factors into their deliberations in a quantitative sense, they can be factored into the calculations of the cost of agreement in a subjective fashion.

SUMMARY OF BARGAINING POWER

In this section, bargaining power has been defined as the ability to secure the other's agreement to one's own terms. When applied to collective bargaining, this definition suggests that a union can increase its bargaining power by increasing management's cost of disagreeing, by decreasing management's cost of agreeing, or through some combination of both approaches. However, it is not always possible to predict the effect of a change in demands on the relative bargaining power of the parties. This is because a change in demands could affect some other variable influencing bargaining power. For example, during a period of rapidly rising prices, the union drops its demand for a cost-of-living agreement. It cannot be assumed that by decreasing management's cost of agreement, the union will necessarily increase its bargaining power. It is necessary also to examine the effect of the decrease in demand on the management's cost of disagreeing. It is possible that by dropping its proposal for a cost-of-living agreement, the membership is no longer willing to strike. Therefore, while decreasing management's cost of agreeing, the union also decreased management's cost of disagreeing. Consequently, the union may not have secured an increase in bargaining power by lowering its demands.

Bargaining power is a deceptively simple concept. It was not presented to allow you to determine definitively where within the settlement range the parties will finally reach agreement. This cannot be done. Bargaining power was discussed to highlight a number of variables that can influence where the final settlement will take place. In a very general sense, this approach also helps identify some of the factors that could cause the final agreement to be more favorable to one party as opposed to another.

In addition to bargaining power, the shape of the final agreement is determined by the negotiating skills of the bargainers. Through the process of negotiations, the parties' perceived costs of agreeing and disagreeing can be clarified and manipulated as the bargainers search for agreement. Attention now turns to an examination of the behavioral aspects of the negotiation process.

Strategy and Tactics of Negotiations

The concept of bargaining power encompasses many of the variables that determine the nature of the final agreement. Many of the variables determining the parties' bargaining power, and therefore, the shape of the final agreement, can be manipulated at the bargaining table. Through the negotiation process, it is possible to alter the perceived costs of agreeing and disagreeing, both one's own as well as those of the other bargainer.

At the outset of negotiations, the positions of the parties are usually far apart. Through the collective bargaining process, the parties change positions and come closer together. This process of change has been described as follows:

> Parties starting far apart must change their positions if there is to be any agreement. But changing a position is difficult because it may harden the other side and create the hope, if not the expectation, that the other party will go all the way and close any gap between the two sides. It is not easy for a negotiator to drop a demand he has been arguing for with great enthusiasm without casting some doubt on positions taken on other issues as well. Changing positions is at the heart of the collective bargaining process and the way in which a negotiator handles these problems distinguishes a skilled veteran from a novice.[20]

The processes by which labor and management attain a mutually acceptable agreement are not completely understood. This is probably because most negotiations take place in private. Once an agreement is reached, attention usually turns to the settlement and not the process that led to the contract.[21] Fortunately, the behavioral aspects of collective bargaining have been intensively examined by Walton and McKersie in their classic book, *A Behavioral Theory of Labor Negotiations*.[22] In order to obtain a better understanding of the process by which labor and management reach agreement, the framework developed by Walton and McKersie will be used.

Walton and McKersie view labor negotiations as a process through which labor and management attempt to define or redefine the terms of their interdependence.[23] They contend that labor negotiations are comprised of four subsystems of activity, each with its own function for the parties, an internal logic, and tactics. They refer to these subsystems as distributive bargaining, integrative bargaining, attitudinal structuring, and intraorganizational bargaining.

DISTRIBUTIVE BARGAINING

Distributive bargaining is most likely to be used by the parties when they perceive themselves pursuing incompatible goals. This probably occurs when they are negotiating over the allocation of a scarce resource such as money. Under such circumstances, the parties believe they are negotiating over a fixed amount that must be allocated between union and management. Since the total amount is fixed, a gain by one party must be matched by a loss to the other. Consequently, the potential for conflict is great. Distributive bargaining is basic to labor negotiations since it can involve issues of vital importance to both the union and the company such as wages, hours, and working conditions.

Distributive bargaining tactics. Before discussing the tactics of distributive bargaining, it is necessary to briefly review the concept of settlement range. A positive settlement range is defined by the parties' resistance points and describes an area in which an agreement is possible without a strike. The tactical assignment for the negotiators is to secure an agreement as close as possible to the other bargainer's resistance point. This is the best contract a bargainer can obtain without having a strike.

Notice that the settlement range depicts a distributive bargaining situation. The settlement range is a fixed amount that is allocated between the parties through bargaining. Whatever one party gets constitutes a loss for the other bargainer.

A number of tactics can be used by negotiators when engaged in distributive bargaining. These tactics are designed to manipulate the other bargainer's costs of agreeing and disagreeing as well as the other bargainer's perceptions of the first party's costs of agreeing and disagreeing. While this section does not provide an exhaustive discussion of the tactics of distributive bargaining, it will highlight some of the factors underlying several of the most frequently observed bargaining tactics.

Padding the initial list of demands. Typically, the parties enter negotiations with a list of demands greatly exceeding their expectations. Both parties know that the other bargainer does not expect to receive all that is requested and that it will be necessary to make a number of concessions. Regardless, the parties will initially put forth a "laundry list" of proposals.

There are several reasons for this. First, there are tactical reasons. At the outset of negotiations, the parties want to be able to disguise their resistance point while searching for the other bargainer's resistance point. While the other bargainers are trying to determine your "real" demands, you have the opportunity to explore for their resistance point. It is important to identify the other bargainers' resistance point since it represents the best contract you can obtain without having to strike.

In addition to the tactical reasons for padding your initial list of demands, there are political reasons, especially for the union. As will be discussed in more detail in Chapter 9, a union typically goes to its rank-and-file membership to determine its bargaining demands. While the rank and file can be the source of many useful suggestions, it can also generate a number of demands which the negotiators know cannot or should not be pursued in the upcoming bargaining sessions. Rather than telling the rank and file that their ideas cannot be used, the negotiators can include them on their initial list of demands. Once negotiations start, the union negotiators can then make concessions on those issues. Later, they can go back to the membership, telling them that they really tried to pursue the rank and file's demands but that the company was just too resistant on those issues. By so doing, the union leadership avoids the political problems associated with telling the rank and file that their demands will not be pursued during negotiations. It should also be noted that the issues that pad the list of demands can also be used as "trading" stock. While it is recognized that the issues are low priority, they might be traded for something else.

Bluffing. Bluffing is an attempt to convince the other bargainer that something is more or less important to you than it actually is. For example, the union could state that if the company does not agree to its wage demand of $.50/hour wage increase, it will strike. In reality, the union's resistance point on the wage issue could be $.25/hour. If the union negotiators can convince the company that its resistance point is $.50/hour, then the union may be able to obtain a settlement more favorable to itself than otherwise may be possible. Cullen cites several advantages of using bluffing tactics as opposed to relying solely on good faith and rational discussion:[24]

- Through the use of bluffing tactics, the parties have room to maneuver during negotiations. This allows both company and union bargainers to work toward the settlement most favorable to their side.
- Many workers join unions because they do not like management unilaterally determining their conditions of employment. The name calling and emotionalism that can be associated with the use of bluffing tactics give the parties the impression they are "winning" something from the determined opposition. This is likely to make the final agreement more acceptable to the parties.
- The "slam-bang" negotiating sessions likely to emerge when the parties rely heavily on bluffing tactics can provide a healthy outlet for the tensions and frustrations that build up between workers and management.

Heavy reliance on the strike threat. Given the importance of the issues such as wages and job security discussed during distributive bargaining, the parties are likely to underscore their demands by expressing their willingness to strike or take a strike. It is known from the discussion of bargaining power that the strike is a major factor affecting the parties' costs of disagreeing. During distributive bargaining, the parties will convey information concerning their preparation for the strike and their willingness to resort to a strike if necessary.

Other considerations. The tactics described above are used in conjunction with rational discussion. During distributive bargaining, both parties will attempt to alter the other parties' perceptions of the costs of agreeing and disagreeing. For example, the union could argue that its wage demands are less costly than they might appear since with the higher wage, productivity will go up, and absenteeism, tardiness, and turnover will decline. Similarly, management could respond to a union's proposal for heavier reliance on seniority when making promotions by arguing that the union, by pushing such an issue, will be creating political problems for itself by alienating the younger workers.

In summary, when engaging in distributive bargaining, the parties have a number of tactics available to them ranging from rational discussion to bluffing and the use of threats. In general, the parties will be motivated to disguise or distort their bargaining positions. This causes them to withhold information or deliberately misrepresent their position to the other side. While such tactics may increase the likelihood of obtaining a settlement more favorable to one's side, the parties run the risk of intensifying the conflict between them.

INTEGRATIVE BARGAINING

Walton and McKersie describe integrative bargaining as a "system" of activities that is instrumental to the attainment of objectives that are not in fundamental conflict with those of the other party and which, therefore, can be integrated to some degree.[25] Integrative bargaining usually involves problems facing the parties. By resolving the problem, both parties may benefit. Alternatively, the resolution of the problem may yield benefits to only one of the parties while the other bargainer experiences limited or no costs. Plant safety could be an issue amenable to integrative bargaining. By improving plant safety, union members secure a safer, healthier work environment. At the same time, the company may benefit by decreased turnover, and perhaps, lower insurance and worker's compensation premiums. Similarly, both parties could benefit by resolving union security problems. For example, by negotiating a union shop provision, a union does not have to devote its resources to organizing new employees continuously. Consequently, the union leadership can spend more time working with management to develop a stronger, more effective collective-bargaining relationship. As a result, both parties can benefit by including a union shop provision in the labor agreement.

Integrative bargaining is a form of problem solving. Consequently, it can be described in terms of a three-step problem-solving model:

1. Identify the problem.
2. Identify alternative solutions to the problem and the consequences of the alternatives.
3. Preference order the solutions and then, select a course of action.[26]

As can be seen, the task before the negotiator in integrative bargaining is basically different than the situation confronting a negotiator involved in distributive bargaining. Instead of competing over the allocation of a scarce resource, the negotiators are attempting to resolve a problem. The solution to the problem has the potential to benefit both parties. Instead of being motivated to withhold or distort information and threaten or intimidate the other bargainer as in distributive situations, there are incentives for the negotiators to utilize a different set of tactics when engaged in integrative bargaining.

When the parties are involved in integrative bargaining, the resolution of the problem confronting the parties requires the negotiators to be open, honest, and willing to share information concerning their preferences for the alternative solutions to the problem. When engaged in integrative bargaining, the parties confront two dilemmas: the dilemma of openness and honesty, and the dilemma of trust.[27]

Dilemma of openness and honesty. For integrative bargaining to take place, there must be an exchange of information. The parties must decide how frank or deceitful to be when communicating with the other side. Integrative bargaining requires the parties to share the information they have. However, being completely frank could commit you to a position from which it is difficult to move later in negotiations. Also, if you are open and honest while the other bargainer is being deceptive, you run the risk of being exploited. For integrative bargaining to be effective, the dilemma of openness and honesty must be resolved in favor of sharing the information needed to explore fully the problems of joint concern.

Dilemma of trust. Related to the dilemma of openness and honesty is the dilemma of trust. It has been written:

> To believe everything the other party says is to place one's fate in his hands and to jeopardize full satisfaction of one's own interests. . . . On the other hand, to believe nothing that the other says is to eliminate the possibility of accepting any relationship with him.[28]

During the collective-bargaining process, both parties will have to make decisions concerning the truthfulness of the other bargainer's statements.

When involved in integrative bargaining, the task for the negotiators is to identify the best solution to the problem confronting them. This requires a free flow of accurate information from both sides. To do so, the parties must resolve the dilemma of openness and honesty as well as the dilemma of trust. The parties need to believe little or no risk is attached to sharing information and accepting the information provided by the other bargainer. Failure to resolve the dilemmas in favor of openness, honesty, and trust will preclude the use of integrative bargaining and force the parties into a distributive bargaining situation. By doing so, the parties lose the opportunity for mutual gain available to them through integrative bargaining.

ATTITUDINAL STRUCTURING

Both distributive and integrative bargaining have outputs. Distributive bargaining results in the allocation of some fixed quantity such as the revenues of the firm between labor and management. Successful integrative bargaining results in the resolution of some mutual problem. In addition to these outcomes, collective bargaining can have a third result—the maintenance or modification of attitudes held by the parties toward each other.[29] These attitudes help define the relationship existing between the parties. Attitudinal structuring refers to the bargaining intended to maintain or change these attitudes, and in turn, maintain or change the nature of the relationship between the parties.

Walton and McKersie argue that the bargaining relationship existing between labor and management can be characterized in several different ways. This approach is similar to one described in Chapter 5 concerning management attitudes toward unions. However, Walton and McKersie go beyond the presentation of categories of behaviors by identifying the factors underlying these categories. Walton and McKersie identify five basic relationship patterns:

- Conflict—the parties deal with each other only because it is legally mandated. They will take full advantage of the opportunity to defeat or destroy the other bargainer.
- Containment-Aggression—while the parties grudgingly accept each other, they tend to be militant in their attitudes toward each other.
- Accommodation—the parties accept each other, have adjusted to each other and have developed ways to perform the required functions and settle disputes.

- Cooperation—characterized by complete acceptance of each other which leads to a willingness to discuss mutual concerns far beyond the traditional areas of wages, hours, and conditions.
- Collusion—labor and management form a coalition through which they pursue common objectives.[30]

The particular relationship pattern established by the parties will be largely determined by a combination of several attitudinal dimensions:

- Motivation orientation—this refers to the general attitude of the parties toward each other. There are three basic orientations:

1. A competitive orientation is indicated by the parties' desire to defeat the other bargainer.
2. An individualistic orientation exists when the parties pursue their own self-interests without motivation to help or obstruct the other bargainer.
3. If a cooperative orientation is present, bargainers are concerned about the welfare of the other party as well as their own.

- Beliefs about the other bargainer's legitimacy; that is, does the other party have a legitimate role to play?
- Feelings of trust toward the other bargainer.
- Feelings of friendliness or hostility toward the other bargainer.[31]

These interrelated dimensions influence the relationship pattern existing between the parties, which in turn, determines the basic nature of their joint dealings. Exhibit 8.2 relates the attitudinal dimensions to the relationship patterns and describes the general nature of each relationship pattern.

Walton and McKersie cite four basic reasons why the relationship pattern is important to the parties. First, the relationship may be valued in its own right. Some parties may take pride in a positive bargaining relationship characterized by friendliness, mutual trust, and cooperation. Others, for personal or ideological reasons, may prefer to maintain a relationship characterized by much conflict.

Second, the relationship pattern can have implications for the administration of the contract. As discussed at the outset of this chapter, collective bargaining is a continuous relationship. What goes on during the negotiation of a new contract will probably have an effect on subsequent labor-management relations. The relationship pattern characterizing negotiations can spill over and influence the manner in which grievances and other disputes arising during the life of the contract are handled.

Third, the relationship pattern can affect future rounds of negotiation. Walton and McKersie state as a general proposition that as the parties move from the competitive end of the scale to the more cooperative end, they tend to limit the areas of distributive bargaining and expand the number of areas subject to integrative bargaining.

EXHIBIT 8.2
Attitudinal Components of the Relationship Patterns

Attitudinal dimensions	Pattern of Relationship					
	Conflict	Containment-Aggression	Accommodation	Cooperation	Collusion
Motivational orientation and action tendencies toward other	Competitive tendencies to destroy or weaken the other bargainer		Individualistic policy of "hands off"	Cooperative tendencies to assist or preserve the existing relationship	
Beliefs about legitimacy of other party	Denial of legitimacy	Grudging acknowledgment	Acceptance of status quo	Complete legitimacy	Not applicable
Level of trust in conducting affairs	Extreme distrust	Distrust	Limited trust	Extended trust	Trust based on mutual-blackmail potential
Degree of friendliness	Hate	Antagonism	Neutralism-Courteousness	Friendliness	Intimacy—"sweetheart relationship"

Source: Richard E. Walton and Robert E. McKersie, A Behavioral Theory of Labor Negotiations (New York: McGraw-Hill, 1965), p.189.

Finally, the internal organization of labor and management could affect and be affected by the relationship pattern. For example, in a situation where a union's leadership is politically insecure, they may pursue bargaining strategies intended to intensify conflict and develop a more competitive bargaining relationship. This would allow the union leaders to rally the rank and file in the face of difficult negotiations, thereby gaining support for their policies.

The relationship pattern characterizing a bargaining situation is a given at a point in time but can be changed over time. If one or both of the parties decide to change their relationship pattern, they can endeavor to do so at the bargaining table. Assume that labor and management have a relationship founded on conflict and competition. Also assume that the union leadership decides a more cooperative relationship pattern is within the self-interest of both parties. What could the union do during negotiations to move the relationship in a more cooperative direction? Walton and McKersie present two ways to help redefine the relationship.

One approach requires the union negotiators to behave in a fashion inconsistent with the management negotiators' expectations. Since the parties are in a competitive relationship, management is likely to expect the union negotiators to be uncooperative, untrustworthy, and inconsiderate of company needs. To help redefine the relationship, the union negotiators should strive to be cooperative, open, honest, trustworthy, and considerate. These behaviors put the management negotiators in a difficult situation. They expected one type of behavior and experienced something else. There is psychological discomfort associated with inconsistencies between beliefs and observations. Therefore, management is under pressure to reestablish a balance between what they believed and what they observed. To do so, it is quite possible that they will replace the beliefs that the union was untrustworthy and inconsiderate with beliefs more consistent with the union's more cooperative behavior. Once management's underlying attitudes toward the union are redefined, it is quite likely that they will interact with the union in a more cooperative fashion.

The second approach for redefining the bargaining relationship outlined by Walton and McKersie focuses on behavior rather than attitudes. This approach is based on reinforcement theory which suggests that behavior rewarded is repeated and behavior not rewarded or punished is less likely to be repeated. During negotiations, both union and company negotiators have a number of rewards that they can dispense ranging from compliments to concessions. These rewards can be used to influence the relationship pattern.

Again, assume the union negotiators want to move their relationship in a more cooperative direction. By using rewards and punishments, they could "train" the management negotiators to be more cooperative. Whenever management negotiators exhibit cooperative behavior, however minor, it could be rewarded. Similarly, conflict-producing acts could be punished. Over time, the reinforced cooperative acts are likely to be repeated more frequently while there would be a decrease in conflict-producing behaviors. As the management negotiators see themselves engaging in a more cooperative relationship pattern, it is quite possible that they will also develop more positive attitudes toward the union and its negotiators.

INTRAORGANIZATIONAL BARGAINING

While distributive and integrative bargaining and attitudinal structuring describe patterns of interaction between labor and management, intraorganizational bargaining takes place within the union and management. Intraorganizational bargaining is especially important to union negotiators. During the course of bargaining, union negotiators are under pressure to deal with factional conflicts created when various groups within their organization seek incompatible objectives during negotiations. While it is desirable to resolve the problems associated with incompatible objectives prior to negotiations, this may not be possible. Therefore, union negotiators will have to take special measures later to resolve the factional conflict and bring about membership ratification of the final agreement. This will require the negotiators to take information back to the membership in an attempt to get them to modify their expectations. By so doing, the negotiators attempt to bring the union's aspirations in line with what can realistically be obtained through bargaining.

As can be seen, the strategies and tactics of labor negotiations will vary depending on the nature of the bargaining situation. What makes collective bargaining so complex and challenging is that the behaviors exhibited in a distributive-bargaining situation may preclude the use of integrative bargaining techniques. For example, it is difficult to be open, honest, and willing to share information as required by integrative bargaining when faced with deliberate attempts by the other side to withhold or distort information as is often found in distributive-bargaining situations. It is important for the parties to keep in mind the nature of the issues being negotiated and vary their bargaining tactics accordingly.

The approach taken by the parties to collective bargaining is a function of the parties' bargaining power and negotiating skills and abilities. While the parties are relatively free to develop a bargaining relationship responsive to their specific needs, collective bargaining is subject to a number of legal restraints. Attention now turns to an examination of the legal environment in which collective bargaining takes place.

The Legal Requirements of Collective Bargaining

GOOD FAITH BARGAINING

Once a union obtains the status of the employees' exclusive bargaining representative, either voluntarily or through an NLRB-conducted certification election, the parties incur the obligation to bargain in "good faith." The mutual obligation to bargain in good faith is created by Sections 8(a)(5), 8(b)(3), and 8(d) of the National Labor Relations Act (NLRA).

Sections 8(a)(5) and 8(b)(3) make it an unfair labor practice for management and the union, respectively, to refuse to bargain collectively. Section 8(d) elaborates on the parties' obligation to bargain. Section 8(d) can be broken down into two components: a general statement of the obligation for good faith bargaining and a list of procedures that must be met. Section 8(d) specifies:

> For the purpose of this section, to bargain collectively is the performance of the mutual obligation of the employer and the representative of the employees to meet at reasonable times and confer in good faith with respect to wages, hours, and other terms and conditions of employment, or the negotiation of an agreement, or any question arising thereunder, and the execution of a written contract incorporating any agreement reached if requested by either party, but such obligation does not compel either party to agree to a proposal or require the making of a concession.

Section 8(d) also specifies that where a labor agreement is in effect, it cannot be terminated or modified unless certain procedures are followed. These procedures include:

- Giving the other party at least 60 days notice of the proposed termination or modification of the agreement.
- Offering to meet and confer with the other party in order to negotiate a new contract.
- Notifying the Federal Mediation and Conciliation Service that a dispute exists within thirty days of notifying the other party of the proposed contract termination or modification.
- Keeping the existing contract in full force without resorting to a strike or lockout for a 60 day period after notice is given to the other party.

The parties to a collective-bargaining agreement typically do not have problems abiding by the four procedural requirements found in Section 8(d). These provisions are straightforward and are designed to provide the parties ample time to negotiate over the proposed contract changes. Also, the procedural requirements of Section 8(d) help insure that the dispute resolution services of the Federal Mediation and Conciliation Service are available to the parties in a timely fashion.

The problems with Section 8(d) are associated with its opening paragraph which outlines in very broad terms the tenets of "good faith" bargaining. An examination of this provision indicates that the parties have an obligation to:

- Meet and confer at reasonable times.
- Negotiate in good faith with respect to wages, hours, or other terms and conditions of employment.
- Execute a written contract.

Additionally, the provision specifies that good faith bargaining does not require either party to agree to a proposal or make a concession.

As can be seen, Section 8(d) uses extremely broad language to define the legal obligations of the parties at the bargaining table. It has become the responsibility of the NLRB through its decisions and the courts to provide meaning to the general language of Section 8(d).

THE TENETS OF GOOD FAITH BARGAINING

Archibald Cox clearly stated the rationale behind the obligation to engage in "good faith" bargaining in the following manner:

> It was not enough for the law to compel the parties to meet and treat without passing judgment upon the quality of the negotiations. The bargaining status of a union can be destroyed by going through the motions of negotiating almost as easily as by bluntly withholding recognition. The NLRB reports are filled with cases in which a union won an election but lacked the economic power to use the strike as a weapon for compelling the employer to grant it real participation in industrial government. As long as there are unions weak enough to be talked to death, there will be employers who are tempted to engage in the forms of bargaining without the substance. The concept of "good faith" was brought into the law of collective bargaining as a solution to this problem. Even with the "good faith" requirement, approximately one-third of the first bargaining situations do not result in a signed labor agreement.[32]

"Good faith" bargaining is more a philosophy or approach to bargaining than a specific set of behaviors. In order for the parties to bargain in good faith, they must:

- Enter negotiations with an open mind, that is, without a predetermined disposition not to bargain.
- Make a sincere effort to reach an agreement on mutually acceptable terms.[33]

It is difficult to determine whether the parties are engaging in good faith bargaining. Typically, it is necessary to examine the behavior of the parties during negotiations to determine whether the parties have an open mind and sincerely want to reach agreement.

When determining whether good faith bargaining exists, the NLRB studies all relevant facts. This is known as the "totality of conduct" standard.[34] How does the NLRB distinguish between legal hard bargaining and bad faith?

> No single factor determines whether an employer or a union are bargaining in good faith with an intent to reach an agreement. Good faith is judged on the totality of a party's conduct. There are, however, certain acts that are usually considered evidence of bad faith bargaining. These include: agreeing on minor bargaining issues, but refusing to give in on any major point (such as agreeing to general contract language but maintaining a fixed position on all major economic issues); refusing to agree to provi-

sions found on most collective bargaining agreements (such as a just cause clause or seniority provision); proposing wages and benefits that are no better than those under the prior contract or before the union was certified; rejecting union proposals without making any counterproposals or indicating why the union's proposals are unacceptable; and delaying meetings.[35]

Therefore, even when no specific act violates the tenets of "good faith" bargaining, "bad faith" may be found if a review of all the facts of the case reveals that a party was not making a sincere effort to find the basis for an agreement.

It must be emphasized that good faith bargaining requires the parties to enter negotiations with an open mind and a desire to reach agreement. It does not require the parties to make a concession or to agree to any proposal. This provision of Section 8(d) gets the NLRB into an examination of the substance of the negotiations. While the NLRB will consider the making of proposals and counterproposals as an element of good faith bargaining, offering a proposal that is obviously unacceptable to the other party does not constitute bad faith bargaining unless it has the effect of precluding future negotiations.

For example, in the *White v. NLRB*[36] decision, the Fifth Circuit Court of Appeals found that an employer's demand for a broad management-rights clause in which the union would surrender the right to strike and give the employer full control over working conditions did not constitute "bad faith" bargaining. The court ruled that the insistence on a broad management rights clause was not a *per se* violation of the act. It was up to the parties to determine whether the broad management-rights clause would be in the contract, not the NLRB. The Fifth Circuit recognized, however, that it was possible for the content of proposals and counterproposals to constitute "bad faith" bargaining. The court stated:

> We do not hold that under no possible circumstances can the mere content of the various proposals and counterproposals of management and union be sufficient evidence of a want of good faith to justify a holding to that effect. We can conceive of one party to such a bargaining procedure suggesting proposals of such a nature or type or couched in such objectionable language that they would be calculated to disrupt any serious negotiations.[37]

Consequently, if the proposals or counterproposals have the effect of precluding future negotiations, or if they are so patently unacceptable as to inhibit future agreement, they are likely to be found as an indicator of bad faith bargaining.

Closely related to the concept of good faith bargaining is another term ill-defined in Section 8(d)—"meet and confer at reasonable times." The parties are expected to be willing to meet and confer at times that will not frustrate or inhibit agreement. For example, a party that repeatedly postponed the bargaining sessions or insisted, as a precondition for bargaining, that negotiations be conducted at a time (e.g., next year) or place (e.g., another city) clearly inconvenient to the other party, would probably be found to have failed in its obligation to "meet at reasonable times and confer in good faith."

SUBJECTS OF COLLECTIVE BARGAINING

As previously mentioned, Section 8(d) does not define the term "wages, hours and other terms of conditions of employment" over which the parties are expected to bargain in good faith. Over the years, this phrase has been provided meaning by board and court decisions. Three categories of bargaining subjects have been defined: mandatory, permissive, and illegal.

Mandatory subjects of bargaining. Mandatory subjects are those over which the parties must bargain in good faith. These include issues that constitute or affect wages, hours, or other terms and conditions of employment. Examples of mandatory subjects include:

- Wages.
- Hours of employment.
- Incentive pay.
- Overtime.
- Lay off and recall procedures.
- Union security clauses.
- Grievance procedures.
- Arbitration.
- Seniority.
- Safety conditions.

The list of items considered mandatory subjects of collective bargaining is lengthy and continues to grow as both labor and management develop new bargaining demands. These topics are discussed in detail in Part Four of this book. However, the mandatory subjects do not include issues typically considered managerial prerogatives such as corporate structure, size of the supervisory staff, or other business practices.[38]

Permissive subjects of bargaining. Permissive subjects of collective bargaining include issues not directly related to wages, hours, or other terms or conditions of employment. Either labor or management can raise a permissive issue during collective bargaining and the other party may voluntarily negotiate over it. However, it is an unfair labor practice to insist that a permissive subject be included in the final agreement if the other party does not want it.[39] In other words, permissive subjects can be discussed but cannot be negotiated until an impasse occurs. However, if the parties agree to include permissive issues in the labor agreement, the agreement is binding and enforceable. Examples of permissive subjects include:

- Benefits for retired employees.
- Union label agreements.
- Performance bonds for either the union or the company.
- Pricing policy.

Illegal subjects of bargaining. The third category of bargaining issues is those that are illegal. Any subject considered illegal under the NLRA or some other piece of legislation would be in this category. Examples include:

- Featherbedding.
- Discriminatory hiring halls.
- Closed shop agreements.

If one bargainer attempts to negotiate over an illegal subject, the other party can refuse to bargain over it.

In sum, the parties to a collective-bargaining relationship are obligated to negotiate in "good faith" over mandatory subjects. While permissive subjects can be discussed during negotiations on a voluntary basis, they cannot be bargained to the point of impasse. Finally, the parties are under no obligation to bargain over illegal subjects.

DURATION OF THE OBLIGATION TO BARGAIN

After a union is recognized as the employees' exclusive bargaining representative, the NLRB has applied its "one-year certification" rule. This means a union is certified for a one-year period. The rule was designed to give a union ample opportunity to demonstrate results to the employees. After that time, the employees could attempt to decertify the union if they no longer wanted the labor organization to represent them. In other words, the NLRB will assume the union represents a majority of the employees for one year. Then, the issue of majority status can again be raised.

A number of employers have attempted to avoid their bargaining obligation by stalling during the initial round of negotiations. By making negotiations appear futile, the employer could undermine the union's support in the bargaining unit. When it appeared that union support had sufficiently dissipated, the employer would then refuse to bargain. The employer would justify this position by claiming the union no longer represented a majority of the employees.

In *Brooks v. NLRB*,[40] the Supreme Court attempted to stop this practice by supporting the board's ruling that even if the union loses its majority status during the "certification year," the employer is obligated to bargain with the union for the entire year. This position was expanded by the NLRB in its *Mar-Jac Poultry Co.*[41] decision. The board ruled that if illegal employer activities delayed the bargaining process, this time would not be counted as part of the "certification year." Instead, the certification year would start after the employer's illegal activities were resolved.

NLRB REMEDIES IN GOOD FAITH BARGAINING CASES

One of the major problems in collective bargaining concerns remedies in situations involving failures to bargain in good faith. Typically, cease-and-desist orders are issued when a party has violated the tenets of good faith bargaining. In other words, the NLRB directs the offending party not to engage in the behavior indicating bad faith and to bargain in good faith.

The timeliness and adequacy of cease-and-desist orders to remedy violations of the good faith bargaining requirements have been questioned. The timeliness issue relates to the length of time it takes to obtain a remedy. On this point, it has been noted that:

> If an employer is determined to defeat the union, he can appeal the Board's decision to the court of appeals, perhaps delaying bargaining for several years. Even if the employer is eventually forced to the bargaining table, the union may have been defeated through delay.[42]

As pointed out, years can go by before an order of the board is enforced by the courts. During this time, workers are denied their basic rights under the law. The old adage, "justice delayed is justice denied," appears to apply in this situation. While the review of the board's cease-and-desist order wends its way through the courts, the employer continues to operate as if it was non-union. Consequently, workers are deprived of the rights and benefits typically associated with working under a labor agreement.

The adequacy of cease-and-desist orders in good faith bargaining cases is the other dimension of the remedy issue. The NLRB has tried to formulate remedies intended to rectify the problems created by a failure to bargain in good faith. In the *Ex-Cello Corporation* decision,[43] the board discussed the inadequacy of remedies in good faith bargaining cases. It stated:

> We are in complete agreement that current remedies of the Board designed to cure violations of Section 8(a)(5) are inadequate. A mere affirmative order that an employer bargain upon request does not eradicate the effects of an unlawful delay of 2 or more years in the fulfillment of a statutory bargaining obligation. It does not put the employees in the position of bargaining strength they would have enjoined if their employer had immediately recognized and bargained with their chosen representative. It does not dissolve the inevitable employee frustration or protect the Union from the loss of employee support attributable to such delay.[44]

In this case, the trial examiner (now called an administrative law judge) ordered the employer to compensate its employees for monetary losses attributable to the employer's failure to bargain in good faith. The compensation was an amount equal to the increase in benefits the employees would have received had an agreement been reached in a timely fashion. The board reluctantly refused to approve the trial examiner's remedy. It was concluded that the board did not have the power to direct such a remedy.

The board's decision in the *Ex-Cello Corporation* case reflected the Supreme Court's *H.K. Porter Co. v. NLRB* decision.[45] In this case, the board concluded the employer's refusal to negotiate over a check-off of union dues provision violated the tenets of good faith bargaining. As a remedy, the board directed the employer to grant the union a contract clause providing for the check-off of union dues. However, the Supreme Court refused to enforce the board's order. The Supreme Court noted:

> The Board's remedial powers under [Section] 10 of the Act are broad, but they are limited to carrying out the policies of the Act itself. One of these fundamental policies is freedom of contract. While the parties' freedom of contract is not absolute under the Act, allowing the Board to compel agreement when the parties themselves are unable to agree would violate the fundamental premise on which the Act is based—private bargaining under governmental supervision of the procedure alone, without any official compulsion over the actual terms of the contract.[46]

In other words, the Supreme Court concluded the board cannot direct an employer to accept a specific contract proposal even if the employer has failed to bargain in good faith.

The Labor Reform Act which was defeated by Congress in 1978 attempted to broaden the board's remedial powers in refusal-to-bargain cases. It was proposed that the board be allowed to award employees compensation for bargaining delays. The amount of the monetary award would equal the average wage settlements negotiated at plants where bargaining was not thwarted by illegal employer practices. The award would be retroactive from the beginning of the illegal bargaining.[47] Since the Labor Reform Act was not passed, the board's remedial powers in good faith bargaining cases are still limited to cease-and-desist orders. It has been argued that this is a serious limitation in our nation's labor laws. While the NLRB has been empowered to protect employer interests in secondary boycotts and jurisdictional disputes by use of the injunction, similar remedies are unavailable to protect worker interests. On this point, it has been noted:

> These prompt and effective remedies available to the employer stand in sharp contrast to the plight of the individual employee and his bargaining agent. This is but another example of the unfortunate tendency of the law frequently to pay more attention to the need for protecting *property* rights than individual rights.
>
> Before it is too late, we must devise remedies which are adequate to enforce the rights granted employees under the law. The lack of effective enforcement in this area can only exacerbate the general loss of respect for our system of laws today.[48]

Summary

Through collective bargaining, labor and management establish the basic terms and conditions under which employees will work. Collective bargaining also establishes a procedure by which the parties will resolve disputes over the interpretation or application of the collective-bargaining agreement. Each union-management situation develops its own collective-bargaining relationship responsive to major factors such as the nature of the environment (e.g., technology, product market, and labor market), the attributes of the union and management officials, and the impact of public policy.

When the parties sit at the bargaining table to define or redefine the terms of their relationship, a number of different alternative settlements are available to them. Each party has a resistance point, that is, a contract value they would rather accept than strike. The parties' resistance points define a settlement range. If the employer's resistance point is higher than the union's, a settlement is possible at a contract value within the settlement range. The concept of bargaining power was introduced to identify the variables influencing one party's ability to have its terms of agreement accepted by the other side. The ability to strike by the union and take a strike by management are key factors influencing the parties' bargaining power.

Like many aspects of labor-management relations, collective bargaining is subject to regulation by the nation's labor laws. The legal obligations of the parties during the collective bargaining process are established by reading Sections 8(a)(5), 8(b)(3) and 8(d) of the National Labor Relations Act together. Section 8(d) defines, in a general way, what the parties must do to avoid violating Sections 8(a)(5) and 8(b)(3).

Section 8(d) was drafted in very general language which has required much interpretation and elaboration by the NLRB and the courts. It was included in the legislation because it was recognized that getting the parties into the bargaining room was insufficient. The intent of Section 8(d) was to impose on the parties the obligation to bargain in "good faith" once they were in the bargaining room. As a result, the parties must enter bargaining with an open mind concerning the possibility of reaching an agreement. Also, the bargainers must attempt to reach an agreement. Once an agreement is obtained, the parties must be willing to put it into writing, if one party requests to do so. Behavior that indicates a predisposition not to reach agreement or precludes or frustrates the process of securing an agreement will be used as indicators that the party is not negotiating in "good faith."

This chapter has provided a general overview of the collective bargaining process and the factors that influence it. With this background in mind, the activities of the parties as they engage in collective bargaining can now be examined.

Discussion Questions

1. What are the major implications for labor and management of collective bargaining being a continuous relationship?
2. Compare and contrast distributive and integrative bargaining. What are the advantages and disadvantages of having both distributive issues and integrative problems on the bargaining agenda?
3. What is bargaining power? What are the major factors determining the bargaining power of labor and management?

4. How can the bargaining skills of the negotiators influence the outcomes of the collective bargaining process?
5. Given the importance of collective bargaining to the parties, why do they utilize "poker table" tactics such as bluffing when negotiating?
6. Given the overview of the collective bargaining process presented in this chapter, what are the attributes needed to be an effective negotiator?

Key Concepts

Bargaining power
Area of interdependency
Direct costs of agreement
Secondary costs of agreement
Nonmarket costs of agreement
Distributive bargaining
Integrative bargaining
Dilemma of openness and honesty
Attitudinal structuring
Intraorganizational bargaining
Good faith bargaining

Strike insurance
Multiemployer bargaining
Coordinated or coalition bargaining
Union resistance point
Management resistance point
Positive settlement range
Negative settlement range
Mandatory subjects
Permissive subjects
Illegal subjects

Notes

1. U.S. Department of Labor, Bureau of Labor Statistics, *Directory of National Unions and Employee Associations, 1979* (Washington, D.C.: Government Printing Office, 1980), p. 73.

2. John T. Dunlop, *Industrial Relations Systems* (New York: Henry Holt and Company, 1958), p. 14.

3. John T. Dunlop, "The Social Utility of Collective Bargaining," in *Challenges to Collective Bargaining,* ed. Lloyd Ulman (Englewood Cliffs: Prentice-Hall, 1967), p. 169.

4. Joseph Shister, "Collective Bargaining," in *A Decade of Industrial Relations Research,* eds. Neil Chamberlain et al. (New York: Harper and Bros., 1958).

5. Benjamin H. Selekman et al., "Power Relations: Corporations and Unions at the Bargaining Table," in *Problems in Labor Relations,* 3rd ed., Benjamin H. Selekman et al. (New York: McGraw-Hill Book Company, 1964), p. 4.

6. Neil W. Chamberlain and James K. Kuhn, *Collective Bargaining* (New York: McGraw-Hill Book Company, 1965), p. 170.

7. Richard E. Walton and Robert B. McKersie, *A Behavioral Theory of Labor Negotiations* (New York: McGraw-Hill Book Company, 1965), p. 19.

8. Chamberlain and Kuhn, *Collective Bargaining,* p. 163.

9. Ibid., p. 170.

10. Ibid., pp. 171–72.

11. "Strike Fund Leaves Baseball's Owners Safe on First Base," *Wall Street Journal,* 15 June 1981.

12. For a thorough discussion of strike insurance in the airline industry, see: S. Herbert Uterberger and Edward Koziara, "Airline Strike Insurance: A Study in Escalation," *Industrial Relations* 29 (October 1975): 26–45 and S. Herbert Uterberger and Edward Koziara, "The Demise of Airline Strike Insurance," *Industrial Relations* 34 (October 1980): 82–89.

13. Chamberlain and Kuhn, *Collective Bargaining,* pp. 171–72.

14. Industrial Union Department, AFL-CIO, "Coordinated Bargaining: Labor's New Approach to Effective Contract Negotiations," in *Readings in Labor Economics and Labor Relations,* 4th ed., Richard L. Rowan (Homewood, IL: Richard D. Irwin, 1980), p. 180.

15. Howard D. Marshall and Natalie J. Marshall, *Collective Bargaining* (New York: Random House, 1971), p. 87.

16. *General Electric v. NLRB,* U.S. Court of Appeals, 412 F.2d 512 (2d Cir. 1969).

17. Archibald Cox, Derek C. Bok, and Robert A. Gorman, *Labor Law,* 8th ed. (Mineola: Foundation Press, 1977), pp. 328–29.

18. This section is based on Chamberlain and Kuhn, *Collective Bargaining,* pp. 182–87.

19. F. Ray Marshall, Allan M. Cartter, and Allan G. King, *Labor Economics* (Homewood, IL: Richard D. Irwin, Inc., 1976), p. 253.

20. John Dunlop and James Healy, *Collective Bargaining: Principles and Cases* (Homewood, IL: Richard D. Irwin, 1953), pp. 60–61.

21. Edwin F. Beal, Edward D. Wickersham, and Philip K. Kienast, *The Practice of Collective Bargaining,* 5th ed. (Homewood, IL: Richard D. Irwin, 1976), p. 202.

22. Richard E. Walton and Robert B. McKersie, *A Behavioral Theory of Labor Neogtiations* (New York: McGraw-Hill Book Company, 1965).

23. Ibid., p. 3.

24. Donald E. Cullen, *Negotiating Labor-Management Contracts* (Ithaca, NY: New York State School of Industrial and Labor Relations, Cornell University, 1965), p. 51.

25. Walton and McKersie, *Behavioral Theory of Labor Negotiations,* p. 5.

26. Ibid., p. 137.

27. Jeffrey F. Rubin and Bert R. Brown, *The Social Psychology of Bargaining and Negotiation* (New York: Academic Press, 1975), ch. 1.

28. H. H. Kelly, "A Classroom Study of the Dilemmas in Interpersonal Negotiations," in *Strategic Interaction and Conflict: Original Papers and Discussion,* ed. K. Archibald (Berkeley: Institute of International Studies), p. 60.

29. Walton and McKersie, *Behavioral Theory of Labor Negotiations,* p. 184.

30. Ibid., pp. 186–88.

31. Ibid., p. 185.

32. Archibald Cox, "The Duty to Bargain in Good Faith," *Harvard Law Review* 1401, 1412–15 (1958).

33. *NLRB v. Montgomery Ward and Co.,* U. S. Court of Appeals, 133 F.2d 676 (No. Cir. 1943).

34. *NLRB v. General Electric,* U. S. Court of Appeals, 418 F.2d 736 (2d Cir. 1970).

35. Bruce Feldacker, *Labor Guide to Labor Law* (Reston, VA: Reston Publishing Co., 1980), p. 121.

36. *White v. NLRB,* U. S. Court of Appeals, 255 F.2d 564 (5th Cir. 1958).

37. Ibid.

38. *NLRB v. American National Insurance,* 343 U.S. 395 (1952).

39. *NLRB v. Wooster Division of Borg-Warner Corp.,* 356 U.S. 342.

40. *Brooks v. NLRB,* 348 U.S. 96 (1954).

41. *Mar-Jac Poultry Co. Inc.,* 136 NLRB 785 (1962).

42. Feldacker, *Labor Guide to Labor Law,* p. 138–39.

43. *Ex-Cello Corp.,* 185 NLRB 107 (1970).

44. Ibid.

45. *H. K. Porter v. NLRB,* 397 U.S. 99 (1970).

46. Ibid.

47. "Controversy Over 'Labor Reform Legislation,'" *Congressional Digest,* January 1978, p. 9.

48. Elliot Bredhoff, "The Scope of "Good Faith" Bargaining and Adequacy of Remedies," Industrial Relations Research Association, *Proceedings of the Twenty-Sixth Annual Meeting* (Madison, WI: n.p., 1973), pp. 117–18.

Suggested Readings

Kochan, Thomas. *Collective Bargaining and Industrial Relations*. Homewood IL: Richard D. Irwin, Inc., 1980.

Peters, Edward. *Strategy and Tactics in Labor Negotiations*. New London, CT: National Foremen's Institute, 1955.

Slichter, Sumner; Healy, James; and Livernash, E. Robert. *The Impact of Collective Bargaining on Management* (Washington, D.C.: The Brookings Institution, 1960).

Stevens, Carl. *Strategy and Collective Bargaining Negotiation*. New York: McGraw-Hill Book Company, 1963.

Walton, Richard and McKersie, Robert. *A Behavioral Theory of Labor Negotiations*. New York: McGraw-Hill Book Company, 1965.

Chapter 9

COLLECTIVE BARGAINING: FROM PREPARATION TO AGREEMENT

Les Payne remembered something that a professor of real estate had said in class one day: "There are three things to remember when buying real estate—location, location, and location." After a couple of months in the labor relations department of a large farm implement parts manufacturer, Les had paraphrased the real estate maxim as follows: "There are three ingredients to successful collective bargaining: preparation, preparation, and more preparation."

After first joining the labor relations department, Les worked handling grievances and helping company attorneys prepare for arbitration. However, his job assignment had recently changed. The company and its union were going to renegotiate their labor agreement later in the year. Les was assigned to work directly for John Hadley, the company's vice president for labor relations. Mr. Hadley would be the company's chief bargainer during the upcoming negotiations. From Les's view, Hadley was the perfect "boss." Hadley realized Les knew very little about collective bargaining and how to prepare for it. Consequently, Les's first assignment was to develop an outline of the steps the company would have to take to prepare for negotiations. Hadley suggested Les do library research, talk to some of the "older hands" in the company, and interview labor relations executives with other firms in town to see how they got ready for collective bargaining. Once the research was finished, Mr. Hadley would review and comment on Les's proposal. Once they agreed on the strategy for preparing for bargaining, it would then become Les's responsibility to implement the plan as much as he could, given his position in the organization. Mr. Hadley explained that Les did not have the authority to implement portions of the plan, such as forming the negotiating team. Whenever Les could not make the decisions, he was instructed to notify Mr. Hadley. In these situations, Hadley expected Les to have a list of options and the pros and cons of each.

Les was really excited about his new job responsibilities. Mr. Hadley had structured the position to provide a real learning opportunity for Les. Also, reporting directly to a vice president gave Les a lot of visibility. If he did a good job, he thought that the position would enhance his career with the company.

Now the problem was to take full advantage of the opportunity made available to him. Les knew what he had to do—develop a strategy to guide the company's preparation for the upcoming negotiations and then implement it. Les's first thought was "Where do I start?"

COLLECTIVE BARGAINING: FROM PREPARATION TO AGREEMENT

This chapter examines the collective-bargaining process from the point where the parties start their preparation for negotiations through the decision to finalize the agreement or strike. The first section of this chapter specifically addresses the problem confronting Les Payne. It takes you through a series of steps the parties can utilize to help insure they are adequately prepared for collective bargaining. Later sections examine the role of the contract expiration date in collective bargaining, the nature of the written agreement, the contract ratification process, and the strike weapon and related tactics including picketing and the consumer boycott.

More specifically, after studying this chapter you should:

- Be able to outline the steps of both the early and final stages of preparation for collective bargaining.
- Describe the role played by the contract expiration date in the collective bargaining process.
- List the reasons a written agreement has become a standard feature in labor-management relations.
- Know why a union submits a tentative labor agreement to its membership for final ratification and the implications of this procedure for the collective bargaining process.
- List the different types of strikes and know how the type of strike influences the rights of striking employees.
- Detail how picketing and consumer boycotts enhance the effectiveness of the strike weapon.

Under Section 8(d) of the National Labor Relations Act (NLRA), a party wanting to renegotiate an existing labor agreement must give the other party at least sixty days notice prior to the contract's expiration date. However, due to the complexity of labor agreements today, the parties would be remiss if they waited until the last two months prior to the contract's expiration date to begin preparation for collective bargaining. As labor agreements become longer and increasingly complex, the parties need more time to prepare for negotiations than in the past. It is quite common for labor and management to start preparing for an upcoming round of negotiations six months to a year in advance. Since preparation for negotiations is such an instrumental part of the collective bargaining process, the parties' preparation for negotiations will be examined in detail. Both labor and management use similar preparation techniques. To simplify the discussion to follow, the focus will be on management's preparation. Where the union's preparation varies sharply from management's, these differences will be pointed out.

Early Preparation for Negotiations

If the parties make mistakes during negotiations, both union and management will have to live with the consequences for the duration of the agreement and perhaps longer. Since it is difficult to undo errors made at the bargaining table, it is important for the parties to be well-prepared when negotiating. Preparations for negotiations require time and money, that is, a commitment of the organization's resources. However, the costs associated with preparation can be viewed as an investment on which there will be a return—a better contract than could have been obtained if the party was not as well prepared.

Management's early preparation for negotiations should be organized with the following objectives in mind:

- Identify potential union demands and alternative management responses to them.
- Identify management's demands and try to anticipate the union's responses.
- Create a data base to support the upcoming negotiations.

If at all possible, an individual or small group of individuals should be responsible for the early stages of preparation. Since preparation is a time-consuming activity, the people responsible for it should be freed from other duties. This will allow them to concentrate their efforts on the upcoming round of negotiations.

IDENTIFYING POTENTIAL UNION PROPOSALS

It is important for management to anticipate the union's proposals. By so doing, it can determine prior to negotiations the potential cost of the demands. Also, being able to anticipate the other party's demands allows counterproposals or rebuttal arguments to be prepared prior to the start of negotiations. While it is difficult to define precisely all the union's proposals months in advance of the negotiations, doing so will help avoid surprises. The more that can be done prior to negotiations, the less research will be needed during negotiations. This will allow the bargainers to concentrate on the negotiations and not worry about having to research "new" demands proposed by the union.

There are a number of information sources that can be tapped to help identify potential union proposals.

Study past negotiations. Assuming the parties have an existing contract, a review of the previous round of negotiations can help identify potential union demands. When the previous negotiations were completed, they should have been summarized to provide a record of that round of bargaining. For each proposal made by the union, its disposition should have been noted. The union's demands only partially included in the contract or totally rejected by management are likely to surface again in the upcoming negotiations.

Examine grievance files and arbitration awards. Such a review can indicate the number of grievances associated with each section of the contract, interpretations of contract provisions as reflected in the grievance settlements and arbitration awards, and weaknesses in contract language brought out through contract administration.[1] The objective will be to identify parts of the contract the union has sought to have interpreted or modified through the grievance procedure and arbitration. These issues could become "hot spots" in the upcoming negotiations. Also, the review of the grievance files provides an opportunity to examine the interpersonal relationships among the union and management officials. Do the grievances indicate a willingness on the union's part to cooperate with management? Are there individuals, both union and management, who do not appear able to work together to resolve problems? The objective of such an analysis is to determine how these relationships could influence both bargaining demands and the negotiating process.[2]

Study the union, its leaders, and its politics. Throughout the life of the contract, the union could be giving clues concerning the demands likely to be proposed during the upcoming negotiations. It has been suggested that management make note of the issues raised by the candidates running for union office, statements made during grievance meetings, and public addresses made by union leaders.[3] Additionally, union newspapers and magazines can be monitored to help identify union concerns that could surface as bargaining issues. Knowledge of the union's internal politics, the presence of dissident groups, and the influence of the political situation on the leadership could provide insights into potential bargaining demands and the diligence with which the union will pursue the proposals at the bargaining table.

Review recently negotiated contracts. By examining contracts negotiated by one's own union with other employers as well as the contracts of other unions in the same locale, it is possible to determine potential contractual goals. Are there trends in the industry or other industries that might indicate the direction of future negotiations? Recently negotiated settlements could influence union members' expectations for the upcoming contract talks.

Talk to the first-level supervisors. First-level supervisors are an often overlooked source of valuable information concerning a union's bargaining demands. Supervisors work closely with the rank-and-file union members. It has been argued that:

> Foremen also give you a feel for the pulsebeat of the shop. What's the union likely to demand this year? What's the rank and file grumbling about this year? Are they talking strike? After all, he's been there for 15 or 20 years and he was once a union man. They'll talk to him. He's an excellent source of feedback.[4]

As had been suggested, there are a number of potentially fruitful sources of information concerning potential union bargaining demands. By anticipating the union's demands, a company will be better able to react to them at the bargaining table. It should be recognized that it is quite likely that a number of the potential demands identified will not be presented by the union in the upcoming negotiations. However, it is probably better to be over prepared rather than ill prepared.

IDENTIFY POTENTIAL MANAGEMENT DEMANDS

Many employers do not put forth a list of their own demands during negotiations. Instead, they simply react to the union's proposals. However, other employers enter negotiations with their objectives clearly stated as a list of their demands. Negotiations are less likely to be conducted solely along the lines proposed by the union when management offers its own demands. By proposing a list of management's demands, the message is conveyed to the union that the company is dissatisfied with aspects of the existing agreement and will need improvements to offset the inevitable higher costs of the new contract. As part of the preparation process, management also needs to anticipate the union's response to management's demands and prepare rebuttal arguments to the union's position.

As when determining potential union proposals, several techniques are available that can be used to identify management's objectives for the upcoming negotiations.

Prepare a clause book. A clause book contains on each page a clause from the current agreement, as well as similar clauses from preceding agreements.[5] It has been suggested that a loose-leaf notebook be made with a page for each contract paragraph; then similar paragraphs from the past three or four contracts can be clipped and pasted on the same page as the clause from the existing contract.[6]

The clause book can give a clear indication of how contract language has changed over the years. By examining changes in contract language, it is possible to identify infringements on management rights or other problems needing to be rectified in the upcoming round of negotiations. Exhibit 9.1 is an example of a clause book page. It summarizes the evolution of contract language affecting the staffing of

---

EXHIBIT 9.1
An Example from a Clause Book

Article 14(c)—Servicing and Operating Equipment

1966–69

It is agreed that an Assistant to Engineer is required on all crawler and rubber-tired, self-propelled, shovel-type equipment of one-half (½) cubic yard and over, scoopers, and on all truck-mounted, shovel-type equipment, cranes, all ditching machines when rigged to dig to a depth of seven (7) feet or more; piledrivers; drill rigs, rotary, churn or cable tools mechanically driven; and all concrete batching pavers, crushers, washing plants, separation plants, asphalt plants and road mixing machines.

It is agreed that an Assistant to Engineer is NOT required on the following types of equipment: front end loaders and farm tractors with backhoes; tower cranes and hydrocrane type equipment self-propelled; and Kolman type screening plants.

Gravel and rock crushers and asphalt plants shall be operated by one or more operators as determined by the Contractor and shall be serviced by

EXHIBIT 9.1 *(continued)*

one or more Assistant to Engineers as may be determined by the Contractor.

Concrete batch plants shall be operated by one or more Operating Engineers, as may be determined by the Contractor. Servicing of concrete batch plants shall be made by one or more Assistant to Engineers but only at such times and for such periods as may be determined by the Contractor.

1969–72

1. All equipment shall be manned as provided in Appendix A and B and in addition to the Manning Provisions therein contained, when an Engineer requires assistance in addition to any that must be provided, he shall be assisted by an Employee covered by this Agreement (Assistant to Engineer, Apprentice).

1972–75

1. With regard to any machine or machines or item or items of equipment described in Schedules 1 and 2 of Appendix B of this Agreement or with regard to any additional item or items of equipment brought under this Agreement pursuant to the provisions of Article XVII (C), the Contractor at his or its option may assign one or more Assistants to Engineers to assist in the operation of the same, provided that Assistants to Engineers shall be required to assist in the operation of those items of equipment where designated in Schedules 1 and 2 of Appendix B.

1975–78

1. With regard to any machine or machines or item or items of equipment described in Schedules 1 and 2 of Appendix B of this Agreement or with regard to any additional item or items of equipment brought under this Agreement pursuant to the provisions of Article XVII (C), the Contractor at his or its option may assign one or more Assistants to Engineers to assist in the operation of the same, provided that Assistants to Engineers shall be required to assist in the operation of those items of equipment where designated in Schedules 1 and 2 of Appendix B.

1978–81

1. With regard to any machine or machines or item or items of equipment described in Schedules 1 and 2 of Appendix B of this Agreement or with regard to any additional item or items of equipment brought under this Agreement pursuant to the provisions of Article XVII (C), the Contractor at his or its option may assign one or more operators to operate the same and may assign one or more Assistants to Engineers to assist in the operation of the same, provided that Assistants to Engineers shall be required to assist in the operation of those items of equipment where designated in Schedules 1 and 2 of Appendix B.

Source: A series of agreements between a local of the International Union of Operating Engineers and a multiemployer contractors' association.

various pieces of equipment in the construction industry. As can be seen, the language was greatly simplified in the 1969 negotiations. However, the employer's association had to staff all the equipment. In 1972, the staffing of certain equipment was made optional, at the employer's discretion. Since 1972, Article 14(c) has remained the same.

Study past arbitration awards. By reviewing past arbitration awards, it is possible to identify sections of the contract that have proved troublesome to administer. Many such problems can be remedied by negotiating new, more workable contract language.

Survey management officials to identify the shortcomings of the existing agreement. Preparation for negotiations should include discussions with both line and staff management concerning life under the existing agreement. What problems are they facing when working under the present contract? How could the agreement be modified to alleviate these problems? Special attention should be given to the problems identified by the first-level supervisors. They are the ones who work with the contract day in and day out. Consequently, they are most aware of the problems associated with the agreement. A side benefit of this approach is that the first-level supervisors gain a feeling of participation in management's decision-making process.[7] A survey of management is likely to yield a number of unrealistic proposals. However, if these proposals are properly screened, a number of specific management bargaining objectives can be identified.[8]

A survey of management could also be a useful way to identify past practices that have developed over the years. In labor relations, a past practice "is ordinarily the unique product of a particular plant's history and tradition, of a particular group of employees and supervisors, and of a particular set of circumstances which made it viable in the first place."[9] Past practices creep into an organization frequently without the knowledge of top management. For example, whenever a particularly dangerous piece of equipment was used, a supervisor may have allowed that employee to record an extra hour of overtime. Or, whenever employees worked four or more hours of overtime, they may have been given a free lunch. Such practices were not required by the labor agreement; they are responses to problems that have been worked out over the years by supervisors and workers.

The problem with past practices is that they can become binding on the parties. A binding past practice develops when:

> In the absence of a written agreement, "past practice" to be binding on the parties, must be (1) unequivocal; (2) clearly enunciated and acted upon; (3) readily ascertainable over a reasonable period of time as a fixed, and established practice accepted by both parties.[10]

When a binding past practice is present, management cannot unilaterally change it. With reference to the examples presented above, it would be difficult for management to stop providing overtime to the employee using the dangerous piece of equipment or to stop providing lunches to employees working overtime. If the union filed a grievance against management's decision to terminate the practices, it is likely that an arbitrator would require the employer to continue them.

To eliminate binding past practices, it is necessary for management to notify the union that it will no longer adhere to the practice after the new contract has been negotiated. Then, it becomes the union's responsibility to get the practice included in the labor agreement. The parties are likely to bargain over the issue. If the parties incorporate the practice into the new contract, the practice will continue. However, failure to do so voids the practice. Therefore, part of management's preparation for negotiations could include discussions with supervisors intended to uncover past practices. Practices likely to be binding that limit managerial flexibility or are costly to management can be considered for discussion in the upcoming negotiations.

It has been suggested that the problems identified by the management survey be screened so that a list of problem contract clauses can be identified. Specifically, clauses creating the following types of problems should be identified for possible improvement in the upcoming agreement:

- Interfere with efficient operations.
- Are costly.
- Limit managerial flexibility.
- Lead to too many grievances.
- Are unclear or ambiguous in their meaning.[11]

Review relevant legislative as well as court and administrative decisions. It is quite possible that the legal environment will have changed since the last contract was negotiated. These changes could require modifications in the labor agreement. For example, it may be necessary to bring the existing contract in line with new legislation such as the Pension Reform Act. Also, government wage-price guidelines, court decisions, and NLRB decisions can impact on the upcoming negotiations.[12]

By using some or all of the techniques outlined above, management will be able to develop a list of contract changes it could propose during the negotiations. It is not essential that management offer its own demands. However, by doing so, a company may secure productivity improvements needed to offset some of the increased costs associated with the new agreement.

DEVELOP THE DATA BASE NEEDED FOR NEGOTIATIONS

The process of developing the information needed for negotiations is one of the most important parts of the prenegotiation preparations. During negotiations, a wide range of data is needed. The pace of negotiations will be greatly enhanced if data are on hand rather than having to generate the information during negotiations. Also, since more time is available to generate the needed information during the prenegotiation period, it is quite likely the data will be higher quality than if quickly compiled during the heat of negotiations.

INTERNAL DATA SOURCES

While some data needed during negotiations will come from external sources, much information needed by the negotiators is already available within the company. The accounting department will probably be able to provide data concerning labor costs. The personnel department would be the source of information describing the work force. Some of the major categories of information likely to be needed during negotiations are discussed below.

A complete description of the work force. Personnel files should allow a profile of the work force to be developed describing it in terms of sex, race, age, number of dependents, job classification, work shift, and seniority.[13] Also, for each employee, a record should be compiled that shows hiring data and wage rate, the date(s) wage increases were given and when job classifications were changed, length of service, and current wage rate.[14] This information will be needed to cost out the new agreement. Also, changes in the composition of the work force can give ideas concerning the problems the union will address during the upcoming negotiations. For example, if the data revealed an increase in female workers, the union might be interested in negotiating over issues such as maternity leave or child care.

Present wage and benefit data. For each job classification in the bargaining unit, average hourly wage rates should be calculated and available to the negotiators. They should also have cost data describing the full range of benefits received by the workers. In other words, the average hourly cost of holidays, vacations, sick pay, pensions, as well as legally mandated benefits such as unemployment insurance and social security should be calculated.

Information describing worker performance. Data describing factors influencing the workers' performance should also be compiled. For example, the number of days lost to absenteeism and layoffs could be useful. Also, negotiators may need to know the number and types of promotions and transfers as well as leaves of absence. Information could also be used describing the costs associated with pay for time not worked, such as rest and cleanup periods, lunch breaks, and paid time for union activities.

While much of the data listed above already exists in many organizations, it will have to be compiled in others. This is a time-consuming and expensive process, especially if an organization's financial and personnel records are not computerized. (See Exhibit 9.2 for a discussion of computer applications in collective bargaining.)

EXHIBIT 9.2
Computer Applications in Collective Bargaining

Much of the time-consuming, expensive preparation for negotiations can be greatly facilitated by the use of computer technology. Several examples of computer applications during the collective bargaining are presented below.

- If the company's personnel records are computerized, the arduous task of describing the work force can be easily handled. Otherwise complex tasks such as finding out the distribution of employees by seniority for each job classification can be performed quickly and accurately by computer.

- The costing out of alternative contract proposals can be done much more efficiently and accurately by computer than by hand. Computer programs can be developed so that the effect of various

> **EXHIBIT 9.2** *(continued)*
>
> wage and benefit packages on overall labor costs can be determined. This is useful during the preparation process as well as during negotiations when accurate and timely cost information is needed.
>
> - Information on grievances can be computerized. For example, New York State has a grievance information system that records all grievance activity by issue, state agency, bargaining unit, salary grade, and contract article. While such a system has a number of useful applications, it can be employed during the preparation for negotiations process. Knowing the contract provisions generating the greatest number of grievances could help identify "hot spots" in the agreement needing to be renegotiated. When there are 57 different agencies and over 11,000 grievances filed per year, as in New York, a computer-based grievance information system is an important tool.
>
> - Unions have used computers to analyze labor contracts. It is possible to compare a large number of contracts to establish patterns by industry, union or key pattern-setting agreements. This is a useful procedure for determining how other unions have approached specific contract provisions.
>
> This is not intended to be an exhaustive list of computer applications in collective bargaining. At the present time, computer usage varies greatly. While many parties do not use computers at all, a growing number of employers and unions are using computer technology to improve the efficiency and accuracy of the bargaining process. As labor relations specialists become more familiar with computers and as the technology improves, greater usage of computers during collective bargaining can be expected.

Once the information is available, it must be organized so that it is readily available to the negotiators. Also, the data should be in a form allowing the rapid calculation of increased costs associated with benefit changes proposed by the union or the impact of wage changes on the company.[15] It should also be noted that much of the data available in the company are historical in nature. In most situations, historical data are used in negotiations. Reliance on historical data does not create serious problems unless the firm is contemplating major changes during the life of the new agreement. However, if the firm is planning to implement major technological changes or some other significant modifications in its operation, estimates of the impact of the changes on the data used in negotiations might avoid miscalculations of the costs likely to be associated with the new agreement.

EXTERNAL DATA SOURCES

While much of the data needed for negotiations is available within the company, some of the information used during collective bargaining is only available from other sources. While the type of information needed varies from company to company, several widely used data sources are discussed in this section.

Area wage data. For many organizations, it is important for their wages and benefits to approximate those offered at other firms in the area. To determine how the wages paid by one company compare with others in the area, an area wage survey is useful. Data describing area wages can be compiled by the company by calling or writing for the information from other organizations. Similar data could be provided by groups such as the local chamber of commerce or the local manufacturers' association. Alternatively, the Department of Labor's Bureau of Labor Statistics can be the source of a wide range of information describing wages and benefits.

Cost-of-living data. The change in the cost of living is likely to be a major determinant of a union's wage demands. Information describing cost-of-living changes since the last contract, as well as changes anticipated during the life of the new agreement, should be available. Also, if the local cost-of-living figures differ from the more readily available national data, an attempt should be made to develop an estimate of the local cost of living. Cost-of-living information is generated by the Bureau of Labor Statistics and can be found in publications such as the *Monthly Labor Review*.

Industry outlook. It is important for the bargaining team to be aware of the economic prospects likely to be confronted by their industry during the life of the new agreement. Are new products being developed that could substitute for the firm's product? What is the likelihood or extent of foreign competition? Non-union competition? Such concerns reflect upon the firm's ability to adequately finance the new labor agreement. Related to the industry's economic outlook, a study of local industry should also be made. Have any local companies failed recently? Are firms moving out of the area? Are these failures or moves attributable to high labor costs? Management could use such information to support its resistance to the union's wage proposals. Also, it could be indicative of general labor market conditions influencing the workers' ability to secure employment elsewhere. Finally, as previously discussed, the firm's ability to hire replacements in the event of a strike can be affected by local labor market conditions.

The union, its politics, its leaders, and the likely negotiators. It is potentially useful to be familiar with both the local union and the national union with which it is affiliated. A union's constitution, by-laws, and its financial reports are on file with the Department of Labor as a result of the Landrum-Griffin Act requirements. Also, an attempt should be made to learn about the union's strike fund and the union's strike history.

Identifying likely union negotiators is a potentially useful activity. A review of their work histories, demographic characteristics, educational backgrounds, and personal interests could provide insights into their negotiating abilities as well as the issues likely to be their greatest concerns. For example, if it appears that the union negotiating team is dominated by older, long-service employees, it is likely that issues such as seniority and pension benefits will receive attention during the upcoming round of bargaining.

Labor-relations reporting services. A number of organizations such as the National Association of Manufacturers, National Industrial Council, Bureau of National Affairs, and Commerce Clearing House publish periodic reports on labor-relations issues. These reporting services should be monitored to keep abreast with current developments that could influence the upcoming negotiations.

As can be seen, the early preparations for negotiations are a time-consuming, expensive process. While it is not necessary for all organizations to use the extensive form of preparation outlined above, organizations that do so are likely to be more effective in bargaining than those which do not. After a union's potential proposals have been identified, potential company demands formulated, and the data likely to be needed during negotiations compiled and organized, the preparations for bargaining can move into the final stages.

Final Preparations for Bargaining

The final stages of preparation include a diversity of activities. In this section, the steps taken by a negotiating team during the final weeks before negotiations begin are examined.

SELECTING THE BARGAINING TEAM

This is not an easy task. Negotiations are physically and mentally demanding. It is important to staff the bargaining team with individuals capable of working effectively under extreme pressures for a prolonged period of time. There is no set of specific rules to follow when selecting a bargaining team. However, some general guidelines used to establish negotiating teams have been developed.

Most bargaining situations can be handled by a negotiating team of about five members. It is useful to select team members from both line management and the labor-relations staff. Somebody on the team should have finance/accounting skills so that issues can be costed out quickly during negotiations. It has been suggested that the team should have a general foreperson or supervisor with ten to fifteen years experience in the plant. The reason for this is that such a team member will be able to respond to the union when it brings up past practices dating back a number of years.[16] One of the basic objectives is to develop a bargaining team with a diversity of skills.

It is also important to balance the bargaining team with respect to the personalities involved. On this point, it has been stated:

> If most of your members are hellfire-and-brimstone types and determined to beat the union at any cost, you've got trouble. On the other hand, you don't want a collection of Walter Mittys and Casper Milquetoasts.[17]

It is difficult to determine the specific set of personal attributes the members of the negotiating team should possess. To a large degree, the nature of the bargaining situation helps determine the type of individuals who should compose the negotiating team. For example, a well-established collective-bargaining relationship in which the parties have a proven track record for reaching agreements, even on the toughest issues, will probably require negotiators with a particular set of skills. A different set of skills could prove useful in situations where the parties are negotiating their first contract.

A review of the literature concerned with the personal attributes of skilled negotiators indicates there is no generally accepted list of characteristics. Exhibit 9.3 summarizes the personal attributes identified by a number of different authors.

EXHIBIT 9.3
Personal Characteristics of Negotiators

Fritz and Stringari[1]
- experienced in previous negotiations
- command respect from other party's negotiators
- common sense
- working knowledge of human relations
- knowledge of the practical and legal implications of the topics covered during negotiations

Miller[2]
- technical knowledge
- experience in collective bargaining
- personality

Roemisch[3]
- imagination
- resourcefulness
- patience
- balance
- objectivity
- forceful
- dynamic

- able to command respect
- impeccable integrity

Constantino[4]
- mutual respect and sensitivity to the other side's thinking and objectives (rapport)
- patience
- honesty/integrity
- sense of timing
- confidence and support of top management for company negotiators and the rank and file for union negotiators

Mills[5]
- patience
- cool-headedness
- good will
- honesty and integrity
- courage
- lack of vindictiveness

Sources:
1. Richard J. Fritz and Arthur M. Stringari, Employer's Handbook for Labor Negotiations (Detroit: Management Labor Relations Service, Inc., 1968).
2. Ronald L. Miller, "Preparation for Negotiations," Personnel Journal, January 1978.
3. Roger Roemisch, "Preparing for Bargaining, Negotiating and Writing the Union Agreement," Personnel Journal 46 (October 1967).
4. George E. Constantino, "The Negotiator in Collective Bargaining," Personnel Journal 54 (August 1975).
5. Daniel Q. Mills, Labor-Management Relations (New York: McGraw-Hill, 1978).

Once the bargaining team has been selected, they should become thoroughly familiar with the information put together during the earlier phase of the preparation process. Also, the team should develop a group of experts from the personnel, accounting, and industrial engineering departments. The support group does not usually get involved in the actual negotiations; instead, they are available to the negotiating team to provide information and expertise needed during negotiations. The negotiating team should get to know the support group and become familiar with their skills and abilities. Effective negotiations require the negotiating team and support group to be coordinated in their activities. This will allow the negotiating team to respond quickly to union proposals that had not been anticipated during the preparatory phase of bargaining.

FORMULATE FINAL DEMANDS

Once the negotiating team has been selected, they can start formalizing the company's position on the various issues likely to be negotiated. While there is no one best way to establish bargaining demands and priorities, the "collective bargaining by objectives" approach[18] offers both labor and management a number of benefits.

During the early phases of preparation, a number of potential union and management demands were identified. Once this is done, the problem becomes: What do you do with this information? Collective bargaining by objectives offers the parties a procedure for organizing demands and preparing a bargaining strategy for each issue. There are a number of steps to the bargaining by objectives approach.

Establishing priorities. At the outset of the final stages of preparation for negotiations, the bargaining team has a list of its own demands and issues likely to be raised by the union. The first step in organizing this information is to establish a list of priorities. This requires the bargaining team to rank the items on their list of demands in terms of importance. Not all the issues will be of equal importance to the negotiators. Establishing the priorities of the demands will highlight the issues of critical concern to the company. The items that should be strenuously pushed for inclusion in the contract, and the union demands that should be seriously resisted, need to be identified. As a result of determining the priorities of the issues, the negotiators will be able to focus their attention on the most important items. Also, they are less likely to be distracted by the relatively less important demands. Establishing the priorities of the items is not a precise science. Richardson states:

> The priority given to the bargaining items need not be a consecutive listing. Some items might have about the same relative priority as others. Ranking the items by relative priority or importance to the bargaining party, therefore, might be done consecutively, with no two items the same, or by groups of items. The key is to establish an identification method that is easily followed, but most of all *to establish the priorities,* whatever the method used. Both the identification of priorities that is so extremely important for strategy considerations and the thinking process necessary to establish a relative priority system are positive steps for successful negotiations.[19]

The priorities established by the negotiators will reflect their organization's value system. The priority attached to a particular demand could reflect its cost, the implications for continued labor-management relations, ease of contract administration, its precedent value in future negotiations or the personal prestige of the parties.[20]

The development of priorities will probably take much discussion. This is a time-consuming process requiring some tough decisions to be made. However, it is important that the priorities be established prior to the opening of negotiations. Not only will the priority system help the negotiators while at the bargaining table, it will also help structure the final stages of preparation. The negotiators and their support staff can concentrate their efforts on collecting data and prepare arguments for the high-priority items.

Establish a range of bargaining objectives. After the priorities have been established, the bargaining team will have to determine the position they will take on the individual items. The collective-bargaining-by-objectives approach suggests that the negotiators develop a range of objectives rather than a single objective. For each issue to be bargained, the negotiators should identify three goals: the most realistic settlement to be expected, the most optimistic objective and the most pessimistic objective. The realistic bargaining objective on an item represents the settlement most likely to emerge from the negotiations given the pattern to the agreements recently negotiated or the bargaining climate as determined by factors such as union politics, economic conditions, and the skills of the negotiators.

The most optimistic bargaining objective (also known as a target point) represents the settlement to be expected if everything works out favorably to the management team. It is the best settlement possible. Relating the collective-bargaining-by-objectives approach with the subject of bargaining power discussed in Chapter 8, management's optimistic bargaining objective approximates the union's resistance point on the issue. The pessimistic bargaining objective is the settlement to be expected if negotiations go worse than expected. In the terminology of the bargaining power discussion, the pessimistic bargaining objective represents a settlement on the issue very close to the party's own resistance point.

Developing a range of acceptable settlements for the various issues requires more effort than identifying a single bargaining objective. However, there are advantages of doing so for the negotiators, including:

- The negotiating team will have a sense of direction provided by the tangible goals and a yardstick to evaluate progress during negotiations.
- The identification of a range rather than a specific goal for each item requires a more detailed and careful preparation for bargaining.
- The range of acceptable settlements provides the parties greater flexibility and allows a broader range of strategies and tactics to be used.[21]

Establish initial bargaining positions. As just discussed, the range of bargaining objectives represents the bargaining team's confidential estimates concerning its expectations for the upcoming negotiations. The initial bargaining position is the one taken by the team at the outset of negotiations on each issue on the agenda. The initial position could be close to the bargaining objectives. However, it is more likely that the initial position will be quite different from what is expected. The union negotiators will initially propose much more than they expect to receive and the management negotiators will usually offer much less.

It has been suggested that the priority, range of bargaining objectives, and initial position for each item likely to be negotiated be recorded on a form. A facsimile

EXHIBIT 9.4
Collective Bargaining by Objectives
(A Guide for Data Preparation, Strategy, and Evaluation of Bargaining Results)

Bargaining Items[a]	Priorities[b]	Range of Bargaining Objectives			Initial Bargaining Position[c]
		Pessimistic	*Realistic*	*Optimistic*	
Holidays	8	8 days	7 days	6 days	6 days
Wages	1	10¢ 1st year 10¢ 2nd year 5¢ 3rd year	5¢ 1st year 10¢ 2nd year 10¢ 3rd year	5¢ 1st year 10¢ 2nd year 5¢ 3rd year	12¢ over three years
—					
—					
—					
Union security	12	Union shop	Modified union shop	Agency shop	Agency shop
Probationary period	20	30 days	60 days	90 days	120 days
—					
—					
—					

[a]Classify items in two groups: financial and nonfinancial.
[b]Relative priority of each bargaining item to all bargaining items.
[c]Actual visible position taken at opening of negotiation (union initial proposal or company response or counter offer).

Source: Reed C. Richardson, Collective Bargaining by Objectives: A Positive Approach, © 1977, p. 141. Reprinted by permission of Prentice-Hall, Inc., Englewood Cliffs, N.J.

of this form is presented in Exhibit 9.4. By so doing, the negotiators will have a concise, usable summary of their bargaining objectives that will be frequently used during negotiations.

KEEPING TOP MANAGEMENT INFORMED

After the bargaining objectives have been finalized, the negotiating team should discuss the upcoming negotiations with top management. It is important that the negotiating team know how their plans fit into the organization's overall plans. Also, top management should know the bargaining strategy to be used. Additionally, a mechanism for keeping top management informed during negotiations should be developed.

DEVELOP A STRIKE PLAN

While it is unlikely that the parties enter negotiations expecting a strike to occur, both union and management negotiators would be remiss if they did not prepare for that eventuality. Consequently, the preparation of a strike plan is a basic part of management's preparation for bargaining. Strike plans vary greatly in terms of their detail but should cover issues such as procedures for building up inventories, preshipping products, the possibility and procedures for hiring replacements for the strikers, consequences of the strike for customer relations, and the training and scheduling of supervisors to run the plant.[22] The strike plan could also include a review of the procedure for obtaining an injunction and procedures for getting nonstriking employees into the plant.[23] In general, the strike plan outlines the procedures to be used in the event of a bargaining impasse. Hopefully, the plan will not have to be used. However, like many aspects of collective bargaining, it is better to be over prepared than ill prepared.

Union Preparation for Negotiations

Many of the steps in the preparation for collective bargaining described above in conjunction with management apply equally to the union's preparation. Also, many of the data sources used by management will be used by the union bargaining team. The collective-bargaining-by-objectives approach can be used with equal effectiveness by both union and management negotiators. However, preparation for negotiations is frequently more complex for the union. This is because the union does not have access to much of the information concerning factors such as workforce characteristics and the company's financial position.

Estimating the company's ability to pay is an especially difficult task for the union. Their ability to pay for the union's demands is likely to be a major factor influencing the final outcome of negotiations. Therefore, it is important for the union to have an accurate picture of the company's financial position. The company's annual report can be a useful source of financial information. Other useful information can be obtained from sources such as the *Wall Street Journal*, the business pages of the local newspaper, and the company's house newspaper or newsletter. The objective is to get an accurate view of the company's financial position and factors likely to bear on the firm's ability to pay in the future. It is not enough simply to evaluate the firm's financial condition at the time of negotiations. Are there projects under consideration likely to influence the firm's future ability to pay? Is expansion being contemplated? Will the company introduce new product lines? Are technological changes being considered? Will foreign competition affect the company's business? Are consumer tastes changing? Answers to these types of questions will have to be found as the union tries to estimate the company's ability to pay.

The company's ability to pay is one matter. The company's willingness to pay is another matter. Companies able to fund union demands may not be willing to. In preparation for negotiations, the union needs to appraise the factors influencing the company's willingness to pay.

A review of recently bargained union contracts is a beneficial exercise for union negotiators. These contracts can be a useful source of union demands. They may also be used to estimate what management may be willing to accept. Management is unlikely to agree with a contract out of line with other contracts recently negotiated in the industry. This is the case for two major reasons. First, the company does not want to be at a competitive disadvantage because of labor costs higher than those paid by other firms in the industry. Second, a more costly contract would reflect negatively on the bargaining skills of the management negotiating team. Management negotiators are likely to resist a contract that will make them look "bad" in the eyes of top management and their counterparts in other companies.

The study of the management negotiating team can aid the union's preparation for bargaining. The inclusion of negotiators with a known anti-union bias is a good indicator that tough negotiations are ahead. In anticipation of this, union negotiators may want to intensify their preparation. Representatives from the functional areas, such as production or personnel, on the bargaining team may indicate the types of issues of greatest concern to management negotiators. For example, the inclusion of someone from production could indicate that management wants to negotiate over work rules limiting workers' productivity. Accordingly, the union can prepare to negotiate such issues.

The political nature of the union organization is a factor contributing to the problems faced by union negotiators as they prepare for bargaining. It is important for union negotiators to reflect the needs and interests of the rank and file in their bargaining demands. Two major techniques can be used to ascertain the rank and file's bargaining objectives. The leaders could hold meetings with the membership at which the workers can express their concerns about the upcoming negotiations. Alternatively, the rank and file could elect representatives who would attend meetings at which the issues for the bargaining agenda would be identified.

While the rank and file can be an excellent source of bargaining proposals, their input must be tempered by the experience of the leadership. It is possible that the union negotiators will have to ignore or moderate rank-and-file demands because the proposals, if accepted, could harm part of the membership or jeopardize the financial position of the firm.

From Initial Proposals to the Final Agreement

Once bargaining begins, the dividends from months of preparation are likely to be received. Typically, bargaining begins with an exchange of bargaining proposals accompanied by an explanation concerning the basic reasons for making the proposals. This is not intended to be a definitive statement about the issues. The preliminary statements are intended to provide the other negotiating team an overview of the package of demands.

After the bargaining proposals have been exchanged, the parties will typically try to establish a bargaining agenda. The agenda establishes, at least tentatively, the sequence in which the bargaining proposals will be negotiated. Once the agenda is established, the parties get down to the business of negotiating an agreement.

Through the process of offering proposals and counterproposals, the differences between the parties on the various issues begin to narrow. The rate at which the parties converge on an agreement and the size of the concessions made by the parties will be a function of the negotiators' skills as well as the variables that determine the parties' relative bargaining power—a topic covered in the preceding chapter.

THE ROLE OF THE CONTRACT EXPIRATION DATE

The discussion of proposals and counterproposals, the emotional tirades, and the occasional modification of positions go on throughout the negotiating period. However, the pace of activities quickens as the contract expiration date approaches. In most negotiations, the parties are free to strike once the existing contract expires. Typically, the parties intensify their efforts to reach agreement when they face the strike deadline.

The final days of negotiating have been described as follows:

> And so the bargaining drama reaches its climax—sometimes in a dignified culmination of piecemeal compromises reached over a period of weeks, sometimes in a frenzied, last minute rush reminiscent of the closing hours of many legislative sessions. For just as legislators faced with adjournment, so labor and management negotiators faced with a contract deadline have reached their Rubicon. Speeches and press conferences are of no help now. If the union negotiator now repeats his strike threats, he had better mean them or his members will be working on management's terms tomorrow; if the employer still talks bravely of standing firm on his latest offer, he must reckon with the losses of a possible strike. In short, all bluffs are called by the contract deadline; there is no place to hide.[24]

THE WRITTEN AGREEMENT

In a vast majority of collective negotiations, the parties reach an agreement without resorting to a strike. Typically, this is done prior to the expiration of the existing contract. However, if the parties are close to an agreement at the time the old contract expires, it is possible for the employees to stay on the job while negotiations continue. Once an agreement is reached on all topics negotiated, the parties will prepare a written contract. The written agreement has become a standard feature in labor-management relations for a number of reasons, including:

- It introduces stability into the collective bargaining relationship by giving each party an assurance that the other side will not renege on its word.
- Because of the complexity of some topics negotiated, it is necessary to put them into writing to insure they are understood and preserved over time.
- In order to use the contract to help resolve individual grievances, it is necessary to have a rather precise statement of the terms of the agreement to be applied.[25]

Once the union and management negotiators reach a tentative agreement on the terms of the contract, the task of trying to sell the agreement to the union's rank and file begins. In some unions, the negotiators are authorized to reach a binding agreement. Under these circumstances, the union leadership is ultimately responsible to the membership the next time they stand for election. In other situations, a special representative body elected by the rank and file union membership has the authority to ratify the tentative agreement.[26] With this approach, there is a separation of authority between the power to negotiate and the power to bind the union finally to the agreement.[27] Granting the negotiators the right to bind or using a representative body to ratify the tentative agreement reached by the negotiators are used infrequently. In most unions, contracts are ratified by the rank and file through a direct vote. For the contract to be ratified, a majority of the voting membership must support its acceptance.

CONTRACT RATIFICATION

Legally it is not necessary for unions to submit tentative agreements to the rank and file for final approval. However, most unions have constitutions requiring rank-and-file ratification. Therefore, the legal function of ratification is to make the agreement binding when the union's internal procedures require a membership referendum. While this may be the legal function of ratification, a membership referendum tests the acceptability of the tentative agreement. It has been stated that:

> The meaningful function of ratification is to test the acceptability of a proposed collective agreement to those who are to be governed by its terms. Acceptability is measured directly by a referendum vote, while it is measured only indirectly, if at all, when it is approved by the negotiators or the vote of delegates.[28]

The basic premise of the contract-ratification procedure is that the collective bargaining agreement should be acceptable to the individuals who will be obligated to work under its conditions. This view is a direct extension of the proposition that trade unions are democratic institutions. Under the democratic model, the union leadership functions as a representative of the workers. Given the democratic character of trade unions, the acceptance of the contract by a majority vote of the membership is "the primary test of the legitimacy of a collective agreement."[29]

Whenever a tentative agreement is submitted to the membership for ratification, there is a risk that the contract will be rejected. Many employers do not like negotiating in situations where the authority to negotiate and the power to make the contract binding are separated.[30] The fear is that if they offer the union negotiators the best contract possible and it is voted down by the membership, they will either have to dig deeper into the company's coffers to fund additional contract provisions or take a strike. Neither alternative is particularly attractive to an employer.

The well-publicized air traffic controllers' strike during 1981 is a good example of the potential problems for negotiators associated with membership ratification. The president of the Professional Air Traffic Controllers Organization, Robert Poli,

Striking air traffic controllers were unsuccessful in pressing the federal government for contract improvements. Strikers were terminated and their union decertified.

agreed to a package valued at $40 million dollars per year. When the tentative agreement was taken to the membership for ratification, 95 percent of those voting rejected the contract, and Mr. Poli returned to the bargaining table. However, the government refused to increase its offer. As suggested above, once a contract is rejected, the employer is expected to "up the ante." If the employer does not, a strike is likely to occur, since the union leadership has a clear message (the negative ratification vote) that the contract is unacceptable to the membership. In this case, a strike occurred that is now history. The government had threatened a harsh response if striking air traffic controllers did not return to work. When the striking controllers refused to do so, they were replaced and their union was decertified.

Not all employers share the view that membership ratification of tentative agreements is a detriment to effective collective bargaining. It is argued that ratification increases the acceptability of the labor agreement to the union membership. Having the agreement acceptable to the rank and file has advantages to both the union leadership and the company. From the union's point of view, contract ratification decreases the likelihood that an unacceptable contract will be negotiated. A contract unacceptable to the membership could lead to internal dissension. This in turn could cause the union leaders to be voted out of office or even lead to the union's decertification.

There are also advantages to the employer of having the union membership ratify a tentative agreement. Summers argues that:

> When negotiators try to bind employees with an agreement that the latter find unacceptable, the employer may obtain neither the productivity nor the peace which he bargained. . . . Ratification gives an employer some added assurance that his employees will comply with the letter and spirit of the agreement.[31]

Several reasons have been cited for the positive effect contract ratification has on collective bargaining. First, union negotiators will keep in closer contact with the membership while preparing and then negotiating the agreement. To insure the agreement is acceptable, the union leadership will have to work to "sell" the contract to the membership. As a result, a potentially unacceptable contract becomes acceptable. Second, a union member's vote in support of the agreement is an expression of a willingness to be bound by the agreement. As a result, the union member incurs a sense of obligation to uphold the agreement. Third, the sense of obligation carries over to those who rejected the agreement. Because of the acceptance of majority rule, individuals voting against the agreement are obliged to follow the will of the majority. It has been noted that "a contract validated by majority vote thereby gains a claim to obedience by a dissenting minority."[32]

CONTRACT REJECTION

As previously mentioned, the risk associated with submitting a tentative agreement to the membership is that it can be rejected. Table 9.1 reports the number of contracts agreed to by the negotiators but later rejected by the union's membership. Research concerning contract rejections has identified a number of factors influencing

Table 9.1 *Number and Percent of Cases Involving Rejection of Tentative Settlement for Fiscal Years 1970 through 1979*

	Total number of cases	Number of rejections	Percent of rejections
1970	7,509	843	11.2%
1971	7,991	795	9.9
1972	7,215	732	10.1
1973	7,238	697	9.6
1974	8,479	1,050	12.4
1975	8,795	976	11.1
1976	8,985	876	9.8
T.Q.[1]	2,507	278	11.1
1977	10,528	1,208	11.5
1978	9,639	1,145	11.9
1979	10,203	1,219	11.9

[1]T.Q. stands for the Transition Quarter, the three months from July 1, 1976 to September 30, 1976 that occurred between fiscal year 1976 and fiscal year 1977 as a result of a change in the beginning of the fiscal year from the first of July to the first of October.

Source: Federal Mediation and Conciliation Service, Thirty-second Annual Report *(Washington, D. C.: Government Printing Office, 1980), p. 19.*

workers' decisions. These factors can be placed into two broad categories: background and ratification procedure. Background causes are the basic reasons for the failure to ratify. Ratification-procedure causes refer to procedural defects after tentative settlement but before ratification.[33]

The belief that an agreement is not as good as contracts obtained elsewhere was the background reason cited most frequently in the research as the cause of a contract's rejection. In other words, the employees felt "shortchanged" relative to some real or alleged standard. This factor was identified in over 30 percent of the contract rejections studied.[34] The importance of the workers' perceptions of the economic aspects of the tentative agreement cannot be minimized. Another study of contract rejections indicated that a definite relationship existed between:

> . . . economic activity and contract rejection. High employee expectations coupled with a reason to question the wage offer, lead to tentative settlement rejections in over one-half of the cases. The hypothesis that economic activity is a major source of rejection, therefore, must be accepted.[35]

Internal union politics was the second most frequently cited background cause for contract rejection. Simkin notes:

> In view of the inherently political nature of union leadership, it is not entirely surprising that this cause is rated so high. In a sizable number of situations, the union leadership handling the negotiations is elected by a narrow majority. A strong minority group in the membership may oppose the agreement primarily because it was negotiated by the

opposition. Or, a quantitatively weak but very vocal minority may rally enough support from others who are dissatisfied for other reasons to promote a negative ratification vote.[36]

Political reasons were cited for 20 percent of the contract rejections studied. Other frequently cited background factors causing a failure to ratify include:

- Dissatisfaction among skilled workers over the agreement.
- Leaders' failure to understand the real feeling of the membership.
- Dissatisfaction of other groups (excluding skilled workers).
- Reaction of membership to prior company policies.

A number of procedural reasons for contract rejection were also identified. In approximately 30 percent of the contract rejections, the union leaders failed to recommend the agreement's acceptance by the membership. However, this figure could be somewhat inflated. It is difficult to distinguish between situations where there is a real tentative agreement between union and management negotiators and situations in which the union membership votes on the company's last offer. In this latter situation, the union leadership has not necessarily agreed to the company's position. Therefore, it is not possible to conclude a tentative agreement exists. Some portion of that 30 percent of the contracts rejected in situations where there was no leadership recommendation (it could be as high as 5 percent) actually involved membership votes on the company's last offer. In other words, the rank and file was not voting on a tentative agreement reached by the union leadership.[37]

The type of vote has also been identified as a factor influencing contract rejection. This was a factor in approximately 13 percent of the rejection cases studied. It has been reported that the circumstances surrounding voice votes or standing votes are less conducive to rational decision making than secret ballots. Although there is no solid empirical evidence to support the conclusion, it appears that a secret ballot is the preferable method for ratifying contracts.[38]

Another procedural factor influencing the contract ratification process is the length of time between reaching the tentative agreement and the membership vote. It is not possible to generalize about this factor. In some situations, a vote can take place "too soon" if the leadership needs time to "sell" the agreement to the membership. At the other extreme, a long time between tentative agreement and the vote could provide a dissident group time to undermine the contract. The ideal timing of the membership vote can only be established by examining all the facts in the situation.[39]

The timing of the disclosure of the tentative agreement's provisions can also influence the outcome of ratification votes. Are the contract's terms publicized prior to a membership meeting or are they kept confidential until the membership meeting is held? Again, it is difficult to generalize about the way this factor influences the outcome of the vote. When announcing contract terms before the meeting, there is the risk that poorly written or inaccurate newspaper accounts could confuse the membership. This could cause misunderstandings and contribute to the contract's rejection. This is an increasingly serious problem as labor agreements become longer and more complex.[40]

Finally, the type of meeting at which the ratification vote takes place has been found to influence the outcome of the vote. It has been stated:

> As a general proposition, a meeting attended by the maximum possible percentage of members is most likely to produce a rational vote. There appears to exist an unfortunate but understandable tendency for the satisfied or neutral member to stay at home and for the unhappy member to attend and bring his friends. For this reason, an increasing number of companies have been willing, when so requested by the union, to permit so-called "stop-work" meetings on company time for explanation of the agreement and the vote.[41]

IMPLICATIONS OF CONTRACT REJECTIONS

Having to submit the tentative agreement to the membership for ratification has potential implications for the negotiators. Fear of contract rejection could force the union negotiators to press for larger demands and be less willing to reach a tentative agreement. From the management negotiator's position, membership ratification could force them to hold something back so they can "sweeten the pot" in the event the tentative agreement is rejected.[42]

If the tentative agreement is rejected, the membership is, in effect, directing the union leadership to go back to the bargaining table to get an improved agreement. Sometimes the negotiators can improve the agreement. In approximately 53 percent of the contract rejection cases studied, a monetary gain was noted when the final agreement was compared with the rejected agreement. However, in the remaining 47 percent of the cases, no appreciable monetary gain was realized by the employees after the tentative agreement was rejected.

One of the implications of contract rejection is that a strike can occur or be extended. In 38.3 percent of the rejection cases studied, strikes were experienced. A correlation of the additional strike days attributable to the contract rejection and subsequent monetary gains in the final agreement indicates that few of the rejections paid off for the employees. While the strikes incurred or extended by the rejection last an average of nineteen days, monetary improvements were found in only 57 percent of the cases studied.[43]

If the parties fail to reach agreement, the possibility is that a strike will occur. Certainly, when the membership rejects a tentative agreement they are saying that they are willing to risk a strike or a prolongation of a dispute in order to achieve a better agreement. The threat of the strike always seems to be part of the collective-bargaining process. In Chapter 8, the strike was discussed as it affects the parties' bargaining power. In the section to follow, the incidence of strikes and factors causing strikes will be discussed.

The Strike and Lockout

The vast majority of all negotiations end in an agreement without any work interruptions caused by a strike or lockout. However, this does not mean the outcome of the negotiations would have been the same if the threat of the strike was not present. The possibility of a strike is a basic part of collective bargaining. The strike is critical to the collective-bargaining process because it induces compromises on the differences existing between the parties. Without the threat of a strike, negotiations could drag on interminably. Exhibit 9.5 presents a brief description of the role of the

---

EXHIBIT 9.5
Some Effects of the Strike on Collective Bargaining

The possibility of a strike and the costs which strike action will place on the union, the employees, and the company are inducements to the parties to bargain effectively. To illustrate: when I used to bargain for a company, there were times when I had made an offer of, say, $.08; but, knowing that the union would indeed refuse if I held at that point, I was willing to move up a little more rather than assume the costs of a strike for the company. Likewise, without the threat of the strike, the union might have held at, say, $.12; but, knowing that I would indeed take a strike if it held at that level, the union was willing to move down rather than face the costs of a strike for it and its membership. Thus, the threat of a strike forced both of us to move from an offer and a demand which we would have preferred to a point where agreement was reached.

The threat of the strike was not always successful in forcing us to reach agreement. On a few occasions both parties felt that the other side was so adamant that we had to take a strike. Then the cost of the strike itself began to put pressure on both of us to settle. The loss of production and sales was translated into a loss of profits for the company. Some of our customers who had to turn to our competitors for delivery might be lost for good. The longer the strike lasted, the greater the pressure within the company to reach a settlement and get back into production.

On the union side, the pressure to settle built up in the same way. The early days of the strike were accepted by the employees with a carnival attitude, but after several paydays without checks, the cost of the strike action to them and their families caused them to put pressure on the union to seek a settlement. Eventually, the pressures forced a retreat from one or both of the previous positions, and with the help of a mediator a settlement was reached.

It is the threat of the strike and, if that is not successful, it is the strike itself which creates the kind of pressures necessary at times to force the parties to reach agreement under our free collective bargaining system. Without the right to strike, our system would not be so effective in bringing about settlements.

Source: Reprinted by permission of the *Harvard Business Review.* Excerpt from ''Freedom to Strike Is in the Public Interest'' by Thomas Kennedy (July/August 1970). Copyright © 1970 by the President and Fellows of Harvard College; all rights reserved.

strike in collective bargaining. A strike is a concerted activity by employees who refuse to work until management agrees with union terms. As previously discussed, the strike is used primarily as a way to increase management's costs of disagreeing with the union. It is also possible for work stoppage to take place because of an employer's lockout. The lockout has been defined as the employer's "withholding of available work from employees hired to perform such work in order to obtain a change, or resist a change, in terms or conditions of employment, or to resist recognition of an employee bargaining agent."[44]

Lockouts are not used very frequently because it is usually to the employer's advantage to have employees working rather than shutting down the facility to underscore its demands. However, situations can develop in which the lockout can be used. For example, if one company from a multiemployer bargaining unit is struck by a union, the other employers could engage in a defensive lockout of their employees in an effort to maintain the integrity of the multiemployer bargaining unit.[45] One of the basic functions of a defensive lockout is to prevent "whipsawing." "Whipsawing" is an attempt by the union to impose demands on one employer and then try to force the same demands on other employers in the multiemployer group. The Supreme Court has held that employers can hire temporary replacements to keep their facilities operational during such a lockout.[46]

Not all lockouts are defensive in nature. It is also possible for an employer to engage in an offensive lockout. In the *American Ship Building* case,[47] the employer locked out a number of its employees when it failed to reach agreement with the union. The Supreme Court examined the issue of whether a company could lay off employees to generate economic pressure on the union to adopt the employer's position after an impasse was reached. It was concluded that the nation's public policy did not preclude such a lockout.

The use of employer lockouts in single-employer bargaining situations is subject to greater scrutiny by the NLRB than multiemployer situations. This is because the primary objectives of lockouts in multiemployer situations, to maintain the integrity of the bargaining unit and to avoid "whipsawing," are absent in single-employer situations. A single employer can use a lockout as a counterweapon to the strike if the contract has expired, and an impasse over mandatory issues of bargaining exists. However, the lockout cannot be designed to discourage workers in the exercise of their Section 7 rights.

While the lockout is an option available to employers, it is not used very often. Therefore, the section to follow focuses on the strike and its role in collective bargaining.

TYPES OF STRIKES

There are a number of different types of strikes. In this chapter, the primary concern is with strikes occurring as a result of the parties' failure to reach agreement while negotiating a contract. These are known as economic strikes. Not all strikes arise out of the collective-bargaining process. Unfair labor practice strikes occur when a union strikes in response to alleged illegal employer conduct as opposed to disputes over wages and other conditions of employment as in economic strikes. In an unfair labor practice strike, the union strikes to exert pressure on the employer to remedy unfair labor practices such as a refusal to bargain.

The distinction between economic and unfair labor practice strikes is important since the rights of the striking employees are determined by the type of strike in which they are involved. Individuals involved in unfair labor practice strikes have greater rights under the nation's labor policy than economic strikers.

During an economic strike, an employer is free to replace striking employees in an effort to keep its facility operational.[48] However, the permanent replacement of striking employees is difficult, especially if the firm requires large numbers of skilled workers. While difficult, it is not impossible. In 1978, Adolph Coors Co., a large brewery located in Golden, Colorado, reopened its facility with strikers desiring to return to work and several hundred new employees. Approximately one year after the brewery reopened, the workers voted to decertify the union which continued to stay out on strike.

If the strike is of the unfair-labor-practice variety, strikers who want their jobs back at the conclusion of the labor dispute must be reinstated. This is the case even if doing so would require the termination of employees hired during the strike. In economic strikes, workers have a right to their jobs as long as the employer has not hired permanent replacements. If permanent replacements are hired, the striking employees do not have to be reinstated at the end of the strike. However, strikers not obtaining substantially equivalent regular employment elsewhere are entitled to be recalled by the employer to jobs for which they are qualified as such positions become available.

In addition to economic and unfair labor practice strikes, several other types occur periodically. Wildcat strikes occur during the life of a collective bargaining agreement without the authorization of the union's leadership. These are usually strikes of short duration frequently caused by factors such as job safety, working conditions, or disciplinary actions. Wildcat strikes typically violate a contract's no-strike provision in which the union agrees not to strike during the life of the agreement. Workers participating in wildcat strikes lose their status as employees under the National Labor Relations Act. Consequently, employers are under no obligation to rehire them at the conclusion of the wildcat strike. While not being liable for monetary damages caused by their unauthorized walkout, wildcat strikers can be discharged or disciplined by the employer. However, the union can be held responsible for monetary damages caused by the wildcat strike.

Jurisdictional strikes occur when a union strikes in an effort to have an employer assign work to its members as opposed to the members of some other union. Labor organizations are encouraged to resolve jurisdictional disputes on their own without resorting to a work stoppage.[49] However, if the unions are unable to resolve the work assignment issue satisfactorily, the NLRB will resolve the dispute by assigning the work in question to one union or the other.[50] The NLRB has been granted such authority to help protect employers and the public from disruptive jurisdictional strikes.

Sympathy strikes occur when one union strikes to express its support for another labor organization involved in a labor dispute. In such situations, which do not occur frequently, the union participating in the sympathy strike does not have a dispute with the employer. It participates in the strike to strengthen the position of another union involved in a labor dispute with the employer. As a result of the Supreme Court's *Buffalo Forge Co. v. the United Steelworkers Union* decision,[51] unions can engage in sympathy strikes without being subjected to court injunctions even if the labor agreement contains a no-strike provision.

CAUSES OF ECONOMIC STRIKES

The primary concern of this section is with economic strikes evolving out of contract negotiations. As previously discussed, economic strikes are used to increase the other bargainer's costs of disagreeing. In an attempt to secure desired improvements in wages or other conditions of employment, a union may strike to increase its bargaining power. Similarly, an employer may take a strike to demonstrate graphically its willingness to resist the union's demands.

Strikes can be deliberate attempts to influence the parties' bargaining power. Additionally, it may be necessary to strike periodically in order to remind the other party of the viability of the strike weapon. Occasionally, a strike can occur to demonstrate to management that a union has the ability to strike. Also, a labor dispute can remind the union membership that striking is a serious matter to be utilized only when necessary.

While strikes are frequently the result of rational decisions, it is quite possible for strikes to occur as a result of errors by the negotiators. The bargainers may miscalculate the commitment of the other side to a position or overestimate their bargaining power vis-à-vis the other side. Sometimes bargainers take positions during negotiations that make strikes inevitable. The negotiators may assume extreme po-

Table 9.2 *Work Stoppages by Major Issue, 1978*

Issue	Number of stoppages	Number of workers involved (in thousands)	Percentage of days idle during the year
All Stoppages	4,827	1,727.1	100.0%
General wage changes	3,190	1,114.2	73.8
Supplemental benefits	62	46.1	1.9
Wage adjustments	103	34.6	3.8
Hours of work	7	2.3	.1
Other contractual matters	279	56.0	2.3
Union organization and security	250	48.1	3.2
Job security	168	109.1	7.1
Plant administration	616	265.8	7.2
Other working conditions	59	16.3	.3
Interunion or intraunion matters	76	32.9	.3
Not reported	17	1.7	.1

Source: U. S. Department of Labor, Bureau of Labor Statistics, *Analysis of Work Stoppages, 1978* (Washington, D. C.: Government Printing Office, 1981), p. 19.

sitions during the heat of negotiations from which it is difficult to back down later. In such situations, a strike, at least a short one, can be necessary to "save face."

Tradition may be another factor influencing a decision to strike. In Chapter 8, reference was made to the United Mine Workers' long-standing tradition of "no contract, no work." As a result of this practice, if a new agreement has not been ratified by the membership before the old contract expires, a strike will occur.

In addition to these background factors, specific causes of strikes can also be identified. Table 9.2 presents the publicly stated reasons for strikes in 1978. It is not surprising, given the factors influencing the workers' decision to unionize, that the most frequently cited reason for striking was disagreements over economic issues, especially general wage changes.

Activities in Support of Strikes

While a union is on strike, it is also likely to be engaging in other activities designed to reinforce its strike activity. These activities include picketing, consumer boycotts, and the new tactics of the "corporate campaign."

PICKETING

Usually, picketing goes hand in hand with a strike. Once the strike begins, striking employees will patrol the employer's facility. The ostensible purpose of a picket line is to publicize the existence of a strike. By doing so, it is hoped that customers will refuse to patronize the employer's business. Some customers refuse to cross a picket line as an act of sympathy for the striking employees or as a matter of principle. Others do so out of a desire to avoid trouble they think they might experience if they crossed the line. It is also hoped that the presence of a picket line will interfere with any employer attempts to keep the facility operational. Employees of other companies could refuse to cross the picket line, thereby disrupting deliveries and pickups and, for example, preventing the installation or maintenance of equipment. Many union contracts allow employees to observe picket lines found at other companies.

Public policy with regard to picketing has undergone dramatic changes over the years. Prior to passage of the Norris–La Guardia Act, picketing was frequently limited by the use of the court injunction. For example, in *Vegelahn v. Guntner*,[52] the Massachusetts Supreme Court enjoined a peaceful picket line on the assumption that picketing necessarily carried with it a threat of bodily harm. However, with changing attitudes and new legislation, the position of the courts toward peaceful picketing changed dramatically. The broadest view of picketing is found in *Thornhill v. Alabama*.[53] In this United States Supreme Court decision, picketing was viewed as a form of constitutionally protected free speech.

Subsequent court decisions began to narrow the view of picketing as free speech. In the *Bakery and Pastry Drivers v. Wohl* decision, the Supreme Court stated:

Picketing by an organized group is more than free speech since it involves a patrol of a particular locality and since the very presence of a picket line may induce action of one kind or another quite irrespective of the nature of the ideas which are being disseminated.[54]

Since picketing involves more than free speech, that is, the exercise of concerted economic activities, the NLRB and courts have allowed some limitations on the employees' rights to picket. For example, peaceful picketing in support of illegal activities can be enjoined. In *Giboney v. Empire Storage and Ice Co.*,[55] an injunction by a lower court was upheld by the Supreme Court in a case where the picketing was designed to prevent the employer from handling non-union products. The union's objective was illegal under the state's anti-trust laws. Additionally, under Section 7 of the National Labor Relations Act, employees have the right to refrain from concerted union activities. This has been interpreted as meaning picketing that prevents employees from working during a strike coerces and restrains workers in the exercise of their Section 7 rights.[56] Consequently, picket line violence and sabotage are illegal activities. However, name calling directed at individuals crossing a picket line is lawful. For example, if picketing employees call fellow workers who cross the picket line "scabs," such actions are protected as free speech. See Exhibit 9.6 for a facsimile of a union leaflet distributed as part of an effort to strengthen its picket line activities.

The location of the picketing. In general, peaceful picketing at the primary employer's facility is a concerted activity protected by the National Labor Relations Act. However, there are limitations on the sites at which legal picketing can take place. The objective of the public policy is to isolate the strike, that is, insure it involves only the primary employer and its union. The public policy strives to buffer secondary employers and employees from involvement in labor disputes. At times, this is quite difficult.

Common situs picketing. Common situs picketing is a problem where two or more employers share the same work location. This is found in the construction industry where a number of different subcontractors can be located on the same job site or where one company has been hired to do work at another company's facility. What happens when a union strikes one employer and attempts to picket the job location? Since secondary employers share the site, they can become involved in the dispute if their employees observe the picket line.

The problem confronted in this type of case involves the conflicting rights of the parties. Under the nation's labor policy, employees have the right to picket the primary employer involved in a labor dispute. Similarly, secondary employers have the right to remain neutral in the dispute between the primary employer and union. In situations involving conflicting rights, the rights of one party must give way to the rights of the other.

The general policy concerning common situs picketing was established in the Supreme Court's *NLRB v. Denver Building and Construction Trades Council*[57] decision. In this case, the trades council struck a construction site to require an electri-

EXHIBIT 9.6
Sometimes Picket Lines Are Not Enough

STALL-IN

SUNDAY, JULY 26, 1970—12:00 NOON—ATLANTA AIRPORT

On May 7, almost 500 Dobbs House workers at the Atlanta airport walked off their jobs in solidarity with their Memphis comrades. As in Memphis, Dobbs House workers voted overwhelmingly in favor of the Teamsters as their union and bargaining agent. As in Memphis (also Louisville, St. Louis, and Chicago) Dobbs management has refused to recognize and negotiate with the union. Here in Atlanta, Dobbs has gotten an injunction restricting the number of pickets at each restaurant to two.

SPEND SEVERAL HOURS ORDERING COFFEE AND COKES FROM SCABBING WAITRESSES WITHOUT HEALTH CARDS. EXPLAIN THE DOBBS HOUSE STRIKE TO CUSTOMERS AND SCABS INSIDE THE RESTAURANT. PEACEFUL! LEGAL! AND EFFECTIVE.

A SCAB

After God finished the rattlesnake, the toad, and the vampire, He had some awful substances left with which He made a scab.

The scab is a two-legged animal with a corkscrew soul, a water logged brain, a combination back bone of jelly and glue. Where others have hearts, he carries a tumor of rotten principles.

When a scab comes down the street, men turn their backs and angels weep in heaven, and the devil shuts the gates of Hell to keep him out.

No man has a right to scab as long as there is a pool of water to drown his carcass in, or a rope long enough to hang his body with. Judas Iscariot was a gentleman compared with a scab. For betraying his master, he had character enough to hang himself. A scab has not.

Esau sold his birthright for a mass of pottage. Judas Iscariot sold his savior for thirty pieces of silver; Benedict Arnold sold his country for the promise of a commission in the British army. The modern strikebreaker sells his birthright, his country, his wife, his children, and his fellow men for an unfulfilled promise from his employer, trust, or corporation.

Esau was a traitor to himself; Judas Iscariot was a traitor to his God; Benedict Arnold was a traitor to his country. A strikebreaker is a traitor to his God, his Country, his Wife, his family, and his class.

STALL IN—CUT BUSINESS—HASSLE SCABS

cal subcontractor to hire union workers. A picket line was established. The workers of the other subcontractors observed the picket line, thereby disrupting the project. The purpose of the strike and picket line was to force the general contractor to terminate its agreement with the non-union electrical subcontractor. The general contractor did so. However, it filed unfair labor practice charges with the NLRB. It was the decision of the NLRB and ultimately the Supreme Court that employers at a construction project are separate entities. Therefore, when the strike and picket line shut down the entire project, the union involved secondary employers. Such activities can be restricted as part of the policy of stopping neutrals from becoming involved in a labor dispute. In this case, it was decided that the union's efforts to get the general contractor to cease doing business with the non-union subcontractor violated Section 8(b)(4)(A) of the NLRA.

"Reserved Gate" doctrine. Additional restrictions were placed on the union's ability to picket by the NLRB's "reserved gate" doctrine. This practice was upheld by the United States Supreme Court in *Local 761, International Union of Electrical Workers v. NLRB*.[58] In this case, General Electric hired a firm that was engaged in construction activities at a G. E. plant. Although a number of gates through which employees gained access to the plant were available, one gate was set aside for use by the employees of subcontractors working at the G. E. plant. The sign stated, "Gate 3A for Employees of Contractors Only—G. E. Employees Use Other Gates." The NLRB held that the union's (the G. E. employee union) picketing of the reserved gate was illegal because it was directed at the employees of secondary employers. The Supreme Court upheld the NLRB's decision. The key concept in this decision was the relatedness of the work performed by G. E. employees and that of the subcontractors' employees who used the reserved gate. If the activities of a contractor's employees are unconnected to the normal operations of a struck facility such as the construction of new facilities or remodeling of existing facilities, then picketing the reserved gate constitutes an illegal secondary activity. However, if the reserved gate is also used by the employees of the primary employer or for plant deliveries, picketing is not restricted. The reserved gate doctrine has been succinctly described as follows:

> There must be a separate gate, marked and set apart from other gates; the work done by the men who use the gate must be unrelated to the normal operations of the employer, and the work must be of the kind that would not, if done when the plant were engaged in its regular operations, necessitate curtailing those operations.[59]

Ambulatory picketing. Ambulatory or "roving" situs picketing involves situations where the location of an employer's business moves from one place to another. The landmark NLRB decision in this area, *Sailor's Union of the Pacific* (Moore Dry Dock Co.),[60] involved a strike and picketing of a shipping company. Since it is difficult to picket a ship while at sea, the union attempted to picket the ship while it was in drydock for refitting. The union notified Moore Dry Dock employees that the strike was directed at the owners of the ship. Also, the picket signs clearly indicated the dispute was with the ship owner. Moore Dry Dock Co. employees continued to work on other ships in dry dock. However, Moore Dry Dock filed unfair labor practice charges alleging that the union violated Section 8(b)(4) of the NLRA. The NLRB concluded the union picketing was legal. The NLRB stated:

> When a secondary employer is harboring the *situs* of a dispute between a union and a primary employer, the right of neither the union to picket nor the secondary employer to be free from picketing can be absolute. The enmeshing of premises and *situs* qualifies both rights. In the kind of situation that exists in this case, we believe the picketing of the premises of a secondary employer is primary if it meets the following conditions: (a) the picketing is strictly limited to the times when the *situs* of dispute is located on the secondary employer's premises; (b) at the time of the picketing the primary employer is engaged in its normal business at the *situs;* (c) picketing is limited to places reasonably close to the location of the *situs;* and (d) the picketing discloses clearly that the dispute is with the primary employer. All these conditions are met in the present case.[61]

Subsequent to this decision, the standards described above known as the "Moore Dry Dock" standards have been applied to establish the legality of situations involving ambulatory picketing.

The Ally Doctrine. For a secondary employer to be protected from a union's picketing, the secondary employer must be neutral in the dispute between the union and the primary employer. The landmark case in this area is *Douds v. Metropolitan Federation of Architects.*[62] In this case, the primary employer with which the union had a dispute transferred work to a secondary employer. The union began to picket the secondary employer. Charges that the union's picketing of the secondary employer constituted a violation of Section 8(b)(4) were filed with the NLRB. Later, the court ruled that when the secondary employer accepted the work of the struck pirmary employer, it was no longer neutral in the dispute. In other words, the secondary and primary employer were allies.

CONSUMER BOYCOTTS

One of the basic purposes of a picket line is to encourage the public not to patronize the struck employer. This effort can be extended by the use of consumer boycotts. A consumer boycott is an organized attempt to encourage the public not to purchase the products of firms with which a union has a labor dispute. Consumer boycotts are most likely to be used when the union is unable to shut down an employer by the traditional use of a strike and related picketing activities. In order to decrease the firm's revenues, the union goes to the employer's customers and requests the customers not to purchase the products of the struck firm.

To a substantial degree, the effectiveness of a consumer boycott is a function of the publicity concerning the dispute. Picketing and handbilling are ways to publicize the existence of a boycott. In the *NLRB v. Fruit and Vegetable Packers, Local 760,*[63] the union was involved in a labor dispute with a multiemployer group involved in the packing and warehousing of Washington State apples. The union initiated a consumer boycott by picketing the retail stores selling Washington State apples. The picket signs and handbills requested the retail customers to refrain from buying Washington State apples. Throughout the picketing, retail store employees continued to work and neither pickups nor deliveries were interrupted. The NLRB found that the union's picketing violated Section 8(b)(4). The Supreme Court disagreed with the NLRB's conclusion. In its decision, the Supreme Court differentiated between consumer boycotts in which the customer is requested not to purchase the product of the primary employer and a situation in which the union requests the customer not to patronize the secondary employer which carries the primary employer's product. The Supreme Court stated:

> When consumer picketing is employed only to persuade customers not to buy the struck product, the union's appeal is closely confined to the primary dispute. The site of the appeal is expanded to include the premises of the secondary employer, but if the appeal succeeds, the secondary employers' purchases from the struck firms are decreased only because the public has diminished its purchases of the struck product. On the other hand, when consumer picketing is employed to persuade customers not to trade at all with the secondary employer, the latter stops buying the struck product, not because of falling demand, but in response to pressure designed to inflict injury on his business generally. In such case, the union does more than merely follow the struck product; it creates a separate dispute with the secondary employer.[64]

Picketing and handbilling the customers of retail outlets requesting them not to purchase struck products is just one form of consumer boycott. Unions can also implement consumer boycotts on a much broader scale. Recent examples of such boycotts include actions against the Adolph Coors Company and J. P. Stevens Company. Through rather widespread publicity and with the support of other unions and occasionally religious groups, unions request customers not to patronize the employer for the duration of the labor dispute.

THE EMERGENCE OF THE "CORPORATE CAMPAIGN"

The lengthy labor dispute between the J. P. Stevens Co. and the Amalgamated Clothing and Textile Workers Union (ACTWU) spawned a new set of union tactics designed to pressure employers to make concessions to the union. These tactics became known as the "corporate campaign." The company resisted NLRB and court decisions and a nationwide consumer boycott of its products organized by the ACTWU. However, in October 1980, the company finally agreed to its first contract with the union after resisting such a move for seventeen years. The effectiveness of the "corporate campaign" orchestrated by the union has been cited as a major factor leading to the union contract.[65] The "corporate campaign" had several dimensions:

- Efforts were made to isolate J. P. Stevens Co. from the business community by forcing James Finley, chairman of J. P. Stevens, off the board of directors of New York Life Insurance Company and Hanover Trust Company. This was done by mobilizing thousands of policy holders and depositors.[66]

The union also pressured other companies to have their executives resign from the J. P. Stevens board of directors.

- More recently, the union went after Metropolitan Life Insurance Company, J. P. Stevens' biggest lender. The union proposed to contest two seats on Metropolitan's board of directors. Under New York State insurance laws, companies have to send election ballots to all policy holders if an election is contested. In the case of Metropolitan Life, an election involving all 23 million policy holders would have cost between $5 million and $7 million.[67] *Business Week* estimated the cost of the election at $9 million.[68] The union, Metropolitan Life and the New York Insurance Department worked out an agreement to postpone a hearing on the election. In the meantime, the union and J. P. Stevens reached agreement on contract terms. An interesting feature of the new contract was that the union was prohibited from trying to remove directors from the J. P. Stevens board and from restricting the availability of financial or credit accommodations to Stevens.[69]

In general, the "corporate campaign" was designed to inhibit J. P. Stevens' operations by making it unprofitable for other firms to deal with it. It is too early to tell whether this marks the beginning of a new set of union tactics. However, given the tremendous amount of money in union treasuries and union controlled pension funds, the potential for unions to flex their economic muscle is always present. For example, it is quite possible for unions to threaten to remove deposits from a bank if the bank lends money to a firm involved in a labor dispute. Similarly, unions can try to elect directors who are sympathetic toward unions and collective bargaining.[70] Used in conjunction with traditional union weapons such as strikes and picketing, the tactics of the "corporate campaign" appear to be potentially potent devices for increasing management's costs of disagreeing.

Summary

This chapter was designed to be a very pragmatic approach to collective bargaining. The first part of the chapter emphasized the "how to" of collective bargaining. The focus was on the steps through which the parties go as they prepare for collective bargaining. The early phase of the preparatory process requires the parties to identify their demands and the anticipated demands of the other side and develop data to be utilized in the upcoming negotiations. Later stages of preparation focus on the selection of the bargaining team, the final compilation of demands and the development of bargaining objectives. Preparation for negotiations may not appear to be an "exciting" activity. However, it is critical to the success of the negotiations. While effective preparation takes much time, effort, and money, it can be viewed as an investment on which there is likely to be a return. The return is an improved labor agreement relative to the contract that would have been negotiated in the absence of such thorough preparations.

After examining the preparation phase of collective bargaining, the chapter moved on to the activities found after the contract has been negotiated. Most unions will take the tentative agreement reached with management to the rank-and-file union membership for final ratification. This step is an extension of the democratic aspects of trade unions. While rank-and-file ratification introduces a measure of uncertainty into the collective-bargaining process, it can also be beneficial. It improves the acceptability of the labor agreement to the individuals obligated to work under the contract—the workers.

The final portion of this chapter examined the activities exhibited by the parties, especially the union, in the event they fail to reach agreement at the bargaining table. These activities included the strike and lockout, picketing, consumer boycotts, and the new "corporate campaign."

Additional space was devoted to the strike in this chapter. The strike weapon was examined in the context of bargaining power in Chapter 8. In Chapter 10, methods for avoiding strikes or limiting their adverse effects will be discussed. This chapter looked at some of the causes of strikes. Three separate discussions of strikes have been included in this book because the strike is one of the most frequently misunderstood aspects of collective bargaining. On the surface, a strike may appear to be economic brute force which is to neither party's advantage. Because of the widespread publicity strikes receive, it may appear that the public is severely inconvenienced by strikes. In response, some people will argue that strikes should be banned. However, to do so would severely undermine the collective bargaining process. Without strikes or the threat of one, collective bargaining would not operate as it does today. It is the desire of the parties to avoid the costs associated with a strike that keeps them bargaining, making concessions, and moving toward agreement. Without the strike, negotiations would probably drag on interminably.

While collective bargaining and strikes go hand in hand, neither party usually wants to strike or take a strike. The next chapter looks at ways the likelihood of a strike's occurring can be minimized. Some of these techniques can be used by the parties without third-party involvement. Other techniques require third parties to get involved in the collective-bargaining process. Chapter 10 also examines forms of government involvement in labor disputes and the efficacy of these efforts.

Discussion Questions

1. Assume you are the president of a local union. Outline the steps you would go through to prepare for an upcoming round of negotiations.
2. What effect does the contract expiration date have on the collective bargaining process?
3. Discuss the pros and cons for both union and management of the union submitting the tentative agreement to the rank-and-file union membership for final ratification.

Would it be better for the collective bargaining process for the union negotiators to be able to bind the labor organization to the contract without rank-and-file ratification?
4. What difference does it make to the workers whether they are involved in an economic or unfair labor practice strike?
5. Why do unions supplement their strike activities with other tactics such as picketing and consumer boycotts?
6. Some members of the business community have labeled the union's "corporate campaign" in the J. P. Stevens case "deplorable." What is your opinion? Should the nation's labor laws be amended to limit the ability of unions to influence traditional management or owner decisions such as the selection of members of the board of directors?
7. What is the significance of each of the following NLRB or court decisions:
   a. *NLRB v. Truck Drivers Local 449* (Buffalo Linen)
   b. *NLRB v. Brown*
   c. *American Ship Building v. NLRB*
   d. *NLRB v. Mackay Radio and Telegraph Co.*
   e. *Buffalo Forge Co. v. United Steelworkers of America*
   f. *Thornhill v. Alabama*
   g. *NLRB v. Denver Building and Construction Trades Council*
   h. *Sailors Union of the Pacific* (Moore Dry Dock Co.)
   i. *Local 761, International Union of Electrical Workers v. NLRB*
   j. *Douds v. Metropolitan Federation of Architects*
   k. *NLRB v. Fruit and Vegetable Packers, Local 760*

Key Concepts

Realistic bargaining objectives
Pessimistic bargaining objectives
Optimistic bargaining objectives
Contract expiration date
Written agreement
Contract ratification
Contract rejection
Economic strike
Unfair labor practice strikes
Jurisdictional strikes
Sympathy strikes

Wildcat strikes
Offensive lockout
Defensive lockout
Picketing
Common situs picketing
"Reserve gate" doctrine
Ambulatory picketing
Ally doctrine
Consumer boycotts
"Corporate campaign"
"Whipsawing"

Notes

1. Ronald L. Miller, "Preparation for Negotiations," *Personnel Journal* 57 (January 1978): 37.
2. Ibid., p. 37.
3. Ibid., p. 37.
4. W. J. Kalb, "Are You Ready for Labor Talks?" *Iron Age,* 28 March 1968, p. 59.
5. Bruce Morse, *How to Negotiate the Labor Agreement* (Detroit: Trends Publishing Co., 1971), p. 4.
6. Roger Roemisch, "Preparing for Bargaining, Negotiating and Writing the Union Agreement," *Personnel Journal* 46 (October 1967):581.
7. Kalb, "Are You Ready for Labor Talks?," p. 59.
8. Roemisch, "Preparing for Bargaining, Negotiating and Writing the Union Agreement," p. 582.
9. Richard Mittenthal, "Past Practice and the Administration of Collective Bargaining Agreement," *Proceedings of the Fourteenth Annual Meeting of the National Academy of Arbitrators* (Washington, D.C.: Bureau of National Affairs, 1961), p. 31.
10. *Celanese Corp.* 24 L.A. 168 at 172 (Justin, 1954).
11. Morse, *How to Negotiate the Labor Agreement,* p. 19.
12. Roemisch, "Preparing for Bargaining, Negotiating and Writing the Union Agreement."
13. Miller, "Preparation for Negotiations," p. 38.
14. Richard J. Fritz and Arthur M. Stringari, *Employer's Handbook for Labor Negotiations* (Detroit: Management Labor Relations Service, Inc., 1968), p. 44.
15. Miller, "Preparation for Negotiations," p. 38.
16. Kalb, "Are You Ready for Labor Talks?," p. 58.
17. Roemisch, "Preparing for Bargaining, Negotiating and Writing the Union Agreement," p. 581.
18. Reed C. Richardson, *Collective Bargaining by Objectives* (Englewood Cliffs: Prentice-Hall, 1977).
19. Richardson, *Collective Bargaining by Objectives,* p. 128.
20. Ibid., p. 128.
21. Ibid., p. 109.
22. Roemisch, "Preparing for Bargaining, Negotiating and Writing the Union Agreement," p. 503.
23. Kalb, "Are You Ready for Labor Talks?," p. 58.
24. Donald E. Cullen, *Negotiating Labor-Management Contracts* (Ithaca, N.Y.: New York State School of Industrial and Labor Relations, 1965), pp. 6–7.
25. Neil W. Chamberlain and James W. Kuhn, *Collective Bargaining,* 2nd ed. (New York: McGraw-Hill Book Company, 1965), pp. 80–81.
26. Derek C. Bok and John T. Dunlop, *Labor and the American Community* (New York: Simon and Schuster, 1970), pp. 77–78.
27. Clyde W. Summers, "Ratification of Agreements," in *Frontiers of Collective Bargaining,* ed. John T. Dunlop and Neil W. Chamberlain (New York: Harper and Row, 1967), p. 79.
28. Ibid., p. 82.
29. Ibid., p. 83.
30. Ibid., p. 81.
31. Ibid., p. 84.
32. Ibid., p. 85.
33. William E. Simkin, "Refusal to Ratify Contracts," *Industrial and Labor Relations Review* 21 (July 1968):527.
34. Ibid., p. 528.
35. Charles A. Odewahn and Joseph Krislov, "Contract Rejections: Testing the Explanatory Hypotheses," *Industrial Relations* 12 (October 1973):296.
36. Simkin, "Refusal to Ratify Contracts," p. 528.

37. Ibid., p. 534.
38. Ibid., p. 534.
39. Ibid., p. 534.
40. Ibid., pp. 534–35.
41. Ibid., p. 535.
42. Ibid., p. 535.
43. Ibid., pp. 536–37.
44. Willard A. Lewis, "The 'Lockout as the Corollary of the Strike' Controversy Reexamined," *Labor Law Journal* 23 (November 1972):660.
45. *NLRB v. Truck Drivers Local 449* (Buffalo Linen), 353 U. S. 87 (1957).
46. *NLRB v. Brown,* 380 U. S. 270 (1965).
47. *American Ship Building v. NLRB,* 380 U.S. 300 (1965).
48. *NLRB v. Mackay Radio and Telegraph Co.,* 304 U.S. 333 (1938).
49. As discussed in Chapter 3, Section 10(k) of the National Labor Relations Act gives the parties ten days to voluntarily resolve jurisdictional disputes before the NLRB gets involved in the dispute.
50. *NLRB v. Radio and Television Broadcast Engineers Local 1212,* 364 U.S. 573 (1961).
51. *Buffalo Forge Co. v. United Steelworkers,* 428 U.S. 397 (1976).
52. *Vegelahn v. Guntner,* 167 Mass. 92 (1896).
53. *Thornhill v. Alabama,* 310 U.S. 88 (1940).
54. *Bakery and Pastry Drivers v. Wohl,* 315 U.S. 769 (1942).
55. *Giboney v. Empire Storage and Ice Co.* 336 U.S. 490 (1949).
56. Benjamin J. Taylor and Fred Witney, *Labor Relations Law,* 3rd ed. (Englewood Cliffs: Prentice-Hall, 1979), p. 456.
57. *NLRB v. Denver Building and Construction Trades Council,* 341 U.S. 675 (1951).
58. *Local 761, International Union of Electrical Workers v. NLRB,* 366 U.S. 667 (1961).
59. Ibid.
60. *Sailors' Union of the Pacific* (Moore Dry Dock Co.), 92 NLRB 547 (1950).
61. Ibid.
62. *Douds v. Metropolitan Federation of Architects,* 75 F.Supp. 672 (1948).
63. *NLRB v. Fruit and Vegetable Packers, Local 760,* (Tree Fruits), 377 U.S. 58 (1964).
64. Ibid.
65. "The Ripples Spreading from the Stevens Pact," *Business Week,* 3 November 1980, p. 107; and "How the Textile Union Finally Wins Contracts at J. P. Stevens Plants," *Wall Street Journal,* 20 October 1980, p. 1.
66. "How the Textile Union Finally Wins Contracts at J. P. Stevens Plants," p. 18.
67. Ibid., p. 18.
68. "The Ripples Spreading From the Stevens Pact," p. 110.
69. "How the Textile Union Finally Wins Contracts at J. P. Stevens Plants," p. 18.
70. "The Ripples Spreading From the Stevens Pact," p. 110.

Suggested Readings

Chamberlain, Neil W. and Schilling, Jane M. *The Impact of Strikes.* New York: Harper and Brothers, 1954.
Connolly, Walter B., Jr. *Strikes Stoppages and Boycotts, 1976.* New York: Practising Law Institute, 1976.

Dereshinsky, Ralph M. *The NLRB and Secondary Boycotts*. Philadelphia: University of Pennsylvania Press, 1972.
Fritz, Richard J. and Stringari, Arthur M. *Employer's Handbook for Labor Negotiations,* 3rd ed. Detroit: Management Labor Relations Service, Inc., 1968.
Goldman, Alvin L. *The Supreme Court and Labor-Management Relations Law*. Lexington, MA: D. C. Heath and Company, 1976.
Gouldner, Alvin W. *Wildcat Strike*. New York: Harper and Row, 1954.

Chapter 10

THE RESOLUTION OF BARGAINING IMPASSES

Les Payne thought a career in labor relations would be challenging and rewarding. It certainly started that way. His first major assignment was to spearhead the company's preparation for negotiations. While that involved a lot of monotonous work, it provided an excellent opportunity to learn about collective bargaining. He also realized that the visibility of the assignment would not hurt his career.

Once bargaining started, Les played a rather minor role on the company's negotiating team. On his more cynical days, he considered himself nothing more than a "go fer." While he wanted more responsibility, he realized he had no experience in negotiations. So, he paid close attention to the chief negotiators. As a result, he learned more about the strategy and tactics of negotiations than he could have ever imagined.

The early stages of negotiations went rather smoothly. The union and management negotiators tackled a number of difficult issues with success. However, the union's wage proposals caused real problems. The union requested an 11 percent wage increase plus a cost of living clause. While the company negotiators were sympathetic to the employees' declining purchasing power, the firm was not in a financial position to allow it to agree with the union's demands. The parties negotiated long and hard. But when the old contract expired, the union went out on strike.

That was two weeks ago. Since then, the negotiating teams met only once. Les went to work every day, but he had very little to do as long as the parties were at impasse. This was not the challenging and rewarding career in labor relations he had expected. In short, he was bored.

Since Les had plenty of time on his hands, he spent lots of it thinking about the negotiations leading up to the strike. Did he do something in the preparatory phase that prevented the parties from reaching agreement? Did something happen during the negotiations that now stood in the way of a settlement? Why wouldn't one side make a move to get negotiations started again? Les could not help but believe there must be some way to get the bargaining back on track. He also knew labor and management had to do something to make sure this didn't happen again in the future. Both sides were being hurt by the strike. The problems were only going to be intensified since there was no agreement in sight.

One of the first things Les was going to do after the strike was settled was to look into techniques that would help prevent strikes in the future. Given the intransigence of the parties, Les couldn't help but wonder when he would get around to the job.

THE COLLECTIVE BARGAINING PROCESS

Les experienced firsthand the problems associated with a strike. At least, he was getting paid during the strike. Others are not so fortunate. The workers are not getting paid. The union is not receiving dues. The company is losing revenues. The company's customers are being inconvenienced. Les seriously wondered why there were any strikes since it appeared that everyone loses. It seemed to Les that no one ever won a strike.

There is little doubt that strikes are costly to all parties involved. Despite this problem, strikes have been and are likely to remain an integral part of the collective bargaining process.

As discussed in the preceding chapter, negotiations could drag on interminably without the threat of a walkout. Even though the strike threat is necessary for effective collective bargaining, strikes are likely to affect the workers, union, employer, and the public adversely. Therefore, the decision to strike is usually a serious one taken only as a last resort.

Because of the extreme costs attached to strikes, a growing number of unions and employers are exploring techniques designed to decrease the likelihood strikes will occur. These techniques can be placed into two broad categories: those designed to improve the collective bargaining process and techniques for more effective third-party intervention into bargaining impasses. This chapter is designed to explore a number of these techniques. Also, the chapter examines procedures for government intervention into labor disputes imperiling the nation's health and safety. After this chapter, you should:

- Know three techniques (continuous bargaining, prebargaining fact finding, and "early bird" negotiations) that the parties can use to improve the collective bargaining process.
- Be able to differentiate between mediation and arbitration.
- Describe the three major roles played by mediators.
- Know what interest arbitration is and why it is being substituted for the strike in some situations.
- Be able to identify the factors underlying national emergency strikes and how the government can intervene in these situations.
- Understand why the strike is so important to collective bargaining and why strikes should be allowed without government intervention.

Techniques for Improving Collective Bargaining

As the parties negotiate a collective-bargaining agreement, they face a number of problems. The exploration of the alternative solutions to these problems takes time and information. It has been argued that:

The strike represents a temporary breakdown in the creative process, not a continuation of the process. When the parties break off and resort to the exercise of naked power, it means they have temporarily abandoned all hope of reaching agreement through creative discussion and have instead resorted to persuasion through punitive action. All that a strike can accomplish is a reevaluation by each side of the other's relative power. Once this reevaluation has occurred, then bargaining must be resumed to find accommodation in light of this new power alignment.[1]

With or without a strike, the parties must address and resolve their differences as they seek a mutually acceptable pact. Techniques are available to the parties that facilitate the exploration of creative solutions to their problems. This section examines some of the major techniques.

CONTINUOUS BARGAINING

Continuous bargaining is an attempt to avoid crisis bargaining precipitated by the contract's expiration date and the threat of a strike. The term "continuous bargaining" is used to contrast this technique with conventional bargaining which takes place in the shadow of the contract expiration date and the strike threat.[2]

Some issues faced at the bargaining table are too complex to resolve in the sixty or ninety days frequently allocated for the renegotiation of a labor agreement. For example, negotiating contract language to minimize the adverse impact of major technological changes on the union's membership is an extremely complex issue. The parties will need to consider how the remaining jobs will be allocated, whether the company will retrain workers, and the roles to be played by the union and company in placing the workers displaced by the technological change in new jobs. In most situations, such complex problems could take months to resolve. The resolution of difficult problems is not possible in the emotionally heated bargaining sessions likely to be experienced as the contract's expiration date approaches. Exhibit 10.1 describes the nature of this problem and the general approach for minimizing these difficulties.

There are no set practices describing continuous bargaining. However, some common features are found when a number of instances where continuous bargaining is used is examined. First, the parties create committees to study the thorny issues confronting them. The committees examine the problems and develop proposals for their resolution. Second, the committees confer for extended periods so that adequate study time is available. Third, the committees make recommendations to the union and management negotiating teams. In other words, the proposals emanating from the committees involved in continuous bargaining are usually not binding on the parties. The committees make recommendations that can be included in the labor agreement if labor and management negotiators decide to do so. Fourth, the committees are made up of union and management representatives but can also include neutral third parties.[3] For example, the Armour Automation Committee, which addressed the problems faced by the closing and subsequent relocation of a number of meat-packing facilities, extensively utilized neutrals. In fact, the use of neutrals has been cited as a major factor contributing to the effectiveness of the committee in dealing with

> **EXHIBIT 10.1**
> **A Discussion of the Need for Continuous Bargaining**
>
> As contract deadlines approach, there is a natural tendency to attempt hasty solutions to remaining issues. Although these solutions could be successful, they are more apt to be temporary in nature and to be poorly developed. In far too many cases, these solutions have become problems of a more serious nature when the parties have tried to administer them. Not only does this create a major problem for the next contract negotiations, but also these irritations can have a very detrimental effect on the overall labor-management relationship.
>
> The benefits in the way of increased understanding and solution of problems to the mutual satisfaction of the parties through day-to-day efforts at improving communications have already been discussed, as have the advantages accruing from thoroughly studying a particular issue away from the time and emotional pressure of actual bargaining. The logical way to capitalize on these benefits and to avoid the dangers cited above is to arrange to study and search out well in advance the facts about the significant problems that may become issues in the next negotiations.
>
> Source: Healy, et al. *Creative Collective Bargaining: Meeting Today's Challenges to Labor-Management Relations*, © 1965, pp. 192–193. Reprinted by permission of Prentice-Hall, Inc., Englewood Cliffs, NJ.

the complex issues faced by the parties.[4] However, equally difficult problems in the longshoring industry were addressed and resolved through joint labor-management consultation and negotiation without any third-party participation.[5]

The advantages of continuous bargaining have been described as follows:

> Developing facts well in advance of negotiations has considerable advantages. . . . By extending the studies to cover almost the entire length of the contract, the parties have even more time in which to conduct their study and explore alternatives. They can maintain contact with a problem area over the length of the contract and can coordinate with other subcommittees. Time is a valuable commodity if used efficiently, but there is a tendency to meet only sporadically until near the bargaining deadline and then to speed up.[6]

PREBARGAINING FACT-FINDING

The need for information and the development of a data base as an integral part of the preparation for collective bargaining was discussed in Chapter 9. Failure to generate needed information or the development of conflicting data by labor and management could inhibit the effectiveness of the upcoming negotiations. Through prebargaining fact-finding, the parties jointly develop data such as agreed-upon production and cost figures. Then, the data are used as the basis for negotiations by both sides.[7] As the collective bargaining process becomes more complex, the volume of information needed has increased dramatically. It is quite possible that joint fact-finding can increase the amount and quality of information available to the negotiators. As a result, the collective bargaining process can be advanced by these improved informational resources.[8]

EARLY-BIRD NEGOTIATIONS

Early-bird negotiations are more like conventional bargaining than continuous bargaining. Whereas continuous bargaining may take place throughout the life of the contract, early-bird negotiations are concentrated during the time period prior to the contract's expiration date as in conventional bargaining. However, early-bird negotiations start earlier than conventional bargaining. If early-bird negotiations are successful, crisis bargaining precipitated by the contract's expiration date can be avoided. However, if the parties are unable to reach an agreement despite the additional time available for negotiations, the pressures created by the contract's expiration date are present as in conventional bargaining.

Advantages of getting a head start on negotiations have been identified as follows:

- The early meetings permit an exchange of demands and a complete review of the proposals.
- There is time to explore background conditions likely to influence the negotiations. These conditions include factors such as the firm's financial condition, wage trends, and area surveys; cost-of-living data; grievances and anticipated operational and manpower problems.
- If the chief negotiators are new to each other, the early meetings can be used to get to know one another. Such early discussions can help alleviate misunderstandings later in negotiations.[9]

With this approach, negotiations are frequently completed well before the old contract is due to expire. One of the interesting features of this approach is that the new contract terms are put into effect once the union membership ratifies the agreement.[10] As a result, the workers receive the contract's new benefits immediately rather than waiting for the old contract to expire. Also, if the negotiations involve concessions or give-backs by the union, the employer achieves the resulting lower labor costs and the related benefits sooner than with conventional bargaining.

The economic recession of the early 1980s has stimulated an increased use of early-bird negotiations. For example, in September 1981, the International Brotherhood of Teamsters urged the negotiating committee for the trucking industry to start negotiations early. Unemployment was high among union members and many trucking companies were ailing financially. The parties started negotiating on December 1, 1981. By January 15, 1982, they had reached tentative agreement on a new contract. This was about two and one-half months before the old contract was due to expire. The resulting contract was marked by moderate wage increases and a relax-

THE COLLECTIVE BARGAINING PROCESS

The UAW leadership announced their willingness to enter into negotiations with Ford and General Motors months before the contract was to expire. It was hoped that a new contract benefiting both labor and management could be negotiated.

ation of some work rules. By negotiating and concluding the agreement early, both the union and employers could realize the benefits of the new contract sooner than if they had followed their traditional bargaining timetable.

A similar approach was taken in the auto industry. Ford Motor Company and the United Auto Workers (UAW) started negotiations of a new contract in January 1982. Even though the old contract was not due to expire until the fall of that year, the parties apparently believed an early start would be mutually beneficial.

In February 1982, Ford and the UAW reached agreement on a new, lower cost agreement months in advance of the old contract's expiration. Later, the UAW and General Motors also reached an early agreement.

Continuous bargaining, prebargaining fact finding, and early-bird negotiations are cooperative efforts by the parties to improve the collective bargaining process. It is hoped that by improving the negotiating process, the parties will increase the likelihood of reaching agreement without a strike. In general, these techniques are utilized by the parties without any outside intervention. In addition to these private efforts, other techniques designed to improve the negotiating process rely on the involvement of a third party. Outside third parties can be employed to help the parties resolve impasses that develop during their negotiations.

Third-Party Efforts to Resolve Bargaining Impasses

During negotiations, it is possible for the parties to reach an impasse which they may need help to resolve. Mediation is a technique for involving neutral third parties in the negotiations. Through third-party involvement, it is hoped the impasse will be resolved and the need to strike avoided. Arbitration is another approach to resolving bargaining impasses discussed in this section.

MEDIATION

Before proceeding to a discussion of mediation in labor disputes, it may be useful to differentiate between mediation and another form of third-party intervention with which it is often confused—arbitration. Ann Douglas differentiates between mediation and arbitration in terms of the degree of independence left to the parties to the bargaining impasse. With arbitration, the parties enlist an outside third party to make a judicial-like decision on the points in dispute. Parties to arbitration agree in advance to bind themselves to the arbitrator's decision. In other words, they have no independence; they must abide by the arbitrator's award.

The situation is basically different when the parties to collective bargaining rely on mediation to help resolve their dispute. With mediation, an outside third party is brought into the dispute but remains involved in the case at the discretion of the parties. Throughout the mediator's involvement in the dispute, the parties retain the right to accept or reject the mediator's counsel. At any point in the process, the mediator can be dropped from the proceedings.[11] Whereas the arbitrator has the authority to decide the disputed issues, the mediator has no such authority,[12] serving instead at the pleasure of the parties.

A mediator is a well-trained professional who has a thorough understanding of the collective bargaining process and dispute resolution techniques. The mediator is not responsible for the specific solutions or outcomes that will resolve the dispute. Rather, the mediator's primary concern is the process through which the parties will secure an agreement.[13]

There is no "right" time to bring a mediator into a labor dispute. At one extreme, the mediator could be present from the first day of negotiations. At the other extreme, the parties could wait until their inability to reach agreement leads to a strike prior to bringing a mediator into the dispute. However, it has been argued that the proper time to involve a mediator is some time between the two extremes. Simkin suggests that the optimal time span in which to bring in a mediator begins "after trouble seems certain to the negotiators and ending before a deadlock on issues is firm and certainly before an actual strike starts. . . ."[14] This time period varies from situation to situation. Some bargainers will know months in advance of the contract expiration date that the parties will not be able to resolve their differences of opinion without outside help. In other situations, there may be only a few days, or even hours, notice that a deadlock will occur.

The mediator's primary responsibility is to create an environment that facilitates the parties' ability to resolve the dispute. The mediator establishes:

> An environment in which all participants sense that they are involved in a problem-solving procedure. The forum created by the mediator is just such an environment, and the mediator himself is a symbol of the problem-solving procedure. The personal style of mediators varies, but it has been our experience that in spite of such variations, the authority of each mediator resides in his ability to convince the parties that he is present to oversee their efforts to reach an agreement. He exudes conviction that the individual spokesmen will devote themselves to this objective. So, he establishes an atmosphere of concern for them as individuals and for their problems and concentrates their attention on solution seeking.[15]

In sum, the parties can bring a mediator into contract negotiations when it becomes apparent they will need outside help in reaching an agreement. Although the mediator does not have the ability to impose a settlement on the parties, he or she can facilitate the dispute resolution process by creating an environment conducive to problem solving. Attention now turns to an examination of how a mediator can help the parties reach agreement.

THE FUNCTIONS PERFORMED BY MEDIATORS[16]

It is difficult to generalize about the functions performed by mediators since they vary sharply from one situation to another. Mediators do not enter the bargaining relationship with a list of tactics they plan on using. Rather, the mediator does whatever is necessary to help the parties reach agreement. However it is possible to place the different activites performed by mediators into three broad categories:

1. Functions that are procedural in nature.
2. Functions intended to improve communications.
3. Functions that allow the mediator to contribute to the substance of the dispute's resolution.

Each of these categories will be examined in the sections to follow to help give better understanding of the mediator's role.

Procedural functions. The procedural activities are primarily concerned with structuring the environment in which subsequent negotiations will take place. While the procedural activities might appear rather inconsequential, they can contribute greatly to the parties' ability to reach agreement.

- *Scheduling meetings*—Mediators will often take responsibility for scheduling future meetings. While this may sound like a clerical task, it is quite possible that the timing of future meetings is part of the bargaining strategy for one or both sides, and therefore can pose an obstacle for agreement. For example, the parties could have negotiated to a stalemate. In such a situation, a request for another bargaining session could be viewed as a sign of weakness. By allowing the mediator to schedule future meetings, the parties can avoid any such stigma.

- *Recessing meetings*—During a negotiating session, the mediator can take the initiative to terminate the meeting. If negotiations are proceeding toward a settlement, it is unlikely that a mediator would destroy the momentum by suggesting the parties take a recess. However, if it appears that progress has stopped or that the discussion has degenerated into endless speeches with little content, the mediator is likely to recess negotiations until some later date. By so doing, the mediator may prevent both sides from hardening their positions, a situation that could interfere with future negotiations.
- *Arrange joint or separate meetings*—While a final agreement usually takes place while both parties are at the bargaining table, there will be times during negotiations when the mediator will want to separate the labor and management negotiators. It may be necessary to have the parties meet separately to prevent personalities or tempers from interfering with negotiations. Also, separate meetings will allow the mediator to confer in private with the parties. By so doing, it may be possible to explore the bases for settlements more quickly than if both labor and management were participating in the discussions.
- *Suggest around-the-clock negotiations*—At some point during the bargaining, the mediator may decide that negotiations should be intensified by increasing the length of the bargaining sessions. This may be because the strike deadline is rapidly approaching. Or, the negotiators may think they must bargain all night at least once during the negotiations in order to demonstrate to top management or the rank-and-file union membership that they have done the best job possible. Since around-the-clock bargaining is demanding, both physically and mentally, it must be properly timed. The mediator works with labor and management negotiators to schedule continuous negotiations at a time when it will facilitate settlement and not stand in its way.
- *Other procedural activities*—In addition to the procedural functions outlined above, there are several other activities through which a mediator can structure a bargaining environment so the likelihood of settlement is increased. On occasion, the room or rooms used for bargaining are inadequate. In such situations, the mediator can facilitate settlement by encouraging the parties to relocate their negotiations. Having the parties use subcommittees is another technique mediators employ to help the parties reach agreement. This is especially useful when the parties have almost reached agreement but a number of details need to be worked out. The mediator can encourage the bargaining teams to create subgroups to study the issue in greater detail and arrive at a solution. The subgroups then report to the bargaining teams which take final action.

As the contract expiration date approaches, the mediator can encourage the parties to extend the existing contract or otherwise postpone the strike. It has been pointed out that the timing of this action is very important because:

If it is made too early, it will tend to destroy the usefulness of deadline pressures. If the parties know that a request for postponement will be made and that both agree to it, they may seize upon this as an excuse for avoiding the difficult last minute decisions that precede a real strike or lockout threat. Conversely, if it is made too late, the strike or lockout procedures may be so far advanced that it is almost impossible to reverse them.[17]

In situations where it appears that the bulk of the issues confronting the parties will be resolved but one or two remain unsettled, the mediator may encourage the parties to finalize the agreement except for the issues still at dispute. Then, additional efforts can be employed to resolve the remaining points of conflict. Also, the negotiator can encourage the parties to try some other form of dispute resolution such as arbitration, fact finding, or the bringing in of another mediator.

Finally, if negotiations and mediation attempts fail and a strike results, it is quite likely that bargaining will be terminated. Another procedural aspect of the mediator's role is to get the parties back to the bargaining table during the strike. Since initiating bargaining after the strike starts could be viewed as a sign of weakness, both labor and management negotiators could be hesitant to propose additional negotiations. In such situations, a mediator can perform a useful function by insisting that the parties renew negotiations.

As can be seen, a number of procedural tasks can be performed by a mediator. While several of them appear on the surface to be rather simple, clerical-type activities, they can be instrumental in the conflict resolution process. In addition to these procedural functions, several activities performed by mediators can improve communications between the parties.

Communication functions. It is quite possible for a stalemate to develop during negotiations, not because of the real differences in the positions of the parties, but as a result of the parties' inability to communicate effectively with each other. For example, a union could demand a union shop and get a definitive "no" from the management negotiators who think a union shop means a closed shop. It is the mediator's responsibility to help the parties communicate effectively. By doing so, the mediator can help labor and management negotiators reach agreement. The mediator can perform several activities to help the parties communicate more effectively:

- *Supplement normal communication channels*—While most communicating goes on at the bargaining table, the mediator can help keep communication channels open between negotiating sessions. It is common practice for the mediator to keep in contact with labor and management bargainers while negotiations are in recess. During these informal conversations, the mediator may obtain information which could facilitate the bargaining process. With the party's permission, the information can be passed on to the other bargainer and serve as the basis for future negotiations.

- *Facilitate the search for agreeable terms*—During negotiations, one bargainer may want to make a tentative offer or concession. However, this is difficult to do for fear of becoming committed to the position. It is difficult to explore alternative solutions to the bargaining problems without becoming committed.

    If a mediator is involved in the negotiations, the search for an acceptable solution can be greatly facilitated. Instead of the parties making the offer or concession, the mediator can put forth the idea. This is known as "trying on for size." For example, the union negotiating team might be willing to lower its wage proposal from a $.50/hour increase to $.42/hour if that would prevent a strike. However, if $.42/hour would be unacceptable and a strike would occur anyway, the union negotiators would probably stay at $.50/hour. If the union negotiators asked the company if $.42/hour would be acceptable, the union would probably be committed to the $.42/hour figure.

    It would be possible for the mediator, after talking to the union negotiators about their willingness to drop their demand to $.42/hour, to then go to a separate meeting of the management negotiators. In this meeting, the management team can "try the $.42/hour offer on for size." Since the mediator has no money to spend or authority to make concessions, the mediator and the management negotiators can explore the principles involved with the union's position. Since the union is not a party to the discussions, it is in no way committed to the $.42/hour figure. If the mediator learns that the offer is acceptable to management, this information can be communicated to the union negotiators who can formally extend the offer. If it is apparent to the mediator that the $.42/hour increase is unacceptable to management, this information can also be conveyed to the union. In this situation, the union is in no way committed to the $.42/hour figure and can explore other options.

- *Identify and communicate rigidities in bargaining positions*—For both management and union negotiators, there are some items that "must" be included in the labor agreement. These are the items over which the parties would be willing to strike or take a strike. At the same time, there will be other provisions they would like to see in the new agreement but which are not worth striking over.

    During negotiations, the identification of the "must" issues is an important task for the negotiators. Sometimes these issues are readily apparent. In other situations, the parties may fail to identify the "must" items. The successful completion of the negotiations could be threatened while one party waits for further concessions, not recognizing they are discussing a "must" issue on which there will be no further concessions.

By observing negotiations and through discussions with the parties, a mediator will be able to identify the rigidities in bargaining positions. By communicating this information to the other bargainer, the mediator can try to convince the negotiators that the other bargaining team is firm in its resolve on a particular issue and that future concessions are unlikely. There is no need for the parties to wait, perhaps until after a strike has begun, for concessions when they are not likely to come. Once the bargainer is convinced no further movement will occur on a particular issue, other bargaining strategies can be pursued, and, it is hoped, a stalemate avoided.

As can be seen, helping the parties maintain good communications is an important part of the mediator's job. It can help avoid or clear up misunderstandings concerning the positions of the parties. The mediator can also serve as a mechanism through which the parties can try out offers without incurring obligations or risking being perceived as weakening in their bargaining positions. Notice that when helping the parties communicate more effectively, the mediator is using information provided by the parties themselves and presenting it to the other bargainer. The mediator is not adding much additional information. In a third dimension of the mediator's role, he or she interjects new information or ideas into the negotiations with the hope that the new information will provide the basis for future negotiations and ultimately a settlement.

The substantive function. The procedural and communication functions are designed to create an environment in which the labor and management negotiators are able to better respond to their own ideas and proposals. By helping structure the environment in which the parties are negotiating, the mediator moves the parties closer to an agreement. However, with the procedural or communications functions, the mediator is not providing input into the substance of the disputes. In other words, the mediator is not suggesting proposals or alternatives not previously considered by the parties. In the substantive function, the mediator gets directly involved in the exploration for an agreement.

- *Offering suggestions on specific issues*—Because mediators are experienced labor relations experts, they may be able to see solutions to the bargaining problems not seen by the negotiators. Sometimes these proposals represent compromises. Other times, they are new poposals not previously considered by the parties. As previously noted, mediators do not have the authority to compel the acceptance of their proposals by the parties. However, union and management negotiators will often voluntarily accept them, or at least use them as the basis for continued bargaining.
- *Clarifying priorities*—As previously discussed, the bargaining teams may not agree between themselves on what is a "must" issue and what is not. This is especially true for the union team which is usually sensitive to the pressures from its constituent groups. The problem may be exacerbated by having representatives from the union's various constituent groups on the

bargaining team. While it is desirable to have a well-established list of priorities when entering negotiations, this is not always the case. There may be items that represent the pet projects of an individual negotiator or that might be important to a major constituent group but are clearly unattainable at the bargaining table. On the role a mediator can play in such situations, it has been written:

> The principal negotiators may welcome the assistance from the mediator in killing off some issue(s). . . . Without being dictatorial or improperly slipping into a decision-making role, a mediator can quite properly influence the priority development by calling on his general labor relations experience, his knowledge of contractual provisions elsewhere, and his specific knowledge of negotiations elsewhere.[18]

- *Helping the parties identify strike costs relative to the remaining unresolved issues*—As the strike deadline approaches, it is quite likely that the parties will have agreed on many issues but will still be negotiating others. In the face of the deadline, the parties must determine if they are willing to strike over the remaining unresolved issues. In such situations, a mediator can perform a valuable service for the parties by reminding them of the costs of striking. While the negotiators should be more aware of strike costs than the mediator, they can lose sight of these costs in the heat of negotiations. The mediator can estimate daily costs of a strike for labor and management and assess the probable length of the strike. By doing so, the mediator can remind the parties of the strike costs relative to the value of the unresolved issues still being bargained.

- *Recommending a "package" settlement*—While many of the mediator's activities will focus on the individual items being bargained by the parties, the mediator may want to suggest a "package" settlement designed to resolve all the remaining issues in dispute. The mediator may see some tradeoffs involving a number of different issues that could be acceptable to both labor and management negotiators.

This section has described a number of rather specific functions a mediator can perform. While the mediator's specific activities are significant, it is important not to lose sight of the mediator's overriding responsibility—to create an environment conducive to problem-solving. Let's look more closely at the environment fostered by having a mediator involved in the bargaining process and the potential benefits for the parties.

THE BENEFITS OF MEDIATION TO THE PARTIES

Without the formal authority to impose a settlement on the parties, mediators must rely on their personal characteristics such as knowledge of labor relations, effective communication skills, integrity, and patience to create a forum that helps the negotiators reach an agreement. In the bargaining environment created by a mediator, the parties should be able to:

- Develop clear and concise statements of their positions, thereby providing order to their discussions.
- Develop an expression of their goals and objectives. While these are usually known, they may not be clearly enunciated in bargaining situations involving inexperienced negotiators.
- Establish an agenda for future negotiations. This helps prevent negotiations from floundering because of the parties' inability to agree on what they will discuss.
- Relieve tensions and help establish a climate more conducive to bargaining. During negotiations, tensions may build. By talking to a mediator who is sympathetic to one's problems and who is willing to help work them out, some of the frustrations and uncertainties may be alleviated.
- Areas of agreement and disagreement may be more precisely defined. Through discussions with the mediator, similarities between the positions of the parties may emerge that were not recognized in their previous negotiations.
- Restate issues for the mediator in a language free from inflammatory rhetoric. By so doing, the true nature of their differences may emerge.
- Develop problem-solving procedures that focus the parties' attention on seeking solutions rather than confrontation.
- Identify solutions to problems when they become available to the parties.[19]

THE FEDERAL MEDIATION AND CONCILIATION SERVICE

Any individual requested by the parties can serve as a mediator. However, the Federal Mediation and Conciliation Service (FMCS), an agency of the federal government, is a major source of mediators. The FMCS was created in 1947 by the Labor-Management Relations Act (LMRA). Section 203(b) of the LMRA describes the functions of the FMCS with respect to mediation. It reads as follows:

> The Service may proffer its services in any labor dispute in any industry affecting commerce, either upon its own motion or upon the request of one or more of the parties to the dispute, whenever in its judgement such dispute threatens to cause a substantial interruption in commerce. The Director and the Service are directed to avoid attempting to mediate disputes which would have only a minor effect on interstate commerce if state or other conciliation services are available to the parties. Whenever the Service does proffer its services in any dispute, it shall be the duty of the Service promptly to put itself in communication with the parties and to use its best efforts, by mediation and conciliation, to bring them to agreement.

Mediation is a technique available to the parties for resolving impasses confronted during collective bargaining. By availing themselves of such a procedure, labor and management negotiators can improve the effectiveness of the collective bargaining process. By doing so, the likelihood that the parties will have to resort to a strike to resolve their differences is decreased.

So far, the techniques described in this chapter are designed to help the parties reach agreement without having to resort to a strike. Continuous bargaining, prebargaining fact finding, and early-bird negotiations are utilized by the parties without third-party involvement. Mediation is also intended to improve negotiations. However, this latter technique requires the parties to invite a neutral third party to help them reach agreement. Despite the use of the techniques discussed thus far, an impasse may continue and a strike could result.

Some parties believe that a strike is dysfunctional to their relationship. Therefore, there is a need to develop alternatives to the strike. In the section to follow, a technique is examined that resolves impasses between labor and management so that a strike is unnecessary.

INTEREST ARBITRATION

In most situations in the private sector, a strike will result if the parties reach the old contract's expiration date without signing a new agreement. As previously discussed, a strike is used to impose costs on the other bargainer. To avoid the costs of a continued strike, one or both sides will usually redefine their positions on the issues at dispute. As this occurs, the parties move toward agreement. However, the costs of striking mount as the parties work toward an agreement. Arbitration has developed as a device for resolving bargaining impasses without having to strike. Interest arbitration is used extensively in the public sector. However, it has potential application in the private sector as well.

Like mediation, arbitration involves a neutral third party. While mediation and arbitration are usually separate processes, it is possible for them to be combined. Exhibit 10.2 describes a procedure known as med-arb which utilizes both mediation and arbitration. When interest arbitration is used in lieu of a strike, the parties submit unresolved contract provisions to an arbitrator. Then, the parties are obligated to abide by the arbitrator's decision which is final and binding.

TYPES OF ARBITRATION

There are two major situations in which arbitration is used. Rights arbitration is used to resolve disputes arising during the life of a labor agreement over its interpretation or administration. In most labor contracts, rights arbitration is the final step of the grievance procedure. Rights arbitration will be discussed in detail in Chapter 15.

The primary concern of this section is interest arbitration. Interest arbitration occurs when disputes arising during the negotiation or renegotiation of a labor agreement are submitted to a neutral third party for a final and binding decision. Interest arbitration can be either voluntary or compulsory. Voluntary arbitration is most likely to be found in the private sector. With voluntary arbitration, the parties are not legally obligated to submit their bargaining impasses to an arbitrator. They do so because both labor and management believe it is in their self-interest to submit dis-

> **EXHIBIT 10.2**
> **Med-Arb—The Combining of Mediation and Arbitration**
>
> The whole point of what we call mediation-arbitration, or med-arb, is to give the parties an opportunity to carry out the negotiation process. Where med-arb differs from orthodox mediation is that the orthodox mediator, as such, does not have any muscle. And orthodox arbitration, in terms of substantive matters or interest arbitration, is not used very frequently; parties are afraid to put their fate in the hands of third parties.
>
> When parties agree to med-arb, they have to agree in advance that all decisions, whether reached by mediation or arbitration, become part of the mediator-arbitrator's award and are final and binding. None of the decisions goes back to the parties for acceptance or rejection. Once having agreed to that, it can be seen immediately that taking off the arbitrator hat and putting on the mediator hat gives a person muscle that he or she doesn't have when exercising orthodox mediation—and that's the whole name of the game.
>
> In carrying out the functions of med-arb, one is in effect negotiating meetings. There are no records; there is no transcript; and each issue is taken up whatever it might be. The parties for the first time really have to bare their souls, because if they are dishonest in the sense of holding back on a particular issue, they know the med-arbitrator is going to make the decision. It really does keep them honest, and that's the whole point in med-arb. Most interest problems are settled by direct negotiations; and since both parties approach the problem with complete honesty, they come within an area of settlement.
>
> *Source: Sam Kagel, "Combining Mediation and Arbitration,"* Monthly Labor Review, 96 (September 1973):62.

putes to arbitration rather than strike. Compulsory arbitration is most likely to be found in the public sector. However, it has had limited application in the railroad industry. The term "compulsory" is used because the arbitration of interest disputes is mandated by law. This section is concerned with voluntary interest arbitration. The use of compulsory arbitration in the public sector will be discussed in Part Six of this book concerned with collective bargaining in the public sector.

THE EXPERIMENTAL NEGOTIATING AGREEMENT

Interest arbitration in the private sector has had only limited applications in the United States. However, the Experimental Negotiating Agreement (ENA) in the steel industry provides an example of the use of voluntary interest arbitration in the private sector.

Origins of the ENA. Over the years, the steel industry had been characterized by labor unrest. For example, the industry incurred a 116-day strike in 1959. During contract negotiation years, a disruptive pattern of behavior developed. In anticipation of a strike, the steel companies and their customers stockpiled large amounts of steel. As a result, union members were able to work large amounts of overtime. However, if an agreement was reached without a strike, partial plant shutdowns and worker layoffs would occur as the companies worked off the stockpiles. In the event the negotiations led to a strike, especially a lengthy one such as in 1959, foreign steel manufacturers gained an opportunity to acquire American customers. In some cases, the United States firms were unable to regain these customers at the end of the strike.[20]

Details of the agreement. To help avoid the "boom-bust" cycle that had developed in the steel industry and the permanent loss of customers to foreign competition, the United Steelworkers of America and the companies comprising the basic steel industry developed the ENA. The ENA was adopted by the parties in 1973 to govern the negotiations of the agreement in 1974. The major feature of the ENA was described in the following terms:

> The most significant provision of the ENA was an agreement not to strike or lockout at the expiration of the contract and to submit all national issues not resolved through collective bargaining to a panel of impartial arbitrators for final and binding decision. Thus the parties guaranteed that there would be no interruption of steel production the following year.[21]

In order for the union to give up the right to strike, the steel companies made the following concessions:

1. The no-strike agreement would not extend to local issues. For the first time in the history of steel negotiations, local unions were given the right to strike over local issues, subject to approval of the international president.
2. Each employee would be given a bonus of $150 "because economic advantages could accrue to the companies by elimination of the effects of hedge-buying and shutdowns."
3. A minimum wage increase of 3 percent per year would be granted at the beginning of each contract year, subject to additional increases which might be negotiated by the parties.
4. The cost-of-living agreement providing a one-cent increase in wages for each .3 increase in the 1967 Consumer Price Index (instead of one cent for each .4 increase in the 1957–59 CPI provided in the 1971 contract) would be continued for the term of the new agreement.
5. If the parties went to arbitration, provisions dealing with local working conditions, union shop, and check-off, the principle of cost-of-living adjustments, wage increases, and the bonus under ENA, management rights, and the no-strike–no-lockout commitment could not be changed.[22]

The right to strike over local issues has been cited as the key concession made by the steel companies. The union would not accept the agreement without the local strike provision. The provision was particularly objectionable to the companies for two major reasons:

- For single-plant companies such as Inland Steel, a local strike shutting down their single facility was like a company-wide strike.
- Multiplant companies were also concerned because a local strike could cause company-wide problems as customers shifted orders from plants on strike to those not on strike.[23]

The local strike issue was a major stumbling block that the parties had to overcome when negotiating the ENA. As noted above, the issue posed serious problems for management. Similarly, the USW negotiators believed it was a necessary part of the agreement. Exhibit 10.3 discusses the significance of this provision from the union's perspective.

Since the signing of the ENA, three contracts have been negotiated (1974, 1977, and 1980). In none of these negotiations have the parties had to utilize the three-person arbitration panel created to resolve disputed contract provisions. It appears the ENA has brought stability to the steel industry. It also appears that I. W. Abel was quite accurate when he described the ENA in the following way:

> The new procedure not only relieves both sides of the pressures of a potential shutdown but also offers us a genuine opportunity to achieve results equal to those obtainable when the threat of a strike exists. We have carefully preserved the nature and role of our bargaining relationship. What we have done is to extend and refine the tools of collective bargaining to solve a special and highly vexing problem afflicting our industry.[24]

As discussed at the outset of this section, voluntary arbitration is a technique available to the parties desiring to avoid the need to strike. However, arbitration is

---

EXHIBIT 10.3
The "Local Strike" Issue: The Union's Perspective

Another positive factor in the 1974 negotiations is the fact that local unions will have the right to strike over local issues. These have always been a festering sore in our negotiations and they often produce demoralizing reactions from our members—even when we negotiate good national economic terms. Since the local unions in 1974 for the first time will have the right to strike over local issues, we expect more effective bargaining and speedier resolution of such issues.

Faced with the genuine possibility of a strike locally—however limited—the companies will have an incentive to bargain out such issues promptly in negotiations. This should help produce a prompt and satisfactory total settlement. It is important to remember that the right to strike over local issues is an essential ingredient of the experimental procedure, and the plan could not succeed without it.

Source: I. W. Abel, "ENA . . . A Better Way," pamphlet published by the United Steelworkers of America.

not likely to be of interest to all collective bargaining situations. It is usually adopted when it becomes apparent to the parties that the traditional strike system is so costly and disruptive that they are forced to explore alternative means of dispute resolution. The significance of substituting arbitration for the right to strike must be recognized. When the parties make such a move, they give up control over the final settlement. Rather than reaching agreement at the bargaining table, the parties delegate the right to resolve the dispute to the arbitrator. From labor's and management's perspectives, this can introduce a measure of uncertainty into collective bargaining which deters many parties from utilizing voluntary arbitration. Instead, the parties attempt to reach a negotiated agreement.[25]

Emergency Disputes

In the vast majority of labor disputes, the parties are left on their own to resolve their differences without government intervention. Under most circumstances, the parties develop their own dispute resolution mechanisms. They also retain the right to strike in the event their negotiation efforts fail. While the services of the FMCS are available to the parties, labor and management negotiators do not have to take advantage of their assistance. This is usually the extent of government involvement in most labor disputes.

However, some labor disputes in the private sector can imperil the nation's health and safety. As a result, emergency dispute procedures have been developed to facilitate the resolution of such disputes. Emergency dispute procedures are found in the Labor-Management Relations Act and the Railway Labor Act.

LABOR-MANAGEMENT RELATIONS ACT PROCEDURES

Section 206 of Title II of the Labor-Management Relations Act states:

> Whenever, in the opinion of the President of the United States, a threatened or actual strike or lockout affecting an entire industry or a substantial part thereof engaged in trade, commerce, transportation, transmission or communication among the several states or with foreign nations, or engaged in the production of goods for commerce will, if permitted to occur or continue, imperil national health and safety. . . .

As a result of this provision, it is possible for government to intervene in labor disputes having a direct effect on either the health or safety of the nation.[26] The rationale underlying the creation of emergency disputes procedures has been described as follows:

> The basic concept underlying emergency disputes procedures in peace-time is that the public interest some times supersedes private interests. While strikes and lockouts nor-

mally are permissible as persuaders in the reaching of voluntary agreements, in some circumstances the exercise of economic sanctions by the parties can inflict irreparable damage on parties not directly involved. Since collective bargaining is an institutional arrangement within a democratic society, the needs of the total economy sometimes must prevail over the interests of a segment of the economy.[27]

An outline of the national emergency strike procedure. The basic objective of this procedure is to delay strikes or lockouts. During the delay, efforts are made to resolve the issues on which the parties disagree. Under this procedure, the public is protected by having the strike or lockout postponed while the parties retain control over the conduct of the negotiations.

Sections 206 through 210 of Title II of the Labor-Management Relations Act outlines the following procedure:

1. When the United States president believes an actual or threatened strike imperils the nation's health or safety, the president appoints a board of inquiry.
2. The board of inquiry examines the issues involved in the dispute and makes a written report to the president. The report includes a statement of the facts of the dispute and statements from each party to the dispute. However, the board's report is to include no recommendations.
3. Upon receiving the report, the president may direct the attorney general to petition a federal district court to enjoin the strike or lockout from occurring or, if in progress, from continuing.
4. The court will issue an injunction if it is established that (a) the dispute affects an entire industry or a substantial part of an industry and (b) the dispute imperils the nation's health and safety.
5. When the injunction is issued, the parties to the dispute are under a duty to make every effort to settle their disagreements with the assistance of the FMCS.
6. The president reconvenes the board of inquiry. After sixty days, the board reports to the president the parties' current positions, the efforts made to reach agreement, statements describing the positions of both sides to the dispute, and a statement of the employer's last offer of settlement. This report is made available to the public by the president.
7. Within fifteen days of the report, the NLRB conducts a secret ballot of the employees on the question of whether they will accept the employer's final offer of settlement. The NLRB has five days to certify the results of the vote.
8. Once the results of the votes are certified or a settlement is reached, whichever comes first, the attorney general must request the court to vacate the injunction. Then, the court must discharge the injunction.
9. Once the injunction is vacated, the president makes a full report to Congress including the board of inquiry findings, the results of the NLRB ballot, and any recommendations the president sees fit to make.

The essence of this procedure is to create an eighty-day "cooling-off" period[28] by means of an injunction. During the cooling-off period, the parties are encouraged to continue their negotiations and reach agreement. However, if the parties do not settle during this period, they can legally strike once the injunction is vacated unless Congress enacts additional controls over the dispute.[29]

Experience under the emergency disputes procedure. Since its passage in 1947, the emergency disputes provision has been infrequently utilized. The procedure has been invoked on only thirty-one occasions. Of these disputes, four were settled before an injunction was issued. In the twenty-seven remaining cases, fifteen of the disputes were settled during the injunction period. However, in six cases, a strike continued after the eighty-day cooling-off period.

Critique of the procedure. The effectiveness of the emergency strike procedure is best evaluated in terms of the provision's objectives. A major reason for the establishment of this procedure was to protect the public from work stoppages imperiling the nation's health and safety. It has been argued that the national emergency strike procedure has not achieved this objective.

It must be remembered that the emergency strike procedure found in the LMRA does not resolve labor disputes. It merely postpones them for up to eighty days, thereby relieving the parties of the obligation to bargain. Cullen argues:

> In effect, it is said, the strike deadline that precipitates most agreements is just moved back eighty days; instead of this being a cooling-off period during which mediation and second thoughts can prevail, it becomes a "warming-up" period for the next deadline.[30]

Another criticism of the procedure is that in six cases in which the labor dispute was enjoined, a strike was experienced after the injunction was vacated. In other words, strikes can be enjoined for up to eighty days because they imperil the nation's health and safety. However, after the eighty days, the strike is allowed to continue unless Congress intervenes through the passage of special legislation. In these situations, the procedure fails to stop emergency strikes.[31]

Other criticisms of the procedure include:[32]

- Rarely is more than mediation needed. More extensive government involvement in labor disputes is usually unnecessary.
- The injunction is a one-sided device. Workers must continue employment under the old contract. Management has 80 more days of production under the old agreement. Also, the injunction is a repressive measure to labor in light of the historical application of the injunction in labor disputes. (See Chapter 2 for a discussion of this issue.)
- The procedure is inflexible, and therefore predictable. For example, when the employer's last offer has been submitted to the employees for a vote, it has been rejected every time. Once an offer is made, it is rarely withdrawn. Therefore, why not reject the offer. You might get more. It is unlikely you will get less.[33]

- The effectiveness of the board of inquiry is severely limited by the legislative prohibition on its ability to make recommendations for settling the dispute. Without recommendations, there is "no point around which public opinion can mobilize."[34]

EMERGENCY STRIKE PROVISIONS UNDER THE RAILWAY LABOR ACT

The Railway Labor Act (RLA) has contained an emergency strike provision since its passage in 1926. While this procedure has some similarities to Title II of the LMRA, there are also a number of important differences.[35]

An outline of the RLA emergency disputes procedure. Under the RLA disputes resolution procedure, the National Mediation Board (NMB) attempts to mediate disputes over issues such as pay, work rules, or working conditions. If mediation efforts fail to secure an agreement and if one or both of the parties refuses to arbitrate the disagreement, the emergency dispute provisions can be invoked. The basic steps of this procedure found in Section 10 of the RLA are as follows:

1. If the NMB believes a dispute threatens to interrupt interstate commerce by denying any section of the country essential transportation service, the NMB will notify the president.
2. The president can create an ad hoc emergency board to investigate the dispute and report its findings to the president with recommendations for resolving the dispute. The board has thirty days from its creation to fulfill its functions.
3. The parties are required to maintain the status quo for thirty days after the emergency board's report has been submitted to the president.

The basic purpose of this procedure is to delay the strike for up to sixty days while the parties continue to negotiate. The rationale behind prohibiting the strike while the emergency board performs its function has been described as follows:

> Without the restriction against strikes throughout negotiations and mediation, the appointment of an Emergency Board under Section 10, after the exhaustion of negotiations, would seem a dubious step. Such a Board is to be appointed where a disruption to commerce threatens. Its purpose is to prevent such disruption. If the strike is not barred during and prior to the appointment of the Board, the disruption may occur regardless of the appointment of the Board—and the Board would seem a futile gesture. The disruption to commerce could be complete before the Emergency Board stage was reached and concluded.[36] (footnotes deleted)

It is hoped the parties with the aid of the ad hoc emergency board will be able to reach agreement during the sixty-day period. However, if the parties fail to agree, the RLA is silent concerning further actions the government can take.[37] At the expiration of the sixty-day period, the parties are free to strike unless special action is taken to prevent the labor dispute.

To prevent strikes subsequent to the exhaustion of the emergency disputes procedure, a number of steps have been taken. For example, President Truman seized the railroads in 1946 and again in 1948 to prevent interruptions of service. Seizure occurs when the government takes over the operation of business threatened with or actually involved in a strike. While seized, strikes and lockouts are prohibited.[38] Also, it is possible for the government to impose a solution to the labor dispute on the parties while the facility is seized. In 1946, President Truman went so far as to ask Congress "for authority to draft the strikers, strip them of their seniority rights, and permit the government to determine the workers' wages and retain the company's profits during the period of seizure."[39] However, it was not necessary for Congress to act on this request since the strike ended. In other disputes, injunctions have been used to delay strikes. Similarly, congressional action has been taken to delay strikes. Congress has also passed a law requiring the parties to submit their dispute to arbitration.

Between 1926 and 1975, 198 emergency boards were appointed and there were 656 strikes in the railroad and airline industries subject to the RLA emergency disputes procedure. It has been argued that the procedure has not effectively prevented interruptions in essential transportation services. Another argument is that the procedure inhibits effective collective bargaining. It has been stated that:

> Preparing for an emergency board proceeding and bargaining are quite different approaches to the task of either winning gains or achieving agreement. If one is doing the former, it is often wiser to ask for more than expected, in both amounts and quantity of demands, in the hope that the emergency board will recommend the maximum possible. Why bargain away anything when it might be granted? This is what happened in the industry. The parties usually go through the procedure of the Act with little or no intention of yielding on anything till the emergency board stage is involved—and then too often, not till after emergency board recommendations are issued.[40]

SUGGESTED IMPROVEMENTS IN EMERGENCY DISPUTE PROCEDURES

Concern about the effectiveness of existing emergency dispute procedures has led to discussions concerning legislative changes that could improve these procedures. Suggestions for improving emergency disputes procedures include:[41]

- Repeal the emergency strike provisions of the Railway Labor Act and bring the transportation industries under coverage of the procedures included in Title II of the Labor-Management Relations Act.
- Extend the coverage of the LMRA procedure to include regional as well as national disputes imperiling health and safety.
- Boards of inquiry could make recommendations if so directed by the president. Also, the president could issue an executive order freezing the status quo for thirty days prior to invoking the court-ordered eighty-day injunction.
- Establish an "arsenal of weapons" approach. If the dispute continues after the eighty-day cooling-off period, the president would be empowered to in-

voke one of three new options. One option is to extend the cooling-off period for up to thirty days. This would give the parties additional time to negotiate an agreement. Alternatively, the president could direct partial operation. Where a shutdown of an entire industry imperils health and safety, the president could require the parties to operate an essential part of the industry or to provide production or services to a critical class of customers. The parties would be free to continue to strike in the nonessential aspects of their operations. Finally, the president would be authorized to direct the parties to submit their dispute to arbitration.

The arsenal of weapons approach. The "arsenal of weapons" approach appears to be an effective way to improve the nation's emergency disputes procedures. The rationale is that the uncertainty of this approach will motivate the parties to reach agreement on their own. Also, including arbitration as one of the options provides a mechanism for resolving strikes or lockouts that truly imperil the nation's health or safety. In support of the "arsenal of weapons" approach, it has been argued:

> The popularity of this approach is therefore understandable, for while the interventionists cannot agree among themselves on any single weapon approach, they can all agree on the premises underlying this plan: most of the single weapons have serious flaws; any intervention should preserve or induce as much genuine bargaining as possible; and yet the public should be protected in the event that bargaining results in a critical stoppage. By thus creating strength out of weakness, the arsenal of weapons approach demonstrates that the whole may indeed be greater than the sum of the parts.[42]

The Nonstoppage strike. Another approach for exercising control over emergency disputes is the nonstoppage strike.[43] With a nonstoppage strike, each side experiences the economic costs of striking without resorting to a strike. For example, the employer could forfeit its profits for the duration of the labor dispute. Similarly, the workers could forfeit their wages while the nonstoppage strike takes place. The advantage of this approach is that the parties experience the costs of disagreeing associated with the traditional strike system. The desire to avoid these costs should keep the parties negotiating. However, these costs are administratively imposed on the parties. There is no interruption in production or services. Therefore, the public is not inconvenienced and there is no threat to the nation's health and safety. When the parties voluntarily negotiate such an arrangement, it is known as a nonstoppage strike. If the procedure is legislatively mandated, it is known as a statutory strike. Exhibit 10.4 provides an overview of the nonstoppage strike.

On the surface, this approach seems very appealing. It protects the public from disruptive labor disputes, while retaining the traditional incentives to negotiate and settle associated with the use of the strike threat system. However, this procedure is very difficult to administer. How much money should each side forfeit? Who will collect the forfeited funds? What happens to the funds after the nonstoppage strike is over? These are just a few of the issues that would have to be resolved if labor and management were to utilize the nonstoppage strike. These problems are not insurmountable but do pose serious obstacles for the widespread adoption of this approach.

> **EXHIBIT 10.4**
> **The Nonstoppage Strike**
>
> The idea of a strike that would hurt no one other than the parties directly involved has long intrigued labor relations experts. The basic idea is to reconstruct the economic pressures of a strike without the loss of production—a nonstoppage strike. It is most often urged for national emergency labor disputes and has recently been suggested for the public sector. The procedure could be imposed by statute or voluntarily agreed to, bit it has rarely been applied. In general, a nonstoppage strike stipulates that, if labor and management cannot agree, the employees stay on the job instead of going on strike. Some, or all, or an increasing proportion of their wages would be placed in a bank to be given to a community service cause. For management, too, some, or all, or an increasing proportion of profits would go to the bank for the same purpose. The rationale of the scheme holds that economic pressure similar to that of a strike would occur (loss of wages, loss of profits) to push the parties toward settlement.
>
> Source: *The Conference Board,* Resolving Labor-Management Disputes: A Nine-Country Comparison *(New York: The Conference Board, Inc., 1973), pp. 71–72.*

The Case for Free Collective Bargaining

Proposals designed to improve the effectiveness of government intervention into labor disputes reflect a concern over the power of certain unions and businesses to engage in strikes that could imperil the nation's health and safety. The most decisive way to avoid such threats is to make strikes illegal and substitute some potentially less disruptive technique such as compulsory arbitration. Except under the most exceptional circumstances, government officials have refused to substitute imposed settlements on labor and management for the right to strike. As previously noted, even the nation's national emergency strike provisions found in the NLRA and the RLA emphasize delaying strikes or lockouts rather than forcing a settlement on the parties. This indicates a commitment to free collective bargaining, that is, "the right to negotiate a labor agreement without the intervention of the government or some other outside force."[44] Exhibit 10.5 describes free collective bargaining in more detail.

The temptation to substitute techniques such as compulsory arbitration for free collective bargaining increases with the inconvenience and risks to health and safety associated with some strikes. Despite the frustrations caused by strikes, relatively few restrictions on private-sector economic strikes have been governmentally imposed. During peace time, there has been an almost unwavering commitment to free collective bargaining in the private sector.

Several arguments favor the maintenance of a system of free collective bargaining even though some inconvenience and uncertainty is attached to such an ap-

> **EXHIBIT 10.5**
> **Free Collective Bargaining**
>
> While it has always been illegal in this country for public employees to strike, in the private sector of the economy strikes have not been illegal except during war time. The National Labor Relations Act of 1935 (NLRA) requires a private employer and the union that has been certified as the bargaining agent for a group of the employer's workers to bargain in good faith with respect to "wages, hours and other conditions of employment." Before a contract terminates, the employer and the union must make an honest attempt to reach agreement. However, no union and no company is forced by the government to work under conditions to which it will not agree. Instead, when the labor agreement terminates and an impasse is reached, either party is free to use its economic power in the form of the strike or the lockout to try to force the other party to terms which it considers more reasonable. We refer to this system as *free collective bargaining*.
>
> Source: Reprinted by permission of the Harvard Business Review. Excerpt from "Freedom to Strike Is in the Public Interest" by Thomas Kennedy (July/August 1970). Copyright © 1970 by the President and Fellows of Harvard College; all rights reserved.

proach. First, free collective bargaining is an important part of a political democracy. In a free society, conflict inevitably develops between groups, including labor and management. The parties are left on their own to resolve differences free from government involvement. Free collective bargaining is an extension of this principle to the workplace. Second, the strike is an essential part of the collective-bargaining process. As previously discussed, the desire of the parties to avoid the costs associated with strikes motivates them to modify their positions during negotiations and reach agreement. It is quite possible that restrictions on the right to strike would adversely affect the collective bargaining process. Exhibit 10.6 discusses two reasons government intervention in the form of compulsory arbitration would adversely affect the negotiating process. Third, the methods of government intervention into strikes attempted to date have not been very successful. They do not appear to improve collective bargaining or deter disruptive strikes. While costs are associated with free collective bargaining, it appears that the system works more effectively than one relying on government intervention. Finally, the costs of strikes have been overestimated. Strikes are very visible to the public. When people drive down the street, they can see the picket lines. Also, strikes make good press. As a result, strikes are discussed in the morning paper and on the television news in the evening. The successful conclusion of negotiations without a strike does not generate the same degree of interest by the news media. It must be emphasized, however, that the vast majority of all negotiations are concluded without a strike. Also, because of the high costs of striking to both labor and management, most strikes tend to be relatively short. Even if a strike is lengthy, the company's ability to stockpile or utilize alternative products or services decreases the adverse impact of the dispute.

> **EXHIBIT 10.6**
> **The Effect of Compulsory Arbitration on Negotiations**
>
> There are two reasons that the companies and unions find it more difficult to reach agreement when the possibility of the strike has been removed:
>
> 1. The parties are not under so much pressure to work out a contract because, while the compulsory settlement may be less desirable than the contract that could have been negotiated, it does not carry a threat of immediate loss of production and wages.
> 2. If the compulsory settlement authority—whether it be a government board, a court, or an arbitrator—has the right to decide on what it thinks is a fair settlement, then the company and the union may well hesitate to make a move toward a settlement, fearing that the other party will hold at its old position and that the board, court, or arbitrator will split the difference. If, for example, the company is offering a $.10-per-hour increase, and the union is asking for $.16 per hour, why should the company move to $.12 when there can be no strike anyhow and when the authority might then decide between $.12 and $.16 instead of between $.10 and $.16? For like reasons, the union hesitates to move down from $.16 to $.14. Thus, compulsory settlement interferes with the process of voluntary settlement.
>
> *Source: Reprinted by permission of the* Harvard Business Review. *Excerpt from "Freedom to Strike Is in the Public Interest" by Thomas Kennedy (July/August 1970). Copyright © 1970 by the President and Fellows of Harvard College; all rights reserved.*

In conclusion, the public desires both the elimination of strikes from vital industries and free collective bargaining.[45] Unfortunately, these are mutually incompatible goals. The ability to strike is a critical part of the collective-bargaining process. Without it, there is a distinct possibility that the parties will be less likely to reach agreement than when they bargain in the shadow of a strike. While free collective bargaining has its problems, it appears to be relatively more effective than alternatives that limit the right to strike.

Summary

While strikes are an integral part of the collective bargaining process, they are usually quite costly to the parties and inconvenient to the public. To avoid these problems without placing constraints on the right to strike, an increasing number of companies and unions are exploring ways to improve the collective-bargaining process. These techniques can be placed into two broad categories: those available to the parties without third-party intervention, and those requiring third-party intervention.

Continuous bargaining, prebargaining fact finding, and early-bird negotiations are techniques labor and management negotiators can use to increase the likelihood they will reach agreement without having a strike. These techniques are designed to "buy" the parties the essential ingredients for successful negotiations—time and information. By making more time available for negotiations through continuous bargaining and early-bird negotiations, the problem associated with crisis bargaining precipitated by the approach of the old contract's expiration date can be avoided. Through prebargaining fact finding, it is hoped that the data base needed for efficient and effective collective bargaining will be developed.

Sometimes the parties get to a point in negotiations where it becomes apparent that outside help will be needed to resolve the impasse confronting them. Mediation is a form of third-party intervention available to the parties. By bringing the third party into the situation, it is hoped the obstacles to successful negotiations can be resolved. Mediation is a rather common form of third-party involvement in labor negotiations. The mediator's job is to help establish an environment conducive to collective bargaining. Although the mediator has no authority to impose a settlement on the parties, the mediation process can help the parties reach agreement on their own.

There are times when the parties reach the conclusion that striking is not within their self-interest. In such situations, another form of third-party intervention can be used. Interest arbitration is rather commonplace in the public sector but used sparingly in the private sector. The Experimental Negotiations Agreement between the United Steelworkers of America and the major steel companies is an example of interest arbitration in the private sector. With interest arbitration, the parties submit unresolved contract issues to an arbitrator rather than striking over them. The arbitrator decides the issues. The parties agree to abide by the arbitrator's decision.

One of the major concerns of Congress when it deliberated the amendments to the National Labor Relations Act in 1947 was that the public needed protection from crippling strikes. In response to this concern, Title II of the Labor Management Relations Act created an emergency-disputes procedure. The Railway Labor Act already contained such a procedure for disputes in the transportation industries. The primary intent of these procedures is to delay a strike or lockout. It is hoped that the parties with the help of mediators will be able to settle. However, once the period of delay is over, the parties are free to strike unless special action is taken by the president or Congress.

An important feature of the emergency-disputes procedure is that these strikes are not banned even though they constitute a threat to the nation's health and safety. This recognizes the importance of the strike to the collective-bargaining process and the risks the government is willing to take to avoid limiting the right to strike. Collective bargaining, including the right to strike free from government intervention, is part of a democratic society. Since very few strikes imperil the nation's health and safety and since the alternatives to a strike are not particularly effective, it is best for government not to place limitations on the right to strike.

This section has been concerned with the collective-bargaining process. The focus was on the process with very little concern for the subjects negotiated by the parties during collective bargaining. In the section to follow, the subjects of collective bargaining will be discussed.

Discussion Questions

1. It has been argued that since mediators have no authority to force the parties to accept their recommendations, mediation is a waste of time. Respond to this argument.
2. If the parties negotiated in good faith there would be no need to use techniques such as continuous bargaining. Do you agree or disagree with this statement? Why?
3. Why have so few parties substituted interest arbitration for the strike as in the public sector?
4. What are the differences between mediation and arbitration?
5. Should the strike be banned in private sector labor relations?

Key Concepts

Continuous bargaining
Prebargaining fact finding
Early-bird negotiations
Mediation
Interest arbitration
Rights arbitration
Voluntary arbitration
Compulsory arbitration

Med-arb
Experimental Negotiating Agreement
"Arsenal of weapons" approach
Free collective bargaining
Nonstoppage strike
Statutory strike
Seizure
National emergency disputes

Notes

1. Donald B. Strauss, "Alternatives to the Strike," *Labor Law Journal* 23 (July 1972): 388–89.
2. Donald E. Cullen, "Recent Trends in Collective Bargaining in the United States," *International Labour Review* 105 (June 1972): 511.
3. For an interesting review of several examples of continuous bargaining, see James J. Healy, ed., *Creative Collective Bargaining* (Englewood Cliffs: Prentice-Hall, 1965).
4. Harold E. Brooks, "The Armour Automation Committee Experience," *Proceedings of the Twenty-First Annual Meeting of the Industrial Relations Research Association* (Madison, WI: n.p., 1968), p. 137.
5. Charles C. Killingsworth, "The Modernization of West Coast Longshore Work Rules," *Industrial and Labor Relations Review* 15 (April 1962): 305.
6. Healy, *Creative Collective Bargaining*, p. 242.
7. Robert Grunsky, "Replacing Economic Weapons With Reason," *Monthly Labor Review* 96 (September 1973): 54.
8. Strauss, "Alternatives to the Strike," p. 389.
9. Walter E. Baer, *Strikes* (New York: AMACOM, 1975), pp. 193–94.
10. Ibid., p. 194.
11. Ann Douglas, *Industrial Peacemaking* (New York: Columbia University Press, 1962), pp. 3–4.

12. William E. Simkin, *Mediation* (Washington, D.C.: Bureau of National Affairs, 1971), pp. 27–28.

13. Ibid., p. 139.

14. Ibid., p. 116.

15. Paul Yager, "Mediation: A Conflict Resolution Technique in the Industrial Community and Public Sector," in *New Techniques in Labor Dispute Resolution*, ed. Howard J. Anderson (Washington, D. C.: Bureau of National Affairs, 1976), p. 124.

16. This section is based on Chapter 5 of *Mediation*, supra.

17. Simkin, *Mediation*, p. 87.

18. Ibid., p. 99.

19. Yager, "Mediation: A Conflict Resolution Technique in the Industrial Community and Public Sectors," pp. 122–30.

20. I. W. Abel, "ENA: The Experimental Negotiating Agreement," pamphlet from the United Steel Workers of America, p. 4.

21. Jack Stieber, "Steel," in *Collective Bargaining: Contemporary American Experience,* ed. Gerald C. Somers (Madison, WI: Industrial Relations Research Association, 1980), p. 180.

22. Ibid., p. 171.

23. Ibid., p. 171.

24. Abel, "ENA: The Experimental Negotiation Agreement," p. 16.

25. Henry S. Farber and Harry C. Katz, "Interest Arbitration, Outcomes, and the Incentive to Bargain," *Industrial and Labor Relations Review* 33 (October 1979): 62.

26. Richard A. Levin, "National Emergency Disputes Under Taft-Hartley: A Legal Definition," *Labor Law Journal* 22 (January 1971): 31.

27. Simkin, *Mediation*, p. 199.

28. The eighty-day period is the maximum amount of time a strike or lockout can be postponed. It is the sum of sixty days after which the board of inquiry reports to the president; fifteen days the NLRB has to conduct a ballot; and five days for the NLRB to certify the ballot results.

29. Donald E. Cullen, *National Emergency Disputes* (Ithaca, NY: New York State School of Industrial and Labor Relations, 1968), p. 54.

30. Ibid., p. 63.

31. Ibid., p. 63.

32. This section is based on Cullen, *National Emergency Disputes,* pp. 61–66.

33. Herbert R. Northrup and Gordon F. Bloom, *Government and Labor* (Homewood, IL: Richard D. Irwin, Inc., 1963), p. 364.

34. Cullen, *National Emergency Disputes,* p. 65.

35. Simkin, *Mediation,* p. 214.

36. Norton N. Newborn, "Restrictions on the Right to Strike on the Railroads: A History and Analysis (1)," *Labor Law Journal* 24 (March 1973): 150.

37. Donald E. Cullen, "Emergency Boards Under the Railway Labor Act," in *The Railway Labor Act at Fifty,* ed. Charles M. Rehmus (Washington, D. C.: Government Printing Office, 1977), p. 153.

38. Gordon F. Bloom and Herbert R. Northrup, *Economics of Labor Relations,* 8th ed. (Homewood, IL: Richard D. Irwin, Inc., 1977), p. 664.

39. Cullen, "Emergency Boards Under the Railway Labor Act," p. 163.

40. Northrup and Bloom, *Government and Labor,* p. 328.

41. This section is based on a review of two pieces of legislation. One piece was proposed by President Richard Nixon and the other by Senator Jacob Javits of New York. Neither piece of legislation was adopted by Congress.

42. Cullen, *National Emergency Disputes,* p. 108.

43. Stephen H. Sosnick, "Non-Stoppage Strikes: A New Approach," in *Critical Issues in Labor,* ed. Max Wortman (New York: Macmillan Company, 1969), p. 395.

44. Thomas A. Kochan, *Collective Bargaining and Industrial Relations* (Homewood, IL: Richard D. Irwin, Inc., 1980), p. 235.

45. Archibald Cox, *Law and the National Labor Policy* (Los Angeles: Institute for Industrial Relations, University of California–Los Angeles, 1960), p. 53.

Suggested Readings

Cullen, Donald E. *National Emergency Disputes*. Ithaca, N.Y.: New York State School of Industrial and Labor Relations, 1968.

Lefkowitz, Jerome, et al., eds. *The Public Interest and the Role of the Neutral in Dispute Settlement* (Reston, VA: n.p., Society of Professionals in Dispute Resolution, 1974).

Simkin, William E. *Mediation*. Washington, D. C.: Bureau of National Affairs, 1971.

The last section was concerned with the collective-bargaining process. At that time very little was said about the topics discussed by the parties while negotiating a labor agreement. Attention now turns in Part Four to an examination of the issues that are the subjects of the collective-bargaining process. These issues constitute the subjects jointly determined by the parties. When put into writing, the topics discussed in this section comprise the collective-bargaining agreement. Chapter 11 looks at wage issues in collective bargaining. The focus is on how wage levels are determined and the importance of wage decisions. Chapter 12 examines supplemental compensation, discusses public policy affecting wages, fringe benefits, and the procedures used to cost out a labor agreement. Chapter 13 examines institutional and administrative issues in collective bargaining. Topics covered in this chapter include union security, technological change, and subcontracting.

PART FOUR

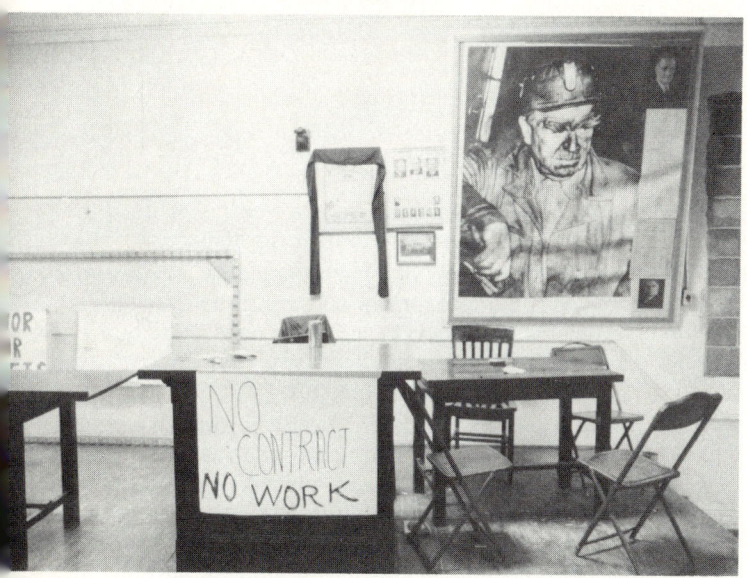

COLLECTIVE-BARGAINING ISSUES

Chapter 11

WAGE ISSUES IN COLLECTIVE BARGAINING

Charles Bradley was beginning preparations for his first round of collective-bargaining negotiations. He had been recently hired as vice-president of personnel and labor relations for the Albany Mining Company. During the past year the American Miners Union had been certified as the bargaining agent for Albany's mining workforce.

Charles had many years of experience in personnel administration in non-union organizations. However, he had no experience in dealing with unions. He did not know what to expect during contract negotiations. Several questions occurred to him:

- Undoubtedly the union negotiating committee would demand substantial wage increases. What arguments would they make to justify their wage demands?
- What information should the management negotiating committee be assembling to be prepared to respond to the union's demands?
- Probably many arguments would be put forward by both management and union representatives at the bargaining table. Which ones would be important and which merely smoke to confuse those sitting across the table?
- Charles knew how the wage structure should be established in a non-union organization. His review of Albany's wage administration practices suggests to him that these practices were probably one of the factors leading to the certification of a union. The company claimed to have had a merit compensation system, but there appeared to be favoritism in granting wage increases. What could be expected from the union given the employees' experience with Albany's compensation practices in the past? What procedures for establishing wage rates should management try to negotiate?

Charles has raised some of the issues concerning wages that must be addressed during contract negotiations. These as well as other questions and issues concerning wages are addressed in this chapter. When you have completed this chapter you should be able to recommend answers to Charles's questions. Specifically, you should:

- Be able to discuss issues concerning each of the determinants of wages listed below:
  a. Ability to pay.
  b. Productivity.
  c. Going rates.
  d. Standard of living.
  e. Cost of living.
- Be able to describe the relative importance of these determinants.
- Know the important factors related to employee satisfaction with pay, and why pay satisfaction is important to both management and union leaders.
- Be able to describe the recommended process for establishing the wage structure of an organization, understand how this process relates to employee pay satisfaction, and know how a union can fit into this process.
- Understand why collective bargaining agreements seldom provide for merit compensation procedures.

This chapter will discuss common criteria that are considered in setting wages. In addition, the procedures usually followed in establishing the wage structure of an organization will be discussed. This chapter will also address some key questions for establishing the wage procedures in an organization.

Determinants of Wage Levels

Several determinants or criteria have been used in establishing the wage level of organizations. The wage level is the average wage for an organization. For example, there may be fifteen job titles within a plant. Each of these jobs may have a different wage rate. The wage level for these jobs is the average of the fifteen different wage rates. Among the criteria that have been used to establish wage levels are: ability to pay, productivity, going rates or comparative norm, standard of living, and purchasing power or cost of living. Each of these criteria will be discussed as well as the considerations that enter into the use of each.

ABILITY TO PAY

A leading criterion in wage determination during contract negotiations is the organization's ability to pay wages. If an organization's profits are high, the union negotiators are likely to demand that wages should be increased substantially. Alternatively, if profit levels of the organization are low, management negotiators are likely to point to this evidence and argue that wage increases should be kept at a minimum. The problem with this criterion is the definition of high- and low-profit levels. What is high in the eyes of union negotiators may be moderate in the eyes of management negotiators.

COLLECTIVE-BARGAINING ISSUES

Management is concerned with insuring that sufficient profits are available to provide a reasonable rate of return to stockholders. In addition, management must insure that capital is available for future investment in equipment and modernization of the organization. If, as a result of agreeing to high demands for wage increases, sufficient profits are not available to meet these obligations, the long-run needs of the organization will not be met. Of course, when an organization does not have the capital to invest in needed capital improvements, the employees of the organization will also suffer in the long run.

FUTURE STABILITY

There are a number of other issues that management should consider in responding to union demands for wage increases based on the organization's ability to pay. The union's arguments that the firm is able to pay higher wages will be based on the historical experience of the organization. However, the organization is making commitments for the future. Judgments must be made by management concerning the stability of future economic conditions and the employer's ability to maintain past levels of profits.

ELASTICITY OF DEMAND

Another consideration is the ability of the employer to pass along to consumers increased labor costs. For example, if wages increase by 5 percent and a corresponding increase in labor productivity does not occur, the employer's options are to accept a reduction in profits or attempt to pass these increased costs along to consumers.

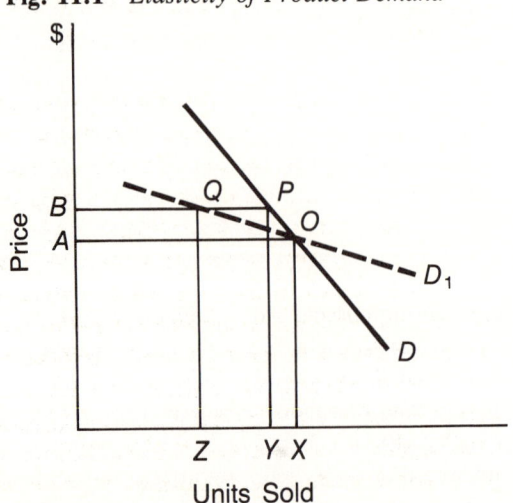

Fig. 11.1 *Elasticity of Product Demand*

Fig. 11.1 represents alternative situations that an organization could face. Assume that an employer is operating at a situation represented by the intersection of price A and X number of units sold. If this is in a highly competitive industry, meaning that it is easy for customers to move to other business organizations to obtain the goods or services sold by this organization, we would say that the demand for that organization's product is elastic. This is represented by the demand curve labeled D_1. On the other hand, if it is difficult for customers to receive comparable goods or services from other organizations, we would describe the organization's demand curve as inelastic. This is represented by the demand curve labeled D.

If an employer faces an inelastic demand curve, increased labor costs can be passed along to customers without substantially reducing the level of sales and the level of profits. Alternatively, an employer with an elastic demand curve would face substantial reductions in the number of units sold if prices are increased and, as a result, profits would be reduced. In the latter case, management must be extremely cautious in agreeing to substantial wage increases keyed on the employer's past profits.

THE TRUITT DECISION

Management representatives in contract negotiations could be tempted to rely on an "inability to pay" argument in responding to union wage demands. In such a situation management could be obligated to produce accounting and financial records to substantiate this claim. In 1956 the United States Supreme Court handed down a decision concerning the legal obligations of employers who argue in negotiations that they are unable to meet union wage demands.[2] In this case, the employer assumed such a position in contract negotiations. The union requested the employer to furnish information substantiating the claim of inability to pay. The company refused.

The Supreme Court held in the Truitt Manufacturing Company decision if an organization argues that it lacks the economic resources to meet a union's wage demand, it must make financial information available to the union. The court's reasoning was that good faith bargaining requires the claims made by either party to contract negotiations to be honest ones. The court reasoned that if such an argument is critical to the negotiation process it is reasonable to require some proof of the argument's accuracy.

The Truitt decision does not mean that an employer must produce proof substantiating every argument or every statement concerning an inability to pay that might be made in contract negotiations. The critical point in the eyes of the United States Supreme Court concerns the employer's obligation to bargain in good faith. In this particular case the court took the position that the employer's refusal to provide economic data substantiating its financial condition plus the argument of inability to meet the union's wage demand constituted a refusal to bargain in good faith. The implication for management is that when one argues an inability to meet union wage demands because of the organization's financial conditions, one must be prepared to present financial information supporting that claim or face the possibility of being charged with an unfair labor practice.

PRODUCTIVITY

Productivity is another wage criterion. Productivity increase is an attractive criterion in theory because it permits increases in real income. In other words, when employees produce more in the same number of hours, the labor cost per unit of output decreases. When labor costs per unit of output decline, more money is available to compensate employees in the form of wage increases and to pay shareholders in the form of dividends.[3] Some evidence is available that supports the position that unionization leads to increases in productivity.[4,5] It appears that these productivity gains result from the introduction of more efficient management personnel and procedures. This evidence can serve to justify union demands for wage increases.

Productivity as a basis for wage increases is seen as the mechanism whereby employee compensation can be increased without producing inflationary pressures. This was the rationale for the wage guideposts of Presidents Kennedy and Johnson. Starting in 1962, the President's Council of Economic Advisors argued that wage increases should be limited to the annual rise in labor productivity. For the years just prior to this time, the annual productivity increase had averaged 3.2 percent. The Council of Economic Advisors argued that contract settlements should remain below this figure.[6]

When total compensation, which includes wages as well as fringe benefits, increases faster than change in output per hour or productivity, unit labor costs increase. For example, in 1978 in the manufacturing sector, productivity grew 2.4 percent. At the same time hourly compensation rose 9.5 percent, and unit labor costs increased 7.0 percent.[7] When unit labor costs increase either profits of the organization decrease or prices to consumers increase.

PROBLEMS WITH PRODUCTIVITY AS A WAGE CRITERION

For the total economy it is relatively easy to obtain a measure of change in output per hour of employment. However, it is more difficult to measure productivity for an organization or for subunits within the organization. Consequently, one factor limiting the use of productivity as a criterion for wage determination is the absence of a satisfactory measure of productivity.

A more difficult issue concerning the use of productivity as a criterion for wage determination is identifying the cause of increased productivity. Is it due to increased effort and skill on the part of employees? Is it due to improved organization on the part of management? Is it due to capital expenditures that permit installation of better equipment and new technology?

Each of the above is a potential explanation for increased productivity. What share of that total increase in productivity should be allocated to providing higher wages for employees? To answer this question, one should distinguish between change in output per hour and change in labor productivity.[8] Overall changes in productivity could be due to any of the factors discussed above. Changes in labor productivity are the result of increased employee effort and skill. While employees are entitled to benefits of the latter, they may not be entitled to all of the benefits of the former. If the change in productivity stems entirely from increased capital investment or new technology, employees may not be entitled to any benefits of increased productivity, even though they may feel they deserve some of the benefits. The question of how to share the benefits of increased productivity is difficult to answer. The proper balance of these benefits between employees and stockholders must be handled carefully.

ANNUAL IMPROVEMENT FACTOR

The productivity criterion, under the label annual improvement factor, has been used as a basis for wage determination in contract negotiations. The annual improvement factor (AIF) criterion for wage determination originated in the General Motors–United Automobile Workers agreement in 1948.[9] Union representatives argued that the increased productivity of the automobile industry should be shared with employees. At that time, productivity was estimated to increase at around 3 percent per year in the automobile industry. Accordingly, automatic pay increases based on improved productivity were negotiated.

While the wage price guidelines of the Kennedy-Johnson era tried to establish changes in output per manhour as the upper limit in wage increases, it is doubtful that this upper limit will ever be adhered to. There are too many other demands placed on employers that require going beyond the upper bound established by productivity.[10]

PRODUCTIVITY BARGAINING

A procedure labeled "productivity bargaining" has been adopted by some industries as a means to introduce productivity issues into the collective bargaining process. Typically these efforts involve removal of inefficient work rules and increased flexibility of assigning work to employees. When such changes bring about increased productivity, unions argue that workers are then entitled to a share of the benefits. Productivity bargaining provides a means to achieve increased cooperation between labor and management.[11]

While productivity bargaining does offer the benefit of increased cooperation between labor and management, it presents problems in application. A major problem is the measurement of productivity. For most jobs it is difficult to arrive at an objective measure of output. Another issue is whether the change in output is attributable to employee skill and effort or to improved technology and organization by management. These problems are very similar to the problems discussed earlier in this section.

Productivity bargaining tends to be used in certain circumstances. Among them is the situation when unionized employers face intense competition either from non-union employers or from foreign competition. Another common situation in which productivity bargaining is used occurs when technology is available that permits substantial increases in productivity. In the construction industry, negotiations between labor and management have attempted to reduce jurisdictional disputes, make-work rules, featherbedding, and the like. In this case, the stimulus for productivity bargaining is the loss of work to non-union contractors and then desire of union members to protect their employment opportunities.[12] Similarly, in the shipping industry, a joint labor-management system has been established to promote increases in productivity. Agreements have resulted in the reduction of restrictive work practices that reduce the work-group size and enable a more flexible use of workers. In return, union members receive improved wages and benefits, reduction of the work force through attrition, and a generous retirement package.[13]

GOING RATES

The essence of the going-rate criterion for wage determination is external equity. There are several dimensions to the external-equity norm. Chapter 6, Why Workers Organize, showed that when employees feel their pay is not as high as it should be, they are dissatisfied. Employees will often compare their wages with those of employees in similar jobs at other organizations.

The primary comparison group that an employer is concerned with is the local labor market. The employer wants employees to feel that the wage offered is fair compared to what they could get from other employers in the community.

A union leader is also concerned that the rank-and-file member feel fairly treated with respect to wages. However, the union leader's focus is not limited to the local labor market. The membership probably expects, following negotiations, a wage increase that is comparable to the increases received by members of the same union in other localities. If the union leader is to be judged acceptable by the membership, he or she has to deliver on that expectation.

There are other dimensions to the external comparisons that are important both to the union leader and to the employer. In addition to meeting member expectations regarding wages, the union leader is concerned because of a desire to take labor out of competition. Recall from the chapter on union structure and government that with the advent of national product markets in the American economy, national unions were formed. A primary reason for forming national unions was to equalize wages across localities. For this reason, during contract negotiations unions encourage comparisons with employers in other localities within the same industry.

Employers are also interested in comparisons with other organizations in the same industry. However, an employer's interest is for a different reason. The employer wishes to keep labor costs below those of other employers in the industry in order to have a competitive advantage in the product market. As a result, management looks upon the average or typical wage level of other employers in the industry as an upper limit for wages. Consequently, the industry comparison takes on a very different meaning to the union leader and to management in contract negotiations. The union leader wants to be at the industry average while management wishes to be below the industry average.

PROBLEMS WITH THE GOING-RATE CRITERION

When using the going-rate criterion for wage determination there are several problems to be dealt with. First, one has to ensure that the jobs being compared are in fact the same. A maintenance mechanic in one organization may be an employee who has completed a four-year apprenticeship program and is a highly skilled journeyman. In another organization a maintenance mechanic may be no more skilled than an individual who can tune up a car at the corner gas station. Consequently, erroneous comparisons can be made if one relies solely on job titles to compare wages of different organizations. Later in this chapter job analysis, job descriptions, and wage surveys will be discussed, and recommendations will be made concerning ways to minimize erroneous comparisons.

Another problem in comparing wages across organizations is that fringe benefits include all forms of compensation other than direct regular wages and thus may vary widely. For example, in 1975 employee benefits as a percent of payroll varied widely across industries. The chemical industry paid an average of 42.2 percent, followed by the primary metal industry which paid 40.6 percent. At the other end of the scale, hospitals paid 24.0 percent and the textile products and apparel industry paid 27.8 percent. Expressing these benefits as dollars per employee per hour, payments ranged from $2.49 for the petroleum industry to $1.07 for hospitals.[14] With such wide variations in fringe-benefit compensation across industries and across employers, wage surveys focusing solely on wage rates can be quite misleading. When conducting a wage survey, it is necessary also to gather information concerning fringe-benefit compensation. This permits estimates of total compensation provided by other employers.

Another factor that makes comparisons across organizations difficult is differences in regularity of employment. For example, people in such occupations as carpenter and plumber in the building trades industry invariably receive higher wages than those in the same occupations who work in other industries.[15] The primary reason for the difference is that employment in the building trades is irregular. An individual carpenter or plumber would probably earn more income in a year when employed by an organization providing regular employment throughout the year.

Another problem in comparing results of wage surveys is differences in wages by region of the country and by industry. At the technical, professional, and administrative job level, average wage rates by region of the country do not vary more than 1 or 2 percent from the national average.[16] However, among occupations characterized by lower levels of geographic mobility, variation in wage rates across geographic regions is much larger. Table 11.1 reports the average wage rates for local truck drivers in building, heavy construction, and highway construction for selected regions of the country. The ratio of average wage rates for a region compared to the average wage rates of all regions indicates the wide differences that can occur. Generally, wages are lowest in the Southeast and highest in the Pacific region of the country. This data makes it clear that in using wage survey data one must be specific as to job and region of the country.

Table 11.2 reports average hourly wage rates for truck drivers by type of delivery. The point we wish to make with this table is that wide differences in wage rates will be observed by industry of employment. For example, those drivers delivering bakery products and beer and other alcoholic beverages were far below the average, while those employed in general freight and parcel services were far above the average. These data make it clear that one must be concerned about industry of employment in reviewing the results of wage surveys.

Table 11.1 *Average Hourly Wage Rates for Local Truckdrivers in Building and Heavy/Highway Construction by Selected Regions, September 3, 1979*

Region	Average wage rate	Ratio*
New England	$ 8.55	.90
Middle Atlantic	9.68	1.02
Border states	9.01	.95
Southeast	7.97	.84
Southwest	9.24	.97
Great Lakes	10.38	1.09
Pacific	11.61	1.22
Combined	$ 9.50	

*Ratio = Wage rate for individual region divided by combined average wage rate.

Source: U. S. Department of Labor, Union Wages and Hours: Local Truckdrivers and Helpers, September 3, 1979, Bulletin 2089, (Washington, D. C.: U. S. Government Printing Office, 1981), p. 3.

Table 11.2 *Average Hourly Wage Rates for Local Truckdrivers by Type of Delivery, September 3, 1979*

Type of delivery	Average wage rate	Ratio*
Bakery	$ 7.20	.80
Beer and other alcoholic beverages	7.97	.88
Building and heavy/highway construction	9.99	1.11
Building materials and supplies	9.17	1.01
General freight	10.32	1.15
Grocery—wholesale and retail	8.66	.96
Meat	8.57	.95
Moving and moving and storage	9.02	1.00
Parcel services	10.20	1.13
Average	$ 9.01	

*Ratio = Wage rate for individual type of delivery divided by the average wage rate.

Source: U. S. Department of Labor, Union Wages and Hours: Local Truckdrivers and Helpers, September 3, 1979, Bulletin 2089, (Washington, D. C.: U. S. Government Printing Office, 1981), p. 2.

DIFFERENCES IN WAGES FOR AN OCCUPATION WITHIN A REGION

Wage contour. The concept of a wage contour is relevant to this discussion. A wage contour is a stable group of wage-determining units, plants, or employers. Factors linking these wage-determining units are: employment of workers with similar kinds of skills, a sector of industry, and a particular geographic location.[17] Factors contributing to the observed variation in wage rates include differences in labor productivity and differences in employing organizations. For example, employers differ in ability to pay because some industries are more profitable than others. In addition, some industries have higher ratios of capital investment to number of employees than others. As a result, the employees in those industries with high ratios of capital equipment to labor are more productive.

STANDARD OF LIVING

Chapter 5 dealt briefly with the living conditions of factory workers in the United States in the late 1800s and early 1900s. At that time factory worker wages were typically below the level necessary to provide the basic necessities of life. At the present time, it is infrequent that wages and benefits are below the level needed to meet minimum standards of decency. Even so, the issue of providing wages that meet the needs for maintaining a reasonable standard of living enters into contract negotiations.

BUDGET ESTIMATES

One set of yardsticks for establishing reasonable standards of living is provided by the Bureau of Labor Statistics.[18] The BLS attempts to estimate how much it costs a family of four persons to live. The family consists of a husband employed full-time, a wife who does not work outside the home, and two children—a girl of eight and a boy of thirteen years of age. The budget estimates are for lower, moderate, and higher levels of living costs in major cities. The lower budget estimate is intended to identify the living costs of families who are at the low end of the income distribution. However, it is not intended to identify the cut-off point that separates families with enough income from those with insufficient income. This budget estimate was developed in an attempt to provide a guide for administrators of such programs as public assistance and workers' compensation programs.

The intermediate or moderate budget estimate is intended to identify the cost of an adequate standard of living. The moderate standard was intended to play a role in collective bargaining by providing an estimate or basis for evaluating the adequacy of earnings of experienced workers.[19]

The higher budget estimate attempts to identify the cost of a standard of living that permits greater variety in foods and higher quality in such purchases as clothing and housing. In terms of relevance to collective bargaining, it is the lower budget estimate and the moderate budget estimate that appear most relevant. The former might be used by union negotiators as establishing a minimum level of income necessary for employees of an organization. The moderate budget estimate might be used as a standard for judging the adequacy of wages provided experienced workers.

Table 11.3 indicates the budget estimates just described for autumn 1979. The lower annual budget implies an hourly wage rate of $6.29 and the intermediate budget an hourly wage rate of $10.26. Comparing these figures to the average hourly wage rates for local truckdrivers reported in Table 11.2 indicates that truckdrivers, regardless of type of delivery, exceed the wage rate for the lower budget estimate. However, with the exception of truckdrivers in general freight, all fall below the intermediate budget estimate.

Table 11.3 *Annual Budget Estimates for an Urban Family of Four, Autumn 1979*

Level	Annual budget estimate	Necessary hourly wage rate*
Lower	$12,585	$ 6.29
Intermediate	20,517	10.26
Higher	30,317	15.16

*The hourly wage rate necessary to provide an annual income equal to the indicated annual budget estimate assuming 2,000 hours of employment per year. For example, $12,585 ÷ 2,000 = $6.29

Source: "Family Budgets," Monthly Labor Review 103, no. 8 (August 1980): 29.

These data show why labor negotiators might argue that increases in wage rates are necessary in order to reach the budget levels necessary to maintain a moderate standard of living. Management, on the other hand, has criticized the content of the moderate budget estimate. They have argued that many of the items used in computing the budget are far too generous for what is described as a moderate standard of living. Another point in the budget that management spokespeople question is the assumption of one wage earner in the family. Labor force participation rates of married women indicate that this assumption simply is not valid. In 1979 the labor force participation rate of married women with spouse present in the family was 49.4 percent.[20]

A definition of minimum standard of living and moderate standard of living satisfactory to both management and labor negotiators will be difficult to achieve. These concepts are very subjective. However, such estimates as prepared by the Bureau of Labor Statistics do provide a guideline for estimating reasonable standards of living. Such estimates are certainly preferable to allowing each individual negotiator to arrive at his or her own estimates independently.

It must be recognized that the standard-of-living criterion is primarily a social-responsibility or an "ethical" criterion. For some employers the wage rates associated with the intermediate budget in Table 11.3 would result in labor costs so high that the organization would not earn a profit. In such cases employers must negotiate wages accordingly.

COST OF LIVING

One factor affecting employee satisfaction with pay is maintaining real wages. Workers' welfare depends on the amount of goods and services they can buy with their take-home pay or money wage. The term real wage is defined as how much the money wage will buy in goods and services.[21] If an increase in money wages is accompanied by corresponding increases in the price of goods and services purchased, real wages have not increased. Alternatively, during periods of rapid inflation, when money wages do not increase, real wages decline. Unions recognize the problems rapid inflation causes for their members and try to help them cope with it.

The typical procedure for doing this is to provide a cost-of-living allowance or adjustment (COLA). The usual way in which a COLA works is that wages are adjusted according to some formula keyed to changes in the consumer price index.

ALTERNATIVE COLA METHODS

There are two principal ways of relating changes in wages to variations in the consumer price index.[22] One is to have a corresponding percentage change in wages. The other is to change wages a specified number of cents per hour given a predetermined change in the price index. Using the percentage method, wages of individual employees are increased by an agreed-upon formula relating wages to changes in the consumer price index. The percentage adjustment technique is easier to understand and does not affect the percentage wage differential among jobs. The cents-per-hour method is more complex and over a period of time can result in narrowing wage differentials among jobs.

A common cents-per-hour formula is that for every .3 point increase in the price index, wages are increased by one cent per hour.[23] Therefore, if the price index moves from 175.0 to 175.9, there is a .9 point increase in the consumer price index which would result in a three-cents-per-hour cost-of-living adjustment.

COLAS IN COLLECTIVE-BARGAINING AGREEMENTS

The use of cost-of-living provisions in collective-bargaining agreements is increasing. A survey of collective-bargaining agreements conducted in 1975 found COLAs in 36 percent of the agreements studied. In 1979, the figure had increased to 49 percent. Nearly all the contracts providing for cost-of-living adjustments contained a clause tying wage increases to changes in the Bureau of Labor Statistics' Consumer Price Index. Eighty-two percent of the escalator provisions called for an hourly increase of one cent for each specified rise in the Consumer Price Index.[24] The most common Consumer Price Index change specified is .3 (43 percent of escalator clauses) followed by .4 (35 percent), .5 (7 percent), and .6 (2 percent).

The frequency of adjustment varies a great deal. Most common is the adjustment of wages at quarterly intervals, found in just under 60 percent of escalator provisions. The next most frequent interval is an annual adjustment, found in 26 percent of cost of living provisions.[25]

For management, an important issue concerning COLAs is controlling the amount of wage increase that can be triggered by changes in the Consumer Price Index. The use of such limits or "caps" is decreasing. In 1975, 28 percent of contracts studied had limitations in the amount of cost-of-living wage increase possible during the life of the agreement. In 1979 this figure had dropped to 16 percent.[26] The most common ceiling in 1979 was twelve cents per hour.

COLLECTIVE-BARGAINING ISSUES

IMPACT OF COLAS

Cost-of-living clauses can have several effects. Some specialists in the field of compensation believe that such automatic adjustments in wages tend to perpetuate inflation.[27] In other words, as labor costs automatically increase throughout the economy, total costs increase and these costs are passed along in the form of price increases. This assumes there is not a corresponding increase in productivity. Another assumption of this point of view is that the employer can easily pass along cost increases to consumers. This depends on the elasticity of product demand, discussed earlier in the chapter. At a time when the economy is experiencing double-digit inflation, the possibility that COLAs perpetuate inflation is an important concern.

One must also keep in mind the reason for instituting such clauses. They are intended to maintain real earnings during the life of the collective-bargaining agreement. With respect to this objective, the typical COLA clause compensates for about half of the increase in the Consumer Price Index.[28] Of course, this might change if ceilings are removed from escalator clauses in collective-bargaining agreements.

Another effect of COLAs is that wage adjustments are made during the life of the agreement. This eliminates or at least reduces the need for unions to bargain for catch-up earnings in the next round of negotiations. On the other hand, the cents-per-hour formula for COLAs will tend to cause wage differentials to become compressed. As a result, negotiators will be faced with the task of trying to restore equity in the wage differentials among jobs.

Table 11.4 presents an example of wage compression. It assumes that the agreement covers a three-year period and that there is a one-cent-per-hour adjustment in wages for each .3 point change in the Consumer Price Index. Further, it is assumed the inflation rate increase is 12 percent each year during the contract. Hope-

Table 11.4 *COLAs and Wage Compression*

Assumptions

1. Three-year contract.
2. Adjustment formula = one-cent-per-hour wage increase for each .3 point change in CPI.
3. Inflation rate of 12 percent annually for the entire contract period; e.g., CPI goes from 160.0 to 224.8.
4. At the beginning of the contract an unskilled job (A) had an hourly wage rate of $4.00 and a skilled job (B) had an hourly wage rate of $8.00.

Given the above, the cents-per-hour adjustment would be 64.8 ÷ .3 = 216

Implications

Given the above assumptions, the cents-per-hour adjustments for both jobs would be 64.8 ÷ .3 = 216.

	Wage Rates		Ratio of
	Job A	Job B	B/A
Beginning of contract	$4.00	$ 8.00	2.00
End of contract	6.16	10.16	1.65

fully, this is an unreasonable assumption. However, in 1979 a 13 percent rate in inflation was attained.[29]

The implication of these assumptions is indicated at the bottom of Table 11.4. At the beginning of the contract, an unskilled job is assumed to have had a wage rate of $4.00 an hour, while a skilled job had a negotiated wage rate of $8.00 per hour. This implies that the skilled job is worth about twice as much as the unskilled job. Because the typical COLA clause will adjust wages for all jobs by the same number of cents, the wage rate for low-skilled jobs increases at a faster rate than that of high-skilled jobs. In this example, at the end of the contract period, the wage rate for the unskilled job would be $6.16 and for the skilled job would be $10.16. The ratio of wage rates if 1.65. Probably wage compression of this magnitude would create feelings of dissatisfaction among those in jobs represented by B. In such a case we would expect negotiators to receive pressure from union members in such jobs to reestablish the previous ratio of wage rates. It would appear that fewer problems would be encountered in the long run by relying on percentage adjustments in wage rates rather than the cents-per-hour method.

In the preceding paragraph we have assumed an agreement containing a "roll-in" provision, which means that wages are modified to include cost-of-living adjustments. Many agreements view COLAs as add-on earnings which are not part of the wage schedule.

WAGE-REOPENER CLAUSES

Wage-reopener clauses are another means of adjusting wages during the life of a contract. This procedure permits reopening bargaining negotiations with respect to wage issues at specified intervals during the contract. For example, if a contract covers a two-year period, negotiations might be reopened after one year.

The major difference between a COLA and a wage-reopener clause is that the former specifies an automatic increase in wage rates, while the latter specifies that the parties can negotiate wage-rate changes. The usual procedure to implement a wage-reopener clause is that the party who wishes to change wages gives written notice of this intention to the other party. Under the terms of Taft-Hartley, sixty days' notice is necessary. Wage-reopener clauses are not as popular as COLAs. In 1979, wage-reopener clauses were found in 8 percent of the contracts studied.[30] This is about the same figure as was observed in 1975.

Relative Importance of Wage Determinants

In a recent study conducted by the Conference Board, an attempt was made to assess the relative importance of wage criteria in setting wages.[31] Respondents to this study were both unionized companies and non-union companies. Fig. 11.2 presents an indication of the relative importance of various criteria investigated in this study. The

Fig. 11.2 *Scale of Company Importance Attached to Different Criteria in Setting Wages and Benefits*

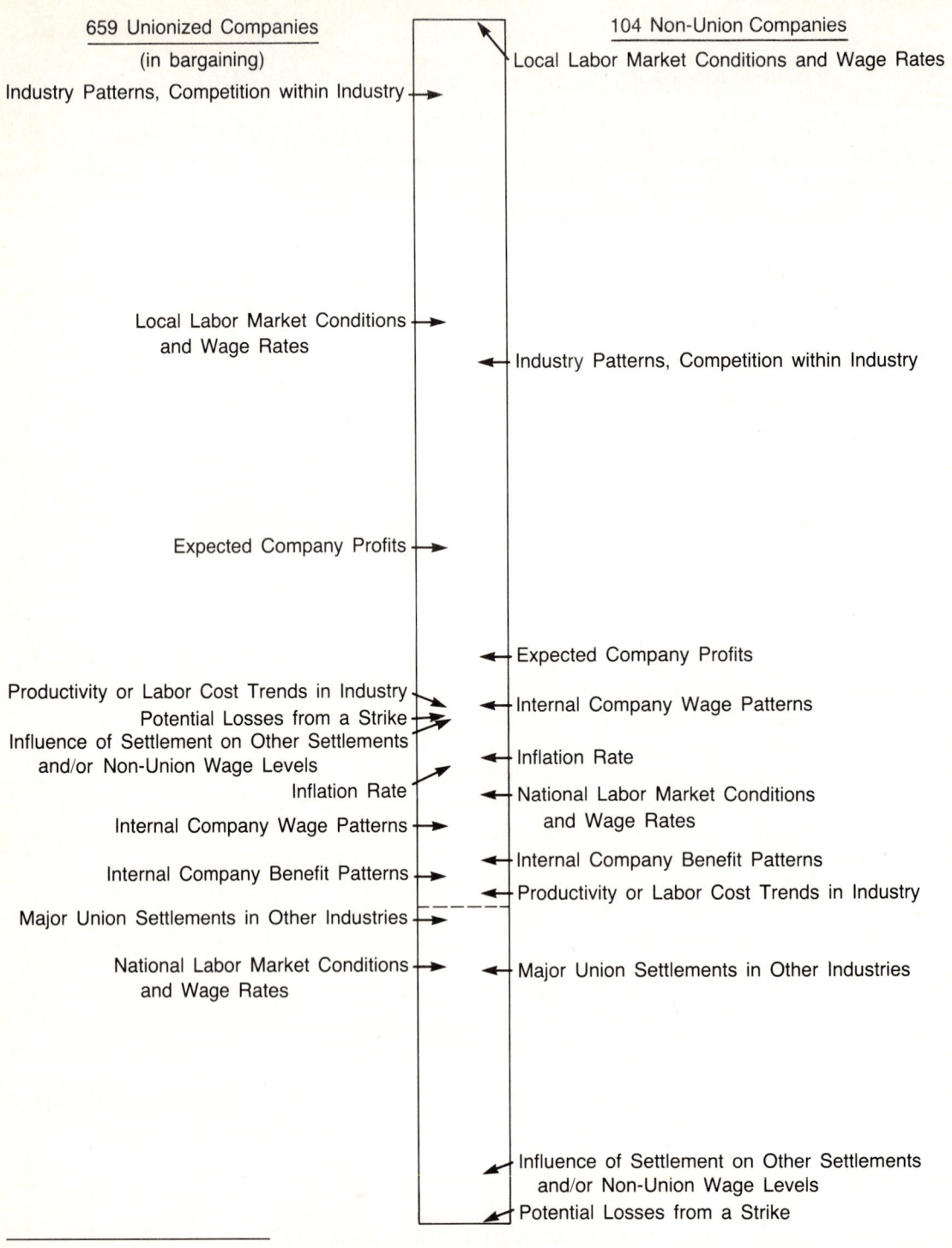

659 Unionized Companies (in bargaining)	104 Non-Union Companies
Industry Patterns, Competition within Industry	Local Labor Market Conditions and Wage Rates
Local Labor Market Conditions and Wage Rates	Industry Patterns, Competition within Industry
Expected Company Profits	Expected Company Profits
Productivity or Labor Cost Trends in Industry	Internal Company Wage Patterns
Potential Losses from a Strike	Inflation Rate
Influence of Settlement on Other Settlements and/or Non-Union Wage Levels	National Labor Market Conditions and Wage Rates
Inflation Rate	Internal Company Benefit Patterns
Internal Company Wage Patterns	Productivity or Labor Cost Trends in Industry
Internal Company Benefit Patterns	Major Union Settlements in Other Industries
Major Union Settlements in Other Industries	Influence of Settlement on Other Settlements and/or Non-Union Wage Levels
National Labor Market Conditions and Wage Rates	Potential Losses from a Strike

Source: Audrey Freedman, Managing Labor Relations *(The Conference Board, Report No. 765, 1980), p. 37.*

labels used in this study are different from those used in the above discussion. However, we suggest that our criterion "going rates" corresponds to "industry pattern," "competition within industry," and "local labor market conditions and wage rates." "Ability to pay" corresponds to "expected company profits." "Productivity" corresponds to "productivity or labor cost trends." Finally, "cost of living" corresponds to "inflation rate." No factor studied in the Conference Board investigation corresponds to standard of living.

UNION AND NON-UNION COMPANIES

Comparison of the rankings of unionized companies and of non-union companies presented in Fig. 11.2 provides an indication of the impact of unions on wage determination. The primary wage criterion in non-union companies is local labor market comparisons. This is also the case in collective bargaining relationships in which the employer is clearly dominant.[32] In such situations employers are free to offer wages at the level necessary to attract and retain the necessary supply of labor. When unions are strong, companies attach greatest importance to industry patterns and competition within the industry. This is the second most important factor for non-union companies.

The top two factors cited in the Conference Board study are various dimensions of the going rates criterion, which was discussed above. This suggests that going rates are the dominant factor in setting wages. The presence of a strong union seems to change the relative importance of the two dimensions of going rates. Industry patterns are the most important factor among unionized companies. Among non-union companies, local labor market conditions are the number-one criterion. This reflects the union goal of taking labor out of competition by obtaining comparable wage settlements in different collective bargaining agreements.

The factor ranked third in importance is expected company profits in both categories of companies. Fourth in importance among unionized companies is productivity or trends in industry labor costs. This factor is relatively unimportant among non-union companies. The importance attached to trends in inflation is about the same in both categories of companies. However, it is ranked higher among non-union companies than among union companies.

It is clear from this study that the primary consideration in setting wages is going rates. Consequently, it is important to address the problems involved in conducting wage surveys. Later in this chapter, recommended procedures for conducting wage surveys will be discussed.

Employee Pay Satisfaction

Thus far this chapter has focused on determinants of wage levels considered by employing organizations. The Conference Board study points out that the most important factor is going rates. This suggests that management, as well as union leaders, are seeking to insure that workers earn as much at where they are employed as could be earned at other places of employment. This section seeks to explain why management and union leaders focus on going rates in setting wages.

Chapter 6 described equity theory. This theory suggests that a worker compares his or her own outcomes, e.g., pay relative to own job inputs, or skill, with the outcomes and job inputs of others. When these ratios are perceived to be about equal, equity theory predicts that the worker will be satisfied.

PAY SATISFACTION MODEL

Fig. 11.3 presents a model that is based on the comparisons implied by equity theory. It attempts to identify key personal inputs and job characteristics that are involved in these comparisons. Skill, experience, training, education, and seniority are individual characteristics that influence ability to perform a particular job. Job performance is how well an employee does perform a particular job.

The cell labeled "Job characteristics" lists outcomes present in varying degrees with different jobs. Examples are responsibility, difficulty, working condi-

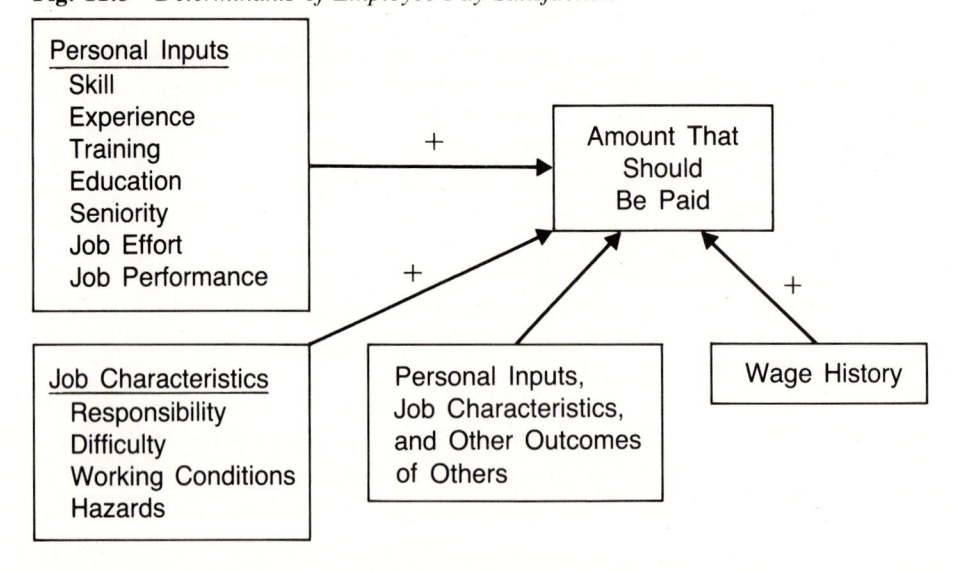

Fig. 11.3 *Determinants of Employee Pay Satisfaction*

Personal Inputs		
Skill		
Experience		
Training	→ + →	Amount That Should Be Paid
Education		
Seniority		
Job Effort		
Job Performance		

Job Characteristics	Personal Inputs, Job Characteristics, and Other Outcomes of Others	Wage History
Responsibility		
Difficulty		
Working Conditions		
Hazards		

If actual pay ≈ Amount that should be received → pay satisfaction

If actual pay > Amount that should be received → guilt

If actual pay < Amount that should be received → pay dissatisfaction

Source: Adapted from: Edward E. Lawler III, Pay and Organizational Effectiveness: A Psychological View *(New York: McGraw-Hill Book Co., 1971), p. 215.*

tions, and hazards. The cell labeled "Personal inputs, job characteristics and other outcomes of others" reflects the comparisons a worker makes with other workers with respect to these variables. The final cell, "Wage history," suggests that an employee's estimate of the amount he or she should be paid is influenced in part by what that person has earned in the past.

Lawler has reviewed the research evidence concerning the relationship between these variables presented in Fig. 11.3 and perceptions of the amount that should be paid.[33] Generally, the evidence indicates that the greater a worker's personal inputs, job characteristics, or wage history the more that person believes he or she should be paid. During periods of rapid inflation the variable, wage history, is probably a significant contributor to increases in perceptions of the amount that should be paid. This is because inflation has the effect of reducing real earnings. With respect to comparisons with others, the relationship is not simply a positive or a negative relationship. Rather, comparisons with others seem to indicate that workers arrive at an estimate of the appropriate amount that should be paid.

Felt fair pay. Jaques has suggested the label "felt fair pay" for this estimate.[34] He defines felt fair pay as the existence of a norm among members of the labor force of the fair payment for any given level of work. Jaques presents evidence indicating that for various measures of level of responsibility, employee estimates of the fair rate of pay range about plus-and-minus 5 percent.

The idea that employees have estimates of the appropriate amount that they should be paid is reflected by the statements at the bottom of Fig. 11.3. First, if actual pay is equal or nearly equal to the employee's perception of the amount that should be received, pay satisfaction follows. We do not mean to imply that actual pay must be exactly equal to the amount that is felt should be received. Rather, there appears to be a range in which employees will feel fairly treated. It has been suggested by one compensation specialist that a difference of about 15 percent is necessary before it is large enough to be recognized.[35]

If actual pay exceeds the amount that is felt should be received, guilt is predicted. Research on satisfaction with compensation very seldom finds employees who perceive they are being overpaid. As a result, one can usually ignore the possibility of this problem in establishing wages.

If actual pay is less than the amount workers feel they should be paid, pay dissatisfaction results. The perception that actual pay is less than the amount that is felt should be received is common.

CONSEQUENCES OF PAY DISSATISFACTION

Pay dissatisfaction is very important both to management and to union leaders. As indicated in Fig. 11.4, it is predicted that pay dissatisfaction leads to a reduction in job performance, more grievances, increased likelihood of strikes, and higher rates of absenteeism. These are outcomes that management wishes to avoid. To the union leader, the existence of pay dissatisfaction may provide the opportunity to demonstrate the effectiveness of the union by negotiating pay increases that remove pay

Fig. 11.4 *Consequences of Pay Dissatisfaction*

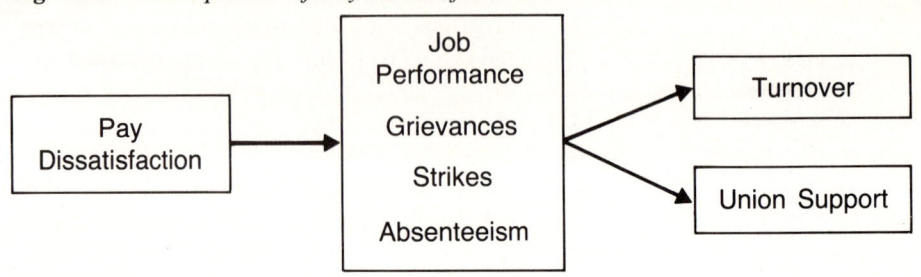

Pay Dissatisfaction → Job Performance, Grievances, Strikes, Absenteeism → Turnover / Union Support

dissatisfaction. However, if the union is not successful in removing pay dissatisfaction or if the union is perceived to have contributed to the existence of pay dissatisfaction, problems will result for the union leadership.

The right side of Fig. 11.4 points out two possible outcomes that can stem from pay dissatisfaction. If pay dissatisfaction continues for a long period of time, it is assumed that turnover is a possibility. With respect to union support, pay dissatisfaction could have either a positive or a negative effect. When the work force of an organization is dissatisfied with pay and the union is successful in negotiating wage increases that remove the pay dissatisfaction, union support should increase. However, if union negotiation efforts are not effective in removing the source of pay dissatisfaction, it is assumed that support of the union could erode.

Establishing the Wage Structure

The first section of this chapter focused on factors influencing wage levels or average wages within a firm. This section will describe recommended procedures for establishing wage rates for specific jobs. This process results in the wage structure of an organization. Topics that will be discussed include: job analysis, wage surveys, job evaluation, pricing jobs, wage progression, and role of union representatives.

JOB ANALYSIS

Job analysis is the process of studying jobs in an organization.[36] The objective is to identify the tasks and duties involved in the performance of a job as well as the employee characteristics necessary to perform these tasks. The product of job analysis is a job description and a statement of worker characteristics needed to perform the job. A job description describes the tasks and behaviors associated with performing the job. The job specification indicates the characteristics necessary to perform the job. Examples of such characteristics are skill, knowledge, and experience. After developing job descriptions and specifications for the jobs in an organization, one has the necessary information to analyze the results of wage surveys and identify the going rates for jobs.

WAGE SURVEYS

The basic options for obtaining wage survey information are to use the information gathered by a third party or conduct one's own survey. Each year the Bureau of Labor Statistics conducts many area wage surveys. Among them are surveys of seventy-two standard metropolitan statistical areas (SMSAs). These surveys focus on clerical and blue-collar occupations and cover many manufacturing and nonmanufacturing industries. They provide pay data for selected jobs. Included among the data reported in these surveys are measures of average wage rates and the dispersion in wages. Exhibit 11.1 provides sample information for maintenance mechanics–machinery and maintenance mechanics–motor vehicles in the Denver-Boulder, Colorado area. Hourly earnings are reported for all workers covered by the survey and for broad industry groupings. Inspection of these data indicates a wide degree of variation in compensation across industries. For example, the median pay for maintenance mechanics–motor vehicles in manufacturing is $8.23 an hour. The correspond-

EXHIBIT 11.1
Hourly Earnings for Maintenance Mechanics: Denver-Boulder, Colorado, December 1979

Occupation and industry division	Mean[1]	Median[2]	Middle range[3]
Maintenance mechanics			
(Machinery)	8.87	9.11	8.14– 9.80
Manufacturing	8.84	9.18	8.14– 9.80
Nonmanufacturing	9.06	8.46	7.62–10.92
Public utilities	9.34	9.10	7.62–11.00
Maintenance mechanics			
(Motor vehicles)	9.46	9.44	7.90–10.94
Manufacturing	8.41	8.23	7.56– 9.21
Nonmanufacturing	9.72	9.69	8.10–11.02
Public utilities	10.23	10.66	9.44–11.02

1. The mean is computed for each job by totaling the earnings of all workers and dividing by the number of workers.
2. The median designates position–half of the workers receive the same or more and half receive the same or less than the rate shown.
3. The middle range or interquartile range is defined by two rates of pay: a fourth of the workers earn the same or less than the lower rate and a fourth earn the same or more than the higher rate.

Source: U. S. Department of Labor, Bureau of Labor Statistics, *Area Wage Survey: Denver-Boulder, Colorado, Metropolitan Area, December 1979* (Washington, D. C.: U. S. Government Printing Office, May 1980), Bulletin 2050–72, p. 10.

ing figure for maintenance mechanics in public utilities is $10.66 an hour. This information reinforces the importance of being aware of the existence of wage contours and obtaining information for specific industries.

The wage data represented by the example in Exhibit 11.1 are collected for SMSAs annually. At three-year intervals, data describing employer practices and supplementary wage provisions are collected. Included in these surveys are information concerning shift differentials, scheduled weekly hours, paid holidays, paid vacations, and health, insurance, and pension plans.

The Bureau of Labor Statistics also conducts industry wage surveys for fifty manufacturing and twenty nonmanufacturing industries.[37] These surveys are conducted on a recurring five-year or three-year cycle. These surveys provide detailed information on wage rates as well as supplemental forms of compensation.

Since the detailed area wage surveys and the industry wage surveys are infrequent, an employer and union involved in negotiations may find the information available from this source somewhat dated. As a result, it is quite likely that both the employer and union would find it necessary to turn to some other source of wage survey information or to conduct their own wage surveys.

Inspection of a BLS area wage survey points out another problem. Information is collected on a limited number of jobs. For example, in the Denver-Boulder area wage survey referred to in Exhibit 11.1, there are only twelve job titles surveyed in the classification, maintenance, tool room, and power plant workers.

Key jobs. Wage surveys focus on benchmark or key jobs. These are jobs that are common in the labor market. In this context, common means that the jobs are found in many different organizations and, in addition, the content of the jobs tends to be similar. For such jobs, wage survey information is available.

Non-key jobs. But what of the non-key jobs? By definition, these jobs are not common in different organizations. As a result, wage survey information on such jobs is not available. Consequently, one cannot rely directly on the results of a wage survey to estimate going rates for non-key jobs.

JOB EVALUATION

Job evaluation is a process used to determine or estimate the relative worth of jobs in an organization. There are different job evaluation methods. The most common method is called "point job evaluation." This approach involves determining the extent to which compensable factors are present in the jobs being evaluated. Four commonly used basic compensable factors are responsibility, working conditions, education and skill, and mental and physical effort. Each basic factor can include several subfactors. For example, subfactors that could be included under the basic factor, responsibility, are responsibility for: money and property; equipment and materials; and safety of others.[38]

Compensable factors (both basic factors as well as subfactors) are closely related to the job characteristics and personal inputs listed in Fig. 11.3. This is because the ultimate purpose of job evaluation is to arrive at a fair wage rate for each job that is evaluated.

A point evaluation system consists of scales or measures for each compensable factor that is to be used to evaluate jobs in the organization. A key step in constructing such a system is arriving at point values to be assigned to each degree of each factor. This is a judgment process. In addition, deciding how much of each degree is present in key jobs as well as nonkey jobs is a judgment process. The success of a job evaluation system must be judged on the extent to which employees feel their jobs are accurately evaluated.

JOB EVALUATION COMMITTEE

The judgments referred to in the previous paragraph are typically made by a job evaluation committee, or a wage committee. A primary objective of this committee is to secure employee acceptance of the compensation system. To attain this objective it is essential that the committee be composed of individuals from different departments who have the respect and confidence of employees in the organization.[39] Given that employees are represented by a union, it is recommended by compensation specialists that management and labor cooperate in administering such programs.[40]

INCIDENCE OF JOB EVALUATION

Concerning the incidence of such programs, a recent study of union contracts found that 40 percent spelled out jobs classification or job evaluation procedures.[41] Such programs are more common in manufacturing than in nonmanufacturing organizations, 54 percent and 18 percent respectively. With respect to union involvement, 34 percent of the contracts contained job evaluation procedures requiring union consultation. Twenty-five percent required the company to negotiate with the union concerning evaluation of new jobs or reevaluation of jobs. Only 14 percent called for joint job evaluation committees.

ESTIMATING WAGE RATES FOR NON-KEY JOBS

After all jobs within an organization have been evaluated, it is possible to estimate the relationship between non-key jobs to key jobs. Once one is able to identify going rates in the market for key jobs, given an estimate of the relative worth of each job in the organization, one is able to estimate accurately the appropriate wage rate for non-key jobs. Fig. 11.5 describes this process. Jobs A, B, C, D, and E represent key jobs. By definition, such jobs are common in the relevant labor market and wage survey information can be obtained that indicates the going rates for these jobs.

Wage curve. The diagonal line labeled "Wage Curve" represents the relationship between job evaluation points within an organization and market wage rates. One can think of this as a simple regression curve in which the independent variable is job evaluation points and the dependent variable is market wage rates.

To estimate the appropriate hourly wage that should be paid for non-key jobs, one simply finds the point value on the horizontal axis corresponding to each non-key

COLLECTIVE-BARGAINING ISSUES

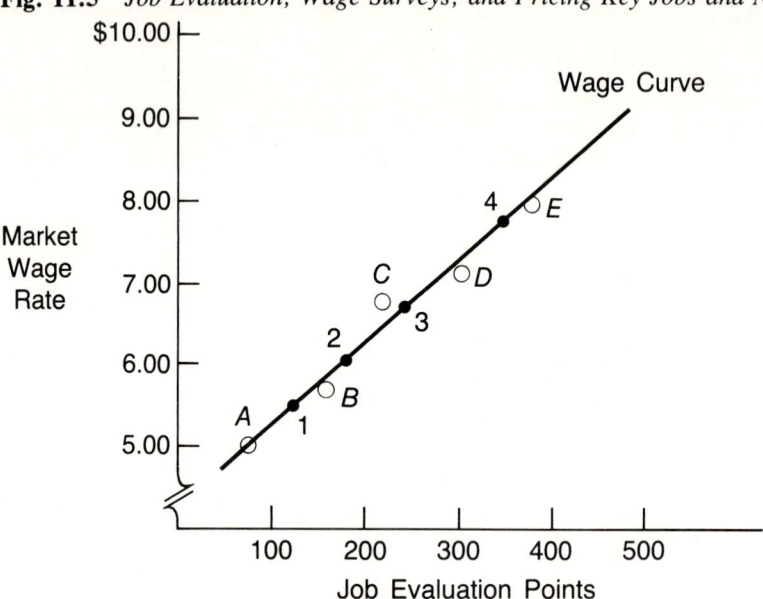

Fig. 11.5 *Job Evaluation, Wage Surveys, and Pricing Key Jobs and Non-key Jobs*

Relative Importance of Jobs

Non-Key Jobs	Key Jobs
Job 1 = 125 points	Job A = 75 points
Job 2 = 180 points	Job B = 160 points
Job 3 = 240 points	Job C = 220 points
Job 4 = 350 points	Job D = 300 points
	Job E = 380 points

job. Then one goes vertically from that point to the wage curve. Next, one goes horizontally from that point on the wage curve to the vertical axis. The point of intersection with the vertical axis is the estimate of the appropriate hourly rate for non-key jobs. For example, Job 3 has a point value of 240. Going horizontally from that point on the wage curve indicates that the estimated appropriate hourly wage rate is $7.00.

ESTABLISHMENT OF PAY GRADES

The discussion of Fig. 11.5 suggests that one could establish a unique wage rate for each job within an organization. In fact, jobs are usually grouped into categories of approximately equal worth; then a single wage rate or a range of wages is established for each of these categories. Fig. 11.6 represents wage rates for various pay grades. Jobs were grouped into categories of 100 points each; any job within a category is assumed to be of equal worth.

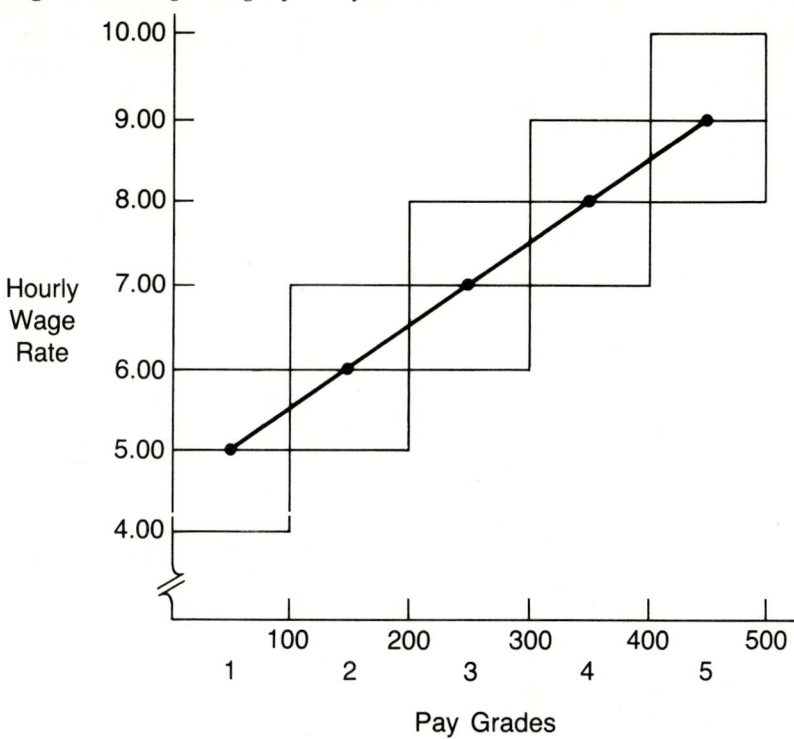

Fig. 11.6 *Wage Ranges for Pay Grades*

SETTING WAGE RATES FOR PAY GRADES

The process of determining the wage rates to correspond to these pay grades is the business of contract negotiations. This discussion has assumed an hourly-wage- or time-based system of compensation rather than an incentive-compensation plan which is based on units of production. The latter requires a work situation in which there is an objective measure of output. Since this situation is somewhat unique, we have assumed a time-based system of compensation in our example. Another factor taken into consideration in assuming a time-based system of compensation is that incentive systems are relatively uncommon. Incentive compensation procedures appear in 29 percent of contracts, while virtually all contracts contain provisions specifying time-based compensation for at least some jobs in the bargaining unit.[42] Also, one study shows that union members prefer time-based or hourly wage rates to incentive wage rates by a ratio of about two to one.[43]

PAY RANGES

Given an hourly wage system, another issue to be addressed is whether there will be a single wage rate or a pay range for each pay grade. Fig. 11.6 presents an example of pay ranges for each pay grade. For example, for pay grade 2 the minimum hourly

Table 11.5 *Basis of Progression through Pay Ranges (Frequency Expressed as Percentage of Contracts)*

Basis for progression	Frequency
Solely on length of service	52%
Length of service given satisfactory performance	25
Combination of length of service and merit	11
Solely on merit	12

Source: Bureau of National Affairs, Basic Patterns in Union Contracts, 9th ed. (Washington, D. C.: BNA, Inc., May 1979), p. 106.

wage is $5.00 an hour, and the maximum is $7.00 an hour. If there were no pay ranges, the midpoint would correspond to the wage rate for each pay grade. In such a case the wage rate for pay grade 2 would be $6.00 an hour. About one-third of collective bargaining agreements provide for rate ranges.[44]

Given pay ranges, the next issue is deciding on a method of progression through the pay range. The alternatives are to progress through a pay range on the basis of seniority, merit, or a combination of seniority and merit. Progression based on merit implies some form of performance appraisal by supervisors. Table 11.5 reports the incidence of these alternative procedures in collective-bargaining agreements. Progression based solely on seniority or on the basis of seniority, given satisfactory performance, appears in three out of four contracts.[45]

MERIT AND INCENTIVE COMPENSATION

The low frequency of contracts calling for pay ranges, as well as for merit-based progression where pay ranges are found, may strike the reader as unusual given the positive relationship between job performance and employee perceptions of the amount that should be paid, as reported in Fig. 11.3. In discussing that figure, it was pointed out that research indicates workers expect to be paid more as their job performance increases. This suggests that workers will demand that wage rates reflect differences in job performance. However, discussions the authors had with a group of workers adamantly opposed to merit-based compensation indicate two themes to their opposition. The reason most frequently mentioned for opposing merit compensation was that at some time in their career they had been subject to an unfair merit system. Supervisors had shown favoritism in completing performance evaluations. As a result, the workers perceived that wage increases more closely reflected who was able to get along with the supervisor than how well they performed their job.

The other theme to this opposition was that merit compensation creates hard feelings among coworkers. It was suggested that cooperation on the job among workers suffers as a result. Admittedly, the above is anecdotal evidence. However, a recent study found that employees who perceived a strong relationship between their level of job performance and the size of their pay raises tended to oppose unionization. Alternatively, employees who perceived a weak or no relationship between their job performance and their pay increases tended to favor unions.[46] The same

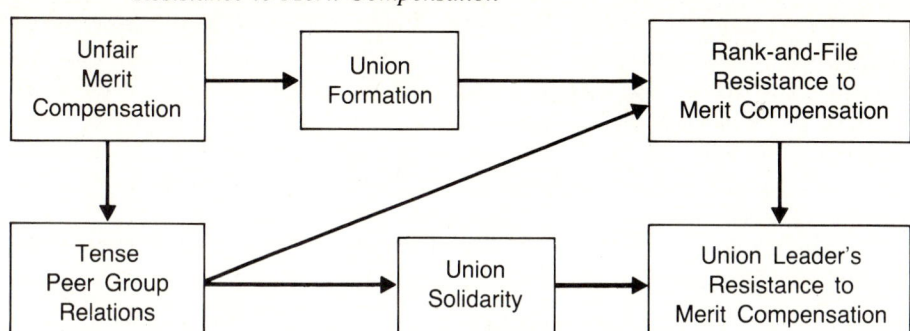

Fig. 11.7 *Unfair Merit Compensation, Union Formation and Solidarity, and Union Resistance to Merit Compensation*

```
┌──────────────┐      ┌──────────┐         ┌──────────────┐
│   Unfair     │─────▶│  Union   │────────▶│ Rank-and-File│
│    Merit     │      │Formation │         │ Resistance to│
│ Compensation │      │          │         │Merit Compensation│
└──────┬───────┘      └──────────┘         └──────────────┘
       │                                          │
       ▼                                          ▼
┌──────────────┐      ┌──────────┐         ┌──────────────┐
│    Tense     │      │  Union   │         │Union Leader's│
│  Peer Group  │─────▶│Solidarity│────────▶│ Resistance to│
│  Relations   │      │          │         │Merit Compensation│
└──────────────┘      └──────────┘         └──────────────┘
```

phenomenon, unfair merit compensation, could be related both to favoring formation of a union and rejection of merit compensation. In addition, unfair merit compensation may be related to poor peer group relations.

Fig. 11.7 suggests how these factors, along with others, may account for the high incidence of single-rate pay structures and the high incidence of seniority progression where pay ranges exist. Unfair merit compensation is assumed to be related both to the formation of unions and to tense peer group relations. Given that unfair merit compensation leads to unionization, it follows that the rank-and-file union member would oppose merit compensation. In attempting to reflect the interests of the membership, union leaders will oppose merit compensation.

The above discussion provides a partial explanation for the low incidence of merit compensation systems in collective-bargaining agreements. However, we suggest that another factor reinforces a union leader's opposition to merit compensation. Tense peer group relations will tend to undermine union solidarity. This is an outcome that union leaders prefer to avoid. In addition, tense peer group relations reinforce worker opposition to merit compensation. In summary, it is our opinion that the low frequency of merit-compensation procedures in collective-bargaining agreements stems from what employees perceived to be unfair merit systems.

UNION-MANAGEMENT COOPERATION: GROUP INCENTIVES

It is our judgment that union leaders and union members are not opposed to merit compensation per se. Rather they oppose merit compensation that is perceived to be unfair. Given cooperative union-management relations, it is possible to install successful incentive systems.

Scanlon Plan. An example of such a system is the Scanlon Plan.[47] The objective of this plan is to increase productivity. There are two basic mechanisms to achieving this objective. One is the establishment of production committees throughout the plant to insure that all members of the organization have the opportunity to participate in improving productivity. The other is the equitable distribution of the financial rewards of improving productivity to all members of the organization.

The Scanlon Plan assumes that workers throughout a plant or organization can suggest ways to increase productivity. As these ideas are implemented, productivity increases. This creates a pool of money available for incentive bonuses. In the Scanlon Plan, all employees, including management, share in the group incentive bonus. Bonuses are usually distributed monthly. Each individual's share of the bonus is equal to his or her monthly earnings as a percentage of total labor costs for the month.[48]

Other group incentive systems which have many of the same features as the Scanlon Plan have been used successfully. Among them are the Rucker Plan and the Kaiser-Steel Union Sharing Plan.[49] An advantage of a group incentive system such as the Scanlon Plan is that group cooperation is encouraged.[50] On the other hand, individual incentive plans tend to discourage group cooperation.[51] Consequently, a group system is less likely to be a threat to union solidarity.

Summary

The principal determinants of wages are ability to pay, productivity, going rates, standard of living, and cost of living. One dimension of ability to pay is an organization's recent profit picture. If profits are high, unions are likely to demand an increased share of the profits in the form of higher wages. Another dimension of an organization's ability to pay is the elasticity of demand for its products and services. As elasticity increases, the organization's ability to pass along increased labor costs to consumers decreases.

Productivity has received a great deal of attention as a determinant of wages. This is because wages cannot increase faster than productivity without reducing profits and/or contributing to inflation. A problem with productivity as a basis for determining wage increases is identifying that portion of increased productivity attributable to labor. Other possible reasons for increased productivity are improved technology and management techniques.

The most important factor in setting wages appears to be the going rates for labor. There are two dimensions to this determinant: local labor market rates and industry wage patterns. These two dimensions are the number-one and number-two factors in setting wages. In non-union organizations, the former appears to be more important. In unionized organizations, the latter is more important. This appears to be due to the union objective of achieving uniform wage rates within an industry.

Providing a living wage does not appear to be an important wage criterion. However, union negotiators may present an argument based on this factor if it supports the union's bargaining objective. One should recognize that such factors as going rates and ability to pay will play a more important role in setting wages.

In recent years, cost of living has increased in importance in determining wages. This is because of the rapid increase in the Consumer Price Index (CPI). An increase in the CPI reduces workers' real income unless wage rates increase. The usual contract provision to adjust wages for increases in the CPI is a cost-of-living allowance or adjustment (COLA).

Both union leaders and management must be concerned with employee pay satisfaction. This is achieved when the amount that a worker feels he or she should be paid is equal, or nearly equal, to the amount actually paid. The amount that should be paid is influenced by personal inputs or skills, job characteristics, and comparisons with other workers.

Pay satisfaction depends largely on how the wage structure is established and administered. Recommended procedures for establishing a wage structure include job analysis, job evaluation, and conducting wage surveys. It is our opinion that union representatives should serve on the job evaluation committee. This implies at least an accommodative relationship between the union and management.

Merit-compensation procedures are seldom called for in collective-bargaining agreements. A possible explanation for this is that management-administered merit-compensation procedures have been perceived as unfair. As a result, efforts to reflect individual job performance in wage rates have been rejected. The Scanlon Plan is a group-incentive system. It is suggested as an incentive system that might be acceptable to management and union leaders, as well as union members.

Discussion Questions

1. With respect to ability to pay, productivity, going rates, standard of living, and cost of living:
   a. On what basis is each put forth as a determinant of wages?
   b. What problems are encountered in trying to use each as a wage criterion?
   c. What is the relative importance of these wage determinants?
2. Why are there difference in wages rates for the same or closely related jobs across industries within a given geographic area?
3. What factors influence employee perceptions of the perceived amount that should be paid?
4. Why is pay satisfaction important to both union leaders and management?
5. What is the role of job analysis, job evaluation, and wage surveys in establishing the wage structure of an organization? How can union representatives fit into this process?
6. Why are single rates so common in collective bargaining agreements? Where pay ranges are found, why is progression usually based on length of service?
7. Why is the Scanlon Plan more likely to be more acceptable to union members and leaders than an individual incentive system or a merit compensation system?

COLLECTIVE-BARGAINING ISSUES

Key Concepts

Wage level
Annual improvement factor
Productivity bargaining
Wage contour
COLA
Wage-reopener clause
Felt fair pay

Key jobs
Nonkey jobs
Wage curve
Pay range
Merit compensation
Scanlon Plan

Notes

1. Herbert G. Zollitsch and Adolph Langsner, *Wage and Salary Administration,* 2nd ed. (Cincinnati: South-Western Publishing Co., 1970), pp. 133–34.

2. *NLRB v. Truitt Manufacturing Co.,* 351 U.S. 149, (1956).

3. Thomas H. Patten, Jr., *Pay: Employee Compensation and Incentive Plans* (New York: The Free Press, 1977), p. 183.

4. Charles Brown and James L. Medoff, "Trade Unions in the Production Process," *Journal of Political Economy* 86, no. 3 (June 1978): 355–78.

5. Kim B. Clark, "The Impact of Unionization on Productivity: A Case Study," *Industrial and Labor Relations Review* 33, no. 4 (July 1980): 451–69.

6. Lloyd G. Reynolds, *Labor Economics and Labor Relations,* 7th ed. (Englewood Cliffs, N. J.: Prentice-Hall, Inc., 1974), p. 221.

7. *Employment and Training Report of the President: 1979* (Washington, D. C.: U. S. Government Printing Office, 1979), pp. 23–25.

8. Patten, p. 183.

9. Ibid., pp. 183–84.

10. Ibid., p. 184.

11. Robert B. McKersie and L. C. Hunter, *Pay, Productivity and Collective Bargaining* (London: Macmillan Press Ltd., 1973), pp. 1–4.

12. William F. Maloney, "Productivity Bargaining in Contract Construction," *Proceedings of the 1977 Annual Spring Meeting: Industrial Relations Research Association* (Madison, WI: Industrial Relations Research Association, 1977), pp. 533–34.

13. Joseph P. Goldberg, "Bargaining and Productivity in the Private Sector," in *Collective Bargaining and Productivity,* Gerald Somers et al. (Madison, WI: Industrial Relations Research Association, 1975), pp. 28–42.

14. Chamber of Commerce, *Employee Benefits 1975* (Washington, D. C., 1976), p. 9

15. U. S. Department of Labor, *Union Wages and Hours: Local Truckdrivers and Helpers—July 1, 1976,* Bulletin 1984 (Washington, D. C.: U. S. Government Printing Office, 1978).

16. H. F. Zeman, "Regional Pay Differentials in White-Collar Occupations," *Monthly Labor Review* 94 (January 1971): 53.

17. John T. Dunlop, "The Task of Contemporary Wage Theory," in *New Concepts in Wage Deter-*

mination, eds. George W. Taylor and Frank C. Pierson (New York: McGraw-Hill Book Company, 1957), pp. 127–39.

18. J. C. Brackett, "New BLS Budgets Provide Yardsticks for Measuring Family Living Costs," *Monthly Labor Review* 92, no. 4 (April 1969): 3–16.

19. Ibid., p. 7.

20. *Employment and Training Report of the President: 1980* (Washington, D. C.: U. S. Government Printing Office, 1979), p. 281.

21. Reynolds, pp. 184–85.

22. Robert H. Ferguson, *Cost-of-Living Adjustments in Union-Management Agreements* (Ithaca, NY: New York State School of Industrial and Labor Relations, Cornell University, Bulletin 65, 1976), p. 15.

23. Bureau of National Affairs, *Basic Patterns in Union Contracts,* 9th ed. (Washington, D. C., 1979), p. 98.

24. Ibid.

25. Ibid.

26. Ibid.

27. David W. Belcher, *Compensation Administration* (Englewood Cliffs, NJ: Prentice-Hall, 1974), p. 485.

28. H. M. Douty, *Cost-of-Living Escalator Clauses and Inflation* prepared for the Council on Wage and Price Stability (Washington, D. C.: U. S. Government Printing Office, August 1975), p. 3.

29. C. Howell, W. Thomas, and E. Lamb, "Consumer Price Rise at 13-Percent Rate for the Third Consecutive Quarter," *Monthly Labor Review* 102, no. 12 (December 1979): 35.

30. Bureau of National Affairs, p. 99.

31. Audrey Freedman, *Managing Labor Relations* (The Conference Board, Report No. 765, 1980), pp. 35–38.

32. Ibid., p. 35.

33. Edward E. Lawler III, *Pay and Organizational Effectiveness: A Psychological View* (New York: McGraw-Hill Book Company, 1971), pp. 217–30.

34. Elliot Jaques, *Equitable Payment* (New York: John Wiley and Sons, 1961).

35. Richard I. Henderson, *Compensation Management: Rewarding Performance,* 2nd ed. (Reston, VA: Reston Publishing Co., 1979), pp. 196–97.

36. Herbert G. Heneman III, Donald P. Schwab, John A. Fossum, and Lee D. Dyer, *Personnel/Human Resource Management* (Homewood IL: Richard D. Irwin, Inc., 1980), pp. 87–88.

37. Henderson, p. 253.

38. Zollitsch and Langsner, p. 228.

39. Ibid., p. 750.

40. Ibid., p. 755.

41. Bureau of National Affairs, p. 105.

42. Ibid., p. 106.

43. Lawler, p. 160.

44. Bureau of National Affairs, p. 105; and U. S. Department of Labor, *Characteristics of Major Collective Bargaining Agreements—January 1, 1978,* Bulletin 2065 (Washington, D. C.: U. S. Government Printing Office, April 1980), p. 36.

45. Ibid.

46. Robert E. Allen and Timothy J. Keaveny, "Correlates of University Faculty Interest in Unionization: A Replication and Extension," *Journal of Applied Psychology* 66 (October 1981): 582–88.

47. Carl F. Frost, J. H. Wakeley, and R. A. Ruh, *The Scanlon Plan for Organization Development: Identity, Participation and Equity* (Michigan State University Press, 1974), p. 5.

48. Henderson, p. 371.

49. Ibid., pp. 371–72.

50. Lawler, p. 130.

51. Ibid., p. 128.

Suggested Readings

Bureau of National Affairs. *Basic Patterns in Union Contracts,* 9th ed. Washington, D. C., 1979.

Ferguson, R. H. *Cost-of-Living Adjustments in Union-Management Agreements.* Ithaca, NY: New York State School of Industrial and Labor Relations, Cornell University, Bulletin 65, 1976.

Freedman, A. *Managing Labor Relations.* The Conference Board, Report No. 765, 1980.

Lawler, E. E., III. *Pay and Organizational Effectiveness: A Psychological View.* New York: McGraw-Hill Book Company, 1971.

McKersie, R. B. and Hunter, L. C. *Pay, Productivity and Collective Bargaining.* London: Macmillan Press Ltd., 1973.

Somers, G., et al. *Collective Bargaining and Productivity.* Madison, WI: Industrial Relations Research Association, 1975.

Zollitsch, H. G. and Langsner, A. *Wage and Salary Administration,* 2nd ed. Cincinnati: South-Western Publishing Co., 1970.

Chapter 12

SUPPLEMENTAL COMPENSATION ISSUES IN COLLECTIVE BARGAINING

Charles Bradley, vice-president of personnel and labor relations for the Albany Mining Company, was continuing his preparations for contract negotiations with the American Miners Union. In addition to attempting to anticipate the union's wage demands, he was concerned about the union's supplemental compensation demands. Because the cost of supplemental benefits typically exceeds 35 percent of direct wages and salaries, such benefits are an important part of an organization's labor costs. Another concern of Bradley's was insuring that the negotiated compensation package was in compliance with the many statutes that govern employee compensation and benefits.

Charles assumed there would be three categories of union demands for fringe benefits. These categories were compensation for inconvenience and unpleasantness for employees in the performance of their jobs, pay for time not worked, and benefits related to employee job security. Charles wanted to know which specific benefits in each category the union negotiators would demand. It would help if Charles knew how frequently various fringe-benefit provisions appear in collective bargaining agreements. This information would indicate which union demands were the "real" demands.

A number of collective bargaining agreements provide for unique fringe benefits. For example, health maintenance organizations and child-care facilities are provided in some organizations. Charles wondered if the American Miners Union would demand these or other unique forms of supplemental compensation.

Finally, Charles was concerned about the cost of the wage-and-benefit proposals that would be negotiated at the bargaining table. Management should know the cost of the alternative proposals being considered before accepting or rejecting any of them.

Charles hoped that the union negotiators shared his concern. It would not be in the interest of union members to have their employer agree to contract terms that reduced the organization's ability to compete in the market. Charles thought that both union and management negotiators should be able to cost out the provisions of collective-bargaining agreements.

Management as well as union negotiators should share the concerns attributed to Charles Bradley. These issues and others will be addressed in this chapter. After you have studied this chapter you should:

- Understand the basic arguments for and against legislation concerning wages and supplemental forms of employee compensation.
- Be able to describe the provisions of the Davis-Bacon Act, Walsh-Healey Act, Fair Labor Standards Act, Equal Pay Act and Civil Rights Act that pertain to employee wages and salaries.
- Know the provisions of the laws that attempt to provide minimum levels of protection for workers in the event of unemployment, injury, illness, retirement, and death.
- Be able to discuss the factors leading to the growth of private forms of supplemental compensation.
- Know examples of supplemental compensation that
  a. Compensate employees for inconvenience and unpleasantness encountered in performing their jobs.
  b. Compensate employees for time not worked.
  c. Provide benefits intended to increase employee security.
- Be aware of emerging forms of fringe benefits.
- Understand the problems associated with supplemental compensation programs.
- Be able to cost out a collective-bargaining agreement.
- Know the problems associated with the typical approach to costing out collective-bargaining agreements.

This chapter will review legislation that pertains to employee compensation and benefits. In addition, common forms of supplemental compensation that appear in collective bargaining agreements will be discussed. Finally, the process of estimating the cost of the provisions of a collective-bargaining agreement will be described.

Public Policy on Wages

Several federal laws pertain to employee compensation. The intent of these laws is to establish minimum standards for wages. The justification for such legislation is that the bargaining relationship between employers and employees is unequal. An employee has relatively little power compared to an employer. Most of the legislation concerning wages was passed during the 1930s. Those opposed to such legislation argued that employees were free to quit or refuse employment under the terms being proposed by employers. The counterargument was that in many situations the hardship imposed on an individual who quit a job was quite severe. For example, a company might be the only major employer in the community. Refusal to work under the conditions proposed by that organization would probably necessitate moving to another community to find work. Also, during periods of high unemployment, such as the Depression years, an individual who was not willing to work at the wage being offered by an employer was quickly replaced by someone who would accept the proposed wage rate.

DAVIS-BACON ACT

This legislation, also known as the Prevailing Wage and Fringe Benefit Law, was passed in 1931. It covers employment on public construction projects that are financed entirely or in part with federal funds. It requires the contractor to provide wages and benefits for employees of the project equal to those prevailing in the geographic area in which the construction is taking place.[1] The Secretary of Labor is required to determine the prevailing wage rates and fringe benefits for the geographic area.

The rationale for this legislation was to protect local contractors and workers from outside contractors employing cheaper itinerant workers. In addition, since contracts are usually awarded to the lowest qualified bidder, it was intended to discourage employers from underbidding competitors by paying lower wages.

In recent years Davis-Bacon has been the object of criticism. One criticism is that since union wage rates and benefits are often specified as those prevailing in a geographic area, non-union contractors paying lesser rates lose their cost advantage in bidding on contracts. Consequently, the cost of federal construction in some cases is higher than would otherwise be the case. A second criticism is that Davis-Bacon retards the growth of non-union construction employment. The available studies of the impact of the Davis-Bacon Act indicate that it does result in higher costs for federal construction.[2]

WALSH-HEALEY ACT

The Walsh-Healey Act, or Public Contracts Act, applies to employers supplying the federal government with goods and services involving contracts of ten thousand dollars or more.[3] It parallels the Davis-Bacon Act in that the Secretary of Labor identifies the prevailing wages and fringe benefits for the relevant occupations and industry in the geographic area of the employer who has the contract. These prevailing rates constitute the minimum standard for wages and fringe benefits of the contractor.

In addition, this legislation has an overtime provision. It specifies that overtime pay at one and one-half times the normal wage rate be paid for work in excess of eight hours a day or forty hours a week.

The Walsh-Healey Act has not been the object of as much criticism as the Davis-Bacon Act. However, when the prevailing wages and benefits for a locality are defined to be those negotiated in relevant collective agreements, the same criticisms would appear to apply.

FAIR LABOR STANDARDS ACT

The principal federal legislation regulating hours and wages is the Fair Labor Standards Act, passed in 1938.[4] It is also known as the Wage and Hour Act. As with the previous legislation pertaining to wages, it was intended to stop employment at substandard wage levels. A second intent of the act was to increase the number of people employed. Establishment of a minimum wage pertained to the former objective. Requiring overtime pay for work in excess of forty hours a week pertained to the latter objective. Concerning overtime, the Fair Labor Standards Act requires pay at one and one-half the regular wage rate for work in excess of forty hours a week. Originally, the minimum wage was 25 cents an hour. This part of the law has been amended frequently over the years. Table 12.1 reports the various minimum wage rates that have been in effect since the Fair Labor Standards Act was originally enacted. During this period the minimum wage rate has typically been at a level equal to approximately 50 percent or one-half the average gross hourly earnings of production workers in manufacturing.[5]

There are two dimensions to coverage by the Fair Labor Standards Act, establishment coverage and occupational coverage. Originally, the act pertained to business organizations engaged in interstate commerce. This aspect of coverage of the act has been modified. There are a number of specific employer exemptions to the act. However, most employers with gross revenues in excess of $362,000 are covered by the act. The occupations excluded from coverage by this act are executive, administrative, professional, and outside sales employees. The latter are sales personnel who call on customers at their place of business, as opposed to those who perform their work on the premises of their employer.

There is a major controversy concerning minimum wage legislation. Some critics argue that it is so high that it discourages the employment of teenagers. Periodically legislation is proposed that would amend the Fair Labor Standards Act to set a

Table 12.1 *Minimum Wage Rates and Year Became Effective*

Year effective	Minimum wage rate	Year effective	Minimum wage rate
1930	$ .25	1968	$1.60
1939	.30	1974	2.00
1945	.40	1975	2.10
1950	.75	1976	2.30
1956	1.00	1978	2.65
1961	1.15	1979	2.90
1963	1.25	1980	3.10
1967	1.40	1981	3.35

Sources: U. S. Department of Labor, Employment Standards Administration, Minimum Wage and Maximum Hours Standards under the Fair Labor Standards Act *(Washington, D. C.: U. S. Government Printing Office, 1976)*, p. 15.
U. S. Department of Labor, Employment Standards Administration, Minimum Wage and Maximum Hours Standards under the Fair Labor Standards Act *(Washington, D. C.: U. S. Government Printing Office, 1981)*, p. 10.

subminimum wage for younger members of the labor force.[6] Anecdotal evidence that the minimum wage causes high rates of unemployment among teenagers is abundant.[7] Further, the rate of unemployment among teenagers has increased dramatically between 1950 and 1980. During the 1950s, teenage unemployment averaged about 11 percent; during the 1960s, about 14 percent; and during the 1970s, about 17 percent.[8] Among nonwhite teenagers, the unemployment rate was about 36 percent in 1979.

Those favoring a subminimum wage for teenagers argue that such workers are typically less experienced and less productive.[9] Their reasoning is that if the minimum wage is more than such workers are worth, employers hire one person instead of two, and so on. Further, employers hire the most qualified applicant available. Those opposed to a subminimum wage for young members of the labor force counter that there simply are not enough jobs for all those seeking employment.[10] In a situation of job scarcity, the least experienced and least qualified individuals seeking employment will be last to be hired.

Evidence concerning the impact of minimum wages on teenage employment is not clear cut. Evidence that such legislation leads directly to a decline in employment opportunities for young members of the labor force is not convincing.[11] However, there is evidence suggesting that such legislation has slowed the growth of those sectors employing young workers.[12]

EQUAL PAY ACT

The Equal Pay Act, enacted in 1963, is an amendment to the Fair Labor Standards Act. It requires equal pay for equal work regardless of sex.[13] The objective was to prohibit lower wage rates for women doing the same work as men. Equal work is defined as work performed by men and women requiring equal skill, effort, and responsibility, and performed under similar working conditions. However, wage differentials are permitted if based on seniority, merit, or measures of quantity and quality of performance.

Labor unions are prohibited from attempting to negotiate contract agreements that are not consistent with the Equal Pay Act. Originally the coverage of the Equal Pay Act was the same as the other provisions of the Fair Labor Standards Act. A 1972 amendment removed the occupational exemption to the Equal Pay Act. The occupational exemption continues to apply for other provisions of the Fair Labor Standards Act.

CIVIL RIGHTS ACT

The Civil Rights Act of 1964 is also relevant for establishing and administering a compensation package. The act prohibits employers from discriminating against any individual with respect to compensation, terms, conditions, or privileges of employment because of an individual's race, color, religion, sex, or national origin.[14] This legislation parallels the Equal Pay Act in that it prohibits different wages and benefits for groups protected by the law that are doing the same work.

In addition, several provisions of the Civil Rights Act address other dimensions of discrimination pertaining specifically to unions. Labor organizations cannot:

- Exclude or expel individuals from membership because of race, color, religion, sex, or national origin.
- Limit, segregate, or classify membership, or refuse to refer to employment, or limit the employment opportunities of individuals because of the individual's race, color, religion, sex, or national origin.
- Cause an employer to discriminate against an individual.
- Utilize discriminatory practices with respect to admission to or employment in apprenticeship programs.[15]

AGE DISCRIMINATION ACT

This legislation prohibits discrimination in terms and conditions of employment against individuals in the age group from 40 to 65.[16] This legislation, originally enacted in 1967, was amended in 1978 to extend its protection to individuals through the age of 70.

These laws provide the basic standards for establishing wages and benefits in a collective-bargaining agreement. With respect to the minimum wage, it is far exceeded by the provisions of most collective-bargaining agreements. With respect to legislation concerning discrimination, these are standards to which collective-bargaining agreements must adhere.

Public Policy on Employee Benefits

The legislation discussed in the previous section focused mainly on wages or direct compensation. This section focuses on legislation concerning employee benefits. This legislation can be grouped in three categories: that concerning worker benefits in the event of death or injury, legislation pertaining to worker retirement, and that providing protection in the event of unemployment.

WORKERS' COMPENSATION

The first legislation involving employee benefits in the United States was workers' compensation laws. These are state rather than federal laws. The intent of these laws is to provide "some protection" in the event of work-connected injury, illness, or death.

Common law defenses. Prior to workers' compensation laws, employees injured on the job had to go to court and bring suit against the employer to receive any compensation for their injuries. Employers were responsible only when their negligence resulted in the injury. Employers had three common-law defenses that they could use in such suits.[17] If any of these defenses applied in the case, the employer was free from any liability. One defense was the assumption-of-risk principle. If the employer could demonstrate that the injury or accident involved in the suit was caused by risks that were common in the particular type of employment, the employer could argue that the employee has assumed that risk when he or she took the job. An extention of the assumption-of-risk defense was that the hazards inherent in the occupation were reflected in the wage rate for the occupation.[18] A second defense was the fellow-servant rule. This doctrine held that if the injury or accident resulted in any way from negligence on the part of a fellow worker, it was this individual and not the employer who was liable for damages. The final defense was contributory negligence. This meant that if the employer were able to demonstrate that the injured worker was in some way responsible for the accident, the employer was free of any liability. Needless to say, with these defenses employers were in a strong position in court to deal with workers trying to receive compensation for industrial accidents.

The beginning of this century was a time of great hazards on the job and many accidents and deaths for industrial workers. The peak years of industrial accidents were 1907 and 1908. The estimated death toll in 1908 was between 30,000 and 35,000. The number of permanent injuries is estimated at 25,000, and the estimated number of temporary disabilities lasting over three days was two million.[19]

PROVISIONS

With so many work-related accidents and injuries and virtually no insurance or compensation for employees involved in these accidents, there was pressure to provide some protection for industrial workers. The first state legislation was passed in New York in 1910. In the years to follow, other states enacted similar legislation. Workers' compensation laws are based on the principle of liability without fault. Under this principle, employers contribute to a fund providing compensation for employees involved in work-connected accidents and injuries. The benefits are not provided because of liability or negligence on the part of the employer; rather, the benefits are provided simply as a matter of social policy.[20]

Workers' compensation provides three types of benefits: payments to replace lost wages while one is unable to work; payments to cover medical bills; and, in the event an individual is unable to return to his or her former occupation, financial assistance for retraining. Regarding payments to replace lost wages, the legislation typically provides some percentage of regular wages up to a maximum amount. The most common percentages are in the range of 60–67 percent. Normally the maximum benefit limit is reached before reaching the limit imposed by the percentage of regular earnings. Typically, benefits actually received are less than half of regular wages.[21]

Experience rating. Workers' compensation funds are financed by employer contributions. Employers pay a percentage of employee wages and salaries to the fund. Most states use an employer experience-rating system to establish the percentage that employers pay. Those employers whose employees make fewer claims for workers' compensation pay a smaller amount to support the fund.

SOCIAL SECURITY

The major social insurance program in the United States was created by the Social Security Act in 1935. The insurance programs provided by Social Security are: 1) Old-Age and Survivors' Insurance; 2) Disability Insurance; 3) Hospital Insurance; and 4) Supplemental Medical Insurance. The abbreviation that reflects these various programs is OASDHI. Until this legislation was passed the only social insurance program in the United States was workers' compensation. This program provided assistance only in cases of work-connected accidents and injuries. The objective of Social Security was to provide assistance in other situations.

RETIREMENT BENEFITS

Under Social Security, the monthly retirement payments to a retired worker begin at age sixty-five. If a worker chooses, he or she can begin receiving reduced payments at age sixty-two. Additional payments will be made if a retired person has a spouse who is sixty-two or older and for children who are under eighteen or who are disabled.

SURVIVOR INSURANCE

The survivor benefits include payments to a widow who is sixty-two or older. In addition, payments will be made to a widow or divorced wife, regardless of age, who is responsible for the care of dependent children. In addition, monthly payments will be made for children who are under age eighteen or who are disabled.

DISABILITY INSURANCE

Most workers' compensation programs provide limited payments for work-connected injuries. There is some maximum amount that will be paid to a worker who is disabled. The disability insurance provisions of Social Security are intended to provide long-term insurance and to cover those situations where the disability does not stem from a work-connected injury. These payments continue as long as a worker is disabled.

HOSPITAL INSURANCE AND SUPPLEMENTAL MEDICAL INSURANCE

There are two dimensions to the medical care provided by Social Security. Both apply to persons over sixty-five. Hospital insurance is provided to help cover the costs of hospitalization, nursing-home care and extended care after hospitalization. The second part of the program is voluntary. It is designed to help those over sixty-five pay for doctor services and other medical expenses not covered by the first phase of the program.

FINANCING

Social Security is financed by employer and employee contributions. Table 12.2 reports the scheduled wage base and tax rate for Social Security. While the taxable wage base appears to be increasing dramatically, in fact it is being adjusted so that the proportion of workers whose entire income is subject to Social Security taxes is about the same as it was in 1935. When the Social Security Act was passed in 1935, the taxable wage base was $3,000. At that level 93 percent of those covered by the program had their entire income subject to tax. It is estimated that the 1981 base of $29,700 will result in 95 percent of all covered workers having their entire incomes subject to Social Security tax.[22]

Problems pertaining to the financing of Social Security were brought to the attention of Americans by the Reagan administration. In spite of the social security tax increases reflected in Table 12.2, it has been estimated that the tax needed to support the system could be short between $10 billion and $111 billion during the first half of the 1980s.[23] The financing problems at this time are minor compared to those expected after the turn of the century. At the present time there are three workers contributing to the Social Security fund for every retiree. By 2030 there may be just two workers for every retiree.[24] Two basic approaches can be taken to address this issue: reduce benefits by such measures as advancing the retirement age or generate additional revenues by such measures as financing part of the benefits from general tax revenues.[25, 26] The United States Chamber of Commerce supports the former approach, while the AFL-CIO supports the latter. At the time this chapter was written it was not clear how the issue will be approached.

Table 12.2 *Scheduled Wage Base and Tax Rate for OASDHI, 1977–2011 and After*

Year	Maximum wage base on which tax is paid	Total tax rate to be paid by both employees and employers
1977	$16,500	5.85%
1978	17,700	6.05
1979	22,900	6.13
1980	25,900	6.13
1981	29,700	6.65
1982	31,800	6.70
1983	*	6.70
1984	*	6.70
1985	*	7.05
1986–1989	*	7.15
1990–2010	*	7.65
2011 and after	*	7.65

*No higher wage base has been yet specified in law.

Source: Social Security Bulletin, *March 1978, p. 18.*

UNEMPLOYMENT INSURANCE

The current system of unemployment insurance in the United States grew out of the Social Security Act. This legislation assessed a tax on employers to support an unemployment-compensation program. However, if the state established an unemployment-compensation program meeting federal guidelines, employers received a tax credit against their tax liability. The Social Security Act "encouraged" states to establish unemployment-compensation programs through this taxing arrangement.

PROVISIONS

Since this is a state-designed and -administered program, there are fifty different unemployment compensation programs in the United States. Consequently, we will describe typical provisions of unemployment-compensation programs. To be eligible, a person must meet the basic conditions: demonstrate an attachment to the work force during the recent past and a continuing attachment to the labor force while unemployed. For example, one measure of attachment to the work force during the recent past is evidence that a claimant has received some minimum amount of earnings during the past year, for example $1,000. Concerning availability for employment while unemployed, normally an individual must register with the state office administering the program and actively seek work or make a reasonable effort to obtain employment as well as be willing to accept suitable job offers.

In addition, the person must be unemployed through no fault of his or her own. For example, an individual who voluntarily leaves his job or is discharged for cause is not eligible for unemployment compensation. In most states unemployment due to a labor dispute disqualifies a worker for unemployment compensation.

Various formulas are used to compute the weekly benefit amount. Typically, individuals receive some percentage of their regular earnings, within a minimum and maximum range. For example, one could be entitled to 50 percent of regular earnings up to a maximum of $150. Typically, the dollar maximum is reached before replacing the specified percentage of regular weekly earnings. The median number of weeks that benefits can be received is twenty-six weeks.

Unemployment compensation is financed by a tax on employers. The tax is based on wages and salaries paid to employees. As with the workers' compensation program, an employer-experience rating is used in setting the tax levied on employers. Consequently, employers with high levels of layoffs will make larger contributions to the program.

EMPLOYEE RETIREMENT INCOME SECURITY ACT

The retirement benefits under Social Security were intended to provide a base for retirement income. Private retirement programs were intended to supplement this base to insure a moderate standard of living during one's retirement years. Private

SUPPLEMENTAL COMPENSATION ISSUES IN COLLECTIVE BARGAINING

pension plans grew during the 1950s and 1960s, without any federal legislation governing the funding and administration of these programs. Problems involving the funding and administration of private pension programs led to the passage of the Employee Retirement Income Security Act, ERISA, in 1974. The problems basically concerned two issues, vesting and funding. These problems stemmed from the high mobility of the American workforce, that is, the tendency for Americans to regularly change jobs or enter and withdraw from the labor force.

Vesting. When pension rights are vested, an employee can receive all due benefits upon retirement regardless of continued employment with one organization.

Funding. Funding of pension plans ensures that an employee will receive pension benefits even if the employer goes bankrupt or for some other reason is out of business when the individual retires. The alternative to funded pension plans is unfunded plans. The latter depend upon the employer having the financial resources necessary to pay benefits at the time they are being drawn. The provisions of ERISA contain tax provisions that make funded pension plans very desirable for employers.

Exhibit 12.1 summarizes the vesting provisions of ERISA. The employer is able to select any of the three alternatives for vesting employer contributions to the pension plan. The effect of any of these three formulas for vesting is that after ten years of service, pension benefits must be 50 percent vested, and after fifteen years of service, pension benefits are 100 percent vested. A study of vesting provisions in a sample of private pension plans indicates substantial improvement in vesting provisions since the passage of the act. Of 131 pension programs studied, all met the vesting provisions of ERISA in 1978. This compares with only 50 percent in 1974.[27]

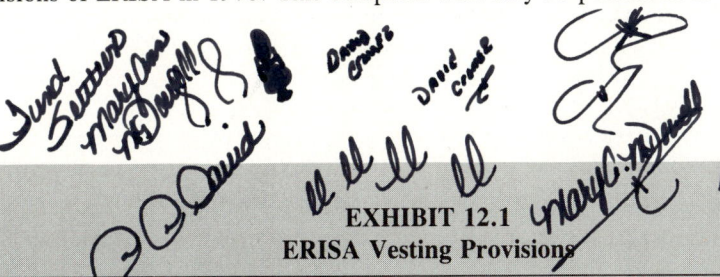

**EXHIBIT 12.1
ERISA Vesting Provisions**

A. Employee contributions: vesting will always be full and immediate.
B. Employer contributions:
  1. Three alternative tests:
    a. 100 percent after 10 years service.
    b. 25 percent after first five years service, 5 percent for each of next five years, 10 percent for next five years.
    c. Rule of 45: 50 percent vested when age + service = 45, 10 percent per year thereafter (provided at least five years service)
  2. Under any of above tests, ten years service must be 50 percent vested (regardless of age) and vest at 10 percent per year thereafter.

History of Supplemental Compensation

In recent years there has been a dramatic increase in the proportion of employee compensation given in the form of fringe benefits or supplemental compensation. We classify any compensation other than direct compensation for time worked as supplemental compensation. The forms that fringe benefits can take are almost endless. In the 1920s some employers sought to provide employees with pension plans and life insurance plans. Typically, these were opposed by the unions because such benefits suggested paternalism.

At the beginning of World War II virtually all compensation was given in the form of direct compensation. At that time fringe benefits made up about 3.4 percent of direct compensation.[28] In 1980, the cost of employee benefits as a percent of payroll dollars was 37.1 percent.[29] Some of the growth in fringe benefits took place during World War II. At that time wage increases were limited under the wartime wage-and-price stabilization program. However, death, retirement, and other security benefits were typically not limited.[30] Consequently, many employers increased employee compensation in the form of fringe benefits in order to be at a competitive advantage in attracting labor. Labor unions sought to increase benefits for their members also.

Tax advantages for both employer and employee have contributed to the growth of fringe benefits over the years. Employer payments to insurance programs on behalf of employees are tax deductible as a business expense. The advantage for employees is that the employer's contribution to a plan is not considered taxable income for employees.

Table 12.3 *Cost of Employee Benefits as A Percent of Payroll Dollars: 1980*

Type of benefit	Percent of payroll
Legally required payments (employer's share only)	8.9%
Pension, insurance and other payments (employer's share only)	12.6
Paid rest periods and lunch periods	3.5
Payments for vacations, holidays, and sick leave	9.9
Profit-sharing payments and bonuses	2.2
Total	37.1%
Total employees' benefits as dollars per payroll hour	$ 2.96
Total employees' benefits as dollars per employee per year	$6084.00

Source: Reprinted with the permission of the Chamber of Commerce of the United States of America from Employee Benefits 1980, *p. 8.*

Table 12.3 reports the total cost of employee benefits as a percent of payroll dollars, as well as for selected categories of benefits. Included among legally required payments are contributions to OASDHI, unemployment compensation and workers' compensation. The most expensive benefit is contributions to pension and other insurance programs. The remaining major category of benefit is payments for vacations, holidays, and sickleave. This category is referred to as pay for time not worked. Factors contributing to the growth of this category of fringe benefit will be discussed later in the chapter.

The bottom section of Table 12.3 reports the cost of benefits both as dollars per hour and dollars per employee per year. The cost of employee fringe benefits becomes more apparent when put in these terms. Some organizations provide larger fringe-benefit packages. For example, in 1980 the cost of fringe benefits for the typical petroleum industry employee was $10,578.[31]

Common Fringe Benefits

This section describes common forms of fringe benefits and discusses issues concerning each benefit. The categories of benefits are compensation for inconvenience, pay for time not worked, benefits to increase employee security, and emerging forms of benefits.

COMPENSATION FOR INCONVENIENCE

Several fringe benefits compensate employees for inconvenience experienced in the performance of their job. Examples include working longer than the normal shift, reporting for work only to find one is not needed that day, working evenings or nights.

OVERTIME

Unions have two basic objectives when they seek to negotiate overtime-pay provisions during negotiations. First, overtime provides a mechanism for encouraging an organization to spread the available work among more employees. When an employer's work force cannot perform all the work required during the standard work week, overtime pay provides an incentive for an employer to hire more workers. The second objective of overtime pay is to compensate workers for the additional fatigue incurred and the nonwork activities given up to work more than the standard work day or work week.

The cost of training new employees and paying fringe benefits that vary as a function of employment rather than the number of hours worked limits the effectiveness of overtime pay in achieving the first ojbective. When the demand for labor in excess of that which can be done by the regular work force during the standard day or week is expected to last only a short time, paying overtime may still be less expensive than hiring more workers.[32]

Virtually all (98 percent) collective-bargaining agreements provide for a five-day work week.[33] About 75 percent provide for a forty-hour work week. Table 12.4 reports common overtime provisions. Daily overtime is very common. It normally begins after eight hours' work and at a rate of time and one-half. Weekly overtime is found in about two of three collective-bargaining agreements. It is also typically

Table 12.4 *Payments Compensating Workers for Inconvenience and Unpleasantness (Frequency Expressed as Percentage of Contracts)*

Overtime provisions (see note)	Frequency	
1. Daily overtime	87%	
a. For work after eight hours		92%
b. At time and one-half		84
2. Weekly overtime	64	
a. For work after forty hours		93
b. At time and one-half		95
3. Premium pay for weekend work	92	
a. For Saturday—not part of regular work week		62
b. For Sunday—not part of regular work week		84
c. For Saturday—part of regular work week		3
d. For Sunday—part of regular work week		12
4. Premium pay for work on holidays	82	
a. Double time		12
b. Double time and one-half		45
c. Triple time		30
Reporting pay	78	
1. Two-hour guarantee		25
2. Four-hour guarantee		56
3. Eight-hour guarantee		9
Call-in/Call-back pay	53	
1. Four hour guarantee		61
2. Rate of pay		
a. Straight time		48
b. Time and one-half		35
Shift differential	83	
1. Money differential		77
2. Time differential		13

Note: When interpreting the percentages, the left column is based on all contracts studied. The right column is based on those contracts having the contract provision in question. For example, 87 percent of all contracts provide for daily overtime. Among those contracts providing for daily overtime, 92 percent pay overtime after eight hours' work, and in 84 percent of these contracts the overtime rate is time and one-half.

Source: U. S. Department of Labor, Characteristics of Major Collective Bargaining Agreements—January 1, 1980 *(Washington, D. C.: U. S. Government Printing Office, May 1981), Bulletin 2095.*

at time and one-half. Premium pay for weekend work and holiday work is found in most agreements. Concerning premium pay for work on holidays, the most common overtime rate is double time and one-half. Other common provisions pertaining to overtime pay can be seen in Table 12.4.

REPORTING PAY

This provision addresses the situation in which an employee is scheduled to work and reports to work but finds that the employer does not need his or her services. Issues that must be addressed in reporting pay provisions are the amount of advance notice that the employer is obligated to give the employee, the amount of compensation the employee is to be guaranteed if he or she reports to work and has not been properly notified, and the designation of those situations that make it impossible for work to proceed and are outside the employer's control. An example of the latter might be power failure that makes it impossible to light the work place and operate equipment. Such provisions attempt to place a reasonable burden on management to plan the organization's need for workers. The incidence of reporting pay provisions and common pay guarantees are also indicated in Table 12.4. Concerning the amount of notice, the two most common provisions are notification before the end of an employee's previous shift and eight hours' advance notice.

CALL-IN AND CALL-BACK PAY

At times it is necessary for an employer to ask employees to report for work at times other than their normal shift. This could be a result of illness or the absenteeism of an employee who is critical to the operation of a shift. There are usually two dimensions addressed in call-in and call-back pay provisions. One is the rate of pay and the other is amount of guaranteed work time. The most common provisions on both dimensions are presented in Table 12.4.

SHIFT DIFFERENTIAL

The normal work day is 8:00 A.M. to 5:00 P.M. for many members of the labor force. At times, however, there are economic advantages for employers to operate facilities sixteen or twenty-four hours a day. Shift work permits the increased use of capital investments. In the case of continuous-process production it is necessary to use shift work to avoid the problems associated with starting up and shutting down operations. For the employee, there are many disadvantages in shift work. Among them are health-related problems such as loss of sleep, disruption of eating patterns, and ulcers.[34] In addition, family and community obligations as well as social activities may suffer. The changing hours of work may prohibit participation in social functions and may create strains for marriage and parent-child relationships. In view of these costs to employees, greater rates of compensation are sometimes negotiated for those working at times other than the normal work day.

Table 12.4 reports the incidence of shift differential provisions. Eight out of ten agreements provide for shift differentials. The alternative ways to provide a shift differential are a money differential or a time differential. Money differentials are by far the most common. The typical money differential calls for an additional 5 percent for those working on the second shift and an additional 10 perent for those working on the third shift. The most common time-differential provision calls for eight hours' pay for seven-and-one-half hours' work on the second shift and eight hours' pay for seven hours of work on the third shift.

COMPRESSED WEEK AND FLEXTIME

Earlier in the chapter it was indicated that the standard work week called for in collective bargaining agreements consists of five eight-hour work days per week. In recent years many organizations have experimented with alternative work schedules. A compressed work week schedules the normal forty hours of work in four days. Flextime is an arrangement which provides that all workers be present for a specified period (core-time) but the remaining hours of work may be completed at the discretion of the employees. For example, core-time may be 10:00 A.M. to 12:00 A.M., and 1:00 P.M. to 3:00 P.M. There are different variations of flextime. With daily flextime, an individual must work the full scheduled number of hours each day but has discretion outside the core-time as to when the hours are worked. With weekly flextime the individual must work the core hours each day but is free to use his or her discretion for completing the scheduled number of weekly hours of work.

There has been a great deal of research concerning the compressed work week. One review of this research concludes that the results are mixed.[35] On the positive side it appears that middle-aged workers are most likely to be satisfied with the compressed work week. Alternatively, older employees find that they tend to become fatigued, especially when the work is physically or mentally taxing. Younger workers appear to find that it interferes with their social life. Working mothers with young children find that this arrangement interferes with their child-rearing responsibilities. In addition, when the work is physically taxing or is machine-paced, it appears that fatigue sets in beyond an eight-hour day and productivity suffers as a result. Union leaders resist returning to a ten-hour day for philosophical reasons. For decades the union movement sought to reduce the work day to eight hours. This work schedule would reverse the attainment of a goal that was sought for many years.

The research on flextime is more limited, but that which is available tends to be positive.[36] One explanation is that the research on flextime has not been conducted over a long enough period of time. Early research concerning the compressed work week was positive; however, it appears that after a time the novelty wears off and negative attitudes toward the compressed work week appear. Possibly a similar pattern would exist in studies concerning flextime that cover a long enough block of time. The alternative explanation is that flextime does genuinely have positive results for employee satisfaction. One of the alleged advantages of flextime is that it enables employees to have greater control over their work life. They are able to schedule their work time and as a result have greater freedom, much as managers and professional employees.

It is our judgment that in some situations it is necessary for unions to recognize that some employees may achieve feelings of satisfaction through these innovations in work scheduling. There is some evidence that unions are pursuing the negotiation of flextime agreements.[37] Where union members would derive increased job satisfaction from either of these alternative work schedules, it is in the interest of union leaders as well as management to experiment with them.

PAY FOR TIME NOT WORKED

Since World War II there has been a dramatic increase in the amount of vacation time and the number of holidays provided in collective-bargaining agreements. An advantage of holidays and vacations for unions as an institution is that they reduce the amount of work done by an individual union member, thereby increasing the number of people employed. This results in a larger number of union members. For the union member, longer vacations and more holidays have the advantage of providing time and money to pursue leisure-time activities. For an employer, providing employees with time off may have the advantage of increasing their productivity when they are working. In addition, vacation time that increases as a function of length of service provides a reward for longevity and serves as a means to reduce labor turnover. For example, a long-service employee who is entitled to four weeks of vacation with pay is probably reluctant to quit that organization and seek employment with another where he or she might be entitled to only one or two weeks of paid vacation.

Table 12.5 summarizes common collective-bargaining agreement provisions concerning pay for time not worked. About three of four collective-bargaining agreements specify length of vacation. Those agreements that do not provide for vacation pay normally involve work in which a union member does not work for a single employer. For example, in the building trades, a carpenter may be employed by several different contractors during a construction season. Most agreements provide for a maximum vacation of four to five and one-half weeks. Normally, vacation time increases as a function of years of service. The most common numbers of years of service associated with varying lengths of vacation are reported in Table 12.5. Concerning paid holidays, the modal number is ten. Also reported in Table 12.5 are other forms of pay for time not worked; for example, paid lunch breaks and rest periods.

Sabbatical vacation. In 1962, the United Steel Workers negotiated an extended vacation of thirteen weeks. These were called sabbatical vacations. Employees with fifteen or more years of service were eligible for a sabbatical every five years. The objectives of these extended vacations were to provide greater leisure time for long-service employees and to create jobs for additional employees in the steel industry. This sabbatical vacation has not been widely adopted outside the steel industry.

Possibly sabbatical vacations may become more common in the future. Extended vacations could serve as a vehicle to facilitate the adjustment to retirement of long-service employees. Research concerning retired workers suggests that a prob-

Table 12.5 *Provisions Pertaining to Pay for Time Not Worked (Frequency Expressed as Percentage of Contracts)*

	Frequency
Vacation pay (percent specifying length)	72%
1. Maximum length vacation	
a. Under four weeks	7%
b. Four to five and one-half weeks	73
c. Six weeks or longer	20
2. Modal length of service for various vacations	
a. One weeks' vacation—one year of service	
b. Two weeks' vacation—three years of service	
c. Three weeks' vacation—ten years of service	
d. Four weeks' vacation—twenty years of service	
e. Five weeks' vacation—twenty-five years of service	
f. Six weeks' vacation—thirty years of service	
Paid holidays	84%
1. Eight holidays with pay	6%
2. Nine holidays with pay	12
3. Ten holidays with pay	25
4. Eleven holidays with pay	22
5. Twelve holidays with pay	11
Other payments for time not worked	
1. Funeral leave	69%
2. Jury duty	67
3. Court witness	25
4. Military service	30
5. Paid meal periods	31
6. Paid rest periods	42
7. Paid wash-up, clean-up, and clothes-changing periods	24

See Note, Table 12.4

Source: U. S. Department of Labor, Characteristics of Major Collective Bargaining Agreements—January 1, 1980 *(Washington, D. C.: U. S. Government Printing Office, May 1981), Bulletin 2095.*

lem for some is a lack of challenging and interesting activities to occupy their time.[38] A program used by some organizations to help resolve this problem is gradual retirement. It involves a gradual reduction of the work week or progressively longer annual vacations.[39] Similarly, sabbatical vacations could be a vehicle to facilitate the adjustment to full-time retirement.

    The most commonly observed holidays and the percentage of contract agreements providing for the indicated holidays are reported in Table 12.6. The reader should note that Table 12.6 is based on a different survey of collective-bargaining agreements than Table 12.5. The latter surveyed a more comprehensive sample of collective-bargaining agreements. However, there were 400 agreements sampled in the survey reported in Table 12.6.

SUPPLEMENTAL COMPENSATION ISSUES IN COLLECTIVE BARGAINING

Table 12.6 *Most Commonly Observed Holidays (Frequency Expressed as Percentage of Contracts)*

Holiday	Frequency
Thanksgiving	98%
Labor Day	98
Christmas	98
Independence Day	97
New Year's Day	97
Memorial Day	96
Good Friday	50
Day after Thanksgiving	49
Christmas Eve	47
Washington's Birthday	36
New Year's Eve	27
Employee's Birthday	22

Source: Bureau of National Affairs, Basic Patterns in Union Contracts, *9th ed. (Washington, D. C.: BNA, Inc., 1979), p. 20.*

BENEFITS INTENDED TO INCREASE EMPLOYEES' SECURITY

Several different fringe benefits have developed over the years that are intended to help workers and their families cope during periods when earnings from employment are interrupted. Factors that can cause disruptions in the flow of earnings are: lay-offs, technological displacement, injury or illness, retirement, and death.

SUPPLEMENTAL UNEMPLOYMENT BENEFITS

In discussing the federal-state system of unemployment compensation earlier in the chapter, we noted that benefit levels are usually less than the median income of members of the labor force. With only unemployment compensation to depend on during a lay-off, there will be severe economic hardships for one's family. In 1955 the United Automobile Workers negotiated a supplemental unemployment benefit plan (SUB). The following year the United Steel Workers negotiated a similar plan with the basic steel corporations.

The typical SUB benefit provides a payment of 60 to 65 percent of take-home pay. When combined with public unemployment compensation, which typically provides benefits of about 30 percent, an employee receives about 90 to 95 percent of normal take-home pay while unemployed. Usually an employee must complete a minimum length of service, e.g., one year, to be eligible for SUB benefits. The length of time one is able to draw benefits is a function of length of service with the employer. As originally envisioned, SUB plans were intended to enable employees to cope with moderate periods of unemployment. In 1975, large-scale lay-offs in the automobile industry placed heavy demands on SUB funds, and they were depleted after a period of time.[40]

SEVERANCE PAY

Another benefit that is intended to help ease the problems of unemployment is severance pay. However, one is eligible for severance pay only when the lay-off is expected to be permanent. Causes of such lay-offs include displacement by technological change, merger of organizations, and permanent reductions in the scale of operations. Typically, employees who are discharged for just cause or who refuse to accept another job offered by the employer are not eligible for severance pay. Usually the amount of severance pay increases as a function of length of service.

The top section of Table 12.7 reports the incidence of SUB plans and severance-pay provisions in collective-bargaining agreements. The reader will note that neither are common.

INSURANCE

The United States is the only industrialized nation without a comprehensive national health care system.[41] As a result, collective-bargaining agreements typically provide for a wide range of insurance programs to provide protection for union members and their families in the event of injury, illness, or death. Table 12.7 reports the percentage of agreements containing various forms of insurance and benefits. These are intended to supplement the limited protection provided by workers' compensation and Social Security programs described earlier in the chapter.

Pension plans are a benefit provided in most collective-bargaining agreements. They became prominent during World War II. Then in 1949, a United States Supreme Court decision held that employers and unions are obligated to bargain over this issue.[42] Other factors have contributed to the growth of pension plans. One factor is the tax advantages of receiving a portion of employee compensation in the form of contributions to pension funds.

Another factor contributing to the growth of pension plans is that in some cases they are a means to reduce the impact of technological change on displaced workers. Some unions have successfully negotiated generous pension benefits and early retirement provisions in return for agreeing to the rapid introduction of technological change.

A third factor contributing to the growth of pension plans is the relatively modest benefits that are available under Social Security. A measure of the adequacy of pension plans is the replacement rate. It identifies the percentage of annual preretirement earnings replaced by pension income. A recent study found the median replacement rate for those dependent solely on Social Security for pension income was 31 percent and for those receiving Social Security plus a second pension, the median replacement rate was 42 percent.[43]

We expect that the combined effect of rapid increases in the cost of living and a desire for early retirement will be increased pressure in collective bargaining for larger pension benefits. While Social Security benefits are automatically adjusted to reflect changes in the cost of living, very seldom do private pension plans adjust benefit levels after an individual has retired. Perhaps union negotiators will attempt to secure cost-of-living adjustments in private pension benefits.

Table 12.7 *Provisions Providing Protection When Not Working or Unable to Work (Frequency Expressed as Percentage of Contracts)*

Unemployment[a]	Frequency
1. Severance pay	34%
2. Supplemental unemployment compensation	14
Sick leave[a]	30
Insurance[b]	
1. Life insurance	95
2. Accidental death and dismemberment insurance	65
3. Sickness and accident insurance	81
4. Long-term disability insurance	35
5. Hospitalization insurance	91
6. Surgical insurance	84
7. Major medical insurance	71
8. Dental insurance	41
9. Prescription drugs	24
Pension plans[b]	
1. Retire at sixty-five	87
2. Noncontributory plans	92
3. Benefit formula	
a. Flat monthly amount per year of service	59
b. Percentage of employee earnings multiplied by years of service	12
c. Choice of a or b, whichever is greater	9
d. Benefits depend on contributions to employee's retirement fund	22

[a]*Source: U. S. Department of Labor, Characteristics of Major Bargaining Agreements—January 1, 1980 (Washington, D. C.: U. S. Government Printing Office, May 1981), Bulletin 2095.*
[b]*Source: Bureau of National Affairs, Basic Patterns in Union Contracts, 9th ed. (Washington, D. C.: BNA, Inc., 1979), pp. 41–50 and 68–72.*

Table 12.7 reports common provisions of private pension plans. The typical retirement age is sixty-five. Since the Age Discrimination Act permits an individual to continue working to age seventy, retirement at sixty-five is voluntary rather than mandatory. The vast majority of pension plans are noncontributory; i.e., the employee does not contribute to the pension fund. The most common benefit formula is a flat monthly amount per year of service. The median monthly amount is $10.50. For example, an employee retiring after thirty years of service would receive a monthly benefit of $315 (30 × $10.50).

Emerging Forms of Employee Benefits

Several forms of employee benefits are emerging or are likely to emerge in the near future. Among them is the provision of prepaid employee legal services. Under some plans the employee is free to select an attorney of his or her choice. Under others the legal services of a particular law firm are retained and the employee must use that law firm.[44] Dental insurance is growing rapidly. In 1972 only 8 percent of major collective-bargaining agreements included a dental plan. Table 12.7 indicates that in 1979, 41 percent of the collective-bargaining agreements surveyed had such coverage.

One might also see growth in health maintenance organizations (HMO). This is a system of health care in which a group of physicians is employed to care for the employees of an organization. The physicians are compensated on a flat fee or salary basis rather than a fee-for-services basis. In an HMO, physicians focus on maintaining the health of patients through regular checkups and preventative medicine.

Abuse of alcohol and the use of addictive drugs by members of the labor force are receiving increased attention.[45] These are large-scale problems. For example, it is estimated that 10 percent of the labor force are alcoholics and another 10 percent are border-line alcoholics. Given the number of workers involved and the recognition that these are treatable problems, we expect increased attention to providing rehabilitative services for such employees.

The labor force participation rate of women with children has increased dramatically over the past three decades. In 1950 the labor force participation rate of those with children under six was 12 percent. In 1978 the corresponding figure was 42 percent.[46] Women who have preschool-aged children are faced with the problem of providing care for them while working. As a result we expect to see increased attention given to negotiating for day-care centers or other means of providing for the welfare of children while their mothers are working.

A recent study involving benefits experts attempted to forecast trends in employee benefits.[47] Among the benefits they anticipated that we have not referred to are increases in private-pension incomes and periodic adjustments in retirement income during retirement to reflect cost-of-living increases.

Problems with Fringe Benefits

Research on the utility of fringe benefits to employees as well as employee awareness of the cost of fringe benefits suggests there are problems with both issues. Employees appear to underestimate greatly the dollar value of the fringe benefits provided by employers, and in addition, some components of the fringe-benefit package are of little value to subgroups of employees.[48] For example, married employees with children may attach great value to medical or dental insurance, while older employees may place little value on these forms of insurance. Older employees may prefer a larger contribution by employers to the pension plan.

This poses a problem both for employers and for unions. Since the employer incurs the cost of providing the fringe-benefit package, the employer wishes to provide a complement of benefits that contributes to employee job satisfaction. Similarly, it is in the interest of the union to be perceived as instrumental in securing such a fringe-benefit package.

One program that is intended to deal with both of these problems is the cafeteria-style benefit plan. In this type of plan an employee allocates the money available for the benefit package to those benefits he or she wants. This process makes the cost of the benefit package clear to employees. It also insures that the money is allocated to those fringe benefits valued by employees.[49] Naturally such a plan presents bookkeeping problems for the employer and results in the inclusion of a high proportion of high-risk employees in various insurance plans. However, it can also counter the problem of a great deal of money being spent for fringe benefits that have little or no utility to the recipients of those benefits.

Costing Out a Labor Agreement

Wages and fringe benefits have been described in the previous chapter and in the initial section of this chapter. Together, wages and fringe benefits make up an organization's compensation package. Both parties to a collective-bargaining agreement should be able to estimate the value of a proposed compensation package. The phrase, costing out a labor agreement, refers to the process of estimating the cost of a particular proposal or component to an agreement, as well as estimating the total cost of a set of proposals or collective-bargaining agreement.

IMPORTANCE OF COSTING OUT A LABOR AGREEMENT

Labor costs are the largest costs incurred by many American organizations. United States corporations spend over four times as much to compensate their employees as is spent on new equipment and facilities.[50] As a result, relatively small changes in labor compensation can have a large impact on profits and the ability of an organization to invest in new equipment and facilities. Both union and management negotiators should be able to estimate the cost of any proposed change in an agreement, and in addition, the effect of that change on an organization's profits. Such estimates should be available before negotiators accept or reject any change in a collective-bargaining agreement.

Both management and union negotiators should have such estimates in order to judge the organization's ability to pay. Obviously management recognizes the importance of this factor. The reader should recognize that union negotiators are typically aware that it is in the long-run interest of union members to insure that the organization achieves reasonable profit levels.[51]

In addition, costing out proposals to an agreement can be an integral part of the negotiating process. When "trading" demands, it is necessary to know the cost of each demand. This information is needed to determine how much is being gained or lost by the trade. Another concern is the point of time that proposals take effect. A wage increase or benefit received in the third year of a contract costs an organization less and is of less value to the membership than a wage increase or benefit received in the first year of an agreement.

Another relevant dimension of costing out proposals is the situation where two alternative proposals may have equal utility to the union members, but different implications for labor costs and organization profits. If management negotiators are able to accomplish a trade in which the less costly prosposal is accepted, they will have exercised some control over labor costs.

HOW TO COST OUT AN AGREEMENT

Fig. 12.1 describes a sample bargaining unit. This unit and its contract agreement provide examples for costing out different contract provisions to be discussed throughout the remainder of this chapter.[52] Fig. 12.1 presents the calculations needed to cost out the labor agreement in the sample bargaining unit.

Fig. 12.1 *Sample Bargaining Unit*

Murray and Miller (M & M) Manufacturing, Inc. is a small company that manufactures wooden kitchen cabinets. The 100 production employees are represented by the United Wood Workers of America. Recently, the union and company officials negotiated a new contract containing the changes listed below. The bargaining unit and the previous collective bargaining agreement had the following characteristics:

a. Employment status and salaries

Job classification	Number of workers	Hourly wage
Unskilled laborers (UL)	20	6.00
Semiskilled machine tenders (MT)	60	7.25
Skilled wood workers (SW)	20	9.00
Total	100	

b. *Hours of work:* M & M Manufacturing, Inc., operates two shifts. One-half of each job classification is assigned to each shift. Each shift is eight hours long. A work week consists of five eight-hour shifts (forty hours per week). The day shift runs from 8:00 A.M. to 4:00 P.M. The evening shift begins at 4:00 P.M. and concludes at 12:00 midnight. Workers assigned to the evening shift receive a $.20/hour shift differential.

c. *Overtime premium:* The labor agreement specifies that any work over eight hours per day will be paid at a rate of one and one-half times the wage associated with the worker's job classification. (In other words, workers are paid time-and-a-half for overtime.) Last year, a total of 2,000 overtime hours were worked. Only employees in the Semiskilled machine tenders category worked overtime.

d. *Vacations:* Vacations will accrue according to the following schedule:

Fig. 12.1 *(Continued)*

Service	Vacation	Number of employees in each category		
		UL	MT	SW
0–3	1 week	4	12	4
4–7	2 weeks	4	12	4
8–12	3 weeks	4	12	4
13–20	4 weeks	4	12	4
20+	5 weeks	4	12	4
		20	60	20

e. *Paid Holidays:* Each worker receives ten paid holidays per year and receives eight hours' pay for each holiday.

f. *Hospitalization*

Type of coverage	Number of employees	Employer's cost per employee per month
Single-coverage	25	$25.00
Family-coverage	75	$50.00

g. *Pensions:* The employer contributes $.35 per hour for all hours worked at straight time plus 4 percent of the payroll (this includes straight-time wages, overtime and shift differentials).

h. *Additional Payroll Costs*:
1. F.I.C.A. = 6.70 percent of total earnings
2. State and federal unemployment insurance tax = 2.5 percent of total earnings
3. Workers' compensation insurance = 2.5 percent of total earnings

ESTIMATING COSTS ATTRIBUTABLE TO THE NEW LABOR AGREEMENT

The following is an example of how to determine the cost of a new contract. The example assumes that Murray and Miller Manufacturing and the United Wood Workers of America negotiated a one-year contract. The new contract contained the following changes:

1. Wages: UL $6.50/hour (from $6.00)
   MT $7.75/hour (from $7.25)
   SW $9.50/hour (from $9.00)
2. Paid holidays: two additional paid holidays
3. Pensions: employer contributes $.50 per hour for all hours worked at straight time plus 4 percent of the payroll (this includes straight-time wages, overtime and shift differentials)

There were no changes in the remaining provisions of the labor agreement.

Fig. 12.2 describes a procedure that could be used to cost out the new labor agreement.

Fig. 12.2 *Costing Out the Existing Labor Agreement*

I. Straight-time Earnings

	(1) ×	(2) ×	(3) =	(4)
	No. of employees in each job class	Straight-time hourly wage	No. hours worked at straight time/ year (2080 hours minus vacation and holiday hours)	Total straight-time earnings
UL	20	$6.00	1,880	$ 225,600
MT	60	$7.25	1,880	817,800
SW	20	$9.00	1,880	338,400
				$1,381,800

II. Night shift differential

(1) ×	(2) ×	(3) =	(4)
No. of employees on evening shift	No. hours worked at straight time/year	Night shift differential	Night shift differential
50	1,880	$.20	$18,800

III. Overtime

(1) ×	(2) ×	(3) =	(4)
No. hours of paid overtime	Hourly wage	Overtime premium	Overtime costs
2,000	$7.25	1.5	$21,750

IV. F.I.C.A. contributions = 6.70 percent of total earnings*

.0670 × $1,569,350 = $105,146.45

V. State and federal unemployment insurance = 2.5 percent of total earnings

.025 × $1,569,350 = $39,233.75

VI. Workers' compensation = 2.5 percent of total earnings

.025 × $1,569,350 = $39,233.75

VII. Vacations

(1) × (2) × (3) = (4)

SUPPLEMENTAL COMPENSATION ISSUES IN COLLECTIVE BARGAINING

Fig. 12.2 *(Continued)*

Weeks of vacation	No. of employees in each category			Weekly wage for each category (hourly wage × 40 hours)			Cost of vacations (no. of weeks × no. of employees × weekly wage)		
	UL	MT	SW	UL	MT	SW	UL	MT	SW
1 (40 hrs)	4	12	4	$240	$290	$360	960	3,480	1,440
2 (80 hrs)	4	12	4	240	290	360	1,920	6,960**	2,880
3 (120 hrs)	4	12	4	240	290	360	2,880	10,440	4,320
4 (160 hrs)	4	12	4	240	290	360	3,840	13,920	5,760
5 (200 hrs)	4	12	4	240	290	360	4,800	17,400	7,200
							14,400	52,200	21,600

$$\begin{aligned}\text{Total cost of vacations} &= UL + MT + SW \\ &= 14{,}400 + 52{,}200 + 21{,}600 \\ &= \$88{,}200\end{aligned}$$

VIII. Paid holidays

$$\underset{\substack{\text{No. of}\\\text{holidays}}}{(1)} \times \underset{\substack{\text{No. of employees}\\\text{in each category}}}{(2)} \times \underset{\substack{\text{Wage for}\\\text{each category}}}{(3)} \times \underset{\substack{\text{No. of hours paid}\\\text{for a holiday}}}{(4)} = \underset{\substack{\text{Cost of paid}\\\text{holidays}}}{(5)}$$

$$10 \times [(20 \times 6.00) + (60 \times 7.25) + (20 \times 9.00)] \times 8$$
$$10 \times (120 + 435 + 180) \times 8$$
$$10 \times 735 \times 8 = \$58{,}800$$

IX. Hospitalization

$$\underset{\substack{\text{Number of employees}\\\text{single-coverage}}}{(1)} \times \underset{\substack{\text{Annual cost of}\\\text{single-coverage}}}{(2)} = \underset{\substack{\text{Cost of}\\\text{hospitalization for}\\\text{single-coverage}}}{(3)}$$

$$(25) \times (12 \times \$25.00) = \$7{,}500$$

$$\underset{\substack{\text{Number of employees}\\\text{family-coverage}}}{(1)} \times \underset{\substack{\text{Annual cost of}\\\text{family-coverage}}}{(2)} = \underset{\substack{\text{Cost of}\\\text{hospitalization for}\\\text{family-coverage}}}{(3)}$$

$$75 \times (12 \times \$50.00) = 45{,}000$$
$$\text{Total annual cost of hospitalization} = \$7{,}500 + \$45{,}000$$
$$= \$52{,}500$$

X. Pensions

$$\underset{\substack{\text{No. hours paid at}\\\text{straight time (no. of}\\\text{employees} \times 2{,}080)}}{(1)} \times \underset{\substack{\text{Per hour}\\\text{employer}\\\text{contribution}}}{(2)} + \underset{\substack{4\% \text{ of total}\\\text{earnings}}}{(3)}$$

$$([100 \times 2{,}080] \times [.35]) + (.04\,[\$1{,}569{,}350])$$
$$(208{,}000 \times [.35]) + (.04\,[\$1{,}569{,}350])$$
$$72{,}800 \quad + \quad 62{,}774 = \$135{,}574$$

XI. Total cost of existing contract

I. Straight-time Earnings	$1,381,800
II. Night Shift Differential	18,800

Fig. 12.2 *(Continued)*

III.	Overtime	21,750
IV.	F.I.C.A. Contributions	105,146.45
V.	Unemployment Compensation	39,233.75
VI.	Workers' Compensation	39,233.75
	Direct Payroll Costs	$1,605,963.95
	(Sum of I through VI)	
VII.	Vacations	$ 88,200
VIII.	Paid Holidays	58,800
IX.	Hospitalization	52,500
X.	Pensions	135,574
	Cost of Fringe Benefits	335,074
	(Sum of VII through X)	
	Total Cost of Contract	$1,941,037.95
	(Direct Payroll + Fringe Benefits)	

*Total earnings = I (straight-time earnings) + II (night shift differential) + III (overtime) + VII (paid vacations) + VIII (paid holidays).

**An example of the calculations to generate these numbers:

No. of weeks × No. of employees in MT category × weekly MT wage =
   (2)   ×   (12)   ×   (290)   = $6,960

SECONDARY EFFECTS OF WAGE CHANGES

The cost of several benefits not altered in a new contract will increase because of wage changes. This is the secondary effect of wage changes.

Roll-up. Roll-up is the term used to refer to the secondary effect of a wage increase on fringe benefits.[53] These costs must be identified and included in determining the cost of a new contract. Refer to the portion of Table 12.8 that identifies the cost of the new pension provision. In this calculation, the cost of overtime under the new contract changed because of the new wage rate. This is an example of the secondary effects of wage changes.

    Similarly, it is necessary to recalculate the cost of other contract provisions not changed by the new contract, but whose cost changes as a result of the higher wages. For example, it is necessary to determine the secondary effects of the higher wage rates on the cost of vacations, F.I.C.A., unemployment compensation, and workers' compensation. This consists of repeating the calculations in Fig. 12.2 pertaining to these benefits, substituting the new total for straight-time earnings reported in Table 12.8. After both the primary and secondary effects of changes in contract provisions have been determined, the cost of the new contract agreement can be established.

Table 12.8 *Determining Costs Attributable to a New Labor Agreement*

1. Cost of change in wages

(1)	×	(2)	×	(3)	=	(4)
No. of workers in each job category		New hourly salary		No. of hours paid each year		Change in wages
UL 20		6.50		2,080		270,400
MT 60		7.75		2,080		967,200
SW 20		9.50		2,080		395,200

               New total straight-time earnings $1,632,800
               Old total straight-time earnings   −1,528,800
               Increase attributable to new contract $ 104,000

2. Cost of change in paid holidays

(1)	×	(2)	×	(3)
Number of holidays		(Number of employees in each category × new wage)		Number of hours paid for a holiday

12 × [(20 × 6.50) + (60 × 7.75) + (20 × 9.50)] × 8 =
12 × (130 + 465 + 190) × 8 =
12 × 785 × 8 =   75,360 Cost of new paid holidays
              −58,800 Cost of old paid holidays
             $16,560 Increase attributable to new contract

3. Cost of change in pension provisions

No. hours paid at straight time (No. of employees × 2,080)	×	Per-hour employer contribution	+	4% of payroll (total wages + shift differential + overtime*)

[(100 × 2,080) × (.50) + .04 ($1,632,800 + 18,800 + 23,250)]

(208,000) × .50 + .04 (1,674,850)

       100,400 + 66,994 = 167,394 new pension cost
                          135,574 old pension cost
                       $ 31,820 increase attributable to new contract

*The cost of the shift differential is taken directly from Fig. 12.2 because the shift differential rate was not changed and it is assumed that the number of employees working the night shift will not change. To estimate the cost of overtime, we assumed the same number of overtime hours as occurred last year. Overtime calculations must reflect the new wage. The estimated cost is:

Number of hours of paid overtime × hourly wage × overtime premium
                   2,000 × 7.75 × 1.5 = 23,250

ESTIMATING THE COST OF CONTRACT PROPOSALS

The above example focuses on estimating the cost of a new contract that has been ratified. To determine the cost of a contract after ratification is analogous to closing the gate to a corral after the horses have escaped. Both management and union negotiators should know what a set of proposals will cost before agreeing to them. It

COLLECTIVE-BARGAINING ISSUES

is in the long-run interest of neither union leaders nor union members to secure a contract that forces an employer out of business. According to a spokesman of the AFL-CIO, the days when a union takes as much as its bargaining power permits have passed.[54] Instead, union leaders recognize the need to base negotiation decisions on relevant economic data.

The costs of proposals should be determined during the negotiation process. Problems encountered and alternative approaches to determining the cost of contract provisions will be discussed in the following sections. The parties involved in contract negotiations must insure that such costs are identified during the negotiation process. Failure to do so makes it possible to stumble into an agreement that is beyond an employer's ability to pay, which in turn has implications for the employment opportunities of union members.

REPORTING THE COST OF A NEW CONTRACT AGREEMENT

There are no general rules for reporting the cost of a new contract.[55] Instead, negotiators are free, within a broad range, to engage in creative arithmetic. The cost of most new contract agreements is reported to the public and to union members in terms of change in cents-per-hour.[56] Another method used in some cases is to report the cost of a new agreement in terms of change in compensation as a percentage of payroll. An alternative seldom used is reporting the total cost of the contract changes. This is probably because it is difficult for the individual union member to understand the implications of a new contract for his or her paycheck if the latter method is used.

Use of the most common method for reporting the costs of a new agreement requires that the cost of the changes be divided by a measure of hours. One of the key questions both in estimating the cost of proposals during negotiations and the cost of a new agreement is the measure of hours to be used.[57] The alternatives are the number of hours of paid employment and the number of hours worked. The former includes vacation and holiday time. The latter does not include pay for time-not-worked benefits.

Table 12.9 presents sample computations based on Murray and Miller Manufacturing. Calculations involved in determining both the number of hours of paid employment plus the number of hours worked are reported. As the example indicates, the two measures of hours are substantially different.

Table 12.10 presents sample computations of the costs associated with changes in the Murray and Miller Manufacturing contract. The calculations assume the choice of using number of hours of paid employment as the measure. This choice results in a lower cents-per-hour increase than basing computations on number of hours worked. The effect of the alternative measure of hours on the change in cost attributable to wages is reported at the bottom of Table 12.10.

Since management negotiators seek to negotiate an agreement that is least costly to the organization, they favor reporting contract terms on the basis of hours paid rather than hours worked.[58]

Table 12.9 *Calculating the Number of Hours of Paid Employment and the Number of Hours Worked*

$$\text{Number of hours of paid employment} = \text{Number of employees} \times 2{,}080 + \text{Number of overtime hours}$$

$$= (100 \times 2{,}080) + 2{,}000$$
$$= 208{,}000 + 2{,}000$$
$$= \underline{210{,}000} \text{ hours}$$

$$\text{Number of hours work} = \text{Total number of hours paid} + \text{Overtime hours} - \text{Number of paid holiday hours and paid vacation hours}$$

$= (100 \text{ employees} \times 2{,}080 \text{ hours}) + 2{,}000 -$

(12 holidays × 100 employees × 8 hours) +
(20 employees × 40 hours) +
(20 employees × 80 hours) +
(20 employees × 120 hours) +   ⎱ Distribution of vacation benefits among employees
(20 employees × 160 hours) +
(20 employees × 200 hours)

$= (208{,}000 + 2{,}000) - (9{,}600 + 800 + 1{,}600 + 2{,}400 + 3{,}200 + 4{,}000)$

$= 210{,}000 - 21{,}600$

$= \underline{188{,}400} \text{ hours}$

Alternatively, when union negotiators present a new contract to the membership, the negotiators wish to make changes in compensation appear as large as possible. This increases member satisfaction with the new contract and increases the probability of ratification.[59] Since management negotiators wish to have the membership ratify the proposed agreement, they do not dispute the union negotiators' computations.

During contract negotiations, the preferences of management and union negotiators for the alternative measures of hours are probably reversed. During negotiations, management wishes to convince union negotiators that their demands are too costly. On the other hand, union negotiators wish to convince management that the union demands are not too costly. Consequently, during negotiations management bargainers would use the calculation that appears most costly while union bargainers would use the calculation that appears least costly.

PROBLEMS WITH THE TYPICAL APPROACH TO COSTING

There are several problems with the traditional approach to costing the provisions of collective bargaining agreements which has been described above. First, the calculations are based on past conditions, or more precisely, a continuation of past con-

Table 12.10 *Computing the Cents-per-Hour Costs of New Contract Provisions*

| Change in costs attributable to wages | ÷ | Number of hours of paid employment |

$104,000 ÷ 210,000 = $.495/hour

| Change in costs attributable to paid holidays | ÷ | Number of hours of paid employment |

$16,650 ÷ 210,000 = $.079/hour

| Change in costs attributable to greater pension contributions | ÷ | Number of hours of paid employment |

$31,820 ÷ 210,000 = $.152/hour

| Change in costs attributable to wages | ÷ | Number of hours worked |

$104,000 ÷ 188,400 hours = $.552/hour

| Change in costs attributable to paid holidays | ÷ | Number of hours worked |

$16,650 ÷ 188,400 = $.088/hour

| Change in costs attributable to greater pension contributions | ÷ | Number of hours worked |

$31,820 ÷ 188,400 = $.169/hour

ditions.[60] In Table 12.9 it was assumed that the number of overtime hours and the category of employees receiving overtime during the coming year would be identical to the past year's experience. Another assumption was that the composition of the work force would not change. For example, the number of employees in each job category and the number of single and married employees were assumed to remain the same. In fact, all of these numbers would probably change. More accurate cost estimates would probably result if they were based on projections of the future work force characteristics.

A second deficiency with the above approach is that it focuses on the direct cost of contract changes rather than on the effects of the changes on profits.[61] The effects of changing contract provisions on profits could be either nonexistent or devastating, and the above method would not reflect either of these extremes. Changes

SUPPLEMENTAL COMPENSATION ISSUES IN COLLECTIVE BARGAINING

in sales volume, prices, product mix, and capital investment are often disregarded in estimating the costs of contract changes.[62] Such changes could completely offset the impact of contract changes or they could greatly intensify the effects of contract changes.

An example involving product mix may clarify this point.[63] Assume that a company produces one product accounting for roughly half of its sales revenue and employment. The remaining half is tied to the production and sales of several other products. If most competitive employers in all these product markets are unionized and agree to similar contract provisions, increased labor costs can probably be passed along to consumers with little impact on profits and employment. Alternatively, assume that competitors in the miscellaneous-products area are typically not unionized and do not face pressure to increase wages and benefits. In the latter case, substantial increases in labor costs reduce the profitability of these products. At some point the employer is likely to phase out these products and the jobs associated with their production.

A related problem is that the traditional approach tends to be rigid in its application. In the example presented in Table 12.8, two additional paid holidays were assumed. The cost of this change was estimated by multiplying the new wage rate times the number of additional holiday hours. However, the cost of these holidays could be substantially different.[64] They could be floating holidays; i.e., days taken at the discretion of each employee such as one's birthday or the opening day of elk-hunting season. In such a case there may be enough slack in the work force or enough flexibility in work scheduling to cover for the employees taking a holiday without any decline in productivity.

Yet another problem that becomes increasingly significant as the time period covered by a contract increases is considering the time value of money.[65] The present value of one dollar either spent or received one year from today is less than one dollar. If the duration of a contract is three years and the total wage adjustment is $1.50, a distribution of 40 cents the first year, 50 cents the second year, and 60 cents the third year is more favorable for management than the reverse sequence. This is a back-loaded agreement. The reverse would be more favorable for union members. This is referred to as a front-loaded agreement. Generally, the longer management is able to delay implementation of a contract provision, the smaller the present value of the cost of the provision. Correspondingly, the smaller the present value of the change to union members.

Table 12.11 compares the change in earnings per worker during a three-year contract. Each worker receives a wage increase of $1.50. However, with the front-loaded example, each worker would receive $832 more earnings ($6656 − 5824). This is because front loading implies that higher wages will be in effect longer during the contract.

Table 12.11 also provides an example of computing the present value of the change in earnings during the contract. The following formula is used to estimate present value:[66]

COLLECTIVE-BARGAINING ISSUES

Table 12.11 *Front Loading and Back Loading a Wage Increase: Change in Earnings Per Worker During a Three-Year Contract*

		Front-loaded wage increase		
Contract year	Raise	Hours*	Change in earnings during contract	Present value of earnings during contract
1	$.60	6,240	$3,744.00	$3,413.95
2	.50	4,160	2,080.00	1,504.95
3	.40	2,080	832.00	687.60
			6,656.00	5,606.50

Difference = $1,050.00

		Back-loaded wage increase		
Contract year	Raise	Hours*	Change in earnings during contract	Present value of earnings during contract
1	$.40	6,240	$2,496.00	$2,275.96
2	.50	4,160	2,080.00	1,804.95
3	.60	2,080	1,248.00	1,031.40
			5,824.00	5,112.31

Difference = $711.60

Cents per hour for entire contract

	Not discounted	Discounted
Front-loaded	107	90
Back-loaded	93	82

*Hours refer to the total number of hours to which the raise would apply. For example, the first-year raise would apply to three years of employment or 6,240 hours (2,080 × 3 = 6,240) and so on.

$$PV = \frac{F}{(1+r)^n}$$

where

PV = Present value of a given sum
F = Equivalent future value n periods hence
r = Discount rate
n = Number of periods

In this example we assumed a discount rate (cost of money) of 10 percent. Consideration of the present value of future wage rates provides further incentive for management to delay wage increases.

RECOMMENDATION FOR COSTING AN AGREEMENT

Our general recommendation is that management negotiators call on the expertise and information available from organization and human-resources planners as well as financial managers in estimating costs of proposed contract provisions. Most, if not all, of the criticisms of the traditional approach to costing out agreements presented here can be addressed by inclusion of these information sources.[67]

Finally, it should be kept in mind that these are estimates of costs. They are based on estimates of the composition of an organization's future labor force, estimates of implications of technological change on productivity, and so on. However, cost estimates based on the best planning information available will certainly result in fewer "bad" collective-bargaining agreements.

Summary

Legislation concerning employee wages and benefits is based on the premise that the bargaining relationship between employees and employers is unequal. As a result, laws establishing minimum wages, workers' compensation and other protective legislation are necessary to protect employees.

The law concerning wages and overtime that has an impact on the largest number of employees is the Fair Labor Standards Act. It specifies the minimum wage and requires overtime pay one and one-half the normal wage rate for work in excess of forty hours per week. The Davis-Bacon Act covers employment on construction projects financed in part with federal funds. The Walsh-Healey Act covers employment in organizations contracting with the federal government to provide goods and services. The laws are parallel in that both require employers to provide wages and benefits comparable to those prevailing in the relevant occupations, industries, and geographic area.

Both the Equal Pay Act and Civil Rights Act prohibit discrimination in compensation and benefits on the basis of sex. The Civil Rights Act extends the protection to include all terms and conditions of employment and prohibits discrimination on the basis of race, color, religion, and national origin. The Age Discrimination Act prohibits discrimination based on age.

Several laws attempt to provide minimum levels of income when one is not working. Workers' compensation laws provide some protection in the event of work-connected injuries and illness. Social Security provides some benefits in the event of disability, death, and retirement. Unemployment compensation programs provide some protection when one is laid off.

The Employee Retirement Income Security Act is intended to protect the private-pension benefits of employees. This act specifies minimum vesting and funding standards for private-pension plans to achieve this end.

Supplemental compensation has expanded rapidly since World War II. The cost of supplemental compensation now exceeds 35 percent of direct compensation. The growth of supplemental compensation can be attributed in part to the tax advantages for employees who receive a part of their pay in this form.

Most fringe benefits can be placed in one of three categories: compensation for inconvenience and unpleasantness connected with a job; pay for time not worked; and benefits designed to increase employee security. New forms of fringe benefits are appearing in collective bargaining agreements. They are designed to meet employee needs. Among such new programs are employee legal services, alcohol and drug treatment programs, and child-care centers.

Labor costs represent the largest single cost of operation for most organizations. The compensation package is determined during contract negotiations. It is important for both union and management negotiators to be able to identify the cost of a proposed agreement. Both parties to a contract should know if a proposed compensation package is consistent with an organization's ability to pay. In addition, when "trading" demands, both parties should be aware of the cost of the demands being traded.

An approach to costing out a labor agreement has been presented in this chapter. It can be described as the standard approach. It is subject to several criticisms. Typically, it is applied in a way that assumes that history will repeat itself. In addition, it focuses on the direct cost of a proposed compensation package. While this is certainly relevant, the impact of the compensation package on organization profits is more important. Finally, the time value of money is not taken into account. This would be important if a multiyear contract is being negotiated. While these are legitimate concerns about the approach presented here, our objective is to provide the reader with a basic approach to costing out a collective-bargaining agreement. Anyone involved in contract negotiations should be aware of the problems we have described and seek out reference materials that provide guidance in addressing them.

Discussion Questions

1. What arguments can be made in favor of and in opposition to legislation establishing minimum wages, requiring overtime pay in specified circumstances, and establishing such insurance programs as workers' compensation, unemployment compensation and Social Security?

2. What are the provisions of the following: Davis-Bacon Act; Walsh-Healey Act; Fair Labor Standards Act; Equal Pay Act; and Civil Rights Act?

3. Discuss the American public policy and programs designed to provide protection for: unemployed workers; disabled workers; retired workers; and the families of workers who have died.

4. What factors have contributed to the growth of private supplemental compensation programs during and since World War II?

5. Identify and describe examples of supplemental compensation that:
   a. Compensate workers for inconvenience and unpleasantness in performing their jobs.
   b. Compensate workers for time not worked.
   c. Provide some protection for unemployed workers, workers displaced by technological change, workers and their families affected by illness, and retired workers.
6. What problems are employers encountering with respect to supplemental compensation programs?
7. What are the problems and shortcomings of the typical approach to costing out collective-bargaining agreements?

Key Concepts

Common-law defenses
Experience rating
Vesting
Funding
Supplemental compensation

Compressed work week
Flextime
Sabbatical
Roll-up

Notes

1. Russell L. Greenman and Eric J. Schmertz, *Personnel Administration and The Law,* 2nd ed. (Washington, D. C.: Bureau of National Affairs, 1979), pp. 55–56.

2. Robert S. Goldfarb and John F. Morrall III, "The Davis-Bacon Act: An Appraisal of Recent Studies," *Industrial and Labor Relations Review* 34 (January 1981): 191–206.

3. Ibid., pp. 51–54.

4. Ibid, pp. 14–44.

5. U. S. Department of Labor, Employment Standards Administration, *Minimum Wage and Maximum Hours Standards Under the Fair Labor Standards Act* (Washington, D. C.: U. S. Government Printing Office, 1976), p. 15.

6. Erik P. Butler, "The Youth Subminimum—A Red Herring?" *New Generation* 61, no. 2 (Winter 1981):8.

7. Adrienne Blum, "$3.35 An Hour? Too Much!" *Nation's Business,* March 1981, p. 90.

8. *Employment and Training Report of the President 1980* (Washington, D. C.: U. S. Government Printing Office, 1980), p. 76.

9. Walter E. Williams, "Minimum Wage—Minimum Employment," *New Generation* 61, no. 2 (Winter 1981): 1.

10. Butler, p. 1.

11. Sar A. Levitan, Garth L. Mangum and Ray Marshall, *Human Resources and Labor Markets,* 2nd ed. (New York: Harper and Row, 1976), p. 59.

12. Ibid.

13. Ibid., pp. 44–51.

14. Ibid., pp. 63–66.

15. Benjamin J. Taylor and Fred Witney, *Labor Relations Law,* 3rd ed. (Englewood Cliffs, N. J.: Prentice-Hall, Inc., 1979), p. 638.

16. Greenman and Schmertz, p. 82.

17. F. Ray Marshall, Allan G. King and Vernon M. Briggs, Jr., *Labor Economics: Wages, Employment and Trade Unionism,* 4th ed. (Homewood, IL: Richard D. Irwin, Inc., 1980), p. 467.

18. John G. Turnbull, C. Arthur Williams, Jr., and Earl F. Cheit, *Economic and Social Security,* 4th ed. (New York: The Ronald Press, 1973), p. 285.

19. Ibid., p. 283.

20. Ibid., p. 288.

21. Marshall et al., pp. 469–70.

22. John Snee and Mary Ross, "Social Security Amendments of 1977: Legislative History and Summary of Provisions," *Social Security Bulletin,* March 1978, pp. 17–18.

23. Barry Crickmer, "Social Security: Is a Patchup Enough?" *Nation's Business,* October 1981, p. 30.

24. Ibid.

25. Ibid., p. 32.

26. Robert M. Ball, "Social Security Cuts: Violating A Trust," *AFL-CIO American Federationist,* June 1981, pp. 12–18.

27. R. Frumkin and D. Schmitt, "Pension Improvements Since 1974 Reflect Inflation, New U. S. Law," *Monthly Labor Review,* April 1979, p. 32.

28. A. Bauman, "Measuring Employee Compensation in U. S. Industry," *Monthly Labor Review* 93, no. 10 (October 1970): 17–23.

29. U. S. Chamber of Commerce, *Employee Benefits 1980* (Washington, D. C.: 1981), p. 8.

30. Turnbull et al., p. 128.

31. U. S. Chamber of Commerce, p. 9.

32. John A. Fossum, "Hire or Schedule Overtime?" *Compensation Review* 2 (1969): 14–22.

33. U. S. Department of Labor, *Characteristics of Major Collective Bargaining Agreements—January 1, 1978,* Bulletin 2065 (Washington, D. C.: U. S. Government Printing Office, April 1980).

34. Herbert G. Heneman III, Donald P. Schwab, John A. Fossum and Lee D. Dyer, *Personnel/Human Resource Management* (Homewood, IL: Richard D. Irwin, Inc., 1980), pp. 552–53.

35. William F. Glueck, *Personnel: A Diagnostic Approach,* rev. ed. (Dallas: Business Publications, Inc., 1978), pp. 126–27.

36. Ibid., pp. 127–28.

37. J. C. Swart and R. A. Quakenbush, "Union's Views Concerning Alternative Work Schedules and Proposal to Alter Federal Overtime Pay Legislation," *Proceedings of the 30th Annual Meeting: Industrial Relations Research Association* (Madison, WI: Industrial Relations Research Association, 1977), p. 378.

38. Wendell L. French, *The Personnel Management Process,* 4th ed. (Boston: Houghton Mifflin Co., 1978), p. 294.

39. Ibid.

40. *Business Week,* 3 February 1975, p. 20.

41. B. Seidman, "Health Security: The Complete Rx," *AFL-CIO American Federationist* 82, no. 10 (October 1975): 10.

42. *Inland Steel Co. v. United Steelworkers of America,* 336 U. S. 960 (1949).

43. A. Fox, "Earnings Replacement Rates of Retired Couples: Findings From The Retirement History Study," *Social Security Bulletin* 42, no. 1 (January 1979): 22.

44. Sandy DeMent, "A New Bargaining Focus on Legal Services," *AFL-CIO American Federationist* 85 (May 1978): 7–10.

45. Glueck, pp. 707–9.

46. U. S. Department of Labor and U. S. Department of Health Education and Welfare, *Employment and Training Report of the President, 1979* (Washington, D. C.: U. S. Government Printing Office, 1979), p. 295.

47. T. J. Gordon and R. E. LeBleu, "Employee Benefits: 1970–1985," *Harvard Business Review,* January-February 1970, pp. 93–107.

48. Edward E. Lawler III, *Pay and Organizational Effectiveness: A Psychological View* (New York: McGraw-Hill Book Company, 1971), pp. 198–99 and 253–54.

49. Ibid.

50. Michael H. Granof, "How To Cost Your Labor Contract," in *New Techniques in Labor Dispute Resolution,* ed. H. J. Anderson (Washington, D. C.: Bureau of National Affairs, 1973), p. 21.

51. Harold H. Jack, "The Accountant's Role in Labor Relations," *Management Accounting,* October 1973, p. 57.

52. The example method of costing out an agreement is based on the following material: Marvin Friedman, *The Use of Economic Data In Collective Bargaining,* U. S. Department of Labor (Washington, D. C.: U. S. Government Printing Office, 1978), pp. 41–51.

53. Granof, "How to Cost Your Labor Contract," pp. 35–36.

54. Jack, p. 57.

55. John G. Kilgour, " 'Wrapping the Package' of Labor Agreement Costs," *Personnel Journal,* June 1977, p. 298.

56. Michael H. Granof, "Financial Evaluation of Labor Contracts," *Management Accounting,* July 1973, p. 38.

57. O. U. Ciller, "Pricing Employment Contracts," *Management Accounting,* November 1973, p. 29.

58. Ibid.

59. Kilgour, p. 313.

60. Granof, "How To Cost Your Labor Contract," p. 47.

61. Ibid.

62. Granof, "Financial Evaluation of Labor Contracts," p. 39.

63. Ibid., pp. 40–41.

64. Granof, "How to Cost Your Labor Contract," pp. 47–48.

65. Ciller, p. 30.

66. Granof, "How To Cost Your Labor Contract," pp. 110–11.

67. Granof, "Financial Evaluation of Labor Contracts," p. 42.

Suggested Readings

Anderson, H. J. *New Techniques in Labor Dispute Resolution.* Washington, D. C.: Bureau of National Affairs, 1976.

Friedman, M. *The Use of Economic Data In Collective Bargaining.* U. S. Department of Labor, Washington, D. C.: U. S. Government Printing Office, 1978.

Granof, M. H. "How To Cost Your Labor Contract," in *New Techniques in Labor Dispute Resolution,* ed. H. J. Anderson. Washington, D. C.: Bureau of National Affairs, 1973.

Greenman, R. J. and Schmertz, E. J. *Personnel Administration and The Law,* Washington, D. C.: Bureau of National Affairs, 1979.

Turnbull, J. G.; Williams, C. A., Jr.; and Cheit, E. F. *Economic and Social Security,* 4th ed. New York: The Ronald Press, 1973.

Chapter 13

INSTITUTIONAL AND ADMINISTRATIVE ISSUES IN COLLECTIVE BARGAINING

Charles Bradley was continuing preparations for his first round of collective-bargaining negotiations. In addition to preparing for wage-and-fringe-benefit negotiations, he recognized that a wide range of institutional and administrative issues would be addressed. Since this was the first contract to be negotiated between the Albany Mining Company and the American Miners Union, he was not sure what to expect from the union. From his discussions with labor relations specialists at other mining companies, he was aware of some issues the union was likely to address. In addition, there were several provisions that could be beneficial to the company, if the union would agree to them.

He anticipated that the union would want a strong union security clause, e.g., a union shop clause. Charles wondered if the company should agree to such a provision. The union was also likely to demand a check-off. What were the long-run implications of such clauses?

Charles recognized that the National Labor Relations Act requires an employer to negotiate with the union on certain issues. However, there are other issues about which management is not required to negotiate, but about which unions prefer to negotiate or at least be consulted. Charles believed that it was in the company's interest to have a strong management-rights clause.

The mining industry faces wide swings in demand. Consequently, large scale lay-offs occur. Also, changes in technology have been taking place. At present Albany Mining Company is a family-owned organization. Years ago such an arrangement was common. However, as time passes, more and more small mining companies are becoming subsidiaries of large corporations. Everyone, including the union leaders and the union members, recognized these facts. Charles wondered what kinds of provisions the union would seek to be included in the collective-bargaining agreement in order to provide some protection for the jobs of union members.

INSTITUTIONAL AND ADMINISTRATIVE ISSUES IN COLLECTIVE BARGAINING

These are some of the institutional and administrative issues addressed in collective-bargaining negotiations and agreements. Employer and union points of view with respect to these and other issues are discussed in this chapter. When you have completed this chapter you should be able to provide recommendations for the problems Charles raised. More exactly, you should:

- Understand why American unions are concerned about union security.
- Be able to describe alternative union security clauses.
- Be aware of legal issues involving union security clauses.
- Understand the significance of management-rights provisions and the basic types of clauses.
- Be able to describe the basic options open to a union that is opposed to technological change.
- Know why unions prefer to base such decisions as lay-offs on seniority.
- Be able to discuss issues of concern when designing a competitive status seniority system.
- Be able to describe the following and discuss issues involving each:
  a. Make work rules.
  b. Jurisdictional rules.
  c. Subcontracting.
  d. Successorship.

This chapter addresses institutional and administrative issues in collective bargaining. Institutional issues pertain to the duties and rights of the institutions that are parties to a collective-bargaining agreement, the labor organization and the employer. Administrative issues pertain to the rights and duties of the employees covered by a collective agreement.

Management is responsible to the owners of organizations to operate efficiently and to earn a profit. For public sector organizations, administrators are responsible to taxpayers and are expected to manage the organizations in a cost-effective manner. In either case, public or private, management is expected to administer organizations efficiently and effectively. In pursuing this goal, management will attempt to include clauses in the collective-bargaining agreement that protect and preserve management's flexibility in administering the organization. Examples of the decisions that management would prefer to be free to make with a minimum of interference from a union include: introduction of technological change; subcontracting work; assignment of work to current employees; hiring and promotion decisions; and lay-off decisions.

For the material discussed in this chapter it is useful to distinguish between the goals of union members as individual employees or members of the labor force and the goals of unions as organizations or institutions. As institutions, the primary goal of unions can be described as continued existence and growth in membership. The primary subgoals in this goal of continued existence and growth could be expressed as representing workers and receiving money in the form of union dues to finance the union's operations.

A union can seek to have included in the collective-bargaining agreement clauses that facilitate attainment of the union's institutional goals. However, the attainment of the institutional goals of unions depends primarily on securing provisions in the collective-bargaining agreement that result in the attainment of the rank-and-file union members' goals. Chapter 6 pointed out that the members' goals that unions appear able to satisfy include extrinsic issues such as wages, promotions, and job security. Also, unions are perceived to be a means of insuring fair treatment in the work place.

Administration and Institutional Issues

There are a wide range of issues that appear in collective-bargaining agreements that are relevant to the goals discussed above. This chapter will describe these clauses and discuss issues relevant to each.

UNION-SECURITY PROVISIONS

The objective of union-security provisions is to insure that workers represented by a union contribute to its support. The stronger security provisions require that workers represented by a union are also members of that union. Exhibit 13.1 highlights reasons why American unions are concerned about union security.

A brief review of the history of union and management relations will help to clarify the intense emphasis on security by unions. In Chapter 5 concerning management organization for labor relations, a number of techniques used by management to resist unionization were described. Among them were blacklisting, yellow dog contracts and the American Plan. The objective of all these techniques was to avoid having a union represent an organization's employees. As a result, unions sought to insure that employees will support the union that represents their interests. This support takes the form of financial contributions, i.e., dues and union membership.

It must be recognized that employer resistance to unionization continues today. This phenomenon was discussed in Chapter 5. It was pointed out that many employers today go to great lengths to unseat a union once it is certified as the bargaining agent for a group of employees. Consequently, unions perceive that it is necessary to take steps to reduce the possibility of being decertified as the result of pressure or actions on the part of management.

Another factor that helps explain why unions are concerned about union security is the threat of raiding by another union. Chapter 4 on union structure and government reviewed the development of the union movement in the United States. That chapter described the period during which dual unionism was a problem. At that time both the AFL and the CIO usually had a member union seeking to organize workers doing the same kind of work. As a result, when a union represented the employees

> **EXHIBIT 13.1**
> **The Need for Union Security Provisions**
>
> *Problem of union security.* The strong and widespread emphasis on union security that is characteristic of American trade unions is a natural result of the conditions under which unions operate in this country. The American environment has produced strongly individualistic and highly competitive employers, who have been aggressively hostile to unions and who have been willing to go to great extremes in order to destroy them. In addition, the labor force in the United States is composed of strongly individualistic persons who have different racial and cultural backgrounds, who lack a tradition of class solidarity, and who are keenly interested in getting ahead. These influences have produced business unionism—that is, unionism which has little or no interest in social reforms but which is frankly out to advance the selfish aims of its members. Furthermore, just as individual union members are eager to get ahead, so the several unions are in competition with one another. Over rivalry between the various business unions the national federation has only limited control. Hence, unions need arrangements to protect themselves and their members from the competition of other unions. Union security, therefore, is needed for three reasons—to protect the union from being undermined by employers, to protect it from so-called "free riders" (workers who accept the benefits of unionism without helping to pay for them), and to protect it from other unions.
>
> Source: S. H. Slichter, J. J. Healy, and E. R. Livernash, The Impact of Collective Bargaining on Management (Washington, D. C.: The Brookings Institution, 1960), pp. 34–38.

of a particular organization, the union had to be concerned about the possibility of some other union seeking to organize the same group of workers. The merger of the AFL and the CIO reduced this threat. However, at the present time there are some independent unions that will seek to unseat a union that represents the employees of an organization. Consequently, while raiding is less of a threat than before the merger of the AFL-CIO, it is still a possibility.

The assumption underlying the use of strong union-security provisions to resist employer efforts to avoid unionization is the same as that for using such clauses to resist raiding. It is assumed that an individual who is a member of a union and contributes to the financial support of that organization is less likely to vote against that union in a certification election or to support a movement to decertify that union.

A third factor contributing to the unions' interest in security clauses is that unions are obligated by the Labor Management Relations Act to represent all employees in a bargaining unit. Given this obligation, unions reason that since employees receive the benefits of having a union represent their interests, such employees should contribute to support the union. For example, all employees of a bargaining unit reap benefits of a collective-bargaining agreement and receive the protection of the grievance procedure. Since the union is providing these services for the employees in the bargaining unit, they should contribute to the support of the organization rendering those services.

Alternative security provisions. Common union-security provisions include the closed shop, preferential hiring, union shop, agency shop, maintenance of membership, and open shop agreements. A closed shop provision requires that an individual be a member of the union as a condition of being hired. In other words, a person must be a union member before being employed by the organization. The provisions of the Taft-Hartley Act make this security provision illegal. However, there are exceptions to this generalization. The closed shop provision is found in industries where the employment relationship between an employee and a particular employer is of short duration. Examples are the building trades, longshoring and merchant shipping.[1] The closed shop provision is usually accompanied by an arrangement in which the union acts as a hiring hall or an employment agency for employers in the industry. In the above-mentioned industries, an employer's demand for workers fluctuates widely. As a result, it is convenient for both employers and workers that the union serve an employment agency function. For example, when an employer requires carpenters, the employer contacts the carpenter hiring hall and the union provides the necessary number of qualified carpenters when needed. This enables the employer to avoid the problems associated with recruiting and screening applicants for employment.

In some industries, unions have been able to secure an agreement that gives preference in hiring decisions to union members. While not requiring that the employer hire only union members, this agreement has the effect of giving union members an edge in securing employment. This particular security provision is referred to as the preferential hiring agreement.

Union shop. The union shop provision requires that an individual become a union member after being employed. The most common requirement is that the individual join the union after thirty days of employment. The legality of this security provision will be discussed below. From management's point of view, the principal difference between this provision and the closed shop provision is that management is free to make hiring decisions without reference to the union membership of applicants for employment.

Another common security provision is the agency shop, or a fair share fee, as it is sometimes called in public-sector collective bargaining. This provision requires all employees who do not join the union to pay a fee to the union. Usually the fee is equivalent to the dues for union membership. The effect of this provision is to provide the union with the equivalent income that would be obtained if all the employees in the bargaining unit were union members.

The maintenance of membership-shop provision requires all employees who choose to become union members remain so as a condition of employment. Some maintenance of membership provisions provide for an escape period after the termination of an existing contract agreement. During this escape period, members would have the opportunity to withdraw from the union.

An open shop agreement permits employers to make hiring decisions without considering the union membership of applicants. Further, no requirements are placed on employees in the bargaining unit with respect to joining the union or contributing to the financial support of the union. From the union's point of view this is the least secure provision.

Legal issues concerning union-security provisions. The Railway Labor Act [1926] provided that unions and employers could enter into a union shop agreement. This provision of the law specified that employees within a bargaining unit could be required to join the union within sixty days after employment.

The Wagner Act [1935] permitted unions and employers in the remainder of private industry to enter into any form of union security clause. In 1946 about one-third of all collective-bargaining agreements provided for the closed shop security provision.[2] Following passage of the Taft-Hartley Act prohibiting the closed shop provision, it disappeared from collective-bargaining agreements. However, the practice continued in some cases. For example, in the building trades, use of the hiring hall and employment of union members continued.[3] The Landrum-Griffith Act recognized that the practice continued and provided for legalized closed shop agreements in such industries as building construction.

The Taft-Hartley Act does not prohibit the union shop provision. However, Section 14(b) of Taft-Hartley does enable states to pass legislation prohibiting the union shop provision. This section specifies that nothing in this act can be construed as authorizing the execution or application of agreements requiring membership in a labor organization as a condition of employment in any state or territory in which such application or execution is prohibited by state or territorial law.

In a recent case involving the constitutionality of union shop provisions, columnist William F. Buckley argued that such provisions amounted to compulsory membership and violated the constitutional right to free speech. The federal courts rejected this charge and stated that the national labor policy is that a union has a right to collect dues from all members who reap the benefits of the unions' representation of them in the bargaining agreement with the employer.[4]

Right-to-work laws. As a result of Section 14(b) of the Taft-Hartley Act, some states enacted legislation prohibiting union shop security clauses in collective-bargaining agreements. Generally, these laws specify that it is illegal for an employer and a union to agree to a contract provision requiring that membership in a labor organization is a condition of employment. At this time twenty states have such laws: Alabama, Arizona, Arkansas, Florida, Georgia, Iowa, Kansas, Louisiana, Mississippi, Nebraska, Nevada, North Carolina, North Dakota, South Carolina, South Dakota, Tennessee, Texas, Utah, Virginia, and Wyoming. Generally these states are in the South and West, and they are largely agricultural states. While right-to-work laws are alike in that they prohibit union membership as a condition of employment, some go further and prohibit agency shop provisions. In effect the latter attempt to require an open shop agreement.

The effect of such laws appears to be minor. Employers who want to have good relations with their unions typically ignore the law. Alternatively, employers who seek to bust the union can use the right-to-work law as an additional tool in the drive against the union. Additionally, employers can locate new plants in "right-to-work" states and be in a better position to resist unionization of these plants. During the 1970s, General Motors Corporation located several plants in the South and was accused by the United Automobile Workers of undertaking an anti-union "Southern strategy."[5] Another issue concerning the effectiveness of right-to-work laws is the penalties imposed for violation of the statutes. Of the nineteen laws existing in 1966, eight provided no penalties for violation of the law, and ten provided for misdemeanor violations.[6]

- *Arguments for right-to-work laws*—Those supporting such legislation argue that union shop provisions are an undue encroachment on the liberty of the individual worker. It is argued that in a free society an individual should not be compelled to belong to a labor organization in order to obtain employment. A worker should have the "right to work" in any occupation and organization in which he or she is qualified to obtain employment.

  It is also argued that if the union is providing a worthwhile service for the employees in a bargaining unit, the employees will voluntarily join the union. Related to this argument is the notion that the union shop clause removes the incentive for union leaders to do a good job of representing the interests of workers in the bargaining unit. This implies that if employees are required to join a union and pay dues as a condition of employment, the union leadership can be lax in representing the members' interests.

  Another argument that is put forth in support of right-to-work laws is that the union shop provision largely makes a union a permanent fixture in a particular place of employment. This suggests that once a union becomes a certified bargaining agent there is little possibility of that union being removed or decertified.

- *Arguments against right-to-work laws*—The validity of the argument that union leaders can be lax in representing worker interests, given a union shop or a closed shop clause, is open to question. The discussion of turnover among local union leaders in Chapter 4 on union structure and government makes the point that union leaders at this level are subject to being voted out of office if they are not meeting the expectations of the members of the local. In addition, trends in union decertification elections that were discussed in Chapter 6 highlight the fact that when a union is not meeting the expectations of the workers in a bargaining unit, they can take action to remove that union.

  One of the arguments unions put forward in favor of stronger security provisions is prevention of "free riders." The essence of this argument is that since everyone in the bargaining unit benefits from the collective bargaining agreement and grievance procedures, it is appropriate for everyone to be a member and contribute to the support of the union.

  Another position is that right-to-work laws are really intended to retard the growth of unions because unions increase wages and operating costs for employers. According to an AFL-CIO publication, the principal objective of right-to-work laws is to keep down wages and salaries by weakening unions and undermining collective bargaining.[7] The essence of this argument is that states with right-to-work laws are low-wage states because of the relatively small numbers of workers represented by unions. No one can dispute the fact that the South and the West are characterized by relatively low wages. However, one can question the assumption that the presence of unions could change the situation. An alternative explanation is that the industry and economic characteristics of these states cause them to be low-wage states.[8] It will be interesting to see if wage levels in the western states affected by the energy crisis change dramatically without a corresponding increase in union membership.

In our judgment a stronger argument for the union shop is that when a union is secure it can afford to cooperate with management with regard to labor-relations matters. If management is unwilling to agree to a union shop provision, union leaders must assume that management has not accepted the presence of the union and seeks to dislodge it. As a result, the union leaders are not likely to assume an accommodative approach to dealing with management. Rather the union leadership are likely to be aggressive. In addition, if the union must continually justify the need for a union to the members of the bargaining unit, the union leaders are likely to manufacture disputes and grievances with management to demonstrate this need.

Another possibility is that union leaders will focus on representing the interests of union members in the bargaining unit and at the expense of those nonmember employees in the bargaining unit. The objective would be to demonstrate to the non-union employees the advantages of being a union member. Such a strategy is likely to create antagonism between union and non-union employees in the bargaining unit. This in turn would reduce the effectiveness and efficiency of the organizations' work force.[9]

Another argument in favor of a strong union security provision is that the majority of union members have historically demonstrated that they want union security. From 1947 to 1951, the NLRB conducted secret ballot elections to determine if workers wanted union shop provisions. In the 46,119 elections conducted the majority of workers voted for a union shop clause in 96 percent of these elections.[10] Because of the overwhelming support for union shop provisions demonstrated by these elections, the section of the Taft-Hartley Act that required these elections was repealed.

Finally, a strong union security provision is of interest to a union because its power during contract negotiations is influenced by the perceived commitment of members of the bargaining unit to the union. During contract negotiations the effectiveness of union negotiators depends in part on the perceived willingness of the membership to go out on strike, and the support that a strike would receive from the rank-and-file employees. If a significant portion of the workers in a bargaining unit do not belong to the union, it is more difficult to convince management negotiators that a strike would have the whole-hearted support of all employees in the bargaining unit. Perceived support of a union by the employees in the bargaining unit will influence the ability of the union to secure concessions from management during contract negotiations. In turn this will influence the membership's commitment to the union.

- *Effects on union membership*—Studies have attempted to assess the effects of right-to-work laws on union membership. Generally, such studies conclude there has been relatively little impact on membership. One investigation found that very few members resign from unions when the laws go into effect. It was also observed that right-to-work laws have not broken or led to the decertification of many unions.[11] Further, it appears that there has been very little rigorous enforcement of right-to-work laws. Another study focused on the effectiveness of the right-to-work statute in Texas. It concluded that in the industries that traditionally had closed shop provisions such as the building trades, the law has generally been disregarded.[12] The same study observed that in those industries where the initial hiring decision remains in the hands of the employer, organization of additional employees has continued to proceed although perhaps not at the rate that might have been attained without the right-to-work law.[13] A study of the auto and steel industries concluded that the union shop provision has brought in an average of one new member for every six voluntary members.[14]

    One must conclude from this evidence that right-to-work laws have had relatively little impact on the growth of unionization and on the percentage of workers covered by collective-bargaining agreements that choose to be members of the union. It appears that other factors explain why there are relatively few union members and few collective-bargaining agreements in those states that have right-to-work laws. Among them are the extent of industrialization and urbanization, and the general attitude of workers towards unions. States having right-to-work laws have much higher proportions of agricultural employment and work organizations that have few employees. Unionization of such employers is low in both right-to-work states and those without such statutes.

Incidence of alternative union-security provisions. The top section of Table 13.1 reports the incidence of selected union-security provisions. The United States Department of Labor study on which these figures are based found that 83 percent of collective-bargaining agreements provide for some form of union security provision. Among those contracts with a union security provision, 72 percent specified a union shop provision. Clearly this is the dominant form of security provision today. It has replaced the closed shop provision that had been the most common form of security provision prior to passage of the Taft-Hartley Act. The second most common provision is the agency shop agreement. Another common provision is the modified union shop agreement. It is a variation of the union shop provision. In this union-security clause, certain employee groups are exempted from the security provision. For example, those employees who were employed by the organization but were not

Table 13.1 *Union-Security, Check-off, Management-Rights, No-Strike Provisions (Frequency as a Percent of Contracts)*

Provision	Frequency	
Union-security provisions	83%	
Union shop		72%
Modified union shop[1]		7
Agency shop		9
Maintenance of membership		4
Other[2]		8
Check-off provisions	85	
Dues check-off only		31
Dues and assessments		3
Dues and initiation fees		43
Dues, assessments, and initiation fees		22
Other[3]		1
No-strike/No-lockout provision	93	
Absolute provision		45
Limited provision[4]		55

[1] A modified union shop is the same as a union shop except that certain employee groups may be exempted, e.g., those already employed when the provision was negotiated, but who had not joined the union.
[2] Composed primarily of combinations of agreements, e.g., both modified union shop and agency shop provisions.
[3] Agreements that provide other combinations of check-off provisions, or refer to check-off but give no details, or make check-offs subject to local negotiations.
[4] A limited provision prohibits strikes or lockouts except under circumstances or for issues specified in the contract.

Source: U. S. Department of Labor, Characteristics of Major Collective Bargaining Agreements—*January 1, 1980 (Washington, D. C.: U. S. Governement Printing Office, May, 1981), Bulletin 2095.*

members of the union at the time the union shop clause was negotiated may not be required to join the union. Maintenance of membership provisions occur in very few agreements.

THE CHECK-OFF

The check-off is a contract provision that is directly related to the financial support of a union by the membership. This is an agreement in which the employer deducts such financial contributions to the union as dues, initiation fees, and other assessments from the employee's paycheck. The employer forwards this money to the union. Table 13.1 reports that 85 percent of collective-bargaining agreements have some form of check-off provision. The most common check-off provision is an agreement in which the employer deducts dues and initiation fees from employee paychecks. Next most common is the deduction of dues only, followed by an agreement in which the employer deducts dues, assessments, and initiation fees.

The incidence of check-off provisions in collective-bargaining agreements has increased dramatically since the mid-1940s. In 1946 about 40 percent of all collective bargaining agreements contained check-off provisions, and by 1954 this figure had increased to about 75 percent.[15] Table 13.1 reports that at the present time about 85 percent of collective-bargaining agreements contain such provisions.

The check-off is of great convenience to unions. It enables the union leadership to avoid the hassle associated with directly contacting union members and collecting union dues and assessments from them. In addition, a check-off agreement ensures that the members do not become delinquent in paying their dues. Check-off provisions and union shop provisions usually coincide. When management agrees to either of these provisions, it can be interpreted as accepting the presence of the union as the representative of the organization's labor force. It also implies acknowledgment that the union has relatively permanent status as the employee representative. On the other hand, strong opposition to the check-off is likely to be found when management's attitude is one of trying to dislodge a union as the representative of the employees of the organization.

An argument for the check-off is that it enables union leaders to spend more time trying to solve problems of union members rather than collecting dues and encouraging union members who are delinquent in the payment of dues to meet their obligations. Of course, if management's objective is to dislodge the union, it is advantageous to have union leaders focus their efforts on collecting dues rather than issues of concern to members of the bargaining unit. Alternatively, if the relationship between the union and management is accommodative or cooperative, it is in the interest of the organization as well as the labor union to reduce the amount of time union leaders must spend on administrative trivia. Instead both parties benefit from expending effort to find creative solutions to mutual problems.

Taft-Hartley requires that when a check-off agreement is in effect, written authorization to make the deduction must be obtained from each employee. Usually such authorization is provided.

Unions in industries characterized by short periods of employment of union members by a particular employer seldom use the check-off procedure. Examples are the building trades and the maritime industry. In such industries union members carry books that are stamped when dues are paid. This procedure works quite well because union members must rely on the hiring hall to be referred to employers for work. Consequently, it is relatively easy to arrange for paying dues at the union hiring hall. In addition, the union has a lever because union members that are delinquent in paying dues may not be referred to a job.

The usual provision for revoking an employee's authorization for the check-off is that it remains in effect for one year. At the end of one year, there is a period during which the union member can revoke the authorization. If the union member does not revoke the authorization during this period, it is automatically renewed for another year.

MANAGEMENT-RIGHTS PROVISIONS

Probably the most important reason management opposes having a union represent the employees of an organization is that the union restricts management's flexibility in decision making. The Labor Management Relations Act requires that when a union represents the employees of an organization, management must meet with the union and negotiate with respect to wages, hours, and other terms of employment. Over the years there has been an increase in the areas over which unions have sought to be consulted or to negotiate with management. Alternatively, over the years management has tried to resist these "intrusions" into the proper functions of management. Examples of decisions that can be involved in such disputes are plant closings and subcontracting of work. Management might conclude that it is economically advantageous to close a plant in one location and open a plant in another location. Similarly, management could find that certain kinds of work can be done cheaper if subcontracted to another organization. For example, maintenance work and plant security are often subcontracted to other organizations. In both cases such decisions have clear implications for employment of workers in a bargaining unit. Arguments pertaining to subcontracting and plant closure are discussed later in the chapter. The fundamental conflict is between the union's wish to be involved in decisions affecting the interests of bargaining unit members and management's wish to be free to make decisions affecting the efficient operation of the organization. In making such decisions management seeks to represent the interests of the owners in the private sector and the interests of taxpayers in the public sector.

Management-rights clause. In order to restrict "intrusion" of unions into the proper functions of management, a management-rights clause commonly appears in collective-bargaining agreements. These clauses seek to define the proper functions of management.

There are basically two approaches to preserving management's flexibility in making decisions. One approach is to specify certain decisions that are vested exclusively in the company. Such contract clauses are referred to as management-rights or management-security provisions. The alternative approach typically states that the right to make all decisions is vested with the company except as limited by the terms of the collective-bargaining agreement. This type of provision is called a savings clause.

Exhibit 13.2 provides an example of a management-rights provision and a savings provision. The latter seems to offer greater protection for management than the former. This is because it is almost impossible to anticipate every decision that could occur about which the union would wish to be consulted and would wish to negotiate. When a management-rights provision does not specifically exclude a type of decision, it leaves open the possibility that the union could argue that it deserves to be consulted. Savings clauses, on the other hand, state that management has the right to make every decision except those issues specified in the agreement as open to negotiation with the union.

> **EXHIBIT 13.2**
> **Example of Management-Rights and Savings Provisions**
>
> *Management-rights provision.* The management of the plant and the direction of the working force, including the right to hire, discipline, suspend, or discharge for just cause, to assign to jobs, to transfer employees, to increase or decrease the working force, to determine products to be handled, produced, or manufactured, the schedules and standards of production, and the methods, processes, and means of production or handling is vested exclusively in the Company, provided this right shall not be used for the purpose of discrimination against any employee or to avoid any of the provisions of this Agreement.
>
> *Savings provision.* The management of the business and the operation of the plants and the authority to execute all the various duties, functions, and responsibilities incident thereto is vested in the Company. The exercise of such authority shall not conflict with this Agreement.

Table 13.2 reports the results of a Bureau of National Affairs study of 400 collective bargaining agreements. These data provide an indication of the incidence of management-rights provisions relative to savings provisions. The incidence of variations in each type of provision is also indicated. The most common decisions reserved for management in the management-rights provisions are: direct the work force and manage the company business. Other decisions mentioned less frequently are: protection of the right to close and relocate plants and to change technology and organization. The alternative forms of savings provisions are indicated in Table 13.2. Management rights provisions were found in 69 percent of the contracts studied

Table 13.2 *Management-Rights and Savings Provisions (Frequency as a Percent of Contracts)*

Provision	Frequency
Management-rights provisions	69%
Direct the work force	79%
Manage the company business	68
Control production methods	38
Frame the company rules	26
Close or relocate plants	17
Change technology	18
Savings Provisions	30
Management retains all rights not modified or restricted by the contract	61
Management rights listed in the contract are not inclusive	36

Source: Bureau of National Affairs, Basic Patterns in Union Contracts, *9th ed. (Washington, D. C.: BNA, Inc., 1979), pp. 62–63.*

while savings provisions were found in 30 percent of the contracts. Summing the two percentages indicates that almost all collective-bargaining agreements contain a provision intended to protect the flexibility of management to make decisions.

NO-STRIKE/NO-LOCKOUT PROVISIONS

Typically, a collective-bargaining agreement contains a no-strike/no-lockout provision. Such a clause states that the union will not go on strike nor will management lock out employees during the life of the labor agreement. The objective is to insure continuity of operations during the life of the agreement. Typically, this provision coincides with or is in trade for a provision calling for the arbitration of disputes concerning the interpretation and application of the collective-bargaining agreement. The arbitration process, which will be discussed in the chapters on the grievance-arbitration procedure, is the means by which disputes that arise during the life of an agreement are settled rather than through reliance on a strike or lockout.

There are two major forms of no-strike/no-lockout clauses. The first is an absolute provision which states that neither management nor union will interrupt the operation of the organization during the life of the agreement. Both parties agree that there will not be a strike or lockout for any purpose or under any circumstance during the time covered by the contract. The second major form of this provision is termed a limited provision. In such a clause the parties agree there will be no interruption of operations except in disputes that involve particular issues. For example, the contract may call for reopening wage negotiations in the event of rapid inflation. Another situation that might be an exception to a no-strike/no-lockout provision occurs when one of the parties refuses to abide by the decision of an arbitrator. Another example is the United Automobile Workers' refusal to give up the right to strike over production standards disputes. The UAW's position is that because of the complex data involved, a union is at a distinct disadvantage in arbitration hearings concerning production standards. Since it cannot effectively represent its members' interests in arbitration of such issues, the UAW does not arbitrate production standards disputes.[16]

The bottom section of Table 13.1 reports the incidence of no-strike/no-lockout provisions. Of the collective bargaining agreements studied, 93 percent contained a no-strike/no-lockout provision. Among those contracts having such a provision, the limited provision occurred in a little more than half and the absolute provision occurred in just under half.

The legal status of the no-strike provisions will be discussed in more detail in the chapter concerning grievance arbitration. However, it should be noted that in the Supreme Court's decision in *Boys Markets v. Retail Clerks* it was held that when a contract contains a no-strike provision as well as providing for arbitration of disputes involving interpretation and application of the collective-bargaining agreement, a federal court may issue an injunction prohibiting a strike called in violation of the collective-bargaining agreement.[17] In the Supreme Court's explanation of the decision it stated that a consistent theme of public policy with respect to collective bargaining had been to promote the peaceful settlement of labor disputes through arbitration.[18] A major implication of the *Boys Market* decision is that employers now have a potent weapon to stop wildcat strikes that violate no-strike provisions of collective-bargaining agreements.[19] It appears that the critical factors necessary to obtain an injunction are that the collective-bargaining agreement contain a no-strike provision and a provision calling for arbitration.

Instability in the Demand for Labor

Some industries are characterized by seasonal variations in the demand for labor. For example, in building construction, employment increases in the spring, is at a high level in the summer months, and tapers off in the fall, resulting in lay-offs among construction workers. In the clothing industry there are two peak periods in demand for labor during the year with slack periods of employment at other times of the year.[20]

Other industries are simply characterized by irregular employment. In longshoring the demand for work at a particular dock depends on which ships happen to arrive on a particular day. When the ships arrive, it is necessary to hire a group of longshoremen to unload the vessel. When the vessel is unloaded the job is done.[21]

In addition to seasonal fluctuations in the demand for labor, there are cyclical variations. Every three or four years there are downturns in the economy and reduction in the demand for labor. In response to the various patterns in the demand for labor, unions have sought to develop mechanisms that fairly ration or distribute the work among the union membership.

The industries characterized by irregular employment; for example, construction, longshoring, and the maritime industries; have relied on the use of the hiring hall as a central clearinghouse for rationing work. The basic rule followed in the referral of individuals for work is that the person unemployed the longest gets the first opportunity to sign up for new employment. For example, in longshoring a list of work teams is maintained at the hiring hall. These teams are dispatched for work in the order they appear on the list at the hiring hall.[22] In the clothing industry, unions have favored a system of reducing the working hours as the demand for labor declines at the end of the season.[23] This permits all union members to share equally in available work.

When there is a cyclical downturn in the economy, in other words, a recession, the demand for labor in virtually all sectors of the economy declines. When this occurs it is necessary to have mechanisms for sharing the work in all affected sectors of the economy. Among the alternatives used are: advancement of vacations; separation of all temporary employees; no scheduling of overtime; no subcontracting; and reducing the work week.[24]

Reducing the number of hours worked per week by employees offers the advantage to the organization of retaining the assembled work force. Typically a large investment in the form of employee training and development will have been made in an organization's work force. Avoiding a lay-off is advantageous because it reduces the probability of employees obtaining a job with another organization. At some point, however, employees reach the conclusion that they would be better off not working a limited number of hours and drawing unemployment compensation. It has been suggested that when the number of hours worked per week drops below thirty, employees become dissatisfied and prefer to be laid off so that they are able to draw unemployment compensation.[25] When it becomes necessary to lay off employees, a procedure must be established for making these decisions. Management typically prefers to make these decisions on the basis of merit or performance, as determined by management. Union members will typically insist that lay-offs be made on the basis of seniority. The argument put forth in support of the union position is that employees with greater length of service are usually more efficient performers. In addition, longer-service employees typically have greater family reponsibilities and their incomes should be protected. Another reason unions prefer to base lay-offs on seniority is that it is an objective-decision rule. Alternatively, merit is a judgment by management that permits the supervisor to play favorites in deciding who stays and who goes. The issues involved in the measurement of seniority and the exceptions to seniority as the basis of lay-offs are discussed later in the chapter.

UNION POLICY TOWARD TECHNOLOGY CHANGE

The response of unions to impending technology change depends in large part on the effect this change will have on job requirements and the number of union members employed. When the proposed change will make relatively little difference in the skills required and have little effect on the number of the jobs, the usual union policy is willing acceptance.[26] In such circumstances it is hardly surprising that unions favor technological change. Whenever technology is changed it is likely to have a positive influence on labor productivity. As a result the union would be in a situation to demand further increases in wage rates in the next round of collective-bargaining negotiations.

Typically, opposition to technological change is observed when employment in the industry is declining and/or the introduction of technological change will result in reduced employment of union members. Basically, three options are open to a union that opposes technological change. First, resist the introduction of change and try to maintain the status quo. Second, the union may recognize that the changes cannot be entirely resisted. In this case the union can try to secure preferential treatment for retraining union members or for transferring them to the jobs that result after the introduction of change. Third, the union can recognize the inevitability of the change and loss of the jobs that will follow, and try to secure compensation for employees affected by the change.[27]

It has been suggested that a union's response to technological change might evolve through the above stages. At first the union seeks to maintain the status quo by refusing to work with the new equipment or by requiring that obsolete employees be retained by the organization. In the second stage the union's focus is on securing preferential treatment of union members after the change is introduced. In the final stage, the inevitability of the loss of employment by some union members is recognized. The union then seeks to obtain compensation for them. Such compensation may take the form of severance pay, dismissal pay, or early-retirement provisions.[28] A final alternative that might appear at this third stage of adjustment to technological change is negotiation for a shorter work week.

When adjusting to technological change, it may be necessary to reduce the work force, limit employee opportunities for training, or provide limited opportunities for transfers to other jobs in the plant or to other plants in the organization. A mechanism must be established for allocating these limited opportunities. As with the response to an economic downturn, the basic preferences are merit on the part of management and seniority on the part of labor unions. The remainder of the chapter discusses common contract provisions that establish procedures for adjusting to technological change and to limited employment opportunities for members of the bargaining unit.

SENIORITY PROVISIONS

Competitive-status and benefit seniority. The two preceding sections point out that seniority is a key factor in rationing employment opportunities among union members. In discussing seniority it is useful to make a distinction between competitive-status seniority and benefit seniority.[29] The former pertains to those situations in which an employee's length of service relative to other employees is a factor in making such decisions as who will be laid off during a period of reduced business activity. The latter is a criterion that is used when making decisions about such benefits as vacation and pension rights. In addition, benefit seniority might be used to determine one's entitlement to sick leave, supplemental unemployment benefits, and automatic progression through a wage structure. Other decisions that may be based on competitive-status seniority include: transfer decisions, work or job assignments, shift preferences, and allocation of overtime.

Why seniority? One reason for using seniority as the criterion on which to base these decisions has already been discussed; i.e., its objectivity. One factor that has contributed to the formation of unions is distrust of management. Seniority is a factor that unions typically prefer to be used in making these kinds of decisions, rather than managerial judgments concerning employee performance and merit.

Chapter 11 presented a model of the factors influencing employees' perceptions of how much they should be paid. One of the factors in that model is the length of service. This is another reason why employees feel seniority or the length of service should be considered in making lay-off and related decisions. In a sense, all of these decisions are related to the amount an employee is paid.

When seniority is used as a criterion for such decisions as promotions and leads to a reduction in worker dissatisfaction and voluntary quits, there are advantages for employers. Lower voluntary separations imply lower staffing and training costs. In addition, reduced voluntary quits provide greater benefits to employers from the training and development of current employees.[30]

Measurement of seniority. To this point the term seniority has been used synonymously with length of service. This definition of seniority is typically satisfactory with respect to eligibility for benefit programs.[31] However, such a definition of seniority is inadequate when making such decisions as lay-off, recall, and promotion.

Seniority unit. Definition of the unit of seniority is a critical factor in measuring competitive-status seniority. Seniority can be company-wide, plant-wide, department-wide, or restricted to a single job classification. The wider the seniority unit the greater the protection provided the senior employee.[32] However, from the point of view of the employing organization, the wider the seniority unit the greater the disruption of working relationships and the greater the number of employees that will be dislocated as a result of laying off a single employee. The disruption occurs because an employee whose services are not required because of a reduction of demand in a particular department or job classification is able to "bump" or displace another employee who has less seniority in the relevant seniority unit.

Unrestricted bumping based solely on seniority could have a detrimental effect on the morale of union members. For example, in such a system an unqualified individual with longer service in a seniority unit could displace a junior qualified employee. Common provisions that address the weight to be assigned to seniority in making lay-off decisions are: seniority is the sole consideration; seniority is the determining factor among those persons qualified for available jobs; and seniority is a secondary factor that enters the decision only when the ability to perform the job and the worker's physical fitness are equal.[33]

The top section of Table 13.3 reports the incidence of selected seniority provisions in lay-off decisions. Over 80 percent of the agreements studied used seniority to some degree in making lay-off decisions. The most common provision that appears in just under half of the contracts provided that seniority would be the sole factor in making lay-off decisions. The second section of Table 13.3 summarizes bumping provisions, or the seniority units in which one is able to exercise seniority rights during a lay-off. The most common provision restricts an employee's bumping rights to his or her own job classification. This is followed by a provision for exercising one's bumping rights throughout the plant.

Exceptions in applying seniority. Normally a contract agreement will provide for exceptions to the application of seniority when making lay-off decisions. Two common exemptions are for employees holding offices in the union and for employees that are critical for the continuation of business operations. The reason for providing "superseniority" for union officials is that these individuals are typically critical to the day-to-day administration of the collective-bargaining agreement. For example, they are probably on the grievance committee or are shop stewards. The roles of these individuals will be discussed in Chapter 14. It is sufficient at this point to stress that the presence of union officials lends stability and continuity to the administration of the collective-bargaining agreement, a situation that is advantageous to both the union membership and to the employer. With respect to the employees critical to the continued operation of the organization, it is also mutually advantageous for such individuals to have superseniority.

Table 13.3 *Seniority in Lay-off, Bumping, Promotion, and Transfer Decisions (Frequency Expressed in Percentage of Contracts)*

Type of decision	Frequency
Seniority in lay-off decisions	
Sole factor	46%
Determining factor	26
Secondary factor	10
Bumping provisions	
Throughout the company	13
Throughout the plant	27
Restricted to one's division or department	24
Restricted to one's job classification	32
Restricted to one's former job classification	2
Seniority in promotion decisions	
Sole factor	9
Determining factor	33
Secondary factor	22
Equal with other factors	3
Seniority in transfer decisions	
Sole factor	8
Determining factor	22
Secondary factor	12
Equal with other factors	1

Source: Bureau of National Affairs, *Basic Patterns in Union Contracts,* 9th ed. (Washington, D.C.: BNA, Inc., 1979), pp. 51, 53, 74, and 75.

Recall decisions. When economic conditions improve and an organization is expanding employment, the question arises as to who will be first to be rehired. Typically, the collective-bargaining agreement calls for employees to be reeemployed in reverse order of lay-off. The principle of this decision is "last off, first in." Clearly the application of seniority to lay-offs and recall decisions places the brunt of economic hardship on the least senior employees in the bargaining unit.

Promotion and transfer decisions. When there is a collective-bargaining agreement, it is a common practice to consider seniority in making a wide range of "promotion" decisions. Normally the term promotion means the movement to a job that requires greater skill, has more responsibility, and provides an increase in compensation. One should recognize that there are a number of other kinds of moves that can take place that in the eyes of an employee involve a more favorable job. Transferring to a job that has the same wages and benefits but which is less hazardous or less demanding in terms of effort or skill requirements is a possible example. Similarly, an individual may look favorably on moving from the "graveyard" shift to the swing shift, or from the swing shift to the day shift. The authors are aware of an organization in the Rocky Mountain region that has a twenty-four-hour operation. In this organization an individual working in the production area must be employed about ten years before having enough seniority to work the day shift.

Common provisions concerning the application of seniority in the making of promotion and transfer decisions are: seniority is the sole factor; seniority is the determining factor, i.e., the most senior employee in the seniority unit is promoted if he or she is qualified for the available job; seniority is a secondary factor, implying that seniority determines the outcome only when ability to do the job is equal; and seniority is given equal consideration along with other factors.[34]

Table 13.3 indicates that the most common provision in both promotion and transfer decisions is that seniority is the determining factor. In other words, the most senior employee qualified to do the job receives the promotion or transfer. The second most common provision in both cases is that seniority is the secondary factor.

The effects of seniority on employee efficiency. Two basic criticisms can be made of placing heavy weight on seniority in making lay-off and promotion decisions. First, it can be argued that basing these decisions on seniority may lead to a departure from considering merit or ability to do the job. A second criticism is that seniority, as a prime criterion in making these decisions, leads to a reduction in the mobility of labor among employers. However, as pointed out above, one can argue that reduced voluntary quits can reduce hiring and training costs, as well as increase the returns to employers of training provided to employees.

The first criticism assumes that management accurately assesses ability to do the job. The available evidence concerning the ability to predict success among those promoted focuses primarily on managerial employees. The evidence suggests that management must expend a great deal of effort and money to achieve a high degree of accuracy in making promotion decisions among managerial employees.[35] Our judgment is that most employers are not willing to expend the necessary effort and money to achieve high levels of validity in predicting who will be successful if promoted. One of the authors has been involved in studies focusing on the ability to predict success among blue-collar employees who have been promoted within the organization. The general pattern in these studies is that one is able to identify measures of ability, for example, scores on a psychological test that are significantly correlated with job success following promotion. However, the correlations are moderate, and the ability of management to accurately predict who will be successful is open to question. In such situations it is our judgment that management is not losing much by basing lay-off and promotion decisions primarily on seniority.

Alternatively, management must avoid getting into the trap created when unrestricted bumping rights are granted. Similarly, management should avoid basing promotion and transfer decisions solely on seniority. Apart from these extreme situations, it appears that the opportunity costs to an employer of agreeing to seniority as the determining factor are minimal.

The effects of seniority on labor mobility. It has been suggested that use of seniority in personnel decisions reduces the voluntary mobility of blue-collar workers among employers.[36] The rationale for this point of view is that, because of the emphasis on seniority in making lay-off and promotion decisions and in providing fringe benefits, employees become tied to a particular employer. This argument is based in part on the view of the labor market that variations in wage rates produce movement of workers among employers. A further assumption underlying this view is that the labor market is frictionless and that the job structure is open.[37] The validity of this view of the labor market is open to question. Rather, there appear to be two broad types of labor markets. One is closely related to the view of the labor market just described. In this market there appears to be free movement by workers among alternative employers, determined by the wage rate.

Internal labor markets. The second type of labor market appears to involve a high degree of structure. In such a market a worker enters an organization at a job described as a port of entry. From this port of entry, the worker progresses through the job hierarchy or line of progression.[38] The term internal labor market is used to describe organizations using this approach to staffing jobs. Plants in the steel and petroleum industries are examples in which there is heavy reliance on the internal labor market to fill jobs. Fig. 13.1 presents a visual representation of such a labor market. Access to the labor market is restricted to the low-skill level of the job hierarchy. Entry to the job hierarchy at levels above the entry port is largely nonexistent. An

Fig. 13.1 *Internal Labor Markets: Closed Internal Submarket*

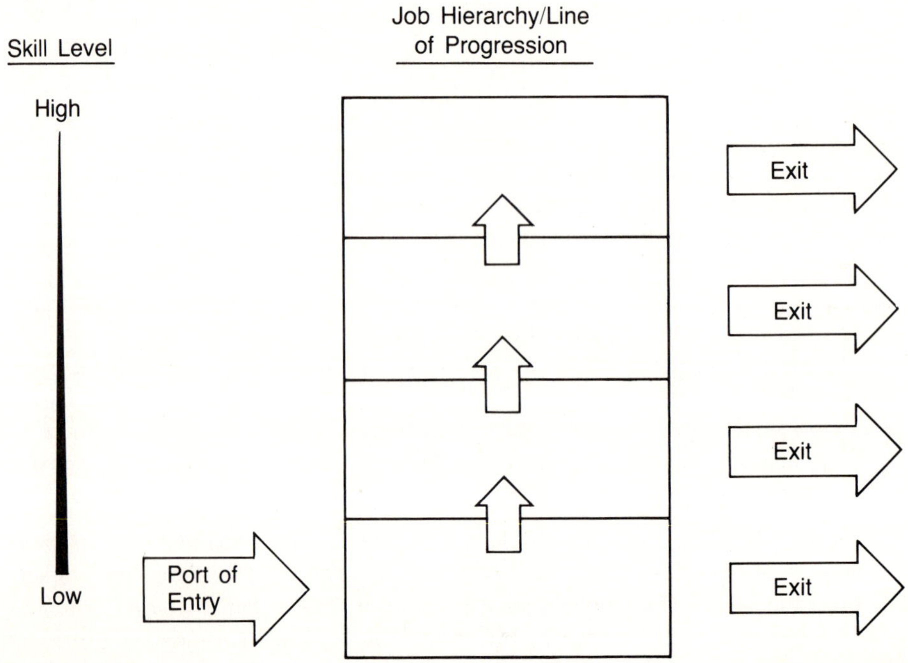

employee is free to exit the hierarchy at any point. It has been suggested that most industrial plants can be represented to some degree as closed internal submarkets.[38] In such a labor market employees are free to leave the job hierarchy at any level. However, to enter the job hierarchy of an organization characterized as an internal labor market, a worker typically must begin at the low-skill level, with the corresponding level of compensation. Alternatively, to progress to higher levels of skill and compensation, it is necessary for an employee to remain with a particular employer.

This phenomenon is pointed out to give a better explanation of why employees may be reluctant to move among employers. Labor immobility may stem in part from the use of seniority as a criterion for making promotion and lay-off decisions and in part from the recognition that leaving a particular employer implies starting at the bottom of the job hierarchy with a different employer. Of course one can argue that it is heavy reliance on seniority as a criterion for making job assignments by other employers that necessitates the restriction of newly hired workers to low-level jobs.

At the beginning of this section it was pointed out that use of seniority to make promotion, transfer, and lay-off decisions reduces voluntary quits. Since use of this criterion is more likely by unionized employers than by non-union employers, it follows that the presence of a union should imply fewer voluntary quits. Early efforts to demonstrate these relationships were not successful.[40] More recent evidence has demonstrated that the presence of a union and a strong seniority provision in a collective-bargaining agreement are both associated with fewer voluntary separations.[41,42]

Seniority systems and equal opportunity. Competitive-status seniority systems can lead to race and ethnic group segregation in employment by job classification or type of work. The following are descriptions of how seniority systems have been used for such discrimination.[43] First, separate seniority lists can be maintained for white and black employees doing the same work. In this system, the most junior white employee has been given preference over the most senior black job holder. Second, in a group of functionally related jobs, lower-level jobs are staffed by either white or black employees. However, only white employees are eligible for promotion to the higher-level jobs. Third, two or more groups of related jobs are organized in separate seniority units. White applicants are given preference in hiring for the more desirable jobs and, effectively, black applicants are hired only into the least desirable jobs. The seniority system can then prohibit transfers and promotions from the seniority unit composed of the least desirable jobs. However, a more common procedure is to permit such transfers and promotions but specify that seniority acquired in one seniority unit does not transfer to another seniority unit.

The latter is a system that one is likely to encounter. It is also the type of seniority system that has been at issue in most court cases involving seniority systems and equal opportunity. Such a system can be a bona fide seniority system. However, when an employer, or an employer and union together, discriminate in hiring applicants in the manner described, they violate the Civil Rights Act.

In *Franks v. Bowman Transportation Co.*, the employer refused to hire two black applicants as over-the-road truck drivers.[44] The Supreme Court directed the company to award the two individuals seniority retroactive to the time of the employment decision because they were the object of race discrimination. Further, they were awarded back pay.

A more recent Supreme Court decision further clarifies how the Civil Rights Act influences seniority systems. In this case, the United States instituted litigation against the Teamsters and T.I.M.E.-D.C., Inc., a nationwide common carrier. The government argued that the company engaged in a pattern of employment discrimination against black and hispanic applicants.[45] They were hired as servicemen or local city drivers. The higher-paying, over-the-road jobs were staffed by whites.

The seniority system permitted transfers from the city driver or serviceman jobs to over-the-road jobs. However, a person making such a move lost all competitive seniority from the previous seniority unit. It was alleged that this system perpetuated the effects of past ethnic group and race discrimination. The Supreme Court ruled that the company had engaged in a pattern of race discrimination in hiring. Employees who were the object of post–Civil Rights Act discrimination (1965 forward) were to be awarded retroactive seniority. In addition, every post–Civil Rights Act minority applicant for an over-the-road driver position was entitled to relief unless the company could show that the earlier refusal to hire the applicant was not based on race discrimintion. Employees who were the object of pre–Civil Rights Act discrimination were not entitled to relief. Although such a seniority system perpetuates race discrimination occurring prior to 1965, Congress intended that seniority rights earned when the Civil Rights Act became effective not be changed. As a result of this decision, a bona fide seniority system by post–Civil Rights Act standards does not become illegal because it perpetuates pre-1965 discrimination.[46]

The above discussion points out the potential for using seniority provisions to discriminate against members of minority groups. In fairness to the American union movement, evidence concerning race discrimination in union and non-union employment in general should be reviewed. It has been found that union membership has a greater positive impact on the wages of black than white workers.[47,48] In a study focusing on factors related to wages and job levels attained by men, it was found that race has far less effect in unionized employment than in non-union employment.[49] Among female members of the labor force, the effect of race on job-level attainment was reduced in the union sector.[50] These studies indicate that generally unions reduce the incidence of race discrimination with respect to wage determination and job assignment.

MAKE-WORK RULES

As pointed out earlier in the chapter, one union response to technological change is to attempt to resist implementation of the change. Another approach that has the same effect is to secure an agreement from the employer to agree to employ more workers than are necessary. Yet another approach is to secure an agreement from the employer for the performance of work that is not needed. For example, wiring of some electrical apparatus can currently be done at the factory while in earlier days this work had been done on the job. In some locals of the International Brotherhood of Electrical Workers such a prewired apparatus is not installed unless the wiring done at the factory is torn out and rewired by union members at the construction site.[51] Another example concerned the crew size of trains in the railroad industry. With the replacement of the steam engines by diesel locomotives, the need for firemen was removed. Unions sought to retain this position on diesel locomotives, primarily as a backup for the engineer. This dispute was not settled until 1972 when the union agreed to the eventual elimination of the firemen of the diesel locomotives through attrition.[52]

Section 8(b)(6) of Taft-Hartley attempted to prohibit a labor union from causing an employer to pay or agree to pay for services that are not performed. This was an attempt to prohibit featherbedding and make-work rules. A Supreme Court decision on this issue largely removed effectiveness of this provision of the act. The court ruled that while the work practices agreed to in the collective-bargaining agreement may indeed not be needed or wanted by the employer, as long as the employees did in fact perform work, it was not prohibited by this provision of the act.[53] The court's position was that the law leaves to the process of collective bargaining the determination of what work shall be compensable.

JURISDICTIONAL RULES

Jurisdictional rules require that certain types of work be done by members of a particular union. The objective of such rules is to protect the jobs of union members. A common provision prohibits supervisors of union members from doing the work of the trade. This prevents a reduction of the amount of work available to union members. In industries characterized by a high degree of unionization by the trade or craft unions, jurisdictional rules often specify which union shall be permitted to do specific kinds of work. The building industry is an example. This industry has experienced a great many technological changes over the years. These changes have resulted in disputes over which union should perform tasks within the industry. This type of dispute follows from the organization of craft unions discussed in the chapter on the structure and government of unions. Recall that craft unions were organized along trade lines and each union affiliated with the American Federation of Labor was granted exclusive jurisdiction over its particular trade. The problem resulting from technological change is that it is not always clear which trade should perform a particular task in a project. The basic argument boils down to which union has "traditionally" performed the work, as opposed to the fact that the work as it exists following the change is different from what it was "traditionally."

While jurisdictional problems are more common among craft or trade unions, they can occur in industrial unions. In this setting, the pattern of events leading to jurisdictional problems is commonly as follows. The technological change simplifies skill requirements permitting the reassignment of work formerly done by skilled employees to semiskilled or to unskilled employees in the same union. To protect jobs in such cases, unions prefer to have written job descriptions that are quite specific concerning the duties and tasks to be performed by job incumbents. Management, on the other hand, prefers to have phrases such as "perform related tasks as directed by management" which provide management with the flexibility in making job assignments.

SUBCONTRACTING

Subcontracting occurs when an organization contracts with a second organization to have work done. This is of concern to union members working for the first organization when they could have done the work. Normally, management chooses to subcontract when it is determined that the work can be done more economically by another organization. For example, janitorial work and cafeteria services are often subcontracted to other organizations. However, other work more central to a business organization can be subcontracted. When the decision is made to subcontract, it means that the amount of work available for members of the bargaining unit will be reduced. This implies a reduction in employment of union members by the contracting organization. As a result, unions have sought to place constraints on or limit the employer's flexibility to subcontract work.

Management usually counters with the view that it should be free to operate the organization efficiently. The union's counterargument is that subcontracting deprives union members of work. As a result, the union is entitled to participate in the decision process concerning subcontracting.

In 1964 the Supreme Court ruled that subcontracting was a matter about which management has a legal obligation to bargain. This dispute involved the Fibreboard Papers Corporation and the United Steel Workers of America. In this case the existing collective-bargaining agreement was to expire on July 31, 1959. Prior to this time the union had sought to establish a time and place for negotiating the renewal of the agreement. The employer responded that it had been determined that subcontracting the work would be more efficient. Consequently, it was not necessary to negotiate a new contract. On July 31, 1959, the company terminated the employees of its maintenance staff. The court held that the company was obligated to bargain with the union before making the decision to subcontract work that otherwise would

Table 13.4 *Selected Job Security Provisions (Frequency Expressed as Percentage of Contracts)*

Provision	Frequency
Work rules	
Limit or regulate crew size	22%
Restriction on work by nonbargaining unit personnel	63
Subcontracting	
Limited restrictions	57
Absolute prohibition	1
Interplant transfers	
Transfers permitted	30
Preferential hiring	11
Relocation allowance	14

Source: U.S. Department of Labor, *Characteristics of Major Collective Bargaining Agreements—January 1, 1980, (Washington, D.C.: U.S. Government Printing Office, May 1981), Bulletin 2095.*

have been performed by members of the bargaining unit. A key point of the Fibreboard decision is that the law does not forbid an employer from making a change in working conditions. Rather, the employer must first bargain with the union concerning the subcontracting decision, and, should an impasse be reached, the change can be made.[54]

The application of the Fibreboard doctrine has presented problems for employers. Before making a change involving subcontracting, employers are obligated to bargain to an impasse. As a result, employers may have not been able to take immediate advantage of economic benefits that would have resulted from a change.[55]

Table 13.4 reports data concerning the incidence of selected job security provisions in collective-bargaining agreements. With respect to work rules, just under two-thirds of the contracts studied place restrictions on work by non-bargaining-unit personnel. About one in five contain provisions limiting or regulating crew size. The most common subcontracting provision places some limitations on the situations in which employers are able to subcontract. Provisions pertaining to interplant transfers are also presented.

SUCCESSORSHIP

What is the obligation of an organization that acquires a plant or facility from another organization when a union represents the employees of the selling organization? This is a question of job security for the members of a collective bargaining unit. Often the motivation for the selling organization is that it is not able to operate the facility efficiently. If the buyer is obligated to abide by the collective-bargaining agreement of the seller, its flexibility in making the acquired facility an efficient operation can be greatly restricted.

Successorship clauses provide that any change in the management of the organization cannot invalidate the contract, and that the new management must assume the contractual obligations of the predecessor. In 1979, 29 percent of agreements sampled in a Bureau of National Affairs study had such a successorship clause.[56] This figure is up 22 percent from 1975.

The legal obligation of the acquiring organization with respect to such clauses has been addressed in three decisions by the Supreme Court. These decisions indicate that the successor employer has little legal responsibility under certain conditions. In the decision of *Livingston v. John Wiley*, the purchaser, John Wiley, acquired Livingston. The employees of the acquired company were absorbed by the John Wiley organization. In this case, the Supreme Court ruled that the successor organization was required to go to arbitration to settle certain disputes that had arisen under the terms of the collective bargaining agreement between Livingston and the union.[57]

In the second case, Lockheed Aircraft contracted with Wackenhut for security services. The United Plant Guard Workers was the certified bargaining agent for Wackenhut employees. The decision was made by Lockheed to award the contract for security services to Burns International Detective Agency. Burns employed forty-two individuals on Lockheed's premises. Twenty-seven of these people had previously worked for Wackenhut. When the Burns agency refused to recognize the United Plant Guard Workers, an unfair labor practice charge was filed against Burns. The Supreme Court ruled that while Burns had no obligation to abide by the contract that had been entered into by Wackenhut, it was obligated to bargain with the union.[58] The reason was that many of the workers who had worked for Wackenhut were retained by Burns. The third decision involved Howard Johnson and Company. In assuming the operation of a motel and restaurant complex, Howard Johnson dismissed the employees of the former organization and hired new employees including a small number of those who had worked for the former employer. In this case the Supreme Court held that the successor employer did not have an obligation to arbitrate its refusal to hire employees of the seller's work force.[59] In this decision the Supreme Court emphasized that the acquiring organization would have assumed inefficient work rules had it been obligated to adhere to the collective-bargaining agreement which the union had with the previous owners.

These decisions suggest that employers are able to get rid of inefficient operations by selling them to other organizations. The acquiring organizations in such circumstances are not obligated to recognize the union that represented the workers of the former employer if there is limited continuity in the employment of the same individuals.

Administrative and Institutional Issues and the Future

Before leaving the topics of union security, management rights, job security, and adjustment to technological change, we must point out that these are not issues of the past. Today they continue to be of critical importance. In the years to come, they are likely to be of even greater significance. It is anticipated that robots and automated equipment will be introduced into American plants and factories at a rapid rate during the coming decade. These changes will probably trigger major conflicts concerning administrative and institutional issues. These issues will be explored more fully in Chapter 19.

Summary

Unions would like to have strong union security provisions for several reasons. Among them is the potential for raiding by another union and a desire by the employer to be rid of the union. Another reason is that a union is required to represent all workers in the bargaining unit, union members as well as nonmembers. Clearly it is in the union's interest to be able to require all workers in a bargaining unit to belong to the union and contribute to its support. In fact, a secure provision such as the union shop is seen as an effective tool in seeking to contend with all of these threats to union security.

The most secure provision, a closed shop, was prohibited by the Taft-Hartley Act. The Landrum-Griffin Act permits the closed shop in situations characterized by employee-employer relationships of short duration. The Taft-Hartley Act permits states to enact legislation prohibiting the union shop agreement. Such laws are called right-to-work laws. Among the union arguments concerning such legislation is the view that it is a tool for union busting. Among the counterarguments is the position that such legislation prohibits workers from being forced to join unions. Research concerning the effects of right-to-work laws on union membership suggests they have had little impact.

A problem for union leaders is the regular and timely collection of fees and dues from members. The check-off is an agreement in which the employer automatically deducts these collections from union member paychecks, on behalf of the union.

Unions typically seek to negotiate with management about issues that management perceives to be the sole function of management. A management-rights clause is an attempt by management to place a limit on those topics open to negotiation.

Fluctuation in the demand for labor makes it necessary to establish procedures to allocate or ration the available work among employees. Also technological change can reduce the number of jobs and at times can eliminate jobs. This also calls for the establishment of procedures for the allocation of the work that is available. Competitive-status seniority is the principal mechanism for achieving this allocation.

Unions favor the use of seniority rather than merit in making such decisions as lay-offs and promotions. The principal reason is that seniority can be objectively measured, while merit is subjectively determined.

In establishing a competitive-status seniority system, the definition of the seniority unit is very important. A system that permits unrestricted or even widespread bumping is inefficient. It leads to large-scale disruption of a work force even when only a few employees are laid off.

There are other mechanisms for rationing work and attempting to protect the jobs of union members. Among them are make-work rules, jurisdictional rules, subcontracting provisions, and successorship clauses. The central theme of all such provisions is an effort by the union to insure that union members are employed.

Discussion Questions

1. What are the threats that account for the intense concern unions have about union-security clauses?
2. What is the distinction between a closed shop and a union shop security provision?

3. Why are closed shop provisions permitted in some industries?
4. What are the arguments for and against right-to-work laws?
5. Why is a check-off clause advantageous for a union and when is management likely to favor such a clause?
6. When is a union likely to favor technological change and when is a union likely to oppose it?
7. What are the alternative approaches a union can take to resist technological change?
8. What are issues that should be considered in establishing a competitive-status seniority system from both the union and management points of view?
9. What is the legal status of make-work rules, jurisdictional rules, subcontracting clauses, and successorship clauses?

Key Concepts

Union-security provisions
Union shop
Right-to-work-laws
Check-off
Management-rights clause
Competitive-status seniority

Seniority unit
Internal labor markets
Make-work rules
Jurisdictional rules
Subcontracting
Successorship

Notes

1. Lloyd G. Reynolds, *Labor Economics and Labor Relations*, 7th ed. (Englewood Cliffs, N. J.: Prentice-Hall, 1978), pp. 464–65.
2. Ibid., p. 465.
3. Ibid.
4. *Buckley, National Review, Inc. and Evans v. AFTRA, NLRB, and American Civil Liberties Union*, 496 F.2d 305 (CA2, 1974); cert. denied 419 U.S. 1093 (1974).
5. *Wall Street Journal*, 23 November 1976.
6. B. S. Warshal, "Right to Work: Pro and Con," Labor Law Journal 17, no. 3 (1966): 135–36.
7. "The Truth About 'Right to Work' Laws," (Washington, D. C.: American Federation of Labor and Congress of Industrial Organizations, 1970), Publication No. 46, p. 12.
8. Albert Rees, *The Economics of Trade Unions*, 2nd ed. (Chicago: University of Chicago Press, 1977), p. 126.
9. Reynolds, p. 467.
10. "The Truth About 'Right to Work' Laws," p. 6.
11. "Right-to-Work Laws," *Fortune* 56, no. 8 (September 1957): 235–36.
12. Frederick Meyers, *Right-to-Work in Practice*, A Report to the Fund for the Republic, Inc. (New York, 1959), pp. 4–5.

13. Ibid.

14. James W. Kuhn, "Right-to-Work Laws—Symbols or Substance?" *Industrial and Labor Relations Review* 14 (July 1961): 592.

15. T. Rose, "Union Security Provisions in Agreements, 1954," *Monthly Labor Review* 78, no. 6 (June 1955): 657.

16. Arthur A. Sloane and Fred Witney, *Labor Relations,* 4th ed. (Englewood Cliffs, N. J.: Prentice-Hall, Inc., 1981), p. 434.

17. *Boys Markets v. Retail Clerks* (398 U.S. 235).

18. Benjamin J. Taylor and Fred Witney, *Labor Relations Law*, 3rd ed. (Englewood Cliffs, N. J.: Prentice-Hall, 1979), p. 426.

19. Ibid.

20. Reynolds, p. 471.

21. Ibid.

22. Ibid., pp. 471–72.

23. Ibid.

24. Bureau of National Affairs, *Daily Labor Report,* no. 42 (March 1975): A–1.

25. Reynolds, p. 473.

26. Sumner H. Slichter, James J. Healy, and E. Robert Livernash, *The Impact of Collective Bargaining on Management* (Washington, D. C.: The Brookings Institution, 1960), p. 348.

27. Jack Barbash, "Union Response to the Hard Line," *Industrial Relations* 1 (October 1961): 25–29.

28. Joseph P. Goldberg, "Bargaining and Productivity in the Private Sector," in *Collective Bargaining and Productivity,* eds. Gerald Somers et al. (Madison, WI: Industrial Relations Research Association, 1975), pp. 15–43.

29. Slichter et al., p. 106.

30. R. B. Freeman, "Individual Mobility and Union Voice in the Labor Market," *American Economic Review* 66 (May 1976): 361–68.

31. Ibid., p. 16.

32. Rees, p. 143.

33. Bureau of National Affairs, *Basic Patterns in Union Contracts,* 9th ed. (Washington, D. C., 1979), p. 51.

34. Ibid., pp. 74–75.

35. Robert Finkle, "Management Assessment Centers," in *Handbook of Industrial and Organizational Psychology,* ed. Marvin D. Dunnette (Chicago: Rand McNally and Co., 1976), pp. 861–88.

36. Rees, pp. 145–46.

37. Peter B. Doeringer, "The Structure of Internal Labor Markets," in *Compensation and Reward Perspectives*, ed. Thomas A. Mahoney (Homewood, IL: Richard D. Irwin, Inc., 1979), p. 146.

38. Ibid., pp. 148–49.

39. Ibid., p. 149.

40. Rees, p. 146.

41. Richard N. Block, "The Impact of Seniority Provisions on the Manufacturing Quit Rate," *Industrial and Labor Relations Review* 31 (July 1978): 474–81.

42. Freeman.

43. Cary D. Thorp, Jr., "Racial Discrimination and Seniority," *Labor Law Journal,* July 1972, pp. 398–413.

44. *Franks v. Bowman Transportation Co.,* 424 U.S. 747 (1976).

45. *International Brotherhood of Teamsters v. U.S.; T.I.M.E.-D.C., Inc. v. U.S.,* U.S. Supreme Court Nos. 75–636, 75–672 (May 31, 1977).

46. Marvin J. Levine, "The Conflict Between Negotiated Seniority Provisions and Title VII of the Civil Rights Act of 1964: Recent Developments," *Labor Law Journal,* June 1978, pp. 352–63.

47. Orley Ashenfelter, "Racial Discrimination and Trade Unionism," *Journal of Political Economy* 80 (May-June 1972): 435–64.

48. D. E. Leigh, "Racial Discrimination and Labor Unions: Evidence From The NLS Sample of Middle-Aged Men," *Journal of Human Resources* 12 (Fall 1978): 568–77.

49. Jeffrey Pfeffer and Jerry Ross, "Union-Nonunion Effects on Wage and Status Attainment," *Industral Relations* 19 (Spring 1980): 140–51.

50. Jeffrey Pfeffer and Jerry Ross, "Unionized and Female Wage and Status Attainment," *Industrial Relations* 20 (Spring 1981): 179–85.

51. Reynolds, p. 492.

52. Reynolds, p. 493.

53. *American Newspaper Association v. NLRB,* 345 U.S. 110 (1953).

54. *Fibreboard Paper Products Corp. v. NLRB,* 397 U.S. 203 (1964).

55. Taylor and Witney, p. 385.

56. Bureau of National Affairs, *Basic Patterns in Union Contracts,* p. 5.

57. *John Wiley and Sons, Inc. v. Livingston,* 376 U.S. 543 (1964).

58. *NLRB v. Burns International Security Service, Inc.,* 406 U.S. 272 (1972).

59. *Howard Johnson Co. v. Hotel and Restaurant Employees International Union,* Supreme Court 73–631 (1974).

Suggested Readings

Bureau of National Affairs. *Basic Patterns in Union Contracts,* 9th ed. Washington, D. C., 1979.

Doeringer, P. B. and Piore, M. J. *Internal Labor Markets and Manpower Analysis.* Lexington, MA: Heath Lexington Books, 1971.

Rees, A. *The Economics of Trade Unions,* 2nd ed. Chicago: University of Chicago Press, 1977.

Reynolds, L. G. *Labor Economics and Labor Relations,* 7th ed. Englewood Cliffs, N. J.: Prentice-Hall, 1978.

Slichter, S. H.; Healy, J. J.; and Livernash, E. R. *The Impact of Collective Bargaining on Management.* Washington, D. C.: The Brookings Institution, 1960.

Taylor, B. J. and Witney, F. *Labor Relations Law,* 3rd ed. Englewood Cliffs, N. J.: Prentice-Hall, 1979.

Part Four
Case Study

AN EXERCISE IN NEGOTIATIONS

**Livingstone Meat Company
and
Slaughterhouse Workers of America
Local No. 731**

THE MEATPACKING INDUSTRY

An Overview

Historically, the meatpacking industry has been quite stable. Old companies such as Swift & Co., Armour & Co. and Wilson Foods Corp. operated profitably over the years. As a result of their consistently profitable performance, a number of the nation's leading meatpacking companies were taken over by conglomerates. However, in recent years, several conglomerates have dropped their meatpacking subsidiaries. According to the *Wall Street Journal,* this is because:

> The fresh meatpacking industry hasn't been reliable for several years. Rising costs and increased competition have turned profits into losses; fluctuating commodity prices have added uncertainty to the gloom. And stockholders see meatpacking units as a detriment to a company.
> (*Wall Street Journal,* 29 May 1981, p. 14)

Companies in the meatpacking industry operate on an extremely narrow profit margin—approximately 1 percent. To make a profit, it is necessary for firms to generate a high volume of sales and then control costs very carefully. Companies have little control over the price of their product since most fresh meat is sold without brand names. Since fresh-meat products are relatively homogeneous and cannot be differentiated by a brand name, meat buyers are very sensitive to price. The fresh-meat portion of the industry approximates a perfectly competitive situation since firms raising their prices can anticipate a substantial decline in sales as their customers start buying from companies able to hold the line on prices.

A Transition Period

The instability in the meatpacking industry comes from two major sources. First, unpredictable swings in hog production and a steady decline in cattle production have created serious problems. It is not possible to generate the high volume needed to make a profit with the uncertain and dwindling supply of the industry's basic raw materials—hogs and cattle.

Of particular concern to the meatpacking industry is the disarray characterizing the cattle industry. Cattle ranchers are losing money because of high interest rates, expensive grain and changing consumer tastes resulting in a substitution of pork and chicken for beef. These conditions have caused a decline in the size of cattle herds. Also, the beef that is available is more expensive. While some cattle operations will survive the currently depressed conditions in their market, a number of cattle ranchers and feed lot operators will go out of business. As a result, a long time will be required for the reduced herds to be expanded when market conditions improve.

The prospects for a prompt turnaround in the cattle industry are not bright. High beef prices caused a number of people to substitute less expensive pork and chicken. Per capita beef consumption has declined from ninety-five pounds to about eighty pounds per year. At the same time, annual per capita chicken and pork consumption has increased to about sixty-five pounds each, up from approximately fifty pounds (*Wall Street Journal,* 8 May 1981, p. 1). Even if beef prices decline, it is unlikely that per capita beef consumption will increase to its old level. As consumers have become more concerned about the presence of fat and cholesterol in their diets, they have cut down on their beef consumption. A Department of Agriculture survey revealed that appoximately two-thirds of American households have changed their diets by decreasing fat and cholesterol intake for health reasons.

It is likely that the reduced supply of cattle will persist for several years. As a result, it will be very difficult for meatpacking facilities to develop the predictable and sufficiently large supply of cattle needed for a profitable volume. The inconsistent profitability record of the meatpacking industry is likely to continue for the next few years.

A second factor contributing to the instability of the meatpacking industry is the emergence of tough new competition. Firms such as Iowa Beef Processors, Inc. and a division of Cargill, Inc. with the unpronounceable name Mbpxl, Corp. have become trendsetters in the industry. These relative newcomers have modern efficient facilities. The older companies with antiquated production facilities are having a tough time competing with these newer plants. To become more competitive, a number of the old-line meatpackers have closed some of their out-dated slaughtering facilities. While an effort has been made to relocate workers displaced by these closings, job insecurity is a growing problem for an increasing number of workers in the beef sector of the meatpacking industry.

In addition to having more efficient production facilities, the newcomers to the industry have also been innovators in the marketing area. Historically, meatpacking companies were not known for their marketing expertise. They viewed themselves as production facilities. The basic view was to produce their meat products and worry later about getting the goods sold. Some of the newer firms in the meatpacking industry have been much more innovative in their marketing. Several of these firms introduced "boxed beef." This involves a process in which a beef carcass is cut into smaller pieces, vacuum-sealed, and then shipped to supermarkets and butcher shops. "Boxed beef" has been widely accepted in the marketplace because it is more convenient and requires less butchering at the retail level. The old-line firms do not have the production facilities to produce "boxed beef" at the present time. As a result, they are having a tough time competing with some of the more aggressive firms in the industry.

Another factor contributing to the success of these new competitors in the meatpacking industry is their approach to labor relations. Historically, the meatpacking industry has been highly unionized. While organized, the newer firms have taken a very tough stance with their unions. These firms have been willing to take long, bitter, and sometimes violent strikes as part of their labor-relations programs. While the labor unrest has been costly to the firms, these factors have kept labor costs approximately 40 percent lower than those of the old-line meatpackers. It has been estimated that the largest newcomer to the industry pays $5.00 to $8.00 per hour per worker less for wages and fringe benefits than the established companies pay to their union workers (*Wall Street Journal,* 29 May 1981, p. 27).

This hard-line approach to labor issues appears to be spreading to some of the older firms in the industry. Montfort, Inc. closed its Greeley, Colorado, facility after a long strike because high labor costs made the facility noncompetitive. This plant reopened two years later on much less costly terms newly established by the company. At another one of its facilities, this same firm entered into a labor agreement with a union which traditionally represents sailors on ocean-going vessels. Labor unions have alleged that this constitutes a "sweetheart" relationship designed to freeze out the union traditionally representing workers in the meatpacking industry. Another old-line company demanded from the union a new, lower-cost labor agreement as a precondition for reopening two noncompetitive plants.

It appears that the meatpacking industry will remain highly unionized. However, conflict between labor and management is likely to intensify as firms try to decrease their labor costs and improve their competitive position by taking a harder line on labor issues.

A Look Ahead

In years to come, the meatpacking industry will look much different than it does today. A number of the larger companies are beginning to take actions to move them away from the high-volume, low-profit part of the industry subject to cyclical fluctuations. To do this, firms are expanding their product lines to include more high-profit processed meats. Luncheon meats, sausage, cooked hams and wieners are examples of the processed meats that will come to be an increasing proportion of the product lines of companies in the meatpacking industry. These lines will be expanded while fresh meat operations will be cut back.

The development of a more balanced (for both fresh and processed meats) product line will be both time-consuming and expensive. While some of the larger firms will be able to survive the transition, others will be forced out of business. The future of the meatpacking industry is highly uncertain, especially for smaller firms.

Smaller companies unwilling or unable to expand their product lines will have to continue to operate on narrow profit margins and face uncertain supplies of raw materials. Firms staying in the fresh-meat business will be forced to become more efficient. If the companies fail to do so, their prospects for survival are not particularly good.

The changes occurring in the product market will have serious implications for labor relations in the meatpacking industry. It can be anticipated that companies will be pressing to hold the line on labor costs in order to help their profit position. As long as some of the new companies entering the market successfully lower their labor costs by taking a tough stance with the unions, pressure is on the other companies to do likewise. Resistance to union wage demands is likely to intensify. Similarly, company demands to eliminate restrictive work rules are likely to increase.

From the unions' perspective, the changes likely to occur in the industry will create a wide range of problems. Union leaders understand the problems that will confront the industry. At the same time, the changes going on in the industry are creating serious problems for the union's rank-and-file membership. Inflation is creating pressures for large wage demands. The closing of antiquated plants and the introduction of new product lines is creating a high degree of anxiety among the rank and file. Job security is becoming a major concern. Pressure from the rank and file is also being felt to resist company efforts to increase the speed of the production line in the fresh meatpacking facilities.

This is not intended to be an exhaustive list of the problems faced by workers in the meatpacking industry. The point is that the workers are experiencing problems that will cost their employers a lot of money to rectify. At the same time, their employers are facing financial problems requiring them to lower labor costs. As a result of these conflicting problems, it is reasonable to expect widespread labor difficulties in the meatpacking industry for the foreseeable future.

LIVINGSTONE MEAT COMPANY

Development of the Company

Livingstone Meat Company was started in 1932 by the Livingstone family. The family had been in the ranching business in eastern Colorado since the 1880s. Because of the depressed economic conditions of the early 1930s, no reliable outlet was available for the family's cattle. Therefore, the Livingstone started slaughtering their own cattle and selling sides of beef to Denver area grocery stores and butcher shops.

As the new business started to grow, Ross Livingstone, the family's youngest son, had to devote his full attention to its operation. While the original impetus was to develop a reliable outlet for the family's cattle, the company soon started turning a profit. By the start of World War II, Livingstone Meat Company was generating greater revenues than the family's ranching operations.

In 1939, the company landed a contract to supply sides of beef to the United States Army. Also, the company picked up contracts to provide beef sides to two large grocery store chains starting to do business in the growing Denver metropolitan area. The little plant and small work force comprising Livingstone Meat Company were no longer adequate to meet the demand for the company's slaughtered beef.

It became apparent in 1939 that the expansion of the physical plant and work force was beyond the financial means of the Livingstone family. Two million dollars were needed to build a new mechanized plant. The family decided to sell two million shares of stock for $1.00 per share. The stock was sold to a small number of family members, friends, and Denver area investors. Ross Livingstone was made president of the company.

World War II was good for the Livingstone Meat Company. Government contracts grew and so did the company. From approximately $1 million in sales in 1941, revenues grew to $17 million in 1945. Along with this growth, the work force expanded. Between 1941 and 1945, the number of employees grew from 65 to 220. The company's expansion was facilitated by the adoption of the newest equipment and procedures available to increase the efficiency of the firm's operation.

After World War II, the company's sales force had problems making the transition from a wartime to a peacetime economy. Government contracts declined. However, the expansion of sales to civilian customers did not occur fast enough to take up the slack. Sales, revenues, and profits all declined. A number of workers had to be laid off. Fortunately, the problems did not last very long. By early 1948, the company's sales were almost back to the wartime level. From this time until the mid-1970s, Livingstone Meat Company grew slowly but steadily.

In 1962, the plant built in 1939 was replaced with a new, larger facility. In order not to dilute the firm's ownership, the new plant was built with long-term debt rather than another sale of stock. The new facility incorporated the most technologically advanced design and equipment available. The plant's design helped keep production costs down and allowed the company a slight price advantage. Since Livingstone Meat Company was selling sides of beef that are difficult to differentiate from the competition and which are not sold with a brand name, the price advantage provided the company a distinct competitive advantage.

From 1962 to the mid-1970s, the success of Livingstone Meat Company was linked to the growth of the Rocky Mountain region. The company's major customers were several large supermarket chains. These companies would buy sides of beef and then butcher the sides into smaller cuts and ground beef. The beef cuts were sold through the chains' retail outlets. As the Rocky Mountain region grew, so did the number of retail grocery outlets and the demand for Livingstone beef.

In 1969, Ross Livingstone retired. He was replaced as president by Victor Webster. While various members of the Livingstone family still owned stock in the company, the family was no longer involved in the active management of the firm. However, since they owned a majority of the outstanding stock, they were still quite interested in the company. The company's stock represented a major component of their wealth and the dividends a major source of their income. Webster wanted to keep family members satisfied. He did not want the family to sell their ownership in the company to interests who might not be as hospitable to Webster and his managerial team.

The Changing Scene

Perhaps success came too easily to the management of Livingstone Meat Company. Except for the couple of difficult years right after World War II, the company had grown steadily and had been profitable. However, by the mid-1970s, the meatpacking industry was starting to see a number of changes in terms of technology; products; consumer tastes; and new, aggressive competition.

Victor Webster had been with the company since 1952. He knew everything there was to know about Livingstone Meat Company. Unfortunately, he and his executive staff were not very observant. They did not pick up on the number of trends emerging in the meatpacking industry. As a result of this, the company's "track record" deteriorated significantly. While the company generated a profit, the profits had been very small in recent years.

As indicated by the company's balance sheets and income and earnings statements (Exhibit I), the company's experience has been rather inconsistent in recent years. The company also started diverting funds that had, in part, gone into plant and equipment into short-term, high-yield treasury bills and money-market certificates. As a result, the plant and equipment were no longer as technologically advanced as they had been.

The Future

Sales and revenues were projected to increase slightly. This was because of rapid population growth in the Rocky Mountain region (see Exhibit I). However, profits were expected to fluctuate widely because of widely varying cattle prices and uncertain cattle supplies. The company was considering three alternatives intended to improve its profitability and lessen its dependence on the volatile beef industry. One option under consideration was to enter the "boxed beef" business. At that time, Livingstone Meat Company only sold sides of beef at the wholesale level. As a result, its customers were limited to companies with butchering facilities. "Boxed beef" would allow Livingstone Meat Company to sell to a much larger number of wholesale and retail establishments since on-site butchering was not necessary. The equipment needed to enter this new business and the plant expansion to house the new operations had a price tag of $7.5 million.

If the company entered the "boxed beef" business, it still faced the problems of uncertain beef supplies, rising beef prices and changing consumer tastes. Also, profit margins were only slightly higher on "boxed beef" products. The second option currently under consideration by company management was to acquire pork-processing and prepared-meat (luncheon meats, wieners, and sausage) operations. Such acquisitions would buffer the company from the vagaries of the beef industry and give the company product lines with higher profit margins. However, these options were very expensive. The company estimated it would cost approximately $6 million to get into the pork business and another $7 million to start marketing processed meat products.

Management considered the reorientation of the firm necessary for its long-run success. However, funding the new ventures was likely to be a problem. The firm's relatively low earnings and poor dividend record made the prospects of a stock sale rather dismal. Since the firm had a relatively large amount of long-term debt, debt financing could be problematic. Even if debt financing were available, it would be at very high interest rates. Livingstone Meat Company would have to "tighten up" its operation so that additional profits could be put into the revitalization program. Otherwise, funds needed to insure the long-run survival of the firm might not be available.

LABOR-MANAGEMENT RELATIONS AT LIVINGSTONE MEAT COMPANY

The Evolution of the Relationship

The Livingstone Meat Company was organized by the Slaughterhouse Workers of America, Local 731, in 1940. Ross Livingstone was making too much money at that time to risk any interruptions because of labor unrest. When the union's international representative told Ross Livingstone that a majority of the company's employees had signed authorization cards, Livingstone verified the claim and then agreed to recognize the union. Within a month of the union's recognition, the initial contract was signed.

This amicable start to the collective-bargaining relationship persisted for several years. However, the downturn in the firm's business after World War II did more than hurt its financial position. During this time period, the workers were experiencing their own financial crunch because of rapidly rising prices and dwindling purchasing power. Union demands for higher wages were met with stiff opposition from the company. At the same time, the company was laying workers off because of the downturn in business. Resistance to the union's pressure for higher wages and decreasing job security led to an eleven-week strike during 1946. The collective-bargaining relationship between Livingstone Meat Company and Local 731 was never the same after this dispute was settled.

The union and management officials never seemed to be as cordial or as trusting after the strike was over. Despite the change in the relationship, the company and Local 731 negotiated a series of contracts over the years without another strike. The management of Livingstone Meat Company was committed to offering the same wage and fringe benefit package as the larger firms in the meatpacking industry in the Denver area. As long as the company maintained this philosophy, the union was satisfied. The company was able to do so until the mid-1970s.

The handling of grievances also changed after the 1946 strike. Before the lengthy dispute, most grievances were handled informally on the shop floor. Rarely was a formal grievance filed. Also, prior to the 1946 strike, the parties never had a grievance go to arbitration. After the strike, the parties relied more heavily on the labor agreement's formal grievance procedure. Every year, they could plan on several cases ending up in arbitration.

It was not as if the relationship between Local 731 and Livingstone Meat Company was rife with open conflict. It was not. The parties did, however, have a more difficult time resolving disagreements through informal discussions than they did in the past. Instead, they developed more of an "arm's-length" relationship in which they relied on formal negotiations, the grievance procedure, and arbitration to resolve their differences.

The More Recent Relationship

In more recent years, labor problems mounted at the Livingstone Meat Company. As can be seen by reviewing the company's financial records (Exhibit I), the firm was very profitable four years ago. Then it had two years when it barely turned a profit. The last contract was renegotiated two years ago. The union had proposed major changes in the wage-and-benefit package. However, the company claimed it could not afford to improve the existing contract substantially. The parties bargained for several months, but when the old agreement expired, it was extended to allow more time for negotiations. When three additional weeks of bargaining failed to yield an acceptable contract, a strike vote was taken. The union's rank and file voted unanimously to strike.

The ensuing strike lasted four weeks. It became apparent to the local's leadership that management was not going to improve its offer. Also, there were rumors that the company might permanently shut down if the strike were not ended soon. Given that most of the rank and file did not have skills allowing them to find comparably paying jobs elsewhere in the Denver area, the union decided to accept the company's last offer. This contract is presented as Exhibit II.

The new contract was very similar to the preceding one. There were no major improvements in fringe benefits and only small wage increases were granted. Across-the-board wage increases of 5 percent and 3 percent were paid in the first and second years of the contract, respectively.

While a majority of the rank and file voted to ratify the agreement, most workers were not very happy with the contract, their union's leadership, or management. Once the employees were back on the job after the strike, the high level of worker unrest became quite apparent. A sharp increase in the number of grievances filed was observed. There were also several civil-rights complaints and NLRB charges filed. Additionally, state and federal agencies responsible for overseeing the plant's sanitation and for monitoring the slaughtering process started receiving anonymous complaints about the company's procedures. There was also an increase in tardiness and absenteeism that some management officials attributed to the general level of dissatisfaction with the new labor agreement.

The union had problems of its own as a result of the new contract. Approximately nine months after the agreement was ratified, the local's officers stood for reelection. In the past, they would not have been challenged. However, because of the way the last round of negotiations was handled, each of the incumbent union officials had opposition in the election. A group of younger members, many of whom were female and hispanic, ran their own slate of candidates. While this insurgent group failed to unseat the local's president, vice-president, and secretary/treasurer, the incumbents' margin of victory was very narrow. The insurgent group did elect two new members to the local's negotiating team, Juanita Alverez and Mike Benson.

From the union's perspective, the last round of negotiations created a situation that could be likened to a good news/bad news joke. The good news was that interest in the local's affairs and attendance at union meetings increased sharply. The bad news was that the increased interest led to widespread unrest in Local 731. Even some of the members who supported the local's leadership let it be known that they were giving the union one more chance. If the union's leadership didn't deliver a good contract next time, something drastic would happen.

The Situation Leading up to the Current Negotiations

The labor relations scene in the Denver area and in the meatpacking industry during the year prior to the upcoming negotiations was very interesting, and, from the union's perspective, quite unsettling. The following events had taken place:

1. A local manufacturing facility replaced its striking employees. It was anticipated that the new workers would move to decertify the union in the near future.
2. The largest meatpacking firm in the area closed its Denver plant and consolidated its operations at other facilities because of a lengthy strike.
3. The management of a medium-sized meatpacking company purchased the firm from its parent organization. The union tried to have the sale enjoined by the courts contending the sale was designed to undermine the union. The company had told its employees they could keep their jobs but with wages and benefits approximately $4.00 per hour less than those stipulated in the labor agreement. The court refused to grant the injunction. In turn, the union tried to block the sale by filing unfair labor practice charges with the NLRB. This effort also proved unsuccessful.
4. As discussed earlier, the two largest meatpacking firms in the nation, although unionized, had labor costs averaging 40 percent less than most other unionized firms. These lower labor costs gave the industry leaders a competitive edge in the product market. One of these firms was just starting to market its products more aggressively in the Rocky Mountain region.

In sum, greater competition in the product market and a more aggressive antilabor stance by a growing number of firms in the Denver area were the two factors dominating the scene during the year prior to the upcoming negotiations between Livingstone Meat Company and Local 731. Most of the company's top management did not want to confront the union with the "strong arm" tactics used by some of the other firms in the industry. While the relationship between Livingstone Meat Company and Local 731 was not ideal, it had worked relatively well over the years. However, management realized a tough stance in the upcoming negotiations might be necessary for the firm to remain competitive. Management was also concerned about the need to get involved with "boxed beef," processed meats, or pork processing. As previously discussed, these proposals were very costly. Also, the firm's financial track record made a stock sale or the use of long-term debt unlikely alternative ways to finance the firm's needed expansion. The company's failure to put money back into plant and equipment for the last three years exacerbated the firm's problems. Even if the company did not expand, funds would have to be put into plant and equipment that had been neglected in recent years. Top management was concerned that higher labor costs could stand in its way when trying to revitalize the firm.

The union, while understanding the company's financial plight and competitive problems, had difficulties of its own. As part of its early preparation for the upcoming negotiations, a review of the existing contract was made. The following list summarizes the major fringe benefits found in the current agreement:

- Group life insurance—$25,000 of term insurance with double indemnity for accidental death. The company pays half ($5.00) of the premium and

the employee pays the other half ($5.00 per month). The employees' portion is automatically deducted from their paychecks.
- Hospital and surgical benefit plan—The employer contributes $40.00 per month to this plan. Cost of individual coverage is $60.00 per month and family coverage is $85.00 monthly. Three-quarters of the rank-and-file union membership are married and subscribe to family coverage. The difference between the employer's contribution and the type of coverage ($20.00 and $45.00 per month for single and family coverage, respectively) is automatically deducted from the employee's paycheck.
- Sick pay—The agreement provides employees with compensation when they miss work due to illness or injury. The amount of sick pay available to employees is a function of their length of service.

Completed years of service	Number of days paid sick leave
0–5	3
6–10	6
11–20	10
21 or more	15

Sick leave is not allowed to accumulate; it must be used during the calendar year. Days not used are lost. To qualify for sick leave pay, the employee must provide a doctor's excuse.
- Retirement—A total of 6 percent of an employee's wages are put into a retirement account managed by a large insurance company. The employer contributes 3 percent and the employee contributes 3 percent which is automatically deducted from his or her weekly paycheck.
- Vacations—The labor agreement contains the following vacation schedule:

Less than 1 year	No paid vacation
1 to 5 years	1 week
6 to 10 years	2 weeks
11 to 15 years	3 weeks
16 to 25 years	4 weeks
Over 25 years	5 weeks

- Holidays—Under the existing contract, employees receive the following paid holidays: New Year's Day, Memorial Day, Fourth of July, Labor Day, Thanksgiving Day, and Christmas Day.
- Pay for other time not worked—Each day employees receive two ten (10)-minute rest periods. Employees are compensated for wages lost due to jury duty. Two days' funeral leave is provided.

This analysis does not provide an exhaustive review of the labor agreement. But the agreement did demonstrate to the leadership of Local 731 that the contract was deficient relative to other unionized firms. To a large degree, the problem was attributable to the poor contract negotiated two years ago. Until that time, the agreement was quite similar to other unionized firms. While recognizing that Livingstone Meat Company had financial problems, the union's leadership believed it was necessary to improve the wage-and-fringe-benefit package during the upcoming negotiations.

Political problems within Local 731 were also likely to affect the next round of bargaining. The younger, more aggressive members of the union's bargaining team were very upset about the procedures for allocating overtime and the heavy reliance on seniority. The older union leadership and its supporters were satisfied with the way things were handled now. The factional splits within the union could make contract ratification very difficult.

The local's leadership had heard rumors that some members of the management negotiating team were ready to play "hardball" with the union. Rumors were spreading that the company was planning to precipitate a strike and then replace the strikers with workers willing to accept lower wages and less costly benefits. While it was not possible to track down the source of the rumors, they were plausible in light of the labor unrest elsewhere in the meatpacking industry.

The Upcoming Round of Negotiations

The stage was set. Both union and management bargaining teams were appointed and preparation for negotiations was under way. A general feeling of apprehension was experienced by both sides. Management negotiators believed the financial future of the company was at stake. The union was rife with internal dissension. The union's negotiating team believed it was necessary to negotiate a contract attractive to a wide range of the rank and file. Failure to do so could intensify the union's political unrest. While there was no way to determine what would happen if an acceptable contract was not negotiated, none of the options was particularly attractive to the union's older leadership.

Ron Martinez, president of Local 731, had to meet with Dan Laird, the company's vice-president for industrial relations, to schedule the first bargaining session, at which the parties would exchange their lists of initial demands.

EXHIBIT I
Financial Records for Livingstone Meat Company

Livingstone Meat Company Statements of Income and Retained Earnings

	Four years ago	Three years ago	Two years ago	Last year before negotiations
Net sales	37,917,420	42,110,680	43,222,890	48,172,368
Costs and Expenses:				
Costs of products sold	27,811,180	38,901,700	39,910,270	43,720,990
Selling, administrative and general	2,291,700	2,643,480	2,900,010	3,280,610
Total costs	30,102,880	41,545,180	42,810,280	47,001,600
Earnings before interest and taxes	7,814,540	565,500	412,610	1,170,768
Interest expense	131,650	159,000	145,000	172,000
Earnings before taxes	7,682,890	412,500	267,610	998,768
Taxes	3,830,460	180,270	110,750	391,000
Net income	3,852,430	232,230	156,860	607,768
Disposition of net income				
Dividends to stockholders	1,600,000	0	0	150,000
Addition to retained earnings	2,252,430	232,230	156,860	457,768
Per share of common stock (2,000,000 shares)				
Earnings per share	$1.92	$0.12	$0.08	$0.30
Dividend per share	$0.80	0	0	0.075

Livingstone Meat Company Balance Sheets for the Last Four Years Preceding Negotiations

	Four years ago	Three years ago	Two years ago	Last year before negotiations
ASSETS				
Current assets				
Cash	2,870,160	3,024,100	3,403,980	3,791,670
Liquid assets (e.g., C.D's and money market funds, including interest income)	0	612,000	1,123,000	2,048,000
Net accounts receivable	2,425,010	2,551,830	2,836,510	3,117,280
Inventories	1,109,500	1,305,310	1,373,460	1,432,770
Prepaid expenses	707,940	745,190	828,110	920,000
Total current assets	7,112,610	8,238,430	9,565,060	11,309,720
Fixed assets				
Land	185,000	189,000	193,000	200,000
Building and improvements (net of depreciation)	3,054,860	2,841,650	2,726,820	2,350,450
Machinery and equipment (net of depreciation)	4,914,740	4,572,440	4,388,440	3,840,100
Other	41,200	43,000	43,500	50,000
Total fixed assets	8,195,800	7,646,090	7,351,760	6,440,550
Total assets	15,308,410	15,884,520	16,916,820	17,750,270
LIABILITIES				
Current liabilities				
Accounts payable	2,219,600	3,174,850	3,285,100	3,749,640
Notes payable	950,000	950,000	950,000	950,000
Accrued wages	324,500	345,220	351,600	375,730
Accrued taxes	1,081,000	424,150	410,450	983,150
Total current liabilities	4,575,100	4,894,220	4,997,150	6,058,520
Long-term liabilities				
Long-term debt	4,171,210	4,195,970	4,968,480	4,282,790
Common stock (2,000,000 shares @ $1.00/share)	2,000,000	2,000,000	2,000,000	2,000,000
Retained earnings	4,562,100	4,794,330	4,951,190	5,408,960
Total long-term liabilities	10,733,310	10,990,300	11,919,670	11,691,750
Total liabilities	15,308,410	15,884,520	16,916,820	17,750,270

Livingstone Meat Company Projected Sales

This year	$50,340,124
Next year	$52,857,713
Year after next	$55,500,598

EXHIBIT II
*Agreement
between
Livingstone Meat Company
and
Slaughterhouse Workers of
America, Local 731*

This agreement is entered into by Livingstone Meat Company (hereinafter referred to as the "Employer") and the Slaughterhouse Workers of America, Local 731 (hereinafter referred to as the "Union"). The Employer and Union agree to be bound by the following provisions covering wages and working conditions:

ARTICLE 1

Recognition. 1.01 The Employer recognizes the Union as the sole collective bargaining representative for all production employees of the Employer, including hourly paid clean-up employees, truck drivers, and dockmen at its plant located at Denver, Colorado, but *excluding* the yardmen; office, professional, and maintenance employees; meat peddlers; shipping and receiving clerks; engineers; salesmen; buyers; clean-up employees of independent contractors; foremen; assistant foremen; superintendents; assistant superintendents; and all other supervisors within the meaning of the National Labor Relations Act.

ARTICLE 2

Management. 2.01 The management of the plant and the direction of the working forces, including the right to hire, transfer, promote, maintain discipline and efficiency, suspend, discharge, and discipline for proper cause, and the right to relieve employees from duty because of lack of work or for other legitimate reasons is vested exclusively in the Employer, except as otherwise provided in this Agreement.

ARTICLE 3

Discharge. 3.01 No employee covered by this Agreement shall be suspended, demoted, or dismissed without just and sufficient cause. Sufficient cause for discharge shall include, among other reasons, persistent tardiness or absence, dishonesty, negligence, incompetence, insubordination, intoxication while on duty, refusal to perform any reasonable work, service, or labor when required to do so by the Employer.

ARTICLE 4

No Discrimination. 4.01 The Employer and the Union recognize that they are required by law not to discriminate against any person with regard to employment or union membership because of his or her race, creed, religion, color, sex, age, national origin, or ancestry and hereby declare their acceptance and support of such laws. This shall apply to hiring, placement, upgrading, transfer, or demotion, recruitment, advertising, or solicitation for employment, training during employment, rates of pay, or other forms of compensation, selection for training including apprenticeship, lay-off or termination, application for, and admission to Union membership.

ARTICLE 5

Hours of Work and Overtime. 5.01 Double time (2×) shall be paid for all work actually performed on Sunday. Overtime at the rate of time and one-half (1½×) the employee's base hourly rate of pay for the classification of work shall be paid under the following conditions:

(a) For all hours actually worked in excess of eight (8) hours per day, exclusive of the lunch period.
(b) For all hours in excess of forty (40) hours per week, exclusive of the lunch periods.
(c) For all work performed on Saturday provided the employees have worked all hours available during the work week. Employees absent because of illness of the employee, death in the immediate family or other excused absences will be considered as having worked for the purposes of qualifying for the above overtime pay for hours worked on Saturday. Probationary employees will not receive time and one-half (1½×) for Saturday as such.

5.02 It is understood and agreed, however, that overtime penalties will not be paid twice for daily and weekly overtime hours worked.

5.03 Employees must give the Employer at least twenty-four (24) hours of notice that they will not be able to work any overtime the next day or on a Saturday should the Employer determine that overtime on a Saturday must be worked.

ARTICLE 6

Reporting for Work. 6.01 On Saturdays and on callback after lay-off, whenever employees are scheduled to report for work and have been notified to report for work, as above set forth, and upon arrival at the plant find no work available, such employee shall be paid for two (2) hours at the hourly rate for his job. If the employees begin work but work less than two (2) hours, through no fault of their own, such employees shall be paid for a minimum of two (2) hours.

6.02 The provisions of this Article shall not apply in any workweek during which normal plant operations are restricted due to causes beyond the reasonable control of the Employer such as acts of God, stoppages of work by any Union, fire, flood, or emergency causing damage to or breakdown of plant equipment, machinery, or other facilities.

ARTICLE 7

Job Classification and Hourly Rates of Pay. 7.01 Job classifications and hourly rates of pay shall be as set forth in Appendix "A," attached hereto and by this reference made a part hereof.

7.02 Any new employee who is hired for a classified job and who is qualified by experience shall receive the classified rate for said job from the date of employment.

ARTICLE 8

Night Premium. 8.01 Employees whose regularly scheduled shift commences between the hours of 1:00 P.M. and 4:00 A.M. shall receive a shift premium of six cents (6¢) per hour for their entire shift.

8.02 Employees whose regularly schedules shift commences between the hours of 4:00 A.M. and 1:00 P.M. are considered day-shift employees and will not receive any shift premium. It is understood that day-shift employees working overtime are not entitled to shift premium.

ARTICLE 9

Fringe Benefit Payments. 9.01 The schedule of wages in Appendix "A" includes compensation for the following fringe items:
(a) Pay for time spent changing clothes.
(b) Pay for furnishing clothes.
(c) Pay for furnishing knives and other materials.
(d) Pay for adjustment of interplant inequities.

9.02 Tools will be prepared and sharpened on the Employer's time.

9.03 Employees must provide the following equipment: safety toe boots, safety helmets, and gloves.

Employees must also provide all the knives needed to perform their assigned functions. Employees are required to wear all required safety equipment. Failure to do so may subject the employee to disciplinary action.

9.04 Employees, without regard to their classification, shall be required to perform any labor or render any services in or about or in connection with the Employer's business provided that when a man is working on more than one (1) classification in a day, the highest classification shall apply for that day.

9.05 Employees now drawing more than the rate set forth in this Agreement for the job which they are performing shall receive an increase over their present rate of pay equivalent to the increase given to their classification of work in this Agreement.

ARTICLE 10

Rest Periods. 10.01 All employees under this Agreement shall be allowed a ten (10)-minute rest period in the morning and a ten (10)-minute rest period in the afternoon. An employee who works in excess of twelve (12) hours in any one (1) day will be allowed an additional ten (10)-minute rest period. Any employee who works seven (7) hours in any one (1) day will be allowed two (2) ten (10)-minute rest periods.

ARTICLE 11

Holidays. 11.01 The following days are recognized as holidays under this Agreement: New Year's Day, Memorial Day, Fourth of July, Labor Day, Thanksgiving Day, and Christmas Day.

11.02 In the event any of the above-mentioned holidays should fall on Sunday, the following Monday shall be observed as the official holiday. The listed holidays will be celebrated on the days celebrated by the federal government.

11.03 Probationary employees are not qualified to receive holiday pay for unworked hours on said holidays or premium pay for work performed on a holiday.

11.04 All regular full-time employees covered by this Agreement shall receive eight (8) hours of compensation at their straight-time hourly rate of pay for each of the holidays set forth above, including holidays falling on Saturday, provided they report for work and work all hours of work available on the regularly scheduled workday before the holiday and on the regularly scheduled workday after the holiday; provided, however, that employees absent because of illness of the employee, death in the immediate family, or absence excused by the immediate supervisor will receive holiday pay.

11.05 Employees laid off for lack of work the week prior to a holiday week and recalled during the holiday week will receive holiday pay.

11.06 Further, an employee will not receive holiday pay unless he performed work for which he receives pay during the pay period in which the holiday occurs.

11.07 Employees who work on Memorial Day will be compensated for hours worked at time and one-half ($1\frac{1}{2} \times$) their hourly rate of pay in addition to the eight (8) hours of compensation at the regular straight-time rate that the employee shall receive for an unworked holiday.

11.08 Employees who work on New Year's Day, Fourth of July, Labor Day, Thanksgiving Day, or Christmas Day will be compensated for hours worked at double time ($2\times$) their hourly rate of pay in addition to the eight (8) hours of compensation at the straight-time rate that the employee shall receive for an unworked holiday.

Holiday Hours Unworked and Worked for the Purpose of Computing Weekly Overtime.
(a) Hours paid for but not worked on a holiday (except holidays falling on Saturday) will be counted as hours worked for the purpose of computing overtime in excess of forty (40) hours in a work week.
(b) In the event an employee is required to work on a holiday, only hours worked in excess of eight (8) will be counted as hours worked for the purpose of computing weekly overtime, as credit for eight (8) hours has already been allowed in paragraph (a).

ARTICLE 12

Vacations. 12.01 All regular, full-time employees covered by this Agreement who have been in the continuous service of the Employer for a period of one (1) year to five (5) years shall be entitled to a vacation of one (1) week with pay. All regular full-time employees who have been in the continuous service of the Employer for a period of six (6) to ten (10) years shall be entitled to a vacation of two (2) weeks with pay. All regular full-time employees who have been in the continuous service of the Employer for a period of eleven (11) to fifteen (15) years shall be entitled to a vacation of three (3) weeks with pay. All regular full-time employees who have been in the continuous service of the Employer for a period of sixteen (16) to twenty-five (25) years shall be entitled to a vacation of four (4) weeks with pay. All regular full-time employees who have been in the continuous service of the Employer for a period of twenty-five (25) years or more shall be entitled to a vacation of five (5) weeks with pay. Employees are not entitled to a paid vacation until they have completed one (1) full year of service.

12.02 Employees begin to qualify for vacation in accord with the establishment of plant seniority.

12.03 Vacations will be scheduled by department, by plant seniority, and in accordance with the needs of the department. Employees will be allowed to schedule vacations in June, July, and August the same as any other months. The Employer reserves the right to schedule vacations so as not to interfere with the efficient operation of the plant.

ARTICLE 13

Continuous Maintenance of Plant Property. 13.01 In the event of work stoppage or strike, the Union agrees to permit such members of the Union or outside maintenance or mechanical workers to maintain the machinery and general property of the Employer in working condition, but such employees will not be used for production work.

ARTICLE 14

Seniority. 14.01 Seniority shall be determined by the length of service in the plant or in a department. There shall be separate department and plant seniority lists.

14.02 *Regular Full-Time Employees.* A regular full-time employee shall be considered as an employee who has completed thirty (30) working days within a sixty (60) calendar day period. When the employee has qualified as a regular full-time employee, his name will be placed on the seniority list and his seniority will date from the date on which the employee was hired within the sixty (60)-day period in which he acquires seniority.

14.03 *Probationary Employees.* A probationary employee is an employee who is not qualified as a regular full-time employee. Probationary employees may be discharged at the discretion of the Employer without recourse by either the employee or the Union. Probationary employees shall be laid off before any regular full-time employees are laid off for lack of work.

14.04 *Department Seniority.* Department seniority is defined as the number of years, months, and days a regular full-time employee has been employed in a department.

14.05 *Plant Seniority.* Plant seniority is defined as the number of years, months, and days from the date an employee qualifies as a regular full-time employee and remains in the continuous employment of the Employer in accordance with paragraph 14.02 above.

14.06 *Posting Seniority Lists.* The Employer will post on the bulletin boards on January 1 and July 1 of each year a seniority list by plant seniority and by department seniority (showing the current job award) of all regular full-time employees and furnish one (1) copy of each to the Union and one (1) copy of each to the Chief Shop Steward.

14.07 *Job Bidding.* When a vacancy occurs in a department or a new job classification is established, notice shall be posted on the bulletin board and employees not employed in the department where the vacancy or new job exists will also be given an opportunity to bid. Employees shall have forty-eight (48) hours, exclusive of Saturdays, Sundays, and holidays, in which to declare their desire to be considered for such vacancy or new job. Departmental seniority shall be established as of the date shown on the job posting. In the event two (2) or more employees have the same departmental seniority, plant seniority shall prevail. Employees who have departmental seniority will be given first (1st) consideration to fill the vacancy or new job.

14.08 In the event no employee in the department expresses a desire to fill such vacancy or new job, then, and in that event, consideration will be given to employees who have signed the posting on a plant-wide basis to fill the job vacancy or new job. The employee with the greatest seniority will fill the job vacancy or new job.

14.09 The employee who is awarded the job shall have a reasonable time to learn the job. (Reasonable time to learn the job will be determined by the Employer.) If after such reasonable time he is not able to perform the duties of the job satisfactorily, he shall be returned to the last job he previously held, and the employee with the next highest seniority who bids for the job shall be given an opportunity to fill the job.

14.10 When no employee in the plant with seniority has indicated a desire to fill such vacancy, and the Employer hires an employee from outside the plant, his plant and department seniority shall commence as provided in paragraph 14.02 of this Article. If the Employer transfers an employee from another department, his department seniority shall start as of the date of transfer.

14.11 *Temporary Vacancies.* The Employer will fill a temporary vacancy of more than one (1) day on the basis of seniority. The Employer has the right to transfer employees in order to fill vacancies without regard to seniority on a temporary basis for one (1) day or part of a day, when such vacancy is caused by absence of employees due to, among other reasons, illness, injury, or leave of absence.

14.12 *Application of Seniority.* Department seniority shall be applied in determining layoffs and rehiring. In the event of a department layoff, meaning that the employees with the least departmental seniority are the first laid off in a reduction of the number of employees in a department, an employee with more than one (1) year of plant seniority shall have the right to displace any one (1) employee in the plant with lesser plant seniority at the rate for such job, provided he can perform the work of such junior employee because that job is a semiskilled, or skilled job, then he shall have the right to displace any unskilled employee in the plant with lesser plant seniority, at the rate of such job, provided such employee is junior to him and provided he can perform the job to the satisfaction of the Employer, or accept the layoff. An employee with less than one (1) year of plant seniority who is laid off shall have the right to displace the employee in the plant with the least seniority at the rate for such job, provided he is qualified to perform such job or accept the layoff. An employee exercising his right to displace another employee by plant seniority must do so in all other departments of the plant before he can displace another employee in the department from which he was laid off. (The layoff procedure will be handled by the designated management representative.)

14.13 An employee displaced because of job elimination shall be handled in accord with layoff procedure of this section.

14.14 When work in the department in which laid-off employees or employees working in other departments who were affected by the lay-off requires additional employees, then the employees on lay-off or who are working in other departments shall be returned to their regular departments by departmental seniority. These vacancies shall not be subject to the bidding procedure.

14.15 *Termination of Seniority.* Seniority shall terminate for any of the following reasons:
(a) Voluntary quitting.
(b) Discharge for cause.
(c) Failure to report to work after a lay-off within three (3) working days after receiving a written registered notice to return to work to the last address furnished the Employer by the employee. The Employer agrees that if an employee complies with the provisions of this paragraph but is unable to

return to work within the three (3) working days herein provided for good and sufficient reasons, it will grant an additional three (3) days for reporting. The employee, however, must notify the Employer within the three (3)-working-day period of his inability to return to work within that period. An employee laid off due to reduction of force must keep the Employer advised of any change in address by means of written notice to the Plant Manager.
- (d) Absence from work for a period of three (3) working days when such absence has not been reported by the employee to the Employer.
- (e) Absence from work for any reason (except occupational or nonoccupational illness or injury) for a period in excess of six (6) calendar months.
- (f) Employees accepting supervisory positions with the Employer for a period in excess of three (3) months.
- (g) Employees accepting full-time Union positions for a period in excess of one (1) term of office.

ARTICLE 15

Breakdowns. 15.01 If a breakdown occurs and more than forty-five (45) minutes are lost, the Employer shall have the right to assign any or all of the men to other jobs in or about the plant for the duration of the breakdown.

15.02 It is agreed by the Union that every precaution shall be used to prevent damage to the hides, carcass, or pelts.

ARTICLE 16

Paycheck. 16.01 The check with which the Employer pays the employees shall include a statement of all deductions, hourly rates, hours worked, straight-time and overtime. Employees shall be paid by Friday of each week for the work week ending the previous Sunday. Paychecks will be available from noon on, or in accord with current practice. If an employee's check is short five dollars ($5.00) or more, the Employer will pay him on request by cash or check or the amount the check is short otherwise the employee will receive the monies due him on the next paycheck.

ARTICLE 17

Hospital and Surgical Benefit Plan. 17.01 A Group Insurance Plan for Hospital and Surgical Benefits is set forth in Appendix "B." The Employer shall contribute a monthly amount of $40.00 on behalf of each eligible employee. The employee will contribute $20.00 per month for single coverage and $45.00 per month for family coverage.

17.02 The contribution on behalf of each eligible employee shall be made to the Omnibus Insurance Company for the insurance package negotiated by the parties.

17.03 The eligibility qualifications set out in Appendix "B" shall continue throughout the term of this Agreement.

ARTICLE 18

Life Insurance Plan. 18.01 It is agreed that all employees covered by this Agreement will be entitled to receive life insurance with a face value of $25,000. That amount is payable in the event of the employee's death from any cause. The life insurance will remain in force if the employee becomes totally and permanently disabled before age sixty (60).

ARTICLE 19

Pension Plan. 19.01 An amount equal to six (6) percent of the employee's hourly wage will be placed into a pension fund maintained by Central Insurance of America. The Employer will contribute one-half of the premium and the employee will contribute one-half. The employees' contribution will be automatically deducted from their paychecks.

19.02 An employee who has reached the age of seventy (70) years may voluntarily retire and receive full pension benefits. The Employer may require an employee who has reached the age of seventy (70) to retire.

19.03 The amount of monthly pension is equal to the employee's number of years of service times $10.

19.04 The employees' contributions vest immediately. Employees are fully vested after participating in the plan for ten (10) years.

ARTICLE 20

Sick Leave. 20.01 Employees in active service who have completed at least one year of regular employment shall receive eight (8) hours pay for each day absent due to illness or injury according to the following schedule:

Completed years of service	*Number of days of paid sick leave per year*
1 to 5 years	3 days
6 to 10 years	6 days
11 to 20 years	10 days
21 or more years	15 days

To receive compensation under this program, the employee must provide the Employer with a doctor's statement documenting the illness or injury.

ARTICLE 21

Jury Duty. 21.01 When an employee is called for jury service, he or she shall be compensated for time lost from his or her job at his or her regular hourly rate less the compensation received for jury duty, but in no case more than eight (8) hours per day or forty (40) hours per week Monday through Friday.

21.02 Employees shall not be expected to report for work on their job if they are required to report for jury duty in the morning and afternoon. In the event they are excused from jury duty prior to noon and are not required to report back after noon, they shall report for work as soon as possible after being released from jury duty and work all hours available.

21.03 Any employee working on the night shift who is called for jury duty and who reports and serves on the jury shall not be required to report on his regular night shift. However, he shall, if at all possible, inform the Employer as to whether or not he is serving on a jury.

21.04 If an employee is excused and does not serve on the jury, he or she will be required to work his or her regularly scheduled shift.

ARTICLE 22

Funeral Leave. 22.01 When a regular full-time employee is absent from work because of the necessity of arranging for and attending the funeral of a member of his immediate family, the Employer will pay him for eight (8) hours at his regular rate of pay for each day of such absence up to a maximum of two (2) workdays.

(a) The employee must be on the active payroll on the date of the death of the member of his immediate family.
(b) The employee must notify his supervisor of the purpose of his absence not later than the first (1st) day of such absence.
(c) Payment will be made for a day of absence only if such day is one of the days during which the gang in which the employee is employed did work and on which the employee would have worked had it not been for the absence.
(d) The employee, when requested, must furnish proof satisfactory to the Employer of the death, his relatonship to the deceased, the date of the funeral, and the employee's actual attendance at such funeral.

22.02   For purposes of this paragraph, a member of an immediate family means only the employee's spouse, child, mother, father, sister, brother, mother-in-law or father-in-law.

ARTICLE 23

Grievances.   23.01   For the purpose of this Agreement a grievance shall mean complaints, disputes, or claims of unfair treatment involving the application or interpretation of the terms of this Agreement.

23.02   For the purpose of adjusting grievances the following procedure shall apply. A grievance not presented as stated hereunder shall be waived and thereafter may not be presented for consideration or adjustment or be made the basis for any action under this Agreement or otherwise.

(a) Each employee and/or the Union representative shall within fifteen (15) days of the date of the incident giving rise to the grievance first seek direct adjustment with the employee's supervisor. The supervisor shall, within three days, give the employee a decision on the grievance; however, the employee has the right to have the complaint heard by the department head if the employee desires. Any grievance or other Union business shall be taken up without undue interruption of work.
(b) If such employee fails to obtain satisfaction from the supervisor, the employee may, through the Union representative, within fifteen days of the date on which the grievance was first filed, submit the grievance to the Plant Manager. Such written grievance shall specify the specific contract clause or clauses allegedly violated, and the details constituting such alleged violation. The third Thursday of each month shall be allotted for grievance meetings between the Company and the Union Committee. Such grievance meetings will commence at 1:30 P.M. The Plant Manager will give the Union Committee a written answer to the grievance within ten days of the grievance meeting, not including the day of the meeting.

23.03   All days referred to in this Article 23 and the succeeding Article 24 shall exclude Saturdays, Sundays, and contract holidays.

23.04   Any individual employee or group of employees shall have the right at any time to present grievances to the Company and have such grievances adjusted without the intervention of the Union, as long as the adjustment is not inconsistent with the terms of this Agreement and providing the Union shall be notified that a conference is to be held and shall have the opportunity of having a representative present at such adjustment.

ARTICLE 24

Arbitration.   24.01   If the Union is dissatisfied with the decision as provided in Section 2.b of Article IV, Grievance Procedure, or if a decision is not rendered within the time limit specified therein, the Union may within forty-five days from the date of such decision, or the expiration of time to render such decision, give the Plant Manager written notice of its desire to carry the matter to arbitration. Said written notice shall designate the representative for the Union and shall be signed by the Chairman of the Union Committee.

24.02   Within ten days following receipt of the Union's request for arbitration the Company shall notify the Union of the name of the representative selected by it. The two representatives so named shall confer within ten days following such notification and attempt to resolve the question. If the two representatives cannot resolve the question within five days following the date of their first conference, the Company will prepare a letter for joint application to the Federal Mediation and Conciliation Service, requesting that a list of seven arbitrators be furnished.

24.03 Within twenty days after receiving the list from the Federal Mediation and Conciliation Service the Company and the Union representative shall select a neutral arbitrator by alternately striking names until one name remains. Thereafter the parties shall notify the arbitrator whose name is not eliminated of the precise issue to be arbitrated and of mutually acceptable dates and places for holding the arbitration.

24.04 As soon after the selection as is reasonably practicable the neutral arbitrator shall choose a date and place for hearing, and at such hearing both Company and the Union shall be permitted to have representatives present, and to present evidence and arguments to the neutral arbitrator. Each party shall have the privilege of crossexamining witnesses presented by the opposite party. The decision of the neutral arbitrator shall be rendered in writing in a decision stating reasons for the award within thirty days of the date of the hearing.

24.05 The only grievances that shall be arbitrable shall be those meeting the following conditions:
(a) Grievances arising between the Union and the Company relating only to the interpretation or performance of this Agreement which cannot be adjusted by mutual agreement.
(b) Grievances specifically designating the express provision or provisions of this Agreement alleged to have been violated, and the manner in which it or they have been violated.

24.06 The sole function of the neutral arbitrator shall be to interpret the express provisions of this Agreement and to apply them to the specific facts of the grievance. The arbitrator shall have no power or authority to change, amend, modify, supplement, fill in, or otherwise alter this Agreement in any respect.

24.07 The decision of the neutral arbitrator shall be final and binding upon both parties.

24.08 The expense of arbitration shall be shared equally between the Employer and the Union, but each party shall bear the expense of their own representatives.

24.09 It is agreed between the Employer and the Union that during the life of this Agreement there shall be no strikes, cessation of work, slowdowns, picketing, boycott, or lockouts.

APPENDIX "A"

	Two years ago (first year of current contract)	Last year (second year of current contract)
Maintenance Department		
Maintenance I	$8.245	$8.50
Maintenance II	7.76	8.00
Maintenance Helper	6.79	7.00
Laborer	6.06	6.25
Clean-up Crew	5.82	6.00
Mechanical Killing Department*		
Labor Grade I	$7.08	$7.30
Labor Grade II	6.94	7.15
Labor Grade III	6.64	6.85
Labor Grade IV	6.16	6.35
Offal Department		
Labor Grade I	$6.84	$7.05
Labor Grade II	6.50	6.70
Labor Grade IIII	6.01	6.20
Cooler Department		
Labor Grade I	$6.94	$7.15
Labor Grade II	6.64	6.85
Labor Grade III	6.30	6.50

*Within the mechanical killing department, different operations require different skills. Under the Agreement, labor grades and wage rates are determined by the number of different operations employees can perform. The mechanical killing department has twenty-one (21) different operations.

Number of operations at which employee is proficient	Labor grade
16–21	I
11–15	II
6–10	III
1–5	IV

EXHIBIT III
Supplemental Information

DISTRIBUTION OF EMPLOYEES BY YEARS OF SERVICE

Years of service	Number of employees	Years of service	Number of employees
<1	22		
1	44	19	11
2	48	20	8
3	39	21	6
4	42	22	7
5	43	23	4
6	34	24	4
7	29	25	9
8	26	26	3
9	21	27	3
10	17	28	4
11	20	29	8
12	14	30	5
13	12	31	5
14	15	32	4
15	16	33	7
16	20	34	3
17	14	35	3
18	9	36	1

DISTRIBUTION OF EMPLOYEES BY JOB CLASSIFICATION

Number of employees

Maintenance Department		
Maintenance I	15	
Maintenance II	15	
Maintenance Helper	15	
Laborer	40	
Clean-up Crew	30	
Total		115
Mechanical Killing Department		
Labor Grade I	20	
Labor Grade II	45	
Labor Grade III	85	
Labor Grade IV	105	
Total		255
Offal Department		
Labor Grade I	10	
Labor Grade II	30	
Labor Grade III	85	
Total		125
Cooler Department		
Labor Grade I	15	
Labor Grade II	30	
Labor Grade III	40	
Total		85
Total number of employees		580

DISTRIBUTION OF EMPLOYEES BY RACE AND SEX

	Male	*Female*	*Total*
White	145	5	150
Black	145	5	150
Hispanic	260	20	280
	550	30	580

BARGAINING UNIT DISTRIBUTION OF EMPLOYEES BY AGE

Age	Number of employees	Age	Number of employees
18 and under	8	41	14
19	6	42	8
20	3	43	8
21	9	44	25
22	15	45	19
23	9	46	12
24	10	47	8
25	15	48	15
26	23	49	16
27	19	50	11
28	24	51	24
29	11	52	19
30	12	53	13
31	16	54	15
32	15	55	3
33	8	56	7
34	12	57	6
35	17	58	2
36	15	59	8
37	11	60	6
38	36	61	7
39	9	62	6
40	12	63	3
		64	6
		65 and over	4

During the life of the labor agreement, disputes over the contract's administration or interpretation may arise. It is possible for the union to strike in order to pressure management into accepting the union's position. Without such pressure, management is likely to prevail in every dispute. However, strikes over contract interpretation problems would be very disruptive. As a result, many benefits of the collective bargaining process would be lost.

To help ensure labor stability during the life of the contract, the parties usually include a disputes resolution procedure in their labor agreement. The chapters in this section examine the processes used to resolve disagreements concerning the contract's interpretation and administration. Chapter 14 discusses grievance procedures used by the parties to settle disputes on their own. Most grievance procedures include arbitration as their final step. Grievance arbitration is the subject of Chapter 15.

PART FIVE

CONTRACT INTERPRETATION AND ADMINISTRATION

Chapter 14

CONTRACT ADMINISTRATION: GRIEVANCE PROCEDURES

Meghan DeGonda was trying to decide what to do about setting up a grievance procedure. She owned a supermarket that employed ninety people. They had recently voted in the Grocery Workers Union. Meghan preferred not to have a union represent the employees of her store, but she had decided that she would do her best to have a cooperative relationship with the union.

In a few days she and her labor attorney would sit down with the union bargaining committee to begin negotiating a contract. Meghan knew that the grievance procedure is an important part of union-management relations. However, she didn't know what kinds of procedures she should try to have established if it is to be an effective grievance procedure.

In addition to having questions about the procedures, she also wondered how much the grievance procedure would be used, what kinds of things about which the employees would grieve, and why grievances would arise. Finally, she was concerned about what could be done to prepare the managers and supervisors in her store to be able to make effective use of the grievance procedure and to keep the number of grievances at a minimum.

The objective of this chapter is to provide answers for Meghan's questions and concerns. In such a situation it is hoped that the union leaders would have corresponding concerns. Labor relations are not simply a matter of negotiating an agreement between a union and an employer. The contract agreement is a crucial part of labor relations, but the heart of labor relations is the day-to-day administration of the contract. The critical process in contract administration is the grievance procedure. During contract negotiations there is no way to anticipate all future situations. As a result, some means is needed to deal with these unforeseen situations. Also, it is not possible to write an agreement so that its meaning is clear to all parties using the contract agreement.

When you have finished studying this chapter you should be able to suggest solutions to the issues raised by Meghan. More specifically you should be able to:

- Describe the typical grievance procedure.
- List the functions of the grievance procedure.
- Describe the historical development of the grievance procedure.
- Discuss factors influencing the frequency of grievances.
- Describe alternative management approaches to handling grievances.
- Discuss legal issues concerning grievance procedures.
- List recommendations for effective handling of grievances.

This chapter will define grievance and will describe the typical grievance procedure, as well as the functions served by a grievance procedure. Determinants of grievances will be discussed and a typical grievance procedure will be described. Legal issues pertaining to grievance procedures will be reviewed and recommendations for an effective grievance procedure will be presented.

What Is a Grievance?

The definition of a grievance depends on the provisions of the particular contract agreement. In other words, a grievance is whatever is defined as a grievance in the contract. Generally, there are two alternative definitions of a grievance. The broad definition of grievance includes any gripe, complaint, or expression of discontent by an employee against the employer, or by an employer against an employee or the union. Given this broad definition of a grievance, the only complaint excluded from the grievance procedure would be one that could result in changing a contract provision. The narrow definition restricts grievances to the application or interpretation of the agreement. Exhibit 14.1 provides an example of each definition of a grievance.

The narrow definition of grievance does not preclude management from hearing complaints that fall outside the provisions of the agreement. In such situations, employees could be free to bring forth their complaints under the grievance procedure and these complaints could be heard in the early steps of the procedure. It is possible that many of these complaints will be resolved. However, when a mutually agreeable solution cannot be reached, management could, at some point, refuse to consider the grievance further. It can be argued that following such a strategy would result in wasting time, but most specialists working in the field of labor relations feel that the long-run benefits in improved employee relations justify the time spent removing a sore spot or resolving a complaint. This approach to handling complaints provides a mechanism for addressing employee problems and yet enables management to restrict the nature of issues going to arbitration.

CONTRACT INTERPRETATION AND ADMINISTRATION

EXHIBIT 14.1
Definitions of a Grievance

Broad: "In the event of any complaints, grievances, difficulties, disagreements, or disputes arising between the Company, its employees . . . , or the Union, there shall be no suspension of plant operations but an earnest effort shall be made to settle such difference, complaints, grievances, difficulties, disagreements, or disputes in the following manner."*

Narrow: "A grievance is a claim that the Employer has violated an express provision of this Agreement. . . . A grievance may be initiated only by an aggrieved employee of the Employer in accordance with the provisions set forth in this Article."†

Sources: *An agreement between Windsor Mfg. Co. and Textile Workers Union.
†An agreement between the Samsonite Corporation and the United Rubber, Cork, Linoleum and Plastic Workers of America.

A Bureau of Labor Statistics study of contract provisions found that 47 percent of the agreements surveyed defined a grievance as any complaint about any subject.[1] The remaining 53 percent defined grievances as disputes arising over the interpretation of the terms of the collective bargaining agreement.

What Is a Grievance Procedure?

Fig. 14.1 describes a grievance procedure. The components of the figure indicate key issues that must be addressed in designing a grievance procedure. The starting point in the grievance procedure is the existence of a grievance or a complaint in the perception of an employee. The first step in the grievance procedure is a meeting between the immediate supervisor and the employee. A union representative, for example, the shop steward, can be present at the first step. The available evidence suggests that usually the shop steward or a union representative can be present at this first step.[2] Management's typical position concerning the first step is that it should include only the supervisor and the immediate employee concerned. Management's argument is that it is in the interest of good employee relations for employees to feel that they can bring their complaints to their immediate supervisor without having to go to a formal procedure. The union argument is that if employees wish to have the union representative present to represent their interests and to insure that they are not intimidated by the immediate supervisor, they should have the right to do so.

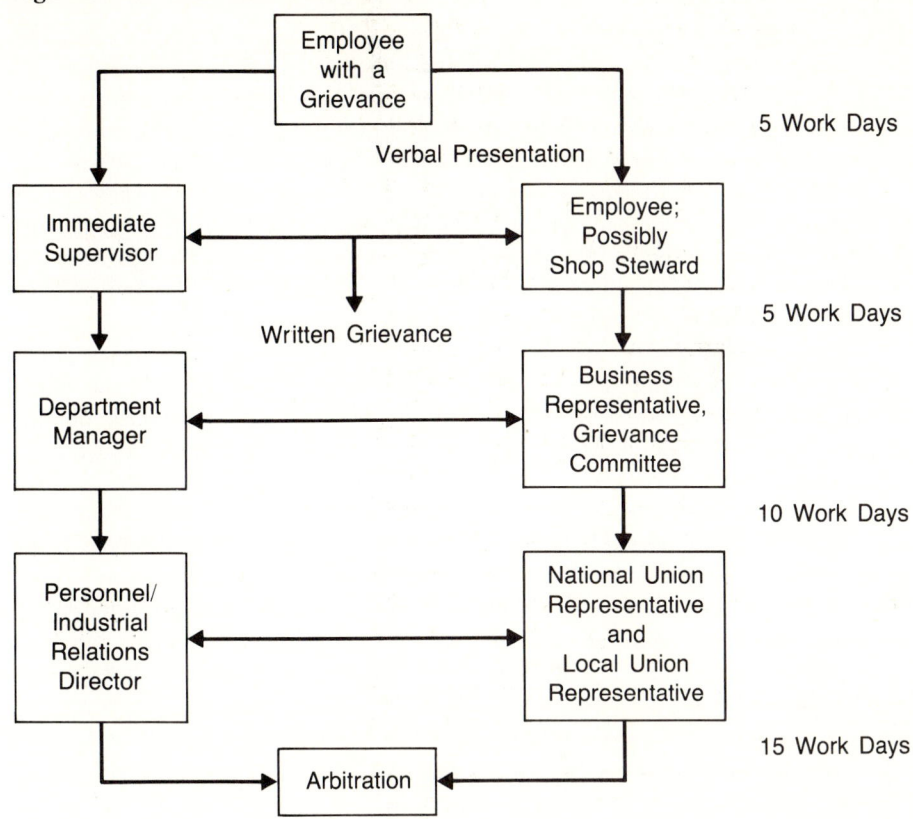

Fig. 14.1 *A Grievance Procedure*

```
                    ┌──────────────┐
                    │  Employee    │
         ┌──────────│   with a     │──────────┐
         │          │  Grievance   │          │
         │          └──────────────┘          │            5 Work Days
         │         Verbal Presentation        │
         ▼                                    ▼
  ┌──────────────┐                    ┌──────────────┐
  │  Immediate   │◄──────────────────►│  Employee;   │
  │  Supervisor  │                    │   Possibly   │
  │              │                    │ Shop Steward │
  └──────────────┘                    └──────────────┘
         │                                                 5 Work Days
         │          Written Grievance
         ▼                                    ▼
  ┌──────────────┐                    ┌──────────────┐
  │  Department  │                    │   Business   │
  │   Manager    │◄──────────────────►│Representative,│
  │              │                    │  Grievance   │
  │              │                    │  Committee   │
  └──────────────┘                    └──────────────┘
         │                                    │           10 Work Days
         ▼                                    ▼
  ┌──────────────┐                    ┌──────────────┐
  │  Personnel/  │                    │   National Union │
  │  Industrial  │◄──────────────────►│ Representative  │
  │  Relations   │                    │      and        │
  │   Director   │                    │  Local Union    │
  │              │                    │ Representative  │
  └──────────────┘                    └──────────────┘
         │                                    │           15 Work Days
         └──────────┐        ┌────────────────┘
                    ▼        ▼
                 ┌──────────────┐
                 │  Arbitration │
                 └──────────────┘
```

WHEN SHOULD THE GRIEVANCE BE WRITTEN?

Another issue concerning this step is whether or not the complaint should be written or whether the complaint should be presented orally. We recommend that an informal or an oral presentation of complaints at this stage be used. When the complaints can be presented in an oral manner it seems that the chances of working out the complaint to a satisfactory conclusion at this level are better. It also seems to facilitate the handling of complaints between the employee and immediate supervisor without having the union representative involved.

The argument for writing out a grievance is to have the facts concerning the incident set down so as to ensure that the information is correct. Those favoring early writing of grievances argue that as time passes, an individual's recollection of the events tends to become less accurate and for this reason a written statement of the incident should be developed as soon as possible.

TIME LIMITS

In the example presented in Fig. 14.1 we indicated that the time limit for the first step is five work days. The specification of time limits is common. A survey of collective-bargaining agreements showed that over 80 percent placed specific time limits on some or all of the steps in the grievance procedure.[3] It is also quite common for extensions of time between steps to be possible by mutual consent of the parties. The amount of time allowed for the various steps varies. Two to three days seems to be the shortest amount of time allowed for the initial step with somewhat longer periods of time for the other steps in the procedure. For example, five to seven days for the second step and ten to fifteen days for later steps in the procedure are common time limits.

The purpose served by specifying limits is to ensure prompt attention to grievances. It is felt that specifying time limits at which one must respond to the grievance prohibits stalling. These time limits have a different meaning from the union's point of view as opposed to the employer's point of view. From the union member's point of view, the five-day time limit in Fig. 14.1 means that from the time at which the employee becomes aware of the incident; for example, his or her reassignment to another job; the employee has five days in which to initiate the grievance. If the employee fails to do so within the five-day period, the employer can refuse to consider the grievance because of the failure to adhere to the time limit specified in the grievance procedure. From the point of view of the employer, however, failing to adhere to the time limit is not an admission of guilt or an agreement that the employee's charge is correct. Rather it is simply a failure to respond in a timely manner and makes it possible for the employee and union to carry the grievance to the next step in the procedure without waiting for that particular employer representative to respond to the grievance.

NUMBER OF STEPS

In Fig. 14.1 we have described a grievance procedure that has three steps prior to arbitration. The number of steps in the procedure prior to arbitration can vary from as little as one step to as many as six or seven. The most common number of steps is three or four.[4] The main factor determining the number of steps is the complexity or size of the work organization.

One can think of a grievance procedure as having two basic levels. The first level can be described as a mechanism whereby an individual employee who feels unfairly treated for some reason can appeal that decision. In Fig. 14.1, one could say that an employee's first level of appeal is to the immediate supervisor and the second appeal is to the department manager. At this level the basic concern is with an individual situation and there is no dimension to the grievance or to the complaint that concerns a basic policy issue either for the union or for the company. Grievances resolved at these levels can be viewed as administering existing policy.[5]

The second basic level in the grievance procedure involves higher-level officials in the organization and in the union. Typically, grievances getting to this level do involve policy.[6] When a grievance does involve matters of policy, it is sometimes possible to skip early steps in the grievance procedure. When such step-skipping procedures are not possible it becomes necessary for higher-level officials to, in essence, dictate that immediate supervisors or department managers, from the view of the company, and shop stewards and grievance committees, from the view of the union, become inflexible in their consideration of the grievance. This forces the grievance up to the policy-making level of the grievance procedure. Examples of such decisions are the determination of work rules and setting production standards. The reason for wanting to force such issues to a higher level in the grievance procedure is that grievances are precedent setting and when such questions as setting production standards are involved it is in the interest of the organization to have higher-level individuals involved in making the decision.

AT WHAT LEVEL SHOULD GRIEVANCES BE SETTLED?

With the exception described in the previous paragraph, the generalization is that grievances should be settled at the lowest level possible. This is in the interest of maintaining good union-management relations. Later in the chapter we will describe recommendations, both for the union and for the employer, to facilitate the settlement of grievances at as low a level as possible. From the point of view of the organization it is desirable to settle grievances at as low a level as possible to preserve the authority of the immediate supervisor and to facilitate employee acceptance. Employees' perceptions of the authority of the supervisor are improved when the supervisor is able to settle grievances that are brought to his or her attention. From the point of view of employee acceptance, when the decision is made close to the employee's level, he or she is more likely to accept the decision than when it is made by levels of union officials and employer representatives that are far removed from that person's work situation.

ARBITRATION

The final step in the grievance procedure is typically arbitration. This step involves referring the grievance to a neutral third party who makes a decision concerning the issue. Arbitration was the terminal step in 94 percent of private-sector collective bargaining agreements that were reviewed in a recent study.[7] The consideration in deciding whether or not to have arbitration as the final step in the grievance procedure will be discussed in detail in the next chapter. The basic issue is whether or not one wishes to have an outside party, a neutral, making decisions concerning one's own work organization. The alternative is having such matters decided by the immediate participants, the union and the employer, and running the risk of having a work stoppage when an agreement cannot be reached. Normally when arbitration is specified as the last step in a grievance procedure there is a clause in the contract agreeing that no work stoppages will occur as a result of grievances during the life of a contract.

Functions of the Grievance Procedure

A grievance procedure is a formal procedure by which grievances, as defined by a collective-bargaining agreement, can be resolved. Thomson has identified several purposes served by the grievance procedure.[8]

1. The grievance procedure permits the application of the contract to many different situations in the day-to-day operation of a work organization. There will be different points of view about the meaning of the clauses in the contract. The grievance procedure is a mechanism that permits working out these differences in points of view.
2. The grievance procedure is a way of controlling conflict. Without a mechanism such as the grievance procedure it is possible that minor differences in the application and interpretation of a contract will become so magnified that work stoppages and wildcat strikes would occur.
3. The grievance procedure permits an employee to make a complaint without fear of retribution.
4. The grievance procedure provides for continuous collective bargaining, in a sense. Differences in the application of the provisions of the negotiated contract can be worked out during the life of the contract.
5. The grievance procedure provides a mechanism that enables the identification of underlying problems in the work organization. When management is sensitive to the nature of grievances being submitted, it can identify the underlying causes and take corrective action.
6. Related to the previous purpose is the fact that the grievance procedure provides a means of communication between employees and managers. Union representatives and management can exchange a great deal of information during meetings discussing grievances. As a result, they obtain a clearer understanding of each other's position on these issues.
7. Finally, the grievance procedure helps insure the consistent application of personnel policies. Because a mechanism is provided for expressing grievances, inconsistent application of rules will be made apparent and these inconsistencies will be removed when management is responsible.

History of Grievance Procedures

During the early years of collective bargaining in the United States, a distinction was not made between negotiating an agreement and administering an agreement. As a result, a dispute concerning the application of an agreement, for example the rate of pay a worker was entitled to receive, could lead to a strike.

Chamberlain and Kuhn point out that while such problems occurred frequently and each incident could potentially have had the same outcome, little was done to establish a procedure to handle such disputes peacefully.[9] At this time, the terms of the agreement were typically established in a unilateral manner. Whichever side had the greater bargaining power at the time dictated the conditions of employment. As a result, the other side would be waiting for the economic advantage to shift so it could try to change the agreement. According to Chamberlain and Kuhn, during the 1800s if union members believed that an employer was not complying with the terms of the agreement, their only option was the show of strength (a strike or the threat of a strike) with which they had secured the terms originally.[10]

The use of a written agreement evolved to which union members and an employer were to adhere for a specified period of time. The existence of a written agreement enabled union and employer representatives to meet and discuss disputes occurring during the life of the agreement. These disputes were settled on the basis of the provisions of the agreement and not on the relative bargaining power of the parties.[11] Unfortunately, when the parties were unable to agree on the interpretation or application of the agreement, their options were to use a strike or lockout to secure their own view or agree to the other side's view. However, by the end of the 1800s, neutrals or third parties were being used to settle such disputes with neither side incurring the costs associated with a work stoppage. The widespread use of grievance-arbitration procedures in strongly organized industries was reported by the Industrial Commission in 1902.[12] At this time, however, well below 10 percent of the nonagricultural workforce was organized.

Following the Wagner Act many employers refused to agree to grievance arbitration. However, with the rapid growth in union membership that occurred there was a shift in attitudes. In 1945, the President's Labor-Management Conference recommended that all labor agreements provide for a grievance and arbitration procedure.[13] Further, Section 203(d) of the Taft-Hartley Act recommended the settlement of disputes arising over the application or interpretation of an existing collective-bargaining agreement by means of a grievance arbitration procedure agreed upon by the parties.[14]

Types of Grievances

Information is not available identifying the kinds of issues about which employees grieve. However, information is available concerning the types of issues that go to arbitration. From this one can infer the types of issues about which employees grieve.[15] The most common issue going to arbitration involves discharge and disciplinary action. Next most common are cases involving seniority. Examples are decisions concerning promotion, layoff, recall, and transfer. The third most common category of arbitration case stems from grievances concerning job evaluation and determining the classification of jobs. Following this are grievances involving overtime, which includes determination of overtime pay, distribution of overtime among employees, and compulsory overtime.

Determinants of Grievances

The frequency of grievances can vary greatly over time and can vary greatly between departments and plants within the same company, and between companies and unions. A rate of about ten to twenty grievances per hundred employees per year, when grievances are written at the first step, is quite common.[16]

Fig. 14.2 shows factors that have an impact on the frequency of grievances. We assume that the primary determinant of the frequency of grievances is dissatisfaction on the part of individual union members. It is suggested that feelings of dissatisfaction result from perceptions of inequity. The latter are assumed to occur when an individual perceives that some condition of employment departs from what should be.[17]

$$\text{Inequity} = f(\text{Is} \neq \text{should be})$$

The conditions of employment in question can take many forms: compensation, job assignment, promotion, overtime, disciplinary action, lay-off, and so forth. The perception of what is corresponds to management's action concerning the particular condition of employment; the perception of what should be can result from an individual

Fig. 14.2 *Determinants of Grievances*

Organization Level

Employer – Union Relations
  Antagonistic/Cooperative
  Experience
  Security Clause

Employer Characteristics
  Personnel Practices
  Centralization
  Leadership Style
  Organization Change

Union Characteristics
  Member Support
  Steward Selection and
    Compensation
  Stability of Leadership

Individual Level

Inequity → Dissatisfaction → Number of Grievances

Instrumentality

Union Power

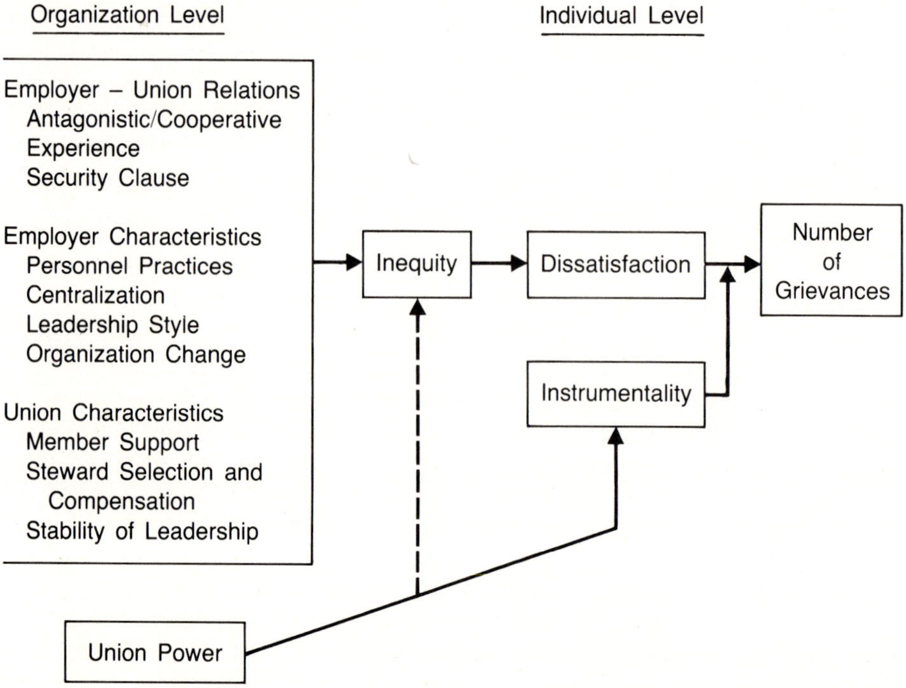

comparing his or her own situation to that of others as specified in the equity model discussed in Chapter 6. In addition, a person's perceptions of what should be can result from comparisons between one's former situation with respect to this condition of employment as well as one's understanding of the terms and conditions of employment specified in the collective-bargaining agreement.

Intervening between feelings of dissatisfaction and the incidence of grievances are the individual's instrumentality perceptions. These are defined as the individual's estimate of the chances of satisfactorily removing the feeling of inequity if a grievance is filed. For example, given some level of dissatisfaction felt by a union member, the greater the person's estimate of removing the source of dissatisfaction by submitting a grievance, the more likely a grievance will be submitted. The key to understanding the frequency of grievances is identifying factors that influence feelings of inequity and instrumentality estimates.

The model presented in Fig. 14.2 focuses on explaining grievances of workers. It must be recognized that some grievances will stem from disputes between union leaders and management over interpretation of the contract.

Slichter, Healy, and Livernash have discussed the complex factors influencing the frequency of grievances.[18] They indicate that an exceptionally low grievance rate does not necessarily mean that employees are satisfied with conditions and that an exceptionally high rate does not always mean that employees are dissatisfied. They also discuss various organizational and institutional conditions that influence the frequency of grievances in detail.

EMPLOYER-UNION RELATIONS

Slichter, Healy, and Livernash state that generally when the relations between a union and an employer are friendly, one can expect to find a low grievance rate.[19] It appears that good relations lead to low grievance rates because employees are less inclined to raise technicalities about the application of the collective-bargaining agreement. In addition, in such an environment employees feel that they are better able to settle complaints orally with supervisors rather than having to submit formal grievances. Similarly, Thomson and Murray conclude that high levels of conflict in the bargaining relationship require more formal processes,[20] while Turner and Robinson found that union and management cooperation was associated with settling grievances at earlier stages of the procedure.[21]

Other dimensions of union-management relations that can have an impact on the frequency of grievances are reflected in Fig. 14.2. One is the amount of experience that a union and its leaders have in dealing with the managers of an organization.[22] Generally, when a new union is representing a group of employees one can expect a higher rate of grievances. This is because the new union is trying to demonstrate to its membership what the union is able to do. As the union becomes more secure, one can expect the number of grievances to decline.

The nature of the union-security clause can have an effect also. Just as the leaders of a new union are concerned about demonstrating that the union is able to be of use to the membership, so also would the leaders of a union that has a weak security clause be motivated to demonstrate to the membership that the union is necessary.[23] When a union is in a secure position, one can expect the union to be more likely to process only those grievances that appear to be justified.

EMPLOYER CHARACTERISTICS

Another category of organization-level factors that Fig. 14.2 assumes to affect the incidence of grievances is the characteristics of the employing organization. Of primary importance are personnel practices and procedures. Basically it is necessary for management to insure that personnel practices are perceived as reasonable and fair. Also, management must insure that personnel practices are applied in a consistent manner over time and across departments within the organization. Inconsistent application of personnel policies and practices is associated with higher grievance rates.[24] To some extent the grievance procedure is the mechanism for correcting this source of grievances. When a rule is perceived to be unfair or when it appears to be applied in an inconsistent manner, grievances will be generated and, as a result of the grievance, these defects in personnel policies should be corrected.

Peach and Livernash also report that as management decision making is increasingly centralized, the incidence of grievances increases.[25] Related to centralization is management's specific policy with respect to handling grievances.

Legalistic vs. clinical approach. A legalistic or formal approach focuses on determining whether a contract violation has occurred and is more likely to elicit the following from one's supervisor: "If you've got a problem, write it up." A clinical approach is the alternative; this involves an effort by the immediate supervisor to resolve the employee's problem—preferably in an informal manner. The leadership style practiced by supervisors is also related to the incidence of grievances.[26] The number of grievances was found to be lower when supervisors were high in consideration, which is defined as a genuine concern for employee welfare, respect for employee opinions, and maintaining two-way communications with subordinates.

On the surface the factors discussed above—consistency in applying personnel policies, a formal versus a clinical approach to handling grievances, and a leadership style high in consideration—appear to place management in a "no win" situation. Permitting supervisors to handle grievances in an informal manner would facilitate their displaying consideration for subordinates but would also appear to invite inconsistent application of personnel policies. It is likely that if supervisors are not well trained in the provisions of the collective-bargaining agreement and in the application of personnel policies, this will be the result. It appears that providing such training for supervisors is the means to avoid this dilemma.

Whenever change is introduced in an organization it is likely to generate grievances.[27,28] The number of grievances generated as a result of introducing change can be reduced by effective communication with employees affected by the change. Resistance to change can also be reduced by giving employees affected by the change an opportunity to participate in the decision. Managers of some organizations try to reduce the frequency of grievances generated by this source by keeping union representatives informed of the factors entering into the decision and by explaining why it is necessary to introduce a particular change. Examples of changes that can generate grievances are changes in piece rates and in production standards as well as introducing new methods of work and technological change.

UNION CHARACTERISTICS

The positions a union can take towards grievances are: encouraging the submission of grievances; a neutral position toward grievances; and discouraging grievances. Factors related to the union's stance are reflected in Fig. 14.2. A union that lacks member support and is trying to demonstrate to the membership that a union is necessary is likely to encourage the submission of grievances. Such a strategy could have the effect of increasing member cohesiveness and reducing the chances of decertification should such an election take place. One of the authors was involved in an arbitration case where a union chose to pursue a relatively weak grievance through to arbitration. The informal word was that the employees of this particular bargaining unit questioned whether the union was doing anything for them and the union pushed this weak grievance because of this attitude among the members.

The way in which stewards and other union representatives responsible for handling grievances are selected can have an impact.[29] When union representatives are elected, there is a tendency for these individuals to search for grievances to submit. The reason for this is that they are able to impress upon the members of the unit what a good job they are doing in handling grievances. Another means that can be used for selecting stewards is for the elected local officials to appoint them. It is felt that the latter technique results in a more rational approach to grievances. The reason is the steward has pressure on him or her to pursue only justifiable grievances and not to encourage any employee in the unit to pursue every grievance he or she may have.

Another factor that appears to generate high numbers of grievances stems from the number and compensation of union stewards and grievance-committee members.[30] It seems that when there are few constraints on the amount of time that committee members and stewards spend on processing grievances and when there are few restraints on the compensation of these individuals, the number of grievances increases. The union argument for compensation of people involved in these activities is that it is in the interest of good management of the organization to solve grievances, and so the employer should compensate people for all time spent on processing them. However, when people are fully compensated for time spent on processing grievances, they have an incentive to spend time doing so. As a result, they can appear to pursue weak grievances or search out grievances in their work unit.

Rivalries within the local union for elected office can result in efforts to generate grievances.[31] In such a situation the incumbent may encourage the submission of grievances to demonstrate the good job he or she is doing for the membership.

The preceding discussion concerning organization-level characteristics and their relationship to the incidence of grievances assumes the intermediate steps of feelings of inequity and dissatisfaction on the part of individual union members. Of particular significance is the nature of employer-union relations and union characteristics in this sequence. When a situation associated with a greater number of grievances is present, we are assuming that union leaders take steps to encourage grievances by contributing to feelings of inequity and dissatisfaction. For example, in a union threatened with decertification the shop stewards could seek out members with gripes and say things that will contribute to their feelings of inequity. Individuals' expectancy estimates are also important. Factors that lead to discouraging the submission of grievances typically stem from the chances of successfully settling a grievance for a union member.[32] A union will probably discourage the submission of grievances when it appears there is little chance of settling the grievance in a way satisfactory to the employee. This is likely when management takes a particularly tough stance on grievances and refuses to make any adjustments in grievances. This implies that the union is relatively weak in dealing with management. The dashed line from union power to inequity is intended to reflect the situation in which the union leader recognizes that the union is in a weak position but the union member does not. We assume that the leader would be inclined to discourage the grievance by suggesting that it does not have merit, rather than point out the futility of submitting a grievance because of the union's inability to secure concessions from management.

Legal Status of Grievance Procedures

There are a number of issues that have been addressed by legislation and the courts concerning the grievance procedure. One of these is whether or not an individual employee can present his or her own grievance or whether that person must rely on the established procedure. Another issue is who controls the decision to pursue a grievance if it is not satisfactorily resolved at a particular level. A third issue is the company's obligation to use the grievance procedure and a final issue is the degree to which the settlement or agreement reached during a grievance procedure is binding on the parties.

INDIVIDUAL PROCESSING OF GRIEVANCES

The concern here is whether or not an individual employee or a group of employees has the right to present a grievance to their employer and to have that grievance adjusted without the presence of a union representative. This issue was addressed by the Labor Management Relations Act.[33] It states that individual employees shall have the right to present their grievance to the employer. The act also states that the union shall have the right to have a representative present at such discussions and that the only limitation on individual submission of grievances is that the adjustment that takes place cannot be in violation of or inconsistent with the collective-bargaining contract.

The decision to handle a grievance on one's own is not without cost. In the case of *Republic Steel Corporation v. Maddox,* an employee who had not attempted to use the grievance procedure to resolve a grievance was prohibited from initiating a court action against the employer when he himself was unable to handle the matter to his own satisfaction.[34] The court stated that an employee wishing to settle a grievance must attempt to use the collective-bargaining grievance procedure as a method of doing so. If the matter is not handled to the employee's satisfaction by the union then it becomes possible to pursue action in the courts. However, the individual employee must afford the union the opportunity to act in his or her behalf before court action can be initiated.

Self-help. A different dimension of individual reliance versus use of the grievance procedure involves self-help. Here we are referring to a situation in which an individual feels unfairly or arbitrarily treated and the person chooses to take matters into his or her own hands at that moment, rather than submit a grievance.

On such issues past arbitration decisions supply some guidance. Arbitrators typically deny or limit requested relief regardless of the merits of the original complaint when an employee resorts to self-help rather than use the grievance procedure.[35] Union members must not take matters into their own hands. They must obey orders and carry out their assignments even if they believe that the orders or assignments are in violation of the agreement. Then such employees should turn to the grievance procedure to seek relief. The exceptions to this general rule are when adherence to orders would involve an unusual risk to one's health and when following commands would involve the performance of an immoral or criminal action.

The rationale for this position is that the grievance procedure is the agreed-upon mechanism for determining if a contract has been violated. Grievance procedures were not destined to handle only doubtful grievances. Rather, the grievance procedure is designed to handle all grievances and the distinction between doubtful and clear violations of the contract agreement is the distinction between clear grievances and doubtful grievances. What appears to be a clear violation to one party may not seem to be a violation at all in the perception of the other party. It is through joint discussions about such matters that grievances will be resolved.

EMPLOYER OBLIGATION TO USE THE GRIEVANCE PROCEDURE

The employer is obligated to use the grievance procedure. One can see that Fig. 14.1 indicates that union representatives become involved in making decisions concerning the resolution of grievances. An employer may feel that union representatives are being unreasonable concerning the grievance and consider bypassing them and going directly to the employee or employees involved in the grievance. Arbitration cases involving this issue have found that employers must adhere to the grievance procedure. When they fail to do so arbitrators typically rule in favor of the employee and grant the relief sought by the employee.

UNION CONTROL OF THE DECISION TO PURSUE A GRIEVANCE

Typically, the union has control over the decision to advance a grievance to a higher step in the grievance procedure. The argument in favor of having the union control the decision to pursue a grievance is to permit the union to separate frivolous grievances. In the eyes of an individual employee, perhaps he or she is right, but in the eyes of a more objective person, the grievance might be frivolous. If the individual had sole right to determine whether or not a grievance would be pursued to higher and higher levels, there would be a great deal of cost to both the employer and the union.

However, giving the union control over determining which grievances will be appealed to higher levels creates the possibility of unfair and arbitrary treatment by union representatives. In *Vaca v. Sipes,* this particular issue was addressed.[36] In this case, the company had ruled that an employee could not be assigned to a particular job for health reasons. There was medical evidence that supported this decision. The union decided that the employee did not have a valid grievance. The matter was pursued in civil court, and Vaca produced medical evidence substantiating his claim. A lower court ruled in favor of Vaca. The Supreme Court stated that an employee may seek relief in the civil courts when the union has sole power under the agreement to carry grievances to higher levels of organization. In such a case, if the employee has been prevented from going through all of the steps in the grievance procedure then that employee has the right to take his or her case into the civil courts. The Court explicitly stated that the individual employee does not have the absolute right to determine which grievances will be taken to arbitration. The Court's reasoning was that the union must have the power to refuse to process frivolous grievances. On the other hand, the Court did state that a union may not ignore meritorious grievances. The Court stated that a wrongful refusal to process a grievance occurs when the union action is arbitrary, discriminatory, and fails to represent the interest of the employee fairly.

Recommendations for Effective Grievance Procedures

Experience has shown that there are a number of things that both a union and an employer can do that will have the effect of reducing the number of grievances and making the grievance procedure function effectively.

UNION PROCEDURES

We discussed earlier why it is advisable for a union to appoint shop stewards and members of the grievance procedure rather than elect such individuals. This is our first recommendation. The union representative has the responsibility not only to pursue legitimate grievances vigorously but also has a responsibility to try to discourage employees from pursuing complaints that are without merit.

A second recommendation is to use a problem-solving approach. The kind of behavior that is recommended is exemplified by a description of one grievance-committee person, Charlie Bragg.[37] Charlie is quoted as saying, "The main function of a committeeman (shop steward) is to settle problems right on the floor." It is pointed out that in an average day Charlie handles about twenty problems, and that he does not use threats in addressing problems. His primary objective is to represent the interests of the union members. However, he recognizes that he must maintain a good working relationship with their supervisors if he is to be effective. He uses his ultimate weapon, the written grievance, infrequently. He uses a problem-solving approach in that he wants to take care of the problem and do so quickly rather than magnify the grievance. If relations between union officials and management are cooperative, if they work together to solve problems, then the number of grievances is likely to be low and those that do occur will be settled at early stages.

To insure the efficient operation of the grievance procedure, it is in the interest of both the employer and the union to have competent individuals involved. A contract provision that facilitates this end is superseniority for union representatives as long as they hold office as shop steward or a grievance-committee person. The underlying purpose of the superseniority provision is to insure that the most qualified representative will be on the grievance committee or act as shop steward.[38]

Plant access is normally provided for union officials who process grievances. Typically, these contract provisions limit free access to those areas that are relevant to investigating a particular grievance. It is essential that union representatives be given reasonable opportunity to investigate the circumstances surrounding a grievance. Without such access the union representative is forced to rely on secondary information in determining the facts surrounding a case. On the other hand, the employer is entitled to ask for information concerning the grievance that the union representative is investigating when he or she seeks entry to a place of work. The plant access provision does not give the union representative the right to roam the place of work to, for example, engage in organizational activities.

Normally, union representatives who are involved in processing grievances have some immunity from disciplinary action as a result of behavior that is normally not acceptable which can occur during the processing of a grievance.[39] The principle underlying this issue is whether or not union representatives feel they can vigorously represent the interests of an employee who is pursuing a grievance. Arbitrator decisions involving such issues imply that a rule of reason must be followed.[40] Zealously pursuing the interests of an employee with a grievance cannot be a basis for disciplinary action nor can a union steward be limited to the language or behavior that would be appropriate for a church social. On the other hand, the union representative cannot engage in behaviors that are completely unreasonable; for example, encouraging employees to engage in a wildcat strike or calling for employees to disobey lawful orders from their superiors. Nor can a shop steward engage in insubordinate actions or actions that serve no other purpose than to embarrass or humiliate supervisors in front of other employees.

RECOMMENDATIONS FOR MANAGEMENT

The general management philosophy will have a major impact on the approach taken with respect to grievances. Generally, if management's objective is to promote good relations with the union, an approach that might be described as cooperative is recommended. In this kind of approach, management recognizes that unions have a legitimate right to represent the interests of their membership and that the goal is to work together to resolve and limit the frequency of grievances. If this is the approach taken by management then the focus will be on first-level supervision and what can be done at this level to limit grievances. Recommendations for first-level supervision are discussed below.

If a hostile approach is being used to deal with unions then the staff function or the industrial-relations function will become more important in handling grievances. In this approach, most grievances that are filed will be vigorously resisted by management and the union's option will be to appeal or not appeal grievances to higher levels. Such a management approach has the effect of centralizing decision making. First-level supervisors and department managers are in effect prohibited from taking an accommodative or cooperative view and those grievances that are appealed end up at the industrial-relations department or personnel department for resolution. This strategy tends to erode the authority of immediate supervision and tends to drive a wedge between management and the employees of the organization. Generally, we recommend avoiding this strategy. Naturally, if the owners or top-level management of an organization do not recognize the right of the union to be present, then this recommendation is not relevant and one must simply recognize the costs that will be incurred with such a strategy.

Effective discipline. Earlier in the chapter the incidence of various issues going to arbitration was discussed. It was noted that employee discipline is the most common grievance ending in arbitration. From this we can infer that an effective system of employee discipline can have an impact on the number of grievances.

There are basically two approaches to employee discipline: authoritarian and corrective.[41] The former implies that disciplinary action is taken to punish an employee for a rule infraction and to serve as an example for other workers, thereby discouraging them from breaking the rule. The latter implies that disciplinary action is taken so that the employee's behavior changes to that expected by the organization.

Employee rule violations can be classified in two broad categories: major violations such as theft, assaulting a superior or failure to obey directions from a superior; and less serious rule infractions such as absenteeism or tardiness. One can infer from decisions of labor arbitrators that employers are justified in discharging employees guilty of major violations without prior warnings or attempts at corrective discipline.[42] Alternatively, when an employee is guilty of some less serious rule infraction, arbitration decisions suggest that employers are expected to engage in a process of corrective discipline.[43]

Corrective or progressive discipline. As indicated above, the objective of corrective or progressive discipline is to change an employee's behavior so that it meets the organization's standards. It involves progressively more severe levels of disciplinary action. The typical sequence for most rule infractions is:[44]

1. Oral or verbal warnings;
2. Written warning;
3. Suspension;
4. Discharge.

When a rule has been broken for the first time by an employee, the supervisor would talk to the employee. The objective is to insure that the employee understands the rule in question and what behavior is expected.

Assuming the oral warning does not bring about a change in behavior, the next step in corrective discipline is typically a written warning. This document should clearly state that a verbal warning has taken place, what behavior is expected from the employee and the next step in the disciplinary procedure if a change in behavior does not take place.

Suspension is the next level of disciplinary action. Should the undesired employee behavior continue, suspension without pay for a limited time, e.g., three days, is likely to follow a written warning.

Finally, if the rule infraction continues, the employee could be discharged. As discussed above, except for major rule infractions, employers should turn to this ultimate disciplinary action only when attempts at corrective discipline have failed.

RECOMMENDATIONS FOR FIRST-LEVEL SUPERVISORS

There appear to be three key suggestions for the immediate supervisor in trying to prevent and reduce the number of grievances. The first is that supervisors must be aware of the provisions of the labor contract and be well trained in the application of personnel policies. Another is that the supervisor should try to establish friendly, cooperative working relationships with the union steward. If the supervisor perceives the steward to be undermining his or her authority then their relationship is likely to be one of hostility and conflict. This is likely to lead to frequent grievances and infrequent settlement of grievances at the first step. A third factor is a supervisor's leadership style.[45] A supervisor who demonstrates a genuine concern for employee welfare and the interests of employees is likely to have fewer grievances.

Recommendations for what an immediate supervisor should do when presented with a grievance have been discussed by Trotta.[46] First a supervisor should insure that he or she gains a clear understanding of the employee's perception of the problem. Then information should be gathered from other sources to insure that the grievant's perception is not biased or inaccurate. After gathering relevant facts and opinions, the supervisor must make a decision. In doing so, an effort must be made to be objective as well as consistent with the collective bargaining agreement and organization practice with respect to the issue in question. Trotta's opinion is that supervisors who implement these suggestions have a high probability of handling most grievances at the first level of the procedure and of minimizing the number of grievances that do occur over the long term.[47]

Summary

The administration of collective-bargaining agreements was introduced in this chapter. During the early years of collective bargaining in the United States a distinction was not made between administering an existing agreement and negotiating a new agreement. Consequently, disputes over interpretation or application of an agreement could lead to demands to modify the agreement and possibly a work stoppage. By the end of the nineteenth century the use of a grievance-arbitration procedure to handle these situations was spreading.

Factors influencing the incidence of grievances were discussed. Of primary importance is the nature of union-management relations. If a cooperative attitude is taken by both parties in which both try to settle problems at the lowest level, the number of grievances can be kept at a minimum.

The use of grievance arbitration is encouraged by Taft-Hartley. Individual employees are expected to use these procedures, where they exist, to resolve grievances rather than relying on self-help or going immediately to the courts. However, the decision to pursue a grievance to higher levels of the procedure when an employee is not satisfied with management's response is controlled by the union. In exercising this control, a union has the responsibility to represent the employee's interests fairly.

Discussion Questions

1. What are the purposes and functions of grievance procedures?
2. How were problems involving the application of an agreement handled prior to use of the grievance procedure?
3. Should grievances be broadly defined or narrowly defined?
4. What approach to handling grievances should be taken by management and by the union?
5. Concerning the grievance procedure:
   a. Should the grievance be presented orally at the first step?

b. Should the shop steward be present at the first step?
c. Should step-skipping be permitted?
6. Should the union control the decision to appeal a grievance to higher levels in the organization?
7. What can the union and management do to improve the effectiveness of the grievance procedure?

Key Concepts

Grievance
Legalistic versus clinical approach to grievances

Grievance procedure
Self-help

Notes

1. U.S. Department of Labor, Bureau of Labor Statistics, *Major Collective Bargaining Agreements—Grievance Procedures,* BLS Bulletin 1425–1 (Washington, D.C.: Government Printing Office, 1964), p. 61.
2. Ibid., p. 18.
3. Ibid., p. 37.
4. Ibid., p. 33.
5. Edwin F. Beal, Edward D. Wickersham, and Philip K. Kienast, *The Practice of Collective Bargaining,* 5th ed. (Homewood, IL: Richard D. Irwin, Inc., 1976), p. 404.
6. Ibid.
7. *Basic Patterns in Union Contracts,* 9th ed. (Washington, D. C.: Bureau of National Affairs, 1979), p. 15.
8. A. W. J. Thomson, *The Grievance Procedure in the Private Sector* (Ithaca, NY: New York State School of Industrial and Labor Relations, Cornell University, 1974), pp. 1–3.
9. Neil W. Chamberlain and James W. Kuhn, *Collective Bargaining,* 2nd ed. (New York: McGraw-Hill Book Company, 1965), pp. 141–42.
10. Ibid., p. 142.
11. Ibid., pp. 142–43.
12. *Final Report of the Industrial Commission,* Reports of the Industrial Commission, vol. 19 (1902), p. 838.
13. *New York Times,* 30 November 1945, p. 17.
14. Labor Management Relations Act, Section 203(d), 1947.
15. J. F. Power, "Improving Arbitration: Roles of Parties and Agencies, *Monthly Labor Review* 95 (November 1972):21.
16. Sumner H. Slichter, James J. Healy, and E. Robert Livernash, *The Impact of Collective Bargaining on Management* (Washington, D. C.: The Brookings Institution, 1960), p. 698.
17. Edward E. Lawler III, *Pay and Organizational Effectiveness: A Psychological View* (New York: McGraw-Hill Book Company, 1971), pp. 205–14.
18. Slichter et al., pp. 701–20.
19. Ibid., pp. 702–703.
20. A. J. W. Thomson and V. V. Murray, *Grievance Procedures* (London: Saxon House, 1976).

21. J. T. Turner and J. W. Robinson, "A Pilot Study of the Validity of Grievance Settlement Rates as a Predictor of Union Management Relationships," *Journal of Industrial Relations* 14 (1972):314–22.

22. Slichter et al., pp. 703–5.

23. Ibid., pp. 707–10.

24. Turner and Robinson.

25. David Peach and E. Robert Livernash, *Grievance Initiation and Resolution: A Study in Basic Steel* (Boston: Graduate School of Business, Harvard University, 1974).

26. Edwin A. Fleishman and Edwin F. Harris, "Patterns of Leadership Behavior Related to Employee Grievances and Turnover," *Personnel Psychology* 15 (Spring 1962):43–56.

27. Slichter et al., pp. 706–7.

28. Peach and Livernash.

29. Slichter et al., pp. 710–11.

30. Ibid., p. 712.

31. Ibid., pp. 711–12.

32. Ibid., p. 703.

33. Labor Management Relations Act, Section 9(a), 1947.

34. *Republic Steel Corporation v. Maddox*, 85 S.Ct. 614, 616; 58 LRRM 2193, (1965).

35. Frank Elkouri and Edna A. Elkouri, *How Arbitration Works* (Washington, D. C.: Bureau of National Affairs, 3rd ed. 1973), pp. 154–59.

36. *Vaca v. Sipes*, 87 S. Ct. 903, 914; 64 LRRM 2369, (1967).

37. W. S. Mossberg, "On the Line: As Union Man at Ford, Charlie Bragg Deals in Problems, Gripes," *Wall Street Journal*, 26 July 1973, p. 1.

38. Chamberlain and Kuhn, p. 156.

39. Ibid., p. 157.

40. Elkouri and Elkouri, pp. 138–41.

41. Hoyt N. Wheeler, "Punishment Theory in Industrial Discipline," *Industrial Relations,* Vol. 15, No. 2, (May 1976):235–43.

42. Elkouri and Elkouri, pp. 630–32.

43. Ibid.

44. *Personnel Policies Forum: Employee Conduct and Discipline,* Survey No. 102, (Washington, D.C.: Bureau of National Affairs, Inc., August 1973), p. 10.

45. Fleishman and Harris.

46. Maurice S. Trotta, *Handling Grievances: A Guide for Management and Labor* (Washington, D. C.: Bureau of National Affairs, Inc., 1976), pp. 48–63.

47. Ibid., pp. 48–49.

Suggested Readings

Elkouri, F. and Elkouri, E. A. *How Arbitration Works*. Washington, D. C.: Bureau of National Affairs, 3rd ed. 1973.

Nash, A. *The Union Steward: Duties, Rights, and Status.* Ithaca, NY: New York State School of Industrial and Labor Relations, Cornell University, Key Issues Series, no. 22, 1977.

Slichter, S. H., Healy, J. J., and Livernash, E. R. *The Impact of Collective Bargaining on Management.* Washington, D. C.: The Brookings Institution, 1960.

Thomson, A. W. J. *The Grievance Procedure in The Private Sector*. Ithaca, NY: New York State School of Industrial and Labor Relations, Cornell University, 1974.

Trotta, M. S. *Handling Grievances: A Guide for Management and Labor*. Washington, D. C.: Bureau of National Affairs, 1976.

Chapter 15

GRIEVANCE ARBITRATION

Today's arbitration hearing had been scheduled for a long time. Even though Tom Perkins had been looking foward to it, he was still quite nervous while he waited to have breakfast with his union's attorney prior to going to the hearing. They were going to go over his upcoming testimony and the events that had led to his discharge one more time before presenting their case to the arbitrator.

Quite a bit had happened to Tom in the last year. He dropped out of college during his sophomore year to get married. Shortly thereafter, he and his wife had a baby girl. To support his family, Tom got a job working for Crosswinds Bus Company as a baggage handler. Part of his job was to process packages people wanted shipped by Crosswinds' buses. In addition to making sure the packages got on the right buses, Tom had to collect payment from the customers.

Tom had been on the job about four months. One morning he was called to his supervisor's office. His supervisor, the director of industrial relations, the head of company security and his union steward were already there. He was told that his cash drawer was short about $104. A review of the company records indicated that there were no bookkeeping errors. Tom was asked where the money was. He didn't know. He was given the opportunity to review the company records that revealed the shortage. After doing so, he acknowledged a shortage existed but denied having taken the money. At this point, his supervisor gave him a previously prepared letter notifying him that he was terminated for the theft of company funds.

Tom was stunned. He needed his job. He also knew that being fired for theft would seriously limit his chances to get employment elsewhere. After leaving the meeting, he talked with the union steward. Tom swore that he hadn't taken the money. The union steward said he would do what he could. Later in the day, Tom received a telephone call from the local union president. He suggested Tom file a grievance. With the help of the union steward, Tom filed a grievance the next day stating that he was not terminated for just and sufficient cause as required by the labor agreement. He requested that he be reinstated and compensated for wages lost due to the improper discharge.

Over the next couple of months, union and company officials had several meetings about Tom's case. However, the company would not change its decision. The union decided to go to arbitration.

Tom had only been in the union for about three months prior to his discharge. While he had heard about grievance arbitration, he really didn't know what it was all about. However, in about an hour, he would learn as his case was presented to the arbitrator. If all went well, he would get his job back. If not, his termination for theft would stand.

Like Tom Perkins, most people have not had personal contact with grievance arbitration. Tom's interest in arbitration was quite limited. He hoped that, through arbitration, he would get his job back. While useful for resolving disagreements between the union and management over discipline and discharge decisions, grievance arbitration plays a much broader role in labor-management relations. This chapter examines the practice and procedure of grievance arbitration. By undertaking such a review, you will gain an understanding of the nature of grievance arbitration, its legal foundation, the way it is used, as well as the advantages and disadvantages of its utilization.

More specifically, by studying this chapter you should be able to:

- Differentiate between interest and rights (or grievance) arbitration.
- Discuss the major NLRB and court decisions that have shaped the evolution of grievance arbitration and the impact of these decisions on the process.
- Understand the advantages and disadvantages of grievance arbitration to labor and management.
- Explain the characteristics of a good arbitration clause.
- Describe how to prepare a case for presentation at an arbitration hearing.
- Identify the major features of an arbitration hearing.

What Is Grievance Arbitration?

As discussed in the preceding chapter, problems related to the contract's interpretation and administration are bound to arise during the life of a labor agreement. The parties usually include a grievance procedure in their labor agreement, which provides a mechanism for resolving disagreements over the contract's meaning and application. Approximately 96 percent of all contracts include arbitration as the final step of the grievance procedure.[1]

Arbitration was initially examined in some detail in Chapter 10. At that time, two types were defined: interest and rights arbitration. Both types of arbitration involve a neutral third party in a labor dispute. The neutral, known as an arbitrator, is brought into the dispute. After an examination of the issues, the arbitrator renders a decision resolving the dispute that is binding on both parties. The basic arbitration process is the same in both interest and rights disputes. It is the nature of the dispute that differentiates the two types of arbitration. Interest arbitration is used to resolve disputes arising out of the negotiation of a new agreement. This approach to dispute resolution is used most extensively in the public sector, as will be discussed in the next chapter. However, interest arbitration has also been used in the private sector in the steel industry and in professional baseball, for example.

Rights arbitration, also known as grievance arbitration, is used as part of a grievance procedure. Grievance arbitration is used to resolve disputes arising during the life of an existing agreement. Since these disputes concern the interpretation and administration of an agreement, the disagreements involve an examination of the parties' rights (hence the name) under the existing contract. Because this type of arbitration is usually the last step of a grievance procedure, it is also known as grievance arbitration.

This chapter examines grievance arbitration. To reiterate, the principle is the same as that involved in interest arbitration. Only the situation leading to arbitration differs. If the parties disagree over the meaning of the labor agreement and are unable to resolve the problem through the grievance procedure, the dispute can be submitted to arbitration. An arbitrator, a neutral third party, examines both sides of the disagreement. Then the arbitrator issues a decision resolving the dispute. Before submitting the dispute to arbitration, the parties have agreed to be bound by the arbitrator's award. As a result of this process, the parties obtain a final and binding resolution to their dispute.

When the parties disagree over the interpretation or administration of the contract, it would theoretically be possible for a union to strike until the company accepts the union's offer to settle the disagreement. Alternatively, a union without the strength to strike could anticipate working under an agreement subject to unilateral interpretations by the employer. However, a procedure relying on strikes for resolving disagreements arising during the life of an agreement would be extremely disruptive from both the firm's and the employees' points of view. The grievance procedure with arbitration as the final step was developed to prevent the need to engage in labor disputes arising during the life of the agreement. By substituting an administrative procedure for the strike, a system was developed to insure that the workers did not lose every dispute. At the same time, the employer is assured an uninterrupted supply of labor for the duration of the contract.

Grievance arbitration is highly acceptable to the parties and is an effective method for resolving contract-interpretation disputes. It has also received support from the NLRB and the courts. Consequently, the national labor policy encourages the parties to utilize arbitrators to resolve contract-interpretation problems. Let's look at the evolution of the national labor policy with respect to grievance arbitration.

Grievance Arbitration and National Labor Policy

Arbitration has been part of the American labor relations scene since approximately 1865.[2] However, this section focuses on arbitration's most recent history. At the present time, the nation's labor policy clearly supports the grievance arbitration process and encourages its usage. For example, the parties may disagree on whether an issue should be arbitrated. This dispute concerns the arbitrability of the issue. To foster the use of grievance arbitration, labor policy holds that any doubts concerning the arbitrability of an issue are to be resolved in favor of arbitration. To insure that the arbitration process is not undermined by the judiciary, the public policy makes it very difficult for the courts to review an arbitrator's decision. By limiting judicial review, the final and binding nature of the arbitrator's decision is protected.

Arbitration did not always have this special status. As will be discussed later, prior to 1947 there were doubts whether an agreement to arbitrate as part of a labor contract was even enforceable in court. This situation changed after 1947 as a result of the Labor Management Relations Act being passed. This section reviews the evolution of public policy toward grievance arbitration since 1947. Examining a series of court and NLRB decisions will show how the nation's labor policy encourages the parties to use grievance arbitration to handle disputes concerning the interpretation and administration of an existing labor agreement.

SECTION 301 OF THE LABOR MANAGEMENT RELATIONS ACT

Section 301 states in part:

> (a) Suits for violations of contracts between an employer and a labor organization representing employees . . . may be brought in any district court of the United States. . . .
> (b) Any labor organization which represents employees . . . shall be bound by the acts of its agents. Any such labor organization may sue or be sued as an entity and on behalf of the employees whom it represents in the courts of the United States. . . .

After passage of Section 301, uncertainty existed over the meaning of the provision. One view of Section 301 was that it was strictly procedural. It simply gave federal courts jurisdiction over disputes involving labor organizations. If a union affecting interstate commerce wanted to sue or was to be sued, a federal court was the appropriate place to pursue the action. Another view of Section 301 was that it was the source of substantive law. This view held that the federal courts would have to identify a source of law for deciding the issues raised in the lawsuits brought under Section 301. With this substantive view, either state or federal law could have been used to resolve the questions arising from Section 301 suits.

THE LINCOLN MILLS DECISION

The United States Supreme Court ruled on the nature of Section 301 in the 1957 *Lincoln Mills*[3] decision. In this case, the parties had as part of the labor contract an agreement not to strike during the life of the contract and to submit unresolved grievances to arbitration. As a result of a disagreement over work loads and work assignments, the union requested the dispute to be settled through arbitration. When the employer refused arbitration, the union brought suit in a federal district court under Section 301 to compel arbitration. While the district court found for the union, the Court of Appeals reversed the decision. Consequently, the employer was not forced to arbitrate.

Upon appeal, the Supreme Court took the opportunity to review Section 301 and the rights of unions to sue and be sued in federal courts. The court decided that the agreement to arbitrate grievances should be enforced.

> Plainly the agreement to arbitrate grievance disputes is the *quid pro quo* for an agreement not to strike. Viewed in this light, the legislation [Section 301] does more than confer jurisdiction in the federal courts over labor organizations. It expresses the federal policy that federal courts should enforce these agreements on behalf of or against labor organizations and that industrial peace can be best obtained only in that way. . . .[4]

In reaching this decision, the Supreme Court ruled that Section 301 did more than give the federal courts jurisdiction over labor organizations. The provision was also a source of substantive law. The court held that federal labor law should be used by the judiciary when deciding cases under Section 301. This means that decisions rendered under Section 301 must be compatible with the nation's labor policy. Since the arbitration of grievances contributes to the goals of national labor policy (that is, industrial peace and stability), the *Lincoln Mills* decision enforced the parties' agreement to arbitrate.

The *Lincoln Mills* decision had a tremendous effect on the use of grievance arbitration. Before 1957, grievance arbitration was relatively widespread but its legal standing was unclear. Even if the parties had included an arbitration clause in their contract, the union was uncertain whether it could require the employer to arbitrate the dispute. However, the *Lincoln Mills* decision specified that when a labor agreement contains an arbitration clause, the parties must arbitrate. Because Section 301 was interpreted as supporting grievance arbitration if required by the labor agreement, an increased number of contracts containing arbitration clauses was negotiated.[5]

THE STEELWORKERS TRILOGY

The *Steelworkers Trilogy* involves three decisions rendered by the United States Supreme Court in 1960. These cases clearly demonstrated that the arbitration of grievances was accepted by the courts as a desirable method for handling disputes during the life of an agreement. Also, the decisions insulated the arbitration process from the review of the courts. In general, the *Steelworkers Trilogy* helped clarify the role of grievance arbitration in the American industrial relations system.

In the *USW v. American Manufacturing Company* case,[6] the company claimed a grievance should not go to arbitration because it did not have merit. An employee who was 25 percent partially disabled claimed his old job when he returned to work after being injured. The union argued that the worker should have gotten his old job back because of his seniority. The employer held that the employee was not physically able to do the job as evidenced by his workers' compensation settlement that acknowledged his partial disability. The company refused to arbitrate the case. The union filed suit in a federal district court seeking enforcement of the labor agreement that called for the arbitration of grievances. The district court held that the employer did not have to arbitrate the grievance. The Court of Appeals upheld the lower court's decision stating that the grievance was "a frivolous, patently baseless one, not subject to arbitration under the collective bargaining agreement."

The Supreme Court reversed the lower court's decision. In its decision, Justice William O. Douglas, writing for the majority, stated:

> The courts therefore have no business weighing the merits of the grievance, considering whether there is in a particular claim, or determining whether there is particular language in the written instrument which will support the claim. The agreement is to submit all grievances to arbitration, not merely those the court will deem meritorious. The processing of even frivolous claims may have therapeutic value of which those who are not a part of the plant environment may be quite unaware. . . . When the judiciary undertakes to determine the merits of a grievance under the guise of interpreting the grievance procedure of collective bargaining agreements, it usurps a function which under that regime is entrusted to the arbitration tribunal.[7]

The *USW v. American Manufacturing Company* decision limited the court's ability to declare a grievance nonarbitrable even in situations where the grievance is considered completely worthless. Through this decision, the Supreme Court insured that arbitrators, not judges, would decide the merits of arbitration cases. While an arbitrator can decide that a grievance is silly or frivolous, the responsibility for resolving the grievance rests with the arbitrator; not the courts.

The second case in the *Steelworkers Trilogy,* the *USW v. Warrior and Gulf Navigation*[8] decision, also concerned the arbitrability of grievances. In this case, the employer subcontracted maintenance work previously performed by bargaining-unit employees. This led to the lay-off of a number of employees. The union grieved the company's decision to subcontract. Since the parties were unable to resolve the conflict through the grievance procedure, the union requested the dispute be arbitrated. The company refused to arbitrate on the grounds that subcontracting was a managerial prerogative. The union filed suit in order to compel the company to arbitrate. The district court decided the employer did not have to arbitrate since an arbitrator does not have the right to review a business decision. On appeal, the district court's decision was affirmed.

The issue before the Supreme Court was whether subcontracting work was a violation of the labor agreement and a subject for arbitration. The Supreme Court reversed the lower court's decision, stating:

> The Congress, however, has by Section 301 of the Labor Management Relations Act, assigned the courts the duty of determining whether the reluctant party has breached his promise to arbitrate. For arbitration is a matter of contract and a party cannot be required to submit to arbitration any dispute he has not agreed so to submit. Yet, to be consistent with congressional policy in favor of settlement of disputes by the parties through the machinery of arbitration, the judicial inquiry under Section 301 must be strictly confined to the question whether the reluctant party did agree to arbitrate the grievance or agreed to give the arbitrator power to make the award he made. An order to arbitrate this particular grievance should not be denied unless it may be said with positive assurance that the arbitration clause is not susceptible to an interpretation that covers the asserted dispute. Doubts should be resolved in favor of coverage.[9]

Since it was not demonstrated that subcontracting had been explicitly identified as a subject excluded from the coverage of the arbitration clause, the Supreme Court decided the dispute should have been arbitrated. The significance of the *Warrior and Gulf Navigation* decision is that the courts cannot find a case nonarbitrable unless clear and specific language exists excluding the issue at dispute from the arbitration clause. As a result of this decision, it is the arbitrator's responsibility, not the court's, to determine the arbitrability of a dispute under most circumstances.

The first two cases of the *Steelworkers Trilogy* concerned the ability of the parties to have the courts enforce a contractual agreement to arbitrate and the arbitrability of grievances. In general, these decisions require the parties to arbitrate grievances as long as an arbitration clause is part of the contract. The third case in the *Trilogy* does not concern the arbitrability of a grievance. Rather, the *USW v. Enterprise Wheel and Car Corp.*[10] decision concerned the ability of the courts to review an arbitrator's decision.

In the *USW v. Enterprise Wheel and Car* case, the parties went to arbitration and the arbitrator rendered a decision. Despite contract language that stated the arbitrator's award would be final and binding, the company refused to comply with the decision. Although the district court directed the employer to comply with the award, the Court of Appeals held that the arbitrator's decision was unenforceable because it contained ambiguities.

On appeal to the Supreme Court, the lower-court decision was reversed. In its opinion, the Supreme Court severely limited the ability of the courts to review an arbitrator's award. Again, Justice Douglas wrote the majority's decision, stating:

> The refusal of courts to review the merits of an arbitration award is the proper approach to arbitration under collective bargaining agreements. The federal policy of settling labor disputes by arbitration would be undermined if courts had the final say on the merits of the awards.[11]

The *USW v. Enterprise Wheel and Car* decision indicated that neither the union nor the company will be able to use the courts routinely to have an arbitrator's award set aside. More specifically, the decision indicated that the courts do not have the authority to set aside an arbitrator's interpretation of the contract.

In summary, the three cases comprising the *Steelworkers Trilogy* demonstrated that the Supreme Court viewed arbitration as an important part of the nation's labor policy. Arbitration was identified as the preferable means for resolving disputes arising during the life of the contract over its interpretation or administration. If the parties included an arbitration clause in their agreement, the *Steelworkers Trilogy* ensured that the arbitrator would be able to determine the arbitrability of the grievance, examine the merits of the case and render a decision relatively free from interference by the judicial system.

WHERE AN ARBITRATOR'S AWARD CAN BE REVIEWED BY THE COURTS

While the *Steelworkers Trilogy* established the integrity of the grievance arbitration process and insulated it from interference by the courts, it is not impossible to have an arbitrator's award set aside by the courts. There are situations where a court can refuse to enforce an arbitrator's award. This section examines the basic conditions under which this can take place.

Arbitrators derive their authority from the labor agreement. Except under limited circumstances, arbitrators cannot exceed the authority granted to them by the agreement. In the *USW v. Enterprise Wheel and Car* decision, the Supreme Court reminded arbitrators about the scope of their authority by stating:

> An arbitrator is confined to the interpretation and application of the collective bargaining agreement; he does not sit to dispense his own brand of industrial justice. He may of course look for guidance from many sources, yet his award is legitimate only so long as it draws its essence from the collective bargaining agreement. When the arbitrator's words manifest an infidelity to this obligation, courts have no choice but to refuse enforcement of the award.[12]

As part of the arbitration process, the parties will usually define the problem they want the arbitrator to resolve. As a result, the arbitrator's authority is limited to resolving only the issue identified by the parties. If the arbitrator exceeds the authority granted by the parties, then the award can be vacated. On this point, Prasow and Peters wrote:

> The most common ground, under state and federal law, for overturning an arbitrator's verdict is that he exceeded the authority prescribed for him [by the parties]. The arbitrator's award becomes vulnerable if he decides matters not presented to him. . . .[13]

In the *Torrington Co. v. The Metal Products Workers, Local 1645*[14] decision, the United States Court of Appeals, Second Circuit, stated:

> It is now well settled that a grievance is arbitrable "unless it may be said with positive assurance that the arbitration clause is not susceptible of an interpretation that covers the dispute." *United Steelworkers of America v. Warrior and Gulf Navigation Co.*, 363 U.S. at 582–583, 80 S.Ct. at 1353. A less settled question is the appropriate scope of judicial review of a specific arbitration award. Although the arbitrator's decision on the merits is final as to questions of law and fact, his authority is contractual in nature and is limited to the powers conferred in the collective bargaining agreement. For this reason, a number of courts have interpreted *Enterprise Wheel* as authorizing review of whether an arbitrator's award exceeded the limits of his authority.[15]

See Exhibit 15.1 for a list of factors providing grounds for vacating an arbitrator's award under the Uniform Arbitration Act.

GRIEVANCE ARBITRATION AND THE NLRB

Typically, an arbitrator's award will provide the parties a final and binding solution to their dispute. However, if the behavior leading to the grievance also constituted an unfair labor practice, the arbitrator's award might not end the conflict. In cases like this, it would be possible for the party losing the arbitration to try to get a more

> **EXHIBIT 15.1**
> **Grounds for Setting Aside an Arbitrator's Award under the Uniform Arbitration Act**
>
> The Uniform Arbitration Act can be adopted by states or used as the basis for state laws. As the name suggests, it is intended to help bring uniformity to state arbitration laws. A number of states have adopted the Uniform Arbitration Act.
>
> The Uniform Arbitration Act lists the following causes for setting aside an arbitrator's award:
>
> *Section 12. Vacating an award*
> (a) Upon application of a party, the court shall vacate an award where:
>
> (1) The award was procured by corruption, fraud or undue means.
>
> (2) There was evident partiality by an arbitrator appointed as a neutral or corruption in any of the arbitrators or misconduct prejudicing the rights of any party.
>
> (3) The arbitrators exceeded their power.
>
> (4) The arbitrators refused to postpone the hearing upon sufficient cause being shown therefor or refused to hear evidence material to the controversy or otherwise so conducted the hearing . . . as to prejudice substantially the rights of the parties.
>
> (5) There was no arbitration agreement and the issue was not adversely determined . . . and the party did not participate in the arbitration hearing without raising the objection.
>
> But the fact that the relief was such that it could not or would not be granted by a court of law or equity is not ground for vacating or refusing to confirm the award.

favorable settlement by filing unfair-labor-practice charges with the NLRB. To limit the possibility a case will be heard twice (arbitration and unfair-labor-practice proceedings), the NLRB will defer to the arbitration process. It should be noted that these situations cannot involve violations of an employee's Section 7 rights.

The conditions under which the NLRB defers to arbitration were originally presented in the *Spielberg Manufacturing Company* decision.[16] The NLRB held that the desirable objective of encouraging the voluntary settlement of labor disputes would best be served by recognizing the arbitrator's award as long as:

- The proceedings are fair and regular.
- All parties agreed to be bound by the arbitrator's award.
- The arbitrator's award is consistent with the purposes and policies of the National Labor Relations Act (NLRA).

The rationale behind the *Spielberg* doctrine was enunciated rather clearly in the *International Harvester Co.*[17] decision. The NLRB stated:

> If complete effectuation of the Federal policy is to be achieved, we firmly believe that the Board, which is entrusted with the administration of one of many facets of national labor policy, should give hospitable acceptance of the arbitration process as "part and parcel of the collective bargaining process itself," and voluntarily withhold its un-

doubted authority to adjudicate alleged unfair labor practice charges involving the same subject matter, unless it clearly appears that the arbitration proceedings were tainted by fraud, collusion, unfairness, or serious procedural irregularities or the award was clearly repugnant with the purpose and policies of the Act.[18]

The NLRB extended the *Spielberg* doctrine in its *Collyer Insulated Wire Co.*[19] decision. In this case, the union filed unfair-labor-practice charges alleging the company violated Sections 8(a)(5) and (1) of the NLRA by making unilateral changes in wages and certain working conditions. The company maintained that it had the authority under the labor agreement to do so. If the union believed the company exceeded its authority, the company argued that the problem should be remedied through the grievance and arbitration procedures, not the NLRB.

The NLRB agreed with the company's position that the dispute was over terms and meaning of the labor agreement. Therefore, the NLRB concluded the controversy should have been handled through the grievance and arbitration procedures. The board maintained that:

> Because this dispute in its entirety arises from the contract between the parties, and from the parties' relationship under the contract, it ought to be resolved in the manner which that contract prescribes. We conclude that the Board is vested with authority to withhold its processes in this case, and that the contract here made available a quick and fair means for the resolution of this dispute including, if appropriate, a fully effective remedy for any breach of contract which occurred. We conclude, in sum, that our obligation to advance the purposes of the Act is best discharged by dismissal of this complaint.[20]

In the *Spielberg* case, the parties had already gone to arbitration before pursuing the unfair-labor-practice charges with the NLRB. When deciding whether to defer, the NLRB was able to review the already completed arbitration process to insure the deferral standards set out in the decision were met. In the *Collyer* case, the parties had not gone to arbitration before going to the NLRB. Since it appeared the parties' grievance-and-arbitration procedure could resolve the dispute, the NLRB decided to defer to arbitration. However, under the *Collyer* doctrine the board retains jurisdiction over the unfair labor practice until it is apparent that the dispute has been resolved through arbitration.[21]

The *Spielberg* and *Collyer* doctrines require the parties, prior to going to the NLRB, to utilize their grievance-and-arbitration procedures in situations where the behavior in dispute also constitutes an unfair labor practice. Nash states:

> Industrial self-government is thus given the opportunity to function and the Board is given the benefit of a determination by an arbitrator skilled in contract interpretation and familiar with the law of the shop. The *Spielberg* standards insure that the unfair labor practice allegation has been properly resolved and the retention of jurisdiction under *Collyer* insures the standards will be applied in cases of pre-award deferral.[22]

IMPLICATIONS OF THE NLRB DEFERRAL TO ARBITRATION POLICY

Most obvious, the NLRB's willingness to defer to arbitration under certain circumstances will lead to an increase in the number of cases going to arbitration. Since the NLRB does not charge for its services and arbitrators do, the costs associated with resolving disputes that are both contract violations and unfair labor practices could increase. Also, it is quite possible that the time required to resolve the disputes will increase. Under the NLRB's deferral policy, the dispute will have to be arbitrated first. In the event that the arbitration fails to meet the *Spielberg* criteria, the case will then be heard by the board. The average case takes months to go through the arbitration procedure. When the NLRB refuses to honor the arbitrator's award, the time and money associated with the arbitration is wasted.[23] Finally, on a more pragmatic level, NLRB deferral to arbitration could lessen the board's caseload.[24] By so doing, the board can decrease the amount of time needed to handle cases for which an alternative forum such as arbitration is unavailable.

ARBITRATION AND THE CIVIL RIGHTS ACT

A number of collective-bargaining agreements include clauses banning discrimination on account of race, color, religion, sex, or national origin. Consequently, it is possible, as an example, for an employee's discharge to violate both the contract's antidiscrimination clause and Title VII of the Civil Rights Act which makes certain discriminatory acts illegal.

As a result of the *Alexander v. Gardner-Denver Co.*[25] decision, arbitration is not buffered from judicial review and possible reversal in discrimination cases as in situations where possible violations of the nation's labor policy have occurred. In this decision, the Supreme Court refused to allow a federal district court to defer to a prior arbitration award in a case involving a grievant who subsequently filed a court suit charging his Title VII rights had been violated. The implication of this decision has been described as follows:

> The Court held that an employee is entitled to a trial *de novo* [a new trial] in the District Court notwithstanding any prior adverse arbitration award rendered in a proceeding under a collective bargaining agreement in which he participated. The High Court did concede that the arbitration award could be received in evidence by the District Court but that the weight which would be accorded to it was within the trial court's discretion in each case.[26]

The Supreme Court decided that the federal labor policy encouraging arbitration did not prevent individuals from filing discrimination charges under Title VII of the Civil Rights Act after losing the arbitration. The court held that Congress intended to give the federal courts the final responsibility for enforcing Title VII.[27] Nowhere in Title VII is arbitration identified as a way to resolve discrimination charges. This is basically different from the Labor Management Relations Act, which identifies private-dispute resolution techniques (Section 201) as an important part of the nation's labor policy. Consequently, the deferral by the courts to an arbitrator's award does not serve the purposes of the Civil Rights Act. However, deferral to arbitration in contract interpretation cases furthers the federal labor policies.[28]

As a result of the *Alexander v. Gardner-Denver* decision, employees charging discrimination have a choice of procedures for redressing the discrimination. Under the labor agreement, an employee can utilize the arbitration procedure. If the employee wins the arbitration award, the case will probably end since the employer has agreed to be bound by the arbitrator's award. However, if the employee loses the arbitration case, he or she can then seek redress of the discrimination through the mechanisms provided by Title VII of the Civil Rights Act.

The Major Advantages of Grievance Arbitration

Grievance arbitration offers labor and management an effective alternative to seeking enforcement of labor agreements through the slow, complex, and expensive court system or by relying on strikes to resolve contract interpretation problems.[29] Reliance on the judicial system to handle disputes arising during the life of a labor agreement would seriously undermine the labor-management relationship. When discussing the judicial system as a method for resolving labor disputes, Supreme Court Justice William H. Rehnquist noted:

> It is extraordinarily costly in terms of attorney's fees and associated expenses, and it is extraordinarily time consuming both in the stage of pre-trial discovery and actual trial, and it is usually several years between the time a lawsuit is begun and the time the last appellate court involved renders its decision.[30]

When compared with striking over contract-interpretation problems, arbitration is the distinctively more attractive alternative. Strikes do not offer a meaningful alternative to parties who do not have the ability to engage in a walkout. For parties able to strike, doing so is expensive and inconvenient for everyone involved. Arbitration precludes the need to strike during the life of the agreement. This ensures steady employment for the worker and a guaranteed labor supply for the employer.

Grievance arbitration that submits the disputes to a neutral third party offers the parties a number of advantages relative to utilizing the court system.

ARBITRATION IS QUICKER AND LESS EXPENSIVE THAN LITIGATION

Although the costs and the amount of time associated with arbitration vary greatly depending on the nature of the case, arbitration is usually less expensive and time consuming than relying on the courts or the NLRB to resolve disputes. This is because it is less important in arbitration to utilize attorneys and court reporters. Also, a fewer number of witnesses is usually required. Grievance arbitration provides the parties the opportunity to obtain a relatively quick solution to their problem. This is an important consideration since unresolved grievances can accumulate and undermine plant morale.[31]

GRIEVANCE ARBITRATION IS RELATIVELY MORE UNDERSTANDABLE TO THE PARTIES

Although grievance arbitration is a judicial-like process in which the arbitrator hears the evidence and makes a decision in a fashion similar to a judge, it can be much less formal than a court of law. Often times, neither party will be represented by an attorney. Also, while many arbitrators are lawyers, many are not. Consequently, the arbitration hearings usually do not rely on hard-to-understand legal terminology or formal procedures. While arbitrators need to maintain control over the hearing, they do not have to rely on strict rules of evidence and courtroom procedures to do so.

ARBITRATION CAN PROVIDE FLEXIBLE REMEDIES[32]

The remedies available through the judicial system are rather inflexible because they are likely to rely on a strict interpretation of the contract language in question. However, arbitration has the potential to formulate remedies designed to meet the specific circumstances of the case. Arbitrators can be selected with special expertise in the subject matter at dispute or with an intensive understanding of the industry. Because of control over the arbitrator-selection process, the parties can choose an arbitrator with the skills needed to resolve the dispute rather than rely on a judge who may not be as well qualified as the arbitrator to settle the particular dispute.[33]

It is interesting to note that the major benefits associated with arbitration, such as minimizing time delays and costs, being understandable to the parties, and yielding flexible solutions to the grievances, have also been the focal points for criticism of the arbitration process. Arbitration is being sharply criticized for becoming too slow, too expensive, and too legalistic. These problems, as well as possible solutions, will be discussed later in this chapter.

Moving from the Grievance Procedure to Arbitration: The Arbitration Clause

In order for the parties to utilize grievance arbitration, they usually write a provision into the labor agreement calling for its use. This is known as an arbitration clause. The arbitration clause authorizes the arbitrator to decide questions of interpretation or administration of the labor agreement.[34] As with grievance procedures discussed in the preceding chapter, arbitration clauses can be placed into two categories: broad or narrow. A labor agreement with a broad arbitration clause excludes very few subjects from arbitration. This allows a wide variety of issues to be reviewed by the arbitrator. A narrow arbitration clause restricts arbitration to disputes involving the interpretation or application of the labor agreement.[35] Regardless of the type of clause used, additional language is usually found restricting the arbitrator's authority. For example, the labor agreement between the Denver Retail Grocers and the United Food and Commercial Workers, Local No. 7, includes the following limitation on the arbitrator's authority: "the award of the arbitrator shall not affect, change, alter or modify any of the terms and conditions set forth in this Agreement."

It is also possible for narrow arbitration clauses to exclude certain types of disputes from the arbitration process. For example, the labor agreement between Continental Trailways Bus Center, Inc. and the Amalgamated Transit Union, District 1001, removes discipline for certain types of behavior from the arbitration process. The contract states: "In the event the final decision in all discipline and discharge cases, *except cases of breach of trust, intoxication or immoral acts,* is not satisfactory either party may submit it to arbitration as provided herein." (emphasis added)

In addition to defining the arbitrator's authority by identifying the type of case that can be arbitrated, a good arbitration clause will also address a number of procedural issues employees face when taking a grievance to arbitration. A good arbitration clause will address issues such as:

HOW THE ARBITRATOR WILL BE SELECTED

Some parties may have a permanent arbitrator who will be requested to decide any grievances going to arbitration. Alternatively, the parties may use an ad hoc procedure; that is, the arbitrator is selected after the parties decide to take the case to arbitration. This procedure is used in approximately one-half of labor agreements with arbitration clauses.[36] When contracts specify the use of ad hoc arbitrators, they will usually specify how the arbitrator will be selected. Typically, it will be specified that either the Federal Mediation and Conciliation Service or the American Arbitration Association will provide a list of arbitrators. Exhibit 15.2 contains a provision for selecting an arbitrator on an ad hoc basis.

If the parties agree, the contract's selection procedure can be waived. In such a situation, the union and management officials can then select an arbitrator upon whom they mutually agree. This is known as the direct appointment of an arbitrator.

HOW QUICKLY THE ARBITRATOR MUST RETURN HIS OR HER DECISION

The time limit written into an agreement serves as a reminder to the busy arbitrator that the parties want a prompt decision. Typically, contracts placing time restrictions on the arbitrator require the decision to be submitted to the parties within thirty days.[37]

> **EXHIBIT 15.2**
> **An Example of an Ad Hoc Selection Procedure**
>
> In the event the parties are unable to reach agreement upon the selection of an arbitrator, the party requesting arbitration with reasonable promptness, requests a panel of five (5) arbitrators from the Federal Mediation and Conciliation Service. From the panel of five names, each party shall strike two names and the remaining arbitrator from the list shall be the impartial arbitrator.
>
> *Source: From the labor agreement between King Soopers, Inc. and the Delivery Drivers, Warehousemen and Helpers Union, Local No. 435.*

THE NUMBER OF ARBITRATORS TO HEAR THE DISPUTE

While most contracts specify that the dispute will be decided by a single arbitrator (about three-quarters of union contracts),[38] the remaining contracts require three or five arbitrators. When multiperson arbitration panels are used, there is a single impartial arbitrator, and the others are appointed by the union and management. Use of a single arbitrator is usually quicker and less expensive than is the case when panels are used. Where multiperson panels are employed, the impartial arbitrator usually benefits from the advice and assistance received from the union and management representatives on the panel. Also, if the panel returns a unanimous decision, that is, the union and management representatives agree with the impartial arbitrator's decision, the award tends to be more acceptable to the parties than if rendered by a single arbitrator.

HOW THE ARBITRATOR WILL BE PAID

The vast majority of contracts with arbitration clauses specify that the costs of arbitration will be shared equally by the parties.[39] A limited number of contracts require the losing party to pay for arbitration. It would also be appropriate for the arbitration clause to address other cost-related issues such as who will pay for a transcript of the arbitration hearing and whether witnesses will be paid for time lost from work while testifying.

The Arbitrability of Grievances

If the parties exhaust the steps in the grievance procedure without negotiating a settlement to the dispute, one or both may want to submit the issue to arbitration. If the dispute is arbitrable in light of the language of the arbitration clause, then the parties will begin preparation for the arbitration hearing. It is possible for the parties to disagree on whether the dispute is arbitrable. An example of a problem concerning the arbitrability of a grievance evolved from the previously discussed contract language in which the parties agreed to arbitrate all discipline cases except those involving a breach of trust, intoxication, or immoral acts. Union and company officials disagreed over the arbitrability of a case involving the discharge of a worker for theft. The company maintained that the case was not subject to arbitration because theft was a breach of trust exempted from the arbitration clause. The union held that the exemption referred to proven breach of trust cases and that the company had not proven its charges. Since the parties could not agree on the arbitrability of the discharge, they requested the arbitrator to rule on that issue. In other words, disputes over the arbitrability of an issue are likely to be resolved through the arbitration process. In the example just described, the arbitrator ruled that the exemption applied to proven or admitted cases of theft. To rule otherwise would seriously undermine the rights to due process of workers accused of serious offenses such as theft.

Let's assume that the parties have a grievance that is eligible for arbitration. It could involve a disagreement over the way in which the company is interpreting a provision in the contract. Or, the issue could involve a discipline or discharge decision thought to be inappropriate or inconsistent with the language of the labor agreement. The sections to follow examine how the parties would prepare to arbitrate the dispute.

DO WE REALLY WANT TO ARBITRATE?

Before proceeding to arbitration, each party must decide whether it is within its best interest to arbitrate the dispute. Under certain circumstances it may be better to negotiate a settlement rather than arbitrate. It has been suggested that the parties ask themselves the following questions to help decide whether to settle or arbitrate:

1. Are we right?
2. Is the issue sufficiently important?
3. Can the case be won?
4. What will be the effect of winning or losing?
5. What negotiated settlement is possible?[40]

After answering these questions, labor and management should be able to make the decision to arbitrate or pursue a negotiated settlement. O'Hara provides some useful guidelines to follow when making this decision. He states:

> If you believe you are "right," if your case is sound on the merits, is sufficiently important to you, and you estimate that there is a 70 percent chance of winning with no adverse long-range effect that will result from your victory, the price of a settlement on your part may be high, but it should be explored. If, on the other hand, your case is not sound, or you think you are not right, or it's not that important, or there is some-

thing to be lost by losing, then you had better avoid the risk of arbitration and take refuge in that old American political axiom that "you can't beat something with nothing."[41]

If you decide to arbitrate rather than settle, then you will have to prepare your case for presentation to the arbitrator.

Preparing Your Case for Arbitration

This section will present a general outline of the steps that can be taken while preparing a case for arbitration. Since the nature of the preparation phase will vary depending on the nature of the dispute, the discussion to follow will focus on the major steps in the process.[42]

KNOW THE CONTRACT

Typically, the written grievance will cite the specific contracts provision allegedly violated. It is important, therefore, when preparing a case for arbitration that the contract be fully understood. It is not enough to know what each provision says. It is also necessary to understand the interrelationships among the contracts's provisions. Does one section of the agreement modify another? Is one provision inconsistent with another? Is the contract language ambiguous? Does the management-rights clause affect the provision in question?

As part of the process of becoming familiar with the agreement, a review of the contract's negotiations could be made. It is unlikely that an arbitrator will modify the specific contract language to reflect the intentions of the negotiators. The parol evidence rule applied by most arbitrators when interpreting contracts holds that written or oral evidence such as notes made during negotiations cannot be used to vary or contradict the labor agreement's unambiguous language.[43] However, in the event the contract language is ambiguous, an arbitrator could give weight to evidence describing the intentions of the parties when negotiating the contract. Consequently, a review of the contract's negotiations could provide useful information that would help clarify the meaning of ambiguous contract language.

Also, a review of company procedures related to the grievance could be made to see if the contract's language has been modified or supplemented by a past practice.[44] When trying to interpret ambiguous contract language, an arbitrator is likely to examine custom or past practice to see if the parties have given meaning to the provision in question. If, whenever a situation is repeatedly faced by the parties, they responded in the same way with such regularity and consistency as to indicate a distinct and accepted pattern of behavior, a binding past practice is said to exist.[45]

For example, a group of workers received a $.51/hour increase in pay whenever they used a relatively dangerous piece of equipment. This was a procedure developed by first-level supervisors and the employees to encourage some workers to use the equipment voluntarily. The "hazard pay" procedure had been in effect for approximately six years before it came to the attention of top management. Top management decided that the company did not grant "hazard pay" under any circumstances since the contract was silent on the issue. Therefore, a memo was issued stating that "hazard pay" for use of the machine would no longer be granted. The next time the machine was used, the workers requested "hazard pay," but their request was denied. The workers grieved. The arbitrator reviewed the situation and sustained the grievance. He concluded that a binding past practice existed because the "hazard pay" procedure had been worked out by management officials and employees; it was used whenever the equipment was utilized for a number of years; and the workers expected "hazard pay" as part of their compensation when using the machine. Despite the contract's silence on the "hazard pay" issue, the arbitrator concluded the company was obligated to grant extra compensation to workers using the machine. In this situation, the past practice had the same effect as clear and unambiguous contract language.

It is possible for past practice to "creep" into an organization as lower-level supervisors and employees work out procedures to fill in gaps found in the labor agreement. It is quite possible that these practices may not come to the attention of top management or the labor relations staff. Consequently, it is important that an effort be made when preparing for arbitration to determine whether contract language has been supplemented or modified by binding past practice.

GET THE FACTS

The second phase of the preparation for the arbitration process is to develop a complete understanding of the events that led up to the filing of the grievance. It is important for union and management representatives when preparing for arbitration to make a first-hand investigation of the case. Such an investigation can help the parties decide whether to arbitrate the case. Alternatively, the investigation could identify a basis for a negotiated settlement. Assuming the case goes to arbitration, the investigation phase should develop all the factual information the arbitrator will need to make a decision. It has been argued that one of the surest ways for a party to pursuade an arbitrator that it has a good case is to enter the arbitration hearing with full and accurate information.[46]

Getting the facts could involve a visit to the scene of the incident leading to the grievance, a review of personnel files and an examination of company records. Also, interviews with the individuals involved in the events under study can be useful. It is important to know what your witnesses will say when they testify at the arbitration. It is very embarrassing to have a witness called by your side provide testimony that strengthens the arguments of the other side. It is also important to determine what prospective witnesses for the other side are likely to say when testifying. Liebes provides the following guidelines for interviewing witnesses prior to arbitration:

It cannot be overstressed that the advocate [union or company representative] must exercise the greatest skill and judgment in talking to potential witnesses. What is the extent of their knowledge of the disputed facts? Does their story conform with the grievant's? Do they have any special ax to grind? How will they behave when it is time for opposing counsel to cross examine? It is a sad time when one's own witness falters on the stand, or comes out with some revelations that were not disclosed during prehearing conversations.[47]

DEVELOP A THEORY OF THE CASE

After reviewing the contract and investigating the situation leading to the grievance, it should be possible to develop a theory of the case. The theory of the case is the "game plan" to be used to convince the arbitrator that he or she should agree with your side when deciding the case. The theory provides the basic argument and the sequencing of evidence to best support your position. Also, it is at this stage of the preparation process that you anticipate what the other side is likely to do. What is their theory of the case likely to be? What evidence do you need to rebut their presentation? How should your case be modified, if at all, in anticipation of the other side's presentation?

As with contract negotiations, preparation is the key to success in the arbitration. While it also helps to be "right," that is, have the contract's language support your theory of the case, a well-prepared case can help insure the arbitrator will issue a decision favorable to your side. If both parties are well prepared, it is quite likely that all the information the arbitrator needs to render a proper decision will be presented. This greatly enhances the effectiveness of the arbitration process.

SELECTING AN ARBITRATOR

As discussed in connection with arbitration clause, many contracts specify the procedure for selecting an arbitrator. The mechanics of selecting an arbitrator will not be reviewed here. Instead, we will focus on the characteristics to look for in an arbitrator. Remember, the arbitrator serves as both a judge and jury. The arbitrator conducts the hearing, analyzes the information presented, and renders a decision final and binding on the parties. Then, the parties have to live with the arbitrator's award. Given the critical nature of the arbitrator's role, it is important for the parties to exercise care when selecting an arbitrator to decide a case. It is difficult to identify a definitive list of characteristics to look for in an arbitrator since the desirable attributes will be a function of the parties' specific needs. However, it is possible to present some general characteristics to look for when selecting an arbitrator.

Objectivity. Both labor and management should be confident that the arbitrator can make a fair and unprejudiced decision. It is important that the arbitrator be objective when conducting the hearing, evaluating the evidence, and writing the decision.

A thorough understanding of labor relations. Given the complexity and importance of the issues to both labor and management, arbitrators should be well versed in labor relations and economics. While rigorous academic preparation can be an important part of an arbitrator's training, experience in labor relations is another important consideration. Many experienced arbitrators have had their awards published so it is possible to review these decisions to develop an appreciation for their approach to the various subjects of arbitration. For arbitrators listed with organizations such as the American Arbitration Association and the Federal Mediation and Conciliation Service, it can usually be assumed they have the technical qualifications to fulfill the arbitrator's role satisfactorily. However, additional investigation such as a review of published awards and conversations with parties that have previously utilized the arbitrator can provide additional insights into the arbitrator's abilities.

An understanding of legal processes. Arbitration is a judicial-like process. While it is not essential for an arbitrator to be a lawyer, an arbitrator should understand legal rules of evidence that can facilitate an orderly hearing.

Ability to communicate clearly. During the hearing, the arbitrator will have to utilize good verbal communication skills in order to maintain control of the procedure and help the parties present the information needed to make a decision. After the hearing, well-developed writing skills are needed to prepare an opinion and award that clearly presents the decision and explains why it was made. The likelihood that the award will be final and binding will be enhanced if the parties understand the decision. Otherwise, it may be necessary to go back to the arbitrator to obtain a clarification of the decision. This can slow the arbitration process and add appreciably to its costs.

Different parties will have different requirements for an arbitrator. The important consideration is that they find someone who can meet their specific needs. Not only must the arbitrator have the technical ability to conduct a hearing and deal with complex issues, the individual must have the acceptance and trust of the parties.

The Arbitration Hearing

All the preparation and the theories developed have been directed toward the arbitration hearing, the climax of the entire arbitration process.[48] At the hearing, both labor and management have the opportunity to present to the arbitrator their versions of the events leading to the grievance. They will also present their arguments intended to convince the arbitrator that the case should be decided in their favor.

There is no single way to conduct an arbitration hearing. The arbitrator will attempt to create an environment in which all the information needed to make a decision resolving the dispute will be obtained. Depending on the arbitrator, the hearing will be either formal or informal. A formal hearing is one which resembles a courtroom trial. Informal hearings have very little structure, resembling a business conference more than a court proceeding.[49]

In an informal hearing, the parties discuss the case with the limited use of witnesses and little concern for rules of evidence. Informal hearings have been described as follows:

There is very little of the courtroom atmosphere in most informal arbitrations. Instead of the systematic presentation of a series of witnesses and cross-examination of them by opposing parties, there is a general interchange of comments, discussion, and argument across the table. The arbitrator usually takes a more active part in these hearings, guiding the discussion and questioning both sides.[50]

As previously mentioned, formal hearings take on the trappings of a courtroom proceeding. While the specific procedures used vary depending on the arbitrator, a number of steps are common to most formal arbitration hearings.

OPENING THE HEARING

After determining that both parties are ready to begin, the arbitrator will make a statement to mark the opening of the hearing. This is more a procedural "nicety" than a substantive contribution to the hearing.

STATING THE ISSUE

This step requires the parties to define rather specifically the issue they would like resolved by the arbitrator. Sometimes this is done prior to the hearing. More likely, however, the arbitrator will request the parties to do so at the outset of the hearing. If the grievance was carefully worded, it can serve as the basis for defining the issue. Alternatively, the parties can work together during the hearing to define the issue. The resulting statement defining the issue is known as a submission agreement. If the parties are unable to reach agreement on the issue to be decided, the arbitrator can define the issue for them.

Identifying the issue is an important concern. If it is defined too narrowly, the arbitrator's award might not resolve the entire dispute. If the issue is defined too broadly, the arbitrator will not receive meaningful guidance from the parties and, as a result, the decision may be unresponsive to the parties' needs.

At this point in the hearing or at some early time, the arbitrator is likely to request the parties to stipulate certain facts that are not in dispute. This will avoid the need later in the hearing to present testimony or evidence on information not in dispute. Also, the arbitrator will probably ask the parties whether they have any joint exhibits. These are pieces of evidence to which both parties will be referring during the hearing. Typically, items submitted as joint exhibits would include a copy of the grievance and the labor agreement.

OPENING STATEMENTS

Each party will usually be given the opportunity to make an opening statement. The opening statements provide the arbitrator an overview of the case. They represent each party's most optimistic view of what it intends to prove during the hearing. Since the opening statement is an overview, it does not include evidence or testimony.[51] The significance of the opening statement has been described as follows:

CONTRACT INTERPRETATION AND ADMINISTRATION

The opening statement should be prepared with utmost care, because it lays the groundwork for the testimony of witnesses and helps the arbitrator understand the relevance of oral and written evidence. The statement, although brief, should clearly identify the issues, indicate what is to be proved and specify the relief sought.[52]

SWEARING IN WITNESSES

The arbitrator has the authority to swear in witnesses. While there is no such thing as perjury in arbitration hearings, it has been suggested that requiring witnesses to take an oath in which they promise to testify truthfully lends more dignity to the hearing.[53]

PROCEEDING WITH THE CASE

Either the union or management can present its case first. In most situations, the complaining party, that is, the one who filed the grievance, moves first. Then the other party presents its case in the form of a defense. In most contract-interpretation cases, the union is the complaining party. Consequently, it presents its case first.

However, in discipline and discharge cases, the employer usually goes first even though the union has filed the grievance. The logic behind the employer moving first in discipline or discharge cases has been described as follows:

> In a discharge situation, the employer has changed the status quo by terminating an employee's employment. Presumably he has done this for good cause, and the basis for such termination is within the purview of the employer. In the arbitration of a discharge case, therefore, the employer should move forward first because ordinarily the union is claiming that the reasons advanced for the discharge or the basis for employer's action is unjust or improper or not in accord with the agreement. Since this is usually the claim of the union, it makes sense to have the employer move first and set forth on the record why he discharged the employee, i.e., the basis for the termination. Then the union assumes the burden to establish that the reasons or basis for the discharge were not proper or fair.[54]

The party presenting its case first will start calling its witnesses. After a witness is called to testify, the party requesting the witness will begin its direct examination. Without interruption or questioning from the other side, the witness will be interrogated in an attempt to bring out testimony and evidence supportive of the party's position. Once direct testimony is completed, a representative from the other party will be given the opportunity to cross-examine the witness. The purpose of cross-examination is to review the evidence offered during direct examination, to test its truthfulness, clarify it or develop it further.[55] If after cross-examination the representative for the side originally calling the witness has additional questions, there will be redirect questioning. Then, the other side can re–cross-examine. This procedure is continued until there are no additional questions from either side. At this point, the next witness is called.

The party moving first will call all its witnesses. When it has completed this process, it will rest its case. Then, the other party will proceed with its case. Its witnesses will be subjected to direct examination and cross-examination by the other side. After the party going second has called all its witnesses, it will rest its case.

CLOSING ARGUMENTS

After all the testimony has been heard and evidence submitted, the arbitrator will give both parties the opportunity to make closing statements. At the discretion of the parties, the closing statement will be made orally at the end of the hearing. Alternatively, the parties may opt for posthearing briefs in which they submit their closing arguments to the arbitrator in writing within a specified time period. Closing arguments have been described as follows:

> The closing argument should avoid details of the case and emphasize points in the chain of reasoning underlying the parties' positions. This will not only tend to clarify the issues for the arbitrator, but it will also give both parties the assurance that they have presented their case as fully as possible.[56]

EXHIBIT 15.3
Checklist for Presenting an Arbitration Case

1. If a party wishes the arbitrator to put the witness under oath, he should request the arbitrator to do so at the beginning of the hearing.

2. If an opening statement is to be presented, it should be clear, concise, and well organized.

3. Exhibits should be presented during the course of the hearing. They should be shown to the other party first before seeking to introduce them.

4. If opposing counsel offers evidence that you believe should not be in the record, make a proper and timely objection.

5. The parties and counsel should avoid unnecessary friction between themselves at the hearing.

6. Direct examination should be to the point, complete, but not repetitive.

7. Cross examination should be used carefully and only in situations where the advocate is almost certain that the testimony obtained through cross examination will weaken the case of the opposing party.

8. Neither party should attempt to introduce irrelevant material into the record. It will not strengthen his case, and it may cloud the issue for the arbitrator. It also provides grounds for objection.

9. The closing argument should compellingly and persuasively present the party's theory of the case. It should be well-organized, and no longer than it absolutely needs to be.

Source: Sam Kagel, *Anatomy of a Labor Arbitration* (Washington, D. C.: Bureau of National Affairs, Inc., 1961), pp. 120–21.

This section was not intended to provide a detailed blueprint to use when presenting a case to an arbitrator. Rather, the material was presented to give an overview of the arbitration hearing, that is, the basic sequence of events. To develop a better understanding of how to present a case, refer to the selected readings listed at the end of the chapter. However, experience is probably the best teacher. If given the opportunity, observe an arbitration hearing. Doing so will help develop a better understanding of the arbitration process and how it can be adapted to meet the specific needs of the parties. Exhibit 15.3 presents a useful checklist to refer to when presenting an arbitration case.

The Arbitrator's Decision

Typically, an arbitration case ends when the arbitrator submits a decision to the parties. A decision usually has two major components: the opinion and the award. The award presents the arbitrator's ruling on the issue submitted by the parties and a remedy, if appropriate. The opinion outlines the reasoning underlying the arbitrator's award.

After the hearing or the receipt of posthearing briefs, the arbitrator can start deliberating. The arbitrator will take a number of factors into consideration before making a decision. Typically, the arbitrator will review the relevant contract language and intensely study the record of the hearing. Sometimes a verbatim transcript of the hearing is prepared. More likely, however, the arbitrator will have to rely on the handwritten notes he or she took during the hearing and the physical evidence to review the parties' positions. Also, if posthearing briefs were submitted, they will be studied to help decide whether the position of the company or union should be accepted. Sometimes the arbitrator will review published arbitration awards to see how others have handled similar situations. In sum, the arbitrator looks to the labor agreement, the issue, the evidence, testimony, and arguments of the parties and, perhaps, published arbitration awards to help make the decision.

The deciding of an arbitration case is not a precise science. In other words, arbitrators have much discretion when making their decisions. However, there are a number of principles or guidelines arbitrators can employ. See Exhibit 15.4 for a discussion of the major decision rules used by arbitrators when deciding contract-interpretation and discipline/discharge cases.

In addition to resolving the specific issue, the arbitrator's decision can serve other purposes.[57] Arbitration decisions can be used for improving contract administration by eliminating problems with the existing contract. The decisions can also be used as educational devices for foreman and union-steward training. For example, the review of decisions can give the parties insights into the arbitrator's decision-making process. This could help the parties improve their negotiations during the grievance procedure, thereby increasing the likelihood they can reach agreement without having to rely on arbitration. Finally, the arbitrator's decisions can pinpoint problem areas in the contract that will have to be addressed in future negotiations.

EXHIBIT 15.4
Guidelines Frequently Used When Deciding Arbitration Cases

The types of issues decided by arbitrators can be placed into two major categories—contract interpretation and discipline/discharge cases. There is no standard procedure guiding the arbitrator's decision-making process. However, principles or guidelines are used that structure the arbitrators' research and guide their thinking on the matters. Contract-interpretation and discipline/discharge cases each has its own set of decision rules.

Contract-interpretation cases. Some of the guidelines have been borrowed from the judicial system. Others have been employed repeatedly by arbitrators over the years and have demonstrated their usefulness. These decision rules facilitate the arbitrator's decision-making process. Also, knowledge of these guidelines gives the parties insights into how decisions are made and, therefore, makes the arbitration process more understandable to them.

A typical contract-interpretation case involves a disagreement between the union and management over the meaning of a provision in the labor agreement. This situation frequently develops because the contract language is ambiguous; that is, it is subject to more than one interpretation.

The arbitrator's basic objective when determining the meaning of ambiguous contract language is to ascertain the intent of the parties when the contract was negotiated. Initially, the arbitrator will try to determine the meaning of the ambiguous language by focusing on the labor agreement itself. Several of the guidelines used to do this include:

1. *View the labor agreement as a whole, not as independent parts.* The arbitrator will interpret the ambiguous language to be consistent with other parts of the contract. Also, an attempt will be made to interpret words in line with the way they are used elsewhere in the agreement.
2. *Provide words their normal meaning.* Unless it is shown the parties intended a special meaning for a word, its dictionary definition is likely to be used. Common word usage is likely to prevail.
3. *Specific language prevails over general language.* If the contract interpretation problem is caused by an inconsistency between general and specific language, arbitrators will typically decide the case in accordance with the specific language.
4. *Arbitrators will try to avoid harsh results.* When faced with two interpretations, one yielding harsh or nonsensical results and the other bringing about a reasonable outcome, the latter interpretation will probably be selected by the arbitrator.
5. *Interpret ambiguous language against the drafter.* When other guidelines do not help the arbitrator determine the intent of the parties, the arbitrator can interpret the provision against the party responsible for the language. The logic behind this guideline is that the drafter of the language had the responsibility to explain the meaning of the language fully. If the drafter fails to do so, the ambiguity is resolved in favor of the other party.

If the arbitrator cannot determine the intent of the parties by reviewing the labor agreement, it is then possible to go outside the contract to find the meaning of the ambiguous contract language. Several factors external to the contract can be examined to ascertain the meaning of the contract provision under review:

1. *Bargaining history.* A review of the negotiations leading up to the inclusion of the ambiguous language may be useful. Testimony from negotiators or bargaining notes may shed light on the parties' intentions.
2. *Past practice.* Arbitrators will look to see how the parties have interpreted the language in practice. If it can be shown that a practice has existed over the years that indicates a mutual agreement between the parties with respect to the practice under review, the arbitrator is likely to interpret the ambiguous language in accordance with the parties' past practice.

EXHIBIT 15.4 (Continued)

3. *Industry practice.* The meaning given the ambiguous language elsewhere in the industry may provide insights into the intent of the parties.

Discipline/discharge cases. Arbitrators typically approach the resolution of discipline/discharge cases differently than contract interpretation cases. In discipline/discharge cases, the arbitrator is usually asked to determine whether the employer had "just cause" for disciplining or discharging the employee. In this type of case, the arbitrator is likely to consider the following types of issues:

1. *Did the company have a rule prohibiting the behavior leading to the employee's discipline?* Employees must know their behavior is unacceptable before they can be disciplined. The company is obligated to demonstrate the existence of the rule. It should be recognized that some behaviors are so unacceptable in the workplace that specific rules are unnecessary. Employees should know that they cannot steal from their employer, be insubordinate or punch their supervisors.

2. *Was the rule communicated to the employees?* Having a rule is one thing. Communicating the rule is another. The employer is obligated to demonstrate that the employees were aware of the rule they were charged with violating.

3. *Has the rule been consistently enforced?* Is everyone who violated the rule disciplined? Lax enforcement of rules can be grounds for setting aside the employer's disciplinary actions. Also, the penalty attached with the infraction must be consistent with that imposed in similar cases involving the violation of the rule.

4. *Did the employee, in fact, violate the rule?* The company is obligated to establish that the employee violated the rule. The arbitrator will review the facts of the case to determine whether the company had sufficient grounds for taking action against the employee.

5. *Have due process requirements been met?* Employees charged with violating company rules must be given a reasonable opportunity to respond to the allegations. Employers are obligated to investigate the matter. Employees should have union representation, if desired. Also, employees should have an opportunity to have their side of the situation heard before disciplinary action is taken. Failure by the company to abide by due-process considerations can provide grounds for the arbitrator setting aside the disciplinary action.

This discussion is not intended to be an exhaustive review of decision rules used by arbitrators. Such a review is beyond the scope of this book. The point being made is that while arbitrators do not have a specific formula for deciding cases, they do have a number of guidelines available to them that facilitate the arbitration decision-making process. For a thorough discussion of these issues, see Frank Elkouri and Edna Elkouri, *How Arbitration Works,* 3rd ed. (Washington, D. C.: Bureau of National Affairs, 1973).

An Evaluation of Grievance Arbitration

By most measures, it must be concluded that grievance arbitration in the private sector has been successful. The fact that arbitration clauses are found in approximately 96 percent of the labor agreements in the United States indicates that arbitration is the method clearly desired by labor and management to resolve disputes arising during the life of the contract. The fact that more and more disputes are arbitrated each year provides further support for the contention that grievance arbitration is meeting the needs of the parties.[58]

Despite the widespread acceptance of grievance arbitration by union and management negotiators, the courts, and the NLRB, problems are associated with the arbitration process that threaten its usefulness. It was mentioned earlier in this chapter that arbitration offers the parties a relatively fast, inexpensive, nonlegalistic procedure for resolving disputes arising during the life of the contract. Arbitration's image has become tarnished as a result of growing criticism that the process has become too expensive, too slow, and too legalistic to effectively resolve labor and management's problems. While the arbitration process does have some problems, they are relatively minor when compared with the benefits associated with arbitration. Also, many of the problems can be minimized if given adequate attention by labor and management. In the section to follow, the major problems will be identified and techniques for avoiding them discussed.

PROBLEM: RISING ARBITRATION COSTS

While it is difficult to argue that arbitration is more expensive than its major alternatives (seeking interpretations of the contract through litigation or striking), arbitration costs have risen over the years. The increasing cost of an arbitration is only an annoyance for large employers and unions because they have the financial resources to handle the problem. However, the increased costs of arbitration have the potential of putting the process beyond the financial capabilities of many small companies and local unions. The rising cost of arbitration is a factor contributing to the use of strikes to resolve disputes during the life of the contract.[59]

Causes of the problem. A number of factors have contributed to the rising arbitration costs. Today, the parties are much more likely to be represented by attorneys than in the past, adding appreciably to the cost of arbitration. For example, legal fees can be more than $1,000 for even the simplest case.[60] Other expenses associated with grievance arbitration include: wages of individuals participating in the hearing; a verbatim transcript of the proceeding; rental of a room for the hearing; and payment of a fee to the American Arbitration Association for providing the parties a panel of arbitrators.[61] The arbitrator's fee and expenses are other major costs. In 1980, arbitrator's fees in FMCS cases averaged $988.76 with an additional $143.55 in expenses.[62]

Decreasing arbitration costs. The parties have a number of ways to reduce the growing cost of arbitration. For example, they could work to improve the grievance procedure and their general handling of contract interpretation problems. The quickest way to decrease arbitration costs is to reduce the number of cases going to arbitration. Even assuming a case goes to arbitration, the parties still have ways to reduce the costs. The parties do not have to rent a room for the arbitration hearing. They could use a room at the plant, the union headquarters or an attorney's office. In most cases, the parties do not need a verbatim transcript of the hearing. While a transcript can be useful in some lengthy, complex cases, it is usually an unnecessary expense in most routine proceedings. Defining the issue to be decided by the arbitrator before the hearing can save valuable time (and therefore money) during the hearing. Also, using oral arguments at the end of the hearing as opposed to written post-hearing briefs can save lawyers' fees. The arbitrator's fee can be reduced if the parties request only an award without a lengthy supporting opinion. As can be seen, a number of approaches can be taken to reduce arbitration costs if the parties are willing to utilize a "no-frills" arbitration procedure. If they are unwilling to utilize cost-cutting techniques, it is quite likely that arbitration costs will continue to rise.

Expedited arbitration. Reducing arbitration costs does not mean the quality of the arbitration process must suffer. It has been demonstrated that expedited arbitration can provide the parties with a relatively quick, less costly procedure for resolving certain types of disputes arising during the life of the agreement. In 1971, the United Steelworkers Union and several large steel companies developed expedited arbitration as an alternative to traditional arbitration procedures.

The procedure found in the steel industry has the following characteristics:[63]

- If the parties fail to reach agreement at the third step of grievance procedure, they can opt for expedited arbitration. If either party objects to expedited arbitration, they will utilize the traditional arbitration procedure.
- The parties schedule the expedited arbitration within ten days.
- The arbitrator is expected to make a decision within forty-eight hours of the hearing.
- The hearings are informal, without legal representation and briefs, and transcripts are not used.

Not all disputes are amenable to expedited arbitration. In complex cases or those having serious implications for the parties, speed in settling the dispute is not the primary concern. However, during the life of the agreement, a number of disputes can be settled quickly and inexpensively without jeopardizing the quality of the labor-management relationship. Typically, expedited arbitration is used in discipline cases because many of these situations are routine. Then, conventional arbitration can be used more efficiently to handle the complex, precedent-setting cases.[64]

PROBLEM: ARBITRATION IS BECOMING SLOWER

One of the potential advantages of grievance arbitration is that it can provide relatively quick solutions to disputes over the interpretation or application of the labor agreement. However, arbitration does not appear to be living up to its potential. The FMCS reports that the average length of time from filing the grievance to receipt of the arbitrator's decision is 247 days. Exhibit 15.5 shows how the 247 days are distributed.

EXHIBIT 15.5
Arbitration Time Delays

Activity	Days
Time Between Grievance Date to Request for Arbitration Panel	79
Time Between Request for Panel and Panel Sent Out	5
Time Between Panel Sent Out to Appointment of Arbitrator	42
Time Between Appointment of Arbitrator to Hearing Date	71
Time Between Hearing Date to Arbitrator's Award	50
Total: Grievance Date to Award	247

Source: Federal Mediation and Conciliation Service, Mini Memo No. 82–1, 8 March 1982.

Causes of the problem. The problems facing grievance arbitration are closely intertwined. Factors contributing to the rising costs of arbitration also tend to delay the process. For example, posthearing briefs will add approximately four weeks to the length of an arbitration proceeding. Not only are verbatim transcripts expensive, but also they add two to four weeks to the arbitration. Another problem adding to the time delays is the shortage of acceptable arbitrators. Notice in Exhibit 15.5 the number of days transpiring after the FMCS provides the parties with a list of arbitrators. Because of the shortage of acceptable arbitrators, those that are acceptable tend to be very busy. The parties must wait to have their case heard and must wait again to receive the arbitrator's decision. This is a problem because both labor and management place a premium on experience when selecting an arbitrator. Even though more than 1,500 arbitrators are listed with the FMCS and the American Arbitration Association, 80 to 90 percent of all grievance arbitration is handled by fewer than 200 arbitrators.[65]

Decreasing delays in arbitration. To hasten arbitration, the parties can decrease the time taken to process grievances. This can be done by negotiating time limits into each step of the grievance procedure, and then observing the limits. During arbitration, the parties can avoid the use of verbatim transcripts and posthearing briefs.

The delays attributable to the heavy case load of the acceptable arbitrators are not so easy to eliminate. It is not irrational for the parties to rely heavily on experience when selecting an arbitrator. They must be able to trust the arbitrator's ability to conduct a fair and impartial hearing and render an informed decision. Despite the research (albeit quite limited) indicating that labor attorneys cannot distinguish between the awards of experienced and inexperienced arbitrators,[66] years of arbitration experience will continue to be a prerequisite employed by many parties when choosing an arbitrator.

However, the length of time needed to arbitrate a case could be shortened greatly if the parties were willing to use relatively less experienced arbitrators. Such individuals can usually schedule a hearing sooner and return a decision quicker than their colleagues in greater demand. Labor and management should cooperate with efforts by organizations such as the FMCS and AAA to train new arbitrators. Also, the parties could facilitate the development of new arbitrators by being willing to hire less experienced arbitrators for their more straightforward cases. As the older, more experienced arbitrators who received their training during World War II as part of the War Labor Board approach retirement, there will be an increasing need to develop a new supply of acceptable arbitrators. The parties can facilitate this process by being willing to "take a chance" and utilize less experienced arbitrators. If the supply of acceptable arbitrators does not grow, the parties will be faced by an increase in the length of time needed to arbitrate a grievance.

PROBLEM: ARBITRATION IS BECOMING TOO LEGALISTIC

According to Fleming, the substance of the criticism that arbitration is too formal (or legalistic) is that:

> The merits of the dispute get lost in arguments over arbitrability, the form of the grievance, technical rules as to the admissibility of evidence, the application of precedent, reliance on transcripts, briefs, etc.[67]

To a degree, formalities in grievance arbitration are necessary. Good posthearing briefs can help the arbitrator's understanding of a complex case. Application of rules of evidence by the arbitrator during a hearing can help the parties stay "on task" and keep the record of the case from being cluttered by irrelevant information. Technical objections, even if they are not sustained, can put the arbitrator on notice that the advocate making the objection has a problem with whatever is going on. This can be useful as a reminder that a potential problem exists in the record when the arbitrator is reviewing his or her notes when making the decision.

Causes of the problem. Arbitration is too legalistic when procedural issues stand in the way of one side's presenting its case to the arbitrator. Another dimension of the problem is that arbitration is too formal when procedural considerations add appreciably to the cost without increasing the quality of the outcome. For example, when one of the parties objects too frequently or too strenuously to what the other party is doing during the hearing, very little is added to the process under most circumstances.

Three factors have been cited as bringing about a shift from informal arbitration hearings to hearings that take on the trappings of the courtroom, including the increased use of attorneys.[68]

- The increase in public sector collective bargaining. Disputes in this area involve the interpretation of complex statutes that invites the use of attorneys.

- The increasing intervention of the courts and administrative agencies such as the NLRB in the arbitration process as a result of previously discussed decisions like *Collyer Insulated Wire* and *Alexander v. Gardner-Denver*.
- The appearance of attorneys and courtroom-like procedures during the arbitration hearing. Today, it is much more likely for the union and management to have attorneys represent them during the arbitration process than in the past. Also, arbitrators are more likely to be attorneys today than in the past.[69]

A review of the above factors suggests that the increased use of attorneys who are likely to introduce more legalistic procedures in the arbitration process has occurred for two reasons: labor and management prefer to have attorneys involved; and the use of attorneys is necessary given the changing nature of the arbitration process. In other words, the use of attorneys and legal procedures is a necessary reaction to the more complicated nature of the arbitration process.[70]

Keeping arbitration understandable. The increased role of attorneys and legal proceedings is not a problem per se. However, it can become a problem if the informal, understandable, and inexpensive nature of arbitration is lost as a result. The parties can realize the potential benefits of increased legalism while maintaining the traditional benefits of arbitration if they exercise some restraint. For example, they can restrict the use of transcripts and posthearing briefs to the most complicated and difficult cases. Similarly, the arbitrator can minimize the use of legal procedures during the arbitration hearing. This can be done without affecting the parties' ability to present their case or decreasing the quality of the record put together by the arbitrator during the hearing.

Summary

Grievance arbitration has been supported as the preferable method for resolving disputes over the interpretation or administration of the labor agreement. As a result of the *Lincoln Mills* decision, Section 301 of the LMRA was interpreted to allow federal courts to enforce labor agreements. Consequently, it is difficult for a party to refuse to arbitrate a grievance if it entered into a labor agreement with an arbitration clause. *The Steelworkers Trilogy* provided additional Supreme Court support for grievance arbitration. This was done by making it difficult for federal courts to decide the arbitrability of an issue and to refuse to enforce an arbitrator's award. The NLRB has also supported the use of grievance arbitration. As a result of its *Spielberg* and *Collyer* decisions, the NLRB is likely to defer to arbitration in situations where an action is both a violation of the labor agreement and an unfair labor practice.

Grievance arbitration has emerged as an important part of the labor agreement because it has proved to be an effective way to resolve disputes arising during the life of the contract. Rather than striking or resorting to court action to resolve disagreements over contract interpretation, the parties submit the dispute to the grievance procedure. If the labor and management representatives are unable to resolve the problem through the grievance procedure, it can be submitted to an arbitrator for a final and binding decision.

Grievance arbitration is a quasilegal procedure in which both labor and management present their views of the dispute to the arbitrator. It offers the parties a relatively fast and inexpensive procedure for resolving problems that could not be resolved in the grievance procedure. While there are problems associated with grievance arbitration, such as its increasing expense and decreasing timeliness, it still serves the parties quite well and is more effective than the alternative methods such as strikes or court action for resolving disputes arising during the life of the labor agreement.

Discussion Questions

1. Most labor agreements specify that the arbitrator's award will be "final and binding." However, there are situations in which the award may not be. After a review of the public policy affecting grievance arbitration, discuss the situations in which the decision of the arbitrator may not provide the final resolution of the dispute.
2. As with contract negotiations, preparation is the key to successful arbitration. Outline the steps you would use to prepare a case for presentation to an arbitrator.
3. What factors would you consider when selecting an arbitrator? Would it make any difference whether the case involved employee discipline as opposed to the interpretation of contract language?
4. How can arbitration awards be used by the parties in their preparation for the renegotiation of the labor agreement?
5. What is the significance of the following NLRB and court decisions:
   Textile Workers of America v. Lincoln Mills
   United Steelworkers of America v. American Manufacturing Co.
   United Steelworkers of America v. Warrior and Gulf Navigation
   United Steelworkers of America v. Enterprise Wheel and Car
   Spielberg Manufacturing Co.
   Collyer Insulated Wire Co.
   Alexander v. Gardner-Denver

Key Concepts

Permanent arbitrators
Ad hoc selection procedures
Arbitration clause

Cross-examination
Closing arguments
Opinion and award

Formal arbitration hearings
Informal arbitration hearings
Direct examination

Expedited arbitration
Opening statement

Notes

1. *Basic Patterns in Union Contracts,* 9th ed. (Washington, D. C.: Bureau of National Affairs, 1979), p. 15.

2. R. W. Fleming, *The Labor Arbitration Process* (Urbana: University of Illinois Press, 1967), p. 1.

3. *Textile Workers Union of America v. Lincoln Mills of Alabama,* 353 U.S. 448 (1957).

4. Ibid.

5. Benjamin J. Taylor and Fred Witney, *Labor Relations Law,* 3rd ed. (Englewood Cliffs: Prentice-Hall, 1979), p. 418.

6. *United Steelworkers of America v. American Manufacturing Co.,* 363 U.S. 564 (1960).

7. Ibid.

8. *United Steelworkers of America v. Warrior and Gulf Navigation Co.,* 363 U.S. 574 (1960).

9. Ibid.

10. *United Steelworkers of America v. Enterprise Wheel and Car Corp.,* 363 U.S. 593 (1960).

11. Ibid.

12. Ibid.

13. Paul Prasow and Edward Peters, *Arbitration and Collective Bargaining* (New York: McGraw-Hill Book Company, 1970), p. 18.

14. *Torrington Co. v. Metal Products Workers, Local 1645,* U.S. Court of Appeals, 326 F.2d 677 (2d Cir. 1966).

15. Ibid.

16. *Spielberg Mfg. Co.,* 112 NLRB 1080 (1955).

17. *International Harvester Co.,* 138 NLRB 923 (1962).

18. Ibid.

19. *Collyer Insulated Wire Co.,* 192 NLRB 837 (1971).

20. Ibid.

21. Peter G. Nash, "Board Deferral to Arbitration and *Alexander v. Gardner-Denver:* Some Preliminary Observations," *Labor Law Journal* 25 (May 1974): 259–60.

22. Ibid., p. 269.

23. Taylor and Witney, pp. 392–93.

24. Arthur P. Menard, "The NLRB—No Longer a Threat to the Arbitral Process," *Labor Law Journal* 23 (March 1972): 143.

25. *Alexander v. Gardner-Denver,* 415 U.S. 36 (1974).

26. Jay S. Siegal, "Deferral to Arbitration Awards in Title VII Actions," *Labor Law Journal* 25 (July 1974): 398.

27. Nash, p. 262.

28. Nash, p. 267.

29. John Zalusky, "Arbitration: Updating a Vital Process," *American Federationist,* November 1976, p. 1.

30. Hon. William H. Rehnquist, "A Jurist's View of Arbitration," *The Arbitration Journal* 32 (March 1977): 3.

31. *Labor Law Course,* 23rd ed. (Chicago: Commerce Clearing House, Inc., 1976), p. 4068.

32. *Labor Law Course,* p. 4069.

33. *Labor Law Course,* p. 4069.

34. Owen Fairweather, *Practice and Procedure in Labor Arbitration* (Washington, D. C.: Bureau of National Affairs, Inc., 1973), p. 54.

35. Frank Elkouri and Edna A. Elkouri, *How Arbitration Works,* 3rd ed. (Washington, D. C.: Bureau of National Affairs, 1973), p. 65.

36. *Basic Patterns in Union Contracts,* p. 16.

37. Ibid., p. 17.

38. Ibid., p. 16.

39. Ibid., p. 17.

40. John F. O'Hara, "Strategy to Settle or to Arbitrate?" *Proceedings of the Twentieth Annual Meeting of the National Academy of Arbitrators* (Washington, D.C.: Bureau of National Affairs, 1967), p. 342.

41. O'Hara, p. 342.

42. This discussion will follow the procedure outlined by Richard Liebes in "Preparing the Case for Arbitration," *Proceedings of the Twentieth Annual Meeting of the National Academy of Arbitrators* (Washington, D. C.: Bureau of National Affairs, 1967), pp. 359–60.

43. Fairweather, p. 166.

44. For a thorough discussion of past practices, see Elkouri and Elkouri, Ch. 12 and Fairweather, Ch. X.

45. *Continental Can Company,* 53 LA 809 (Sidney L. Cahn), 1969.

46. *Labor Law Course,* p. 4152.

47. Liebes, p. 363.

48. Sam Kagel, *Anatomy of a Labor Arbitration,* (Washington, D. C.: Bureau of National Affairs, 1961), p. 79.

49. *Labor Law Course,* p. 4175.

50. *Labor Law Course,* p. 4177.

51. Kagel, p. 83.

52. Donald P. Rothschild, Leroy S. Merrifield and Harry T. Edwards, *Collective Bargaining and Labor Arbitration* (Indianapolis: Bobbs-Merrill Company, Inc., 1979), pp. 227–8.

53. Kagel, p. 85.

54. Ibid., pp. 80–1.

55. Ibid., p. 101.

56. *Labor Law Course,* p. 4187.

57. Harold W. Davey, "Third Parties in Labor Relations—Negotiation, Mediation, Arbitration," *Employee and Labor Relations* ed. by Dale Yoder and Herbert G. Heneman, Jr., (Washington, D. C.: Bureau of National Affairs, 1976), pp. 7–200.

58. Richard D. Mittenthal, "Grievance Arbitration in the Private Sector," in *Broader Perspectives in Dispute Resolution* (Proceedings of the Sixth Annual Meeting of the Society for Professionals in Dispute Resolution, 1978), p. 26.

59. W. J. Usery, "Some Attempts to Reduce Arbitration Costs and Delays," *Monthly Labor Review* 95 (November 1972):3.

60. Zalusky, p. 2.

61. Usery, p. 3.

62. Federal Mediation and Conciliation Service, Mini Memo No. 82-1, March 8, 1982.

63. Zalusky, p. 5.

64. Ben Fischer, "Arbitration: The Steel Industry Experiment," *Monthly Labor Review* 95 (November 1972): 9.

65. "Arbitration is No Bargain," *Nation's Business,* October 1979, p. 87.

66. Patrick R. Westerkamp and Allen K. Miller, "The Acceptability of Inexperienced Arbitrators: An Experiment," *Labor Law Journal* 22 (December 1971): 763.

67. Fleming, p. 57.

68. J. A. Raffaele, "Labor Arbitration and Law: A Non-Lawyer Point of View," *Labor Law Journal* 28 (January 1978): 27.

69. Henry K. Brown, "Structural Change in the Labor Arbitration Profession," *Personnel Journal*, December 1976, p. 618.

70. Ibid., p. 619.

Suggested Readings

Elkouri, Frank and Elkouri, Edna Asper. *How Arbitration Works,* 3rd ed. Washington, D. C.: Bureau of National Affairs, 1973.
Fairweather, Owen. *Practice and Procedure in Labor Arbitration*. Washington, D. C.: Bureau of National Affairs, 1973.
Fleming, R. W. *The Labor Arbitration Process*. Urbana: University of Illinois Press, 1965.
Harrison, Allan J. *Preparing and Presenting Your Arbitration Case*. Washington, D. C.: Bureau of National Affairs, 1979.
Hays, Paul R. *Labor Arbitration: A Dissenting View*. New Haven: Yale University Press, 1966.
Hill, Marvin, Jr. and Sinicropi, Anthony V. *Evidence in Arbitration*. Washington, D. C.: Bureau of National Affairs, 1980.
Hill, Marvin, Jr. and Sinicropi, Anthony V. *Remedies in Arbitration*. Washington, D. C.: Bureau of National Affairs, 1981.
Kagel, Sam. *The Anatomy of a Labor Arbitration*. Washington, D. C.: Bureau of National Affairs, 1961.
Prasow, Paul and Peters, Edward. *Arbitration and Collective Bargaining: Conflict Resolution in Collective Bargaining*. New York: McGraw-Hill Book Company, 1970.
Scheinman, Martin F. *Evidence and Proof in Arbitration*. Ithaca, NY: New York State School of Industrial and Labor Relations, Cornell University, 1977.

Part Five
Case Studies

ARBITRATION CASES

This section contains two cases that are based on actual arbitration proceedings. These cases provide examples of the types of issues addressed by grievance arbitration—discipline/discharge and contract interpretation. The major facts are provided for these cases. Answering the discussion questions will simulate a procedure like that used by the arbitrator when deciding these cases.

Sunshine Supermarkets Inc.
vs.
Truckdrivers Union, Local No. 1079

STATEMENT OF THE CASE

Sunshine Supermarkets Inc. is a retail supermarket chain operating in fifteen western states. Its regional distribution center is located in Denver, Colorado. From its warehouses, meat-cutting facilities, and bakeries in Denver, 279 stores located in Colorado, Wyoming, Montana, North Dakota, and South Dakota are serviced. Typically, orders are received from the stores and filled at the company's warehouse complex. Then, the orders are loaded into trucks for delivery to various destinations in the five-state region.

On Friday, August 31, 1979, Ian McDermott* was discharged for striking a supervisor. The incident leading to Mr. McDermott's discharge took place on Sunday, August 26, 1979, at approximately 1:00 P.M. At about that time, Jim Sandler went to the dispatch window to pick up his trip ticket for a run to Rapid City, South Dakota. (A trip ticket is the paperwork that specifies the driver's destination for an upcoming delivery as well as the type of equipment (tractor and trailer) to be used.) He noticed he was assigned a White 300 Series Freightliner tractor. Mr. Sandler did not want to make the run in that make of tractor since he thought the White Freightliner was an extremely rough-riding vehicle. Previous to August 26, 1979, he had circulated a petition that was signed by a number of drivers calling the tractor's problems to the company's attention.

Mr. Sandler returned to the dispatch window and asked Robert Davey, a relief dispatcher, if another tractor was available. As a dispatcher, Mr. Davey was considered to be a supervisor. Mr. Davey responded that Mr. Sandler would have to make the run in the White Freightliner. Mr. Sandler threw the trip ticket through the dispatch window and said someone else could take the run. Also, he complained that the tractor was rough riding and that he had taken his last thirteen runs in a White Freightliner. In response, Mr. Davey asked

---
*The names of all individuals are fictitious.

Mr. Sandler why he was the only driver to complain about the tractor.

While the above-described interchange was taking place, a number of other drivers were in the room and overheard the conversation between Mr. Davey and Mr. Sandler. When Mr. Davey implied that Mr. Sandler was the only driver to complain about the White tractors, Mr. McDermott interjected himself into the discussion. Mr. McDermott stated that Mr. Sandler was not the only driver to complain; a number of other drivers had also complained about them.

At this point, there is a major discrepancy in the testimony offered by company and union witnesses. Mr. Davey testified that he said: "God damn it, Ian, someone has to drive it." In his written description of the events of August 26, 1979, which was submitted as evidence, Mr. Davey stated: "God damn, Ian, someone has to run them." Supporting Mr. Davey's testimony (that he said "God damn it. . . .") was that of Robert Toughy, another dispatcher on duty on August 26, 1979.

Mr. McDermott testified that Mr. Davey said: "God damn you, Ian. It isn't your problem. Stay out of it." In general, Mr. McDermott's testimony was supported by that offered by Mr. Sandler and two other drivers in the room at the time the statement was made.

After the statement directed at Mr. McDermott by Mr. Davey was made, Mr. McDermott moved quickly from the table at which he had been seated to the dispatch window. Mr. McDermott made a statement that, in effect, told Mr. Davey not to curse him. He then reached through the dispatch window and grabbed Mr. Davey by the upper part of his tie and shirt. As a result of this action, Mr. Davey was raised from his chair and moved toward the window. Mr. Davey testified that he broke the grievant's grasp with his hands and said, "Ian, this is none of your business." It appears that other drivers quickly intervened to break up the incident. At this point, Mr. McDermott returned to his table and finished his preparation for the run he was scheduled to make. Prior to leaving on his trip, Mr. McDermott checked with another dispatcher to determine whether there was anything he could do in reference to the incident with Mr. Davey. Since no suggestions were made, he left on his trip. Additionally, Mr. Sandler decided to make his run to Rapid City, South Dakota.

After the incident in the trucking department involving Mr. McDermott, Mr. Davey attempted to contact other supervisory personnel. First, he tried to call Jerry Taylor, manager of the trucking department. However, no one answered the telephone at Mr. Taylor's residence. Then, Mr. Davey attempted to call Sam Greene, the trucking superintendent. Although Mr. Greene was not at home at the time Mr. Davey telephoned, he returned Davey's call about thirty minutes later. After hearing the details of the incident, Mr. Greene told Mr. Davey that he should have suspended McDermott at that time. Mr. Davey, however, did not know he had the authority to do so.

On Monday morning, August 27, 1979, Mr. Truman Spitzer, manager of the Sunshine Supermarket's Denver Warehouse, learned about the incident involving Mr. McDermott and Mr. Davey from Mr. Taylor. Mr. Spitzer told Mr. Taylor to get the facts of the case and report back to him. Mr. Taylor had Mr. Davey, Mr. Toughy, and Tony Randolf, another dispatcher on duty at the time of the incident, prepare written statements describing the events of August 26, 1979. These statements were submitted as evidence by the company during the arbitration hearing. Also, Mr. Taylor tried to contact Mr. McDermott, but Mr. McDermott did not return from his run until after Mr. Taylor had left work on Monday evening.

Mr. Taylor reported back to Mr. Spitzer on Tuesday, August 28, 1979. He gave Mr. Spitzer the written statements prepared by Mr. Davey, Mr. Toughy, and Mr. Randolf. With this information, Mr. Spitzer tentatively decided that Mr. McDermott should be terminated, but before doing so, Mr. McDermott should be heard. He asked Mr. Taylor to contact Mr. McDermott to hear his description of the incident. He also told Mr. Taylor that if Mr. McDermott did not provide any additional information, he should be terminated.

Mr. Taylor had a meeting with Mr. McDermott and Mr. Sandler, the union steward, late Tuesday afternoon. From descriptions of this meeting, it did not appear that a thorough review of the incident took place. Mr. McDermott did not deny grabbing Mr. Davey. Mr. McDermott said that Mr. Davey cursed him. Mr. Sandler claimed some responsibility for the situation. During the meeting, Mr. Taylor informed Mr. McDermott that he was suspended pending further investigation. On Friday, August 31, 1979, Mr. Spitzer notified Mr. McDermott that he was terminated. Mr. McDermott grieved the discharge. Attempts to resolve the grievance failed and the company and the union decided to arbitrate the matter.

POSITION OF THE COMPANY

The company argued that the arbitrator should deny the grievance for two reasons. First, it was the unrebutted testimony of Mr. Spitzer that it was a uniform policy of the company to discharge for insubordination any employee who lays his hands on supervisory personnel. Second, the language of Mr. Davey directed at Mr. McDermott was not so inflammatory or provocative to justify the act of grabbing Mr. Davey. The company maintained that the arbitrator should deny the grievance and sustain the discharge. To do otherwise, the company contended, the arbitrator would be rewriting the law of the industrial setting as found in the company.

POSITION OF THE UNION

The union argued the grievance should be sustained for two reasons. First, the incident did not constitute insubordination. The union maintained that the incident was minor and over quickly. Also, Mr. Davey was at fault in the matter because of his statement to Mr. McDermott. The grievant thought he was cursed in a manner that was offensive to him. In response, Mr. McDermott took appropriate action; i.e., he did not hit Mr. Davey; he told him that he would not tolerate being cursed, and then sat down. Because of the provocation and the minor nature of the incident, the union contended the grievance should be sustained.

Second, the union maintained that the grievance should be granted because the company violated the tenets of industrial due process. The union urged that industrial due process requires that the grievant should have been given the opportunity to present his side of the case before the decision to terminate was made. The union contended that the termination decision was made on August 27, 1979 based on the written statements of Mr. Davey, Mr. Toughy, and Mr. Randolf. Mr. McDermott and Mr. Sandler did not have the opportunity to present their full description of the events of August 26, 1979 until a grievance meeting sometime after the discharge. Since the investigation of the incident included only input from management's side, industrial due process was denied the grievant. Consequently, the union argued the grievance should be sustained.

RELEVANT CONTRACT PROVISIONS

The following contract provision is relevant to this decision:

ARTICLE 3

Seniority. An employee's seniority date shall be his most recent date of hire or rehire within the bargaining unit by the Employer, which has not subsequently been interrrupted by a termination of seniority.

Seniority shall be terminated for any of the following reasons:

1. Discharge for just cause . . .

ISSUE

The parties requested the arbitrator to decide the following issue: Did the Company have just cause for discharging Mr. Ian McDermott?

DISCUSSION QUESTIONS

1. What is insubordination? Did Mr. McDermott's behavior on August 26, 1979 constitute insubordination? Why?
2. Did Mr. Davey provoke Mr. McDermott? Justify your position.
3. If you were the arbitrator in this case, would you deny the grievance or would you put Mr. McDermott back on the job? Why? If you sustained the grievance, would you grant back pay to Mr. McDermott? Why?

Purco Packing Company
vs.
The Packinghouse Workers of America, Local 1201

STATEMENT OF THE CASE

Purco Packing Company is a meat-packing and rendering company located in Rapid City, South Dakota. On the morning of October 26, 1976, at approximately 3:30 A.M., a fire occurred in an electrical transformer that is a basic part of the power distribution system for the company. The fire department arrived at 4:13 A.M. and remained on the scene until 4:44 A.M. According to Donald Bell* of Electrical Technologies, Inc., an electrical consulting company, the most probable cause for the fire was "moisture, in, on or around the phase A primary conductor" attributable to the rain, snow, and wind occurring at the time of the fire. The transformer fire caused a power outage in various sections of the company's facility.

The power outage interrupted the work of the Offal Department employees who started work at 4:00 A.M. The Offal Department is responsible for taking the hide off the slaughtered animal and removing the viscera and trimmings from the recently butchered animals. By about 5:20 A.M., power was restored to the Offal Department. Other employees began arriving at the plant at approximately 5:30 to 6:00 A.M. The power outage that still affected much of the plant delayed these workers from starting their jobs.

Henry McBride, vice-president for operations, arrived at work at approximately 5:40 A.M. At about 5:50 A.M., he decided that the Kill Floor (the area where the animals are killed) would not operate. Cooler Department workers, however, were told to start work at approximately 6:00 A.M. or shortly thereafter. After about fifteen to twenty minutes on the job, another phase of the transformer "blew up" and cut off power to the coolers.

According to the plant engineer, William Haywood, the fire did damage to a number of parts of the transformer. Some of the damage was not apparent until the Cooler Department employees began work, thereby increasing the transformer's workload. In Mr. Haywood's opinion, the plant should not operate that day because he could not guarantee there would not be additional power outages, the transformer could be further damaged and repairs could take place at a quicker pace if the transformer could be completely shut down.

Mr. McBride knew there was some work Offal Department employees could do just to "keep busy" for the rest of the shift, but he thought it would be better if the entire plant shut down as suggested by Mr. Haywood. At approximately 6:20 A.M., Mr. McBride called two foremen, Frank Padak and Donald Wiltberger, into his office. Mr. McBride told the foremen to tell the employees that the plant could not operate that day because of the power problem and that the workers should go home.

Because the employees began their jobs at different times, the work force was differentially affected by the decision not to operate the plant on October 26, 1976. The Offal Department employees who started at 4:00 A.M. finished cleaning up at approximately 8:00 A.M. and were paid for four hours of work. The Cooler Department employees who started work at approximately 6:00 A.M. and worked for about twenty minutes were paid for the twenty minutes they worked. Other workers were told to wait until a decision was made whether the plant would operate. The workers who did not start work prior to the decision not to operate the plant received no compensation for reporting or the time they spent at the plant waiting for the decision to be made. Most of the workers waited about twenty to thirty minutes before being told to go home.

The union requested that the company pay all workers four hours' reporting pay under Article 9 of the labor agreement, and that the Offal Department employees receive eight hours' pay for their efforts on October 26, 1976 under Article 16 of the agreement. As a result of the company's re-

---

*The names of all individuals are fictitious.

fusal to make the requested pay adjustments, grievances were filed that ultimately led to this arbitration.

RELEVANT CONTRACT PROVISIONS

The following provisions contained in the labor agreement between the parties are pertinent to the decision:

ARTICLE 9
Reporting for Work

9.01: On Saturdays and on call-back after layoff and whenever employees are scheduled to report for work and have been notified to report for work, as above set forth, and upon arrival at the plant, find no work available, such employees shall be paid for four hours at the hourly rate for his job. If the employees begin work but work less than four hours, through no fault of their own, such employees shall be paid for a minimum of four hours.

9.02: The provisions of this article shall not apply in any work week during which normal plant operations are restricted due to causes beyond the reasonable control of the Employer such as Acts of God, stoppages of work by any union, fire, flood, or emergency causing damage to or breakdown of plant equipment, machinery or other facilities, and failure to receive necessary livestock.

ARTICLE 16
Guaranteed Work

16.01: The weekly guarantee for all regular full-time employees for 46 weeks each year during the term of this agreement shall be 40 hours of work, except for a holiday week, in which the hereinafter named holidays occur where the guarantee shall be 32 hours at 40 hours pay. The 40 hours guarantee, as above set forth, shall be worked in the first five days of the employees' work week, which shall start Monday through Friday, consisting of five eight-hour days, namely, Monday, Tuesday, Wednesday, Thursday, and Friday.

16.12: The provisions of this article shall not apply in any work week during which normal operations are restricted due to causes beyond the reasonable control of the employer, such as Acts of God, stoppages of work by any union, fire, flood, or emergency causing damage to, or breakdown of plant equipment, machinery, or other facilities.

POSITION OF THE UNION

The union argued that the reporting-for-work (Article 9.01) and the guaranteed-work (Article 16.01) provisions of the labor agreement provide basic job security to the employees and that there are only very narrowly defined exceptions to the company's obligations under these articles. Both Article 9.02 and Article 16.12 provide an exception for situations where "normal plant operations are restricted due to causes beyond reasonable control of the Company, such as Acts of God, stoppages of work by any union, fire, flood, or emergency causing damage to, or breakdown of, any equipment, machinery, or other facilities."

The union contended the transformer fire was not beyond the reasonable control of the company, because the company should have anticipated such problems and taken steps to prevent them. Also, the union argued that the cause for the unavailability of work October 26, 1976 was not "fire" within the meaning of Article 9.02 and Article 16.12, but was attributable to a power failure, which is not contained in the list of exceptions contained in Article 9.02 and Article 16.12.

Finally, the union contended the company is obligated to pay the Offal Department employees for a full eight hours and the Cooler Department employees, who began work, a minimum of four hours' pay. Regarding the Offal Department employees, the union argued that the power failure did not affect the jobs and a full day's work was available. Since the Offal Department employees could have worked all day, they were entitled to eight hours' guaranteed pay as specified in Article 16.01.

The union also maintained that the Cooler Department employees, some of whom received pay for the fifteen to twenty minutes they actually worked, or no pay if they did not start work, should get four hours' pay because the company instructed workers to stay at the plant while attempts were made to get the plant operational. The union relied on a previous arbitrator's award, which involved the same parties. The union argued that the workers should be paid for, at least, the time spent at the plant. Because the company failed to properly notify employees not to report and did not unequivocally release the employees who had reported to work, the union believed four hours' pay should be granted.

POSITION OF THE COMPANY

The company argued that Article 9.02 and Article 16.12 are applicable as exceptions to their obligations under Article 9.01 (Reporting for Work) and Article 16.01 (Guaranteed Work). The company also contended that it fulfilled its responsibilities to attempt to notify employees not to report to work, an issue that had been the subject of an earlier arbitration. For these reasons, the company requested the grievance be dismissed.

THE PREVIOUS ARBITRATION AWARD

The union argued that the company failed to abide by the provisions of an earlier arbitration award. The previous case took place in December 1973. The arbitration arose out of a snow storm. Because of adverse weather conditions, most of the company's supervisors were unable to report for work. A number of employees, however, called the plant to determine whether or not it would be operational. Those calling early in the morning (at approximately 5:15 A.M.) were encouraged to report to the plant. Later, the company decided not to operate that day and subsequently refused to pay four hours' reporting pay to the employees who showed up at the plant. In this case, the union argued that the employees should have been paid four hours for reporting to work because the company made no effort to notify the workers not to report to the plant. On the contrary, the company actually encouraged some employees to come to the plant. The arbitrator in this case decided for the union. In his decision, he stated that the company was under an obligation to attempt to notify employees if it was apparent that the plant would not be operational. The fact that the company did not have an up-to-date list of its employees and their telephone numbers, which made the task of notification very difficult, was not considered by the arbitrator to be an adequate defense for the company's lack of effort.

The earlier case is relevant to the case at hand because of questions raised by the union concerning the company's level of effort with regard to the notification of employees. The union argued that the company knew as early as 4:00 A.M. that it had a power problem. The fact that Mr. McBride did not report to work until approximately 5:40 A.M. was not of any concern to the union. They felt that the company should have notified the employees that the plant would not be operational. Because it failed to do so, the company was obligated to pay the workers who reported to work on October 26, 1976.

In the present case, the company did the following in an attempt to notify employees that the plant would not operate. The foremen had the employees sign a list as they reported to work. Then the foremen attempted to telephone the workers not reflected on the list. These efforts began at approximately 6:15 to 6:20 A.M. The notification attempt was rather futile since most workers had already left for the plant by the time the telephoning began. However, workers whose shifts began later in the day were properly notified not to report to work.

THE ISSUES

The parties requested the arbitrator to decide the following issues: (1) Were the Offal Department workers eligible for eight hours' pay under Article 16 of the labor agreement, and (2) were the other employees who reported to work on October 26, 1976 entitled to four hours' reporting pay under Article 9?

DISCUSSION QUESTIONS

1. Was the unavailability of work on October 26, 1976 attributable to factors that make the exceptions to the reporting-to-work and guaranteed-work provisions contained in Article 9.02 and Article 16.12 operative?

2. Assuming the company's decision not to operate was protected by Article 9.02 and Article 16.12, was the protection extended by these articles negated by the company's failure to promptly instruct employees that work would not be available on October 26, 1976?

3. How would you decide this case?

The preceding sections of the book have been built around two related assumptions. First, the focus was on labor-management relations in the private sector under the coverage of the National Labor Relations Act, as amended. Second, the discussions of labor-management relations were limited to the American scene. This was primarily because labor relations cannot be fully explored without considering the effects of public policy. The discussions in preceding chapters emphasized labor-management relations as structured by United States public policy.

This section expands the book's perspective by examining labor-management relations outside the American private sector. Chapters 16 and 17 look at a rapidly growing area of union activity—the American public sector. A number of similarities exist between labor-management relations in the private and public sectors. However, other factors differentiate the two sectors. As a result, many practices effective in the private sector cannot be applied in the public sector or need to be adapted to meet the special concerns of public employment. Chapter 16 looks at the factors differentiating the labor-management relations in the private and public sectors. The implications of these differences for effective collective bargaining in the public sector are also examined. Chapter 17 reviews the evolution of public policy concerning labor-management relations. Then, the impact of collective bargaining on the public sector is reviewed.

Chapter 18 also broadens the book's perspective by looking at labor-management relations in other countries. Expanding opportunities in international business and the growth of multinational corporations requires that a better understanding of union-management relations in foreign countries be developed. Chapter 18 examines labor-management relations in several other countries. It also looks at the implications for the American trade-union movement of expanded foreign competition and trade.

Chapters 1 through 18 have examined the evolution of labor-management relations in the United States and have discussed the current state of affairs. Chapter 19 looks at the future of the American labor movement. Trends likely to challenge unions in the future are identified. Also, the possible implications of these changes for labor-management relations in the years to come are reviewed.

PART SIX LABOR RELATIONS: AN EXPANDED PERSPECTIVE

Chapter 16

PUBLIC EMPLOYEE COLLECTIVE BARGAINING: AN OVERVIEW

Kate Summers was in no mood to be hassled by her children this morning. At the last moment, her babysitter called. The sitter said she was sick and couldn't take care of Kate's children that day. Although Kate was ready to leave for work, she couldn't go until she lined up another sitter. The last thing Kate wanted to do was stay home with the children. Weekends were long enough. She was also concerned about losing a day's pay.

On most days, Kate had no problems taking care of her two children who were in the first and second grades. She didn't have to leave for work until after they left for school. The school took care of the kids all day. After school, they went to a neighbor's house until Kate got home from work. Being a single parent, she had enough problems. However, having her children in school all day helped Kate balance her career and child-rearing responsibilities. However, the school wasn't much help when it wasn't open. The school district had been shut down for two weeks because of a teacher's strike. According to the newspaper, there was no settlement in sight. Until the dispute was over, Kate had to make other arrangements to care for her kids.

Kate wasn't that old—in her early thirties. She couldn't remember missing any school when she was a student due to strikes by teachers. For the last few years, it seemed she heard about teacher strikes every time she picked up the newspaper. And it wasn't just teachers: firefighters, police, nurses, and municipal employees had all been involved in strikes within the last year. It was certainly easier to handle teacher strikes when they involved school districts other than the one her kids attended. This was the first time Kate was directly affected by such strikes.

Kate had a tough time accepting the notion of teachers' strikes. To her, it seemed unprofessional. She was also disgusted by the teachers' disregard for the children and their families. Those were her thoughts this morning: all dressed up with no place to go. If the strike didn't end soon and her babysitter get better, there would be more mornings like this.

In her more objective moments, Kate tried to understand why a dedicated group of people like teachers would resort to strikes. It was not as if Kate was unfamiliar with strikes. Her father had been a Teamster for over thirty-five years. Kate saw the benefits of the union. She also knew the problems associated with striking. Also, her ex-husband was a union carpenter, and Kate had enjoyed the benefits of her husband's well-paying union job. While he was never on strike during the time they were married, Kate's "ex" talked strike every time the union contract was renegotiated.

Kate couldn't explain her feelings on the

strike issue. What was perfectly acceptable for truck drivers and carpenters seemed, somehow, inappropriate when it involved her children's teachers. She didn't know why teachers had to resort to the strike. They never used to. She also didn't know why teachers were unionizing in such large numbers. They never had when Kate was in school. She knew many public employees had joined unions. Again, she didn't know why. Frankly, this morning she didn't really care. Kate just wanted the strike to be settled so that she could go to work and her children could go to school.

It is not surprising that Kate could not remember her teachers striking. Collective bargaining among public employees such as teachers is a relatively recent phenomenon. Some groups of public employees such as firefighters have been involved in union activities for decades; however, for most public employees, unionization and collective bargaining did not come about until the 1960s. Since that time, public employee collective bargaining has been the most rapidly growing segment of the trade union movement. As a result, government (local, state, and federal) has had to deal with unionization by its employees. The rapid transition from non-union to union status in government employment has not been without its strains. However, as the government managers and unions have become more experienced, many problems faced by the parties in the early years of their relationship appear, today, to be less severe.

The purpose of this chapter is to provide an overview of public-employee collective bargaining. After this chapter you should be able to:

- Explain why collective bargaining in the public sector lagged behind collective bargaining in the private sector.
- Discuss the factors causing the rapid growth of public-sector collective bargaining since the 1960s.
- Be able to identify the factors differentiating labor relations in the public and private sectors and understand the implications of these differences for public-sector collective bargaining.
- Understand the reasons why strikes have been limited in the public sector and the implications of these restrictions for the collective-bargaining process.
- List the steps in a typical public-sector impasse procedure and understand the impact of impasse procedures on the collective-bargaining process.
- Discuss why bargaining-unit determination and the scope of negotiations issues in the public sector have had to be handled differently than in the private sector.

The Growth of Government Employment

The rapid growth of government as an employer has been one of the most dramatic changes in the American labor market. In recent years, government has been the fastest growing sector of the economy. Table 16.1 presents information concerning the changes in employment by major sectors of the economy for selected years between 1920 and 1979. The table reveals that in 1920, government employed 9.5 percent of nonagricultural employees. By 1960, this had increased to 15.4 percent and to 19.0 percent by 1979.

Table 16.1 also reveals that the bulk of the growth in government employment has been at the state and local levels. Between 1960 and 1979, total government employment increased 104 percent. During this same time period, employment with the federal government increased 22.2 percent while state and local government employment increased by 113 percent. The data presented in Table 16.1 also indicate that while the federal government has been relatively stable in recent years, state and local governments have expanded dramatically.

Concomitant with the growth of government employment since the 1950s has been the rapid increase in union membership among government workers. Table 16.2 presents union membership in national unions by economic sector for selected years between 1956 and 1978. The table indicates that since the mid-1960s, the proportion of union membership employed in manufacturing has declined. During this same time period, the proportion of union membership employed in the nonmanufacturing sector increased, but only minimally. However, unionization among government employees increased substantially in absolute numbers and as a proportion of union membership. In 1978, the most recent year for which data is available, 16.7 percent of all union members were employed by government. When members of professional associations are added to union membership, the growth of government

Table 16.1 *Employees on Nonagricultural Payrolls by Industrial Division for Selected Years (in thousands)*

Year	Total	Goods producing	Service producing	Total government	Government as % of total employment	Government Federal (civilians only)	Government State and local
1920	27,340	12,760	14,605	2,603	9.5%	—	—
1930	29,409	11,958	17,481	3,361	11.4	526	2,622
1940	32,361	13,221	17,304	4,202	13.0	996	3,206
1950	45,197	18,506	26,690	6,026	13.3	1,928	4,098
1960	54,189	20,434	33,756	8,353	15.4	2,270	6,083
1965	60,765	21,926	38,838	10,074	16.6	2,378	7,696
1970	70,880	23,577	47,302	12,554	17.7	2,731	9,823
1975	76,945	22,600	54,345	14,686	19.1	2,748	11,973
1979	89,482	26,574	62,909	17,043	19.0	2,773	12,839

Source: U. S. Department of Labor, Bureau of Labor Statistics, Handbook of Labor Statistics *(Washington, D. C.: Government Printing Office, 1980), p. 151.*

Table 16.2 *Distribution of National Unions by Economic Sector for Selected Years, 1956–1978*

Year	Manufacturing Members (in thousands)	Manufacturing % of all membership	Non-manufacturing Members (in thousands)	Non-manufacturing % of all membership	Government Members (in thousands)	Government % of all membership
1956	8,839	48.2	8,350	45.6	915	5.0
1958	8,359	46.5	8,574	47.7	1,035	5.8
1960	8,519	47.6	8,375	46.4	1,070	5.9
1962	8,050	45.8	8,289	47.2	1,225	7.0
1964	8,342	46.6	8,125	45.3	1,453	8.1
1966	8,769	45.9	8,640	45.2	1,717	9.0
1968	9,218	45.6	8,837	43.7	2,155	10.7
1970	9,173	44.3	9,198	44.5	2,318	11.2
1972	8,920	42.8	9,458	45.4	2,460	11.8
1974	9,144	42.4	9,520	44.1	2,920	13.5
1976	8,568	40.6	9,549	45.2	3,012	14.3
1978	8,119	37.3	9,997	46.0	3,625	16.7

Source: U. S. Department of Labor, Bureau of Labor Statistics, Directory of National Unions and Employee Associations, 1979 *(Washington, D. C.: Government Printing Office, 1980), p. 66.*

employee unionism is even more dramatic. When professional associations are added to union membership, 25 percent of all union and professional employee membership is in the government sector. Traditionally, professional associations have been more willing to use political action and professional sanctions such as blacklisting employers to bring about desired changes than have unions. Public-sector unions, like their private-sector counterparts, have always relied more heavily on collective bargaining. Professional organizations and unions have been contrasted in the following way:

> Because associations have strongly supported the merit principle and believed that collective bargaining weakened that principle, they, in sharp contrast to unions, generally opposed collective bargaining. In general, associations appear to be more conservative, less militant, and more hindered by their past attitudes than are unions.[1]

However, professional associations have started relying more heavily on collective bargaining, including the strike, to achieve desired goals. As a result, the basic differences between unions and professional associations are not as distinct as they have been in the past.

Referring again to Table 16.2, it is apparent that, in the past, unionization among government employees lagged behind labor-union membership in the other sectors of the economy. For example, in 1956, only 5 percent of union membership was held by government employees. Workers in the private sector had been utilizing collective bargaining to bring about shared decision making with respect to wages, hours, and other conditions on a wide scale since 1935 and passage of the National Labor Relations Act. This was not the case in the public sector. In the following section, the factors contributing to the lag between public- and private-sector unionization are discussed.

Factors Inhibiting Public-Sector Unionism Prior to the 1960s

A number of factors deterring unionism among public employees prior to the 1960s have been identified. Some of these factors are related to the legal environment in which public employees work. Other factors describe the attributes of public employees and their jobs. Both sets of factors are discussed below.

THE RESTRICTIVE LEGAL ENVIRONMENT

As in the private sector, the unionization of public employees does not take place in a vacuum. It takes place in an environment subject to numerous legal restraints. Until these legal barriers were removed or modified, the organization of public employees by labor unions was quite difficult.

The sovereignty of the state. One of the major factors inhibiting public-sector unionism prior to the 1960s was the belief that "representatives of the sovereign authority (that is, government) cannot share authority with employee representatives by engaging in collective bargaining with the latter."[2] The sovereignty issue differentiated labor relations in the private and public sectors. Sovereignty can be defined as the "supreme, absolute, and uncontrollable power by which any independent state is governed . . ."[3] In the United States, sovereignty rests with the people. However, out of necessity, sovereignty is exercised by the government through the people's elected representatives and executives.[4] The sovereign power has the ability to make and enforce laws within constitutional and statutory limits.[5]

The implications of the government's sovereignty for public-sector labor management relations have been described as follows:

> To the extent that collective bargaining entails joint determination of conditions of employment, such bargaining with government is seen as unavoidably creating an interference in the sovereign's affairs. Unionization is similarly thought to involve intolerable splitting of the civil servant's loyalty between the government of which he is a part and his union. Furthermore, such practices as exclusive recognition, the closed or union shop, the checkoff of union dues are thought not only to invite organized interference with the conduct of public business but to involve improper preference for one group at the expense of others in society. The use of arbitrators to resolve disputes is seen to entail an improper abandonment by the sovereign of a portion of his authority. And the strike, needless to say, involving, as it does, concerted coercion of the employer, falls little short of insurrection when the employer is the government.[6]

As a result of this traditional view of sovereignty, only government was permitted to establish terms and conditions of employment. Since unionization and collective bargaining necessitate the joint determination of wages, hours, and other conditions of employment, public-sector collective bargaining was considered incompatible with the sovereignty of the government.[7] On a more practical level, sovereignty was used to justify the denial of collective bargaining rights to public employees by individuals who feared unionization would adversely affect government operations. In other words, sovereignty was used as an excuse not to bargain in the public sector by government officials who believed they would be inconvenienced by collective bargaining.[8] This is nothing more than a traditional management-rights argument. That is, management has the right to run the organization with minimal union involvement and minimal shared decision making. On this point, it has been argued that:

> Government officials often have wished to continue unilateral determination of conditions of employment. They feared that collective bargaining would infringe on management prerogatives, weaken authority, and affect adversely the efficiency of government operations. In addition, many feared that collective bargaining in government would inevitably lead to strikes against the government.[9]

As long as the sovereignty of government argument was applied to collective bargaining by public employees, it was unlikely that unionization would lead to meaningful participation in the decision-making process. It was not until the traditional view of sovereignty gave way to a more flexible approach that public-sector collective bargaining took hold.

Anti-union legislation. To bolster the traditional view of sovereignty discussed above, a number of laws were passed restricting the public employees' right to join unions, engage in collective bargaining, or strike. Also, the courts have tended not to be supportive of public-employee collective bargaining. With near unanimity prior to 1960, the courts held that public employees did not have a constitutional right to join or form unions.[10] It was not until 1968 that it was held by the courts that public employees have the right under the First Amendment of the United States Constitution to join and form unions.[11] In addition to the restrictive environment created by the courts, legislation was also in effect that limited public employee unionism. For example, in 1912, the federal government passed a law that gave postal employees the right to organize. However, they could not strike. Similarly, the Labor-Management Relations Act of 1947 forbade federal employees from striking and outlined severe penalties for violating the strike ban.[12] Widespread unionization by public employees would have to wait until a less restrictive legal environment emerged.

The need to protect the public from public-employee strikes. Bans on strikes by public employees were justified on two grounds. One has already been discussed. It was considered intolerable to have public employees strike against the sovereign power of the state. The second argument was that work stoppages by public employees would deprive the people of essential services provided by government. President Calvin Coolidge made a national reputation for himself while governor of Massachusetts for his actions in a 1919 strike by Boston policemen. In conjunction with that work stoppage, Coolidge stated: "There is no right to strike against the public safety by anybody, anywhere, at any time."[13] The belief the public should not be deprived essential government services provided additional grounds for passing legislation depriving public employees of the right to strike.

The role of civil service commissions. The civil service concept developed "to protect public employees from political attack and job insecurity, as well as to establish and maintain high standards of competence and professionalism in the public service."[14] Over time, civil service commissions began handling a full range of personnel matters. As civil service commissions became an intregal part of the government's personnel function, a widespread belief developed that the civil service concept was incompatible with collective bargaining. It was the conventional wisdom "that the standards of individual merit would clash with the traditional aspects of collective action and more particularly with certain maintenance of membership practices."[15] On a more practical level, it has been argued that civil service commissions have resisted public-employee collective bargaining on the grounds that unionization would infringe on their operations. It has been maintained that civil service commissions "have not taken kindly to trade union challenges to their authority to set down, unilaterally, rules and regulations relative to standards of competence, hiring, firing, tenure and so on."[16]

ATTRIBUTES OF PUBLIC-SECTOR EMPLOYEES AND EMPLOYMENT LIMITING UNIONIZATION

In addition to the restrictive legal environment, several other factors limited trade union growth in the public sector. These factors are related to the perceived nature of public-sector employment and the characteristics of public employees.

The nature of public employment. Traditionally, employment in the public service was characterized by fringe benefits, job security, and status greater than that found for comparable jobs in the private sector. These positive job attributes frequently compensated public employees for receiving wages lower than their private-sector counterparts. By offering terms of employment considered superior to the private sector, government employers did not have a difficult time attracting and maintaining a work force. Unions did not have much to offer many government employees since they were already working under conditions more favorable than those experienced by many unionized workers.

Another aspect of government employment has been a spirit of public service.[17] Many government employees took pride in providing essential services to the public. The tradition of service provided a deterrent to concerted activities by many public employees. On this point, it has been written:

> To engage in concerted action at the expense and pain of the public was to deny the tradition—to violate one's sense of pride and identification with that tradition. Plainly, so long as the tradition ruled, unionism and public employee strikes were inhibited.[18]

Characteristics of public employees. Male blue-collar workers employed in an industrial setting had traditionally been the backbone of the American labor movement. There were basic differences between the characteristics of traditional union members and many public employees. Government employers hire large numbers of white-collar, professional, and female employees. These groups expressed little interest in unionization. Also, as long as there were large numbers of industrial workers to be organized, labor unions expressed little interest in unionizing public employees.

As indicated in Table 16.2, barely one million public employees were unionized in 1960. The bulk of these workers were found in federal employment in the post office, in navy yards and arsenals (as craftsmen), in the Tennessee Valley Authority, the Government Printing Office, and the Panama Canal Zone. At the state and local level, organized employees fell into several major occupations: firefighters, some police and sanitation workers, skilled maintenance crafts, municipal transit workers, and some other industrial-type jobs. Only a limited number of clerical and administrative personnel were unionized in 1960.[19] Despite the limited inroads made by public employee unionism by 1960, the situation changed dramatically during the 1960s. A number of factors have been cited for this rapid change.

Factors Contributing to the Growth of Public-Employee Unionism

Throughout the 1960s and 1970s, public-employee unionism grew at an impressive rate. The factors bringing about this growth are many and varied. This section discusses some of the major reasons for the rapid spread of unionism among public employees.

THE EROSION OF THE FAVORABLE JOB CONDITIONS OF PUBLIC EMPLOYEES RELATIVE TO WORKERS IN THE PRIVATE SECTOR

During the 1960s, it became apparent that the traditional advantages of public employment relative to private-sector employment were deteriorating. Two major factors contributed to this shift. First, wages received by public employees were not increasing as rapidly as those in the private sector. Taxpayers were becoming increasingly resistant to the continued funding of wage increases.[20] Second, unions in the private sector were successful in securing improved wages and benefits for their members. To improve their economic position, many public-sector employees turned to unionism.

THE INDIFFERENCE OF PUBLIC-SECTOR MANAGERS TO THE NEEDS AND INTERESTS OF PUBLIC EMPLOYEES

In the public sector, there was a long tradition of unilateral and perhaps authoritarian decision making in personnel matters by public managers. As a result of this approach, many public managers were slow when responding to worker complaints.[21]

The implications of the indifference demonstrated by public managers to worker problems have been described as follows:

> For years public employees have felt that many of their grievances have gone unheeded. Prolonged periods of time lapse and still they do not receive a satisfactory solution to their job-related complaints. This leaves them frustrated and helpless, apathetic and angry. Many employees have become convinced that management does not care about their problems. . . . This development has further convinced public employees that individually they are ineffectual against the amorphous, monolithic system known as government; however, were they to collectively unite through a designated spokesman and act as one unified whole, they would have a much larger voice to air their grievances.[22]

The new interest by public employees in unionism appears to have reflected a belief that public managers would be made more responsive to worker needs with collective bargaining and a formal grievance procedure.

THE GENERAL ACCEPTANCE OF UNIONISM AND COLLECTIVE BARGAINING BY SOCIETY

By the 1960s, the United States had had over 150 years of experience with unions in the private sector. Since the 1930s, unionism had been on a relatively large scale. By the 1950s, unionism was widely accepted. Also, the public accepted collective bargaining as an appropriate way for making decisions concerning wages, benefits, and working conditions. By the 1960s, the legitimacy of collective bargaining began to transfer to public employees.[23] In other words, there was a recognition that the collective-bargaining rights afforded private-sector employees should be extended to government employees.[24]

The major implication of this change in attitude is found when the legal environment is examined. At the federal level, executive orders were issued. The most notable of these was Executive Order 10988 issued by President John Kennedy in 1962. This established the basis for collective bargaining by employees of the federal executive branch. Executive Order 10988 also had spill-over effects. It served to legitimize unionism and collective bargaining at the state and local levels.[25] By 1969, thirty-eight states enacted legislation recognizing the right of at least some public employees to engage in collective negotiations.[26] By removing restrictive laws from the books and passing legislation protecting the public employees' right to organize and engage in collective bargaining, a climate more conducive to union organizing activities was created. The changing legal environment will be discussed in greater detail in the next chapter.

INCREASED INTEREST BY UNIONS IN ORGANIZING PUBLIC EMPLOYEES

By the 1960s, union organizing in the private sector began to slow down. The large industrial plants of the north, which were most amenable to unionization, were already organized. If the American labor movement was going to continue to grow, unions would have to organize workers such as white-collar employees and professionals. It has been argued that:

> Labor unions with experience primarily in the private sector were eager to seize upon the new organizing possibility. Declining union membership and prospects of lower employment in traditional strongholds because of automation threatened to weaken these unions economically and politically. Public employees, largely unorganized, provided a new opportunity.[27]

It appears that unions took full advantage of the organizing opportunities available to them. Unions made efforts to diversify their appeal by broadening the issues over which they expressed concern.[28] For example, in addition to bargaining over the traditional economic issues, other concerns such as class size, professionalism, and tenure were addressed.

An interesting aspect of increased organizing efforts in the public sector was the rivalry that developed between unions and professional associations. Unions were trying to organize white-collar, female, and professional employees, groups historically resistant to union organizing. At the same time, professional associations, which had already been active in the public sector, began to take on the trappings of unions while attempting to maintain their image of being independent of the labor movement.[29] The competition between professional associations and unions vying for the allegiance of the same worker groups led to aggressive organizing and militant bargaining stances.

THE EFFECTIVENESS OF CONFRONTATION TACTICS

American society went through a change in mood during the 1960s. It has been argued that during this period, there was "a general societal deterioration in respect for all forms of constituted authority. Aggressiveness and militancy appeared to be everywhere, as a variety of protest groups engaged in direct confrontation with institutional forms of power, governmental and other."[30] Unrest was found on the college campuses and in the city streets. On many occasions, the use of confrontation tactics led to desired results.

The success of public demonstrations to advance one's position did not escape the notice of public employees. Despite the illegality of strikes in most government jurisdictions, a number of public employees engaged in such activities. Strikes, slowdowns, work-to-rule campaigns, and other concerted activities designed to pressure government employers to improve wages and working conditions were used with increasing regularity. Over time, the lesson became clear. Confrontation tactics such as the strike led to positive results. Unorganized workers turned to unions as a way to increase the likelihood that they could successfully utilize pressure tactics against their public employers.

For the reasons outlined above, public employee unionism spread rapidly. This development was not without its strains. Public employers had traditionally made unilateral decisions. There was a widespread reluctance to share this decision-making authority with their employees. The concept of collective bargaining was relatively foreign to most public managers. Similarly, many union officials were inexperienced with public-sector collective bargaining. While unions had decades of experience with organizing and collective bargaining in the private sector, this experience did not carry over, in total, to the public sector. In the section to follow, the differences between the public and private sectors will be examined. Also, the implications of these differences for collective bargaining in the public sector will be discussed.

Differences Between the Public and Private Sectors

The differences between the public and private sectors are more than just an academic concern. These differences need to be identified and understood because they can serve as obstacles to the effective application of techniques developed in private-sector labor-management relations to the public sector. Where private-sector procedures are not applicable, new approaches need to be developed to accommodate the nuances of public-sector labor-management relations. With reference to the differences between public and private sectors, it has been argued:

> In any public jurisdiction, unless all of the organizations can accept the existence of this difference, the road of labor management relations will be too perilous for the public to travel. The government involved and the public which supports it will be too suspicious of unionism to permit it to play its proper and important role in public service. Conversely, if the government and the public it serves believe that the union recognizes and accepts the essential difference, then all of the problems of equality of status, methods of operation, and particular aspects of the relationship have a good chance of resolution.[31]

In other words, for an effective system of labor-management relations to develop in the public sector, it is necessary to recognize and accommodate the specific characteristics of public employment. A number of differences exist between the private and public sectors; and several of the more significant ones are discussed below.

DIFFUSED MANAGERIAL AUTHORITY IN THE PUBLIC SECTOR

In the private sector, business organizations are characterized by a well-defined hierarchy of authority and responsibility. In these firms, "[t]he subordinate organization and delegations of authority are clearly drawn and the scope and magnitude of responsibility in labor relations can be defined with a reasonable degree of precision."[32] This is not the case in the public sector. As a result of the constitutional system of checks and balances, authority is distributed among the three branches of government—the legislative, judicial, and executive. With the diffusion of authority in the public sector, decisions concerning wages and working conditions could rest with the executive branch. However, the authority to establish budgets and make the financial decisions needed to fund labor agreements could be granted to the legislative branch. The essence of this problem has been described in the following terms:

> It is argued that the public sector presents a unique problem, in that authority in government is often divided among various departments. This argument raises a host of problems. The central one is: with whom is the public employee to bargain? Public employees, for example, may be forced to bargain with a government official in the executive branch of government, even though the money for settlement must come from the legislative body. Divided authority can cause other serious problems in bargaining structure concerning programs that are locally administered but state funded—such as state educational systems. This difference between the private and public sectors raises the question of how to structure the bargaining relationship so as to avoid multiple and inconsistent negotiations, lapses of good faith, and overexpenditure of governmental budgets.[33]

The practical implication of the diffusion of authority in the public sector is that the union may be negotiating with a management representative who does not have the authority to reach a final agreement. Unions often complain that they are unable to deal with the source of "yes" or "no" authority.[34] After reaching an agreement with the public manager, it may be necessary for union negotiators to wait to see if the legislative branch will finance the new contract. Technically, this can also be the case in the private sector. The management negotiator may require the cooperation and consent of top management. However, this consent can either be delegated before the start of negotiations or obtained quickly once a tentative agreement has been secured. The organization's hierarchy of authority and the general acceptance of the profit motive provides a unity of interest that allows for the speedy approval of labor agreements by top management officials.[35]

Another way to view this problem is that collective bargaining in the private sector is a bilateral process whereas it is a multilateral process in the public sector. When collective bargaining is viewed as a bilateral process, it involves "the interaction of representatives of employees on one side and management on the other."[36] However, collective bargaining in the public sector is more complex. It is a multilateral process, that is, involves more than two parties, since the decision-making powers on the management side are shared.

IMPACT OF COLLECTIVE BARGAINING ON THE POLITICAL PROCESS

In addition to differences between the public and private sectors with respect to dispersion of authority, differences also exist in terms of the way in which management authority is exercised.[37] In the "normal" American political process, the probability is high that active and legitimate interest groups in society will be able to make themselves heard during the political decision-making process.[38] With this view, a union can be viewed as an interest group much like groups such as senior citizens and welfare mothers.

It has been argued that the danger of the political process being perverted exists if public employees are granted collective bargaining rights as found in the private sector. This is because decisions concerning the allocation of resources are political in the public sector, not economic as in the private sector. It is possible that with collective bargaining, organized workers can obtain a disproportionate amount of power relative to less organized interest groups funded by government.[39] The mayor of a city, when faced with a strike by firefighters over wages and a request from the local senior citizens' group for funding of recreational programs, is in a real dilemma. Because of the dangers associated with the firefighters' walkout, the major might decide to fund a larger wage package for the firefighters with money that would otherwise go to the senior citizens. Theoretically, groups such as senior citizens should have the same opportunity to have their views represented to government officials as do organized city employees. However, groups such as senior citizens have no weapon comparable to the strike by which they could impose costs on city management thereby forcing city officials to listen to their budget requests. Because of the power held by unionized public employees, government officials may not be able to balance effectively the divergent needs of the various interest groups within the community. On the potential distortion of the American political process by public employee collective bargaining, it has been written:

> But there is trouble in the house of theory if collective bargaining in the public sector means what it does in the private. The trouble is that if unions are able to withhold labor—to strike—as well as to employ the usual methods of political pressure, they may possess a disproportionate share of effective power in the process of decision. Collective bargaining would then be so effective a pressure as to skew the results of the " 'normal' American political process."[40]

As a result of this potential, pressures exist in the public sector to limit the employees' right to strike.

INELASTIC DEMAND FOR GOVERNMENT SERVICES

In the private sector, decisions made at the bargaining table are influenced by market considerations. Both labor and management negotiators know that if bargaining outcomes lead to higher costs, and therefore, higher prices, a decline in the demand for the company's goods or services may result. This could lead to a loss in sales and revenues to the firm, and possibly a loss of jobs for the union's membership. Also, the use of the strike weapon is an economic device in the private sector. The strike is designed to impose costs of disagreeing on the other negotiator, thereby redefining the parties' relative bargaining power. As a result of these economic forces, there is a natural limit on collective bargaining in the private sector.[41]

It is argued that similar economic restraints or limits are not found in the public sector. Government, typically, offers essential services for which there are no, or only limited, substitutes. These services are typically supplied free, financed out of tax revenues. The differences between the public and private sectors with respect to the nature of their services and how the services are purchased have important implications for collective bargaining. These implications have been succinctly described in the following terms:

> Unlike the private sector, no loss of revenue follows from a work stoppage, an advantage that lowers management's cost of disagreement with the union. At the same time, however, if the service affected is essential and used by many people, public opinion can enter as an influence of major importance as both sides reckon their costs of agreement or disagreement. Furthermore, since the service need not be financially self-liquidating, the management is free of the discipline of having to balance costs against revenues. Costs remain a problem, but taxes and subsidies permit them to be shifted to third parties without fear of the losses that might result from raising prices. Instead the risk takes the form of possible political reprisal at the polls.[42] (footnotes deleted)

The above quote suggests the economic restraints operating in public-sector collective bargaining are probably not as strong as in the private sector. While this difference affects the bargaining process, it is not as if no restraints are influencing the negotiators in the public sector. However, the restraints are political, not economic. It has been argued that there is a limit on union demands in the public sector and that this limit rests with the electorate:

> The limit is imposed by the public itself. It is reached when the union's demands are exposed and are outrageous enough to raise public anger to the point where the public is not willing to accede to them. From experience, the limit is seldom reached. Still its presence serves as a significant deterrent to immoderate union demands.[43]

Similarities Between the Public and Private Sectors

The issues discussed in the preceding sections have been cited as factors differentiating the collective-bargaining situations in the public and private sectors. These differences have caused sufficient concern among policymakers to insist that the private-sector model of collective bargaining not be carried over, in total, to the public sector. However, it should be noted that a number of similarities between public- and private-sector employment are also present. These similarities argue in favor of granting employees in the public sector the same collective-bargaining rights as their private-sector counterparts. Exhibit 16.1 presents two views of the similarities between public and private employment.

> **EXHIBIT 16.1**
> **Two Views of the Similarities Between Public and Private Employment**
>
> Many believe that there are many similarities between private and public employment; in both there are: (1) an employer and employees; (2) attitudes which do not differ markedly from the attitudes in the private sector; (3) employers who want to be free from restrictions and to secure a work force as cheaply as possible; (4) employees who want to improve their living standards, to have legal rights, and to resolve grievances on their merits. Unions in both sectors have comparable goals for their members and in both instances they believe they should have the same rights.[1]
>
> Most unions . . . see little difference between employment in the private and public sectors. They focus upon the individual employee, his economic needs, his job and his fundamental rights as a citizen in a democratic society. Since public employees do not differ from those in private industry in terms of their economic requirements and the desire to have a voice in determining their conditions of employment; since almost every job in public employment has its counterpart in private industry; and since management behaves the same way vis-à-vis employees, union leaders see no reason for different laws, procedures and institutions governing labor-management relations in the public and private sectors of the economy. They sum it up by calling for "first class citizenship" for public employees.[2]
>
> Sources: [1]Arthur J. Goldberg, New York State Governor's Conference on Public Employment (1968), quoted by Harry T. Edwards, "Labor Relations in the Public Sector," in Collective Bargaining in Public Employment (Washington, D.C.: Bureau of National Affairs, Inc., 1975), p. 35.
> [2]Jack Stieber, "Collective Bargaining in the Public Sector" in Challenges to Collective Bargaining, ed. Lloyd Ulman, p. 77, published by Prentice-Hall, 1967.

The similarities and differences between collective bargaining in the public and private sectors have been the topic of much discussion in the literature. The focus of these discussions concerns the prospects for taking the private-sector model of labor relations and extending it to the public sector. Certainly, collective bargaining in both sectors is a method for resolving differences of opinion over issues such as wages, fringe benefits, and working conditions.[44] However, because of the differences between the sectors, it is necessary to modify many procedures and institutions found in the private sector to accommodate collective bargaining in the broader framework of political decision making. With this view, several questions come to mind. What aspects of private-sector collective bargaining can be carried over to the public sector? What needs to be modified? Are there procedures with marginal effectiveness in the private sector that can be improved through application in the public sector?[45] In the section to follow, several major differences in labor relations as found in the private and public sectors will be discussed.

Bargaining Arrangements in the Public Sector

With the emergence of public employee collective bargaining, it was necessary to develop a system of collective bargaining compatible with the political process. This section focuses on problems specific to the public sector requiring the modification of private-sector collective-bargaining procedures or the development of new ones. These issues include the role of the strike, alternative dispute resolution procedures in the absence of the strike, bargaining unit determination, and the scope of negotiations.

THE ROLE OF THE STRIKE IN PUBLIC-SECTOR COLLECTIVE BARGAINING

The question whether public employees should have the right to strike has been one of the more perplexing issues confronting those involved in public-sector collective bargaining. As discussed in earlier chapters, the strike is an integral part of the collective-bargaining process in the private sector. Without the strike, there would be little pressure to negotiate, modify positions or reach agreement. A distinct possibility exists that talks between the parties would be interminable in the absence of the strike weapon. Recognizing the essential role of the strike in the collective-bargaining process, the national labor policy protects the right of private-sector employees to engage in concerted activities, including the strike.

The approach to the strike issue has been basically different in the public sector. Historically, strikes by public employees have been outlawed and such action was subject to court injunction. The prevailing attitude of the government toward public employee strikes is captured in the following statement by President Franklin Roosevelt:

> A strike by public employees manifests nothing less than an intent on their part to prevent or obstruct the operations of government until their demands are satisfied. Such action looking toward the paralysis of government by those who have sworn to support it is unthinkable and intolerable. (August 16, 1937)[46]

The "hard line" taken against strikes reflects several concerns. First, public employees offer essential services of which the public cannot be deprived. Such services include police protection, firefighting, and garbage collection. The second major argument against the strike relies on the sovereignty argument discussed at the outset of this chapter. It holds that no one has the right to strike against the government which embodies the desires of the people.[47] Third, the strike cannot serve its intended function since the government employer is not deprived revenues. The strike weapon is effective only to the extent it inconveniences the public. This, in turn, generates political pressure on the government managers.[48] Related to this argument is that public managers might capitulate to reasonable union demands to avoid political "heat" created by the strike. As previously discussed, such action could give organized workers a disproportionately "loud" voice in government decision making relative to other, less organized interest groups.

Proponents of the right to strike by public employees argue that meaningful collective bargaining is impossible without the right to strike. A corollary of this argument is that strike substitutes such as arbitration or a public referendum impede the collective-bargaining process. Often times, these arguments will acknowledge that public employees in essential services such as police work and firefighting should be denied the right to strike. However, individuals making this argument will usually contend that public employees in nonessential services such as teachers, recreation workers, or sanitation employees should not be denied the strike weapon.

Public policy with respect to the strike. As mentioned earlier, the right to strike is denied by legislation in most jurisdictions. Strikes are banned in the federal sector and under most state public-employee bargaining laws. However, the ban is not complete. For example, some public employees in Alaska, Pennsylvania, Vermont, and Hawaii can strike. Alaska's legislation places public employees into three categories: (1) employees such as firefighters and police who cannot strike; (2) workers who can strike for limited periods of time such as teachers and sanitation employees; and (3) employees in nonessential services who have no limitations on the right to strike. Vermont denies the right to strike to state employees and some local employees (e.g., firefighters). However, other local employees such as teachers can strike as long as the work stoppage does not endanger the public's health or safety. Teachers in Vermont are subject to another stipulation that states that work stoppages cannot undermine a sound educational program.[49] Public employees in Hawaii can strike but only after certain conditions are met. The preconditions for strikes by public employees in Hawaii are that "the statutory impasse procedures have been complied with and their exclusive representative has given a ten-day notice of intent to strike to the HPERB [the Hawaii Public Employee Relations Board] and the public employer."[50] In Pennsylvania, there is a limited right to strike. Police, firefighters, prison, and mental-hospital guards and employees directly involved in the functioning of the courts cannot strike. However, other public employees in Pennsylvania have the right to strike as long as they have exhausted the impasse resolution procedures available to them.[51]

Frequency of public-employee strikes. Despite the general policy banning public-employee strikes, a marked increase in strike activity in the public sector has taken place. In 1950, only 15 strikes involving 1,720 employees took place. By 1969, there were 409 strikes involving 159,400 employees.[52] In 1978, 193,700 public employees participated in 481 strikes.[53] As would be expected given that the bulk of public employees are employed by local government, most strikes also occur at that level. Of the 481 strikes in 1978, 435 (90.4 percent) occurred at the county and city levels. Almost 70 percent of public-employee strikes are over wage issues. This should not be surprising. All levels of government have been confronted with an increasing demand for services and rapidly rising costs. In order to avoid tax increases, a very sensitive issue for most politicians, there has been pressure to limit government spending. This has led to an era of tight budgets. Faced with increasing employer opposition to improved wages and benefits and a rapidly rising cost of living, public employees have had a difficult time maintaining their purchasing power. An apparent reaction to their eroding economic position vis-à-vis their private-sector counterparts is the rising militancy of many public employees. This militancy has prompted some public employees to resort to strikes despite the illegality of such tactics in most political jurisdictions.

ALTERNATIVE DISPUTE RESOLUTION PROCEDURES IN THE PUBLIC SECTOR

A number of factors have been cited justifying limitations on the ability of public employees to strike legally. Several of these reasons have been discussed earlier in this chapter including the essentiality of government-provided services and concerns that strikes by public employees could distort the political process. In response to these concerns, most states and the federal governments have declared strikes by public employees illegal.

From earlier discussions of the role of the strike in private-sector collective bargaining, it should be remembered that strikes are an integral part of the process. It is the desire to avoid the costs and inconveniences of strikes that makes labor and management negotiators willing to bargain, make concessions, and ultimately, reach a mutually acceptable agreement. However, it is unlikely that negotiations will take the same form in the absence of the strike threat as in most public-sector bargaining situations. Certainly, the banning of strikes does not prevent the disputes from occurring.

Many government jurisdictions outlawing strikes have developed alternative procedures for resolving impasses arising during the negotiations of a new labor agreement. These impasse procedures are similar to those discussed in Chapter 10 intended to decrease the likelihood of a strike in the private sector. Frequently used procedures to resolve bargaining impasses found in the public sector include mediation, fact finding and compulsory arbitration. A bargaining impasse occurs when the parties conclude they are unable to reach agreement. Declaring that an impasse exists triggers the implementation of the impasse procedures found in many public-employee bargaining laws. The general characteristics of these impasse procedures will be discussed in the sections to follow.

Mediation. Mediation, as found in the public sector, is very similar to that employed in the private sector. Once the parties declare an impasse, a mediator can be brought into the dispute. As discussed in Chapter 10, the mediator's role is to help the labor and management negotiators create an environment conducive to effective negotiations. While there are a number of similarities between mediation as found in the public and private sectors, several differences exist. The incentive to utilize mediation is one factor differentiating public- and private-sector mediation.

In the private sector, the parties' use of mediation is voluntary. In the public sector, it is often mandated by law. Even when not legally required, the use of mediation may not be voluntary. For example, it may be used "to satisfy the public that every meaningful effort is being made to resolve the impasse."[54]

In addition to the incentives to utilize the procedure, several other factors that make public-sector mediation somewhat different than that found in the private sector have been identified. These factors include:[55]

- The mediator cannot assume the public-sector negotiators can make final and binding decisions at the bargaining table as in the private sector. The implication of this difference has been described as follows:

    [I]n conveying offers or positions of the parties at various times or in obtaining guidance from the parties on potentially fruitful areas of exploration, the mediator must exercise great care. He must be sure that he knows the extent of the parties' authority and what strings are attached. Is an offer firm if the budget people have final say and may not approve? Who has the power to veto a settlement? Does the union's bargaining committee have authority to act, subject to membership ratification, or is there no ratification vote unless the executive board of the union first approves the settlement? What are the political and power structure problems on both sides? These and similar questions are constantly with the mediator and he is foolish, indeed, if he does not have a clear understanding of the problems before he attempts to interpret the position of the other side.[56]

    In other words, the multilateral nature of public-sector collective bargaining can make the situation more complex than in the private sector where bilateral negotiations prevail.

- The subjects of collective bargaining are different than bargainable issues in the private sector. The scope of negotiations in the public sector will be discussed in detail later in this chapter. However, it can be said at this point that fewer subjects can be negotiated in the public sector than in the private sector. For example, some important issues such as wages may be determined by the state legislature. Similarly, a civil service commission could establish job classifications. As a result of this situation, disagreements may occur over the subjects to be bargained. This adds to the complexity of the mediator's job. Not only are disputes over the substance of the parties' positions likely, disagreements could take place over whether the issue is even negotiable.

- In the public sector, the mediator cannot ignore fiscal and taxation problems. Negotiations in the private sector are largely economic. The parties are free to strike or take a strike to avoid undesirable contract provisions. This flexibility is not usually available in the public sector. There is pressure on the parties (legal and political) not to interrupt important services by striking. At the same time public employees are striving for higher wages and improved benefits, the public employer's ability to raise taxes to fund the new agreement may be limited. As a result, it may be necessary to put larger portions of the economic package in the second and third years of multiyear contracts. This is done to provide the public employers the opportunity to accommodate the increased costs of the agreement by increasing taxes or reallocating available resources. It is necessary for mediators to be aware of and able to respond to such complexities found in public-sector collective bargaining.

These differences between public- and private-sector mediation tend to make the mediation process more difficult and complex. However, the basic nature of the process remains the same. The overriding objective is to help the parties reach a settlement with which the parties can "live."[57]

Fact finding. Fact finding is a procedure found in a number of impasse procedures. Connecticut, Massachusetts, Michigan, New York, and Wisconsin have had extensive experience with fact finding.[58] While several different types of fact finding are available, one type is most likely to be found in the public sector—fact finding with recommendations.[59]

Once it becomes apparent that mediation is not going to be able to successfully resolve the impasse, fact finding with recommendations may be invoked. It should be noted that there is considerable variation to fact-finding procedures because the procedures are a function of state legislation. One approach to fact finding has been described as follows:

> Upon a report by the mediator that his efforts have failed, either party or the top official could request appointment of a fact-finding board to study the issues and prepare recommendations for settlement. In my judgment this board should be composed of neutrals, to increase the probability of a unanimous report. Here it seems desirable to provide for a two-step sequence. In the first step the board would investigate the issues and submit a confidential report to the parties, to give them a further opportunity to reach a settlement. If a settlement were not reached within a specified time, then the second stage would begin: the board would make public its findings and recommendations. Thereupon the struggle for public opinion would start, interest groups could mobilize, and the whole question would move into the arena of a political decision. Perhaps, too, there should be one last effort to break the deadlock, by appointment of a small ad hoc committee which, working quietly and privately, would try to persuade the side that is holding out to accept the board's recommendations. The composition of this committee would depend upon which side was obstructing settlement.[60]

With fact finding, a neutral third party enters the impasse to determine, after an analysis of the facts of the case as presented at a hearing by the parties, an appropriate resolution of the dispute.[61] The fact finder's recommendations can be used by the parties as the basis for a negotiated settlement of the impasse. The theory behind the use of fact finding is that "if the findings and subsequent recommendations of the fact-finder are well reasoned, they will be persuasive in whole or, at least, in part."[62] It should be recognized that the fact finder's recommendations are not binding on the parties. Like mediation, the parties are free to accept or reject the fact finder's input into the bargaining process.

However, if the union and public employer negotiations fail to reach an agreement, the fact finder's report can then be made public in some states. The public plays an indirect but important role in the fact-finding process. It has been argued that "the goal here is not primarily one of using public opinion to influence the parties, but rather to enlighten the public so that it, in turn, can bring pressure on the lawmakers to adopt the [fact finder's] recommendations."[63]

Advantages of fact finding. There is not unanimous support for the use of fact finding as part of public-sector impasse procedures. However, several potential advantages are associated with its use. These advantages include:

- Like mediators, fact finders, because of their expertise, can offer suggestions not previously considered by the parties. These suggestions can provide the basis for a negotiated solution. Also, when mediation has failed, fact finding provides another opportunity for third-party involvement to facilitate the negotiations process. If it is believed a negotiated solution is preferable to an imposed resolution of the impasse or to capitulation by one side, then fact finding has definite advantages for the parties.
- Extreme positions taken during negotiations can be defused through fact finding. Rather than having to back down from demands made during negotiations, the parties can "save face" by deferring to the fact finder's recommendations. Along the same lines, accepting the fact finder's recommendations can be used to "sell" a mediocre agreement to the rank-and-file union membership or top management. Rather than accepting blame for the weak contract, the negotiators can "pass the buck" on to the fact finder.
- Once the fact finder's recommendations are made public, they can help generate political pressure on the parties, especially the one rejecting the recommendations, to reach agreement. Fear that the fact finder's recommendations will lead to undesirable political pressure and adverse publicity can motivate the parties to negotiate and reach agreement.
- The fact finder's report can be very useful when the public gets involved in the negotiations. The report can help alleviate the fear of tax increases or concerns over injustices likely to be experienced by some groups in the community as a result of the negotiations. "In such a situation the explanation set forth by the fact finder as to why the settlement should be as recommended can do much to educate and to assuage the community ire."[64]

Disadvantages of fact finding. It has been argued that fact finding is an unnecessary step in impasse procedures that creates more problems than it resolves. The potential disadvantages of fact finding include:

- Fact finding may undermine the effectiveness of the mediation process. The parties may hold back from making some concessions in anticipation of getting a better deal from the fact finder. As will be discussed in the following section, this argument is similar to the "chilling" effects of arbitration.
- Some argue that fact finding is an unnecessary step. Fact finding and arbitration are alike to the extent that both processes yield proposals for the reso-

lution of the impasse. The major difference is that a fact finder's recommendations are advisory whereas an arbitrator's proposals are binding on the parties. Disputes not resolved through fact finding will, typically, go to arbitration. Therefore, it is argued that fact finding is a time-consuming and expensive step that adds little to impasse procedures.

Compulsory arbitration. In a number of government jurisdictions where the strike is banned, compulsory arbitration is substituted as a mechanism for resolving the dispute. As in the private sector, interest arbitration is a procedure in which issues unresolved through negotiations are submitted to a neutral third party for decision. The primary difference between public- and private-sector arbitration is that it is compulsory in the public sector, that is, mandated by law as part of the impasse procedure whereas the process is voluntary in the private sector.

Arbitration, as part of an impasse procedure, is supported on the grounds that it will reduce the incidence of strikes. It has been argued that "arbitration reduces strikes because its binding award eliminates almost any opportunity for one side to provoke or conduct a work stoppage for terms more favorable than those provided by the arbitrator."[65] Four factors have been cited supporting the use of compulsory arbitration in public-sector interest disputes.

- The arbitration process provides a final and binding resolution of the dispute.
- It reduces the need to strike.
- Arbitration tends to equalize the bargaining power of labor and management. Absent the right to strike, it is quite likely the government employer could win every dispute.
- The arbitration of interest disputes provides a face-saving device similar to that described above in connection with the discussion of fact finding.[66]

Problems with compulsory arbitration. There are two major thrusts to the criticism of compulsory arbitration. First, it is argued that compulsory arbitration has an adverse effect on the negotiation process. The arbitration of interest disputes has the potential to "chill" negotiations. Exhibit 16.2 presents a concise description of the "chilling" effect of compulsory arbitration in the public sector. Second, compulsory arbitration can also have a "narcotic effect" on the bargaining process. It has been stated that:

> A statuatory requirement that labor disputes be submitted to arbitration has a narcotic effect on private bargainers. . . . They will turn to it as an easy and habit-forming release from the . . . obligation of hard, responsible bargaining.[67]

With the availability of arbitration, it is argued that negotiators can become "addicts who habitually rely upon arbitrators to write their labor contracts."[68] Furthermore, some empirical evidence supports the contention that the parties are less likely to reach agreement through negotiations when compulsory arbitration is required than when it is not. After a review of negotiations involving firefighters under different types of impasse procedures, Wheeler concluded:

> **EXHIBIT 16.2**
> **The "Chilling" Effect of Interest Arbitration**
>
> The most publicized criticism [of compulsory arbitration] involves the "chilling" or deterrent effect that conventional arbitration allegedly has on the parties' incentives to bargain in good faith. If either party, the argument goes, anticipates that it will get more from the arbitrator than from a negotiated settlement, it will have an incentive to avoid the trade-offs of good faith bargaining and will cling to excessive or unrealistic positions in the hope of tilting the arbitration outcome in its favor. This lack of hard bargaining will occur because of a significant reduction in the costs of disagreement. Not only will there be no strike costs, the uncertainties associated with continued disagreement are reduced because of the usual compromise outcome: the arbitrator gives less than the union has asked for and more than the employer has offered. In other words, since conventional arbitration imposes much smaller costs of disagreement than strikes, there is little incentive to avoid it.
>
> Source: Peter Feuille, "Final Offer Arbitration and the Chilling Effect," Industrial Relations 14 (October 1975):304.

The data were consistent with the "narcotic effect" argument. Under compulsory arbitration, an average of 37.3 per cent of the firefighter negotiations per year in each state resulted in the institution of arbitration proceedings. In those states which had fact finding laws, 21.5 per cent of the firefighter negotiators went to fact finding. In those states which had voluntary arbitration, only 2.1 per cent of the negotiations resulted in the use of these impasse-resolution procedures.[69]

Final-offer arbitration. Final-offer arbitration is a technique being used in several states (Wisconsin, Massachusetts, Minnesota, and Michigan) to avoid the negative consequences of traditional arbitration. There are two basic forms of final-offer arbitration used in the public sector—package selection and issue-by-issue selection. With package selection, the arbitrator must select one party's entire offer on all issues. With issue-by-issue selection, the arbitrator examines each issue separately and chooses one party's final offer on each issue. It has been argued that:

> Package selection yields an "all or nothing" outcome and does not allow the arbitrator flexibility in balancing the parties' positions on separate issues; issue selection gives the arbitrator some flexibility in handling multi-issue disputes but reduces the parties' incentive to reach agreement on the entire package of bargainable issues.[70]

The theory behind final-offer arbitration is that the uncertainty associated with the chance of losing "everything" in arbitration acts as an inducement to the parties to negotiate a settlement on their own. After a review of the early experience under final-offer arbitration, Feigenbaum concluded:

> The theory of final offer arbitration promises more than its actual performance delivers, based on admittedly limited experience. There is no showing that fewer negotiations

reach impasse than would occur under conventional arbitration. There is evidence, however, that final offer arbitration does tend to produce awards less equitable than warranted by the positions and strengths of the parties, particularly when there are multiple issues at impasse and when arbitrators may select only one overall package or the other. This tendency is built into the process, since the whole point of final offer arbitration is deterrence with little or no concern for getting a good settlement through arbitration.[71]

After a more recent review of the literature concerning the differential impact of conventional and final-offer arbitration on the bargaining process, Kochan tentatively concluded:

> No significant differences in the number of initial impasses were found in cases where final-offer arbitration was compared to conventional arbitration. However, fewer cases resulted in an arbitration award under final-offer arbitration.[72]

This conclusion indicates that the parties are more likely to continue negotiating after invoking final-offer arbitration than conventional arbitration. If one of the objectives of public-sector impasse procedures is to induce "good faith" bargaining that will lead the parties to agreement without third-party involvement, then final-offer arbitration appears to offer advantages over the conventional procedure.

Choice of procedures. In recent years, there has been an addition to public-sector impasse procedures known as choice of procedures. With this approach, one or both of the parties can select either arbitration or a strike if they fail to reach agreement through negotiations and mediation. This approach can be found in impasse procedures in the Canadian federal civil service, British Columbia, Wisconsin, and Minnesota.

Choice of procedures developed as a result of the criticisms that arbitration decreases the likelihood the parties will reach a negotiated settlement. At the same time, it is recognized that the strike-threat system induces negotiated agreements as the parties bargain in good faith to avoid the costs associated with a strike. In other words, the parties work toward a negotiated agreement because the costs of disagreeing are greater than the costs of agreeing.

With choice of procedures, the party selecting the impasse procedure (strike or arbitration) can manipulate the costs of disagreeing. It has been argued that the selecting party will most likely choose the procedure believed to yield the best possible labor agreement for its constituents.[73] A review of the experience of political jurisdictions operating under choice of procedures yielded several interesting results:

- When a choice of procedures is allowed, public managers favored a strike-based system whereas public employees or unions preferred arbitration.
- The rate of negotiated settlements is greater when the strike option is selected.
- Jurisdictions with a choice of procedures have a low incidence of strikes.[74]

After their examination of choice of procedures as an approach to public-sector dispute resolution, Ponak and Wheeler concluded:

> Impasse procedures which culminate in arbitration seem to preordain an excessive usage of arbitration. This is said to violate the norms of voluntarism in collective bargaining, ultimately damaging the relationship between the parties. Impasse procedures anchored in work stoppages, although more likely to produce agreements negotiated by the parties themselves, risk service disruptions that are unacceptable to many policymakers.
>
> Our findings suggest that choice of procedures may be capable of resolving this apparent dilemma. . . . Choice of procedures systems thus seem to have fulfilled multiple objectives: (1) fostering negotiated agreements; (2) avoiding work stoppages; and (3) providing unions with the right to strike, . . . a right of considerable philosophical importance to many unions.[75]

As indicated by this lengthy discussion of strikes in the public sector and impasse-resolution procedures, these constitute important issues in public-sector labor relations. Because of differences between public- and private-sector labor relations, it has been necessary to develop dispute-resolution procedures accommodating the needs of the public sector. In addition to the strike and impasse procedures, two other aspects of labor-management relations pose special problems in the public sector: bargaining-unit determination and the scope of negotiations.

BARGAINING-UNIT DETERMINATION IN THE PUBLIC SECTOR

The term "bargaining unit" refers to the workers covered by a collective bargaining agreement. In the private sector, the National Labor Relations Board determines the bargaining unit most appropriate for collective bargaining. Chapter 7 included a discussion of the factors considered by the NLRB when establishing appropriate bargaining units. Community of interest is the primary criterion used by the NLRB when establishing bargaining units. This means that the NLRB strives to create bargaining units in which there is mutuality of interests among the employees with respect to wages, hours, and working conditions.

Bargaining-unit determination is a more complex issue in the public sector. First, there is no set of criteria found in the public sector analogous to the NLRB's guidelines for bargaining-unit determination. Bargaining-unit determination is an issue addressed by state-level legislation. As a result, wide variation is found in the criteria used to establish bargaining units across the country. Second, a tremendous variety of occupations is represented in public employment. Think about the types of workers employed by your state government. Occupations ranging from custodians to psychiatrists are found in government employment.

When examining bargaining-unit determination in public employment, two problems emerge requiring this issue to be handled differently than in the private sector. The first problem concerns the scope of the bargaining unit; that is, what types of workers should be included in the same bargaining unit. The second problem concerns the inclusion of supervisory personnel in bargaining units. In other words, there are problems with both the size and composition of bargaining units in the public sector. Exhibit 16.3 contrasts the nature of the bargaining-unit-determination issue as found in the public and private sectors.

> **EXHIBIT 16.3**
> **The Implications of Bargaining-Unit Determination in the Public and Private Sectors**
>
> It is becoming increasingly clear that of the numerous problems which complicate the practice of collective bargaining in the public sector, none is more important than the appropriate unit question. In the public sector as well as in private industry, determination of the size and composition of the bargaining unit at the initial stages of organization and recognition can be decisive of the question of which employee organization will achieve majority recognition, or whether any organization will win recognition. Save for the employee organization which limits its jurisdiction along narrow lines such as the craft practiced by its members, the normal tendency may be to request initially a unit whose boundaries coincide with the spread of the organization's membership or estimated strength. The public employer, on the other hand, may seek to recognize a unit in which the no-union votes will be in the majority, or a favored employee organization will have predominant strength; or the employer may simply seek to avoid undue proliferation of bargaining units.
>
> The problem in the public sector, however, is of far greater depth than the initial victory-or-defeat aspect of recognition. In the private sector, it is clear that the scope and nature of the unit found to be appropriate for bargaining has acted as an important determinant of the union's basic economic strength—that is, its bargaining over bread-and-butter economic issues. In the public sector, it seems clear that the scope and nature of the unit found to be appropriate will also affect the range of subjects which can be negotiated meaningfully, the role played in the process by the separate branches of government, the likelihood of peaceful resolution of disputes, order versus chaos in bargaining, and ultimately, perhaps, the success of the whole idea of collective bargaining for public employees.
>
> Source: Eli Rock, "Bargaining Units in the Public Service: The Problem of Proliferation," Michigan Law Review, Vol. 67, March 1969, p. 1001. Copyright by The Michigan Law Review Association 1969.

The scope of the bargaining unit. The size and composition of the bargaining unit is a problem because of the large number of occupations found in the public sector. If the community-of-interest criterion, used frequently in the private sector, is employed in the public sector, it is quite likely that a proliferation of bargaining units will result. The community-of-interest criterion could lead to placing workers in a craft, job classification, or department into separate bargaining units. This would lead to a relatively large number of small bargaining units.

There is nothing inherently wrong with small bargaining units. They can facilitate the union-organizing process. Also, it is probably easier to establish labor agreements responsive to worker needs when the bargaining unit is composed of a relatively small, homogeneous group of workers. Along the same line, it has been argued that "like-situated employees will better understand their own problems and press their unique needs, but it also recognizes the instinct of exclusiveness which causes employees to *want* to form their own organization rather than become part of a larger organization in which they may feel themselves strangers."[76]

At the same time there are strong arguments in favor of a large number of small bargaining units in public employment, a strong case can be made in the other direction. The major arguments favoring broad units composed of a number of different job classifications include:

- Since employment policies are frequently common for a large number of workers, it makes little sense to negotiate over these issues with different unions.
- The government employer has a common source of revenue—taxes. This argues in favor of limiting the number of bargaining units competing for the scarce tax dollars.
- The proliferation of bargaining units can lead to complicated, expensive negotiations.
- Public employers usually keep a "hands off" policy during the representation election campaign. Consequently, unions do not have to resist broader bargaining units because they believe they are at a disadvantage when trying to organize. When not faced with employer resistance, the scope of the bargaining unit should not be a factor in the union's organizing campaign.[77]

The implications of the arguments concerning bargaining-unit determination have been described as follows:

> The larger the employee units selected for representation, the fewer the number of elections, negotiations and possible rivalries among organizations to influence settlements. However, the larger the units, the more likely it is that minorities within a group will feel that their special interests have not been adequately recognized; the possibilities of internal friction increase. Then, too, though fewer strikes may occur in large bargaining units, those that do take place are likely to have greater disruptive impact.[78]

There are three basic types of bargaining units found in the public sector. The vertical or industrial unit is composed of all employees in a governmental unit such as a department. The horizontal or craft units include workers in particular job classifications, professions, or crafts. The tier unit is composed of "all employees for whom specific conditions of employment (e.g., pensions, health and hospitalization insurance, or leave allowances) must be uniform.[79]

It appears to be within the interest of public employers to avoid a proliferation of small bargaining units by pressing for the establishment of vertical or industrial units. However, the response among government jurisdictions to the bargaining unit determination issue has not been uniform. On this point, it has been written that:

> Some jurisdictions have prescribed boundaries, particularly for state employees, in the form of broad statutory units. Most jurisdictions, however, have not followed the policy of mandating broad units but have used a "case-by-case" approach and utilized criteria such as a community of interest, similar skills and duties, employee desires, history of bargaining, etc. in making unit determinations. The two policies are of course, not mutually exclusive and one of the criteria applied may be the effects of over-fragmentation of units.[80]

Inclusion of supervisors in bargaining units. In the private sector, supervisory personnel are clearly exempted from coverage by the National Labor Relations Act. As a result, bargaining units in the private sector do not include supervisors as well as the employees they supervise. Unfortunately, the issue is not so clear-cut in the public sector.

The treatment of supervisors under public-sector labor legislation varies from state to state. Some states exclude supervisors from bargaining units while others allow them full bargaining rights. Several factors have been cited as explaining the lack of uniform treatment of supervisors:

- Rather than being governed by a single law, public-sector labor-management relations is governed by a patchwork of state laws, executive orders, and municipal ordinances. These reflect the pecularities of each jurisdiction.
- Public-sector collective bargaining is a rather recent development which has not achieved stability as has the private sector.
- The definition of the term "supervisor" and the rights associated with such a status is determined by state legislation. This leads to diverse definitions unlike the single definition found in the NLRA.[81]

In the public sector, it is quite likely that some supervisors will be included in bargaining units. The reasons for this divergence between the public- and private-sector models of collective bargaining with respect to the bargaining rights of supervisors rest in the history of public-sector collective bargaining. First, groups such as teachers, firefighters, and police officers have historically been at the front of public-sector organizing. Such groups are characterized by a strong community of interest between the rank and file and their supervisors. For example, both teachers and school principals have joined the National Education Association because of similar professional interests. Second, the term "supervisor" has been pushed farther down the organizational hierarchy in the public sector. As a result, the distinction between supervisor and employee tends to become blurred in the public sector. Third, supervisors and middle managers are less likely to act like managers than their private-sector counterparts. To a degree, this is because state and local civil service commissions handle many managerial responsibilities in the public sector.[82]

Two major approaches have been taken to provide bargaining rights to supervisors in the public sector. States including Wisconsin, Oregon, and Connecticut exclude only bona fide supervisors from coverage of bargaining laws. This approach recognizes the point made above that many public-sector supervisors have limited supervisory responsibilities. If it is concluded after an examination of the supervisors' responsibilities they are not really managers, they will be put in the same bargaining unit with rank-and-file workers.[83]

The second approach is exemplified by states such as Hawaii, Minnesota, New York, Massachusetts, and Michigan. In these states, supervisors have full bargaining rights. However, bona fide supervisors are placed in autonomous bargaining units while less than bona fide supervisors are included in units with rank-and-file employ-

> **EXHIBIT 16.4**
> **Factors Causing the Divergent Policies Affecting Supervisors'**
> **Bargaining Rights in the Public and Private Sectors**
>
> Several factors have contributed to the divergent direction taken by the states vis-à-vis the private sector and the federal government. Perhaps foremost among them is the desires of the supervisors themselves. In several jurisdictions public sector supervisors have demonstrated a strong desire to be included in the bargaining process. This desire is manifested in elections and unit determination petitions and also was no doubt felt through lobbying activities when much of the legislation was developed. This activity, coupled with the questionable managerial status of many supervisors in public employment, has undoubtedly weighed heavily upon the decisions of the various state legislatures and administrative agencies.
>
> The early stage of development of public sector collective bargaining must also be considered a critical factor. In many public sector bargaining relationships the major emphasis has yet to shift from contract negotiation to contract administration. In the private sector, the grievance procedure is well institutionalized, and the supervisor's key role in contract administration is widely recognized. Since successful contract administration has not yet become the focus of the labor relations program in the majority of public sector jurisdictions, the role of the supervisor in those labor relations structures has not been clearly delineated. Therefore, the role ambivalence felt by public sector supervisors has not yet emerged as a major concern which their superiors have considered in depth.
>
> *Source:* Stephen L. Hayford and Anthony V. Sinicropi, "Bargaining Rights Status of Public Sector Supervisors," Industrial Relations 15 (February 1976): 59–60.

ees. Exhibit 16.4 discusses the factors that have contributed to the evolution of different practices concerning the bargaining rights of supervisors in the public and private sectors.

THE SCOPE OF BARGAINING ISSUES

The scope of bargaining issues concerns the number and type of subjects negotiable by the parties to a labor agreement. As discussed in Chapter 8, three categories of issues are identified in the private sector: mandatory, permissive, and illegal. The key category is composed of mandatory issues that concern the traditional concerns of unions: wages, hours, fringe benefits, and working conditions. To a substantial degree, the issues subject to collective bargaining in the private sector are defined by the National Labor Relations Act.

The scope-of-bargaining issue is much more troublesome in the public sector than in the private. In general, the scope of bargaining issues is narrower in the public sector relative to the private sector. However, there is a great deal of variability on this issue among the various government jurisdictions. As previously noted, wages, hours, and other terms and conditions of employment are mandatory subjects of negotiations in the private sector. In the public sector, a threefold division is made in the subjects that can be negotiated: (1) topics determined by legislation; (2) issues determined by civil service commissions and public managers; and (3) those determined by the collective bargaining process.[84] The scope of bargaining in the public sector is narrowed relative to the private sector to the extent the legislative branch of government and civil service commissions decide issues that could be negotiated by labor and management. For example, in the federal government, Congress determines many important issues such as wages and benefits. As a result, unions and professional associations cannot negotiate over such items. Similarly, the decisions by state legislatures and civil service commissions limit the scope of bargaining among state-level government employees. However, the scope of bargaining is usually much broader at the local level.[85]

The practical significance of the scope-of-bargaining issue concerns the role public employees will have in determining the conditions under which they work: the broader the definition of bargainable issues, the greater potential impact unions will have. It is safe to assume that unions and professional associations will press for a broad definition of bargainable items as in the private sector. From the public employer's position, the obligation to bargain with unions can be limited by a narrow definition of bargainable issues. When issues are decided unilaterally by management, legislatively determined, or established through the civil service system, the ability of workers and their unions to influence such decisions is sharply limited. Rather than negotiating such issues, the employees may be consulted by the public employer. However, the public employer is under no obligation to respond to the union's position. Similarly, when matters are legislatively determined, the unions are limited to lobbying in an effort to have their input reflected in the decision.

Summary

In recent years, collective bargaining in the public sector has grown more rapidly than in the private sector. It is quite likely that union-organizing efforts will continue to focus on the public sector for the foreseeable future. With the spread of public-sector collective bargaining, there has been increased worker unrest and media attention given to the situation. It is difficult to pick up a newspaper or watch televised news coverage without seeing reports of public-sector negotiations or groups such as firefighters and teachers being on strike. The purpose of this chapter was to provide insights into the reasons why public employees organize and some of the problems associated with collective bargaining in the public sector.

Several factors have influenced the rapid increase in the number of public employees joining unions. In part, public employees have turned to unionism in an attempt to improve their wages and fringe benefits. Historically, public employees worked under more favorable conditions than their private-sector counterparts. However, their economic position deteriorated during the 1960s and 1970s. Many workers turned to unions in an effort to reverse this trend. Public employees were also motivated to unionize by a desire to make public managers more responsive to their needs. Because public managers traditionally exercised unilateral control, there was a tendency to be unresponsive to worker complaints. A number of workers unionized to provide themselves the bargaining power needed to influence managerial decisions. Additionally, the workers' urge to organize was facilitated by a change in public policy toward unionism. At both federal and state levels, laws were passed protecting the right of public employees to organize and engage in collective bargaining. Another factor stimulating union growth in the public sector was the increased attention by labor organizations to the unionization of public workers. The public sector offered labor organizations a tremendous source of workers potentially interested in their organizing efforts. Finally, changes in society encouraged the use of confrontation tactics to secure desired objectives. Public employees realized confrontation tactics such as strikes would be more effective if they were organized.

Differences have developed between labor-management relations as found in the public and private sectors. Limitations on the right to strike are one of the major factors differentiating labor-management relations in the public sector from the private sector situation. In many government jurisdictions, strikes have been outlawed. This has been done because strikes deny the public essential government services. Also, strikes can give public employees relatively more power than other less organized groups in the community.

The widespread banning of strikes in the public sector has a disruptive effect on the collective-bargaining process. The desire to avoid the costs associated with strikes motivates the parties to bargain, make concessions, and ultimately reach agreement. When strikes are prohibited, pressures to negotiate are removed. To avoid a breakdown in the bargaining process, it has been necessary to develop dispute-resolution mechanisms commonly known as impasse procedures. The most comprehensive impasse procedures include meditation, fact finding and compulsory arbitration.

Other problems that have caused public-sector labor-management relations to evolve differently than in the private sector are the bargaining-unit determination and scope-of-bargaining issues. The bargaining-unit determination issue has two components. First, the diversity of jobs found in the public sector generates pressures for the creation of a large number of small bargaining units. However, the proliferation of bargaining units is frequently incompatible with efficient and effective government. As a result of these divergent pressures, the commality-of-interest criterion frequently used when determining bargaining units in the private sector is not religiously applied in the public sector. Second, the inclusion of supervisors in bargaining units is another factor differentiating bargaining-unit determination in the public and private sectors. In the private sector, supervisors are not employees under the law and are excluded from bargaining units. The situation is not as clear-cut in the public sector. Under certain circumstances, public-sector supervisors will be included in bargaining units with workers they supervise.

The scope-of-negotiations issue concerns the number and types of issues subject to collective negotiations. The scope of negotiations is narrower in the public sector than in the private. This is because many issues such as wages and retirement benefits, which are legislatively determined, are not negotiable in the public sector. As a result, public sector unions must employ lobbying techniques in addition to collective bargaining in order to influence the full range of issues in which they are interested.

With this general background in mind, the next chapter provides a detailed examination of two important aspects of public-sector collective bargaining. First, the legal environment influencing public-sector labor-management relations will be discussed. Then, the impact of collective bargaining on public employees and government operations will be scrutinized.

Discussion Questions

1. In 1960, 5.9 percent of government employees as compared with 47.6 percent of manufacturing employees were unionized. What factors caused the unionization of public employees to lag behind that found in the private sector?
2. The rapid growth of public-employee collective bargaining was one of the most dramatic changes in the American labor force during the 1960s. What factors contributed to the rapid spread of unionization of public employees since 1960?
3. It has been argued that labor-management relations as found in the private sector can be carried over and applied on the public sector. Do you agree with this position? What differences exist between the public and private sectors warranting the modification of the private-sector model of labor-management relations when applying it to the public sector?
4. Discuss the pros and cons of prohibiting public employees from striking.
5. What effect does banning public employee strike have on the collective-bargaining process? Does substituting an impasse procedure including mediation, fact finding and conventional arbitration encourage collective bargaining in the absence of the strike threat?
6. Discuss the pros and cons of final-offer arbitration.

Key Concepts

Professional association
Sovereignty of the state
Multilateral bargaining
Impasse procedures
Mediation
Fact-finding

Arbitration
Compulsory arbitration
Final-offer arbitration
Choice of procedures
Scope of the bargaining unit
Scope of bargaining

Notes

1. James E. Martin, "State Employee Affiliation and Attitude Differences," *Journal of Applied Psychology* 63 (1978):654.
2. Abraham Gitlow, "Public Employee Unionism in the United States: Growth and Outlook," *Labor Law Journal* 21 (December 1970):769.
3. *Black's Law Dictionary,* 4th ed. rev. (St. Paul: West Publishing Co., 1968).
4. Murray B. Nesbitt, *Labor Relations in the Federal Government Service* (Washington, D. C.: Bureau of National Affairs, 1976), p. 83.
5. Kurt L. Hanslowe, *The Emerging Law of Labor Relations in Public Employment* (Ithaca, NY: New York State School of Industrial and Labor Relations, 1967), p. 14.
6. Ibid., p. 14.
7. Michael H. Moskow, J. Joseph Loewenberg, and Edward C. Koziara, *Collective Bargaining in Public Employment* (New York: Random House, 1970), p. 17.
8. Neil W. Chamberlain, "Public vs. Private Sector Bargaining," in *Collective Bargaining in Government,* eds. J. Joseph Loewenberg and Michael L. Moskow (Englewood Cliffs, NJ: Prentice-Hall, 1972), p. 10.
9. Ibid., p. 18.
10. Lee C. Shaw, "The Development of State and Federal Laws," in *Public Workers and Public Unions,* ed. Sam Zagoria (Englewood Cliffs, NJ: Prentice-Hall, 1972), p. 21.
11. Ibid., p. 21.
12. Gitlow, "Public Employee Unionism in the United States: Growth and Outlook," p. 769.
13. Quoted by Anne M. Ross, "Public Employee Unions and the Right to Strike," *Monthly Labor Review* 92 (March 1969):15.
14. Gitlow, "Public Employee Unionism in the United States: Growth and Outlook," p. 770.
15. John W. Macy, Jr., "The Role of Bargaining in the Public Service," in *Public Workers and Public Unions,* ed. Sam Zagoria (Englewood Cliffs, NJ: Prentice-Hall, 1972), p. 9.
16. Gitlow, "Public Employee Unionism in the United States: Growth and Outlook," p. 770.
17. Ibid., p. 770.
18. Ibid., p. 770.
19. Derek C. Bok and John T. Dunlop, *Labor and the American Community* (New York: Simon and Schuster, 1970), pp. 312–13.
20. Morton R. Godine, *The Labor Problem in the Public Service* (New York: Russell and Russell, 1967), pp. 6–7.
21. Gitlow, "Public Employee Unionism in the United States: Growth and Outlook," p. 772.
22. Charles S. Bunker, *Collective Bargaining: Non-Profit Sector* (Columbus: Grid, Inc., 1973), pp. 12–13.
23. Everett Kassalow, "Perspective on the Upsurge of Public Employee Unionism," in *Collective Negotiation for Public and Professional Employees,* eds. Robert T. Woodworth and Richard B. Peterson (Glenview, IL: Scott, Foresman and Co., 1969), p. 21.
24. Bunker, *Collective Bargaining: Non-Profit Sector,* p. 12.
25. Kassalow, "Perspective on the Upsurge of Public Employee Unionism," p. 21.
26. Gitlow, "Public Employee Unionism in the United States: Growth and Outlook," p. 772.
27. Moskow et al., *Collective Bargaining in Public Employment,* p. 221.
28. Alan E. Bent and T. Zane Reeves, *Collective Bargaining in the Public Sector* (Menlo Park, CA: Benjamin/Cummings Publishing Company, Inc., 1978), p. 13.
29. Ibid., p. 14.
30. Gitlow, "Public Employee Unionism in the United States: Growth and Outlook," pp. 772–73.
31. Macy, "The Role of Bargaining in the Public Service," p. 10.
32. Ibid., p. 10.
33. Harry T. Edwards, "Labor Relations in the Public Sector," in *Problems in Collective Bargaining in Public Employment* (Washington, D. C.: Bureau of National Affairs, 1975), p. 33.

34. Macy, "The Role of Bargaining in the Public Service," p. 10.

35. George H. Hildebrand, "The Public Sector," in *Frontiers of Collective Bargaining,* eds. John T. Dunlop and Neil W. Chamberlain (New York: Harper & Row, 1967), p. 127.

36. Thomas A. Kochan, "A Theory of Multilateral Collective Bargaining in City Governments," *Industrial and Labor Relations Review* 27 (July 1972):525.

37. Macy, "The Role of Bargaining in the Public Service," p. 11.

38. Robert A. Dahl, *A Preface to Democratic Theory* (Chicago: University of Chicago Press, 1956), p. 145.

39. Edwards, "Labor Relations in the Public Sector," p. 34.

40. Harry H. Wellington and Ralph K. Winters, "The Limits of Collective Bargaining in Public Employment," in *Readings in Labor Economics and Labor Relations,* 4th ed., ed. Richard L. Rowan (Homewood, IL: Richard D. Irwin, Inc., 1980), p. 210.

41. Edwards, "Labor Relations in the Public Sector," p. 39.

42. Hildebrand, "The Public Sector," pp. 126–127.

43. Edwards, "Labor Relations in the Public Sector," p. 34.

44. Clyde W. Summers, "Public Employee Bargaining: A Political Perspective," in *Government Labor Relations: Trends and Information for the Future,* ed. Hugh D. Jascourt (Oak Park, IL: Moore Publishing Co., 1979), p. 216.

45. Jack Stieber, "Collective Bargaining in the Public Sector," in *Challenges to Collective Bargaining,* ed. Lloyd Ulman (Englewood Cliffs: Prentice-Hall, 1967), p. 79.

46. Quoted by Bok and Dunlop, *Labor and the American Community,* p. 331.

47. Bunker, *Collective Bargaining: Non-Profit Sector,* p. 131.

48. Bok and Dunlop, *Labor and the American Community,* p. 335.

49. Joel Siedman and Paul Standohar, "The Hawaii Public Employment Relations Act: A Critical Analysis," *Industrial and Labor Relations Review* 26 (April 1973):933.

50. Jack E. Klauser, "Public Sector Impasse Resolution in Hawaii," *Industrial Relations* 16 (October 1977):284.

51. Kurt Decker, "The Importance of Impasse for Pennsylvania's Public Employees and Employers," *Journal of Collective Negotiations in the Public Sector* 9 (1980):277.

52. Marvin J. Levine and Eugene C. Hagburg, *Public Sector Labor Relations* (St. Paul: West Publishing Co., 1979), p. 88.

53. U. S. Department of Labor, Bureau of Labor Statistics, *Analysis of Work Stoppages, 1978* (Washington, D. C.: Government Printing Office, 1980), p. 36.

54. Eva Robbins, "Some Comparisons of Mediation in the Public and Private Sector," in *Collective Bargaining in Government,* eds. J. Joseph Loewenberg and Michael H. Moskow (Englewood Cliffs, NJ: Prentice-Hall, 1972), p. 323.

55. This section is based on Robbins, "Some Comparisons of Mediation in the Public and Private Sector," pp. 326–28.

56. Ibid., p. 326.

57. Kenneth Kressel, "Labor Mediation: An Exploratory Survey," in *Public Sector Labor Relations,* eds. David Lewin, Peter Feuille, and Thomas Kochan (Glen Ridge, NJ: Thomas Horton and Daughters, 1977), p. 258.

58. Jean T. McKelvey, "Fact Finding in Public Employment Disputes: Promise or Illusion," in *Collective Bargaining in Government,* eds. J. Joseph Loewenberg and Michael H. Moskow, (Englewood Cliffs: Prentice-Hall, 1972), p. 332.

59. Arnold M. Zack, "Impasses, Strikes and Resolutions," in *Public Workers and Public Unions,* ed. Sam Zagoria (Englewood Cliffs: Prentice-Hall, 1972), p. 113.

60. Hildebrand, "The Public Sector," p. 146.

61. McKelvey, "Fact Finding in Public Sector Disputes: Promise or Illusion," p. 331.

62. Bent and Reeves, *Collective Bargaining in the Public Sector,* p. 248.

63. McKelvey, "Fact Finding in Public Sector Disputes: Promise or Illusion," p. 331.

64. Zack, "Impasses, Strikes and Resolutions," p. 115.

65. David Lewin, Peter Feuille, and Thomas Kochan, *Public Sector Labor Relations: Analysis and Readings* (Glen Ridge, NJ: Thomas Horton and Daughters, 1977), p. 228.

66. Ibid., p. 228.

67. Robert Howlett, "Arbitration in the Public Sector," *Proceedings,* Southwest Legal Foundation, 15th Annual Institute of Labor Law (1969), p. 234.

68. Peter Feuille, "Final Offer Arbitration and the Chilling Effect," *Industrial Relations* 14 (October 1975):304.

69. Hoyt N. Wheeler, "Compulsory Arbitration: A 'Narcotic Effect,' " *Industrial Relations* 14 (October 1975):316.

70. Feuille, "Final Offer Arbitration and the Chilling Effect," p. 305.

71. Charles Feigenbaum, "Final Offer Arbitration: Better Theory Than Practice," *Industrial Relations* 14 (October 1975):316.

72. Thomas Kochan, "Dynamics of Dispute Resolution in the Public Sector," in *Public Sector Bargaining,* eds. Benjamin Aaron, Joseph R. Grodin, and James L. Stern (Washington, D. C.: Bureau of National Affairs, 1979), p. 175.

73. Allen Ponak and Hoyt N. Wheeler, "Choice of Procedures in Canada and the United States," *Industrial Relations* 19 (Fall 1980):299.

74. Ibid., pp. 301–5.

75. Ibid., p. 305.

76. Eli Rock, "Bargaining Units in the Public Service: The Problem of Proliferation," in *Collective Bargaining in Government,* eds. J. Joseph Loewenberg and Michael H. Moskow (Englewood Cliffs: Prentice-Hall, 1972), p. 120.

77. Lee C. Shaw and R. Theodore Clark, Jr., "Determination of Appropriate Bargaining Units in the Public Sector: Legal and Practical Problems," *Oregon Law Review* 51 (Fall 1971):173–76.

78. Bunker, *Collective Bargaining: Non-Profit Sector,* p. 86.

79. Thomas P. Gilroy and Anthony C. Russo, "Bargaining Unit Issues: Problems, Criteria, Tactics," in *Trends in Public Sector Labor Relations,* eds. Arvid Anderson and Hugh D. Jascourt (Chicago: International Personnel Management Association, 1975), p. 77.

80. Ibid., p. 78.

81. Stephen L. Hayford and Anthony V. Sinicropi, "Bargaining Rights Status of Public Sector Supervisors," *Industrial Relations* 15 (February 1976):44–45.

82. Harry T. Edwards, "The Impact of Private Sector Principles in the Public Sector: Bargaining Rights for Supervisors and the Duty to Bargain," in *Union Power and Public Policy,* ed. David Lipsky (Ithaca, NY: New York State School of Industrial and Labor Relations, 1975), pp. 56–57.

83. Hayford and Sinicropi, "Bargaining Rights Status of Public Sector Supervisors," p. 59.

84. Bok and Dunlop, *Labor and the American Community,* p. 326.

85. Ibid., p. 326.

Suggested Readings

Hamermesh, Daniel S., ed. *Labor in the Public and Nonprofit Sectors.* Princeton, NJ: Princeton University Press, 1975.

Jascourt, Hugh D., ed. *Government Labor Relations: Trends and Information for the Future.* Oak Park, IL: Moore Publishing Co., 1979.

Levine, Marvin J. and Hagburg, Eugene C. *Public Sector Labor Relations.* St. Paul: West Publishing Co., 1979.

Moskow, Michael H., Loewenberg, J. Joseph, and Koziara, Edward C. *Collective Bargaining in Public Employment.* New York: Random House, 1970.

U.S. Department of Labor. *Understanding Grievance Arbitration in the Public Sector.* Washington, D. C.: U. S. Government Printing Office, 1980.

Chapter 17

PUBLIC-SECTOR COLLECTIVE BARGAINING: LEGAL ENVIRONMENT AND IMPLICATIONS

Joe Malleck is a firefighter with the Laramie Fire Department. He is also president of the local firefighters union. To say the bargaining relationship between the city and the firefighters union is "interesting" would be a serious understatement. They entered the bargaining relationship in 1967 under new state legislation that extended collective bargaining rights to firefighters in Wyoming. Rather than bargain, the city challenged the constitutionality of the legislation in the courts. However, the Wyoming Supreme Court upheld the constitutionality of the legislation.

Since 1967, the city and firefighters union have negotiated annual contracts. While not providing a "textbook" example of public-sector collective bargaining, the relationship between the city and the union appeared to work. However, in 1980, problems developed. The city refused to send anyone to the bargaining table with the authority to reach a final agreement with the union. The authority to do so rested with the city manager. The union refused to bargain until the city manager got involved in the negotiations. In Wyoming, there was nothing much the union could do. The firefighters believed the state law as interpreted by the courts required the city manager to negotiate. But the union had no recourse short of time-consuming and expensive court action. Although the union and city finally reached agreement without going to court, the 1980 negotiations raised many questions concerning public-sector collective bargaining in Wyoming.

In addition to his job and union responsibilities, Joe was also taking labor-relations courses at the local university. One day while talking with his collective-bargaining instructor, Joe expressed concern over Wyoming's public-sector bargaining legislation. The legislation was very broad and contained no enforcement provisions. Joe wondered if public employees in other states had similar problems. Joe's instructor suggested that Joe investigate state-level, public-sector bargaining laws and draft a "model" piece of legislation as a term paper. Joe thought that was a good idea and got started on the project.

A couple of weeks later, Joe was talking to his instructor about the project. Joe had started examining state as well as federal policy concerning public-sector collective bargaining. The conversation went something like this:

Joe: You've got to be kidding.
Instructor: What are you talking about?
Joe: That "hodge-podge" of state bargaining laws.

Instructor:	What's the problem?	Instructor:	I don't mean to be callous. Each state has the right to establish its own legislation, if any. As a result, there is tremendous diversity to state-level public-sector bargaining laws.
Joe:	I've started looking at the state bargaining laws. They're all different.		
Instructor:	No one said it would be an easy assignment.		
Joe:	Thanks for the encouragement.	Joe:	So I'm finding out.

Joe Malleck experienced the basic difficulty confronted when one gets involved in a review of public-employee bargaining legislation—there are about fifty different approaches to public-employee collective bargaining as well as federal legislation. This chapter examines the evolution of public-sector bargaining legislation at the federal and state levels. Then, the effects of this legislation on labor-management relations will be discussed. The chapter concludes with an examination of the impact of public-sector collective bargaining legislation on government operations. After studying this chapter, you should:

- Be able to trace the evolution of labor-management relations in the federal sector.
- Identify the different types of state-level public-sector bargaining laws and understand the factors associated with the passage of state laws.
- Describe the relationship between the type of bargaining law in effect and the results of the collective bargaining process.
- Explain how public-sector collective bargaining has influenced government operations.

Labor-Management Relations in the Federal Sector

Collective bargaining among employees of the federal government has gone through three distinct phases. Prior to 1962, no comprehensive guidelines regulating labor-management relations existed. In 1962, President John Kennedy issued an executive order granting bargaining rights and establishing the basic pattern for labor-management relations in the federal sector. Finally in 1978, the executive orders structuring federal-sector labor-management relations were replaced by legislation. Each of these time periods will be discussed in the sections to follow.

THE PRE-1962 SITUATION

The federal government supported workers' right to organize and engage in collective bargaining in the private sector since passage of the National Labor Relations Act in 1935. However, similar protections were not extended to federal employees until 1962. On the contrary, federal government employees were explicitly excluded from coverage by the nation's labor laws. Despite the absence of enabling legislation, federal employees engaged in union activities for a number of years.

Union activities by federal employees date back to the 1830s. In 1835, workers at the Navy Yard in Washington, D. C. struck for shorter hours.[1] For a number of years, shipyard workers pressed for the ten-hour day, and later the eight-hour day. In 1863, bookbinders employed by the Government Printing Office struck to bring their wages in line with those prevailing in private employment.[2] Trade unionism has been part of the post office since the inception of free city delivery service in 1863. That same year, letter carriers in New York City organized. Within ten years, most larger cities had associations or societies of letter carriers.[3] In 1890, the first national association of postal employees was formed—the National Association of Post Office Clerks of the United States.[4]

The Civil Service Act of 1883 established the Civil Service Commission and substituted the merit principle for the "political spoils" system of federal government employment. With the development of a professional civil service, some interest was expressed in union activities. In 1896, the National Civil Service Association was established. This organization was primarily concerned with retirement issues.[5]

Early associations of federal workers concentrated their efforts on lobbying Congress for improved wages and working conditions. However, Presidents Theodore Roosevelt and William Taft attempted to limit the employees' lobbying efforts by issuing executive orders which became known as "gag orders." "Gag orders" forbade federal employees from engaging in political activities intended to secure legislation to improve their working conditions. During this same period, government officials interfered with the employees' attempts to join organizations of which the authorities disapproved.[6]

Interference by government officials with the workers' lobbying efforts and organizing attempts led to relatively widespread discontent. In an effort to resolve these problems, federal workers under the leadership of unionized post office employees pressed for legislative action. In 1912, the Lloyd–La Follette Act[7] was passed. This legislation allowed federal employees to lobby; that is, it outlawed "gag orders" and established the right of postal employees to unionize, but not to strike.

Subsequent to passage of the Lloyd–La Follette Act, union membership by federal employees increased. While post office employees became the most heavily organized, interest in trade unions varied widely depending on the type of federal employee involved. Membership in organizations representing federal employees outside the post office has been described as follows:

> The membership of these general government work organizations fluctuated, depending upon the temper of the times, the policies and politics of the individual organizations, and the personnel issues before Congress. They never represented more than a small proportion of the total eligible employee force. This is not surprising, considering the wide distribution of employees in function, grade classification, geographic area, and attitudes. The only thing shared by many of these workers was their common employer. Unions have long had difficulty with organizing white-collar professional workers, and many of these employees fit that category.[8]

To a degree, the luke-warm response to unionism by federal employees can be explained in terms of the nature of employment. Historically, white-collar workers have exhibited an anti-union bias. Partly, this is because many lower-level white-collar employees identify with management. It has been argued that joining a union represents a rejection of this identification. Also, some white-collar employees may view joining a union as being beneath their status.[9]

The legal environment was another factor contributing to the uneven response to unionism by federal employees. From the president on down the government bureaucracy, public officials resisted unionism and collective bargaining. As discussed in the preceding chapter, the prevailing view was that government was a sovereign employer, without any obligation to share decision-making authority with workers or their organizations. Even President Franklin Roosevelt, a supporter of organized labor, had serious reservations concerning collective bargaining by public employees. In a letter to the National Federation of Federal Employees, Roosevelt stated:

> All government employees should realize that the process of collective bargaining, as usually understood, cannot be transplanted into the public service. It has its distinct and insurmountable limitations when applied to public personnel management. The very nature and purposes of government make it impossible for administrative officials to represent fully or to bind the employer in mutual discussions with government employee organizations. The employer is the whole people, who speak by means of laws enacted by their representatives in Congress. Accordingly, administrative officials and employees alike are governed and guided, and in many cases, restricted, by laws which establish policies, procedures, or rules in personnel matters.[10]

The general opposition by government officials to widespread unionization and collective bargaining by federal employees was indicated by the exclusion of federal workers from coverage of the National Labor Relations Act. Further, the Labor-Management Relations Act prohibited federal employees from participating in strikes or asserting the right to strike against the federal government. Violation of this provision could lead to termination, a $1,000 fine, and imprisonment for up to one year.

Prior to 1962, federal employees could belong to unions. However, the government employers were not obligated to bargain with the unions. In other words, labor-management relations in the federal sector were on a voluntary or permissive basis. This led to the development of inconsistent labor-management practices across the various federal agencies.

THE EXECUTIVE ORDERS

The President of the United States can issue executive orders to most departments and agencies comprising the executive branch of the federal government. Executive orders are similar to laws passed by Congress. However, executive orders cannot appropriate money and cannot be challenged in the courts unless a question of constitutionality is involved.[11]

In 1962, President John Kennedy issued Executive Order 10988 extending to all federal employees the right to join or not join unions and the right to bargain and enter into written agreements with agencies of the federal government. This order was the result of a task force study that revealed widely divergent practices with regard to labor-management relations among federal agencies.[12] Also, it was increasingly difficult to justify not extending collective-bargaining rights to public employees since most private sector-employees had enjoyed these benefits since 1935.

MAJOR FEATURES OF EXECUTIVE ORDER 10988

Executive Order 10988 was intended to set the pattern for labor-management relations within federal agencies much like the National Labor Relations Act does in the private sector. Because of the perceived differences between public and private employment, Executive Order 10988 differed from private-sector legislation in a number of ways. This section reviews the major features of Executive Order 10988. From this discussion, the differences between the executive order and private-sector legislation will become apparent.

Types of recognition. Under Executive Order 10988, there were three types of union recognition.

- Exculsive recognition—If a majority of the employees voted for the union in a secret ballot representation election, exclusive recognition would be granted to the union. With exclusive recognition, the union was obligated to represent all the workers in the bargaining unit. This was the only meaningful form of recognition since it allowed the union to participate in decision making through collective bargaining.[13] This form of recognition is similar to that granted unions in the private sector.
- Formal recognition—If more than 10 percent of the employees supported the union but fewer than the 50 percent needed for exclusive recognition supported it, formal recognition would be granted. With formal recognition, unions had the right to be consulted by agency management about personnel practices. Also, the union had the right to submit its views on subjects of concern. However, agency officials were not obligated to bargain as under exclusive recognition. It should be noted that it would be possible for more than one union to obtain formal recognition in a bargaining unit.
- Informal recognition—Informal recognition would be awarded to any labor organization that could demonstrate it represented some of the agency's employees. This form of recognition allowed the union to share its views on issues of concern to federal employees with agency management. However, agency management was under no obligation to solicit these views or act upon them.

Scope of negotiations. In the private sector, workers have the right to bargain over wages, hours, and other terms or conditions of employment. Under Executive Order 10988, the scope of negotiations became much narrower. Section 7 of the Executive

Order severely circumscribed bargainable issues by reserving certain matters as strictly management decisions. The rights reserved for management included the rights to:

- Direct the agency's employees.
- Hire, promote, transfer and retain agency employees.
- Relieve employees from their duties for lack of work or other legitimate reasons.
- Maintain the agency's efficiency.
- Determine methods, means, and personnel needed to operate the agency.
- Take whatever actions are needed to run the agency in emergency situations.

Also, subjects determined by law were not negotiable. This meant that important factors such as salaries, pensions, insurance, and a number of fringe benefits legislated by Congress fell outside the purview of the bargaining process. As can be seen, issues that are central to the collective-bargaining process in the private sector were not negotiable in the federal sector.

Under Executive Order 10988, negotiations focused on issues such as hours of work, holiday pay, rest periods, safety and jury duty.[14] Even on issues such as hours of work, the scope of negotiations was narrower in the federal sector than in the private sector. Unions could not (and still cannot) bargain over shorter hours and the amount of holiday pay. Such matters are legislatively determined. Bargaining was limited to issues such as the scheduling of hours and who would work holiday hours.

Bargaining units. As in the private sector, a "community of interest" was the key factor when establishing bargaining units. However, some types of employees were excluded from bargaining units in which the union had exclusive recognition. For example, supervisors could not be included in bargaining units including the workers they supervise. Similarly, professional employees could not be included in bargaining units with nonprofessional employees unless the professional employees chose to be included.

There were two major avenues available to the union to establish its status in the bargaining unit. The union could request a secret-ballot election. Alternatively, the union could establish its status by obtaining written authorization from the employees designating the union as their bargaining agent.

Dispute resolution. With respect to rights disputes, Executive Order 10988 allowed for the advisory arbitration of grievances. However, the arbitrator's award was subject to final approval by the agency's head. In other words, the arbitrator's award in grievance disputes was not final and binding as in most private-sector situations. In interest disputes, unions were prohibited from striking. They were also denied the use of interest arbitration. The parties relied on techniques such as mediation and fact finding without recommendations. However, without the right to strike and unable to submit disputes to arbitration, agency management had a definite advantage during negotiations.

A critique of Executive Order 10988. Executive Order 10988 was a landmark action because it extended collective-bargaining rights to federal employees. It also served as an example for state governments. Subsequent to Executive Order 10988, a number of state governments extended collective bargaining rights to the employees of state and local governments. However, the order was not without its problems. The major complaints involved the following issues:

- Public managers issued too many rules and regulations rather than allowing negotiations on issues.
- There were too many exclusions from grievance procedures. For example, a number of agreements prevented discipline cases from being grieved through union-negotiated grievance procedures. Additionally, where there was advisory arbitration, management occasionally refused to abide by the arbitrator's award.
- Scope of negotiations was too narrow. Many believed wages and salaries should be subject to negotiations.
- Unions had little bargaining power because they could not strike and they did not have arbitration available to them.
- In unfair-labor-practice cases, the individuals hearing the cases had frequently "rubber stamped" the decisions of management. There was a perceived need for a more objective procedure in these cases, such as that offered by the National Labor Relations Board.[15]

EXECUTIVE ORDER 11491

After approximately five years of operating under Executive Order 10988, President Lyndon Johnson decided it was time to review federal labor-management relations. To this end, a review committee was established. However, President Johnson did not act upon the committee's recommendations. When President Nixon took office, another study committee was created. The conclusions of this committee were similar to the review committee's work during the Johnson administration. The work of this later committee led to Executive Order 11491 issued by President Nixon in October 1969. Executive Order 11491 updated and modified the basic patterns of labor-management relations in the federal sector. New features found in Executive Order 11491 included:

The elimination of formal recognition. As a result of Executive Order 11491, exclusive recognition was the principal form of union recognition. It was no longer possible to have two or more unions representing different groups of workers within the same bargaining unit. However, a new form of recognition was created—national consultation rights. In situations where no union had exclusive recognition at the national level, a union that represented 10 percent of an agency's employees could request national consultation rights. Such unions were entitled to be notified by the agency of upcoming personnel changes. Unions with national consultation rights also had the right to comment on these changes. The primary difference between exclusive bargaining and national consultation rights was that agencies were obligated to negotiate with unions holding exclusive recognition and were not obligated to do so with unions granted national consultation rights.

Major changes in administration. Under Executive Order 10988, many important decisions concerning the administration of federal labor-management relations rested with individual agencies. This led to the development of widely differing practices. Executive Order 11491 centralized decision making by creating three new agencies. The *Federal Labor Relations Council* (FLRC) was a body analogous to the NLRB. The FLRC was responsible for the general administration of the order. This body administered the executive order, decided major policy issues, prescribed regulations, determined criteria for national consultation rights and made reports and recommendations to the president.[16]

Executive Order 11491 also created the *Federal Service Impasses Panel* (FSIP). As its name suggests, this seven-person body was created to help the parties resolve bargaining impasses, that is, interest disputes. After the parties exhausted the bargaining process, including mediation, they could turn to the FSIP for assistance. The FSIP had several options available to it as a result of the "arsenal of weapons" approach. It could recommend procedures for resolving the dispute such as arbitration or fact finding. Alternatively, the FSIP could impose a settlement on the parties if they were unable to reach agreement after fact finding. The advantages of the flexibility available to the FSIP have been described as follows:

> Because the Panel has many options available, including the discretion not to act on any dispute, neither party has assurance that it can obtain more than was possible at the bargaining table. It is hoped that this availability of a number of techniques for settling disputes will create enough of an air of uncertainty as to which one will be employed so that the two parties will be forced to re-evaluate their position and engage in further bargaining.[17]

Finally, Executive Order 11491 created the office of the *Assistant Secretary of Labor for Labor-Management Relations*. This office was similar to the Office of the General Counsel found in the NLRB. It was responsible for day-to-day operations under the executive order including decisions concerning appropriate bargaining units, conducting representation elections, determining whether unions are granted national consultation rights, and issuing complaints in unfair labor practice cases.[18]

Increased use of arbitration. Under Executive Order 10988, arbitration of an advisory nature was available in rights disputes. Executive Order 11491 allowed for binding arbitration of rights disputes if called for by the labor agreement. Also, arbitration was an option available to the Federal Service Impasse Panel for the resolution of interest disputes.

Executive Order 11491 brought federal-sector labor-management relations more in line with that found in the private sector. In 1978, the executive order was replaced by the Civil Service Reform Act as the basis for labor-management relations in the federal sector.

THE CIVIL SERVICE REFORM ACT

With passage of the Civil Service Reform Act (CSRA), labor-management relations in the federal sector became even more like that found in the private sector. The CSRA is a very broad piece of legislation designed to restructure personnel practices in the federal sector. Title VII of the CSRA is concerned with labor-management relations. This provision replaces Executive Order 11491 as the foundation for federal-sector labor-management relations. By providing a legislative basis, a permanent system of labor-management relations could develop. There would no longer be the potential threat of dramatic modifications or unilateral termination by the president as was possible under executive orders.[19] Additionally, a legislative basis allows for judicial review of most orders issued by the agency responsible for administering the labor-management relations program. With executive orders, the only alternatives to parties challenging decisions under the order were to appeal to the president to change the order or enforce it. Alternatively, it was possible to appeal to Congress to prohibit the order. Neither option for seeking redress of decisions made under executive orders was conducive to effective labor-management relations. Judicial review is a better procedure with a proven record of effectiveness in the private sector.

The basic objective of civil service reform was to improve the efficiency and effectiveness of government management. Title VII of the CSRA is part of the effort to improve government operations by establishing a balanced program of labor-management relations in the federal sector.[20] Title VII states that its provisions will "be interpreted in a manner consistent with the requirement of effective and efficient government."[21] This mandate is important to an understanding of the CSRA since it provides a general guideline for decisions made under the legislation. In other words, decisions by the administrative agencies created by Title VII, arbitrators and the courts, must promote efficient and effective government. It has been argued that through Title VII:

> Congress and the Administration have crafted a labor relations program that will do just that. At the same time, the preamble (of Title VII) recognizes that "labor organizations and collective bargaining in the civil service are in the public interest." The intent of this language was to acknowledge the important and constructive role federal employee unions have in the civil service and the contributions they make to good government. They, too, have a responsibility for an effective and efficient government.[22]

Exhibit 17.1 presents the text of the preamble to Title VII. This provision describes the general purpose of the legislation.

Much of Executive Order 11491 was carried over into Title VII of the CSRA. For example, the rights of workers under Title VII and Executive Order 11491 are quite similar. Exhibit 17.2 presents the statement of employee rights found in Title VII. Notice how this provision parallels Section 7 of the Labor-Management Relations Act. Also, both Executive Order 11491 and Title VII contain very strong management-rights clauses. While there are a number of similarities between Executive Order 11491 and Title VII, a number of important changes were incorporated into the legislation.

EXHIBIT 17.1
Preamble to Title VII of the Civil Service Reform Act

Findings and Purpose

a. The Congress finds that—

1. Experience in both private and public employment indicates that the statutory protection of the right of employees to organize, bargain collectively, and participate through labor organizations of their own choosing in decisions which affect them—

   A. Safeguards the public interest.

   B. Contributes to the effective conduct of public business, and

   C. Facilitates and encourages the amicable settlements of disputes between employees and their employers involving conditions of employment; and

2. The public interest demands the highest standards of employee performance and the continued development and implementation of modern and progressive work practices to facilitate and improve employee performance and the efficient accomplishment of the operations of the Government.

Therefore, labor organizations and collective bargaining in the civil service are in the public interest.

b. It is the purpose of this chapter to prescribe certain rights and obligations of the employees of the Federal Government and to establish procedures which are designed to meet the special requirements and needs of the Government. The provisions of this chapter should be interpreted in a manner consistent with the requirement of an effective and efficient government.

Source: Section 7101 of the Civil Service Reform Act.

EXHIBIT 17.2
Employee Rights Under Title VII of the Civil Service Reform Act

Each employee shall have the right to form, join, or assist any labor organization, or to refrain from any such activity, freely and without fear of penalty or reprisal, and each employee shall be protected in the exercise of such right. Except as otherwise provided under this chapter, such right includes the right—

1. To act for a labor organization in the capacity of a representative and the right, in that capacity, to present the views of the labor organization to heads of agencies and other officials of the executive branch of the Government, the Congress, or other appropriate authorities, and

2. To engage in collective bargaining with respect to conditions of employment through representatives chosen by employees under this chapter.

Source: Section 7102 of the Civil Service Reform Act.

Administrative changes. Title VII placed primary responsibility for administering the legislation with a new federal agency—the *Federal Labor Relations Authority* (FLRA). This organization replaces the Federal Labor Relations Council (FLRC) and the Assistant Secretary of Labor for Labor-Management Relations. Three major complaints had been leveled at the FLRC. First, its membership did not elicit the confidence of federal employees. The FLRC was composed of three persons—chairman of the Civil Service Commission, secretary of labor, and the director of the Office of Management and Budget. Each of these individuals had other responsibilities as federal managers. Consequently, the FLRC was criticized for being run by "part-time" administrators. Second, many union groups believed the federal government labor-management relations program was being administered by management representatives. Third, much of organized labor believed that a sound labor relations program could not be administered by an agency appointed by and answerable to the president.[23]

The Federal Labor Relations Authority (FLRA) was established as an independent, neutral, bipartisan agency designed to perform functions similar to the National Labor Relations Board. The FLRA is composed of three individuals appointed for five-year terms by the president with Senate approval. Its members can only be removed for cause. This agency has the responsibility for interpreting Title VII and overseeing labor-management relations in the federal sector. Specifically, Title VII describes the FLRA's major functions as follows:

- Determine appropriate bargaining units.
- Supervise elections to determine whether a labor organization has been selected as the exclusive bargaining representative by a majority of employees in an appropriate bargaining unit.
- Establish criteria and resolve issues concerning national consultation rights.
- Resolve issues related to the duty to bargain in good faith.
- Establish criteria for granting consultation rights.
- Conduct hearings and resolve unfair labor practice complaints.
- Resolve exceptions to arbitration awards.

In general, the FLRA provides leadership in establishing the policies and procedures needed to develop a system of labor-management relations conducive with the efficient operation of the federal government.

As part of the government reorganization that went along with Title VII, a General Counsel was established. The General Counsel investigates alleged unfair labor practices and decides what cases to prosecute before the FLRA. These are functions similar to those performed by the General Counsel within the NLRB framework. Like the members of the FLRA, the General Counsel is appointed by the president with the Senate's consent.

Finally, the Federal Service Impasses Panel (FSIP) created by Executive Order 11491 was continued under Title VII of the CSRA. The basic purpose of this agency, which was described in the preceding section, remained the same. The FSIP provides assistance to unions and agency management in resolving negotiation impasses. As before, Title VII requires the parties to avail themselves of the services of the Federal Mediation and Conciliation Service. If these efforts are unsuccessful, either party can request the FSIP to get involved in the dispute. As was the case under Executive Order 11491, the FSIP is empowered to utilize an "arsenal of weapons" approach to achieve an agreement. As part of its authority, the FSIP can direct a settlement, that is, impose a solution to the dispute on the parties, if other techniques do not successfully resolve the bargaining impasse.

Scope of negotiations expanded. As a result of the broad management-rights provision found in Title VII of the CSRA, the scope of negotiations is narrower in the federal sector than in the private sector. Labor organizations and federal agencies are free to bargain over a wide range of working conditions. However, a number of important issues in addition to pay and retirement which are legislatively determined are not subject to negotiations. The limitations on negotiable issues have been summarized as follows:

> In effect, federal agencies are prohibited from negotiating away the rights of management to: hire, assign, direct, remove, discipline, or take other specified personnel actions; make determinations with regard to contracting out; make selections in filling jobs through promotion or any other appropriate source; or take necessary steps in emergencies. Nor are agencies permitted to bargain on their mission budget, organization, number of employees, and internal security. In addition, management is not obligated to bargain with respect to: the number, types, and grades of employees assigned to any subdivision, project, or tour of duty; or the technology, methods, and means of performing work.[24]

While the management-rights provision in Title VII is similar to that found in Executive Order 11491, changes found in Title VII serve to broaden the scope of bargaining relative to Executive Order 11491. Important new rights available to labor organizations under Title VII include:

- Check-off of union dues were permitted at no cost to the union for exclusive bargaining representatives.
- Unions were permitted to bargain over agency rules and regulations to an extent not inconsistent with federal law or government-wide rules and regulations.
- Union members were granted paid time off to negotiate agreements and for attendance at impasse proceedings.
- Exclusive unions were granted the right to be present during investigative interviews of employees, that is, interviews designed to determine whether an employee has violated agency rules and regulations.
- Grievance procedures including arbitration as the final step were required in labor agreements. Grievances were broadly defined. However, the parties are able to negotiate a narrower provision.

Judicial review. Under Title VII, an aggrieved person (an individual, labor organization, or agency) can seek judicial review of an FLRA final order.[25] Similarly, the FLRA can seek judicial enforcement of its orders. The FLRA can also obtain injunctive relief in unfair-labor-practice cases. As in the private sector with the review of NLRB decisions, judicial review offers an independent examination of public policy being forged by the FLRA. Judicial review of FLRA orders has the potential to be an important source of public policy as has been the case in the private sector. However, there is some uncertainty concerning the effects of judicial review in federal-sector labor-management relations. It has been written:

> Clearly, it is too early to tell where judicial review will lead us. It can add another layer (or two) of third party review where multiple layering was already recognized as a problem. Related to this concern, it can result in further delays, because based on private sector experience it can add 1–4 years to the time it now takes to resolve disputes. It may tend to encourage litigation rather than bilateral resolution of problems. It may result in an increase in the commitment of finite and, for some unions at least, very dear resources in legalistic battles. Finally, it could give rise to different interpretations and different governing principles in the various circuits, thereby creating to some extent a patchwork of different labor relations rules to be applied in the same or similar circumstances in different sections of the country, until the Supreme Court agrees to resolve any differences that might exist among the circuits.[26]

Grievance procedures and arbitration. As previously mentioned, the redefinition of the term "grievance" and the mandatory inclusion of grievance procedures in collective-bargaining agreements represent important additions to the scope of negotiations found in the CSRA relative to the executive orders. Under Title VII, a grievance is defined as any complaint by an employee. This is an extremely broad definition of a grievance in that it relates to alleged violations of the labor agreement as well as any other matters relating to the employees' employment.

Title VII requires that each collective-bargaining agreement in the federal sector include a procedure for settling grievances, including questions of arbitrability. Under Executive Order 11491 as amended, questions of arbitrability had to be submitted to the assistant secretary of labor for labor-management relations. Under the statute, the collective agreements will include a procedure for resolving questions of arbitrability. This will tend to decrease the amount of time between the filing of a grievance and the final disposition of the case. The statute also provides that any grievance not resolved through the grievance procedure will be submitted to arbitration. Subjects not arbitrable must be explicitly specified in the labor agreement or the statute. The broad grievance and arbitration procedures are important features of Title VII. It has been argued that "from the viewpoint of the individual employee, the wide-open grievance procedure and arbitration offers the greatest assurance of fair treatment by immediate superiors in accordance with the collective agreement and governing rules and regulations."[27]

Review and conclusions. The development of federal-sector labor-management relations lagged behind that found in the private sector primarily because of the lack of enabling legislation. With passage of Executive Order 10988, Executive Order

11491, and amendments to these provisions in the 1960s and early 1970s, the basis for an efficient and effective system of labor-management relations was established. Passage of the Civil Service Reform Act established a legislative foundation for collective bargaining in the federal sector. This legislation had many parallels between labor-management relations in the private and federal sectors with respect to the rights of the parties and limitations on their behavior. Also, an independent agency similar to the NLRB—the Federal Labor Relations Authority—was established to oversee the development of public policy under the new legislation. Perhaps most important, the CSRA demonstrates the continued commitment by Congress to collective bargaining as a means for resolving labor-management disputes.

While there are many similarities between labor relations in the private sector and in federal government, the private sector model was not fully implemented by the Title VII of the CSRA. Federal-sector labor-management relations must promote efficient and effective government relations. Therefore, the scope of negotiations in the federal sector is much narrower than that found in the private sector. This is because the parties cannot negotiate over issues such as wages and retirement which are determined by Congress. Also, the right to strike is curtailed in the federal sector. This has led to an increased emphasis relative to the private sector on the use of arbitration and other third-party techniques for the resolution of interest disputes.

At the present time, there has been only limited experience under Title VII of the CSRA. Therefore, it would be premature to try to evaluate the effectiveness of this legislation. Like private-sector legislation, Title VII is a rather sketchy provision which needs further elaboration by FLRA and court decisons. As this occurs, a comprehensive public policy regarding federal-sector labor-management relations will emerge. As in the private sector, this evolution is likely to take a number of years.

Title VII of the CSRA is the foundation for a uniform, comprehensive system of labor-management relations in the federal sector of government. As mentioned at the outset of this chapter, there is no such legislation governing labor-management relations at the state and local levels. This has led to a "patchwork" of public policy. The next section reviews the maze of state laws regulating labor-management relations at the state and local levels of government.

Labor-Management Relations at the State and Local Levels

The roots of state- and local-level labor-management relations can be traced to the late 1800s. During this time period, firefighters and police were organizing into fraternal or benevolent societies. During the early 1900s, unions and professional associations emerged to represent the interests of the uniformed services. With the formation of unions, the focus shifted from the fraternal and benevolent aspects of the organizations to an emphasis on economic issues. Firefighters are represented by the International Association of Fire Fighters (IAFF), formed in 1918. Two organizations represent many unionized police officers. The Fraternal Order of Police (FOP) was formed in 1915. In 1953, the International Conference of Police Associations was founded. Unions representing other public employees also developed during the early 1900s. The American Federation of State, County and Municipal Employees was formed in 1936 claiming jurisdiction over all types of public employees except teachers and firefighters.[28] With the growth of public-sector employment, several unions active in the private sector such as the Service Employees International Union and the Teamsters expressed a strong interest in organizing state and local employees.

Despite the interest in unionism by state and local employees, the legal environment was not very favorable. Prior to 1960, the courts, almost unanimously, held that public employees did not have a constitutional right to unionize. Also, the right of legislative bodies to forbid their employees from joining unions was upheld by the courts.[29] However, the legal environment affecting labor relations at the state and local levels began to change in 1959. In that year, Wisconsin became the first state to grant public employees (except those employed by the state) the right to organize and engage in collective bargaining. President Kennedy's issuance of Executive Order 10988 in 1962 appears to have stimulated other states to pass public-employee collective-bargaining legislation. Since that time, a number of states have implemented legislation allowing at least some public employees the right to organize and engage in collective bargaining.

A REVIEW OF STATE-LEVEL COLLECTIVE-BARGAINING LEGISLATION

Since the regulation of labor-management relations at the state and local levels is within the jurisdiction of the states, a wide range of collective-bargaining legislation can be found. The pressures leading to the development of this "patchwork" of state laws have been described as follows:

> When it became impossible to prevent strikes or to ignore the demands of public workers for participation in the setting of their terms of employment, policy makers turned hesitantly to the private sector model. At a loss for workable alternative policy instruments, they diluted, stretched, and bent the system in attempts to make it fit government needs and employee expectations in hundreds of public agencies and dozens of states. The result has been piecemeal adoption of traditional procedures.
>
> The process has not been smooth or complete. The history of labor relations in the public sector is characterized by continuing tension between the drive for collective bargaining, interpreted as equity by public employees, and the resistance of government as it strives to protect and guarantee its right to make unfettered decisions. From this comes the overriding "labor relations problem" in the public sector: the need to separate or reconcile the sovereign authority of government and the bilateral authority inherent in the grant of collective bargaining rights.[30]

As the various states worked to establish policies regarding public-sector labor-management relations, a number of different types of laws developed. Some states

Table 17.1 *State Collective Bargaining Laws*

Coverage	States
1. All-inclusive laws	Florida,[a] Hawaii, Iowa, Massachusetts, Minnesota, Montana,[b] New Hampshire, New Jersey, New York,[a] and Oregon
2. "All" employees, separate laws	Alaska, California, Connecticut, Delaware, Kansas, Maine, Nebraska, North Dakota, Pennsylvania, Rhode Island, South Dakota, Vermont, and Wisconsin
3. Some employees covered:	
Teachers	Indiana and Maryland
Police and fire	Kentucky, Oklahoma and Texas
Fire	Alabama,[c] Georgia,[c] and Wyoming
All but state civil service	Michigan[d] and Washington
Local employees and teachers	Nevada
Fire and teachers	Idaho
Local employees and police	Missouri
4. No laws	Arizona, Arkansas, Colorado, Illinois,[d] Louisiana, Mississippi, New Mexico,[d] North Carolina, Ohio, South Carolina, Tennessee, Utah, Virginia, and West Virginia
5. Employees covered by separate laws (even if other employees covered by other laws):	
Teachers	Alaska, California, Connecticut, Delaware, Indiana, Idaho, Kansas, Maryland, Nebraska, North Dakota, Oklahoma, Rhode Island, Vermont, and Washington
Police and fire	Kentucky, Oklahoma, Pennsylvania, Rhode Island, South Dakota, and Texas
Fire	Alabama, Georgia, Idaho, and Wyoming
State service	California, Connecticut, Maine, Rhode Island, Vermont, and Wisconsin

[a] Allow local governments to have own systems if in conformity with state laws.
[b] Except separate law for nurses.
[c] Law operative only upon enactment of local ordinances.
[d] State service under nonstatutory system.

Source: Hugh D. Jascourt, "Recent Trends and Developments," Government Labor Relations: Trends and Information for the Future, ed. Hugh D. Jascourt (Oak Park, IL.: Moore Publishing Co., 1979), p. 10. Copyright © 1979 by Public Employment Relations Research Institute and Moore Publishing Co.

have passed comprehensive laws. Comprehensive laws are those applying to most public employees that extend the right to organize and engage in collective bargaining. Such legislation will also establish procedures for selecting bargaining representatives and handling unfair labor practices.[31] Also, comprehensive public-employee collective-bargaining legislation will include an administrative agency analogous to the NLRB in the private sector and the Federal Labor Relations Authority (FLRA) in the federal sector. The administrative agency is responsible for interpreting and enforcing the legislation. By so doing, the agency plays a major role in developing the state's public policy toward labor-management relations. At the other extreme from comprehensive laws are states not having laws concerning public-employee collective bargaining. Between these two extremes, several other categories of laws can be identified. Some states have "comprehensive" laws but apply them to a limited number of occupations such as teachers or firefighters. In other states, most public employees are subject to bargaining laws, but different laws have been passed to cover major occupational groups. Table 17.1 categorizes states by the type of bargaining legislation found. The table indicates that twenty-three states have passed comprehensive laws, that is, all-inclusive laws or separate laws covering all employees. The table also reveals that thirteen other states have legislation governing labor-management relations for at least some occupational groups. The remaining fourteen states have no laws.

Why some states have comprehensive bargaining laws and others do not has been the subject of limited empirical research. Kochan examined the relationships between a number of environmental factors and the type of policy toward public-employee collective bargaining found in different states. Comprehensive public-employee collective-bargaining laws were more likely to be found in states with:

- Relatively higher per capita expenditures by the state government.
- Relatively larger changes in per capita income.
- Relatively more innovative state legislatures.[32]

At the present time, it appears quite unlikely that federal legislation will be passed regulating labor-management relations at the state and local levels of government. See Exhibit 17.3 for some arguments in favor of a federal bargaining act for state and local employees. Exhibit 17.3 also discusses the major factors working against the passage of such legislation.

The Impact of Public Policy on Bargaining Outcomes

Research has indicated the characteristics of the law under which collective bargaining takes place influences the results of the bargaining process. Bargaining outcomes refer to the wage and nonwage issues addressed in the labor agreement. These out-

EXHIBIT 17.3
Arguments Favoring Passage of a Federal Bargaining Law for State and Local Employees

Ralph J. Flynn, Executive Director
Coalition of American Public Employees

The need for federal legislation has been well documented. . . . That two-thirds of the states have felt impelled to enact legislation governing employee-employer relations in the public sector within their own states reflects the ground swell of pressure to grapple with labor relations in the public sector. More important, the substantive variety of the state laws which have been enacted have produced chaos rather than healthy diversity. Noble experiments with "meet and confer" laws such as those originally enacted in Oregon and California have either been discarded, such as that in Oregon, or thoroughly discredited by their initial sponsors, as is the case in California. Primitive antistrike laws have imprisoned public employees on questions of conscience.

W. Howard McClennan, President
International Association of Fire Fighters

It is our belief, based on a half century of experience, that the very long period of "experimentation" we have already had should be brought to an end, and that minimum standardization should replace the broad and essentially meaningless variations in the present state laws. Furthermore, our experience has indicated no important variations based on regional needs that override the need for a common sense federal law for governing the collective bargaining process throughout the states, counties, cities and towns of this nation. Let us move ahead to that kind of federal law . . . one that reflects the reality of public employment at state and local levels today.

Helen D. Wise, President
National Education Association

In some states, teachers are engaged in rather sophisticated bargaining regarding "union security," severance pay, class size, and other matters. At the same time, other teachers are still fighting a "foot-in-the-door" battle and merely are attempting to have the school boards sit down and talk to them. The interpretation of identical statutory language has varied considerably and all too often necessary procedures for recognition, impasse resolution, and enforcement of administrative decisions are either nonexistent or inadequate. . . .

In this milieu of confusion, uncertainty and inequity, the stability so vital to a constructive employer-employee relationship has been difficult to achieve. We believe that this pattern will continue unless the federal government acts to bring some order to the situation.

Jerry Wurf, Late President
American Federation of State, County and Municipal Employees

No pattern prevails among the 50 states and 80,000 local governmental units, but there is a single, over-riding theme: that public employees are nowhere the equals of workers in private industry. They are second-class citizens.

We find that government employers, many of whom are "pro-labor" and would vigorously defend the right of workers in the private sector to organize, are hostile to and even afraid of dealing with their own employees through collective bargaining. I am not here today to tell you that collective bargaining is a perfect process. It is frequently sloppy. It often drags on and on. Sometimes there are excesses in the behavior or the demands put forth by *both* management and the workers' representatives.

The system can and does break down. When that happens in private industry, certain rules and procedures come into play to bring the parties together and work out their differences. Generally, no such machinery exists in the public sector, however. As a result, public employee disputes frequently are lengthy and painful to all parties.

Several factors are working against passage of federal legislation designed to establish a uniform policy for labor-management relations at the state and local levels. First, while unions are in basic agreement over the need for such legislation, there is not agreement over the type of legislation needed. Some argue for the extension of the Labor-Management Relations Act to cover public employees. Others press for the passage of new legislation specifically covering state and local government employees. Still others contend that federal legislation establish-

> **EXHIBIT 17.3** *(Continued)*
>
> ing minimum standards is needed. Then, states could pass their own laws as long as minimum conditions were present.
>
> Second, in 1976 the U.S. Supreme Court handed down a decision in the matter between *National League of Cities v. Usery*. This decision rendered unconstitutional the application of the Fair Labor Standards Act to local governments. With this case as precedent, it is quite possible that it would also be unconstitutional for the federal government to regulate labor-management relations at the state and local level.
>
> Third, it is doubtful that the political climate is "right" for the passage of such legislation. At the present time, there appears to be more concern for limiting the power of public employee unions than passing legislation which could enhance the unions' bargaining power.
>
> *Source of comments on the need for federal legislation:* "A Federal Bargaining Act for State and Local Employees: Testimony in Support of H. R. 8677" (Washington, D. C.: The Coalition of Public Employees).

comes represent the dimensions of the employee-employer relationship subject to shared decision making by labor and management. Typically, researchers have measured the concept of bargaining outcomes by examining the content of labor agreements. Contract provisions are identified and assigned values according to the favorableness of the provision to the union. The values for each contract provision are summed to yield a single value representing total bargaining outcomes found in the agreement. The higher the contract value, the more favorable the labor agreement from the union's perspective.

An early study of bargaining outcomes in the public sector indicates that for firefighters, a relationship existed between the characteristics of collective-bargaining laws and bargaining outcomes. It was concluded that "the characteristics of the legal environment—the comprehensiveness of the collective-bargaining laws and the existence of either a fact-finding or a compulsory-arbitration provision—have the strongest effect on bargaining outcomes. . . ."[33]

A later study of bargaining outcomes indicates that the characteristics of the public policy environment are more important determinants of bargaining outcomes than the bargaining laws.[34] Gerhart defined "public policy environment" as what the public believes the legislation should be rather than what it is. This view presumes that the collective-bargaining legislation lags behind the will of the people. It was found that variables defining the public policy environment are better predictors of bargaining outcomes than the nature of the bargaining laws. Gerhart concluded:

> There is support for the proposition that the public policy environment is more important in determining bargaining outcomes than actual bargaining statutes. One implication of this finding is that legislatures that react to voter sympathy with respect to public sector bargaining laws have less influence on the relative bargaining power of the parties than is apparent on the surface. This is not to say the statutes are irrelevant; on the

contrary, statutes probably have a leveling influence, because agreements in states with bargaining statutes tend to be more homogeneous than those in states without laws.[35]

It is quite likely that the impact of bargaining laws on bargaining outcomes is greater in political environments hostile toward labor organizations. Kochan states that:

> One interpretation of these findings is that the effects of collective bargaining law in a supportive political environment are rather marginal. However, the law serves as a significant source of union power in communities where it is difficult to build political influence and bargain effectively in the absence of a law.[36]

Some evidence indicates the effects of bargaining laws on bargaining outcomes may change over time. A study of bargaining outcomes in twenty-six major Canadian municipalities found that the comprehensiveness of the labor relations statutes was not associated with more favorable bargaining outcomes.[37] More specifically, laws may play an important role in determining bargaining outcomes when the collective-bargaining relationship is relatively new. However, in long-established, more stable relationships as found in Canada, the comprehensiveness of bargaining laws may be a relatively unimportant determinant of bargaining outcomes. It was concluded that:

> This suggests that stability in the system and the maturity of the relationship between the parties may change the nature of the process. Over time, bargaining may tend to move from a reliance on hard core tactics and political pressure to an emphasis on more rationalized and professional negotiations.[38]

OTHER DETERMINANTS OF BARGAINING OUTCOMES IN THE PUBLIC SECTOR

While bargaining laws influence the collective-bargaining process, especially in the earlier years of the relationship, other factors also affect bargaining outcomes. Exhibit 17.4 presents a summary of the three major studies examining the determinants of bargaining outcomes in the public sector. Several observations can be made about these findings. First, Anderson found little overlap between the factors associated with high wages and nonwage outcomes. This indicates that the parties make tradeoffs between wages and benefits while at the bargaining table. This finding also points up the importance of examining wage and nonwage outcomes separately when studying the factors influencing the results of the collective-bargaining process. Second, there is a conspicuous absence from the list of factors influencing bargaining outcomes of variables describing union tactics. While these studies included variables describing union structure and pressure tactics, such factors were not powerful determinants of bargaining outcomes. Environmental factors such as age of the bargaining relationship, the nature of the bargaining laws, level of strike activity, and the manufacturing base of the community were better predictors of bargaining outcomes. Also, variables describing the management side of the relationship and its

EXHIBIT 17.4
Summary of the Research Concerning the Determinants of Bargaining Outcomes in the Public Sector

Kochan and Wheeler[a] reported favorable bargaining outcomes from the union's perspective are associated with:

- The presence of comprehensive bargaining laws.
- The existence of either fact finding or compulsory arbitration.
- Management's negotiator has relatively more power than other management officials.
- A lack of compatibility between the goals of the mayor and the city council.
- Elected officials become involved in negotiations when an impasse occurs.

Gerhart[b] reported that bargaining outcomes favorable to the union were associated with:

- Negotiations taking place in a small Standard Metropolitan Statistical Area (SMSA) rather than large SMSAs or in jurisdictions outside SMSAs.
- Bargaining units composed of workers in certain functional areas such as sewer departments.
- The presence of a statutory bargaining obligation.
- The absence of a bargaining law imposing automatic penalties in the event of a strike.
- An affiliation with the American Federation of State, County, and Municipal Employees (a wholly public employee union).
- A favorable public policy environment.
- Relatively high level of strike activity in the state.

Anderson[c] examined a number of factors influencing wage and nonwage bargaining outcomes. The factors influencing each category of bargaining outcomes were appreciably different. Higher wages were associated with:

- Low unemployment.
- High demand for city services.
- Negotiations taking place in a municipal election year.
- The city having a greater per capita man-days cost due to strikes.
- The local union is autonomous from task environment support.
- The presence of a mayor-council form of city government.
- The absence of a professionally trained city negotiator.
- Low level of conflict within management.
- The parties have been bargaining for a number of years.

Higher nonwage bargaining outcomes were associated with:

- The city's ability to pay is low.
- The demand for city services is high.
- Relatively higher proportion of the workers living in the city are employed in manufacturing.
- Low strike activity.
- Support from the task environment.
- Management has a low commitment to the industrial relations function.
- Absence of a professionally trained negotiator for the city.

[a]*Thomas A. Kochan and Hoyt N. Wheeler, "Municipal Collective Bargaining: A Model and Analysis of Bargaining Outcomes,"* Industrial and Labor Relations Review *29, October 1975.*
[b]*Paul F. Gerhart, "Determinants of Bargaining Outcomes in Local Government,"* Industrial and Labor Relations Review *29, April 1976.*
[c]*John C. Anderson, "Bargaining Outcomes: An IR System Approach,"* Industrial Relations *18, Spring 1979.*

preparation for negotiations were better predictors of bargaining outcomes than union variables. This raises questions about the union's ability to influence the results of the collective-bargaining process. However, at the present time, no definitive conclusions about the impact of union factors relative to management and environmental characteristics can be made. On this point, Anderson noted:

> It may be that the measures of union structure, process and tactics were not designed with a specific enough reference to collective bargaining, weakening the results. On the other hand, the unions interviewed relied heavily on changes in environmental conditions as a basis for demands, and hence, the results may to some extent reflect the ability of the union to use that information in the bargaining process.[39]

THE IMPACT OF UNIONISM AND COLLECTIVE BARGAINING ON GOVERNMENT

The research concerning bargaining outcomes discussed in the preceding section examined the content of labor agreements and the factors associated with the results of the bargaining process. This section broadens the discussion by looking at bargaining outcomes in terms of the impact of the collective-bargaining process on government operations. Also, the effect of collective bargaining on unionized workers relative to their non-union counterparts will be examined.

Wages. Research has consistently reported significant differences in wages between union and non-union employees. This line of research attempts to estimate the degree unions raise the wages of their members relative to comparable non-union wages.[40] These studies have yielded widely varying estimates of the union/non-union wage differential. However, most studies report that unionized public employees are higher paid than their non-union counterparts. After a review of the literature, Lewin concluded that the "average" wage effect is in the order of 5 percent. However, when specific occupations were examined, the union/non-union wage differential varied greatly. The impact of unions on wages for teachers ranged between 1 and 4 percent. For other occupations, the wage differential favoring union workers was between 6 and 15 percent. The union/non-union wage differential appeared to be the greatest for firefighters. Union firefighters received wages 16 to 18 percent higher than their non-union counterparts.[41] It is interesting to note that the average wage effect attributable to unionism in the public sector is less than that reported in the private sector (10 to 15 percent).[42]

Fringe benefits. As discussed in Chapter 12, fringe benefits include a wide variety of issues such as paid holidays, vacations, health and life insurance, pensions, and paid leaves. As in the private sector, fringe benefits in the public sector have been greatly liberalized in recent years. However, it is difficult to determine the extent to which the expansion of public-sector fringe benefits is attributable to unionization. This is because market pressures are requiring the increased usage of fringe benefits. Also, the public sector has had a long tradition of offering more liberal fringe benefits than the private sector. Despite these problems, limited evidence indicates unions have had a positive effect on the fringe benefits received by public employees. It has been stated that:

> Fringe benefits have become more liberal under union pressures, as well as other pressures, and costs of government have risen some more. The gains consist of longer vacations, additional holidays, slightly more generous sick leave, larger government payments for health benefits and group life insurance, and more generous pensions.[43]

The merit principle. Decreased reliance on the merit principle is one of the most significant implications of unionism in the public sector. The merit principle and civil service systems designed to implement and administer personnel practices based on merit were intended to buffer public employment from political favoritism and patronage.[44] After reviewing several definitions of the merit principle, Helburn and Bennett describe the principle as follows:

> All persons in public employment should be treated in an impartial and unbiased manner with regard to certain types of personnel activities, based on their demonstrated competence and ability. It is important to note that the only types of personnel matters mentioned in the definitions are those involving the movement of persons into, within, and out of the organization. Such movements include the hiring process (recruitment, selection and appointment), assignments, promotions, demotions, transfers, layoffs and discharges. Thus, personnel movements constitute the heart of the merit principle which, in the strictest sense, may be defined as the belief that the criterion of relative competence should be the controlling factor in decisions involving personnel movements.[45]

The impact of collective bargaining on the merit principle has not received much attention from researchers. The little existing evidence indicates that collective bargaining has had a "diversity of impacts" on the merit principle. This means that, in some instances, bargaining has strengthened the merit principle while weakening merit in other situations.[46]

With respect to the hiring of new employees, unions appear to have had little or no effect on the process.[47] Public-sector unions have expressed greater interest in promotions than initial employment. With respect to promotions, unions press for giving preference to employees in the unit over outsiders, emphasizing specialized job content as material for promotion so that employees in the unit have an advantage, decreasing the weight given to oral examinations and performance ratings that involve the subjective evaluation of management, and making seniority a factor in the promotion decision.[48] While it can be argued these efforts are inconsistent with the merit principle, union objectives concerning promotions can actually strengthen the merit principle. For example, many civil service systems allow management to use a "rule of three"; that is, management can choose any of the top three qualifiers on a civil service examination. While providing for greater managerial flexibility, the "rule of three" is less consistent with the merit principle than the "rule of one" frequently sought by public-sector unions. The "rule of one" requires management to select the top qualifier for promotion, thereby reducing management's freedom. On this point, Lewin and Horton state "if the unions were victorious on this issue in collective bargaining, it could hardly be cited as an example of inherent conflict between bargaining and merit. Indeed, in this instance, collective bargaining appears to strengthen merit."[49]

The procedures for handling employee complaints are a subject of great concern to public-sector unions. Typically, unions press for grievances to be handled as part of the contractual relationship rather than unilaterally by management representatives as in most civil service systems. As a result, the trend is away from civil service grievance procedures to those found in the labor agreements. Also, third-party arbitration would replace civil service decisions as the last step of grievance procedures.[50]

Control of the work organization.[51]   As in the private sector, the day-to-day operations of public-sector organizations are still controlled by management officials. Public-sector unions have not challenged the basic right of management to run government operations. However, the unions insist upon the opportunity to influence, through the collective-bargaining process, managerial decisions concerning wages, hours and conditions of employment.[52] To this end, unions have attempted to influence work management in several ways.

Subcontracting is an issue attracting interest of many public-sector unions. To save money, various government jurisdictions have subcontracted functions such as trash collection and building maintenance to private firms. As in the private sector, unions are interested in this issue because subcontracting can decrease employment opportunities for union members and weaken the labor organization. Some unions have negotiated contract language requiring management not to contract out work or requiring management to consult with the union prior to doing so. The implications of such contract language are discussed in Exhibit 17.5.

EXHIBIT 17.5
The Impact of Restrictions on Subcontracting on the Public Employer

Such largely successful union efforts to prevent or limit the contracting out of urban government functions add an important element to an understanding of the employment transaction. They mean that governments have agreed to retain work for employees even though there may be otherwise sound management reasons for having the work done by outsiders. Governments have thus surrendered some of their rights to determine management policies. They are obliged, under these anti-contracting pressures, to do their work in such a way as to protect the jobs of certain groups of citizens.

Source: David T. Stanley, Managing Local Government Under Union Pressure (Washington, D. C.: The Brookings Institution, 1972), pp. 92–93.

Job assignments and work loads are other areas in which public sector unions have infringed on decisions historically subject to unilateral managerial control. The factors motivating union interest in these issues are complex. To a degree, there is a concern over the quality of services being provided the public. Negotiations over issues such as the case load for social workers or class size for teachers reflect a desire to maintain quality services in the face of a burgeoning demand for services and tight budgets. There is also a concern over the ability of public employees to easily and safely perform their jobs. Unions have attempted to negotiate contract language determining the number of firefighters assigned to a piece of equipment and requiring that two police officers be assigned to each patrol car.

Work assignments are another area in which public managers have had to share decision making with the employees' bargaining representative. While the right to assign overtime has basically remained with management, unions have pressed for some changes in the policies affecting overtime. In a number of jurisdictions, paid overtime has replaced compensatory time off. Also, employees working overtime are more likely to receive an overtime pay premium (e.g., time and one-half). Despite these changes, the assignment of overtime has remained a managerial prerogative. If discussed in a labor agreement, management is usually directed to distribute overtime opportunities equally.

Similarly, the assignment of shifts has remained largely a managerial prerogative. Shift differentials are found in many labor agreements as an attempt to make the less desirable shifts more attractive. Also, a number of agreements allow seniority to be used as the basis for employees requesting a shift assignment.

As can be seen, the spread of collective bargaining has led to a number of changes in the public sector. While the effect of public-employee unionism on issues such as wages has been the subject of a number of studies, its impact on the merit principle or working conditions has received much less attention. Consequently, many questions concerning the impact of collective bargaining on the public sector are still unanswered. Also, very little attention has been given to the relationship, if any, between public sector unionism and the efficiency and effectiveness of governmental operations. Much additional work needs to be done before a complete understanding of unionism in the public sector is obtained.

Summary

This chapter provided a detailed examination of the legal environment regulating public-sector labor-management relations. In the federal sector, collective bargaining is governed by Title VII of the Civil Service Reform Act. This legislation provides a basis for labor-management relations in the federal sector that, to a degree, parallels private-sector labor relations. Provisions concerning employee rights, union recognition, unfair labor practices and administration of the legislation found in the Civil Service Reform Act are quite similar to provisions found in the National Labor

Relations Act. While a number of features differentiate federal and private-sector legislation, the major differences concern the scope of negotiations and the right to strike. In the federal sector, the scope of negotiations is narrower than in the private sector because subjects such as wages that are established by Congress are outside the purview of the bargaining process. While the right to strike is protected in the private sector, it is specifically denied federal employees. Instead, an impasse procedure relying on an "arsenal of weapons" approach is found.

Title VII of the Civil Service Reform Act has provided the legislative foundation for the development of an effective and efficient system of labor-management relations in the federal sector. With the creation of an autonomous administrative agency (the Federal Labor Relations Authority), the basis for a uniform policy throughout the federal sector was established. However, this is not the case at the state and local levels of government.

At the state and local level, collective bargaining is subject to state and/or local legislation. As a result, a "patchwork" of legislation has developed. While some states have no bargaining laws, others have comprehensive regulations covering almost all state and local employees. The diversity of laws makes it very difficult to generalize about the legal environment affecting collective bargaining at the state and local levels.

There is evidence indicating the nature of the bargaining legislation can influence the results of the negotiating process. Bargaining outcomes have been found to be more favorable to the union where comprehensive legislation exists and either fact finding or arbitration is available to the parties. The impact of bargaining laws on bargaining outcomes appears to be greater in situations hostile toward labor organizations. Other evidence indicates that the impact of bargaining laws on the results of the negotiating process lessens as the bargaining relationship matures.

In addition to the legal environment, other factors have been found to influence bargaining outcomes. Other determinants of bargaining outcomes in the public sector include: age of the bargaining relationship, level of strike activity, the community's manufacturing base, the characteristics of the management negotiator and management's preparation for negotiations. Little evidence supported the position that union structure or bargaining tactics led to relatively more favorable contract provisions from the union's perspective.

Collective bargaining has left distinct marks on the public sector. Unionized workers in the public sector tend to receive higher wages than their non-union counterparts. However, the union/non-union wage differential is narrower in the public sector than in the private. Unionization also appears to be associated with more liberal fringe benefits. Additionally, unions have made important inroads into the area of management prerogatives. Many public-sector unions have negotiated contract language limiting subcontracting, increasing the use of seniority, and governing job assignments and workloads.

It is unlikely that the rapid growth in public employment will continue as it has in the past. However, this will probably not deter the interest by labor organizations in unionizing public employees. As labor organizations try to keep pace with the expanding work force, they will continue to focus on the public sector as a source of growth. However, continued growth of public-sector unionism will require labor organizations to focus their attention on workers such as women, professionals and clerical employees who have, historically, been resistant to union organizing efforts. To a degree, the ability of labor organizations to expand and thrive in the 1980s will depend on their ability to continue to attract public employees into the trade union movement.

The major concern of this book has been the examination of labor-management relations in the United States private sector. Chapters 16 and 17 expanded this perspective by reviewing the collective bargaining process as practiced in the public sector. The next chapter also broadens the book's perspective by looking at union-management relations in other countries. Increased foreign competition, the growth of multinational firms and expanded employment opportunities overseas increase the need to understand labor-management relations in other parts of the world.

Discussion Questions

1. Discuss the factors leading to the passage of Title VII of the Civil Service Reform Act. What were the major differences between this legislation and the executive orders it replaced?
2. What factors have prevented the passage of a uniform policy regulating labor-management relations at the state and local levels? What are the major implications for public-sector collective bargaining of not having a uniform policy?
3. Some states have comprehensive public-employee collective-bargaining laws, while other states do not. What factors are associated with states passing comprehensive labor laws?
4. What effect does collective bargaining have on the wages and fringe benefits received by public employees?
5. It has been argued that public-sector collective bargaining has seriously undermined the merit principle as found in public management. What is the merit principle? What effect has collective bargaining had on the merit principle?

Key Concepts

Gag orders
Executive order
Executive Order 10988
Executive Order 114911
Exclusive representative

Formal recognition
Informal recognition
Federal Labor Relations Council
Federal Service Impasse Panel
National consultation rights

Assistant Secretary of Labor-Management Relations
Civil Service Reform Act
Federal Labor Relations Authority
General counsel
Comprehensive bargaining laws
Bargaining outcomes
Merit principle

Notes

1. Sterling D. Spero, *Government as Employer* (New York: Remsen Press, 1948), p. 79.
2. Ibid., p. 85.
3. Ibid., p. 106.
4. Ibid., p. 112.
5. Ibid., p. 170.
6. Ibid., p. 3.
7. 37 *Stat*. 555.
8. Michael H. Moskow, J. Joseph Lowenberg, and Edward C. Koziara, *Collective Bargaining in Public Employment* (New York: Random House, 1970), pp. 30–31.
9. Alan E. Bent and T. Zane Reeves, *Collective Bargaining in the Public Sector* (Menlo Park, CA: Benjamin/Cummings Publishing Co., 1978), p. 7.
10. Quoted by David Ziskind, *One Thousand Strikes of Government Employees* (New York: Columbia University Press, 1940), p. 187.
11. Bob F. Repas, *Collective Bargaining in Federal Employment*, 2nd ed. (Honolulu: University of Hawaii, Industrial Relations Center, 1973), p. 3.
12. Jack Stieber, "Executive Order 10988," in *Collective Bargaining for Public Employees,* ed. Herbert L. Marx, Jr. (New York: W. W. Wilson Company, 1969), p. 135.
13. Repas, *Collective Bargaining in Federal Employment,* p. 22.
14. Steiber, "Executive Order 10988," p. 137.
15. Ibid., pp. 137–38.
16. Repas, *Collective Bargaining in Federal Employment,* p. 24.
17. Ibid., p. 28.
18. Ibid., p. 29.
19. Henry B. Frazier III, "Labor-Management Relations in the Federal Government," *Labor Law Journal* 30 (March 1979): 131.
20. Anthony F. Ingrassia, "Reflections on the New Labor Law," *Labor Law Journal* 30 (September 1979): 539.
21. Civil Service Reform Act, Title VII, Section 7101.
22. Ingrassia, "Reflections on the New Labor Law," p. 540.
23. Kenneth A. Kovach, "The FLRA and Federal Employee Unionism," *Public Personnel Management* 9 (January–February 1980): 8.
24. Ingrassia, "Reflections on the New Labor Law," pp. 541–42.
25. There are two exceptions to the types of cases reviewable by the courts—arbitration cases appealed to the FLRA, and appropriate-bargaining-unit determinations.
26. Frazier, "Labor-Management Relations in the Federal Government," pp. 135–36.
27. Frank Elkouri and Edna Aspen Elkouri, *Legal Status of Federal-Sector Arbitration,* supplement to *How Arbitration Works,* 3rd ed. (Washington, D. C.: Bureau of National Affairs, 1980), p. 11.
28. Jack Stieber, *Public Employee Unionism: Structure, Growth Policy* (Washington, D. C.: The Brookings Institution, 1973), p. 2.
29. Lee C. Shaw, "The Development of State and Federal Laws," in *Public Workers and Public Unions,* ed. Sam Zagoria (Englewood Cliffs, NJ: Prentice-Hall, 1972), p. 21.

30. B. V. H. Schneider, "Public Sector Labor Legislation—An Evolutionary Analysis," in *Public-Sector Bargaining,* eds. Benjamin Aaron, Joseph R. Grodin and James L. Stern (Washington, D.C.: Bureau of National Affairs, Inc., 1979), p. 192.

31. Jack Stieber, "Collective Bargaining in the Public Sector."

32. Thomas A. Kochan, "Correlates of State Public Employee Bargaining Laws," *Industrial Relations* 12 (October 1973): 335.

33. Thomas A. Kochan and Hoyt N. Wheeler, "Municipal Collective Bargaining: A Model and Analysis of Bargaining Outcomes," *Industrial and Labor Relations Review* 29 (October 1975): 60–61.

34. Paul F. Gerhart, "Determinants of Bargaining Outcomes in Local Government." Taken with permission from *Industrial and Labor Relations Review,* Vol. 29, No. 3 (April 1976). Copyright 1976 by Cornell University. All rights reserved.

35. Ibid., p. 349.

36. Thomas A. Kochan, *Collective Bargaining and Industrial Relations* (Homewood, IL: Richard D. Irwin, Inc., 1980), p. 474.

37. John C. Anderson, "Bargaining Outcomes: An IR Systems Approach," *Industrial Relations* 18 (Spring 1979).

38. Ibid., p. 143.

39. Ibid., pp. 142–43.

40. David Lewin, Peter Feuille, and Thomas Kochan, *Public Sector Labor Relations: Analysis and Readings* (Glen Ridge, NJ: Thomas Horton and Daughters, 1977), p. 359.

41. David Lewin, "Public Sector Labor Relations," *Labor History* 18 (Winter 1977): 138–39.

42. H. Gregg Lewis, *Unionism and Relative Wages in the United States: An Empirical Inquiry* (Chicago: University of Chicago Press, 1963).

43. David T. Stanley, *Managing Local Government Under Union Pressure* (Washington, D. C.: The Brookings Institution, 1972), p. 83.

44. Moskow et al., *Collective Bargaining in Public Employment,* p. 87.

45. I. B. Helburn and N. D. Bennett, "Public Employee Bargaining and the Merit Principle," in *Trends in Public Sector Labor Relations,* eds. Arvid Anderson and Hugh D. Jascourt (Chicago: International Personnel Management Association, 1975), p. 60.

46. David Lewin and Raymond D. Horton, "The Impact of Collective Bargaining on the Merit System in Government," in *Public Sector Labor Relations: Analysis and Readings,* eds. David Lewin et al. (Glen Ridge, NJ: Thomas Horton and Daughters, 1977), p. 418.

47. Stanley, *Managing Local Government Under Union Pressure,* p. 33.

48. Ibid., p. 36.

49. Lewin and Horton, "The Impact of Collective Bargaining on the Merit Principle," p. 418.

50. Stanley, *Managing Local Government Under Union Pressure,* p. 50.

51. This section is based on Stanley, *Managing Local Government Under Union Pressure,* ch. 3.

52. Ibid., p. 22.

Suggested Readings

Aaron, Benjamin, Grodin, Joseph R., and Stern, James L., *Public Sector Bargaining* (Washington, D. C.: Bureau of National Affairs, 1979).

Bent, Alan E., and Reeves, T. Zane, *Collective Bargaining in the Public Sector* (Menlo Park, CA: Benjamin/Cummings Publishing Company, 1978).

Lewin, David, Feuille, Peter, and Kochan, Thomas, *Public Sector Labor Relations: Analysis and Readings* (Glen Ridge, NJ: Thomas Horton and Daughters, 1977).

Stanley, David T., *Managing Local Government Under Union Pressure* (Washington, D. C.: The Brookings Institution, 1972).

Chapter 18

UNION-MANAGEMENT RELATIONS IN OTHER COUNTRIES

Barry War Bonnet was vice-president of personnel and labor relations for the K. Q. Foster Clothing Company. This organization had several plants located in the southeastern United States. Foster's manufactured men's, women's, and children's clothing. Most of the goods manufactured by Foster were marketed in the United States and Canada. However, sales in other nations, particularly Europe, represented a growing share of Foster's sales.

Some of Foster's plants were unionized, but the employees of most plants were not represented by a union. Prior to 1950, Foster's plants had been located in the northeastern United States. All plants had been unionized at that time. In 1950 the decision was made to close the plants in the northeast and move to the southeast.

This morning Barry had received a memo from Foster's chief executive officer. The memo requested that Barry have a report prepared. The report was to address the following issues:

- What were the probable implications of having some plants located in other nations for union-management relations at the American plants? These plants in other nations would be parallel operations capable of manufacturing the same goods as turned out in the United States.

- Which foreign nations were likely to provide a favorable climate for a corporation which prefers a minimum of interference from unions and employee organizations? Specifically, what were the implications of opening plants in Great Britain and West Germany?

- If Foster opened plants in other nations it would become a multinational corporation. What was the likelihood of being faced with an effective multinational union in the clothing industry? How could the likelihood of this event be minimized if plants were opened in another nation?

The material presented in this chapter could aid Barry in responding to the questions that were presented to him. These and related issues are faced in American industry and the American labor movement. After studying this chapter, in addition to being able to respond to the issues presented to Barry, you should:

- Be aware of the basic nature of union-management relations in Brazil, Great Britain, West Germany, the Soviet Union, and Japan.
- Understand the programs or problems that are unique to these countries, specifically:
  a. Describe the role of Brazilian unions.
  b. Discuss the comparatively "laissez faire" approach to labor relations by the government in Great Britain.
  c. Discuss differences between worker representation on supervisory boards and on works councils in West Germany.
  d. Describe general differences in collective bargaining between Western Europe and the United States.
  e. Know the key functions of unions in the Soviet Union.
  f. Explain the impact that traditional employer-employee relations have had on the industrial relations systems of Japan.
- Explain the threat presented by horizontal expansion of multinational corporations to jobs of union members and the bargaining power of their unions in a base country.
- Discuss the alternative strategies available to unions in dealing with multinational corporations and the effectiveness of each strategy.

The topic of this book is union-management relations in the United States. We believe an understanding of this topic will be enhanced by familiarity with union-management relations in other countries. There are virtually as many systems of union-management relations as there are nations of the world. As a result, it is not possible to cover this topic exhaustively in one chapter. Instead, this chapter will address selected issues pertaining to union-management relations in other countries. First, union-management relations in selected countries and regions of the world will be discussed. This section will, in addition to other topics, discuss selected unique approaches to worker-management relations. Then the impact of multinational corporations on labor relations and the prospects for multinational collective bargaining will be reviewed.

Descriptions of Labor Relations in Other Countries

The number of nations whose approach to union-management relations is discussed here must be limited because of space. In selecting the countries to be described, three criteria were considered. One factor was the magnitude of trade between the

Table 18.1 *Major American Trading Partners 1980*

	Exports		Imports
Rank	Country	Rank	Country
1	Canada	1	Canada
2	Japan	2	Japan
3	Mexico	3	Mexico
4	United Kingdom	4	Federal Republic of Germany
5	Federal Republic of Germany	5	United Kingdom

Source: Adapted from *"Foreign Trade of the United States,"* Survey of Current Business, *May 1981,* pp. S-18 to S-20.

United States and the particular country. The justification for this criterion is that international business is becoming more common. Those of you who embark on a business career are likely to find that an understanding of union-management relations in other countries will be useful.

A second criterion considered in selecting a nation's labor relations system for discussion in this chapter was the presence of unique dimensions in the approach to union-management relations. The rationale for this criterion is that an understanding of different approaches to labor relations is of value not only for its own sake, but for the further insights it can provide concerning the American system.

Finally, we have sought to provide an example of labor relations in each of three common political systems that exist around the world: communism, democracy, and right-wing military government.

With reference to the first criterion, Table 18.1 presents the rank order of the top five American trading partners in 1980. The rankings for both exports and imports are in order of dollar value of goods. The two rankings are very similar. These five nations accounted for 43 percent of the goods exported from the United States and 44 percent of the goods imported to the United States during 1980.[1] Discussions of union-management relations in Japan, the United Kingdom, and the Federal Republic of Germany are presented. Further, all three are democratic nations, but each has a system of labor relations very different than the American system.

The two remaining nations discussed in this chapter were selected primarily because their labor-relations systems provide examples of nations with different forms of government. From the industrialized communist nations of the world, the Soviet system is described. It was selected because it provides the model for union-management relations in the communist nations in the Soviet sphere of influence. The description of Brazil's system of labor relations provides an example of labor relations under a strong right-wing military government. In addition, Brazil represents a developing nation that is making major strides toward being a major industrialized power.

BRAZIL

A discussion of Brazilian union-management relations is included for two reasons. Brazil is a large country whose resources are largely undeveloped. However, it is a developing nation that is well on the way to becoming an industrial power. In 1980,

Brazil ranked ninth in terms of receiving American exports and ranked tenth in terms of imports received by the United States.[2] The second reason is that it is an example of a noncommunist nation in which labor-management relations are largely determined by the government.

Background. Modern Brazilian labor-management relations are strongly influenced by the events and legislation of the late 1930s. In 1937, President Getúlio Vargas cancelled the elections to select his successor, threw out the democratic constitution, and proclaimed a new system of government.[3] This system was modeled after the Fascist government of Italy. A new system of labor unions was established. Unions were to apply to the Ministry of Labor for recognition. Without recognition a union was not permitted to use the labor courts, could not bargain with employers and did not receive financial support from the state.

Once recognized, unions were under the control of the Ministry of Labor. For example, elections could not be held without the approval of the Ministry. Further, the Ministry had the right to approve the qualifications of all candidates and could veto any candidate or elected official who was judged subversive.

The Vargas regime ended in 1945. However the government still plays a dominant role in labor-management relations. Unions play a relatively minor role and are subject to the dictates of the Ministry of Labor. Labor's right to organize is recognized by the government but is vigorously controlled by the original provisions of the Labor Code established by the Vargas regime.[5] Further, the government's role in establishing wages, benefits, and conditions of employment leaves virtually no major functions for labor unions.

Government determination of terms of employment. Brazil's labor legislation is unique in the degree to which the terms of employment are stipulated by legislation. These regulations are so detailed that there is little room for bargaining between unions and management.[6] Working conditions covered by federal legislation include: hiring requirements, work hours, compensation, employment of women and minors, vacations, and dismissals.

Prior to 1965, rates of compensation were virtually the only issue subject to union-management negotiations. At that time the government took control of the wage adjustment process. The result was that labor unions in Brazil were effectively excluded from collective bargaining.

In 1979 Brazilian unions were again granted the right to bargain collectively with employers.[7] The principal goal of these negotiations is to secure salary increases in excess of those mandated by the government.[8] In 1978 the law prohibiting strikes was modified. The modification permits strikes if they are: in nonessential activities, nonviolent, nonpolitical, and address only economic issues.[9] Between 1968 and 1978 there were virtually no major strikes. With the change in legislation there have been several major strikes since 1978.[10] The government reaction to these strikes is not clear. A United States Department of Labor publication asserts that the government did not interfere in the strike activity.[11] However, several *Wall Street Journal* articles have reported that strike leaders were jailed as a result of the strikes.[12, 13, 14]

Resolution of disputes. Labor disputes, including grievances of individual workers, are resolved through a two-stage system of government intervention. In the first stage administrative personnel in the Ministry of Labor attempt to work out conciliations between workers and employers involved in disputes. When these administrative authorities are unable to resolve a dispute, it goes to the labor courts, the second stage. These courts initially attempt to conciliate disputes. If agreement is not reached, the courts arbitrate the dispute. The Brazilian Labor Courts have three levels. Decisions of lower courts can be appealed to higher levels. It should be noted that the courts decide most cases in favor of workers. In 1974, 72 percent of the cases heard by the Superior Labor Court (the highest level) were partially or entirely in favor of labor. This places pressure on management to settle disputes at the conciliation stage.

Union finances. The equivalent of one day's pay is withheld from employee earnings each year. The tax or fee is paid by all employees, union members or not. Receipt of this income by unions is subject to approval of their budgets by the Ministry of Labor and adherence to Brazilian labor legislation.

Functions of Brazilian unions. The above discussion makes clear that Brazilian unions do not perform the functions normally performed by unions in the United States. Prior to 1978 unions exercised three functions:

1. providing employees with legal representation before conciliation and arbitration authorities.
2. performing a watch-dog function, ensuring that employers comply with the provisions of legislation establishing the terms and conditions of employment.
3. performing social-welfare functions such as providing vocational training, medical and dental facilities, and recreation and vacation facilities.[15]

The events since 1978 indicate that some Brazilian unions are again engaged in collective bargaining. The focus of these activities is to secure more favorable wage and benefit packages. While it is too early to be certain, there are signs that with the lifting of government controls some Brazilian unions appear to be following the American model of business unionism rather than the European model of political action to secure social reform.[16]

UNION-MANAGEMENT RELATIONS IN WESTERN EUROPE

In North America and Great Britain collective bargaining is the primary procedure for determining the terms and conditions of employment. In other parts of the world the role of collective bargaining in this process is comparatively insignificant. The Western European nations discussed in this chapter are Great Britain and West Germany. The latter provides an example of an approach to industrial relations that departs in major ways from the American approach. Before discussing each nation's system specifically, we believe that it would be useful to present the main differences in union-management relations between Western Europe and the United States.

As indicated above, with the exception of Great Britain, in Western Europe, legislation and government regulation establish the terms and conditions of employment to a far greater degree than in the United States.[17] Collective agreements typically add supplements to legally established minimum standards.

Typically collective bargaining in Western Europe is more centralized than in the United States.[18] An agreement usually covers all employers in an industry. In some cases an agreement covers groups of industries or even an entire nation. The parties to such an agreement are employers' associations and a union or group of unions. As a result an agreement addresses only basic conditions of employment. In some countries collective agreements are negotiated on a confederation level. France is an example. Using United States organizations to draw an analogy, it would mean that the AFL-CIO would reach an agreement with an employers' association representing most or all nonagricultural employers. Such negotiations involve supplemental fringe benefits going beyond legally required benefits and/or involve minimum wage increases.

Usually the employers' association appearing at the bargaining table is unified and disciplined.[19] Often multiple unions are represented during negotiations. The principle of exclusive bargaining agent is not employed. As a result there are numerous minority unions that participate in the bargaining process.

To supplement this centralized system of bargaining is a highly decentralized system.[20] At each work place an employee organization or workers' council exists that meets with management to determine the detailed employment conditions. The employee organizations at the plant level are usually not associated with a union and consequently are outside union control.

GREAT BRITAIN

Two factors entered into the decision to include a discussion of British union-management relations. There exists a great deal of trade between British and American organizations and the legal environment in Great Britain is the extreme case among industrialized democracies in that comparatively few legislative constraints are placed on unions and management.

Means to attain goals. British unions rely on direct collective bargaining with employers to establish the terms and conditions of employment in the work place. With respect to broader objectives such as social welfare programs, they rely on political and legislative means.[21] In the political sphere, the British trade union approach has been somewhat different than that of American unions. Britain has had for the last fifty years a two-party system of government, the Conservative Party and the Labour Party. The trade union movement is officially affiliated with the Labour Party and provides much of its financial support.[22]

However, it appears that a third major political party will emerge in Great Britain. An alliance between the Social Democratic party and the Liberal party is developing. The Conservative party represents the right and the Labour party represents the left. The Social Democratic and Liberal parties are moderates. Because of the extreme positions taken by the Labour party, it appears possible at the time we are writing that such an alliance could supplant Labour as the responsible party of the left.[23]

Union structure and membership. In 1978 there were 462 British unions, and 255 of these unions had fewer than 1,000 members[24]. The twenty-six largest unions accounted for more than 80 percent of all union membership. About one-half of the British labor force were trade union members in 1978.[25] However, about 75 percent of Britain's wage earners were covered by a collective bargaining agreement.[26]

There are three types of British unions: craft, industrial, and general. The latter restricts membership neither on the basis of craft nor industry of employment. Most British unions are affiliated with the Trades Union Congress (TUC). The TUC has no formal authority over the affiliated unions. The principle of "exclusive bargaining agent" has never been adopted in Great Britain. This coupled with the diversity in types of unions results in a multitude of jurisdictional disputes.[27] In recent years the understanding or norm is that when a union has established majority membership in a particular work place, no other union will attempt to recruit members in that work place without the permission of the union having majority membership.[28]

British labor law. Union-management relations have functioned virtually without law.[29] This changed for a time in 1971 when the Conservative party secured the enactment of the Industrial Relations Act. This act provided a legal framework for union-management relations much like that in the United States. Included were provisions concerning the right to join or not to join a union; the right to form a union; protection against unfair discharge; definition of unfair employer and union practices; creation of a National Commission on Industrial Relations; a "cooling-off" period for national or strategic strikes; and a balloting of members before strikes.[30] In 1974 the Labour party succeeded in repealing the Industrial Relations Act.[31] Until passage of the Employment Act in 1980, British labor relations again functioned with few legislative constraints.

The Employment Act represents a second attempt by the conservatives to reform British labor relations law in a ten-year period. The principal provisions of the Employment Act pertaining to union-management relations are:[32]

1. Restricting pickets to the premises of the employer directly involved in a dispute, thereby prohibiting secondary picketing.
2. Limiting sympathy strikes by restricting immunity from civil court proceedings to those involved in secondary activities targeted at direct or first suppliers and customers of the primary employer in a dispute.
3. Requiring that new closed shop agreements be supported by 80 percent of the affected workers in a secret ballot election.
4. Protecting the right of individual workers not to join a union where a closed or union shop agreement exists when a worker objects on grounds of conscience or personal conviction.
5. Protecting workers from unfair expulsion from a union as well as unfair coercion of a worker to support or join a union.

The collective-bargaining process. Collective bargaining in Great Britain has typically been on an industrywide level.[33] Minimum wage rates and employment conditions are established and serve as a base for local negotiations. In recent years there has been a shift from national bargaining to local bargaining.[34]

The negotiation process functions as follows. At the industry level formal agreement is reached concerning wages and benefits. At the plant level informal, often verbal, agreements modify the formal agreement. The result has been that effective earnings exceed formally agreed upon wages. This phenomenon is defined as *wage drift*. The gap occurs because of three factors.[35] Piece rates are common. As workers' experience increases, earnings increase although piece rates are not changed. Some workers are guaranteed ten or more hours of overtime per week. As a result effective wages are increased. Finally, pay supplements to the industry wage rates may be negotiated by individual organizations or plants. This *two-stage system of negotiations* has been blamed in part for Great Britain's inability to control inflation through wage controls.[36]

Strikes are employed to achieve bargaining objectives in the British negotiation process. Following the early 1960s, British industry became particularly strike prone.[37] A unique characteristic of British labor relations is the widespread incidence of "unofficial" strikes. These are strikes not sanctioned by the national union. Rather they are called by local union leadership during the informal negotiation process. The overwhelming majority of strikes in Great Britain have been unofficial.[38] These unofficial strikes have been effective in securing better terms of employment than those agreed upon in national negotiations.

Most Western European unions do not address the issue of work rules.[39] However, in Great Britain elaborate work rules have been established, often effectively amounting to featherbedding and make-work rules. With government pressure to control wage increases in recent years, *productivity bargaining* has become a common practice.[40] This consists of trading restrictive work rules for improvements in wages and benefits.

FEDERAL REPUBLIC OF GERMANY

Germany is a major trading partner with the United States. However, the primary reason for including a discussion of German industrial relations is its system of providing for employee participation in decisions at the work place. This system is referred to as codetermination.

Union structure and bargaining procedures. In 1978, trade union membership was 9.1 million.[41] This represented about 35 percent of the West German labor force. Just over 83 percent of the union members belonged to one of seventeen industrial unions.[42] These seventeen unions make up the German Trade Union Federation.

German unions are usually industrial unions. The lowest level of the union is typically a local organization that deals with several employers. The union is seldom involved in employee-employer relations within a particular plant.[43] This is the domain of the workers' council that will be discussed below.

As in the Western European countries already discussed, bargaining takes place at the industry level. Typically an agreement is concluded between a union and an employers' association. Two types of agreements are negotiated.[44] One addresses such issues as hours of work, holidays, vacations, overtime pay, and bonus pay. Such agreements are in effect without modification for several years. The second type of agreement concerns only wages. These agreements typically are renegotiated after twelve or fifteen months.

Because these contracts apply to several and sometimes all employers within a given industry, wages and benefits are set at a level acceptable to the least efficient employers.[45] Consequently another round of quasiformal agreements exists at the plant level. These agreements are usually between a particular employer and the workers' council for that organization. These agreements determine actual wage rates. As in Great Britain, this leads to wage drift. In Germany, there is a difference in the employers' obligation to abide by these agreements. Industry-level agreements are legally binding. Agreements concluded at the plant level are not. During periods of recession employers can reduce wages to the level specified in the industry agreement.

The legal environment. As indicated above, a collective agreement between a union and employers' association is legally binding. In addition, unions and employers are obligated to avoid strikes and lockouts during the life of the agreement.[46] If a union goes on strike during the life of an agreement it can be found in breach of contract and held responsible for damages caused during the strike. Strikes can be called during contract negotiations. However most unions require that a secret ballot of members be conducted and that 75 percent favor going on strike. These procedures and requirements probably account for Germany's relatively low incidence of strikes.

A feature of German industrial relations that parallels the French system concerns the extension of contract agreements.[47] The government can extend an agreement to employers in the industry and geographic area covered by an agreement that are not members of the employers' association involved in the negotiations. The agreement may be extended if at least 50 percent of the relevant workers are already covered by it or if extension of the agreement is determined to be in the public interest by the government.

CODETERMINATION AND WORKERS' COUNCILS

Employee participation is receiving increased attention both in the United States and in Western Europe. Several West European nations have legislation concerning employee participation, but the Federal Republic of Germany has led the way in enacting such legislation. Employee participation in German organizations has been at two levels, the supervisory board, which is analogous to the board of directors for an American corporation, and works councils.

Employee representation on the supervisory board. In 1951 legislation was passed requiring companies in the coal and steel industries to set up supervisory boards consisting of eleven members.[48] Five members were selected by the shareholders, five by the employees, and one member was elected by both shareholders and employees. The following year legislation was enacted that applied to all other stock corporations with more than 500 employees. It required that one-third of the members of the supervisory board be worker representatives. The Codetermination Act of 1976 modified the latter legislation.[49] It provides for equal worker and stockholder representation on supervisory boards of corporations with over 2,000 employees. Owners still have an edge because one employee representative must be a member of management.

Exhibit 18.1 presents a brief discussion of the effectiveness of the German system for employee representation. The principal advantage appears to be improved communications and conflict resolution.[50] Decisions that are unpopular among em-

---

EXHIBIT 18.1
Effects of Codetermination in the Federal Republic of Germany

When this law was passed (Corporate Management Law–1952) the general feeling was that it meant the end of German industry. The coal and steel law was passed by Parliament only after the unions threatened a general strike, and the 1952 law was passed against the wishes of the unions as a holding measure. German and foreign management soon found, however, that having one-third of the seats on the Supervisory Board filled by workers made no real difference in the running of the company. In the wholly owned German subsidiary of an American company, for example, two-thirds of the Supervisory Board could be made up of American employees of the company. It was soon discovered that the workers' minority could be overcome in any voting situation, allowing management to protect its interests. It became clear that the general codetermination law really did not give the workers any rights at all at the board level. It was necessary to listen to the workers, but their votes did not really count. The worker representatives were also frequently kept in the dark about the company's operations in order to further limit their power. They were often kept out of special committees formed by the Board, on the grounds that company secrets had to be kept from them.

Management soon realized, however, that codetermination had certain advantages. Codetermination has helped many German firms avoid strikes. The presence of workers on boards has allowed management to discover what impact its decisions will have on employees and unions, thus minimizing conflicts. Worker representatives have even helped management reduce the size of its work force in times of recession, and have suggested means of reducing production when necessary. Open battles are rare in German Supervisory Boards and many votes are unanimous; the neutral eleventh man is almost never called upon to break a tie. Thus, management found that it could live with a board where one-third of the seats belonged to workers.

Source: Reprinted from "The Influence of European Workers Over Corporate Strategy," by Renato Mazzolini, *Sloan Management Review,* Spring 1978, Vol. 19, No. 3, pp. 59–81, by permission of the publisher. Copyright © 1978 by the Sloan Management Review Association. All rights reserved.

ployees are easier to implement if the employee representatives are convinced that they are in the best interest of everyone. Also the employee representatives bring employee concerns to the attention of top management while they are still minor.

Works councils. The 1952 legislation also called for employee participation in the form of works councils in firms with five or more employees.[51] The works council is made up of individuals elected by the organization's employees. The council negotiates/discusses a wide range of issues with management; for example, working hours, vacation schedules, employee discipline and grievances, wage rates, and vocational training.

There are no direct or formal links between German unions and employees serving on supervisory boards or works councils. As a result German unions are not involved in many functions performed by American unions. It has been suggested that works councils prevent German unions from operating at the plant level.[52]

American reaction to codetermination. The term codetermination usually refers to employee representation on bodies such as supervisory boards. American managers typically are opposed to codetermination.[53] Arguments for this opposition include such notions as intrusion in the rights of owners, distortion of the free enterprise system, and loss of freedom. A more basic criticism is that codetermination undermines the ability of unions to confront management.[54] If employee representatives on supervisory boards or boards of directors are also union leaders, the union is no longer able to confront management concerning decisions which are made. It is thought that such a system may not always be in the best interest of workers.

THE SOVIET UNION

The above discussion makes clear that the role of government and functions of unions in the industrial relations process can be very different than the American system. All of the countries discussed to this point have been market-oriented societies. In this section union-management relations in a communist society will be described.

The Soviet Union's system of industrial relations serves as a model for most of Eastern Europe.[55] As a result it was selected from among the numerous communist countries of the world. A second factor is that the Soviet Union's economy is the largest of communist nations, although it ranks about twentieth in terms of America's trading partners.

THE SOVIET ECONOMIC SYSTEM

The Soviet Communist system rejects private ownership of the means of production. It advocates state ownership and central planning and management of the economy. This system of managing the economy relies on directives and administrative orders from state planning authorities to determine production goals of enterprises throughout the economy.[56]

Union structure and organization. In theory Soviet labor unions are independent organizations. In fact they are subordinate to the state, follow state directives, and execute tasks assigned by the state.[57] The trade union structure is centralized. Higher levels of trade unions have a great deal of control over subordinate levels. Alternatively, lower trade union levels have limited autonomy. Union leaders are members of the party and their primary allegiance is to the party rather than the membership. The number of unions is small. In the early 1970s there were twenty-five Soviet labor unions. The unions are organized along industry lines. All workers in a plant are represented by the same union. Typically over 90 percent of eligible workers are union members.

Union functions. Soviet trade unions have two functions: to exhort workers to produce more on the job and to defend the rights and interests of union members against the bureaucratic excesses of management.[58] Some western authors argue that these are inconsistent goals.[59] These writers state that if increased productivity is a primary goal of Soviet unions, they cannot defend workers' rights. Others argue that Soviet unions have done much to improve the working conditions of Soviet workers. Further, they point out that increased productivity, in turn, improves the material well-being of the entire population, including union members.

Plant safety is an example of the protective function of Soviet unions. Factory administrators are required by law to provide safe working conditions and to take reasonable preventative measures. Trade union officials are responsible for organizing plant inspections to insure that such measures are taken.

Collective agreements. The factory trade union leader, representing the workers, and the factory director, representing management, consent to a collective agreement. However these agreements are not the result of collective bargaining as it is known in Western nations.[60] The content of these agreements is regulated by legal norms and directives specified by state authorities. Although the same label is used, the content and role of Soviet collective agreements differ entirely from Western collective agreements. Soviet agreements specify what is expected of employed persons and what they can expect to be allocated to them as a result of their employment.

Basically these agreements state that workers agree to fulfill the production goals of the factory while administrators agree to improve the working and living conditions of all employees and their families.[61] Sample provisions of an agreement may include agreed-upon plant production goals, wages, worker participation in factory management, safety programs, social-insurance programs, and youth programs.

It appears that factory administrators wish to fulfill the provisions of these agreements that are designed to improve working and living conditions. However the demands on factory administrators to meet production quotas often preclude abiding by the provisions of these agreements.[62]

Defense of worker rights and interests. Unions have limited options in attempting to represent the interests of workers. Strikes are prohibited.[63] This fact coupled with the obligation to encourage higher productivity usually compels union officials to accept factory administrators' decisions. The one managerial decision that Soviet unions are forceful and effective in countering is the decision to discharge a worker.

If management wishes to discharge a worker, that decision is reviewed by the factory union committee. Factory administrators can ignore the committee's recommendation and proceed with the discharge. However the worker has the right to appeal the decision directly to the Soviet courts. The courts have consistently enforced the right of unions to protect a worker from dismissal. They usually reinstate a worker discharged without the approval of the factory union committee.[64] In this area it appears that union officials aggressively protect the rights of workers, even when their actions jeopardize production goals.

Pressure for change. The notion of workers' councils that are elected by and responsible to employees of the work place is opposed by Soviet leaders.[65] Such a system would undermine the Soviet system of centralized authority and control. However there are pressures for change.[66] Demonstrations, riots, and wildcat strikes do occur in the Soviet work place. There have been attempts to form unofficial unions. Possibly there will be changes in the future. Two types of change may take place. One is to provide greater autonomy for enterprise managers and union officials. The second is to increase the authority of factory union committees so that they are better able to represent the interests of workers.

DEVIATION FROM THE SOVIET MODEL

As indicated above, the Soviet system serves as the model for Eastern European industrial relations. However, Yugoslavia's system is an anomaly among Communist nations.

THE YUGOSLAVIAN ECONOMIC SYSTEM

In the Yugoslavian system fiscal and monetary policies are determined by central authorities. Control of enterprises throughout the economy is decentralized. *Workers' management* is the term used to describe the system.[67] Enterprises are not nationalized as in the Soviet Union or as utilities such as electricity are nationalized in Great Britain. They are social or public property managed by representatives elected by the enterprises' employees. The organizations are to be managed within the framework of the nation's fiscal and monetary policies.

More precisely, there are two levels of management or authority in an enterprise.[68] One level has authority to establish policy. The other has authority to make decisions and direct the enterprise in accordance with policy. The former corresponds to the board of directors of a corporation in a capitalistic system. The latter corresponds to the managerial staff. Since employees elect the members of the managing board, the employees of an enterprise roughly correspond to the stockholders of a corporation.

A question with workers' management is how unions fit into the system. In a capitalistic system they represent employees in negotiations with employers. In a traditional communist system (Soviet style) they promote employee productivity and protect employee interests from managerial excesses. In the capitalistic system, management is responsible to the stockholders/owners of the organization. In the communist system, management is responsible to central planning authorities. In both cases management is responsible to a body that does not represent employee interests. However, in the Yugoslavian system, managers are responsible to a policy-making body elected by the employees of the enterprise. As a result there appears to be no need for a union to represent employee interests.

In this setting unions play a minor role. Unions do conclude wage agreements with industry associations.[69] These agreements set minimum and maximum wages for various jobs. Unions assist individual workers in handling grievances and nominate candidates for election to workers' councils.

It appears that authority within unions is centralized much as in the Soviet Union. If local union leaders become too involved in promoting worker interests, they come into conflict with higher authorities of all types—union, party and government.[70] In addition, union officials are expected to promote worker production.[71]

POLAND

A brief discussion of the Polish system of labor relations is included because it represents an example of an Eastern European system that attempted to depart from the Soviet model. Following a series of strikes by Polish workers during the summer of

Although the Polish labor movement was unsuccessful in pressing its demands, its actions represented a sharp challenge to traditional labor relations in Eastern Europe.

1981, an agreement was reached that drastically changed the Polish system. The strikers were members of Solidarity, a union not controlled by the Polish Communist party. This agreement was noteworthy for two reasons. First, the agreement gave all Polish workers the right to join unions whose leadership was independent of the Polish Communist party. Second, they had the right to strike and to agitate for economic policies different than those established by the Polish government. For a fleeting moment, about sixteen months, Poland's communist government provided such freedoms.[72] With this exception, trade unions in communist countries have been and continue to be controlled by the Communist party and workers do not have the right to strike.

During December 1981, the Polish government imposed martial law.[73] Civil rights were temporarily suspended and many Solidarity leaders were detained by the Polish armed forces. At the time of this writing, it appears that the Solidarity agreement reached in August 1981 has been set aside and that the role of unions in Poland will be that prescribed by the Soviet model.[74]

The Yugoslavian and Polish experiences point out that the Soviet model is not always found to be satisfactory. Alternatively, the Polish experience suggests that communist nations in the Soviet sphere of influence are not likely to tolerate free trade unions, and are willing to use military force to oppress such movements.

JAPAN

In addition to being America's second largest trading partner, Japan's system of union-management relations has several unique features. Further, Japan provides a third example of union-management relations in a democratic society. For these reasons, Japan's system of union-management relations is included in our discussion.

Japanese labor law. The right of workers to organize is guaranteed by law.[75] The Trade Union Law provides that unions must be free and independent of employers. This is a critical issue in Japanese union-management relations because most unions are organized on an enterprise basis. Under Japanese law employees who represent the employer's interest are prohibited from union membership. Further, the employer cannot provide any financial support for the union.

The Trade Union Law requires that unions be democratic organizations. Election of officers and decisions to strike are made by secret vote of the membership. In addition, unions cannot be engaged primarily in political action. Japanese unions can, however, support political candidates.

Japanese labor legislation was enacted following World War II. It was heavily influenced by the Wagner Act, in large part because the legislation was enacted during the American occupation of Japan. For example, the guarantee of the right to organize and bargain with the employer is enforced through a set of unfair labor practice provisions.

Union structure and membership. In the late 1970s there were about 12.4 million union members in Japan.[76] They made up about 22 percent of the Japanese labor force and one-third of Japan's wage and salary earners.

The basic unit in the Japanese union structure is the enterprise union.[77] An *enterprise union* is an autonomous organization of workers within a given enterprise or company. It usually includes all regular employees regardless of job, through lower-level management. Employees automatically join the union even when it is an open shop. Dues are usually collected through an automatic check-off.

Because of this system of union organization, Japan has numerous unions. The 12.4 million union members belong to more than 70,000 unions.[78] Unions in an industry form industrywide federations. These industry federations often affiliate with one of the four national labor centers.

When an employer has more than one plant, workers are usually organized in a unit union at each plant. These units typically combine to form an enterprise union. In the case of multiplant employers, the federation of unit unions is the center of union activities for collective bargaining and strikes.

National craft and industrial unions as we know them in the United States are rare in Japan. A different form of industrial union is common. It is an industrywide federation of enterprise unions within a given industry. Generally, such industrial unions are loosely organized. They do not play a central role in collective bargaining as in the United States.

Union-management relations. A brief description of the traditional Japanese employer-employee relationship is necessary to understand Japanese union-management relations.[79] The traditional relationship is not one between equals but between a master and servant. It is a relationship of control and subordination. Employment conditions are determined by the employer.

This traditional relationship influences union-management relations. For example, the grievance procedure seldom works well because of this traditional employer-employee relationship. The Japanese worker finds it very difficult to demand satisfaction for a personal grievance and to interact with the employer on an individual basis.

However the Japanese worker can confront the employer as a member of a group. This influences the nature of collective bargaining in Japan. It is better described as a system of confrontation and group pressure rather than negotiation and compromise. Consequently strikes play a unique role in Japanese collective bargaining.

A strike often takes place during contract negotiations. A union will usually prepare its strike schedule at the same time demands are prepared. It is common for the employer not to negotiate seriously until a strike takes place. Consequently in the Japanese system, strikes are usually not the result of a bargaining impasse. Rather they are a means to bring about legitimate negotiations. Strikes in this system are typically prescheduled, of short duration, e.g., a half day or a day, and serve to convince the employer of the union's resolve.

Because of the large number of enterprise unions, labor unity and bargaining strength is an issue for Japanese unions. In an effort to promote labor unity and bargaining strength, the national labor centers try to coordinate bargaining activities and mobilize organized labor during the period March to May of each year.[80] As a result the label *spring offensive* has been applied to this strategy.[81]

The objective of the spring offensive is to achieve uniform increases in wages and benefits for all union members. Usually an agreement is reached with a key industry early in the spring offensive and this becomes the pattern for settlements throughout the economy.[82]

Negotiations involve two categories of issues.[83] One concerns union recognition, membership eligibility, union security, strike procedures, and so forth. The other concerns working hours, employee compensation, vacations, retirement allowances, and so forth. The former is usually spelled out in great detail while the latter is poorly defined and ambiguous. Such issues as job assignment, transfers, and promotion are treated in an ambiguous manner. As a result, employers can make decisions about these matters at will.[84] In addition, while general increases in wages stem from negotiations, wage determination for the individual employee is usually left to the employer's discretion.[85] In essence the Japanese union plays a limited role in day-to-day work activities. Decisions about such matters are usually left to management.

Multinational Collective Bargaining

A multinational corporation (MNC) is one that has affiliates in more than one nation. During the past three decades MNCs have experienced unprecedented growth. United States–based corporations have been actively involved in this growth. The number of United States–based MNCs rose from just over 10,000 in 1957 to over 23,000 in 1966.[86] In 1970 United States subsidiaries accounted for 15 percent of the consumer goods produced in the European Economic Community.[87] The value of United States investment abroad increased from $52 billion in 1965 to $133 billion in 1975, and annual expenditures for plant and equipment in foreign countries increased from $8.6 billion in 1966 to $27.1 billion in 1976.[88]

PROBLEMS PRESENTED UNIONS

Chapter 4 discussed the historical development of unions in the United States. Recall that national unions followed the development of national companies. Union expansion typically cannot follow the expansion of a company across national boundaries. A notable exception is Canada. However, excluding Canada, legal differences, feelings of nationalism, and differences in union structure and industrial relations practices present effective barriers to such an expansion. The barriers and problems faced by multinational unions will be discussed in detail below.

In the following discussion it is necessary to distinguish between host and base countries. The term "host" is used to refer to other countries. The term "base" is used to refer to the country in which corporate headquarters are located. The inability to follow a company across national boundaries presents a major threat to the job security of union members and the bargaining power of unions. Before discussing these threats it must be noted that the nature of foreign investment by MNCs has changed.[89] In the past an MNC typically invested in foreign sources of raw materials. As a result the number of processing and manufacturing jobs in the base country of the corporation was not threatened, and possibly was enhanced. The shift in investment has been toward horizontal expansion or the development of parallel, or nearly parallel, operations in other countries.

THREAT OF JOB LOSS

Foreign investment of this type threatens union members in the base country with loss of jobs or a slower rate of growth in jobs, if their wages are higher than the wages of workers in the host country. A recent study investigated unit labor costs of United States–based corporations in seven host countries.[90] The host countries were Canada, Great Britain, Belgium-Luxembourg, France, West Germany, Brazil, and Mexico. It was found that unit labor costs were lower in the host countries than in the United States. Further the difference in unit labor costs was greatest for companies operating in Brazil and Mexico. These and other less-developed countries may in future years present a challenge to American unions along the lines of the southern United States. The major difference is that it is more difficult to unionize a subsidiary located outside the United States.

One threat to American union members presented by the MNC is the loss of jobs. The difference is that in earlier years the runaway shop went to a southern state within the United States. Now it appears that MNCs have an incentive to move operations to less-developed countries in particular. Note that a condition of this argument is that the foreign investment involves operations that are parallel or nearly parallel to those in the United States. It does not hold when the foreign investment involves vertical operations, e.g., extraction of raw materials to be shipped to the United States for processing.

THREAT OF REDUCED BARGAINING POWER

When an employer has parallel operations in other locations, the firm's ability to switch production from one location which is shut down by a labor dispute to another location is increased.[91] This assumes that the same union does not represent the workers at each plant, or if different unions are involved, they do not coordinate their efforts and strike at the same time. Another assumption is that the various plants are sufficiently parallel that their products are interchangeable.

There are parallels for a union representing employees at one plant of a multiplant operation within the United States, and a union representing all American employees of an MNC with parallel operations in other countries. To the extent that the union is unable to achieve the union coordination and cooperation described above, the "cost of disagreement" that can be imposed on the employer is limited.

Barriers to Multinational Bargaining

A solution to the problems that MNCs pose for union members is multinational bargaining. The coordination of efforts and cooperation of unions described above is needed. In effect what is called for is an "international union" with the centralization of authority characteristic of American national unions. Numerous problems stand in the way of such an international union movement.

ATTITUDES OF UNION LEADERS AND MEMBERS

One of the conditions that would have to exist before multinational bargaining could exist is the willingness of national and local labor leaders to relinquish their autonomy to an international level. This is a significant barrier because, as discussed in the previous section on union movements of other nations, the local union or enterprise union is essentially an autonomous organization. (See the discussions of Great Britain and Japan for examples.)

In addition, the willingness of labor leaders to relinquish authority to an international level would be limited by political and philosophical differences. For example, a French labor leader committed to a communist form of economic organization is not likely to relinquish his authority willingly to an international union patterned after the United Auto Workers. Alternatively, would the leaders of the UAW relinquish their autonomy to a communist international labor union? Virtually all American labor unions are committed to business unionism and the capitalistic economic system. Compared to labor unions in other countries, American unions are at the extreme in this regard. The union movement in many other countries is committed to syndicalism, socialism, or communism and relies on government action to secure benefits for workers.

Exhibit 18.2 contrasts the centralization that exists within an MNC and that of labor unions in different countries. It makes clear that unions within a nation must be structured in such a way and pursue goals that are consistent with the needs, attitudes, and interests of that nation's workers. As a result it is virtually impossible for unions from different countries to permit centralization of authority on an international level approximating that which can exist within a nation.

WORKER ATTITUDES IN LESS DEVELOPED COUNTRIES

Studies have been made of wage structures in less-developed countries and in industrially advanced countries. The results indicate that workers in an international firm located in a low-wage underdeveloped economy typically stand higher on their own country's wage ladder than workers of that firm located in an industrialized country stand on their country's wage ladder.[92] This suggests that there should be little in-

> **EXHIBIT 18.2**
> **Barriers to Multinational Collective Bargaining**
>
> The most important impediment to successful use of traditional forms of collective bargaining on an international scale is inherent in the structure of union organization, which reflects the wide disparity of interests and concern that exists among national unions. Union organization is anything but monolithic. Even when joined together in common purpose, the international union organization is no more than a loosely knit group of divergent organizations from a variety of countries. The MNC's, on the other hand, are always monolithic, centrally controlled, and with a single purpose—the maximization of profits. Among both developed and less developed countries, national economic, social, and political environments will shape the goals and needs of local work forces in different ways, making workers and their unions especially vulnerable to the tactics of the multinationals.
>
> The attitude that a national union develops toward its own problems relative to the problems of unions in other nations is strongly influenced by background economic conditions. In a country like the United States, with a relatively high unemployment rate, the union will be concerned with keeping the multinational investment and plant within its borders. The union may very well be willing to accommodate its demands in order to persuade the MNC to invest further. In countries where labor is in tight supply, on the other hand, the union can afford to deal more sharply with the multinationals.
>
> The problem in bringing off a coordinated response to the multinational becomes even more acute when the company is operating in the less developed countries, which are generally characterized by very low standards of living and a chronic oversupply of labor. Wherever unemployment is the normal way of life, the labor movement will find it difficult to build a coordinated approach to multinational management, as is illustrated by one experience of the IMF (International Metalworkers' Federation). When the Chilean subsidiary of British Leyland Motors ordered the president of the local union either to accept a job as foreman (and join the management side) or be fired, the IMF tried to handle the situation through a coordinated approach. However, although the British union agreed to support any action taken by the Chilean union, the Chilean workers would not take a stand. Instead they asked their president to give in so that they would not lose their jobs.
>
> Finally, even if these barriers did not exist and unions were able to formulate a coordinated approach to the multinational, the chances are that it would not serve the needs of high-wage workers. Since bargaining would have established conditions that fit the marginal plant or the marginal country, the result would not be acceptable to unions in countries like the United States, with relatively high wages and standards of living.
>
> *Source: Stanley H. Ruttenberg, "The Union View of Multinationals: An Interpretation,"* Bargaining Without Boundaries, *eds. R. J. Flanagan and A. R. Weber (Chicago: The University of Chicago Press, 1974), pp. 189–90.*

centive for employees of MNCs in less-developed countries to raise their wages through supporting multinational bargaining.

Another factor involving worker attitudes in less-developed countries is present if the country was at one time a colony. In such cases, a common attitude among the population is that the country had been the victim of exploitation by foreigners. In such cases it is even more unlikely that such employees would participate in multinational bargaining because it implies that they may strike in support of bargaining demands made by American or West European workers.

WAGE-DETERMINATION PROCEDURES

Yet another set of problems is presented by the various wage-and-benefit determination procedures of different countries. Earlier in this chapter the industrial relations systems of selected countries were described. In certain countries such as Brazil and the USSR, such decisions are made by the government and employee unions have little or no role in the process.

In other countries characterized by Great Britain and West Germany, industry-level negotiations determine minimum standards. Then negotiations at the company or plant level determine actual wages and benefits. However, national union leaders have no role in the latter negotiations. Additionally, unions in some cases are not even formally involved in plant level negotiations. Major changes in bargaining procedures would be necessary to make the American procedures compatible with West European procedures.

PUBLIC POLICY

Public policy with respect to union-management relations presents yet another set of barriers to multinational collective bargaining. Of the nations we have discussed, only those with free collective bargaining would appear to have the potential for multinational bargaining. But even in these societies, legal barriers to multinational bargaining exist. For example, wage controls of a nation may preclude wage increases of the magnitude agreed to in collective negotiations. Another example is legislation in several countries prohibiting sympathy strikes and strikes during the life of a collective agreement.[93]

The Experience with Multinational Bargaining to Date

The preceding section makes clear that major barriers stand in the way of multinational bargaining. In this section the existing multinational union structure is described and the efforts to engage in multinational bargaining are reviewed.

MULTINATIONAL UNION STRUCTURE

The most active multinational labor organizations are the International Confederation of Free Trade Unions (ICFTU) and the international trade secretariats (ITS's).[94] The ICFTU is composed of national federations. Members include the Trade Union Congress of Great Britain and the Canadian Labour Congress. The AFL-CIO was at one time a member of the ICFTU.

The ITS's are composed of national industrial or trade unions. For example the United Auto Workers and the United Steel Workers are members of the International Metalworkers' Federation, the largest ITS.[95] Table 18.2 lists the ITS's, the combined membership of affiliated national unions, and the number of countries represented.

The international trade secretariats are autonomous organizations that are loosely linked to the ICFTU.[96] These organizations have agreed upon a division of responsibilities. The ITS's have the primary responsibility for relations between multinational corporations and unions. The ICFTU has the primary responsibility for dealing with governments and intergovernmental organizations on behalf of the multinational union movement.

Table 18.2 *International Trade Secretariats*

		Total membership of affiliates
International Metalworkers' Federation	(IMF)	11,500,000 in 65 countries
International Transport Workers' Federation	(ITF)	6,500,000 in 80 countries
International Federation of Commercial, Clerical and Technical Employees	(FIET)	6,000,000 in 46 countries
International Textile, Garment and Leather Workers' Federation	(ITGLWF)	5,250,000 in 40 countries
International Federation of Plantation, Agricultural and Allied Workers	(IFPAAW)	3,999,359 in 45 countries
Public Services International	(PSI)	3,932,319 in 61 countries
Postal, Telegraph and Telephone International	(PTTI)	3,150,000 in 82 countries
International Federation of Chemical and General Workers' Unions	(ICF)	3,100,000 in 32 countries
International Federation of Building and Woodworkers	(IFBWW)	3,000,000 in 44 countries
International Union of Food and Allied Workers' Associations	(IUF)	2,150,000 in 54 countries
Miners' International Federation	(MIF)	1,500,000 in 33 countries
International Federation of Free Teachers' Unions	(IFFTU)	1,500,000 in 37 countries
International Federation of Petroleum and Chemical Workers	(IFPCW)	1,176,089 in 58 countries
International Graphical Federation	(IGF)	840,000 in 31 countries
International Secretariat of Entertainment Trade Unions	(ISETU)	470,000 in 29 countries
International Federation of Journalists	(IFJ)	60,300 in 23 countries
Universal Alliance of Diamond Workers	(UADW)	10,350 in 6 countries

Source: Adapted from David C. Hershfield, The Multinational Union Challenges the Multinational Company, *Conference Board Report No. 658 (New York: The Conference Board, 1975), p. 4.*

MULTINATIONAL BARGAINING EFFORTS

In 1975, a survey of 134 United States–based MNCs found that 10 percent had experienced some type of multinational union contact with the corporation.[97] An additional 14 percent reported that interunion cooperation across national boundaries had occurred. Combining these percentages suggests that about one-fourth of American MNCs had experienced some type of multinational union activity.

Responses of MNCs based outside the United States indicate that they have encountered more multinational union activities.[98] Of the foreign MNCs surveyed, 21 percent had experienced multinational union contacts and 24 percent reported interunion activities that had not as yet developed into management contacts.

Exhibit 18.3 presents examples of union contacts with employers. It also presents examples of interunion activities of which management was aware. The number of times each type of union contact occurred is also indicated.

Analysis of company characteristics indicates that certain types of MNCs are more likely to be the object of union contacts. Those that have been the object of multinational union activities: have more employees, have a larger proportion of em-

---

EXHIBIT 18.3
Examples of Multinational Union Activities

Examples of contacts with corporations:

- Higher management is asked to change company policy toward employees in another country (eleven instances).
- Company's labor dispute in another country is publicized with the objective of reducing company's sales (four instances).
- Union officials from another country join local company employees at serious negotiating sessions with company (eight instances).
- Union officials from another country join local company employees in arbitration or court proceedings against the company (four instances).
- Company employees refuse to work overtime to compensate for production lost by foreign strike (one instance).
- Company employees refuse to make shipments to company's struck foreign operations (three instances).
- Company employees refuse to handle shipments from the company's struck foreign operations (three instances).
- Company employees strike in sympathy with foreign strike (one instance).

Examples of interunion activities:

- Exchanges of information about the company's policies in different countries.
- Meetings between unions of company employees in different countries.
- Formation of "world councils" of unions of company employees in different countries.

Source: Adopted from David C. Hershfield, The Multinational Union Challenges the Multinational Company *Conference Board Report No. 658 (New York: The Conference Board, 1975) pp. 9–10.*

ployees outside the base country, have more centralized labor relations programs, and are often members of employer bargaining associations.[99] The first three characteristics suggest that multinational unions are focusing on the larger targets.

EFFECTIVENESS OF MULTINATIONAL UNION BARGAINING EFFORTS

Several case studies have been completed of multinational union bargaining efforts. These investigations have found that such bargaining efforts typically place little pressure on management.[100-104] When labor has been successful in attaining its objectives, the causal factor has usually been action by a critical national union. Further, that union would probably have engaged in the same action without multinational union coordination and cooperation. In particular the effectiveness of the international trade secretariats in influencing bargaining outcomes is questioned.

Alternative Union Strategies

The barriers to multinational collective bargaining faced by unions and the extent of multinational bargaining activities to date have been described. Since the prospects for effective multinational bargaining in the near future are not promising, unions must consider alternative strategies. The basic options are that unions bargain independently with an MNC within each country, secure legislation protecting union members' jobs within each country, or try for coordinated multinational collective bargaining.

BARGAINING DIRECTLY WITHIN EACH COUNTRY

Dealing directly with an MNC can take different forms. It can involve negotiating for an agreement to invest in new or additional facilities within a nation or for an agreement not to close an existing facility.

Another approach to dealing with a corporation within a nation is increased worker involvement and authority in management.[105] An outcome of worker representation on boards of directors can be to influence such management decisions. However, our discussion of codetermination in West Germany suggests that management retains control of board decisions. Consequently one must question the effectiveness of this approach.

Another variation in bargaining directly with an MNC concerning investment decisions and plant closings is parallel to union approaches to dealing with technological change. A union can acknowledge that jobs within a country will be lost and seek to obtain the best adjustment possible for the affected workers. Options include retraining, preferential hiring at the remaining plants, severance pay, and early retirement.

Given the economic advantages of location in some other country, our opinion is that this set of approaches represents a short-term solution. Decisions to close less efficient facilities can be delayed by direct negotiations. Eventually such facilities will be closed given sufficient economic advantages at other locations. This process will be accelerated as the number of relatively efficient facilities in other nations increases because of the reduced bargaining power of the union or unions representing workers at less efficient plants.

PROTECTIVE LEGISLATION

Legislation to protect jobs of workers within a nation can take different forms. Trade barriers and import duties can be established that eliminate competition from other nations. In addition government regulations can be established that govern large-scale lay-offs and plant closings.[106] For example France and West Germany require that mass lay-offs be authorized by a public authority.

The effectiveness of this strategy is limited. If the cost of producing a category of goods is less in some other country, protective legislation can eliminate that advantage only within the nation with the legislation. The country with the lower production costs retains that advantage in other countries that do not have trade barriers. If such countries make up a major portion of the world market for the goods in question, protective legislation is a limited solution.

In the case in which protective legislation is effective in protecting jobs of workers within a nation, an interesting anomaly may occur.[107] The national union and the workers in question will support the protective legislation. However the MNC in question will oppose such legislation. Instead the MNC may support coordinated bargaining across national boundaries because it represents a more favorable alternative.

WHICH ALTERNATIVE WILL BE USED?

We expect that independent national bargaining coupled with protective legislation will be relied upon in the near future by unions in most parts of the world. A major force contributing to the selection of these alternatives is also a major obstacle to multinational bargaining—national union authority.[108] A national union can reasonably expect to protect existing jobs within a nation in the short term by relying on the strategies we have suggested. By so doing such unions increase the barrier to multinational collective bargaining.

However, as nations without trade barriers make up more and more of the world market for a given product, the effectiveness of these strategies declines. Further, the incentive for MNCs that are affected by these strategies to support multinational collective bargaining increases. In such cases we expect that eventually effective multinational collective bargaining will emerge.

Summary

Union-management relations in most other nations are quite different than in the United States. The role of unions in Brazilian industrial relations is minor compared to that of unions in the United States. In Brazil the terms and conditions of employment are determined in great detail by legislation and government regulation. Further, it was only in 1979 that unions were again permitted to engage in collective bargaining, following the military takeover in 1964.

In Western Europe a two-stage system of collective bargaining exists. In the first stage, contracts establishing minimum conditions of employment are typically negotiated on an industry basis. The second round of negotiations at the plant level determines the actual conditions of employment. Unions participate in the first round of negotiations. However, they do not formally participate in the second round of negotiations in some nations, e.g., West Germany.

The Soviet Union provides an example of an industrial-relations system in a communist society. It represents the model for the traditional communist system. Yugoslavia, on the other hand, has been described as a decentralized socialist market system. It provides for worker management of enterprises. In both systems unions have little authority to participate in decisions concerning the rules governing the work place. Events in Poland during 1980 and 1981 were described to provide an example of a communist nation that attempted to depart from the Soviet model of industrial relations.

Multinational corporations based in the United States are becoming more common. Insofar as the foreign facilities of these corporations are parallel to those in the base country, i.e., the United States, they present a threat to the job security of employees in the base country as well as to union bargaining power. Alternatives available to unions in dealing with multinational corporations include direct negotiations conducted by independent national unions, protective legislation, and multinational collective bargaining. Unions will probably rely on the first two alternatives in the short term. However, as the world market for a corporation's products and services increases, multinational bargaining is expected to become the more attractive alternative.

Discussion Questions

1. What functions are served by Brazilian unions and why is their role in collective negotiations so different from what we are familiar with in the United States?
2. Contrast the legal constraints on British union-management relations with the constraints in the United States.
3. What is wage drift and why does it occur?

4. Why do unions play a minor role in plant-level industrial relations in West Germany?
5. What is codetermination and what problems would it pose for union-management relations American-style?
6. Describe how modern Japanese industrial relations are affected by the traditional relationship between employers and employees in Japan.
7. What threats do multinational corporations pose for American workers? Evaluate the alternatives available to deal with multinational corporations.

Key Concepts

Two-stage bargaining
Wage drift
Productivity bargaining
Codetermination
Workers' management

Enterprise union
Spring offensive
Multinational collective bargaining
International trade secretariats

Notes

1. "Foreign Trade of the United States," *Survey of Current Business,* May 1981, pp. S–18 to S–20.
2. Ibid.
3. Robert J. Alexander, *Labor Relations in Argentina, Brazil and Chile* (New York: McGraw-Hill Book Company, 1962), p. 59.
4. Ibid., p. 66.
5. James L. Schlagheck, *The Political, Economic, and Labor Climate in Brazil* (Philadelphia: Industrial Research Unit, The Wharton School, University of Pennsylvania, 1977), p. 66.
6. Ibid., pp. 54–55.
7. Edwardo B. Gentil, "Brazil's Labor Movement, Resurging, Could Stress Wages Instead of Politics," *Wall Street Journal,* 11 November 1980, p. 34.
8. U.S. Department of Labor, Bureau of International Labor Affairs, *Country Labor Profile: Brazil* (Washington: U. S. Government Printing Office, 1980), p. 5.
9. Ibid.
10. Ibid.
11. Ibid.
12. "Brazilian Metalworkers Strike at 2,000 Firms," *Wall Street Journal,* 30 October 1978, p. 8.
13. "Metalworkers in Brazil Vote an End to Strike Affecting 500 Concerns," *Wall Street Journal,* 28 March 1979, p. 37.
14. "Striking Metalworkers in Brazil Return to Work," *Wall Street Journal,* 13 May 1980, p. 35.
15. Ibid.
16. Gentil.

17. Adolf Sturmthal, *Comparative Labor Movements: Ideological Roots and Institutional Development,* (Belmont, CA: Wadsworth Publishing Company, 1972), p. 51.

18. Ibid.

19. Ibid., p. 52.

20. Ibid.

21. A. W. J. Thomson, "Trade Unions and The Corporate State in Britain," *Industrial and Labor Relations Review* 33, no. 1 (1979):37.

22. C. Balfour, *Industrial Relations in The Common Market* (London: Routledge and Kegan Paul, 1972), p. 2.

23. "Alliance or Bust," *The Economist,* September 1981, pp. 10–11.

24. U.S. Department of Labor. Bureau of International Labor Affairs, *Country Labor Profile: United Kingdom* (Washington, D.C.: U.S. Government Printing Office, 1980), p. 4.

25. Ibid., p. 1.

26. Efren Cordova, "A Comparative View of Collective Bargaining in Industrialized Countries," *International Labour Review* 117, no. 4 (1978):424.

27. Sturmthal, p. 57.

28. Ibid., p. 58.

29. Balfour, p. 4.

30. Ibid., p. 5.

31. Brian Weeks et al., *Industrial Relations and the Limits of Law* (Oxford, England: Blackwell, 1975).

32. "Employment Law Changed Again," *European Industrial Relations Review,* September 1980, pp. 5–8.

33. Sturmthal, p. 60.

34. Balfour, p. 3.

35. Sturmthal, pp. 122–23.

36. Ibid., p. 60.

37. Balfour, p. 6.

38. W. E. J. McCarthy, "The Nature of Britain's Strike Problem," *British Journal of Industrial Relations* 8, no. 2 (July 1970):224–36.

39. Sturmthal, p. 52.

40. Ibid., p. 61.

41. U. S. Department of Labor, Bureau of International Labor Affairs, *Country Labor Profile: Federal Republic of Germany* (Washington, D. C.: U. S. Government Printing Office, 1979), p. 1.

42. Ibid., p. 4.

43. Sturmthal, p. 67.

44. Balfour, pp. 61–62.

45. Sturmthal, p. 67.

46. Balfour, p. 61.

47. Ibid.

48. Renato Mazzolini, "The Influence of European Workers Over Corporate Strategy," *Sloan Management Review,* Spring 1978, p. 60.

49. David G. Garson, "The Codetermination Model of Workers' Participation: Where Is It Leading?" *Sloan Management Review,* Spring 1977, pp. 64–65.

50. Mazzolini, pp. 62–63.

51. Garson, p. 64.

52. Sturmthal, pp. 96–97.

53. Mazzolini, p. 63.

54. Garson, p. 66.

55. J. L. Porket, "Industrial Relations and Participation in Management In The Soviet-Type Communist System," *British Journal of Industrial Relations,* March 1978, p. 70.

56. Ibid., pp. 71–72.
57. Ibid., pp. 72–73.
58. Blair A. Ruble, "Dual Functioning Trade Unions in the USSR" *British Journal of Industrial Relations*, July 1979, p. 235.
59. Blair A. Ruble, "Factory Unions and Workers' Rights," *Industrial Labor in the USSR*, eds. A. Kahan and B. A. Ruble (New York: Pergamon Press, 1979), p. 59.
60. Porket, p. 74.
61. Ruble, "Dual Functioning Trade Unions in the USSR," p. 236.
62. Ibid., p. 237.
63. Ibid., p. 238.
64. Ibid.
65. Porket, p. 78.
66. Ruble, "Dual Functioning Trade Unions in the USSR," p. 240.
67. Sturmthal, p. 156.
68. Joop Ramondt, "Workers' Self-Management and Its Constraints: The Yugoslav Experience," *British Journal of Industrial Relations*, March 1979, p. 83.
69. Ibid., p. 157.
70. Ibid., p. 158.
71. Ibid., p. 90.
72. Daniel Seligman, "Poland Might Be Only the Beginning," *Fortune*, 1 December 1980, pp. 103–104, 112.
73. W. E. Smith, "The Darkness Descends: Freedom Is Extinguished And A Nation Is Held Hostage By Its Own Army," *Time*, 28 December 1981, pp. 8–14, 18.
74. T. A. Sanction, "Turning Back The Clock: 'Normalization' Seems To Mean A Return To The Practices of 1960," *Time*, 25 January 1982, pp. 32–34.
75. Toru Ariizumi, "The Legal Framework: Past and Present," *Workers and Employers in Japan: The Japanese Employment Relations System*, eds. K. Okochi, B. Karsh and S. B. Levine (Princeton University Press and University of Tokyo Press, 1973), pp. 116–17.
76. U. S. Department of Labor, Bureau of International Labor Affairs, *Country Labor Profile: Japan* (Washington, D. C.: U. S. Government Printing Office, 1979), p. 5.
77. Hisashi Kawada, "Workers and Their Organizations," *Workers and Employers in Japan: The Japanese Employment Relations System*, eds. K. Okochi, B. Karsh, and S. B. Levine (Princeton University Press and University of Tokyo Press, 1973), pp. 235–38.
78. *Country Labor Profile: Japan.*
79. Taishiro Shirai, "Collective Bargaining," *Workers and Employers in Japan: The Japanese Employment Relations System*, eds. K. Okochi, B. Karsh, and S. B. Levine (Princeton University Press and University of Tokyo Press, 1973), pp. 269–72.
80. *Country Labor Profile: Japan*, p. 7.
81. *Labor-Management Relations in Japan*, (New York: Japan Trade Center, JETRO Business Information Series No. 4), p. 11.
82. *Country Labor Profile: Japan.*
83. Shirai, p. 288.
84. Kawada, p. 237.
85. Ibid.
86. David C. Hershfield, "The Multinational Union Challenges the Multinational Company," (New York: The Conference Board, 1975), Report No. 658.
87. Ibid.
88. M. H. Finley, "Foreign Trade and U.S. Employment," *The Impact of International Trade and Investment on Employment*, U.S. Department of Labor, Bureau of International Labor Affairs, (Washington, D. C.: U.S. Government Printing Office, 1978), pp. 129–34.
89. Robert J. Flanagan, "Introduction, Bargaining Without Boundaries: The Multinational Corporation and International Labor Relations," eds. R. J. Flanagan and A. R. Weber (Chicago: The University of Chicago Press, 1974), p. xiii.

90. United States Congress, Senate, Committee on Finance, *Implications of Multinational Firms for World Trade and Investment for U. S. Trade and Labor,* 93rd Congress, 1st Session, 1973, pp. 626–27, 637, 643.

91. Lloyd Ulman, "Multinational Unionism: Incentives, Barriers, and Alternatives," *Industrial Relations* 14, no. 1 (1975):7.

92. Ibid., p. 15.

93. Ibid., p. 20.

94. Hershfield, p. 3.

95. Ibid., p. 22.

96. Ibid., p. 3.

97. Ibid., p. 9.

98. Ibid.

99. Ibid., p. 10.

100. Ibid., pp. 17–39.

101. Herbert R. Northrup and Richard L. Rowan. "Multinational Bargaining Approaches in the Western European Flat Glass Industry," *Industrial and Labor Relations Review,* October 1976, pp. 32–46.

102. Herbert R. Northrup and Richard L. Rowan, "Multinational Collective Bargaining Activity: The Factual Record in Chemicals, Glass and Rubber Tires," *Columbia Journal of World Business,* Summer 1974, pp. 49–63.

103. Herbert R. Northrup and Richard L. Rowan, "Multinational Union-Management Consultation: The European Experience," *International Labour Review* 116, no. 2 (1977):153–70.

104. Herbert R. Northrup and Richard L. Rowan, "Multinational Union Activity in the 1976 U. S. Rubber Tire Strike," *Sloan Management Review* 18 (Spring 1977):17–28.

105. Ulman, p. 28.

106. Ibid., p. 29.

107. Ibid.

108. Ibid., p. 3.

Suggested Readings

Bronstein, A. S. "Collective Bargaining in Latin America: Problems and Trends." *International Labour Review* 117 (September–October, 1978):583–96.

Okochi, K., Karsh, B., and Levine, S. B., eds. *Workers and Employers in Japan: The Japanese Employment Relations System.* Princeton University Press and University of Tokyo Press, 1973.

Peach, D. A. and Kuechle, D. *The Practice of Industrial Relations.* Toronto: McGraw-Hill Ryerson Limited, 1975.

Porket, J. L. "Industrial Relations and Participation in Management in the Soviet-Type Communist System." *British Journal of Industrial Relations,* March 1978, pp. 70–85.

Ramondt, J. "Workers' Self-Management and Its Constraints: The Yugoslav Experience." *British Journal of Industrial Relations,* March 1979, pp. 83–94.

Schlagheck, J. L. *The Political, Economic and Labor Climate in Brazil.* Philadelphia: Industrial Research Unit, The Wharton School, University of Pennsylvania, 1977.

Sturmthal, A. *Comparative Labor Movements: Ideological Roots and Institutional Development.* Belmont, CA: Wadsworth Publishing Company, 1972.

Ulman, L. "Multinational Unionism: Incentives, Barriers and Alternatives," *Industrial Relations* 14, no. 1 (1975):1–31.

Chapter 19

THE FUTURE OF THE AMERICAN UNION MOVEMENT

Molly Brown, a college student, was nearing the end of a course in labor relations. During the course she had developed a greater interest in the field and had noticed several articles in newspapers and newsmagazines concerning union-management relations. In addition to the usual articles pertaining to contract negotiations and strikes, she had noticed articles concerning trends in union membership and the state of the union movement in general.

Many of these articles conveyed the notion that the American union movement was in trouble. For example, one major newsmagazine had the caption, "Unions On the Run" on the cover of one issue. These articles suggested that several factors were contributing to the situation in which unions found themselves. Included were technological change and foreign competition.

Molly wondered about the future of the American union movement. Her study of labor relations this semester had convinced her that unions had been necessary to protect worker interests in the past and she was quite sure they would continue to be necessary. She wondered why unions had been losing membership as a percent of the labor force in recent years. She also wondered what unions could do to reverse this trend in the years to come.

This chapter attempts to address Molly's questions systematically. Specifically, when you finish studying this chapter you should be able to:

- Identify how each of the following is related to union membership as a percent of the labor force:
  a. Changing patterns of employment.
  b. Projected reindustrialization of the American economy.
  c. Recent and projected patterns of foreign competition.

d. Employer actions to resist increases and to reduce levels of unionization.
   e. Changing worker values.
- Describe what unions are doing or can do to minimize the loss of union jobs.
- Discuss union efforts to organize the following:
   a. Employees of the south and west.
   b. Minority workers.
   c. Women workers.
   d. White-collar workers.

In this chapter we attempt to present a look at the future of the American labor movement. Our focus is on union membership as a proportion of the labor force in America. At the time we are writing it is 1981, the centennial of the Federation of Organized Trade and Labor Unions, the forerunner of the AFL-CIO. In 1881, the dominant organization in the American labor movement was the Knights of Labor. Within a few years the Knights ceased to be a major force because the principles and approaches espoused by that organization were not consistent with the challenges facing American trade unions of that time. As history has demonstrated, the principles and approaches followed by the American Federation of Labor enabled it to meet those challenges.

Another Challenge

Today the American union movement faces another major challenge. Changing employment patterns, technological change, non-union employers, and foreign competition are combining to erode union membership. Fig. 19.1 reports union membership as a percent of nonagricultural employment for 1930 to 1978. Union membership increased dramatically between 1930 and 1945. Between 1945 and 1954, union membership as a percent of nonagricultural employment remained stable at approximately 35 percent. Since 1954 union membership as a percent of nonagricultural employment has been declining. In 1978 the figure was 23.6 percent.

Commenting on the challenges faced by American unions in the past, Thomas Donahue, secretary-treasurer of the AFL-CIO, said that it is no different today; organized labor is embattled and in danger.[1] Lane Kirkland, president of the AFL-CIO, stated, "What we in American labor face is not a passing period of acute crisis. Rather we face a permanent challenge to our basic role in American life."[2] Despite the magnitude of the problems facing American unions, labor leaders feel their problems are no more serious than those facing other American institutions. Further, labor leaders are confident that the American union movement will successfully meet these challenges. Glen Watts, president of the Communications Workers of America, has stated that it might take longer to get through these struggles, but once there, the movement will be stronger.[3]

Fig. 19.1 *Union Membership as Percent of Nonagricultural Employment*

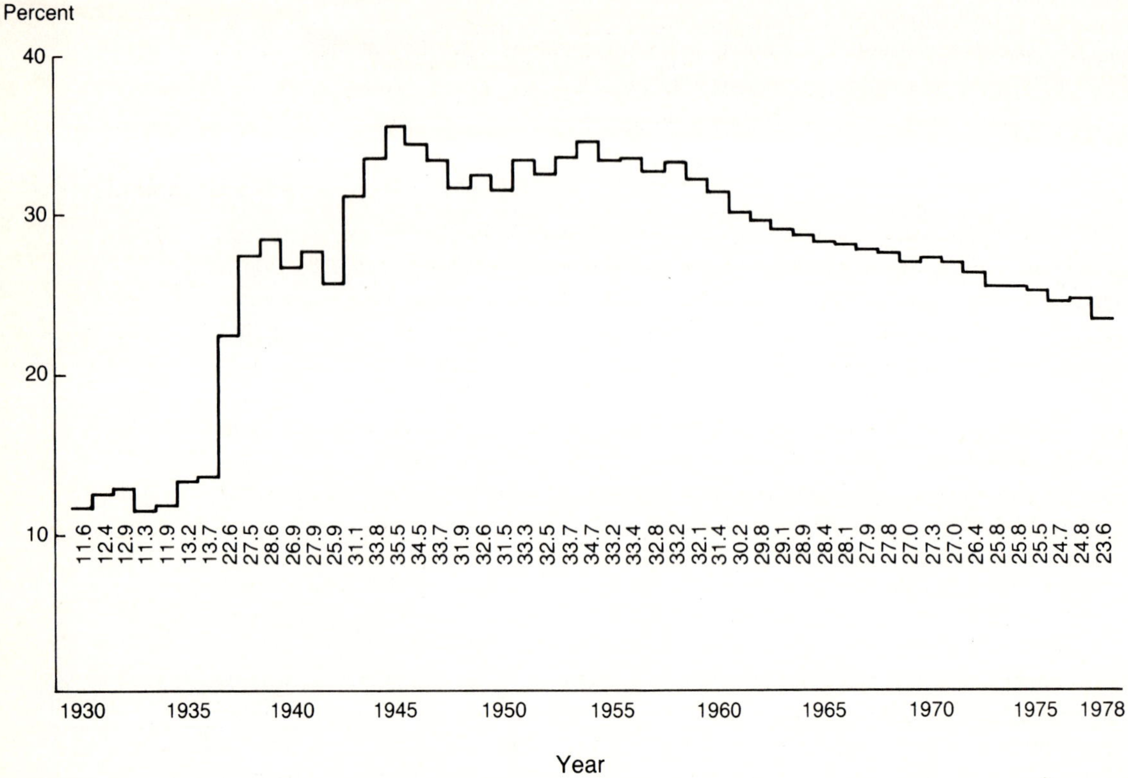
Percent
40
30
20
10
11.6
12.4
12.9
11.3
11.9
13.2
13.7
22.6
27.5
28.6
26.9
27.9
25.9
31.1
33.8
35.5
34.5
33.7
31.9
32.6
31.5
33.3
32.5
33.7
34.7
33.2
33.4
32.8
33.2
32.1
31.4
30.2
29.8
29.1
28.9
28.4
28.1
27.9
27.8
27.0
27.3
27.0
26.4
25.8
25.8
25.5
24.7
24.8
23.6
1930
1935
1940
1945
1950
1955
1960
1965
1970
1975
1978
Year

Source: U.S. Department of Labor, Bureau of Labor Statistics, Bulletin 2070 Handbook of Labor Statistics *(Washington, D. C.: U. S. Government Printing Office, December 1980), Table 165, p. 412.*

Relevant Trends and Forces

There are several factors that have contributed to the declining membership in unions and that may contribute to further reductions in union membership. The most important factor appears to be the changing patterns of employment by industry and by occupation. Related to these changes are two forces that could cause major reductions in union membership during the remainder of this century. These forces are rapid introduction of technological change by American employers and major increases in imports of goods from foreign nations.

In addition, there are a set of forces involving actions by employers that are reducing union employment and membership. Non-union employers are becoming more important in traditionally unionized sectors of the economy. There are signs that employers are willing to go to great lengths to resist unionization, to reduce existing levels of unionization, and to avoid further increases in the unionization of their labor forces.

Finally, a shift in the values and attitudes of American workers appears to be taking place. As a result workers in increasing numbers may perceive that unions that focus on bread-and-butter issues such as wages and job security no longer provide a product worth the cost of union membership.

CHANGING PATTERNS OF EMPLOYMENT

The industry and occupational patterns of employment in the United States are changing. During the coming decade employment in white-collar occupations, which include professional and technical workers, managers and administrators, salesworkers, and clerical workers, is expected to increase at above-average rates.[4] Alternatively, employment in blue-collar occupations is expected to increase, but at a pace below the average change in employment.[5] Since white-collar workers are less likely to favor joining a union than blue-collar workers, the changing occupational makeup of the labor force presents an obstacle for unions seeking to maintain or increase union membership as a proportion of the nonagricultural labor force. A recent study found 39 percent of blue-collar workers favored joining a union, compared to 28 percent of white-collar workers.[6]

A related challenge is presented by changes in industrial patterns of employment. Table 19.1 classifies industries according to growth in employment and extent of unionization during the period 1966 to 1976. Only one industry, state and local government, was highly unionized and also a high-growth industry. Most industries that were highly unionized experienced low rates or growth in employment. Included were mining, construction, transportation, manufacturing, and federal-government employment. In 1976, union members in these industries made up 63.5 percent of

Table 19.1 *Employment Growth by Industry and Level of Union Membership by Industry—1966 to 1976*

Percent of industry workers union members (1966–1976)	*Actual growth in employment by industry (1966–1976)*	
	High (above 25%)	*Low (below 25%)*
High (above 45%)	State and local government	Mining Construction Transportation Manufacturing Federal government
Low (below 15%)	Services Finance Trade	

Source: Ronald Berenbeim, The Declining Market for Unionization *(New York: Conference Board Information Bulletin No. 44, August 1978), p. 3.*

Table 19.2 *Projected Growth in Employment by Industry—1979 to 1990 and Past Level of Union Membership by Industry—1966 to 1976*

Past level of union membership 1966–1976[1]	Projected growth in employment by industry[2]			
	1979–1985		1985–1990	
	High	Low	High	Low
High	Construction Mining	Transportation Manufacturing State and local government Federal government	Mining	Transportation Manufacturing Construction State and local government Federal government
Low	Trade Finance Services		Trade Finance Services	

Source: [1]Ronald Berenbeim, The Declining Market for Unionization *(New York: Conference Board Information Bulletin No. 44, August 1978), p. 3.*
[2]*Valerie A. Personick, "The Outlook for Industry Output and Employment Through 1990," Monthly Labor Review, August 1981, p. 39.*

union members in the United States.[7] These figures demonstrate that union membership is concentrated in low-growth industries. Alternatively, among high-growth industries, high proportions of union membership occurred only in state and local government. In 1976, state and local government employees made up 18.7 percent of union members.[8]

Table 19.2 classifies industries according to past levels of unionization and projected increases in employment. It appears that the rapid increases in employment will continue to be concentrated in industries that have in the past been hard to organize. Through 1985, the industries expected to experience high rates of growth that have had high rates of unionization in the past are construction and mining. Between 1985 and 1990, mining is the only industry with high rates of unionization that is expected to experience above-average increases in employment. In 1976, only 1.7 percent of union members were employed in the mining industry and 11.2 percent were employed in construction.[19] Clearly, unless dramatic changes in patterns of unionization take place, union members will continue to be concentrated in low-growth industries.

REINDUSTRIALIZATION

In manufacturing, job prospects for blue-collar workers are threatened by the anticipated rapid introduction of computer-controlled systems of robots and other machines. In 1979, 1,300 robots were in operation in American manufacturing.[10] By 1981, the figure was 5,000 and it is predicted that by 1990, the figure will be 120,000. Further, it is estimated that robots in existence today could displace one million workers in manufacturing by 1990, and some time after 1990, robot capabilities will be such that all 7.9 million operative employees in manufacturing will be replaceable.[11]

It appears certain that the spread of computerized machines will reduce the number of jobs available in the next few decades and alter the nature of the work that is available.[12] Normally unions have sought to ease the impact of technological change on the workers affected by such means as slowing its introduction and providing retraining. However, in this second industrial revolution, the advantage will be with those nations that introduce the new technology most rapidly.[13] The reason is that the computerized machines will enhance productivity to such an extent that those with the new technology will have a major competitive advantage in international markets. As a result such nations will experience comparatively small reductions in employment stemming from technological change.

FOREIGN COMPETITION

Imports to the United States have increased in recent years. Imports equalled 3.6 percent of gross national product in 1955, 7.4 percent in 1979, and are projected to be in the range of 9.1 to 9.7 by 1990.[14] More importantly for the future of the American labor movement, imports of raw materials are expected to become less significant compared to imports of finished goods. At present the largest category of imported finished goods is motor vehicles and parts. Further gains in the import of motor vehicles are expected during the 1980s.[15]

The major source of imported motor vehicles is Japan. Studies comparing the costs of auto production in the United States and Japan demonstrate that the latter has a major advantage. During 1980, a car could be built in Japan and shipped to the United States for $1,300 to $1,700 less than an equivalent car could be built in Detroit.[16] Estimates of the proportion of the Japanese cost advantage that can be traced back to differences in labor costs have been made. One study comparing Toyota with General Motors and Ford estimated Toyota's total cost advantage, after shipping, at $1,350 per car. Of this total figure, $785 stemmed from lower labor costs.[17] There were two dimensions to Toyota's advantage: one-third fewer man-hours were required to build a Toyota, and, in 1981, auto workers averaged $11.57 per hour in the United States compared to $6.15 per hour in Japan.[18]

During the slump in auto sales in 1980, a great deal of attention in the mass media was devoted to the increase in Japanese auto imports. Chapter 18 reported the nations from which most imports to the United States originate. They are other industrialized countries. During the next decade we can expect imports from newly industrializing countries to increase.

Brazil is expected to be a leading exporter among third-world countries. Among the examples of manufactured goods exported from Brazil are eighteen-passenger airplanes used by many American commuter airlines, pistons for United States light aircraft engines, high-strength steel for use in the undercarriages of American jumbo jets, and rubber-tired armored vehicles.[19] Brazil is second only to the Soviet Union in the production of such armored vehicles and they are used by the armed forces of more than 30 countries.

Table 19.3 *Hourly Compensation: Industrialized Countries and Newly Industrializing Countries (Hourly compensation in U. S. dollars mid-1979)*

Industrial countries		Newly industrializing countries	
United States	$ 9.09	Spain	$5.62
Canada	7.97	Mexico	2.31
Japan	5.58	Brazil	1.80
Germany	11.33	Hong Kong	1.25
France	8.17	South Korea	1.14
Great Britain	5.46	Taiwan	1.01

Compensation data are estimates of average compensation per hour worked by production workers in manufacturing except in Mexico where an average for selected manufacturing industries is shown.

Source: U. S. Bureau of Labor Statistics cited in "Rising Labor Costs Trigger Global Shifts in Industry," World of Work Report 6, no. 3, (March 1981): 23.

Table 19.3 presents average hourly wages for production workers in manufacturing for selected countries in 1979. Among the industrialized countries listed are America's major trading partners. Two countries, Japan and Great Britain, have relatively low wage rates. As the above discussion of Toyota indicates, these nations should enjoy an advantage in the international market as a result.

However, the wage advantage of Japan and Great Britain is small compared to that of newly industrializing countries, excluding Spain. It would seem that given the technology of industrialized nations, the newly industrializing nations will have an even greater advantage in the production of finished goods.

These two factors, reindustrialization and foreign competition, place American labor unions in a dilemma. If unions encourage rapid introduction of technological change, it appears that many union members will be displaced. Alternatively, if unions seek to retain existing technology and delay the introduction of new technology, it appears likely that many union members will lose jobs due to a combination of competition from goods manufactured in newly industrializing countries and in industrialized countries that rapidly introduce new technology.

Employer Actions Having an Impact on Union Membership

Several courses of action can be taken by employers that would have the effect of restricting the growth and of reducing existing levels of unionized employment. Efforts to reduce the perceived need for a union on the part of employees are widespread. Consultants are available to assist employers in designing and implementing such programs.[20] These programs focus on implementing personnel policies and practices that make unions unnecessary in the eyes of employees.

Another approach is to resist unionization vigorously during organization and certification election campaigns. An example is DuPont's effort to defeat the Steelworkers in certification elections in 1981.[21] It has been alleged that some employers make widespread use of illegal practices in their attempts to defeat unions in certification elections.[22]

Other approaches can be used by employers that have the effect of reducing unionized employment. One is for unionized employers to establish non-union subsidiaries that compete with the unionized part of the corporation. In the construction industry such organizations are referred to as "double breasted" companies. This practice is becoming increasingly common in the construction industry. It is estimated that the proportion of construction workers represented by unions fell from 40 percent in 1973 to 35 percent in 1980.[23] The practice of establishing non-union subsidiaries appears to be spreading to other industries such as trucking, tire manufacturing, and air transportation.[24,25,26]

In some cases the establishment of a non-union subsidiary involves relocation of that facility to a part of the country in which unions are less common. This appears to be a part of the problem facing the United Rubber Workers. Due largely to the movement of American tire companies to the South, as well as the establishment of Michelin plants in the United States, the proportion of American tire production capacity that is unionized fell from 91.5 percent in 1976, to 82.7 percent in 1981.[27]

Employers are introducing the threat of relocation in negotiations with unions. In 1981, the Timken Company planned to build a new plant. To build the plant in Canton, Ohio, rather than another part of the country, it demanded major concessions from the Steelworkers.[28]

Relocation of jobs outside the United States is also a possibility. The data presented in Table 19.3 make clear the potential for major labor cost advantages of such moves. In preparing for the 1982 round of negotiations with the UAW, General Motors and other United States auto makers stated that if the Japanese labor cost advantage was not reduced, manufacturing operations would be moved to lower-wage countries.[29]

Changing Workers' Values

In Chapter 6 we pointed out that young workers appear to be more opposed to authoritarianism than older workers.[30] It has been predicted that as these young workers grow older, their antiauthoritarianism will not diminish. Other differences between the work values of younger and older workers have been observed.[31] Young workers place more importance on interesting work, the opportunity to develop their own abilities and on their chances for promotion. Age does not appear to be related to the importance of pay, job security, and fringe benefits.[32] Such factors were equally important to all age groups.

These differences in worker values are relevant because "bread and butter" issues have historically been the focus of American union bargaining efforts. The emergence of these other issues as relatively important among young workers would seem to suggest that a shift in the objectives sought by unions would increase the attractiveness of union membership to young workers.

Alternative Courses of Action

American labor unions have two basic courses of action in their efforts to alter the trend in union membership. One approach involves efforts to slow or minimize the loss of jobs for union members. A number of techniques that can be used in following this strategy will be discussed. The other approach is to organize more workers. Several groups within the American labor force have been suggested as points of focus in union efforts to expand their membership. These groups and issues involving each one will also be discussed.

MINIMIZE THE LOSS OF UNION JOBS

Five different approaches to slowing or minimizing the loss of union jobs are presented in this section. Other approaches can be employed to effect this end. The ones here were chosen because there is evidence that each is being used or considered at this time and some of the techniques described represent innovations in American labor relations.

BARGAINING STRATEGIES

During 1980 and 1981, examples of unions relaxing bargaining demands and accepting reductions in existing agreements were abundant. Unions representing Conrail employees approved deferral of pay increases to help keep the railroad operating.[33] The United Auto Workers agreed to major concessions to help keep Chrysler Corporation out of bankruptcy.[34] The Air Line Pilots Association agreed to a contract with United Air Lines that resulted in a restructuring of wages and work rules.[35] The changes were to enable United to compete more effectively with non-union airlines. The United Rubber Workers found it necessary to agree to work rule changes and alteration in pay structures in order to keep some tire plants open[36]. Several major industries, including auto, rubber, and trucking, negotiated contracts in 1982. In each industry moderate union demands were expected [37,38,39]. The building trades unions also experienced pressure to relax wages and work rules[40]. The common theme in each case was that unionized employers were facing economic difficulties, and to preserve union jobs, unions would have to agree to changes that reduced labor costs. With the exception of Conrail, these employers faced severe competition from non-union employers or from foreign employers.

A possible outcome of these difficult times is more cooperative relations between unions and management. A labor leader of the United Rubber Workers stressed the need to cooperate with union employers so that they are better able to compete with non-union tire manufacturers.[41] Similarly in the building trades there are signs of a willingness on the part of some unions to cooperate with contractors in an effort to compete with non-union employers.[42]

Naturally union negotiators have sought to protect the jobs of union members. The Air Line Pilots Association secured a commitment from United not to start a non-union subsidiary airline.[43] Similarly, in the 1982 round of negotiations, the Teamsters were expected to press for an agreement from union employers not to establish non-union subsidiaries[44]. The Rubber Workers have an agreement from the major tire companies to give six months' notice of intended plant shutdowns and to bargain with the union in an effort to keep such plants operating[45].

UNION MERGERS

Another approach unions appear to be using is consolidation and unification. In 1981, the UAW was again affiliated with the AFL-CIO, and the Teamsters were invited to do so. The rationale is that through reunification, there will be a reduction in jurisdictional disputes and increased political influence.[46]

At the national and international level, several union mergers are taking place or being considered. Among those being considered are a merger of the United Auto Workers and the International Association of Machinists. One factor leading to this proposed merger is the expectation that members of these unions are among those most likely to be affected by the introduction of robots by American manufacturers.[47] The Auto Workers and the United Rubber Workers are also exploring the possibility of a merger.[48] Through such mergers it is expected that unions will be better able to mount more effective organization drives and be more effective in representing member interests at the bargaining table.

PLANT-CLOSURE LEGISLATION

Legislation to regulate plant closings has been proposed in several states with concentrations of heavy industry; for example, Ohio, Pennsylvania, Michigan, Illinois, Indiana, and New York.[49] In 1979 and 1980, federal legislation to regulate plant closings was proposed. The legislation would require employers to give workers and communities advance notice of plant closings; provide workers with some form of job and income security, for example, transfer rights and severance pay; and compensate local communities for tax losses.

Unions representing manufacturing employees favor federal legislation because their concern is not localized. The UAW has supported such legislation for several years. This represents an approach, other than through collective bargaining, by which unions seek to limit the impact of plant closings and relocation of plants on union members.

EFFORTS TO INFLUENCE CORPORATE DECISIONS

American unions are exploring alternative methods of participating in and influencing management decisions. Some techniques focus on influencing top level management. In some cases employees have assumed ownership of a plant or company, thereby influencing management decisions. Finally, some organizations, and unions representing their employees, have established procedures for rank-and-file workers to participate in decisions concerning their work environment.

TOP-LEVEL DECISIONS

Two new methods of influencing top-level management have recently been proposed, and have been implemented on a limited basis. One of these approaches is new to American labor-management relations; however it has been employed for many years in European labor relations. It is an adaptation of the German codetermination model. The other approach involves union representation on boards responsible for managing the investment of pension funds.

In West Germany employees have nearly 50 percent representation on the supervisory boards of firms employing more than 2,000 workers. The primary objective of employee representation on such boards is to provide a formal procedure for employee participation in decision making.[49] This mechanism has been effective in reaching a consensus on such issues as plant relocation and technological change, issues of major importance to American unions representing today's manufacturing employees.

The first instance of union representation on the board of a major American corporation occurred in 1980, when Douglas Fraser, president of the UAW, was elected to the Board of Directors for Chrysler Corporation.[51] Shortly after this, the UAW made the same demand of General Motors, Ford, and American Motors.[52] Several other union presidents have expressed interest in joining corporate boards. Among them is Glenn Watts, president of the Communications Workers of America, who has an interest in joining the board of AT&T. Another is the president of the United Rubber Workers, who is especially interested in board membership at Uniroyal and Firestone.

The prospects for widespread application of this modified version of codetermination appear dim. Both Lane Kirkland, president of the AFL-CIO, and Thomas Donahue, secretary-treasurer of the AFL-CIO, have emphasized their rejection of the codetermination model and their commitment to an adversarial relationship with management.[53] They prefer not to be partners in management and do not favor a blurring of the distinctions between the role of management and the role of labor.

Strong resistance to union representation on corporate boards is expected from management. It has been suggested that the American managerial philosophy views employee participation of limited value at any organizational level, but particularly at the board level.[54] Union representation on corporate boards is perceived by managers and executives as a threat to the conventional power-and-authority employee-employer relationship. However, given the problems that many corporations will face during the coming decade, risk-taking chief executive officers may be willing to experiment with this form of employee participation.

Another approach to influencing top-level management decisions is through exercising control over the availability of investment funds. In 1981, American private pension funds were valued at $580 billion and represented the largest source of private investment capital in the world.[55] The importance of pension funds as a source of capital will continue. It is predicted that private pension fund assets will increase to $889.5 billion in 1985 and $2.9 trillion in 1995, at which time they will account for one-third of corporate debt.[56,57]

Pension funds have not always been invested in enterprises consistent with the best interests of union members. Union interest in exercising control over the investment of pension funds has been limited in the past; however this is changing. Many unions are demanding such control over pension funds in order to direct capital toward such socially desirable investments as home mortgages for union members, job-creating investments in the union's geographic region or industry, and investments in companies with good histories on job safety, labor relations, and equal employment opportunity.[58] An example of the effective use of power stemming from control of pension funds was the signing of a collective bargaining agreement by J. P. Stevens in 1980.[59] A four-year boycott of the textile company's products had been unable to bring about an agreement. However, through ownership of banks, insurance companies, and the firms with which Stevens had interlocking directorates, the union movement was able to isolate Stevens financially.

Naturally, protection of workers' retirement income would be the primary concern of unions. Some experts in pension-fund investment assert that one does not have to give up anything in terms of return on investment by excluding companies linked to anti-union activities and job discrimination.[60] Presumably through influencing pension-fund investment decisions, unions can facilitate the attainment of goals of interest to union members and the union movement without jeopardizing the pension income of the membership.

EMPLOYEE OWNERSHIP

During the 1970s there was renewed interest in worker-owned and -controlled enterprises in industrialized western economies.[61] The dominant factor creating interest and leading to employee ownership of enterprises has been the decision of conglomerates to close subsidiary operations. A common procedure by which employees become owners of a company is that the employees accumulate company stock which is placed in a special trust by the company.[62] The company deducts the fair-market value of the stock from employee income. Plans leading to employee ownership have been proposed in several Western European nations.[63] The Swedish plan calls for 20 percent of pretax profits to be contributed to a worker-controlled fund. The payments would be in the form of company shares. Local trade unions would control the shares and would be entitled to place members on company boards when 20 percent of a company's shares are held by the employee fund. If such a plan were adopted it is estimated that the unions would have a majority of shares in Swedish industry within twenty years.

A 1977 report indicated that 472 companies had employee-ownership plans.[64] There is limited information on the position of organized labor toward employee ownership. Apparently union leaders take a negative view toward employee ownership.[65] However, one can find examples of employee ownership in which the local union played the key role in establishing the plan and supports employee ownership.[66]

Employee ownership is expected to facilitate the attainment of several goals. Specifically, in comparison with conventional firms of the same or similar size, industry, and geographical area, the employee-owned firm will have:

- Better profits.
- A better growth record.
- Increased productivity or lower unit labor costs.
- Fewer work stoppages.
- Lower employee turnover.

While limited, the available evidence pertaining to employee ownership suggests it might be a viable alternative for union members faced with plant or company closings.

A NEW LABOR-MANAGEMENT RELATIONS SYSTEM

The slow growth in productivity in the United States during recent years has created a great deal of concern about this issue. This factor coupled with the expectation that the United States will soon embark on a period of rapid technological change appear to have led to a recognition of the need for more cooperation between management and labor.[67] Thomas R. Donahue, secretary-treasurer of the AFL-CIO, has called for developing an approach to implementing change that humanizes the work place and the work itself.[68]

It has been suggested that a new system of employee-employer relations is evolving in the United States.[69] This system could replace the adversarial system that is characteristic of most American union-management relationships. The motivation for replacing the old system is that it has contributed to the poor competitive position of many unionized employers. The cornerstone of the system is the development of a cooperative working relationship between management and employees that addresses such issues as production and efficiency. The second element involves a reduction of adversary or distributive bargaining and an increase in cooperative or integrative bargaining. Signs of this shift emerged in 1980 and 1981. Some examples of cooperative stances taken by union negotiators have been described above. The third element involves a major shift on the part of management. There must be a willingness to permit participation in the decision process.

QUALITY-CONTROL CIRCLES

A mechanism for accomplishing employer-supervisor cooperation on the shop floor is receiving increased attention. Quality-control (QC) circles are employee decision-making teams. They are widely used in Japan, with apparent success. These groups meet regularly, for example once a week, on company time to discuss problems in their work area pertaining to productivity and product quality.

A study of American worker attitudes concerning the declining rate of productivity in the United States was conducted in 1979. It was a nationwide sample, representative of all workers over eighteen years old. This study found widespread commitment to improving productivity.[70] Most workers taking part in the study would like to be involved in deciding how to do a better job and over 80 percent said that more involvement in decision making would be a definite incentive for them to work harder.

In 1980 it was estimated that 400 American organizations were using the QC concept.[71] In 1981, it was estimated that 1,000 organizations were using QC circles.[72] Numerous case histories pertaining to results of QC circles have been reported.[73,74,75,76] Although the reports are not always favorable, a common theme of most reports is that productivity increases and employee satisfaction, as well as related indexes such as absenteeism and turnover, improve.

Generally labor leaders have not openly advocated and supported QC circles. However the emerging AFL-CIO strategy is to participate in QC circles rather than to oppose them.[77] Selected national unions do support QC circles and are working with employers to establish them.[78,79,80] Among them are the United Auto Workers, United Steel Workers, United Rubber Workers, and the Communications Workers of America. For example, the 1980 contract between the Steelworkers and major steel producers called for the establishment of labor-management participation teams.[81] The teams were at the department level and addressed such issues as health and safety, absenteeism, product quality, and efficiency.

Some labor leaders take the position that in addition to increasing worker efficiency and job satisfaction, QC circles and similar programs increase member satisfaction with the union. Irving Bluestone, UAW vice president, has stated that in every plant where the UAW has a successful program, local UAW leaders who supported it have been reelected.[82] A United Rubber Worker leader explained the advantage of such programs to unions as follows.[83] About 90 percent of union members who are not "perennial grievers" see little relevance of the union to their day-to-day work lives. These are the workers who want to do a good job and will be helped most by QC circles. When the union helps establish these programs it is doing something important for such workers.

UNION INVOLVEMENT IN QUALITY OF WORKLIFE

The essential component of efforts to improve the quality of working life is direct involvement of workers in the decision-making process.[84] Thomas Donahue, secretary-treasurer of the AFL-CIO, has recommended that unions can be the focal point for establishing programs for employee participation in efforts to improve productivity and job satisfaction, if unions are accepted as equal partners in such efforts.[85] This implies a recognition on the part of management for unions to participate in such programs. It also implies that management rejects the idea that worker participation is the latest technique for circumventing the union or for keeping the union out. Resistance to QC circles and worker participation programs on the part of union leaders quite often stem from these perceptions of management motives.[86,87,88]

Irving Bluestone has suggested a list of principles to guide the establishment of a worker participation program. The success of a program of worker participation in decision making involving a union calls for a cooperative collective-bargaining relationship. There must be a climate of mutual respect in which solving problems supersedes beating the other side.[85]

WORKER INCENTIVES

The study of worker attitudes toward productivity referred to above also investigated workers' views concerning rewards and incentives for hard work. Many of those participating in the study felt their pay was less than the value of their work and that working harder would go unrewarded.[90] These views were especially prevalent among union members and among black and women workers.

This suggests the need for an additional dimension to worker participation programs, financial reward. The Scanlon Plan, described in Chapter 11, incorporates both participation and reward for increased productivity. The experience of the Dana Corporation with the Scanlon Plan has been favorable, as has been the reaction of unions representing the Dana employees.[91] Possibly the next decade will witness the inclusion of a mechanism for providing bonuses based on increased productivity in worker participation programs.

Organize More Workers

The previous section focuses on efforts to provide job security for union members by minimizing the loss of union jobs. While this is clearly in the interest of the membership, it does not reverse the trend in union membership as a percent of the labor force presented in Fig. 19.1. The potential for replenishing the membership rolls of organized labor is present in our opinion. It remains to be seen if America's labor movement is equal to the task.

Several shifts in focus of union organization efforts appear necessary.[92] The first shift we will discuss reflects the geographic movement of Americans to the South and West. It is expected that this region will continue to attract people and industry during the next decade. The remaining suggested shifts in focus reflect changes in the composition of the labor force. It is recommended that unions concentrate organization efforts on minority, women, and white-collar members of the labor force.

EFFORTS TO ORGANIZE THE SOUTH AND WEST

Research evidence concerning willingness to join a labor union suggests that both blue- and white-collar workers in the West are as likely to join as those in the Northeast.[93] Contrary to the common assumption that southern workers are less interested in unionization, the same study found that southern blue-collar workers are just as willing to join unions as workers in the Northeast. These data are consistent with a Conference Board report that anticipates that organizing efforts in the next decade will be as successful in the South and West as in other parts of the country.[94]

There have been successful organization efforts in recent years that may be signs of things to come. In 1980, the Amalgamated Clothing and Textile Workers reached a settlement with J. P. Stevens covering 3,500 employees at plants in North Carolina, South Carolina, and Georgia.[95] In 1981, the American Federation of State, County, and Municipal Employees (AFSCME) was certified as the bargaining agent for 23,000 clerical and administrative employees of the state of Florida.[96] The election brought the total number of Florida public employees represented by AFSCME to over 100,000.

In order to facilitate the organization of some major corporations' plants in the South, unions have sought pledges from employers to remain neutral.[97] For example, General Motors made such a pledge in the 1976 contract with the UAW, and the United Rubber Workers have such pledges from three of the major tire companies. Goodyear refused to agree to such a pledge. The objective of such pledges is to counter the "southern strategy" of avoiding unionization by locating new plants in the South.

In 1981, the AFL-CIO embarked on a multiyear campaign to organize workers in the Houston area.[98] It is anticipated that several million dollars will be spent on this effort to sign up new members in some forty affiliated unions participating in the project. Houston holds the potential for substantial gains in union membership. In 1977, it was estimated that only 13 percent of Houston's 700,000 "organizable" workers were union members.

EFFORTS TO ORGANIZE MINORITY WORKERS

A number of factors contribute to the recommendation that unions focus on organizing minority workers. Forecasts through 1995 predict that the minority labor force will grow at about twice the rate of the white labor force.[99] Consequently this group represents an increasing portion of the labor force. A second, and probably more important, factor is the willingness of minority workers to join a union. Kochan's study found that 67 percent of all black and other minority workers would vote to unionize.[100] This compares to a figure of 33 percent among all nonmanagerial employees taking part in the study. Apparently the union movement is taking note of the willingness of minority workers to organize. Part of the rationale for selecting the Houston area for the AFL-CIO's focal point in the effort to organize the South was that Houston's large black and hispanic population is favorably disposed toward unions.[101]

EFFORTS TO ORGANIZE WOMEN WORKERS

Projections of the 1995 labor force indicate that women will account for two-thirds of the anticipated growth in the labor force.[102] As a result, women will make up a larger proportion of the labor force in the future. In 1979, women made up about 42 percent of the labor force. By 1995, women are expected to compose about 47 percent of the labor force.[103] These data make clear that women will make up a larger segment of the labor force. Additionally women are as likely to favor joining a union as men.[104] As a result women represent a potential focus of unionization drives.

Efforts to organize this increasingly important sector of the labor force appear to be increasing.[105] The Teamsters, Communications Workers of America, and Service Employees International unions have mounted successful drives to organize occupations with high concentrations of women, for example, retail and clerical workers. The Communications Workers are participating in a labor education project to increase the awareness of union functions and activities among clerical workers. Some union organizers believe that such educational and consciousness-raising activities among clerical workers are a necessary, preliminary step to unionization.

COMPARABLE WORTH

About 1980, the issue of comparable worth began to receive attention. The Equal Pay Act requires that men and women performing the same or essentially the same job receive equal pay. Since women are concentrated in a limited number of occupations, their pay has not been affected by the Equal Pay Act. An alternative concept provides for equal pay for work of comparable worth or value to the employer. This approach requires that employers evaluate and classify jobs on the basis of such criteria as skill, effort, and responsibility. Alternative approaches to job evaluation were discussed in Chapter 11.

Comparable worth studies have found numerous examples of salary inequities between female-dominated and male-dominated occupations.[106] For example, women operators of complex word processing equipment earn less than male truck drivers, whose only requirement is a driver's license; registered nurses earn less than tree trimmers and tire servicemen; school teachers earn less than liquor-store clerks. A 1981 Supreme Court decision permits women to bring suit under the Civil Rights Act when they are paid less than men holding jobs of comparable worth or less than comparable worth, as determined by job evaluation.[107]

The recommendations and reactions to this decision presented in two journals whose audience is professional personnel managers suggest there will be great resistance to providing equal pay for comparable worth. One recommendation is that the pay differential between men and women be removed by encouraging women to enter nontraditional occupations. This "go slow" approach, in addition to requiring decades to change the male-female pay differential, asks a great sacrifice, in some cases, from those women going into nontraditional jobs. Numerous examples of the harassment encountered by women in nontraditional jobs can be cited.[108]

A second recommendation is that employers cease performing job evaluation studies and instead establish wages and salaries on the basis of wage and salary surveys.[109] This approach ignores the practical difficulties presented by having to evaluate non-key jobs or jobs unique to an organization. By definition one cannot survey the going rates for such jobs. More importantly, this approach recommends that employers evade the moral and legal obligation of employers to compensate women fairly.

If the managers of many organizations choose to vigorously resist efforts to provide equal pay for comparable worth, this issue alone could be sufficient to achieve a dramatic increase in the unionization of women workers. To achieve this end, unions will have to focus on the comparable-worth issue. There are signs that the American union movement intends to do just that. The AFL-CIO has passed a resolution urging equal pay for comparable worth.[110] The American Federation of State, County, and Municipal Employees (AFSCME) has negotiated for comparable-worth studies in several agreements, which have resulted in job reclassification and wage increases for clerical positions.[111] In addition AFSCME has successfully concluded a strike of San Jose municipal employees that resulted in substantial pay increases for traditionally female jobs on the principle of equal pay for comparable worth.[112] Jerry Wurf, former president of AFSCME, has stated that comparable worth is the economic issue of the '80s.[113]

EFFORTS TO ORGANIZE WHITE-COLLAR WORKERS

Occupational employment projections through 1990 indicate that employment among white-collar occupations will increase at above-average rates while employment among blue-collar occupations will increase at below-average rates.[114] As white-collar workers will continue to make up more and more of the labor force, unions should adopt strategies that will increase the attractiveness of unions to white-collar workers.

In our judgment three trends already in motion provide the nucleus around which such a union strategy can be built. Kochan's study of workers' attitudes toward unions found that two important factors related to supporting a union among white-collar workers were satisfaction with the nature of work and ability to influence work conditions.[115] It is our view that if unions would make a major effort to bargain for and participate in establishing quality-of-worklife programs and QC circles, unions would be perceived by white-collar workers as instrumental in attaining highly important outcomes. Recall that it has been found that perceptions of union instrumentality are the best predictors of union support.[116]

A second trend that is already in motion will, in our opinion, also influence the support for unions among white-collar workers. This trend is the increased use of automated equipment in white-collar occupations. Of 50 million existing jobs, it has been estimated that 20 to 30 million will be affected by 1990, and that eventually 38 million will be affected.[117] About 40 percent of those affected are in secretarial and clerical positions and just under 40 percent are in professional occupations.

The impact of technological change on the occupants of white-collar jobs can vary. Some of the possibilities are displacement and discharge as well as retraining and transfer. There is some evidence that introduction of automated equipment in clerical jobs is associated with establishment of higher performance standards and pressure for increased productivity.[118] These outcomes are mentioned in order to point out some of the human costs of technological change. We expect that employers will tend to overlook or disregard the human costs of technological innovation. Past experience has been that it is labor unions who attempt to cushion the impact of technological change on workers. In discussing the impending widespread introduction of change, Thomas Donahue, secretary-treasurer of the AFL-CIO, has argued that worker adjustment costs must be viewed as part of the cost of innovation.[119]

We expect that many employers will introduce change among white-collar workers in such a way that a need for job security and protection from arbitrary treatment and speedups will become common. In essence, we expect management to aid unions in the organization of white-collar workers.

The final current trend that is relevant to the organization of white-collar workers is union efforts to organize women. About half of all white-collar workers are clerical workers and sales workers.[120] Within these groupings fall many traditionally female occupations. By increasing efforts to organize women, unions are also increasing efforts to organize white-collar workers. In summary, it is our view that the combined impact of these trends will be substantial increases in the unionization of white-collar employees.

Summary

Union membership as a percent of the American labor force has been declining since 1954. Unions are less a force in the American political and economic scene today than was true twenty or thirty years ago. Several factors have influenced this trend, and will continue to create a force toward a reduction in union membership.

Changing patterns of employment by industry and occupation have tended to reduce union membership. Growth in employment in highly unionized sectors of the economy has been low during recent years. Instead rapid growth has been in industries and occupations with historically low levels of unionization. These patterns of change in employment by industry and occupation are projected to continue.

During the next decade or so, rapid changes in technology are expected. It is possible that in ten years automated equipment capable of performing virtually all operative manufacturing jobs will be available. Consequently technological change represents a threat to union membership because it could eliminate many blue-collar jobs. In addition, manufacturing jobs are threatened by foreign competition. Import of finished goods as a proportion of GNP has increased substantially in recent years and is expected to continue increasing.

Other forces that influence union membership are employer efforts to resist unionization and decrease existing levels of unionization. Also worker values are changing. As a result unions are perceived to be less instrumental in attaining outcomes important to workers.

Unions have a number of courses of action available to them that can slow or minimize the loss of jobs for the membership. Included are moderation of bargaining demands in order for employers to meet non-union and foreign competition. Unions can also merge so that greater cooperation among unions is achieved. Unions can also attempt to influence corporate decisions. Approaches to influencing corporate decisions include union representation on the board of directors, control of the availability of capital from pension funds, and employee ownership.

Another approach involves union-employee-employer cooperation at the level of the shop floor. In the last few years many employers have established QC circles and QWL programs which encourage worker participation in decisions concerning the work environment, productivity, and efficiency. It is possible that such programs may lead to a shift from adversarial to cooperative labor relations as the dominant pattern in the United States.

Shifts in efforts to organize workers are needed to reverse the trend of declining union membership as a percent of the labor force. The changes needed are increased efforts to organize the South and West, minority workers, women workers, and white-collar workers. Some unions are changing their organization efforts in order to focus on these segments of the labor force. Also some unions are implementing programs that will increase the instrumentality of unions among white-collar and women employees. If such programs and efforts become widespread among American unions, we anticipate that union membership ranks will be replenished. At a minimum, we expect those unions such as the UAW and AFSCME to survive the challenges facing them. As for the unions that do not change with the times, we expect them to go the way of Tyrannosaurus Rex.

Discussion Questions

1. Describe the relationship between projected change in employment by industry and existing levels of union membership by industry.
2. Discuss the impact that technological change is expected to have on employment in the United States during the next ten to fifteen years and how this may influence union membership.
3. Why are changing worker values relevant to trends in union membership?
4. What impact would plant closure legislation have on job security for union members?

5. Describe alternative approaches unions can use in efforts to influence top-level management decisions.
6. How can QC circles help protect union members' jobs as well as promote cooperative labor relations?
7. Describe steps that are being taken by some unions to organize women members of the labor force.
8. Discuss programs and trends that are likely to increase the unionization of white-collar workers.

Key Concepts

Reindustrialization
Double-breasted shops
Plant closure legislation
Pension fund power
Employee ownership

QC circles
Southern strategy
Neutrality clause
Comparable worth

Notes

1. Jeffery L. Sheler, "Unions on the Run," *U. S. News and World Report,* 14 September 1981, pp. 61–63, 65.
2. Ibid.
3. Ibid.
4. Max L. Carey, "Occupational Employment Growth Through 1990," *Monthly Labor Review,* August 1981, pp. 42–55.
5. Ibid.
6. Thomas A. Kochan, "How American Workers View Labor Unions," *Monthly Labor Review,* April 1979, pp. 23–31.
7. U. S. Department of Labor, Bureau of Labor Statistics, *Directory of National Unions and Employee Associations, 1977,* Bulletin 2044 (Washington D. C.: U. S. Government Printing Office, December 1979), p. 71.
8. Ibid.
9. Ibid.
10. Joann S. Lublin, "As Robot Age Arrives, Labor Seeks Protection Against Loss of Work," *Wall Street Journal,* 26 October 1981, pp. 1, 17.
11. Ibid.
12. "Microelectronics Revolution Will Result in Worldwide Job Loss, Predicts Report," *World of Work Report* 6, no. 1 (January 1981): 2, 7.
13. Ibid.

14. Valerie A. Personick, "The Outlook for Industry Output and Employment Through 1990," *Monthly Labor Review,* August 1981, pp. 28–41.

15. Ibid.

16. "Japan's Edge in Auto Costs," *Business Week,* 14 September 1981, pp. 92, 97.

17. Ibid.

18. Ibid.

19. Everett G. Martin, "Brazil Raises Exports of High Technology to Pace Third World," *Wall Street Journal,* 6 October 1981, pp. 1, 18.

20. Charles L. Hughes, *Making Unions Unnecessary* (New York: Executive Enterprises Publications Co., 1976).

21. Ronald Alsop, "DuPont, Steelworkers Step Up the Intensity of Unionization Battle," *Wall Street Journal,* 28 July 1981, pp. 1, 5.

22. *Fabric of Injustice: The Struggle at J. P. Stevens* (New York: Economic Justice, NCC, 475 Riverside Drive, Room 572, New York, N.Y., 10027, July 1978).

23. "Building Trades Lose Ground," *Business Week,* 9 November 1981, pp. 103–4.

24. "A Pilot Contract that Sets a New Course," *Business Week,* 17 August 1981, pp. 27–29.

25. "The IBT Pact Could Be a Model of Moderation," *Business Week,* 28 September 1981, p. 38.

26. "Why the URW Will Be More of a Team Player," *Business Week,* 28 September 1981, pp. 97, 99.

27. "Building Trades Lose Ground."

28. "Timken Talks Tough to Win Concessions," *Business Week,* 9 November 1981, pp. 43–44.

29. Robert L. Simison, "GM Talks Tough on Labor Costs, Seeking Gains in 1982 Negotiations," *Wall Street Journal,* 27 October 1981, pp. 25, 40.

30. H. L. Sheppard, and N. O. Herrick, *Where Have All the Robots Gone?* (New York: Free Press, 1972), pp. xx, 122–43.

31. Ibid., p. 118.

32. Ibid.

33. Robert S. Greenberger, "Economic Gloom Cuts Labor-Union Demands for Big 1982 Contracts," *Wall Street Journal,* 30 September 1981, pp. 1, 21.

34. Sheler.

35. "A Pilot Contract That Sets a New Course."

36. "Why the URW Will be More of A Team Player."

37. Greenberger, "Economic Gloom Cuts Labor-Union Demands for Big 1982 Contracts."

38. "The IBT Pact Could Be a Model of Moderation."

39. Simison.

40. "Building Trades Lose Ground."

41. "Why the URW Will Be More of a Team Player."

42. "Building Trades Lose Ground."

43. "A Pilot Contract that Sets a New Course."

44. "The IBT Pact Could Be a Model of Moderation."

45. "Why the URW Will Be More of a Team Player."

46. Jerome M. Rosow, "American Labor Unions in the 1980s: Reading the Signs," *Proceedings of the Thirty-Second Annual Meeting* (Madison, WI: University of Wisconsin, Industrial Relations Research Association, 1980), p. 3.

47. "Changing 45 Million Jobs," *Business Week,* 3 August 1981, pp. 62–63, 66–67.

48. "Why the URW Will Be More of a Team Player."

49. "Plant Closure Legislation," *BNA Collective Bargaining Negotiation and Contracts,* 21 August 1980, p. 4.

50. Clark G. Ross, "Labor's Role in Corporate Decision-Making," *The Collegiate Forum,* Fall 1981, p. 1.

51. "Unions On the Board," *BNA Collective Bargaining Negotiation and Contracts,* 15 May 1980, p. 4.

52. Jerome M. Rosow, "Labor Directors in U. S. Boardrooms? Chrysler Experiment May Lead the Way," *World of Work Report,* 6, no. 2 (February 1981): 9, 12–13.

53. Ibid.

54. Ibid.

55. Andrew M. Wallace, "Unions Seek Control of Pension Funds to Create Jobs, Advance Social Goals, Face Practical and Legal Obstacles," *World of Work Report* 6, no. 1 (January 1981): 1, 5–7.

56. Ibid.

57. "Targeting Pension Investments," *Business Week,* 7 September 1981, pp. 87–88.

58. Wallace.

59. Ibid.

60. Ibid.

61. D. C. Jones, "Producer Co-operatives in Industrialized Western Economics," *British Journal of Industrial Relations* 18 (July 1980): 141–54.

62. T. C. Jochim, "Employee Stock Ownership Programs: The Next Economic Revolution?" *Academy of Management Review,* 4, no. 3, (1979): 439–42.

63. R. Mazzolini, "The Influence of European Workers Over Corporate Strategy," *Sloan Management Review,* Spring 1978, pp. 59–81.

64. Survey Research Center, University of Michigan for the Economic Development Administration, U. S. Department of Commerce, *Employee Ownership,* unpublished report, 1977. Cited by T. C. Jochim, "Employee Stock Ownership Programs: The Next Economic Revolution?" in *Academy of Management Review* 4, no. 3 (1979): 439–42.

65. Jochim.

66. Penny Singer, "Employees Buy Majority Interest in Rath; Plan Staves Off Company Bankruptcy," *World of Work Report* 5, no. 9 (September 1980): 57, 60–61.

67. "Conference on Productivity Urges Constructive Dialogue Between Sectors," *World of Work Report* 5 no. 6, (June 1980): 41, 44–45.

68. T. R. Donahue, "AFL-CIO Leader Calls for 'Creative' Approach to Technological Change," *World of Work Report* 5 no. 6, (June 1980), pp. 43–44.

69. "The New Industrial Relations," *Business Week,* 11 May 1981, pp. 85–87, 89–90, 92–93, 96, 98.

70. "U. S. Chamber of Commerce Finds Workers Want to Raise Productivity; Seek Recognition, Decision-Making Role," *World of Work Report* 5, no. 11 (November 1980): 73, 79.

71. Frank K. Plous, "The Quality Circle Concept: Growing by Leaps and Bounds," *World of Work Report* 6, no. 4 (April 1981): 25–27.

72. Robert S. Greenberger, "Quality Circles Grow, Stirring Union Worries," *Wall Street Journal,* 22 September 1981, p. 25.

73. David Soyka, "Honeywell Pioneers in Quality Circle Movement," *World of Work Report* 6, no. 9 (September 1981): 65–67.

74. Plous.

75. "A Try at Steel-Mill Harmony," *Business Week,* 29 June 1981, pp. 132–33.

76. "The New Industrial Relations."

77. Greenberger, "Quality Circles Grow, Stirring Union Worries."

78. Ibid.

79. "A Try at Steel-Mill Harmony."

80. "The New Industrial Relations."

81. "A Try at Steel-Mill Harmony."

82. "The New Industrial Relations."

83. Greenberger, "Economic Gloom Cuts Labor-Union Demands for Big 1982 Contracts."

84. Irving Bluestone, "Emerging Trends in Collective Bargaining," *Work in America, The Decade Ahead,* eds. Clark Kerr and Jerome M. Rosow (New York: Van Norstrand Reinhold Co., 1979), pp. 231–52.

85. Fred Solowey, "They Did It in San Jose!!!," *Public Employee,* 46, no. 8 (August 1981): 4.

86. Thomas Donahue, "Productivity Through Equal Partnership," *World of Work Report* 6, no. 4 (April 1981): 25, 27–28.

87. Greenberger, "Quality Circles Grow, Stirring Union Worries."

88. "A Try At Steel-Mill Harmony."

89. "Quality of Worklife at GM," *BNA Collective Bargaining Negotiations and Contracts,* December 1979, p. 4.

90. "U. S. Chamber of Commerce Finds Workers Want to Raise Productivity; Seek Recognition, Decision-Making Role."

91. Andrew M. Wallace, "Workplace Reforms Involve Employees, Increase Productivity in Dana Plants," *World of Work Report,* 5, nos. 7 and 8 (July/August 1980): 49, 54–55.

92. Rosow, "American Labor Unions in the 1980s: Reading the Signs."

93. Kochan.

94. "Outlook for Labor in the 1980s," *BNA Collective Bargaining Negotiations and Contracts,* 20 August 1981, p. 4.

95. "Unions in the Sunbelt," *BNA Collective Bargaining Negotiations and Contracts,* 25 December 1980, p. 4.

96. "23,000 State Office Workers Vote AFSCME in Florida," *Public Employee,* 46, no. 7, (July 1981): 3.

97. "The Neutrality Issue," *BNA Collective Bargaining Negotiations and Contracts,* 26 July 1979, p. 4.

98. "Labor's New Campaign to Crack the Sunbelt," *Business Week,* 19 October 1981, pp. 43–44.

99. H. N. Fullerton, "The 1995 Labor Force: A First Look," *Monthly Labor Review,* December 1980, pp. 11–21.

100. Carey.

101. "Labor's New Campaign to Crack the Sunbelt."

102. Carey.

103. Ibid.

104. Kochan.

105. Jill Casner-Lotto, "Unions Renew Efforts to Organize Office and Service Workers with an Assist from Women, Women's Groups," *World of Work Report* 5, no. 2 (February 1980): 9, 12–13.

106. Jill Casner-Lotto, "Equal Pay for Work of Comparable Worth Urged by Women's Groups, Unions, EEOC; Cite Fair Job Evaluation as Problem," *World of Work Report* 5, no. 12 (December 1980): 81, 84–85.

107. M. F. Carter, "Comparable Worth: An Idea Whose Time Has Come?" *Personnel Journal,* October 1981, pp. 792–94.

108. Carol Hymowitz, "Women Coal Miners Fight for Their Rights to Life, Shovel, Lug," *Wall Street Journal,* 10 September 1981, pp. 1, 20.

109. J. T. Brinks, "The Comparable Worth Issue: A Salary Administration Bombshell," *Personnel Administrator,* November 1981, pp. 37–40.

110. Casner-Lotto, "Equal Pay for Work of Comparable Worth Urged by Women's Groups, Unions, EEOC; Cite Fair Job Evaluation as Problem."

111. Ibid.

112. Solowey.

113. Ibid.

114. Carey.

115. Kochan.

116. Ibid.

117. "Changing 45 Million Jobs."

118. Ibid.

119. Donahue, "AFL-CIO Leader Calls for 'Creative Approach to Technological Change."

120. Carey.

Suggested Readings

Bluestone, I. "Emerging Trends in Collective Bargaining." In *Work in America: The Decade Ahead,* edited by Clark Kerr and Jerome M. Rosow. New York: Van Norstrand Reinhold Co., 1979, pp. 231–52.

Kochan, T. A. "How American Workers View Labor Unions." *Monthly Labor Review,* April 1979, pp. 23–31.

Rosow, J. M. "American Labor Unions in the 1980s: Reading the Signs." In *Proceedings of the Thirty-Second Annual Meeting.* Madison, WI: University of Wisconsin, Industrial Relations Research Association, 1980, pp. 1–11.

Name Index

Aaron, Benjamin, 570, 599
Abel, I.W., 328, 340
Abel, Theodore, 121
Adams, J. Stacy, 182
Alderfer, Clayton P., 162, 182
Alexander, Robert J., 626
Allen, Fredrick Lewis, 159
Allen, Robert E., 168, 182, 373
Alsop, Ronald, 651
Anderson, Arvid, 570, 599
Anderson, Howard J., 340, 413
Anderson, John C., 183, 590, 591, 592, 599
Antos, Joseph R., 182, 183
Ariizumi, Toru, 628
Ashenfelter, Orley, 443

Baer, Walter E., 339
Bakke, E. Wright, 160
Balfour, C., 627
Ball, Robert E., 412
Barbash, Jack., 28, 443
Bauman, A., 412
Beal, Edwin F., 268, 491
Belcher, David W., 373
Bennet, N.D., 593, 599
Bent, Alan E., 568, 569, 598, 599
Berenbeim, Ronald, 633, 634
Berger, M., 121
Berman, Harold J., 60
Berman, M., 182
Bigoness, William J., 168, 182
Blandin, J., 182
Block, Richard N., 443
Bloom, Gordon F., 340
Bluestone, Irving, 28, 643, 644, 652, 654
Blum, Adrienne, 44
Bok, Derek C., 60, 88, 268, 308, 568
Bornstein, Tim, 88, 152
Boyle, Tony, 116
Brackett, J.C., 373
Bragg, Charlie, 487, 492
Brandeis, Louis, 43, 44
Bredhoff, Elliot, 268
Brett, Randall, 152
Bridwell, L.G., 182
Briggs, Vernon M., 412
Brinks, J.T., 653
Brittain, Jack, 122
Bronstein, A.S., 629
Brooks, Harold E., 339
Brooks, Thomas R., 59, 121, 133, 151, 153
Brown, Bert R., 268
Brown, Charles, 372
Brown, Henry K., 527
Buckley, William F., 419
Bunker, Charles S., 568
Busman, Gloria, 183
Butler, Erik P., 411

Cahn, Sidney L., 526
Campbell, John P., 182
Carey, Max L., 650, 653
Carnegie, Andrew, 132, 133
Carter, M.F., 653
Cartter, Allan M., 268

Casner-Lotto, Jill, 653
Chafetz, I., 183, 184
Chamberlain, Neil W., 59, 237, 246, 267, 268, 308, 309, 479, 491, 492, 568
Chandler, Mark, 182, 183
Cheit, Earl F., 181, 412, 413
Ciller, O.U., 413
Clark, Emily C., 60
Clark, Kim B., 372
Clark, R. Theodore, Jr., 570
Cohen, Frederick C., 88
Cohen, Sanford, 28
Coleman, John R., 28
Coleman, John S., 122
Commons, John R., 28
Connolly, Walter B., 309
Constantino, George E., 282
Coolidge, Calvin, 45, 541
Cordova, Efren, 627
Cox, Archibald, 60, 64, 88, 260, 268, 340
Crickmer, Barry, 412
Crowley, James C., 183
Cullen, Donald E., 252, 268, 308, 331, 339, 340, 341

Dahl, Robert A., 569
Davey, Harold W., 526
Debs, Eugene V., 132
Decker, Kurt, 569
DeCotiis, Thomas A., 182, 184
DeMent, Sandy, 412
Dennis, Barbara D., 183
Dereshinsky, Ralph, 310
Doeringer, Peter B., 443, 444
Donahue, Thomas, 631, 640, 642, 643, 648, 652, 653
Donnelly, James H., Jr., 151
Douglas, Ann, 317, 339
Douglas, William O., 498, 499
Douty, H.M., 373
Driscoll, J.W., 152
Dubinsky, David, 101
Dulles, Foster Rhea, 60, 94, 96, 101, 122, 131, 151
Dunlop, John T., 19, 20, 22, 25, 26, 29, 267, 268, 308, 372, 568
Dunnette, Marvin D., 182, 443
Dyer, Lee, 183, 373, 412

Edwards, Harry T., 526, 568, 570
Elkouri, Edna A., 492, 518, 526, 527, 598
Elkouri, Frank, 492, 518, 526, 527, 598
Estey, Martin, 121, 122

Fairweather, Owen, 526, 527
Fanning, John H., 137, 151
Farber, Henry S., 340
Feigenbaum, Charles, 558, 570
Feild, Hubert S., 183
Feldacker, Bruce, 71, 73, 87, 268
Ferguson, Robert H., 373, 374
Feuille, Peter, 182, 558, 569, 570, 599
Finkle, Robert, 443
Finley, M.H., 628
Fischer, Ben, 526

Flanagan, Robert J., 619, 628
Fleishman, Edwin A., 492
Flemming, R.W., 522, 525, 526, 527
Flynn, Ralph J., 588
Fossum, John A., 373, 412
Fox, A., 412
Frankfurter, Felix, 36, 59
Fraser, C.R.P., 183, 184
Fraser, Douglas, 640
Frazier, Henry B., 598
Freedman, Audrey, 141, 145, 147, 148, 152, 153, 373, 374
Freeman, John, 122
Freeman, Richard, 182, 183, 184, 443
French, Wendell L., 412
Frey, John P., 101
Friedman, Marvin, 413
Fritz, Richard J., 282, 308, 310
Frost, Carl F., 373
Frumkin, R., 412
Fuller, Melville W., 40
Fullerton, H.N., 653
Fulmer, William E., 152, 183

Garson, David G., 627
Gentil, Edwardo B., 626
Gerhart, Paul F., 589, 591
Getman, Julius E., 168, 182, 184, 188, 206, 208, 214, 215
Gibson, James L., 151
Gilman, T.A., 183
Gilroy, Thomas P., 570
Gitlow, Abraham, 568
Glueck, William F., 412
Godine, Morton R., 568
Goldberg, Arthur J., 122, 550
Goldberg, James P., 372
Goldberg, Joseph P., 87, 443
Goldberg, Stephen B., 182, 184, 188, 206, 208, 214, 215
Goldfarb, Robert S., 411, 412
Goldman, Alvin L., 60, 310
Gompers, Samuel, 43, 94, 95, 97, 100
Gordon, T.J., 413
Gorman, Robert A., 60, 88, 268
Gouldner, Alvin W., 310
Granof, Michael H., 413
Green, William, 100, 103, 104
Greenberger, Robert S., 651, 652, 653
Greene, Nathan, 36, 59
Greenman, Russell L., 411, 412, 413
Greer, Charles R., 138, 152, 153
Gregory, Charles O., 33, 59
Greiner, William R., 60
Grob, Gerald N., 121
Grodin, Joseph R., 570, 599
Grunsky, Robert, 339

Hackman, J.R., 183
Hagburg, Eugene C., 569, 570
Hamermesh, Daniel S., 570
Hammer, T.H., 182
Hanna, Mark, 133
Hanslowe, Kurt L., 568
Harbison, Fredrick H., 28
Harris, Edwin F., 492
Harrison, Allan J., 527
Hayes, Rutherford, 131

655

NAME

Hayford, Stephen L., 564, 570
Hays, Paul R., 527
Haywood, William, 98, 99
Healy, James J., 159, 181, 268, 269, 314, 339, 417, 443, 444, 481, 491
Helburn, I.B., 593, 599
Henderson, Richard J., 373
Heneman, Herbert G., III, 182, 373, 412, 526
Herman, Jeanne B., 182, 184, 188, 206, 208, 214, 215
Herrick, Neal Q., 176, 178, 183, 184, 651
Hershfield, David C., 621, 622, 628, 629
Heckman, Charles W., 122, 182
Hildebrand, George H., 569
Hill, Marvin, Jr., 527
Hillman, Sidney, 101
Hoffa, James, 247
Hoffman, Fredrick L., 181
Holley, William H., 183
Horton, Raymond D., 593, 599
Howard, Charles P., 101, 373
Howlett, Robert, 570
Hoxie, Robert F., 97
Hughes, Charles L., 152, 183, 651
Huhn, Kenneth C., 87
Hunt, James W., 215
Hunter, L.C., 372, 374
Hutcheson, William L., 101
Hutchinson, John, 121
Hyclack, Thomas, 182
Hymowitz, Carol, 653

Imberman, Woodruff, 152
Ingrassia, Anthony F., 598
Ivancevich, John M., 151

Jack, Harold H., 413
Jackson, John H., 151, 152
Jackson, L., 215
Jacques, Elliot, 373
Janus, Charles J., 122
Jascourt, Hugh D., 569, 570, 586, 599
Javits, Jacob, 340
Jochim, T.C., 652
Johnson, Lyndon B., 348, 577
Jones, D.C., 652

Kagel, Sam, 326, 515, 526, 527
Kahan, A., 628
Kahn, Robert L., 122
Kalb, W.J., 308
Karsh, B., 628, 629
Kassalow, Everett, 568
Katz, Harry C., 340
Kawada, Hisashi, 628
Keaveny, Timothy J., 151, 168, 182, 373
Kelly, H.H., 268
Kennedy, John F., 56, 83, 348, 544, 574, 585
Kennedy, Thomas, 295, 336, 337
Kerr, Clark, 652, 654
Kienast, Philip K., 268, 491
Kilgour, John G., 413

Killingsworth, Charles C., 339
King, Allan G., 268, 412
Kirkland, Lane, 118, 631, 640
Kistler, Alan, 152
Klauser, Jack E., 569
Kochan, Thomas A., 152, 168, 169, 170, 177, 182, 183, 184, 269, 340, 559, 569, 570, 587, 591, 599, 645, 647, 650, 653, 654
Kovach, Kenneth A., 598
Koziara, Edward C., 268, 568, 570, 598
Kressel, Kenneth, 569
Krislov, Joseph, 175, 183, 308
Kuczynski, J., 181
Kuechle, D., 629
Kuhn, James W., 59, 246, 267, 268, 308, 443, 479, 491, 492

Lamb, E., 373
Langsner, Adolph, 372, 373, 374
Lawler, Edward E., III, 161, 182, 360, 361, 373, 374, 413, 491
LeBleu, R.E., 412
Lefkowitz, Jerome, 341
Lelouarn, J.Y., 182, 184
Levin, Richard A., 340
Levine, Marvin J., 433, 569, 570
Levine, S.B., 628, 629
Levitan, Sar A., 411
Levy, Moses, 59
Lewin, David, 28, 569, 592, 593, 599
Lewis, H. Gregg, 599
Lewis, John L., 100, 101, 102, 104
Lewis, R., 215
Lewis, William, 309
Lieberman, Elias, 38, 59
Liebes, Richard, 510, 526
Leigh, D.E., 444
Lipset, Seymour M., 121, 122
Lipsky, David B., 183, 570
Livernash, E. Robert, 159, 181, 269, 417, 443, 444, 481, 491, 492
Loewenberg, J. Joseph, 568, 569, 570, 598
Lublin, Joann S., 650

McCarthy, W.E.J., 627
McClellan, John L., 88
McClennan, W. Howard, 588
McCulloch, Frank W., 88
McDonald, Lois, 115, 121, 122
McDowell, Douglas M., 87
McGregor, Douglas, 128, 151
McGuiness, Kenneth C., 87, 214, 215
McKelvey, Jean T., 569
McKersie, Robert B., 233, 250, 252, 254, 255, 256, 257, 267, 268, 269, 372, 374
McLaughlin, Doris B., 80, 88
Macy, John W., Jr., 568
Mahoney, Thomas A., 443
Maloney, William F., 372
Mangum, Garth L., 411
Marshall, F. Ray, 268, 411, 412, 569
Marshall, Howard D., 268
Marshall, Natalie J., 268
Martin, Douglas, 152

Martin, Everett G., 651
Martin, James E., 568
Martin, Stanley A., 138, 152, 153
Marx, Herbert L., Jr., 598
Maslow, Abraham H., 161, 179, 181
Mazzolini, Renato, 609, 627, 652
Meany, George, 103, 104, 117, 118, 119, 137, 152
Medoff, James, 372, 373
Mellow, Wesley, 182, 183
Menard, Arthur P., 525
Merrifield, Leroy S., 526
Merry, R.W., 215
Meyers, Frederick, 442
Michels, Robert, 114
Miller, Glenn W., 29
Miller, Ronald L., 282, 308
Millis, Harry A., 60, 135, 151
Mills, Daniel Q., 282
Mills, T., 152
Miner, John B., 151
Miner, Mary B., 151
Mittenthal, Richard, 308, 526
Montgomery, Royal E., 135, 151
Moore, B.E., 152
Morgan, Cyril P., 152
Morrall, John F., 411
Morris, Charles J., 60, 88
Morse, Bruce, 308
Moskow, Michael H., 568, 569, 570, 598, 599
Mossberg, W.S., 492
Murray, Phillip, 101, 103, 104
Murray, V.V., 481, 491
Myers, M. Scott, 152, 153

Nash, Alan, 492
Nash, Peter, 502, 525
Nesbitt, Murray B., 568
Newborn, Norton N., 340
Nixon, Richard, 56, 83, 340, 577
Northrup, Herbert R., 340, 624

Odewahn, Charles A., 308
O'Hara, John F., 508, 526
Okochi, K., 628, 629
O'Reilly, Charles A., III, 183

Page, Charles, 121
Parnes, Herbert S., 182
Patten, Thomas H., Jr., 372
Peach, David A., 492, 629
Perlman, Richard, 569
Perlman, Selig, 91, 121, 122, 129, 151
Personick, Valerie A., 174, 634, 651
Peters, Edward, 269, 500, 525, 527
Peterson, Richard B., 568
Pfeffer, Jeffrey, 444
Pierson, Frank C., 373
Piore, Michael J., 444
Plous, Frank K., 652
Poli, Robert, 290
Ponak, Allen M., 559, 570
Porket, J.L., 627, 628, 629
Powderly, Terence V., 92, 93, 94, 97
Powell, L.B., 140, 152
Power, J.F., 491

NAME INDEX

Prasow, Paul, 500, 525, 527
Prichard, Robert D., 182
Pullman, George, 132, 133

Quakenbush, R.A., 411
Quinn, Robert P., 183

Raffaele, J.A., 527
Ramondt, Joop, 628, 629
Rand, James H., Jr., 134, 135
Reagan, Ronald, 383
Reede, Arthur H., 181
Rees, Albert, 442
Reeves, T. Zane, 568, 569, 598, 599
Rehmus, Charles M., 60, 340
Rehnquist, William H., 504, 525
Repas, Bob F., 598
Reuther, Walter, 103, 104, 118, 119
Reynolds, Lloyd G., 372, 442, 443, 444
Richardson, Reed, 283, 285, 308
Robbins, Eva, 569
Robinson, J.W., 481, 492
Rock, Eli, 561, 570
Roemisch, Roger, 282, 308
Roosevelt, Franklin, 551, 574
Roosevelt, Theodore, 573
Rose, T., 443
Rosen, Hjalmar, 121, 181
Rosow, Jerome M., 651, 652, 653, 654
Ross, Anne M., 568
Ross, Clark G., 651
Ross, Jerry, 444
Ross, Mary, 412
Ross, Philip, 66
Ross, T.L., 152
Rothman, Stuart, 87
Rothschild, Donald P., 526
Rowan, Richard L., 268, 569, 629
Rubin, Jeffrey F., 268
Ruble, Blair A., 628
Ruh, R.A., 373
Ruhl, J., 152
Russo, Anthony C., 570
Ruttenberg, Stanley H., 619

Sanction, T.A., 628
Sangerman, Harry, 152
Sayles, Leonard, 121, 122
Scheinman, Martin F., 527
Schilling, Jane M., 309
Schlagheck, James L., 626, 629
Schlossberg, S.I., 214, 215
Schmertz, Eric J., 411, 412, 413
Schmitt, D., 412
Schneider, B.V.H., 598
Schoomaker, Anita W., 80, 88
Schriesheim, Chester A., 168, 182
Schulman, Harry, 237
Schwab, Donald P., 182, 373, 412

Seidman, B., 412
Selekman, Benjamin M., 126, 151, 267
Seligman, Daniel, 628
Shaw, Lee C., 568, 570, 598
Shaw, Lemuel, 34, 35
Sheler, Jeffrey L., 650, 651
Sheppard, Harold L., 176, 178, 183, 184, 651
Sherman, F.E., 214, 215
Shirai, Taishiro, 628
Shister, Joseph, 267
Siedman, Joel, 569
Siegal, Jay S., 525
Simison, Robert L., 651
Simkin, William E., 292, 317, 340, 341, 388
Singer, Penny, 652
Sinicropi, Anthony V., 527, 564, 570
Slichter, Sumner H., 159, 181, 268, 417, 443, 444, 481, 491, 492
Sloane, Arthur A., 29, 443
Smith, W.E., 628
Snee, John, 412
Solowey, Fred, 653
Somers, Anne R., 158, 181
Somers, Gerald C., 178, 340, 373, 374, 443
Somers, Herman M., 158, 181
Sosnick, Stephen H., 340
Soyka, David, 652
Sparks, Phillip, 152
Spero, Sterling D., 598
Stagner, Ross, 122, 181
Staines, Graham, 183
Standohar, Paul, 569
Stanley, David T., 594, 599
Stephens, Uriah, 92
Stern, James L., 183, 570, 599
Stevens, Carl, 269
Steiber, Jack, 340, 550, 569, 598
Strasser, Adolph, 96, 97
Strauss, Donald B., 339
Strauss, George, 121, 122, 179, 183
Stringari, Arthur M., 282, 308, 310
Sturmthal, Adolf, 627, 629
Summers, Clyde W., 291, 308, 569
Suttle, J.L., 183
Swart, J.C., 412
Sylvis, William, 92
Szilagyi, Andrew D., 182

Taft, Philip, 88, 103, 121, 122, 129, 151, 153, 158, 181
Taft, William H., 573
Tannenbaum, Arnold S., 122
Taylor, Benjamin J., 43, 59, 84, 88, 151, 308, 443, 444, 525
Taylor, George W., 373, 412
Thomas, W., 373

Thompson, Mark, 183
Thomson, A.W.J., 478, 481, 491, 492, 627
Thorp, Cary D., 443
Tobin, Daniel J., 101
Trotta, Maurice S., 489, 492
Trow, M.A., 122
Turnbull, J.G., 181, 412, 413
Turner, J.T., 481, 492

Ulman, Lloyd, 550, 569, 629
Usery, W.J., 526
Uterberger, S. Herbert, 268

Vargas, Getúlio, 603
Vroom, Victor H., 162, 182

Wahba, Mamood A., 182
Wakeley, J.H., 373
Wallace, Andrew M., 652, 653
Wallace, Marc J., 182
Walton, Richard E., 233, 250, 252, 254, 255, 256, 257, 267, 268, 269
Ware, Norma J., 121
Warshal, B.S., 442
Watts, Glen, 631, 640
Weber, A.R., 619, 628
Weeks, Brian, 627
Wellington, Harry H., 569
Westerkamp, Patrick, R., 526
Wheeler, Hoyt N., 492, 557, 559, 570, 591, 599
White, J. Kenneth, 152
Wickersham, Edward D., 268, 491
Williams, C. Arthur, 181, 412, 413
Williams, Walter E., 411
Winpisinger, William W., 178
Winters, Ralph K., 569
Wise, Helen D., 588
Witney, Fred, 29, 43, 59, 84, 88, 151, 308, 412, 443, 444, 525
Witte, Edwin E., 59
Woll, Matthew, 101
Woodworth, Robert T., 568
Wurf, Jerry, 588, 647

Yablonski, Joseph, 116
Yager, Paul, 340
Yoder, Dale, 526

Zack, Arnold M., 569
Zagoria, Sam, 568, 569, 598
Zalusky, John, 525, 526
Zeman, H.F., 372
Zimand, S., 152
Ziskind, David, 598
Zollitsch, Herbert G., 372, 373, 374

Subject Index

Ability to pay, 345-347, 370
   elasticity of demand and, 346-347
   future stability, 346
   Truitt decision and, 347
Accident rates, 381
Accommodation, 126-127
Adair v. U.S., 38
Adversarial labor-management relations, 6-7
Age Discrimination Act, 380, 395, 409
Agency shop, 418
   incidence of, 423
Air Line Pilots Association, 638-639
Air Traffic Controllers Organization, 290-291
Airline Deregulation Act, 245
Alexander v. Gardner-Denver Co., 503-504, 523
Allen-Bradley v. Local Union No. 3, 48
Ally doctrine, 303
Amalgamated Clothing and Textile Workers Union, 304, 645
Ambulatory picketing, 302-303
American Arbitration Association, 506
American Federation of Labor, 90, 94-102, 119, 416-417
   basic principles of, 95-98
American Federation of Labor-Congress of Industrial Organizations, 119, 417, 420, 621, 631, 639, 640, 642-643, 645-648
   committee on political education, 106-107
   executive council of, 104-106
   functions of, 108-109
   general board of, 106
   local unions and, 107
   merger of, 102-104
   national unions and, 107
   standing committees of, 106
   state and local bodies and, 107-108
   structure and government of, 104-108
   trade and industrial departments of, 106
American Federation of State, County and Municipal Workers, 645, 647, 649
American Motors, 640
American Plan, 134, 416
American Ship Building case, 296
Annual improvement factor, 349
Anti-trust legislation, 39-45, 541
   double standard, 43-44
   rule of reason and, 43-44
Anti-trust prosecution, 132
Apathy, union member, 114, 120
Appropriate bargaining unit, 195-197
Arbitration, 325-329, 477
   combining mediation and, 326
   types of, 325-326
Arbitration clause, 505-506
Arbitration, compulsory, 326, 557-560
   chilling effect of, 557-558
   effects on negotiations, 337
   narcotic effect of, 557-558
   problems with, 557-558
Arbitration decisions, 516-518
   contract interpretation cases, 517-518

discipline/discharge cases, 518
   guidelines for, 517-518
Arbitration, final-offer, 558-559
   impact of, 559
   issue by issue, 558
   package selection, 558
Arbitration, grievance, 494-495
   advantages of, 504-505
   Alexander v. Gardner-Denver Co., 503-504
   Civil Rights Act, 503-504
   Collyer Insulated Wire Co., 502
   contract clauses and preparation for, 509-510
   evaluation of, 518-523
   expedited arbitration, 520
   factors in decision to arbitrate, 508-509
   facts of the grievance and preparation for, 510-511
   International Harvester Co. decision, 501-502
   Labor Management Relations Act and, 496
   legalistic, 522-523
   length of, 520-522
   Lincoln Mills decision and, 496-497
   national labor policy and, 495-496
   National Labor Relations Board and, 500-502
   number of arbitrators, 507
   payment of arbitrators, 507
   preparation for, 509-512
   problems with, 519-523
   rising costs of, 519-520
   selection of arbitrator, 506, 511-512
   Spielberg Manufacturing Company decision, 501-503
   Steelworkers Trilogy and, 497-500
   theory of the case and preparation for, 511
   Torrington Co. v. The Metal Products Workers, Local 1645, 500
   Uniform Arbitration Act, 500-501
   USW v. American Manufacturing Company and, 497-498
   USW v. Enterprise Wheel and Car, 499-500
   USW v. Warrior and Gulf Navigation, 498-499
Arbitration hearing, 512-516
   checklist for, 515
   closing arguments, 515
   opening of, 513
   opening statements, 513-514
   presentation of cases, 514-515
   stating the issue, 513
   swearing in witnesses, 514
Arbitration, interest, 325, 494-495
Arbitration, rights, 494-495
Arbitration, voluntary, 325
   Experimental Negotiating Agreement and, 326-329
Arbitrators
   desired characteristics of, 511-512
   selection of, 506, 511-512
   training of, 522
Area of interdependency, 239-240

Armour automation committee, 313
Arsenal of weapons, 333-334, 596
Attitudes toward unions, management, 126-127
   accommodation, 126-127
   collusion, 126-127
   controlled hostility, 126-127
   cooperation, 126-127
   open hostility, 126-127
Attitudinal structuring, 254-257
Authority, functional, 143-144
Authority, staff, 142-143
Authorization cards, 186-188
   uses of, 186-188
Authorization card campaign, 186
   limits on unions, 189-191
   management response to, 188
Autonomy of national unions, 95

Bad faith bargaining, 260-261
Bakery and Pastry Drivers v. Wohl, 299-300
Bargaining impasses, third party efforts to resolve, 317-329
   arsenal of weapons, 333-334
   benefits of mediation, 323-324
   emergency disputes, 329-335
   Experimental Negotiating Agreement, 326-329
   Federal Mediation and Conciliation Service and, 324-325
   government intervention, 329-335
   interest arbitration, 325
   Labor-Management Relations Act and, 329-332
   mediation, 317-318
   mediator's functions, 318-323
   statutory strike, 334
Bargaining issues, 158-160
   child labor, 159
   discipline, 160
   historical view of, 158-160
   hours, 159
   job security, 158-159
   public sector bargaining and, 564-566
   safety, 158-159
   wages, 158-159
Bargaining outcomes in the public sector, determinants of, 590-592
Bargaining power, 239-249, 266
   area of interdependency, 239-240
   costs of agreeing, 241-242
   costs of disagreeing, 241-242
   settlement range, 240-241
   summary of, 249
Bargaining range, definition of, 241-242
Bargaining, responsibility for, 145-146
Bargaining team, 281-283
   personal characteristics of, 282
Bargaining unit
   problems with in the public sector, 561-562
   types in the public sector, 562
Bargaining unit determination
   issues in public sector unionism, 566
   public sector and, 560-564
Bargaining unit, public sector
   horizontal, 562

SUBJECT INDEX

inclusion of supervisors, 563-564
tier, 562
vertical, 562
Baseball strike, 245
Bedford Cut Stone Co., 46-47
Bedford Cut Stone Co. v. the Journeyman Stone Cutters' Association, 43-44
Blacklisting, 38, 92, 133, 416
Boys Market v. Retail Clerks, 48, 427-428
Brazil, 635
Brazilian labor relations, 602-604
  background, 603
  functions of unions, 604
  government role in, 603-604
  resolution of disputes, 604
  union finances, 604
Bread and butter unionism, 96. *See also* Business unionism
Brooks v. NLRB, 263
Budd Mfg. Co., Edward G., v. NLRB, 202
Budget estimates, 353-354
Buffalo Forge Co. v. the United Steelworkers Union, 298
Bumping, 431
Bureau of Labor Statistics, 280, 353, 354-355, 363-364, 474
Bureau of National Affairs, 280, 426, 439
Business agent, 111-112
Business unionism, 95, 97

Cafeteria benefit plan, 397
Call-back pay, 389
Call-in pay, 389
Canadian Labour Congress, 621
Captive audience speeches, 203-204
Carnegie Steel Corporation, 132-133
Cease-and-desist orders, 263-265
Centralized decision making, in labor relations area, 145-146
Certification election procedures, 191-208
  appropriate bargaining unit, 193, 195-197
  bargaining order, 212
  challenged ballots, 209
  conduct during the pre-election period, 200
  contract and election bars, 194-195
  discrimination, 202
  election, 209
  election petition, 191-193
  employer behavior during the organizing campaign, 200-204
  interrogation and polling, 202
  NLRB election orders, 198-200
  NLRB investigation, 193-195
  NLRB jurisdiction, 193
  objections to the election, 210-212
  promise of benefit, 203
  qualifications of the employee representative, 193
  question of representation, 193
  run-off elections, 209-210
  show of interest, 193
  union behavior during the pre-election period, 204-205
Certification elections, 175-176
Chamber of Commerce, 383
Check-off, 423-424
Chief steward, 111
Choice of dispute resolution procedures, 559-560
Chrysler Corporation, 149, 638, 640
City central, 91
Civil Rights Act, 379-380, 409, 435-436, 646
  grievance arbitration and, 503-504
Civil Service Act, 573
Civil Service Commission, 573
Civil service commissions, 542
Civil Service Reform Act, 56-57, 579-584, 595-596
  arbitration, 583
  employee rights under, 580
  General Counsel, 581
  grievance procedures, 583
  judicial review, 583
  scope of negotiations, 582
Clause book, 274
Clayton Act, 41-42
Closed shop, 133, 418
Closed shop agreements, 263
Coalition, 160
Codetermination, 149, 608-610, 640
  American reaction to, 610
  effects of, 609
COLA. *See* Cost of living allowance
Collective bargaining
  continuous nature of, 236-237
  diversified relationships and, 237-238
  evolutionary nature of, 238
  group relationships and, 235-236
  objectives of, 233-234
  private relationship, 238-239
Collective bargaining, free, 335-337
Collective bargaining, legal requirements of, 258-265
  duration of obligation to bargain, 263
  good faith bargaining, 258-261
  illegal subjects, 263
  mandatory subjects, 262
  NLRB remedies, 263-264
  permissive subjects, 262
  subjects of bargaining, 262-263
  tenets of good faith bargaining, 260-261
Collective bargaining legislation, state level, 585-587
Collective bargaining, public sector, 537-565
  role of strikes, 551-553
Collective bargaining, techniques for improving, 312-316
  continuous bargaining, 313-314
  early-bird negotiations, 315-316
  prebargaining fact finding, 314-315
Collusion, 126-127
Collyer Insulated Wire Co., 502, 523
Commerce Clearing House, 280
Committee on political education (COPE), 106-107
Committees, employee, 139-140
Common law, 31
Common situs picketing, 300-302
Commonwealth v. Hunt, 34-35, 129-130. *See also* Criminal conspiracy doctrine
Communications Workers of America, 631, 640, 646
Company union, 64
  and employee committees, 139-140
Compressed work week, 390-391
Concession bargaining, 13-15
Conditional autonomy, 104
Conference Board, 141, 144, 146, 357-359
Congress of Industrial Organizations, 90, 98-102, 119, 416-417
Conrail, 638
Conservative Party, 605
Conspiracy doctrine, 129-130
Consumer boycott, 271, 303-304, 306
  handbilling and, 303-304
  picketing and, 303-304
Consumer Price Index, 355-356, 371
Continental Baking decision, 196
Continuous bargaining, 313-314, 325, 338
  need for, 314
Contract administration, responsibility for, 145-146
Contract and election bars, 194-195
Contract proposals, cost of, 403-404
Contract rejection, 291-296
  implications of, 294-296
  internal union politics and, 292-294
  number of, 292
Controlled hostility, 126-127
Cooling-off period, 330-331
Cooperation, 126-127
  union-management, 148-149
Coors Co., 297, 304
Coppage v. Kansas, 38
Coronado Coal Co. v. the United Mine Workers of America, 43
Corporate campaign, 304-306
Costing out a labor agreement, 397-409, 410
  cost of a new agreement, 399-403
  cost of proposed changes, 403-404
  end loading and, 407-408
  front loading and, 407-408
  how to, 398-403
  human resource planning and, 405-406
  impact on profits, 406-407
  importance of, 397-398
  present value of money and, 407-408
  problems with typical approach, 405-408
  recommendations for, 409
  reporting cost of, 404-405
  roll-up, 402
  secondary effects of wage changes, 402-403
Cost-of-living, 280
Cost-of-living allowance, 355-357, 371
  alternative methods, 355
  impact of, 356
  use in bargaining agreements, 355
  wage-reopener clauses and, 357
Cost of new contract, 404-405

SUBJECT INDEX

Costs of agreeing, 242, 248-249
   direct costs of, 248
   nonmarket costs of, 248-249
   secondary costs of, 248
Costs of disagreeing, 242, 305
Council of Economic Advisors, 348
Court injunctions, 35-37, 48, 57, 132
Craft union, 90, 99, 119
Criminal conspiracy doctrine, 32-33, 57

Dana Corporation, 644
Danbury Hatters case, 39-41. *See also Loewe v. Lawler*
Darlington Manufacturing Company, 137
Davis-Bacon Act, 377, 409
Day-care centers, 396
Decertification, 147, 149
Decertification elections, 175-176
Demand for labor, 109-110
   instability in, 428-429
Demand, inelastic, government services and, 548-549
Department of Labor, 280
Discipline, authoritarian approach to, 488
Discipline, corrective, 488-489
Discipline, progressive, 489
Discount rate, 408
Dispute resolution in the public sector, 553-560
   choice of procedures, 559-560
   compulsory arbitration and, 557-560
   fact finding and, 555-557
   final-offer arbitration, 558-559
   mediation and, 553-555
Dissatisfaction with pay, 361-362
Distributive bargaining, 250-252
   attitudinal structuring and, 254-257
   bluffing, 251-252
   padding demands, 251
   strike threat and, 252
   tactics, 250-251
Double-breasted shops, 148, 637
Douds v. Metropolitan Federation of Architects, 303
Dual unionism, 102
Duplex Printing Press Co. v. Deering, 42-43, 46-47
DuPont, 637
Duty to bargain, 66

Early-bird negotiations, 315-316, 325, 338
Elasticity, 109-110
Elasticity of demand, 346-347
Employee ownership, 641-642
Employee Retirement Income Security Act, 384-385, 409
   funded pension rights, 385
   vested pension rights, 385
Employee security, 393-395
Employer discrimination because of union activities, 64-65
Employment Act, 606
Employment, government, growth of, 538-539
Employment by industry, projections of, 633-634

Employment by occupation, projections of, 633-634
Enterprise union, 615
Equal opportunity, seniority provisions and, 435-436
Equal Pay Act, 379, 409, 646
Equity theory, 165-167, 179-180
   inputs and, 165-166
   outcomes and, 165-166
Erdman Act, 38-39
Evolution of labor-management relations, 7-10
Ex-Cello Corporation decision, 264
Excelsior Underwear rule, 204-205
Exclusive jurisdiction, 95
Exclusive recognition, 575
Exclusive representation, principle of, 71-72
Executive Order 10988, 544, 575-577, 585
   bargaining units, 576
   critique of, 577
   dispute resolution, 576
   scope of negotiations, 575-576
   types of recognition, 575
Executive Order 11491, 577-578
   union recognition under, 577-578
   use of arbitration under, 578
Exempt employees, 141
Expectancy, 162-163
   decision to support a union and, 164-165
Expectancy theory, 162-165, 179-180
   decision to support a union and, 163-165
Expedited arbitration, 520
Experimental Negotiating Agreement, 326-329, 338
   Consumer Price Index and, 327
   local strikes and, 328
   United Steelworkers and, 327-328
Expiration date, common, 246
Expiration date, contract, 246, 271, 288
Extrinsic job satisfaction, 167-168

Fact finding
   advantages of, 556
   disadvantages of, 556-557
   dispute resolution in the public sector and, 555-557
   prebargaining, 314-315
Fair Labor Standards Act, 378-379, 409
Featherbedding, 69, 263
Federal Anti-Injunction Act, 46-48. *See also* Norris-LaGuardia Act
Federal Labor Relations Authority, 583, 587, 596
Federal Labor Relations Council, 578, 581
Federal Mediation and Conciliation Service, 259, 324-325, 330, 506-507, 521-522
Federal Republic of Germany, labor relations in, 607-610
   codetermination, 608-610
   Codetermination Act, 609
   employee representation on the super-

visory board, 608-609
   German Trade Union Federation, 607
   legal environment, 608
   union structure and bargaining, 607-608
   works councils, 610
Federal Service Impasses Panel, 578, 581-582
Federation of Organized Trades and Labor Unions, 94, 631
Felt fair pay, 362
Fibreboard doctrine, 438-439
Flextime, 390-391
Ford Motor Company, 316, 635, 640
Foreign competition, union membership and, 635-636
Formal recognition, 575
Franks v. Bowman Transportation Co., 435-436
Fraternal Order of Police, 585
Free collective bargaining, 335-337
Free speech, 70
Fringe benefits, 387-397
   cafeteria benefit plan, 397
   call-back pay, 389
   call-in pay, 389
   compensation for inconvenience, 387-391
   compressed work week, 390-391
   day-care centers, 396
   emerging forms of, 395-396
   employee security, 393-395
   flextime, 390-391
   health maintenance organizations, 396
   holidays, 391-393
   insurance, 394-395
   overtime, 387-389
   pay for time not worked, 391-393
   pensions, 394-395
   problems with, 396-397
   reporting pay, 389
   sabbatical vacation, 391-392
   severance pay, 394-395
   shift differential, 389-390
   supplemental unemployment benefits, 393
   vacations, 391-392
Functions and decisions, responsibility for, 144-146
Funding, 385

Gag orders, 573
General Electric, 246-247, 302
General Knit of California decision, 207
General Motors, 316, 349, 420, 635, 637, 640, 645
General Shoe Corp. decision, 200
Giboney v. Empire Storage and Ice Co., 300
Globe Machine and Stamping Co. doctrine, 196
Goals, employee, 160-161
Goals of union negotiations
   change in, 176-179
   union leaders' views of, 178-179
Going rates, 350, 370
   differences by region, 351-352

SUBJECT INDEX

differences within a region, 352-353
problems as a wage criterion, 350-351
wage contour, 352-353
Good faith bargaining, 70, 258-261, 266, 347
   employer, 65
   totality of conduct and, 260-261
   union, 67
Goodyear, 645
Government Printing Office, 543
Government of unions
   bureaucracy and, 113-114
   change in, 117-118
   democracy and, 113
   oligarchy and, 114-117
Great Britain, 636
Great Britain, labor relations in, 605-607
   British labor law, 606
   collective bargaining process, 607
   Employment Act, 606
   Industrial Relations Act, 606
   means to attain goals, 605-606
   productivity bargaining, 607
   two-stage system of negotiations, 607
   union membership, 606
   union structure, 606
   unofficial strikes, 607
   wage drift, 607
Grievance committee, 111
Grievance procedure, 474-479
   arbitration and, 477
   corrective discipline and, 488-489
   employer obligation to use, 485
   establishing policy and, 476-477
   functions of, 478
   history of, 478-479
   legal status of, 484-486
   number of steps, 476-477
   recommendations for, 486-490
   rights of individual worker and, 484-485
   self-help and, 485
   shop steward and, 474-475
   steps in, 474-475
   time limits, 476
   union control of, 486
Grievance procedures, effective
   corrective discipline and, 489
   first-level supervision and, 489-490
   management approach to discipline and, 488-489
   management procedures and, 488-490
   union procedures and, 486-487
Grievances, 473-474
   arbitrability of, 507-508
   broad definition of, 473-474
   clinical approach to, 482-483
   decision to process, 486
   determinants of, 480-484
   employee dissatisfaction and, 480
   employer characteristics and, 482-483
   employer-union relations and, 481-482
   legalistic approach to, 482-483
   narrow definition of, 473-474
   types of, 479-480
   union characteristics and, 483-484
   union instrumentality and, 483-484

union power and, 483-484
written, 475

Handbilling, 303-304
Hanover Trust Company, 304
Haymarket Square Riot, 131-132
Health maintenance organizations, 396
Hierarchy of needs, 161-162, 167, 179-180
Hiring halls, 263
Hitchman Coal and Coke Co. v. Mitchell, 37, 134
Holidays, 391-393
   estimating cost of, 399-403
Hollywood Ceramics doctrine, 207
Homestead Strike, 132-133
Hot cargo agreement, 70-71
Hot cargo clauses, 86
Hotel and Restaurant Employees and Bartenders International Union, 118

Illegal subjects of bargaining, 263
Impact of unions on control of public sector organizations, 594
Impact of unions on the merit principle, 593-594
Impact of unions on public employee fringe benefits, 592-593
Impact of unions on public employee wages, 592
Incentive compensation, 368-370
   Kaiser-Steel Plan and, 370
   Rucker Plan and, 370
   Scanlon Plan and, 369-370
Industrial Relations Act, 606
Industrial spies, 126
Industrial union, 99
Industrial Workers of the World, 98
Informal recognition, 575
Initiation fees and dues, 69
Injunctions and labor disputes, 48
Inland Steel, 328
Instrumentality, 162-163
   decision to support a union and, 164-165
Insurance, 394-395
   estimating cost of, 399-402
Integrative bargaining, 252-254
   attitudinal structuring and, 254-257
   honesty and, 253
   trust and, 254
Internal labor markets, 434-435
Internal union affairs,
   problems with, 55
   regulation of, 54-56
International Association of Fire Fighters, 584-585
International Association of Machinists, 639
International Brotherhood of Electrical Workers, 436-437
International Confederation of Free Trade Unions, 620-621
International Conference of Police Associations, 585
International Harvester Co. decision, 501-502

International Longshoremen's Association, 118
International Metalworkers' Federation, 621
International Trade Secretariats, 620-621
International union, 107
International Union of Electrical Workers, 247
Interrogation and polling, 202
Intraorganizational bargaining, 258
Intrinsic job satisfaction, 167-168

Japan, 635-636, 642
   labor relations in
      bargaining issues, 616
      enterprise union, 615
      labor law, 614
      negotiations, 615
      spring offensive, 615-616
      union structure, 614-615
Job analysis, 362
Job enrichment, 178-179
Job evaluation, 364-366
Job evaluation committee, 365
Jurisdictional disputes, 77
Jurisdictional rules, 437
Jurisdiction dispute, 102

Kaiser-Steel Plan, 370
Key jobs, 364
Knights of Labor, 90, 92-94, 97, 119, 631

Labor dispute, definition of, 47-48
Laborers Union, 118
Labor Management Relations Act, 53-54, 324, 329-333, 338, 417, 425, 484. *See also* Taft-Hartley Act
   federal employees right to strike and, 574
   grievance arbitration and, 496, 498, 503-504, 523
   national emergency strike procedures, 329-331
Labor-management relations in the federal sector, 572-584
   arbitration under the Civil Service Reform Act, 583
   Assistant Secretary of Labor for Labor-Management Relations, 578
   bargaining units under Executive Order 10988, 576
   Civil Service Reform Act, 579-584
   critique of Executive Order 10988, 577
   dispute resolution under Executive Order 10988, 576
   employee rights under the Civil Service Reform Act, 580
   Executive Order 10988, 575-577
   Executive Order 11491, 577-578
   executive orders and, 574-584
   Federal Labor Relations Authority, 581
   Federal Labor Relations Council, 578, 581
   Federal Service Impasses Panel, 578, 581-582
   General Counsel, 581

SUBJECT INDEX

Labor-management relations *(cont.)*
  grievance procedures under the Civil Service Reform Act, 583
  judicial review under the Civil Service Reform Act, 583
  legislative basis for, 579
  overview of, 583-584
  pre-1962, 572-574
  scope of negotiations under the Civil Service Reform Act, 582
  scope of negotiations under Executive Order 10988, 575-576
  types of recognition under Executive Order 10988, 575
  union recognition under Executive Order 11491, 575
Labor-management relations at the state and local levels, 584-595
  bargaining outcomes and public policy, 587-590
  determinants of outcomes in the public sector, 590-592
  federal legislation for, 588-589
  impact of unionism on, 592-595
  impact of unionism on control of public sector organizations, 594
  impact of unionism on fringe benefits, 592-593
  impact of unionism on the merit principle, 593-594
  impact of unionism on wages, 592
  overview of state level legislation, 585-587
Labor-Management Reporting and Disclosure Act, 54-56. *See also* Landrum-Griffin Act
Labor Reform Act, 56, 138, 204, 265
Labor relations, 16
  approach to the study of, 19-20
  historical view of, 23-24
  phases of, 20-22
Labor relations in other countries, 601-616, 625
  Brazil, 602-604
  Federal Republic of Germany, 607-610
  Great Britain, 605-607
  Japan, 614-616
  overview of, 601-602
  Poland, 613-614
  Soviet Union, 610-612
  Western Europe, 604-605
  Yugoslavia, 612-613
Labor relations staff, authority of, 142-143
Labor relations staff, responsibilities of, 144-146
Labor relations, why study, 18-19
Labor's Magna Carta, 42
Labour Party, 605-606
Landrum-Griffin Act, 54-56, 58, 65, 78-82, 85-86, 70-71, 112, 117, 280, 441. *See also* Labor-Management Reporting and Disclosure Act
  background and holding union office, 81-82
  bill of rights, 79

  controls on picketing, 82
  election of union officers, 81
  financial accountability of union leaders, 81
  penalties under, 80
  reporting requirements, 79-80
  trusteeships, 80-81
  union democracy, 81
Lay-offs, 431
Legal means and ends doctrine, 34-35
Liberal Party, 605
Lincoln Mills decision, 496-497, 523
Little Steel strike, 135
Livingston v. John Wiley, 439
Lloyd-LaFollette Act, 573
Local 761, International Union of Electrical Workers v. NLRB, 302
Local union, 91
  functions of, 110-111
  government of, 112
Lockout, 295-296, 306
  defensive, 296
  multi-employer bargaining unit and, 296
  offensive, 296
  single employer bargaining unit and, 296
  whipsawing and, 296
Loewe v. Lawler, 39-41. *See also* Danbury Hatters case

McClellan Committee, 54-55, 81
Maintenance of membership, 418
  incidence of, 423
Make-work rules, 436-437
Management
  attitudes toward unions, 126-127, 146-147. *See also* philosophy toward unions
  authority of, 142-144
  centralization of labor relations, 145-146
  cost effective to engage in unfair labor practices, 136-138
  current approach to be non-union, 135-140
  historical approach to unions, 129-135
  levels of, 125-126
  line, 138-139
  negative approach to prevent unionization, 136-138
  philosophy toward unions, 146-147. *See also* attitudes toward unions
  positive approach to prevent unionization, 138-140
  role of, 125-126
  why oppose unions, 127-128
Management-rights provisions, 425-427
  example of, 426
  incidence of, 426
Mandatory subjects of bargaining, 262
Mar-Jac Poultry Co. decision, 263
Med-arb, 326
Mediation, 317-325, 338
  combining with arbitration, 326
  differences between public and private sectors, 554-555

  dispute resolution in the public sector and, 553-555
  functions of mediators, 318-323
Mediators, functions of, 318-325
  communications function, 320-322
  procedural functions, 318-320
  substantive function, 322-323
Merger, union, 118-119
Merit compensation, 368-369
  union formation and, 368-369
  union solidarity and, 368-369
Merit principle, 593-594
Michelin, 637
Midland National Life Insurance Co. decision, 207
Minimum wage, 378-379
Minority workers, efforts to organize, 645-646
Mohawk Valley Formula, 134-135
Moore Dry Dock, 302-303
Multinational collective bargaining, 616-624
  bargaining efforts, 622-623
  barriers to, 618-620
  effectiveness, 623
  examples of, 622-623
  multinational union structure, 620-621
  protective legislation and, 624
  public policy and, 620
  union leader attitudes and, 618
  wage-determination procedures and, 620
  worker attitudes and, 618-620
Multinational corporations, 616-617, 625
  alternative union strategies toward, 623-624
  base country, 616
  host country, 616
  problems presented unions, 616-617
  protective legislation and, 624
  threat of job loss, 617
  union bargaining power and, 617
Multinational labor organizations, 620-621
Multiemployer bargaining, 247-248, 296
Mutual aid agreement, 245

National Association of Manufacturers, 280
National Association of Post Office Clerks of the United States, 573
National Civic Federation, 101
National Civil Service Association, 573
National Education Association, 563
National emergency dispute, 77
National emergency strike procedures
  arsenal of weapons, 333-334
  cooling-off period, 330-331
  critique of, 331-332
  experience with, 331
  Federal Mediation and Conciliation Service and, 330
  National Labor Relations Board and, 330
  statutory strike, 334
  suggested improvements in, 333-335
National Labor Relations Board, 330

SUBJECT INDEX

National Industrial Council, 280
National Industrial Recovery Act, 48-49
National Labor Relations Act, 49-52, 56, 75, 82, 126, 136-138, 140, 186-187, 193, 195-198, 201, 203, 205, 212, 258-263, 266, 271, 296, 297, 300, 302, 336, 338, 539, 541, 563-564, 572, 574, 595-596. See also Wagner Act
  grievance arbitration and, 495, 501-502, 523
National Labor Relations Act, as amended, 63-75, 84-86
  basic employee rights under, 63
  employer unfair labor practices, 64-65
  unfair union labor practices, 65-70
National Labor Relations Board, 50-51, 57, 85, 137, 140, 148, 186-205, 207-208, 209, 212, 258, 260, 261, 263-266, 277, 296, 300, 302-304, 421
  administrative law judges, 78
  bargaining unit determination in the public sector and, 560-561
  cease and desist orders, 72-74
  court injunctions, 74
  enforcement of orders, 74
  functions of, 75, 77
  general counsel, 77
  grievance arbitration and, 500-503
  make whole orders, 72-74
  members of, 77
  organization chart of, 76
  prevention of unfair labor practices, 72-75
  procedures in unfair labor practice cases, 72-75
  regional offices, 78
  responsibilities under the Postal Reorganization Act, 83
National Labor Union, 90, 92, 97
National Mediation Board, 332-333
National Trades Union, 91
National union, 107
  emergence of, 91-92
  functions of, 109-110
  government of, 111-112
Need deprivation, 167
Need importance, 167
Needs, employee, 160-162
  categories of, 161-162
Negative approach to remaining non-union, 149
Negotiations, contract, 288-305
  contract expiration date and, 288
  contract rejection, 291-294
  implications of contract rejection, 294-296
  ratification, 289-291
  written agreement and, 288-289
Negotiations, preparation for, 272-287
  administrative decisions and, 277
  arbitration awards and, 273, 276
  area wage data, 279-280
  bargaining objectives, 284-285
  clause book and, 274
  computer applications and, 278-279
  cost-of-living and, 280
  court decisions and, 277
  data sources and, 277-281
  description of workforce, 278
  establishing priorities, 283-285
  final demands, 283-286
  first-level supervisors and, 273
  grievance files and, 273
  identify potential management demands, 274-277
  identify potential union demands, 272-273
  initial bargaining positions, 284-286
  internal data sources, 277-279
  legislation and, 277
  recent contracts and, 273
  selecting the bargaining team, 281-283
  shortcomings of existing agreement and, 276-277
  strike plan, 286
  study past negotiations, 272
  union leaders and, 273
  union preparation, 286-287
  wage and benefit data, 278
  worker performance and, 278
Negotiations, strategy and tactics of, 249-258
Neutrality clause, 645
New York Life Insurance Company, 304-305
NLRB election orders, 198-200
  expedited elections, 198-200
  formal election procedures, 198
  informal election procedures, 198
NLRB v. Babcock and Wilcox, 189, 204
NLRB v. Denver Building and Construction Trades Council, 300-302
NLRB v. Exchange Parts Co., 203
NLRB v. Fruit and Vegetable Packers, Local 760, 303-304
NLRB v. Gissel Packing Co., 187-188
NLRB v. Jones and Laughlin Steel Co., 51, 85
NLRB v. Savair Manufacturing Co., 205
No-distribution rules, 188-189
No-lockout provisions, 427-428
  incidence of, 423
Nonexempt, employees, 141
Non-stoppage strike, 334-335
Non-union employers, 136-140
Non-union, negative approach to remaining, 136-138
Non-union, positive approach to remaining, 138-140
No-raiding agreement, 102, 106
Norris-LaGuardia Act, 46-48, 57, 299. See also Federal Anti-Injunction Act
No-solicitation rules, 188-189
No-strike provisions, 427-428
  incidence of, 423

Obligation to bargain, duration of, 263
Oligarchy, 114-117, 120
One-year certification rule, 263
Open hostility, 126-127
Open shop, 418
Open shop drive, 133-134
Operating Engineers, International Union of, 274-275
Organizing campaigns, 205-209
  board regulation of, 208
  campaign propaganda, 206-207
  channels of communication, 206
  impact of, 208-209
  issues discussed, 205-206
Outcomes, valences of, 165-167
Overtime, 387-389
  common provisions, 388
Overtime pay, 377-379
  estimating cost of, 398-402

Panama Canal Zone, 543
Pay grades, 366-367
Pay ranges, 367-368
  methods of progression, 367-368
Pay for time not worked, 391-393
Peerless Plywood decision, 203
Pension funds, 640-641
Pension Reform Act, 277
Pensions, 394-395
  estimating cost of, 399-402
  private, 384-385
Permissive subjects of bargaining, 262
Philadelphia Cordwainers, 33-34, 158. See also Criminal conspiracy doctrine
Philadelphia and Reading Railroad, 129
Picketing, 82, 299-303, 306
  ally doctrine, 303
  ambulatory, 302-303
  common situs, 300-302
  location of, 300
  Moore Dry Dock, 302-303
  reserved gate doctrine, 302
  restrictions on, 70
Pinkerton Detective Agency, 126
Plant-closure legislation, 639
Poland, labor relations in, 613-614
  Solidarity, 614
Porter Co., H.K., v. NLRB, 264-265
Positive approach to remaining non-union, 149
Postal Reorganization Act, 83
  right to strike, 83
  unfair labor practices, 83
Prebargaining fact finding, 325, 338
Preferential hiring, 418
Present value of money, 407-408
Prevailing Wage and Fringe Benefit Law, 377
Productivity, 348-350, 370
  annual improvement factor and, 349
  as a wage criterion, 348-349
  productivity bargaining and, 349-350
Productivity bargaining, 349-350, 607
Public Contracts Act, 377
Public employees, number unionized, 538-539
Public employee strikes, 541
  frequency of, 552-553
Public employee unionism
  anti-union legislation, 541
  bargaining unit determination, 560-564

Public employee unionism (cont.)
  characteristics of public employees and, 542-543
  civil service commissions and, 542
  effectiveness of confrontation and, 545-546
  factors contributing to growth of, 543-546
  factors inhibiting, 540-543
  general acceptance of unionism and, 544
  indifference of public sector managers and, 543-544
  job conditions of public sector and private sector workers and, 543
  nature of public employment and, 542
  public employee strikes, 541
  scope of issues, 564-565
  sovereignty of the state and, 540-541
  unions' interest in organizing public employees and, 544-545
Public policy on employee benefits, 380-385
  Employee Retirement Income Security Act, 384-385
  Social Security Act, 382-383
  unemployment insurance, 384
  workers' compensation laws, 380-381
Public policy toward unions, sources of, 31-32
Public policy on wages, 376-380
  Age Discrimination Act, 380
  Civil Rights Act, 379-380
  Davis-Bacon Act, 377
  Equal Pay Act, 379
  Fair Labor Standards Act, 378-379
  Walsh-Healey Act, 377
Public sector
  differences from the private sector, 546-549
  diffused managerial authority, 546-547
  impact of collective bargaining, 547-548
  inelastic demand for services, 548-549
  similarities with the private sector, 549-550
Pullman Strike, 132

Quality circles, 642-644, 647, 649
Quality of work life, 15-17, 643-644, 649
Quality of work life and adversarial labor relations, 16-17
Quality of work life and collective bargaining, 16

Railway Labor Act, 45-46, 57, 82-83, 329, 332-333, 338, 419
  emergency strike provisions of, 332-333
  National Mediation Board, 82-83, 332-333
  National Railway Adjustment Board, 83
Railroad strikes of 1877, 130-131
Ratification, contract, 289-291
Real wages, 354-355

Refusal-to-bargain, 265
Reindustrialization, 634-635
Reporting pay, 389
Representation elections, 71-72, 85
Republic Aviation Corp. v. NLRB, 189
Republic Steel Corporation v. Mattox, 485
Reserved gate doctrine, 302
Resistence points, 240-241, 266
Right to strike in the public sector, 541, 551-553
  arguments regarding, 551-552
  public policy regarding, 552
Right-to-work, 66-67
Right-to-work laws, 419-422
  arguments against, 420-421
  effects on union membership, 422
Roll-up, 402
Roving picketing. *See* Ambulatory picketing
Rucker Plan, 370

Sabbatical vacation, 391-392
Sailor's Union of the Pacific. *See* Moore Dry Dock
Satisfaction with pay, 359-362
  consequences of dissatisfaction, 361-362
  felt fair pay and, 361
  model of, 360-361
Savings provisions, 425-427
  example of, 426
  incidence of, 426
Scab, 300-301
Scanlon Plan, 149, 371, 369-370, 644
Schecter Corp. v. U.S., 48-49
Secondary boycott, 39-41, 86
  illegal activities, 68-69
  illegal objectives, 68-69
  legal description of, 67-69
Secondary effects of wage changes, 402-403
Self-help, 485, 490
Seniority provisions, 430-436
  benefit, 430
  competitive status, 430
  effects on labor mobility, 433-434
  equal opportunity and, 435-436
  exceptions in applying, 431
  incidence of, 431-432
  internal labor markets and, 434-435
  lay-off decisions and, 431
  measurement of seniority, 431
  promotion decisions and, 432-433
  reasons for, 430
  recall decisions and, 432
  seniority unit, 431
  transfer decisions and, 432-433
Seniority unit, 431
Service Employees International Union, 646
Settlement range, 240-241
  negative, 241
  positive, 240
  resistence points, 240-241
Severance pay, 394-395
Sewell Manufacturing Co. decision, 207

Sherman Anti-Trust Act, 39-40, 47, 57.
  See also Anti-trust legislation
Shift differential, 389-390
  estimating cost of, 400-402
Shopping Kart Food Market, Inc. decision, 207
Shop steward, 111, 474, 486-487
Sit-down strike, 102
Social Democratic Party, 605
Social Security, 395, 409
Social Security Act, 382-383
Social security tax, estimating cost of, 399-402
Solidarity, 614
Southern strategy, 645
Sovereignty of the state, 540-541
Soviet Union, 635
  labor relations in, 610-612
    collective agreements, 611
    pressure for change, 612
    union functions, 611
    union structure, 611
    worker rights, 611-612
Spielberg Manufacturing Company decision, 501-503
Spring offensive, 615-616
Staff ratio, 143-144
Stale card rule, 189-191
Stall-in, 301
Standard of living, 353-354, 370
  budget estimates of, 353-354
  levels of, 353-354
State labor laws, 84
Statute law, 31-32
  and labor relations, 44-57
Stevens Co., J. P., 137, 304-305, 641, 645
Strike, 242-248, 306
  common expiration date and, 246
  company financial position and, 244
  composition of bargaining team and, 247-248
  contract expiration date and, 246
  critical workers and, 246
  increased inventories and, 243
  internal union politics and, 242-243
  labor market conditions and, 245
  membership savings and, 243
  other unions' impact on, 243
  product market conditions and, 245
  strike funds and, 243
  strike insurance and, 244-245
  trained supervisors and, 243
Strikebreakers, 130
Strike insurance, 244-245
Strikes, 295-305
  activities in support of, 299-305
  effects of, 295
  types of, 296-298
Strikes, economic, 297
  causes of, 298-299
Strikes, jurisdictional, 297
Strikes, local, 328
Strikes, sympathy, 297-298
Strike, statutory, 334
Strikes, unfair labor practice, 296-297
Strikes, wildcat, 297

SUBJECT INDEX
665

SUB. *See* Supplemental unemployment benefits
Subcontracting, 438-439
Successorship clauses, 439-440
Superseniority, 431
Supervisors' bargaining rights, 564
Supplemental compensation, 386-387. *See also* Fringe benefits
  cost of, 386-387
Supplemental unemployment benefits, 393
Surpass Leather Co., 191
Sweetheart contract, 127
Syndicalism, 92. *See also* Workers' cooperatives

Taft-Hartley Act, 53-54, 57-58, 65, 75, 201, 418-419, 422, 437, 441, 479, 490. *See also* Labor Management Relations Act
  balanced labor policy, 53-54
  major changes brought about by, 53-54
Teamsters, International Brotherhood of, 118, 215, 247, 646
Teamsters and T.I.M.E.-D.C., Inc., 436
Technological change, union policy toward, 429-430
Tennessee Valley Authority, 543
Texas and New Orleans Railroad Company v. Brotherhood of Railway and Steamship Clerks, 45-46
Textile Workers Union of America, 137
Theory X, 128-129
Theory Y, 128-129
Thornhill v. Alabama, 299
Timken Company, 637
Torrington Co. v. the Metal Products Workers, Local 1645, 500
Totality of conduct standard, 260-261
Toyota, 635-636
Trade union. *See* Craft union
Trade Union Congress, 620-621
Trilogy, Steelworkers, 497-500, 523
Truitt decision, 347
Trusteeships, 80-81. *See also* Landrum-Griffin Act
Twenty-four-hour rule, 204

Unemployment compensation, 409
Unemployment insurance, 384
Unemployment insurance tax, estimating cost of, 399-402
Unfair employer labor practices, 85
Unfair labor practices, 77
  cost effective to engage in, 137-138
  prevention of, 72-75
Unfair union labor practices, 85
Uniform Arbitration Act, 500-501
Union busting, 137
Union corruption, 117-118
Union discrimination against employees, 66
Union dues, 117
Union finances, 117
Unionization, extent of, 141-142
Union membership, 180
  bargaining strategies intended to influence, 638-639
  certification elections and, 175-176
  changing industry composition and, 173-174
  changing industry patterns of employment and, 633-634
  changing occupational patterns of employment and, 633-634
  changing workers' values and, 637-638
  codetermination and, 640
  comparable worth and, 646-647
  control of investment funds and, 640-641
  corporate decisions and, 639-644
  decertification elections and, 175-176
  efforts to organize minority workers and, 645-646
  efforts to organize white-collar workers and, 647-648
  efforts to organize women workers and, 646
  employee ownership and, 641-642
  employer actions and, 636-637
  employer efforts to reduce the need for a union and, 174
  forces influencing, 631-638
  foreign competition and, 635-636
  incentive plans and, 644
  organization of workers in the South and West and, 645
  plant-closure legislation and, 639
  quality circles and, 642-643
  quality of worklife and, 643-644
  reindustrialization and, 634-635
  trends in, 172-176, 631-632
  union efforts to influence, 638-648
  union mergers and, 639
Union mergers, 639
Union representation election, 77
Union security provisions, 416-423
  agency shop, 418
  alternative security provisions, 418-419
  closed shop, 418
  incidence of, 422-423
  maintenance of membership, 418
  need for, 416-417
  open shop, 418-419
  preferential hiring, 418
  right-to-work laws, 419-422
  union shop, 418-419
Unions, federal employees' lack of interest in, 574
Union shop, 418-419
  incidence of, 422-423
Union shop clause, 77
United Air Lines, 638-639
United Auto Workers, 149, 246, 316, 349, 393, 420, 427, 621, 637, 638-639, 640, 645, 649
United Mine Workers, 98, 299
United Rubber Workers, 637, 638-639, 640
United Steelworkers of America, 327-328, 338, 391, 393, 438, 621, 637
U.S. Department of Labor, 118, 603
U.S. v. Hutcheson, 47

USW v. American Manufacturing Company, 497-498
USW v. Enterprise Wheel and Car, 499-500
USW v. Warrior and Gulf Navigation, 498-500

Vaca v. Sipe, 486
Vacations, 391-392
  estimating cost of, 398-402
Valence, 162-163
  decision to support a union and, 163-165
Vegelahn v. Guntner, 299
Vesting, 385
Violence in labor relations, 130-131

Wackenhut decision, 439-440
Wage compression, 356-357
Wage contour, 352-353
Wage curve, 365-366
Wage and Hour Act, 378-379
Wage level, 345
  determinants of, 345-359, 370-371
    ability to pay, 345-347
    cost of living, 354-357
    going rates, 350-353
    productivity, 348-350
    relative importance of, 357-359
    standard of living, 353-354
    union and non-union companies, 358-359
Wage-reopener clauses, 357
Wage structure, 362-370
  establishing wages for non-key jobs, 365-366
  job analysis and, 362
  job evaluation and, 364-365
  job evaluation committee and, 365
  key jobs, 364
  non-key jobs, 364
  pay grades and, 366-367
  pay ranges and, 367-368
  wage curve and, 365-366
  wage surveys and, 363-364
Wage survey, 363-364
Wages, estimating cost of, 398-402
Wages and fringe benefits, union influence on, 171-172
Wagner Act, 49-52, 57, 65, 419, 479. *See also* National Labor Relations Act
  constitutionality of, 51. *See also NLRB v. Jones and Laughlin Steel Co.*
  criticisms of, 52
  enforcement of, 50
  implications of, 52
  key provision of, 50
  objectives of, 49
Wall Street Journal, 603
Walsh-Healey Act, 377, 409
Welfare secretary, 133-134
Westinghouse, 247
Whipsawing, 296
White-collar workers, efforts to organize, 647-648

SUBJECT INDEX

White v. NLRB, 261
Why workers organize, 180
   feelings of equity and, 172
   research evidence, 167-172
Why workers unionize
   differences between white-collar and blue-collar workers, 168-169
   extrinsic and intrinsic job satisfaction and, 167-168
   instrumentality of unions and, 170
   model of, 163-165
   satisfaction with administrative procedures and, 169-179
   union influence on wages and fringe benefits and, 171-172
Women workers, efforts to organize, 646
Workers' compensation, 380-381, 409
   common law defenses and, 380-381
   estimating cost of, 399-402
   experience rating, 381
   provisions, 381
Workers' cooperative, 92. *See also* Syndicalism
Workers' councils, 610
Workers' management, 612
Workers' values, 637-638

Yellow dog contract, 37, 47, 132, 416
Yugoslavia, labor relations in, 612-613
   workers' management in, 612

AMERICAN LABOR HISTORY HIGHLIGHTS*

1941 Actions by the Carpenters' union in jurisdictional disputes were held to be protected by the Clayton Act from prosecution under the Sherman Anti-Trust Act. These actions were construed in light of Congress' definition of "labor dispute" in the Norris-La Guardia Act. (*U. S.* v. *Hutcheson*.)

1942 The United Steelworkers of America was organized. It replaced the Steel Workers Organizing Committee, which was first established by the CIO in 1936.

The President established the National War Labor Board (NWLB) to determine procedures for settling disputes.

The NWLB laid down the "Little Steel" formula for wartime wage adjustments (i.e., based on a 15-percent rise in living costs from January 1, 1941, to May 1, 1942).

1943 The War Labor Disputes (Smith-Connally) Act, passed over the President's veto, authorized plant seizure if needed to avoid interference with the war effort.

1944 The Railway Labor Act, authorizing a labor union chosen by a majority to represent a craft, was held to require union protection of the minority in the class. Discrimination against certain members on ground of race was held enjoinable. (*Steele* v. *Louisville & Nashville Railroad*.)

1947 The Labor Management Relations (Taft-Hartley) Act was passed (June 23) over President Truman's veto. It outlaws the closed shop, jurisdictional strikes and forms of secondary boycotts. It opens the door to state open-shop laws.

1949 The United States Supreme Court, by denying review of a lower court's action, upheld a decision that the Labor Management Relations Act requires employers to bargain with unions on retirement plans. (*Inland Steel Co.* v. *United Steelworkers of America*.)

The CIO anti-Communist drive culminated in expulsion of two unions at its annual convention. Trial and expulsion of nine other unions followed early in 1950.

1952 Presidents of two principal labor federations, Philip Murray of the CIO and William Green of the AFL, died in November. The AFL Executive Council elevated George Meany, former secretary-treasurer of the Federation, to the presidency. Walter P. Reuther, president of the United Automobile Workers, was named president of the CIO by the CIO convention.

1953 The Supreme Court of the United States upheld the right of the International Typographical Union (AFL) to compel a newspaper to pay for the setting of type not used, and of the American Federation of Musicians (AFL) to demand that a local "standby" orchestra be employed when a traveling orchestra was hired for an engagement. The Court said that neither practice violated the "featherbedding" ban in the Labor Management Relations (Taft-Hartley) Act.

1955 The founding of the American Federation of Labor and Congress of Industrial Organizations (AFL-CIO) on December 5, 1955, brought into one center unions representing approximately 16 million workers—over 85 percent of the membership claimed by all unions in the United States. The first convention of the AFL-CIO elected George Meany its president.

1957 The December 1957 biennial convention of the AFL-CIO expelled the Teamsters, Bakery Workers, and Laundry Workers, with a combined membership of approximately 1.6 million, on charges of domination by corrupt influences.

1959 The Labor-Management Reporting and Disclosure Act of 1959, designed to eliminate improper activities by labor or management, was passed by the Congress. The act provides certain protection for the rights of labor organization members; provides for the filing of reports describing the organization, financial dealings, and business practices of labor organizations, their officers and employees, certain employers, labor relations consultants, and unions in trusteeship; safeguards union election procedures; sets standards for the handling of union funds; amends the Taft-Hartley law to eliminate the "no-man's land" in NLRB cases; closes previously existing loopholes in the protection against secondary boycotts; and limits organizational and jurisdictional picketing. The statute is administered by the Department of Labor.